CONSCIOUSNESS AND BEHAVIOR

fifth edition

BENJAMIN WALLACE
Cleveland State University

BARBARA B. OSWALD
Miami University

LESLIE E. FISHER
Cleveland State University

Kendall Hunt
publishing company

Cover image © Shutterstock, Inc.

Kendall Hunt
publishing company

www.kendallhunt.com
Send all inquiries to:
4050 Westmark Drive
Dubuque, IA 52004-1840

To Roni, Jacob, Sara, and Adam

To Ken and Erin

To Swagata

Meditation 187

PREFACE

The first edition of this book appeared in 1983. In the three decades that have passed, great advances have occurred in the psychology of consciousness. Since the fourth edition was released in 1999, increases in technology, coupled with renewed interest in understanding the neural correlates and applications of consciousness and altered states, have led to tremendous improvements in our understanding of how the brain produces consciousness, and how humans might harness this knowledge for clinical benefit. It was time for a fifth edition.

Based on positive comments from students and professors who used earlier editions, our goal in this edition is to maintain the integrity and focus of the original text, while updating to include the most recent evidence on the topics covered in each chapter. Thus, users of previous editions will find the structure, outline, and focus of the text familiar. However, each chapter contains a thorough update of contemporary research. Given that a major focus in the last decade has been on elucidating the neural correlates of consciousness and altered states, each chapter contains fully updated sections on the current state of research on brain and genetic factors motivating consciousness and behavior. The fifth edition also offers the most recent information regarding clinical efficacy of each of the potential therapeutic techniques addressed in the book. These include clinical applications of hypnosis, biofeedback, meditation, and sensory deprivation.

Each chapter in the fifth edition has received comprehensive updates, while retaining much of the content of the original text.

Information that has been disproven or deemed irrelevant has been removed. We have added over 380 new references, 30 percent of which have been published within the last two years. Important changes in each of the chapters include the following:

Chapter 1 (Introduction) contains a streamlined discussion of the definitions of consciousness, and a description of Ned Block's frequently used taxonomy of phenomenological and access consciousness. A new section on qualia and the binding problem have been added. Discussions of the "classic" theories of consciousness, including those of Weil, Tart, and Jaynes remain, but an updated section on contemporary theories of consciousness has been added. This section introduces readers to the modern Global Workspace Theories of Baars and Dehaene, Higher-Order Theories of Byrne and Rosenthal, and Biological Theories, including that of Crick and Koch.

Chapter 2 (The Physiology of Consciousness) remains an excellent introduction to physiology for students who need this basic understanding to study consciousness. This chapter contains updated information on brain imaging technology including fMRI, PET, SPECT, DTI, and MEG, which are frequently used to assess the neural correlates of consciousness. To complement the section on split-brain patients, we have added a detailed discussion of recent research on brain laterality and consciousness. This section includes reviews of research on the effects of handedness on consciousness, and how promoting bilateral hemispheric activity may affect consciousness. The chapter concludes with an in-depth review of our current knowledge regarding the neural correlates of consciousness.

Chapter 3 (Consciousness-Altering Drugs) thoroughly updates knowledge regarding many popularly abused drugs. The fifth edition adds discussions of benzodiazepines (including sections devoted to the "date rape drugs" GHB and rohypnol), amphetamines (including methamphetamine and stimulant drugs used in the treatment of attention-deficit/hyperactivity disorder), and MDMA ("Ecstasy").

Chapter 4 (Hypnosis) systematically updates research on hypnosis. We have added information on of each of the hypnotic susceptibility scales and induction tests currently in use. The chapter summarizes the most recent information regarding cognitive, personality, and neural correlates of hypnosis and hypnotizability. The chapter contains an updated discussion on the clinical efficacy of hypnosis.

Chapter 5 (Biofeedback) contains a comprehensive update on the clinical efficacy of biofeedback. Special attention is given to biofeedback in the use of anxiety and stress-related disorders, attention-deficit/hyperactivity disorder, and pain management for migraine and tension headaches. Detailed descriptions are provided for the most commonly used types of biofeedback today, including skin temperature, skin conductance, muscle activity, heart-rate variability, and neurofeedback.

Chapter 6 (Meditation) includes comprehensive updates on meditative styles, psychological and physiological correlates of meditation (including neural correlates), and clinical uses for meditation.

Chapter 7 (Sleep and Dreams) adds recent research on the relationship between sleep and obesity, and optimal sleep levels for maintaining optimal health. New sections examine the effects of napping, and the role of sleep on memory formation, including the neural correlates of sleep and memory. The chapter includes updates on theories of why we sleep, and adds discussions of two new theories of dreaming: Hobson's AIM model and Continuity Theory proposed by LaBerge. A section updating why we daydream has been added.

Chapter 8 (Sensory Deprivation) contains updates on newer sensory deprivation techniques including extended blindfolding, neural correlates of sensory deprivation, and a recent theory of sensory deprivation that proposes that perceptual distortions induced by minimal environmental input is the result of increased reliance on top-down processing in the absence of bottom-up processing. The chapter ends with a summary of the latest information regarding the clinical applications of sensory deprivation, especially the flotation-REST technique.

Chapter 9 (Parapsychology) presents the most recent findings on this contentious area of study. A thorough discussion of Bem's (2010) controversial paper reporting significant psychic ability in normal undergraduate students is provided, including a review of criticisms and responses. Although closed in 2007, the chapter includes a discussion of the Princeton Engineering Anomalies Research (PEAR) lab, due to continued interest in applying quantum theory to explain paranormal ability. The chapter includes a new discussion of anomalies in science applied to paranormal phenomena, to facilitate discussion regarding replication and validation of paranormal ability. The chapter contains updates on research on out-of-body and near-death experiences, and includes a new section on "distant healing." Descriptions of two new theories of paranormal phenomena are offered (Houtkooper's Observational Theory and May's Decision Augmentation Theory), and an added section on neural correlates of paranormal phenomena reviews the current status of knowledge regarding neural and genetic aspects of psi.

We hope you enjoy reading the fifth edition of *Consciousness and Behavior*. Our goal of previous editions remains: to introduce students to those controversial yet popular areas of psychology that are typically neglected or given very little attention in traditional course offerings. As an introductory text, our intention remains to keep the presentation of topics at a level that does not necessitate prerequisites for reading and understanding. We hope that we have accomplished these goals in this edition.

ACKNOWLEDGMENTS

We would like to thank Scott Perrine, acquisitions editor for Kendall Hunt, for convincing us that a fifth edition of our book was necessary and long overdue. We also thank Angela Puls and Abby Davis for doing an extraordinary job of editing this edition. We thank our many colleagues, especially Jim Appel, Shaun Youngstedt, and Ruth Propper, for offering helpful comments on portions of earlier chapter drafts. We offer thanks to our numerous students over the years, who offered helpful feedback and insightful discussions to help formulate the content of the current edition. Special thanks are offered to two students who were particularly helpful in preparing the fifth edition, Morgan Kiamy and Sarah Simpson. The second author (BBO) would like to especially thank my co-authors (BW and LEF) for inspiring within me an early interest in the scientific study of consciousness and the physiology of behavior. Finally, as with previous editions, we thank our families for having the patience to put up with us while we prepared and completed this book.

B.W.
B.B.O.
L.E.F.

Introduction

There is a renewed interest in the scientific study of consciousness and altered states. Although at one time criticized for the lack of experimental rigor afforded by "introspection" or the study of conscious contents, advances in science and technology make it an exciting time to study consciousness and behavior.

The contemporary study of behavior has been greatly influenced by the principles, laws, and theories of behaviorism (Skinner, 1964, 1974; Watson, 1913). Whenever psychologists were interested in studying an aspect of behavior, they generally obeyed certain modes of collecting data, making certain that behavior was observable and, therefore, measurable.

This is not a difficult rule to follow, nor is it necessarily one that we will try to change. However, in being so rigid, data collection in many psychology experiments may be incomplete. If we are concerned only with studying and reporting observable behavior or behavior that can be mutually shared, we may be sidestepping a great deal of human behavior that obviously is not observable. For example, should we ignore totally an individual's thoughts or feelings because they are not directly observable or capable of being mutually shared? Should we fail to study dreams because we cannot share them with the dreamer? Should we fail to study hypnosis or meditation because these phenomena are not directly measurable in the true behavioristic sense?

The answer to these questions, obviously, is *no*. Yet psychology has downplayed the importance of studying some of these interesting phenomena because of a bias still present, to an extent, among many contemporary psychologists. We believe that it is time to do away with the philosophical biases of behaviorism but not yet time to entirely abandon that school of thought, science, and methodology.

Today, the influence of behaviorism is declining, replaced by an interest in cognitive psychology. Compared to the behaviorists, cognitive psychologists have not been as rigid in defining what is permissible in data collection (Kihlstrom, 1994, 1996). These scientists are recovering the tools of psychology that existed before the advent of behaviorism, albeit at a slow pace (see Banks, 1993).

Although we are well aware that behaviorism emerged as a reaction to the sloppiness and poor experimental control of such processes as introspection (Hamilton, 1880; Malcolm, 1964), it also did away with other ramifications of structuralism (Titchener, 1909). For example, during introspection, a process of self-observation developed by Wilhelm Wundt (1832–1920), subjects were taught to verbalize everything that they experienced during their participation in an experiment. In other words, they were to give a complete phenomenological report of their experiences with a stimulus event and with the environment. This reporting served as a means for the scientist to gain access to a subject's mental episodes.

In agreement with the behaviorists we believe that much imprecision existed during introspective assessments of experience. However, in reacting against this method of data assessment, behaviorism also reacted against most behavior not directly observable or that, at minimum, could not be mutually shared. This tainted the use of individual verbal reports in psychological research (or, for that matter, in all behavioral research). Psychology as a science witnessed a considerable decline in the use of such reports in research because they were supposedly not scientific. In fact, many psychology and behavioral science instructors still hold to this belief and try to proselytize their students to the "party line."

This strict adherence to behavioristic philosophy has been at the expense of much important data collection and of hypothesis, law, and theory construction. Not to deviate from strict behaviorism is to accept the dictum that thoughts or mental processes are not scientifically testable. We and contemporary cognitive psychologists (e.g., Eysenck & Keane, 1995; Reed, 1996;

Sternberg, 1996) believe that such a view is untenable. All behavior is acceptable for study, whether it is directly observable or is speculated to exist via an individual's verbal report.

One area of research that has made great strides in attempting to assess unobservable behavior through verbal reports and other means, and which therefore falls outside the legitimate realm of study by strict behaviorists, is what is now referred to as the **psychology of consciousness** (Farthing, 1992; Ornstein, 1972, 1986). Although psychologists and philosophers have studied consciousness for many years (see Boring, 1929), it was not until recently that this area of psychology reemerged as an important area of concern.

What exactly is the psychology of consciousness, and when did the study of this area commence? Why is it reemerging as an area for psychologists to study after being in limbo for nearly three-quarters of a century? Most important, will science gain knowledge as a result of its reemergence? Let us examine these issues.

What Is Consciousness?

Although philosophers have studied consciousness for nearly 400 years (see Natsoulas, 1978b), the psychology of consciousness can trace its beginnings only to the writings of William James (1842–1910). James, who founded the school of functionalism, saw consciousness as a tool that enabled individuals to select their own courses of action. He defined *consciousness* as the "function of knowing" (James, 1890, 1904). To James, knowing or the ability to know was a personal thought; therefore, what one individual knew or thought differed from what everyone else knew or thought.

James also believed that consciousness was forever changing. By this he meant that every conscious state is a function of the entire psychophysical totality and that the mind is cumulative and not recurrent. Implicit in this is the belief that objects can recur but sensations or thoughts cannot. James also urged that consciousness is a continuous process. There are time gaps, such as sleep, but when an individual awakens from sleep, he or she has not become someone or something else.

Finally, James believed that consciousness had the important characteristic of being selective. Only a small part of the potentially effective world of stimuli could come to consciousness. The principle of selecting the effective stimuli was highly dependent on relevance. That is, we attend to stimuli that are most relevant to us at a given time and place. Thus, consciousness is a highly selective process that is both logical and rational.

From the early thoughts of James we come to more recent considerations of the concept of consciousness.

One difficulty with the scientific study of consciousness has been the lack of agreement on an accepted definition of consciousness. As noted by Nat-soulas (1978a, 1987), and emphasized by Baruss (1987), at least 29 separate definitions of consciousness can be found. Seven commonly accepted definitions include the following:

1) Joint or mutual knowledge—the expression (usually verbal) of our inner experiences, to promote a shared understanding by others

2) Internal knowledge or conviction—being a witness to one's own behavior and internal state

3) State of awareness—the knowledge of unobservable, private events, as well as knowledge of external events

4) Direct awareness—a condition of all thought, feeling, and volition, or what John Locke (1690/1975) referred to as what passes in man's mind. Indeed, Hunt (1995) views direct, perceptual awareness as the core of consciousness.

5) Direct awareness without sensory stimulation/"Personal unity"—in addition to direct awareness that may be promulgated by external stimuli (for example, a photon of light stimulates our eye, so we have the perception and awareness of seeing a light), we may also be aware of thoughts or experiences without direct sensory stimulation. In this view, consciousness is the totality of the impressions, thoughts, and feelings that make up a person's conscious being, an "internal awareness" that is not necessarily triggered by external stimuli.

6) Normal waking state—Possibly the most common definition, this suggests that consciousness is a state of wakefulness with attentiveness to stimuli or events in the environment (*Oxford English Dictionary,* 1933). We will often refer to this definition in our discussion of various altered states (e.g., Tart, 1972; 1977a), the major theme of this book.

7) "Double Consciousness"—the multiple states of information processing that may occur, including subliminal

For instance, if a light source at a very low level of intensity is present and subjects are requested to indicate when they are first able to see it, we notice that they do not give their indication immediately. There are several reasons for this delay in response. For instance, the retinal receptor system may not be physically capable of detecting light at this low level. Or the subjects may think they see the light but are not quite certain; thus, they may choose to be conservative and delay the response, or the delay maybe due to a combination of these two reasons.

However, light *is* being emitted from a source, and photons are impinging on the retinal photoreceptors of the subjects' eyes; they simply are not able to detect the light. Does this mean the light is really not present? This question is basically a philosophical one, just like the question Does a falling tree make noise when no one is around to hear it? No, obviously a crash and resultant noise occur physically, but they are not perceived.

In the case of the light we might simply say that, for a given individual at the normal state of awareness and processing, the light was not present because the subject did not perceive it. However, we know that it is physically present, and therefore, it could have been perceived, if not by the subject, then by someone else. Thus, the normal waking state of awareness or consciousness may differ from one individual to the next.

At the same time it is also possible for an individual to perceive the light at one level of consciousness and not at another. An excellent example of the existence of such multiple levels of consciousness or awareness is illustrated in the work of Ernest Hilgard (1973, 1976, 1977a, 1977b, 1979), discussed in chapter 4. Briefly, he showed experimentally that with the aid of hypnosis it is possible to separate at least two levels of consciousness. At one level, a subject perceives an event, while at another level, he or she is totally unaware of the event.

More recent definitions of consciousness also focus on this idea of "multiple states" or different forms of "consciousness" we may experience. For example, Block (1995) distinguishes among four types:

1) **Access consciousness**—the contents of information. Access consciousness includes perceiving, reporting, and acting on information. Access consciousness is available for verbal report, and can be used to make judgments and plan actions. Furthermore, access consciousness allows us to gather and filter sensory and other information (e.g., learned memories and reflexes) to allow us to successfully plan and perform behaviors. For example, access consciousness permits us to drive a car: Not only can we see, integrate, and respond to road conditions (signs, other cars, pedestrians, construction areas, sirens, etc.), but access

consciousness allows us to put that information together with our learned memories (on what side of the road we should drive, how much muscle tension is needed in our arms and hands to adjust the steering wheel, how to adjust the lights, turn signals, radio, etc.) so that driving is accomplished successfully.

2) **Phenomenal consciousness**—our qualitative experience of information. For example, phenomenal consciousness refers to the subjective differences in our experiences of "red" and "green," or "loud" and "soft," or "a little pain" and "a lot of pain." Many people describe this aspect of consciousness as "qualia," which will be defined more fully below. Phenomenal consciousness, like access consciousness, is available for verbal report, although the language necessary to explain the experience may not be available. For example, try explaining how "loud" is perceptually different from "soft" without using the words "loud" and "soft."

3) **Self-consciousness**—thoughts and concepts about oneself. Self-consciousness, and Block's next type, monitoring consciousness, have yet to receive the full attention devoted to access and phenomenal consciousness. However, Block proposes that self-consciousness is a distinct and separate type of consciousness, although it may only be represented in man and nonhuman primates. Nonetheless, even animals that may not possess self-consciousness or self-awareness (as in being able to recognize themselves in a mirror) cannot be denied having phenomenal consciousness, for example, phenomenal awareness of pain. Thus, self-consciousness should be viewed as distinct from phenomenal consciousness.

4) **Monitoring consciousness**—"internal perception" or "self-scanning." This type of consciousness is also qualitatively different from phenomenal consciousness. Indeed, it has been suggested that computers regularly engage in "self-scanning," yet clearly are not conscious. Humans probably also engage in monitoring consciousness that does not reach phenomenal or access consciousness, although this (perhaps obviously) has been difficult to verify empirically.

Our definition comes close to another delineated by Natsoulas (1978a): *processing of information at various levels of awareness.* (As you can readily see, we are equating the terms **consciousness** and **states of awareness**.) In fact, we will go one step farther than Natsoulas and Hilgard: Consciousness exists at *many* levels. We define a **level** as one state of awareness that is distinguishable, either empirically or experientially, from another state.

Hilgard has demonstrated two of these levels. However, there is evidence to indicate that more than two levels of consciousness or awareness exist. For example, we can count the several stages of sleep (discussed in chapter 7) as different levels of awareness. Also, as you will see in other chapters, there are different levels of hypnosis (chapter 4) and meditation (chapter 6). Many more levels may also exist during other states of consciousness. One of our goals is to deal with consciousness using a multilevel approach. Another goal is to show that we have only begun to touch the surface in our understanding of consciousness, especially of the different levels of consciousness and what takes place in them.

And What About Qualia?

Qualia refers to the quality of our conscious experiences, for example the "redness" of red, the "blueness" of blue, the "painfulness" of pain, etc. Although some people like the philosopher Daniel Dennett (1988) may be described as "qualiaphobes," or disbelievers in qualia, other people (such as the philosopher David Chalmers) have been described as "qualiaphiles," or advocates of not only acknowledging, but scientifically studying qualia. One of the most difficult obstacles to the scientific study of consciousness is the "hard problem" of qualia (Chalmers, 1995): How might we adequately describe—or measure—the redness of red, the painfulness of pain, etc. Try it now—imagine you must explain the color "red" to a blind person who has never seen red. As if that isn't difficult enough, now try to imagine how a friend might describe "red." Do you think your two descriptions would match?

While obviously verbalizing and measuring qualia is indeed a challenge to the scientific study of consciousness, the hard problem or "explanatory gap" as Block (2009), Byrne (2006), and others have called it, suffers from an additional problem: There is yet no plausible explanation for how the experience of "red" ("redness" of red, or even any other emotions or memories evoked by red, etc.) could arise from the actions of the brain. Although these issues are addressed more fully in chapter 2, it is assumed that if we could reduce qualia to a population of neurons in the brain, we may be able to understand or explain better how our conscious perceptions occur. It could also permit us to study consciousness in other animals that cannot verbalize their conscious experiences (e.g., Dennett, 1995; Nagel, 1974).

The belief that the perception of qualia may be reduced to populations of neurons in the brain has led to an interest in the search for "neural correlates of consciousness" (NCCs). An *NCC* is defined as the minimal set of neuronal events that give rise to a specific, conscious percept. For example, it would be the minimum number of neurons needed to fire for us to be conscious of "red" (Crick & Koch, 2003). If we could identify the neural mechanisms underlying the conscious awareness of our perceptions, we could possibly explain qualia (e.g., the "redness of red"), consciousness, and altered states of consciousness more clearly.

Classic and Contemporary Theories of Consciousness

It is generally not difficult to communicate what consciousness in the normal waking state means. We are well aware of what being awake feels like. We also can describe what we are minimally capable of doing while awake. However, what does it feel like to be in an altered state of consciousness, or not awake? What are we capable of doing in an altered state? Does performance in such a state differ from performance in the waking state?

To begin to answer such questions, it is necessary to enumerate what we believe to be altered states of consciousness or awareness. Then we must decipher existing experimental evidence to determine whether behavior changes or is different in such states. Finally, if behavior does differ, it is necessary to summarize the evidence to formulate laws and theories of cognition, information processing, or neurophysiology that will help explain the psychology of consciousness.

Classic Theories of Consciousness

In the early 1970s, Andrew Weil (1972) attempted to theorize about the concept of consciousness. Although his theory was not formal in any sense of the word, he did elaborate on many observations and hypotheses that ultimately could lead to a formal and comprehensive theory of consciousness. His observations and hypotheses were based primarily on his own personal experiences as well as on laboratory experimentation. The major points Weil made were as follows:

1) The drive to experience modes of awareness other than the normal waking state is innate. In other words, we are born with a desire or urge to experience altered states.

2) Individuals experiment with methods or techniques of changing consciousness. These experimental methods in essence define the topics of the majority of chapters in this book.

3) Altered-state experiences are normal, and individuals spend a certain amount of time each day in such experiences. If you cannot conceive of individuals doing this, just think, for example, of the last time you had a daydream (perhaps a few seconds ago?).

4) Individuals may not always be aware that they are experiencing or have experienced behavior in an altered state. Again, even if you had a daydream, were you aware of it? Or was awareness something that occurred after the conclusion of the daydream?

5) Altered states form a continuous spectrum from ordinary waking consciousness. That is, altered states are not all or none; they flow naturally from the waking state.

6) Artificial agents (e.g., drugs) may elicit altered states but do not cause them (Weil, 1996). As an example, while many may believe that consciousness-altering drugs (see chapter 3) produce altered states, Weil does not believe this to be the case. Rather, the drugs only bring out altered states.

7) It is important to learn how to enter an altered state, because experiences in this state may lead to a more comprehensive understanding of the workings of our central and peripheral nervous systems (see chapter 2). Such experiences also lead to the realization of untapped human potentials and to a better understanding of the functioning of our ordinary waking state of consciousness. As is evident, Weil believes that altered states are beneficial and that we should learn to make greater use of their potential.

As we will see throughout this book, many of Weil's observations are indeed valid premises for a potential theory of consciousness. However, more experimentation is necessary to test his hypotheses before these points can constitute an established theory.

In a more formal sense, Charles Tart (1975, 1977a) also proposed a theory of consciousness. He viewed consciousness as a construction or something that requires learning or experience. As such, it is not automatic or given.

According to Tart, a number of concepts lead to this construction. These include what he referred to as attention/awareness, structure, the interaction of structure and attention/awareness, and the interaction of structures with structures. Let us examine each of these concepts.

Attention/awareness involves the following: Consciousness begins with a *basic awareness* or some kind of rudimentary ability to know or realize that something is happening (in one's environment, broadly defined). Thus, we are cognizant of being conscious. In addition, we are often aware of being aware, which is what Tart referred to as *self-awareness*. This varies from moment to moment. As a result, there are different degrees of being aware. Further, this attention/awareness can be voluntarily directed to some extent. Thus, we can ask someone to pay attention to our right hand, and attention is focused on that part of the body (although as Tart points out, focused attention is never complete).

Tart (1977a) further stipulates that "attention/awareness constitutes the major phenomenal energy of the consciously experienced mind" (p. 162). **Energy** is defined here as the ability to do work, the ability to make something happen. Finally, the total amount of attention/awareness energy available varies from time to time, but there is probably a fixed upper limit on it at any given moment. On some days, we seem to concentrate or attend well; on other days, we appear incapable of focusing our attention.

Tart's concept of **structure** referred to the idea that consciousness consists of a relatively stable organization of component parts that perform one or more related psychological functions. Such a structure may show variation in the intensity and/or the quality of its activity, but it still retains its basic pattern or quality of organization and its function. And, as such, it remains recognizably the same.

Some structures are essentially permanent. These are biological/physiological givens or the **hardware** of our mental system (some of these are discussed in chapter 2). Other structures are determined by the individual's developmental history. These are **software**, and they are created by learning and by living within the culture. According to Tart, the essentially permanent structures create limits on what can be done with programmable (software) structures. Thus, in some respects the hardware constrains the software.

An **interaction of attention/awareness and structure** exists because many structures function totally autonomous of attention/awareness. An example is a physiological structure such as the liver. We do not have a direct awareness of this structure; we infer it from other kinds of data.

On the other hand, according to Tart, psychological structures must use a certain amount of attention/awareness energy (1) to be formed or created, (2) to be operable, (3) to have their operations inhibited, (4) to have their structure or operation modified, and (5) to be dismantled. And although Tart postulates that attention/awareness energy is capable of activating and altering psychological structures, this is not always easy. For example, we may be asked to attend to something, but this does not necessarily mean that we do so. Some of you may recall an experience like this when a teacher asked you to pay attention to something and this command went in one ear and out the other without any (or with little) cognitive processing.

Tart also postulates that, insofar as the amount of attention/awareness energy available at any given time has a fixed upper limit, some decrements should be found when too many structures draw on this energy simultaneously. Also, once a structure has been formed and is operating, the attention/awareness energy required for its operation may be tapped automatically.

As for the **interaction of structures with other structures**, individual structures have various kinds of properties that limit and control their potential range of interaction with one another. For example, they may not interact because there is no direct or mediated connection between them. Interaction is also precluded if the codes of output and input information are incompatible or if the output signal from one is too weak. Also, interaction may not occur if the output signal from one overloads the other. Finally, two structures are prevented from interacting if the action of a third structure interferes with them.

Tart also discusses the terms **discrete state of consciousness (d-SoC)** and **discrete altered state of consciousness (d-ASC)**. The first concept refers to such phenomena as sleep, dreams, hypnosis, drug intoxication, and various forms of meditation (topics discussed in later chapters of this book). The second concept refers to the difference in observable, and perhaps measurable, behavior between some baseline state of consciousness (waking state) and a d-SoC. Therefore, Tart's views of consciousness are very much in line with the multilevel concept that we advocate in this book. It is true that Tart discusses only two levels of consciousness, but it is certainly a good start toward a theory of consciousness.

Perhaps the most controversial theory of consciousness was proposed by Julian Jaynes (1976). On the basis of many laboratory experiments involving brain laterality or hemispheric specialization of the brain (e.g., Galin & Ornstein, 1972; Gazzaniga, Bogen, & Sperry, 1965; Gazzaniga & Sperry, 1967; Gordon & Sperry, 1968; Milner, 1965) and a close reading of existing archeological and historical evidence, Jaynes proposed that people in ancient civilizations could not independently process information or think as we do today. In other words, individuals appeared to be obeying commands that they heard inside their heads. Jaynes (1986a) believed that early peoples interpreted these so-called voices, or possible auditory hallucinations, as commands from the gods that told them what to do and how to behave and basically presented them with everything they needed to maintain their existence. The ultimate source of authority (the voice of the commands of the gods) was tradition. Being so dependent on their gods, people from these cultures were not conscious. According to Jaynes, many examples of obeying these inner voices can be found in both the Old and New Testaments, as well as in writings such as the *Iliad* by Homer.

Because of the catastrophes and cataclysms of many centuries, especially during the second millennium BCE, and because humans were beginning to perform complex activities such as reading and writing, individuals living in those times were forced to become more independent in their thinking and, perhaps to survive, to learn consciousness. Thus, the heart of Jaynes's (1976) theory is that consciousness is a model of the real world composed of words. The model is used to carry out experiments concerning various possible courses of action. The results of these invisible experiments are then used to make decisions and to choose the course of action that appears to be most promising.

More recently, Jaynes (1986b) referred to consciousness in terms of the development of a "mind space." Therefore, consciousness did not evolve in the strict biological sense but was produced via our experiences with history and with different cultures and races. Furthermore, according to Jaynes, consciousness is grounded in the physiology of the brain's right and left hemispheres. (We discuss brain laterality and its role in consciousness in chapter 2).

Three forms of human awareness exist within Jaynes's theory. He refers to these as the *bicameral* or *god-run man*, the *modern* or *problem-solving man*, and the contemporary forms of *throwbacks to bicamerality*. The god-run man was controlled by

Figure 1.1 • Jaynes's God-Run Man

and within the right hemisphere, which told the left hemisphere (especially the auditory and speech centers of that hemisphere) what to do and how to behave (see Figure 1.1). As civilization became more independent, there was less and less god-run control by the right hemisphere over the left hemisphere. In becoming more independent, people acquired consciousness.

However, Jaynes stipulates that, on occasions, the god-run man reemerges and exhibits himself in what is referred to as throwbacks to bicamerality. These include such states as hypnotism, schizophrenia, and poetic and religious frenzy. As part of these throwbacks, modern humans relegate their consciousness to obey the commands of an individual, group, or higher power that gains control for a period of time (specified, as in hypnosis, or unspecified, as in schizophrenia).

An examination of Jaynes's radical theory suggests that all altered states of consciousness are throwbacks to bicamerality. This suggests further that such states temporarily produce a loss of wakeful and controllable awareness in an individual. If this is the case, then men or women at least temporarily give up some control to another individual. Although this may be true to some extent, we will see in the remaining chapters that this is not as straightforward as Jaynes would have us believe. For example, an individual who is hypnotized does not really lose control. Similarly, when one meditates or experiences biofeedback, there is no loss of control. Thus, we do not agree with Jaynes's premise that altered states are necessarily indications of a throwback to bicamerality. We will present our case in detail in the various chapters that deal with the areas of consciousness.

Contemporary Theories of Consciousness

One theory of consciousness that has gained support in recent years is the Global Workspace Model of consciousness, originally developed by Baars (1988, 1993, 1997) and taken in a more neural direction by others (e.g., Dehaene & Nacchache, 2001; Dehaene, Changeux, Nacchache, Sackur, & Sergent, 2006). So while a Global Workspace Model itself does not require specifically neuronal connections (it merely requires something capable of sending and receiving signals), recent models tend to describe the global workspace in neural terms (and probably represent Tart's "hardware").

Global Workspace theories suggest that neural "coalitions" in sensory areas in the back of the brain compete to form dominant coalitions. Sensory areas are activated in most cases by external stimulation (although they can be activated without external stimulation, in the case of dreams, certain drug-induced states, and other altered states addressed in later chapters). Dominant coalitions form as the result of whatever sensory area in the brain is most activated. The dominant coalition then sends information to the frontal cortex, which integrates perception of the stimulus with memory, emotion, planning, etc. This frontal activation can then be "globally broadcast" to all cognitive areas in the brain, which permits integration with other sensory systems, memories, and motor responses.

For example, imagine seeing a guitar. The visual stimulus prompts dominant activation in your visual cortex, which promotes frontal lobe activation of emotions, memories, and plans related to guitars. The visual stimulus and any recollections or behaviors elicited by frontal lobe activation will then be globally broadcast all over the brain. This "global broadcast" facilitates activation among other neural networks devoted to many aspects of "guitar," such as remembering how it feels to hold and play a guitar, what a guitar sounds like, your favorite guitar solo, your favorite guitar musician, the time you were in "Battle of the Bands" in high school, motivation to purchase a guitar, plans to earn and save money to make the purchase, and so on. Consciousness then IS that "global broadcasting"—becoming aware of all of the sensations/memories/experiences of "guitar."

In addition to Global Workspace Theory, Ned Block (2009) suggests that there are two other "major" theories of consciousness today. One of these is Higher-Order Theory, advanced more recently by Byrne (1997) and Rosenthal (2000). Higher-order theories suggest that we are only conscious of an experience *if* we have another state to promote that experience. For example, to be conscious of "red," we have to simultaneously have a visual perception of something red (there must be a physical stimulus of approximately 700nm electromagnetic radiation presented with enough magnitude for our visual system to detect), *and* we have to also *think* that we're seeing something red. This definition minimizes confounds caused by limitations imposed by our perceptual system (it does not include stimuli presented below our threshold for awareness), as well as limitations of our sensory memory (which, according to the Atkinson-Shiffrin (1968) model of memory, is very brief: one to two seconds, and of which we only process a small amount of information). So, for example, our visual system may receive and process information presented above our threshold of awareness. However, if we don't pay attention to the stimulus, that information is lost, even before we become conscious of it. According to higher-order theories, we are not conscious of information in sensory memory, unless we also have the opportunity to "think" about it, that is, notice it, pay attention to it, and so forth.

Block (2009) notes a major criticism of Higher-Order and Global Work-space theories: "[G]lobal broadcasting and higher-order thoughts are what consciousness *does* rather than what consciousness *is*" (p. 1113). Therefore, a third contemporary (and potentially superior) theory is Biological Theory. Although the idea that consciousness derives from a biological function of the brain is not a new one, advances in technology have permitted scientists to begin to elucidate biological underpinnings to consciousness (discussed more fully in chapter 2). Modern biological theories suggest that consciousness is the result of the specific requirements of neural activity: electrical stimulation, followed by chemical stimulation, followed by electrical activity, and so on (which, as described more fully in chapter 2, is how neurons generate action potentials: an electrical charge causes the release of chemical neurotransmitters, which stimulates receptors on other neurons, which causes their electrical charge to reverse). Select neurons appear to regulate consciousness, and much work is being done to isolate these populations of neurons. One likely target is neurons in the thalamus, which have extensive projections to the frontal cortex.

Indeed, there is evidence that a "Thalamic Switch" (proposed by Alkire, Hair, & Fallon, 2000) may promote consciousness. As summarized by Block (2009), anesthetics, which disrupt consciousness to make surgical incisions possible, "disable" neural connections between brain stem and thalamic areas and the frontal lobe. Secondly, functional magnetic resonance imaging (fMRI) studies (described in chapter 2) demonstrate that brain stem/frontal connections sometimes show little to no activity in people in vegetative comas (totally unconscious and nonresponsive), but are active in people in minimally conscious states ("comas" where people can respond at some level, like blinking eyes). However, while the thalamic switch may regulate consciousness, consciousness itself is likely not located in the thalamus (or any primary sensory cortical structures; e.g., Crick & Koch, 1995; Chalmers, 2000). Additional information on the neural correlates of consciousness can be found in chapter 2.

In summarizing our sampling of theories of consciousness, we can find many commonalities. Consciousness appears to develop through a learning process (defined broadly). Many individual differences are found in states of consciousness, and these differences help us to learn about the process. Human potential can be tapped through knowledge of consciousness and experiencing altered states of consciousness. It is also possible to find commonalities between various states or altered states of consciousness. Finally, states of consciousness are to be considered positive in the development of humankind

15

and civilizations and, as such, can help to improve the quality of life and its accomplishments.

The psychology of consciousness, as it is presented here, is a step in the advancement of a study of states and levels of awareness. It is also an attempt to integrate the many diverse areas that define the psychology of consciousness. Many refer to these areas as the peripheral areas of psychology. Yet they are popular areas for discussion by scientists and nonscientists alike. They are also very important areas of study in their own right.

A Taxonomy of States of Consciousness

Before beginning an in-depth study of the various states of consciousness as defined in the remaining chapters, we would like to present an organizational theme.

First, from the general theories of consciousness previously presented, it should be clear that states of consciousness contain an element of variability. That is, regardless of any predictions in a theory or in the many experiments that you will read about in the remaining chapters, individual differences will always exist. This is one reason why states of consciousness are so difficult to study. Individual differences are abundant in all the areas we discuss. Therefore, we cannot generalize as liberally as we would wish about any of the states of consciousness or phenomena that are presented. There will always be individuals for whom the described results will not seem to fit. Thus, what appears on the surface to be a robust effect may not be nearly so potent. We would hope that the results would be predictive for a large segment of the population.

Second, as you will see throughout the various chapters describing the many states of consciousness, consciousness is not a single state or level. In general, if we equate the concept of consciousness with awareness or alertness, it is possible to form a type of hierarchy of consciousness with *wakefulness* at the top of the hierarchy. Drug-altered states (chapter 3), hypnosis (chapter 4), biofeedback (chapter 5), meditation (chapter 6), daydreaming and perhaps night dreaming (chapter 7), sensory deprivation (chapter 8), and perhaps paranormal experiences (chapter 9) form altered states of consciousness that differ clearly from wakefulness. The lowest level of consciousness might be sleep (chapter 7).

Third, within each state of consciousness to be discussed, there exists a further delineation. That is, each state may consist of many levels. As examples, you will see that various levels of consciousness alteration can be produced by the influence of some of the drugs described in chapter 3. And the effects of one drug may be different for one individual than for another; that is, individuals may experience drugs at different levels of consciousness. Similarly, you will find that hypnosis, meditation, biofeedback, daydreaming, night dreaming, and sensory deprivation can be experienced at different levels of awareness or consciousness.

Fourth, altered states of consciousness must contain an element of pleasure. We believe this because so many individuals (all of us, perhaps) seek to attain altered states, often on a regular basis. These altered states must also be more pleasurable than the waking state. Perhaps Weil (1972) was correct: We have an innate drive to experience modes of awareness. Although the drive may be innate, we must learn to use the drive, perhaps in a manner similar to what Ornstein (1986) described as deautomatization, a detachment from the normal or usual manner by which we experience our environment, a concept we describe in detail in chapter 6. Thus, altered states can be experienced through experimentation with drugs, meditation, hypnosis, biofeedback, daydreaming, and sensory deprivation. A good night's sleep with a few fantastic dreams might accomplish this.

Finally, many (e.g., Kokoszka, 1992; Springer & Deutsch, 1997) have speculated that altered states of consciousness are dictated by the right hemisphere of the brain or the *right brain*. That is, altered states are somehow related to a shift in electroencephalographic, or EEG, activity from the left hemisphere of the brain to the right hemisphere. Some evidence suggests that this may be correct (Bakan, 1969; Greenwood, Wilson, & Gazzaniga, 1977; Hoppe, 1977; MacLeod-Morgan & Lack, 1982). However, this area is in its infancy, and very little evidence is yet available to solidly substantiate this conjecture. Nonetheless, research continues to determine the loci and neurological correlates of consciousness. And perhaps we will discover that many of the altered states of consciousness are right-brain phenomena.

What unites all of these phenomena under a single rubric is the notion that each is a tool for demonstrating the possible existence of a state of consciousness or awareness, with accompanying levels of strength, discernible from the ordinary waking state of consciousness. Specifically, each phenomenon can potentially show us that humans are capable of processing various types of information at different levels of control. These levels can differ in both their exhibited behavior and the consequences that result from a change from the normal waking state. It is the variability and diversity of this behavior and accompanying experiences that we explore in the remainder of the book.

For Further Reading

Baars, B. J. (1997). *Consciousness regained: The new science of human experience.* Oxford: Oxford University Press.

Dennett, D. C. (1991). *Consciousness explained.* New York: Back Bay Books/ Little, Brown and Company.

Farthing, G. W. (1992). *The psychology of consciousness.* Englewood Cliffs, NJ: Prentice-Hall.

Goleman, D., & Davidson, R. J. (1979). *Consciousness: Brain, states of awareness, and mysticism.* New York: Harper and Row.

Jaynes, J. (1976). *The origin of consciousness in the breakdown of the bicameral mind.* Boston: Houghton Mifflin.

Kurzweil, R. (1999). The age of spiritual machines. New York: Penguin Books.

Ornstein, R. (1986). *The psychology of consciousness.* New York: Penguin Books.

Searle, J. R. (1997). *The mystery of consciousness.* New York: New York Review of Books.

Tart, C. T. (1975). *States of consciousness.* New York: Dutton.

Weil, A. T. (1972). *The natural mind: A new way of looking at drugs and the higher consciousness.* Boston: Houghton Mifflin.

Wolman, B. B., & Ullman, M. (Eds.). (1986). *Handbook of states of consciousness.* New York: Van Nostrand Reinhold.

The Physiology of Consciousness

In chapter 1 we learned that the early interest in the psychology of consciousness faded quickly in response to the scientific rigors demanded by behaviorism, the philosophical approach adopted by most physiological psychologists. The research efforts in physiological psychology have been labeled reductionistic, rather than holistic. The physiological psychologist, in his research efforts, views the organism not as an integrated whole but in terms of its component parts: receptors, transducers (those parts of the system that change stimuli energies into neural energy), integrators (the brain and spinal cord in higher organisms such as humans), and effectors. Such a research stance is not conducive to the study of a holistic concept such as consciousness.

However, while trying to reduce a holistic function like consciousness is challenging, research into the neuroscience of consciousness has virtually exploded in the last two decades. A quick search in Medline yields 837 returns for the keywords "neuroscience and consciousness," with nearly 60 articles published in 2010 alone. Summarized recently by Duggins (2010), while many neuroscientists remain "confident that subjective experience lies outside the domain of neuroscience ... enlightened neuroscientists, prepared to acknowledge sentience as a phenomenon in need of explanation, seek the neural correlates of consciousness" (p. 1).

A concerted effort is under way, aimed at developing a physiological explanation of conscious states. Certainly, some earlier research programs pointed to the cerebral hemispheres as possible physiological loci of consciousness, and later in this chapter we focus our attention on the results of one such effort that uses the "'split-brain'" procedure. Other research is focusing on cortico-thalamic projections as likely correlates of consciousness (e.g., Alkire, Hudetz, & Tononi, 2008; Chalmers, 2000; Crick & Koch, 1995, 1998; Leopold & Logothetis, 1996; Milner, 1995; Tong, Meng, & Blake, 2006). We evaluate this research more fully later in this chapter as well.

First, it is necessary that we discuss some microscopic and gross structures and functions of the nervous system, as many of these are ultimately involved in consciousness and are referred to in a number of subsequent chapters of this book.

Microscopic Neuroanatomy

The basic anatomical unit of the nervous system is the single nerve cell, often referred to as the **neuron**. There are roughly 12.5 billion neurons in the human adult nervous system. These cells come in a variety of shapes and sizes, but in one form or another they usually have a cell body or **soma, dendrites**, an **axon**, and a **terminal arboration** (see Figure 2.1).

Within the cytoplasm of the cell body the **nucleus** and other **organelles** can be found, which assist in carrying out the life functions of the cell. The nucleus is the central mass of the cell that controls all cellular functions and contains the genetic material, **deoxyribonucleic acid (DNA)**. The most important organelles found in the cytoplasm of the soma and in the axoplasm (the corresponding substance in the axon) are the small, rod-shaped structures called **mitochondria**, which are responsible for the energy-producing reactions of the cell.

The **dendrites** are treelike structures attached to the soma. There may be a single dendrite, as in the case of the **bipolar neuron**, or many, as in the case of the **multipolar neuron**. Dendrites receive information from other neurons and conduct these messages with decrement down their structure to the soma.

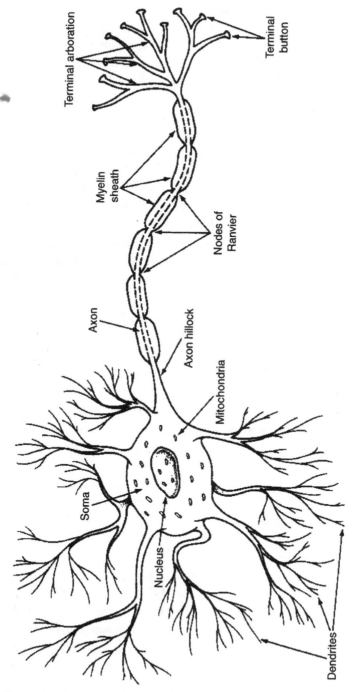

Figure 2.1 • Major Structures and Regions of a Multipolar Neuron

While a neuron can have one or more dendrites, it can have but a single axon. That portion of the neuron where the cell body and the axon connect is called the **axon hillock**. It is here that **action potentials**, the neural impulses that are conducted down the axon, are usually initiated. The axon can be covered with a white, fatty substance called **myelin**. The myelin sheath is segmented rather than continuous. The myelin segments are separated by bare spaces called **nodes of Ranvier**. The myelin serves as a kind of electrical insulation preventing crosstalk between myelinated axons. Myelination also results in a more rapid rate of information conduction. At its distal end (the end away from the center, i.e., the soma), the axon divides and branches a number of times. Collectively, these branches are referred to as the **terminal arboration**. On the end of each of these little branches is a rounded swelling called a **terminal button**. The function of these buttons is the storage and, when conditions are right, the release of a chemical called a **neurotransmitter substance**.

Neurotransmission is accomplished by **neural conduction** and **synaptic transmission**. Since these processes play an integral role in influencing how psychoactive drugs affect consciousness (discussed in chapter 3), we feel it necessary to present a brief discussion of how they function.

Neural Conduction

Generally, the conduction of information in the form of a neural impulse proceeds in one direction from the dendrite, across the soma, and down the axon to the terminal buttons. Such conduction depends on the passage of specific charged molecules, **ions**, across the semipermeable membrane of the cell. Conduction along the dendrite is accomplished with decrement. This means that as the graded potential (a potential that varies in amplitude according to the intensity of the initiating stimulus) is conducted along the dendrite, it decreases in strength until it reaches the axon hillock.

In addition to connecting the axon to the soma, the axon hillock is that region of the neuron that has the lowest threshold value. If the strength of an impulse is sufficient to reach or exceed this threshold level, then a full-blown **action** or **spike potential** will be initiated and will be conducted down the axon at full strength and at a rate or speed determined by the neuron. This is the **all-or-none law** of axonal conduction. If the strength of the impulse is not sufficient to reach threshold, then the impulse may summate (add its strength to that of other graded potentials at the hillock), or it may simply die out. When the action potential finally reaches the terminal buttons, the neurotransmitter substance is released and we have the beginning of synaptic transmission.

Synaptic Transmission

The junction between the terminal button of an axon and the membrane of another neuron, muscle, or gland is the **synapse**. The neuron that contains that terminal button is called the **presynaptic element**, and the neuron, muscle, or gland on which the terminal button synapses is the **postsynaptic element**. Such an anatomical arrangement clearly requires a communication system that differs considerably from that which operates within the neuron.

Synaptic transmission involves a number of separate but interrelated steps. The first of these steps involves the synthesis of the neurotransmitter substance. It is believed that over 20 such chemical molecules serve as neurotransmitters in the human nervous system.

Acetylcholine, norepinephrine, dopamine, and serotonin are the most common of these chemical transmitters. In chapter 3 we see that scientists are becoming increasingly convinced that dopamine plays an important role in a broad range of drug addictions (Nash, 1977); in chapter 7 we uncover the role of serotonin in sleep and dreams.

Generally, the chemical molecule is synthesized from its precursor elements in the presence of an appropriate **enzyme**, a protein molecule that facilitates the biochemical reaction without entering into it. This synthesis typically takes place in the soma of the neuron and is then transported down the axon to the terminal button.

The second step involves the storage of the neurotransmitter substance in the synaptic vesicles located in the cytoplasm of the terminal button. With the arrival of the neural impulse at the terminal button and a sudden influx of calcium ($Ca++$) into the area from the extracellular fluid, we have the beginning of the third step. These two events must occur before a number of the synaptic vesicles migrate to the presynaptic membrane, adhere to it, rupture, and spill their contents into the synaptic cleft.

Once the neurotransmitter substance is released into the synaptic cleft, it must cross the 200–500-Ångstrom space (a distance measurement with 1 Ångstrom = 10^{-10}m) to the receptor sites on the membrane of the postsynaptic element. This is the fourth step. The fifth step involves an interaction of the transmitter substance with a specific postsynaptic receptor to produce a physiological reaction. This results in a change in the permeability of the postsynaptic membrane with a consequent flow of ions through it and the initiation of a graded potential. Just what this mechanism is and how it works are as yet unknown.

Step six, the final step, is vital if we are to avoid having a postsynaptic element in a continual state of firing. The activity of the neurotransmitter must be stopped. To accomplish this, the system must somehow remove the active transmitter molecules from the synapse. **Enzymatic degradation** and **reabsorption** are the mechanisms employed. In the former case an enzyme is released into the synapse, usually at sites on the postsynaptic membrane. This enzyme destroys the neurotransmitter and renders it ineffective. Reabsorption, or what is also known as the **reuptake process**, is the extremely rapid removal of transmitter substance from the synaptic cleft by the terminal button. The exact mechanism by which reuptake is accomplished is still poorly understood. Any understanding of how drugs in general, and particularly the psychoactive drugs discussed in chapter 3, produce their effects depends on a knowledge of neural conduction and transmission.

Gross Neuroanatomy

Together with supportive cells called neuroglia, or simply **glial cells**, neurons combine to form the major structures of the **nervous system**. This system can be divided into two major components: the central nervous system and the peripheral nervous system.

The **central nervous system (CNS)** is the portion of the nervous system housed in a bony skeletal covering, the skull and the spinal column. In turn, the CNS can be divided into two structures: the brain and the spinal cord.

The **peripheral nervous system (PNS)** is the part of the nervous system that lies outside this bony protective covering and allows the structures of the CNS to communicate with the sensory receptors, muscles, glands, and other organs of the body. The PNS can be divided into two components: the somatic and autonomic divisions.

The **somatic division** of the PNS carries sensory information to the CNS from the skin and musculature and contains motor fibers responsible for body movement. The **autonomic nervous system (ANS)**, the other part of the PNS and the one integrally involved in learning biofeedback (see chapter 5), is directly involved in the action of those muscles and glands not ordinarily under conscious control: smooth muscles, cardiac muscles, and glands. Examples of smooth muscles are those found in the eye that control curvature of the lens for focus size and pupil size during changes in light intensity. Other smooth muscles are found in the skin (associated with hair follicles), in the walls of blood vessels, and in the walls and sphincters of the digestive and urinary system. Cardiac muscles, as is obvious, are found exclusively in the heart.

Studies of the ANS have clearly demonstrated that it has two major branches that appear to be both anatomically and functionally distinct: the **sympathetic branch** and the **parasympathetic branch**. These two branches exit and enter the CNS via the spinal cord and brain stem at different levels. Cell bodies that give rise to the fibers of the sympathetic nervous system are located in the thoracic and lumbar segments of the cord, and for this reason the sympathetic nervous system has often been referred to as the *thoracicolumbar system*. Similarly, the parasympathetic nervous system is often referred to as the *craniosacral system* because the cell bodies that give rise to the fibers of this autonomic branch are located in the nuclei of the cranial nerves located in the brainstem and the gray matter in the sacral region of the cord.

The shorter, preganglionic motor fibers of the sympathetic branch exit the spinal cord via the ventral root and shortly afterward pass into the **spinal sympathetic ganglia**. At this point, one of three things can occur. First, the preganglionic motor fibers can synapse on cell bodies that make up the ganglia. Second, they can ascend or descend in the sympathetic ganglia and then synapse. Finally, they can pass completely through the spinal sympathetic ganglia and synapse in one of the **sympathetic prevertebral ganglia**. The longer postganglionic motor fibers then proceed to the **target organ**, the organ that they innervate.

The preganglionic motor fibers of the parasympathetic branch do not synapse in a chain of ganglia but rather synapse on cell bodies that make up ganglia that lie very near their target organs. Thus, the postganglionic fibers that arise from these cells travel only a short distance to reach the organ to be innervated. The preganglionic motor fibers of the parasympathetic nervous system are thus long, while the postganglionic fibers are short. This is in contrast to the situation found in the sympathetic branch, where preganglionic fibers are short and the postganglionic fibers are long.

Besides these anatomical differences, a chemical distinction can also be drawn between these two branches of the ANS. Specifically, they use different neurotransmitter substances at the point where they make synaptic contact with the target organ. The preganglionic fibers of both branches are cholinergic. However, most postganglionic fibers of the sympathetic branch are adrenergic, while those of the parasympathetic division are cholinergic. One major exception to this rule involves the sympathetic innervation of the eccrine sweat glands. The sympathetic postganglionic fibers that innervate these glands are cholinergic rather than noradrenergic, as the rule would predict.

Finally, the branches of the ANS differ functionally. Pupil dilation, pi-loerection (the standing up of hair on the back of the neck), increased blood flow to the skeletal muscles, and the release of epinepherine by the adrenal glands (which produces increased heart rate and a rise in blood sugar levels) are but some of the effects mediated by activation of the sympathetic branch. These effects suggest that the sympathetic branch is involved in *catabolic*, or energy-using, processes. Among other effects, stimulation of the parasympathetic branch will result in an increased blood flow to the digestive system, decrease in heart rate, increased salivation, and pupil constriction, all of which are energy-conserving, or *anabolic*, processes. Much more is said about the ANS in chapter 5 when we discuss biofeedback.

The Central Nervous System

Earlier in this chapter we observed that the brain and the spinal cord, the two components of the CNS, were the best-protected structures in the nervous system.

The Spinal Cord

Lying within the spinal column, the spinal cord consists of a butterfly-shaped inner core (gray matter) of cell bodies, dendrites, and unmyelinated axons and an outer layer (white matter) of ascending and descending myelinated axons called **tracts**. These ascending sensory tracts and descending motor tracts act as a conduit, carrying information between some of the sensory organs of the body and the brain and between the brain and the body's motor apparatus.

Research Techniques

Advances in X-ray techniques and computers have led to the development of several methods for studying the structure and function of the living brain. For years, X-rays were used to detect changes in the brain as a function of trauma or disease. However, a single X-ray of the brain was extremely difficult to interpret because it presented us with a two-dimensional view of a three-dimensional structure.

What would happen, however, if you could get the X-ray to take many separate pictures through the head at many different angles and then feed these pictures to a computer that could assemble these many pictures into a single composite? Such a marriage of the X-ray to the advanced computers resulted in the development of **computer-assisted axial tomography** in 1973, better known as the **CAT scan**. The word *axial* refers to the procedure of rotating the X-ray around an imaginary axis running through the patient's head. *Tomography* literally means "written in cuts or slices," referring to the fact that this technique creates a pictorial representation of the brain slice by slice (Graham, 1990). The CAT scan provides us with a clear and accurate picture of any particular area of the brain.

An even more detailed view of the brain's structure can be provided by a process called **magnetic resonance imaging (MRI)**. Although the MRI scanner resembles the CAT scanner, it does not use X-rays. Instead, the person's head is placed in a strong magnetic field, and radio waves are passed through the brain to reveal the distribution of specific types of atoms within a brain area by using the magnetic properties of the nuclei of the different atoms to make clear pictures of the structures of the brain (Pykett, 1982).

Traditional MRI scans can distinguish between white and gray matter, but only on a large scale, like the large fiber tracts of the corpus callosum. Diffusion tensor imaging (DTI), using a modified MRI scanner, can reveal greater detail and small bundles of myelinated axons, by measuring the amount of water molecules moving in parallel to fiber tracts. DTI technology is increasingly used in the study of the neural correlates of consciousness and altered states. DTI research has led to tremendous advances in our knowledge of the commissures, as well as other smaller fiber tracts within the brain (Gazzaniga, 2005).

CAT, MRI, and DTI scans are all good for visualizing a static image of the brain. However, metabolic brain scans provide analyses of the functioning brain. One such metabolic measure is the positron emission tomography (PET) scan, developed in 1979. PET allows the researcher to assess the amount of metabolic activity in various parts of the brain. This information, in turn, is helpful in determining brain function. In a PET scan, a radioactive form of glucose, **2-deoxyglucose (2-DG)**, is injected into the bloodstream of the subject and is allowed to accumulate in the most active cells of the brain. The individual's head is placed in a PET scanner, and as the radioactive isotopes decay, they emit positively charged subatomic particles called **positrons**. These positrons react with other particles to generate gamma rays, which are detected by a series of detectors in the PET scanner (Li & Shen, 1985). It is the function of the PET scanner to determine from where those gamma rays come. The more gamma rays are detected in a certain area of the brain, the more glucose is being used in that area and the more neural activity is occurring there (Phelps & Mazzietta, 1985). A major emerging research application of the PET scanner has been to provide information concerning two of the most fundamental but least well-understood aspects of human behavior, emotion and consciousness (Reiman, Lane, Ahern, Schwartz, & Davidson, 1996).

Similar to PET is SPECT, or single-photon emission computed tomography. SPECT also uses a radioactive tracer, but directly detects gamma particle emission (unlike PET, which provides an indirect measure of gamma activity, by detecting the "precursor" positrons). SPECT scans are used frequently to assess the neural correlates of consciousness and altered states, likely due to lower cost; the radioactive isotope required for SPECT has a longer half-life and is more easily obtained than that required for PET.

However, problems exist for both SPECT and PET scans. One problem is the poor spatial resolution and "blurry" pictures offered by the scans. A second concern, especially in the use of these scans to delineate the neural correlates of consciousness, is the long sample time—up to 30 seconds or longer—required to detect positrons and gamma particles. This not only limits the rate at which stimuli can be presented, the scans may fail altogether to detect rapid neural activity.

A newer technique, **functional MRI (fMRI)**, offers improvements over particle-detection scans in both spatial and temporal resolution. fMRI measures oxygen use across blood vessels in the brain, or **BOLD—the blood oxygen level-dependent** signal. Because the brain cannot store oxygen or glucose, blood must travel to the brain to supply areas when needed. Areas of high activity have demonstrable increases in cerebral blood volume and oxygenated blood flow. The BOLD signal detects the amount of hemoglobin-rich, oxygenated blood compared to hemoglobin-depleted, deoxygenated blood. If exposed to a magnetic field, oxygenated blood is diamagnetic—it will repel the magnet slightly, while deoxygenated blood is paramagnetic—it will attract the magnet. Thus measuring BOLD, along with magnetic activity in an MRI scanner, allows for greater precision in localizing neural activity. Since the oxygen-dependent response for neural activity typically occurs within 4–5 seconds, the temporal resolution of fMRI is greater than that offered by PET scan. fMRI also produces an image with somewhat greater spatial resolution than PET.

Nonetheless, there are criticisms of fMRI. One main concern is that a whole host of stimuli—external events, as well as internal thoughts, perceptions, emotions, and so on—can trigger brain activity, which can lead to increases in BOLD. Indeed, rarely is the brain *not* active, especially in awake, conscious organisms. Thus careful controls must be devised to reveal clear differences between stimuli- or state-evoked changes in neural activity, and ambient neural firing. A second criticism of fMRI is the fact that BOLD is only an indirect measure of neural activity; animal studies have shown that fMRI activity does not always correspond to single-unit activity (e.g., Logethetis, Pauls, Augath, Trinath, & Oeltermann, 2001). However, the accuracy of fMRI in humans may be enhanced by combining with other, more direct measures of neural activity, such as EEG or MEG.

Earlier in this chapter we noted that axons produce action potentials and the synaptic vesicles of the presynaptic neuron release neurotransmitters that interact with receptor sites on the postsynaptic neuron to create postsynaptic potentials. In 1929 an Austrian psychiatrist, Hans Berger, discovered that patterns of this electrical activity could be recorded from electrodes placed at various points on the scalps of human beings. The recorded combined electrical activity from large numbers of neurons and synapses was called an **electroencephalogram**, or **EEG**. The instrument used to record such activity is an **electroencephalograph**. Electrical activity in the form of a voltage increase produces an upward deflection of the recording pen, and a decrease produces a downward movement. This back-and-forth movement of the pen on a moving paper strip of the electroencephalograph gives these changes the appearance of waves. Today, real-time EEG activity can also be monitored in a paperless environment on a computer screen.

In chapter 7 we have much more to say about the electroencephalograph and the typical brain wave activity seen in humans. For now it is sufficient that you understand that what is being recorded is the electrical activity of thousands of neurons and synapses lying in the area below the electrode placed somewhere on the skull. It is also important to point out that brain waves differ in at least two respects: **amplitude** (the height of the wave) and **frequency** (the rate of occurrence).

If an electrode is placed on the skull, perhaps over the auditory or visual cortex, and the subject is presented with an appropriate stimulus, such as an auditory click or a flash of light, we would observe a wave in the EEG record that is distinguishable from the surrounding waves in that it appears just after the stimulus and is of greater amplitude. This large wave is called an **evoked potential**. Had the stimulus been a click and had the electrode been placed over the auditory cortex, the response, called an **auditory-evoked potential**, would represent the voltage changes occurring in the cortex as the burst of impulses enters it from the auditory nucleus of the thalamus.

Similar voltage waves are created by each nucleus in the auditory pathway to the cortex as the stimulus signal travels through the nervous system. The problem with these other evoked potentials is that they are much weaker and remain hidden in the mass of electrical activity reaching the electrode from all simultaneously active brain areas. So while these other evoked potentials existed in theory, it was impossible until recently to observe them.

To solve this problem, electrophysiologists reasoned that while these potentials evoked by a stimulus would always be present, the other potentials in the brain related to other ongoing events were only randomly related to the click-evoked potentials. This would suggest that if the stimulus were presented repeatedly instead of just once and if the results of these repeated records were stored and combined by a computer, the random activity should cancel out, leaving only the click-evoked potentials. The process by which the various records are combined is called **signal averaging** even though it really consists of simply adding the voltages together algebraically. Typically, this process of signal averaging is carried out over a period of 500 milliseconds (msec). The records are termed **averaged evoked potentials** (Carlson, 2009; Graham, 1990). As more records are averaged, the random activity does drop out and the smaller potentials are clearly seen. As researchers have become more familiar with these evoked potential waves, they have given each its own designation, such as P-300 (the positive wave form that occurs about 300 msec following stimulus onset) or N-80 (the negative wave form that occurs about 80 msec following stimulus onset).

Magnetoencephalography (MEG) measures the minute magnetic field produced by the transfer of ions that occurs during action potentials. Physicists have developed super-conducting quantum interference devices (SQUIDs) that can detect even these tiny magnetic fields. Although EEG and MEG are essentially measuring the same thing—actions potentials generated by populations of cortical neurons—there are advantages to MEG. One main advantage is that MEG can provide greater spatial resolution, primarily due to its enhanced ability to detect activity in neurons farther removed from the scalp. MEG detects activity in deep sulci, while EEG is limited to detecting activity only in neurons directly beneath the skull.

The Brain

The brain is the central character in our continuing story of the biological basis of consciousness. In describing its organization as that part of the CNS that is most integrally involved in consciousness, it would be helpful to include some artificial boundaries. For our purpose it will be sufficient to divide the brain into two parts: the **brainstem** and the **cerebrum**.

If you look closely at Figure 2.2, you will note that the lowest part of the brain retains roughly the shape of the spinal cord, although it enlarges somewhat as you move upward. This part of the brain, from the most inferior level to the superior end of the thalamus, constitutes the brainstem. At this point the tubular form appears to be lost, and the brain becomes greatly enlarged. This part of the brain that lies superior to the thalamus is known as the cerebrum.

In both of these divisions we will find a large number of structures that in turn are composed of **nuclei** (clusters of cell bodies) and **fiber tracts** (groups of axons). As you read the remainder of this section on the brain, keep in mind that this boundary between the brainstem and the cerebrum is an artificial one, something that we have concocted but for which nature has little or no regard. One final suggestion to the reader is in order: Refer frequently to Figures 2.2, 2.3, and 2.4 as you read the following section to help you better understand both the structure and organization of the brain.

The Brainstem

Beginning at the most inferior end of the brain and moving upward, the first major structure we find is the **medulla oblongata**. Here, some of the cranial nerves exit and enter the CNS. Here also are located a number of nuclei that regulate many of the life-support systems, including the cardiovascular

Figure 2.2 • A Midsagittal View of the Human Brain

system, the respiratory system, and skeletal muscle tonus (Smith, Ellenberger, Ballanyi, Richter, & Feldman, 1991). From Figure 2.2, it should be clear that all fibers passing between the brain and the spinal cord must pass through this division.

As the motor fibers of the corticospinal tracts, which originate in the motor region of the cerebral cortex, approach the spinal cord, they **decussate**, or cross over to the contralateral (opposite) side. This means that information arising in the left hemisphere (left side of the brain) controls movement on the right side of the body. Similarly, information arising in the right hemisphere controls movement on the left side of the body. We say more about this later in this chapter as we discuss the left-brain/right-brain phenomenon.

Finally, deep in the center of this part of the brainstem lie the beginnings of the **ascending reticular activating system (ARAS)**. Anatomically, it begins as a tight, complex network of nuclei, axons, and dendrites and retains this form until it reaches the tegmentum. At this point, it branches out, sending projections to the thalamus and the cerebral cortex. Functionally, the ARAS is involved with sleep and arousal, selective attention, muscle tonus, and vital reflexes. We say more about the role of the reticular formation in sleep and arousal in chapters 7 ("Sleep and Dreams") and 8 ("Sensory Deprivation") (Turner & Knapp, 1995).

Immediately rostral (toward the head) to the medulla lies the **pons**, which is exactly what its name implies (in Latin): a "bridge" between the spinal cord, the medulla, and higher brain centers and between the brainstem and the cerebellar cortex. The cranial nerves serving the face also exit and enter the CNS here. Several nuclei that are thought to have a sleep-regulatory function are located in the pons.

Although it forms approximately one-third of the brain volume, the **cerebellum**, which lies dorsal (toward the back) to the pons, does not play a significant role in consciousness. Its function is primarily that of making certain that movements are made smoothly and accurately, with appropriate speed and direction.

Ascending fiber tracts continue to the next major structure, the midbrain, which is usually divided into two parts: the dorsal **tectum** and the ventral **tegmentum**. The principle structures found in the tectum are the *superior colliculi* and the *inferior colliculi*. Collectively, these structures are referred to as the *corpora quadrigemina*. The superior and inferior colliculi function as primitive processing centers for visual and auditory information, respectively. In addition to several important motor nuclei, the tegmentum also contains the superior end of the reticular formation.

As we ascend to the higher levels of the brain, it is clear that the brain expands, losing the tubelike form it had in the lower brainstem and the spinal cord (see Figure 2.2). At this point, the upper part of the brainstem is surrounded by the beginnings of the cerebrum. The **hypothalamus** is located at the base of this region just superior to the pituitary stalk and gland. It is composed of a number of nuclei and, although it is a small structure, its nuclei have been implicated in a wide range of behavioral functions. The *hypothalamus* is important in such diverse behavioral functions as hunger, thirst, maintenance of water and salt balance in the body, temperature regulation, and sexual behavior. Most important, the hypothalamus is central in the study of consciousness, sleep, and waking (discussed in chapter 7). The hypothalamus also controls, in part at least, the autonomic nervous system (discussed in regard to biofeedback in chapter 5).

Lying just dorsal to the hypothalamus is the bilobed structure called the **thalamus**. Like the hypothalamus, the thalamus is composed of a number of nuclei. Some of these nuclei receive sensory information from the various sensory tracts and project fibers to the appropriate sensory projection area of the cortex. These are sometimes called *sensory relay nuclei*. Separate sensory relay nuclei are found here for all of the sensory modalities except olfaction, the sense of smell. Other thalamic nuclei receive input from other fibers within the thalamus and project to specific regions of the cortex. Finally, a third type of thalamic nuclei projects diffusely to widespread regions of the cortex and to other thalamic nuclei.

The Cerebrum

Leaving the thalamus and moving upward, we next locate the cerebrum, which is the most highly developed division of the human brain. It consists of three primary structures: the **limbic system**, the **basal ganglia**, and the **cerebral hemispheres**.

The basal ganglia are badly misnamed. Because they lie deep in the brain and are therefore a part of the CNS, they should have been called the basal nuclei. At any rate, the basal ganglia consist of nuclei involved in the control of motor responses. The limbic system is also composed of a large number of interconnected structures involved in emotional behavior, motivation, and memory. Both the basal ganglia and the limbic system have minimal effects on consciousness.

Earlier, we observed that the entire CNS was essentially bilateral in symmetry. The left and right halves of the brainstem actually do not separate, however, until we reach the level of the thalamus. The cerebrum looks like separate, mirror-image halves connected by bundles of transverse fibers. These halves of the cerebrum are called the **cerebral hemispheres**. The bundles of fibers that serve as connectors between the hemispheres are commissures, the largest of which is the **corpus callosum**. The precise role of the cerebral commissures is as yet unknown. Our best guess at this point is that they serve as a communication channel between the hemispheres through which hemispheric function is synchronized and duplication of effort is prevented (Springer & Deutsch, 1997).

The surface of the hemispheres is covered by **cortex,** which in humans is highly convoluted. These convolutions are composed of **sulci** (small grooves), **fissures** (large grooves), and **gyri** (bulges between adjacent sulci or fissures). By using these landmarks, it is possible to divide the surface into four lobes: **frontal, parietal, temporal,** and **occipital.** Figure 2.3 shows the division of the surface of one hemisphere. The **central sulcus,** or the fissure of Rolando, separates the frontal and parietal lobes. The other major fissure, called the **lateral sulcus** or **Sylvian fissure**, separates the temporal lobe from the frontal and parietal lobes.

Besides looking at the hemispheres in terms of lobes, we can also view them in terms of *projection areas,* or *zones.* At least a part of each of these lobes is known to serve a different sensory or motor function. The anterior part of the parietal lobe is associated with a somatosensory function, while the

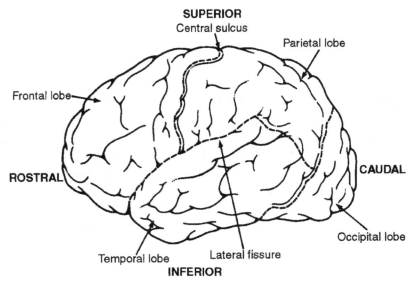

Figure 2.3 • Dominant Lateral Cortical Surface with Lobes

Figure 2.4 • Dominant Lateral Cortical Surface with Lobes and Projection Areas

posterior part of the frontal lobe is concerned with motor function. The occipital lobe is a visual center; the temporal lobe is the auditory cortical center (see Figure 2.4).

Not all the human cortex, however, is committed to the specific senses or to motor function. That part of the cortex not so committed is generally called the *association*, or *silent, cortex*. Some researchers, such as A. R. Luria (1966), make a distinction between secondary and tertiary association cortex. Found adjacent to the primary projection areas, the *secondary association cortex* areas are higher-level processing centers for the specific sensory information coming into the primary areas. These secondary association areas are believed to be sense-modality specific; thus, damage to one of them produces perceptual disorders restricted to a specific sensory modality.

Sensory modality specificity is lost in the *tertiary association areas,* which are located at the borders of the parietal, temporal, and occipital secondary association areas (see Figure 2.4). Here the various sensory areas overlap, and combinations of sensations become higher-order perceptions such that tactile and kinesthetic impulses are built up into perceptions of form and size and then associated with visual information from the same objects (Springer & Deutsch, 1997). Of more interest to us, perhaps, is the fact that this is the level at which asymmetries in the cerebral hemispheres occur. Such asymmetry may account for the fact that the left and right hemispheres handle different processes.

As the parietal, temporal, and occipital lobes are to the sensory modalities, so the frontal lobe is to the motor system. The posterior (rear) portion of the frontal lobes contains the **primary motor cortex**. Immediately anterior (front) to the primary motor cortex, or **motor strip**, lies the secondary motor area, more generally referred to as the **premotor cortex**. Higher-level motor organization is thought to be the role of this area of the cortex. Clinical support for this theory comes from the fact that damage to the premotor area results in disturbances in the organization of movements. As we demonstrate shortly, damage to a particular part of this premotor cortex on the left side, called Broca's area, produces a disorganization of speech called Broca's aphasia. The remainder of the frontal lobe is often referred to as the **prefrontal area** or **frontal granular cortex**. Clinical findings, by no means conclusive, suggest that this area is involved in intellectual functions, such as the planning and control of actions, and in the control or inhibition of emotional tendencies.

Toward a Biological Basis of Consciousness

In the beginning of this chapter we noted that psychologists, in discussing the concept of consciousness, rarely refer to its physiological basis. Despite this fact, it has long been recognized that states of awareness or consciousness are products of the brain. Most people who have watched boxing matches, for example, know that a single blow delivered to the head may be sufficient to render the recipient unconscious for several minutes. Medical professionals have observed that severe brain damage, such as might result from an accident or major illness, may reduce the individual to little more than a vegetable—an organism with a series of simple reflexes but with no awareness or consciousness. Finally, more focal damage to specific regions of the brain has been shown to produce a loss of particular functions, abilities, and even some aspects of awareness or consciousness.

Historical Background

To arrive at the point at which a scientist could suggest, without fear of being excommunicated from the scientific community, that "both the structure and function of ... two 'half-brains' underlie in some part the two modes of consciousness that coexist within each one of us" (Ornstein, 1986, p. 20) has had to await considerable philosophical speculation and scientific endeavor over the years. It would first have to be shown that the assignment of particular mental functions, such as consciousness, to specific regions of the brain, *cerebral localization*, was a scientifically legitimate enterprise. Second, if we assume that two different modes of consciousness are housed in these two cerebral hemispheres, then logic dictates we should see evidence of differences both in function, *cerebral specialization*, and in structure, *cerebral asymmetry*. Time and space do not permit an exhaustive litany of these developments. However, some of the most important advancements in this area can be recounted.

Pinning consciousness to some biological structure has long been a favorite pastime for scientists and philosophers alike. For example, over four centuries ago, French philosopher René Descartes (1596–1650) concluded that the pineal gland, a small gland located at the base of the brain, was the seat of consciousness. His selection of the pineal gland appears to have been based on a belief in the unity of consciousness, and Descartes's anatomical observations that the pineal gland was the only brain structure that was not bilaterally represented as two separate structures.

The concept of cerebral localization, the idea that a particular function could be assigned to a specific region of the brain, began to receive serious attention by the early 1800s. Although he was dismissed as a quack in many scientific circles, Franz Gall (1758–1828), a German anatomist, and his student Johann Spurzheim (1776–1832) were among the first to suggest that specific psychological traits should reside in specific brain locations. More specifically, Gall and Spurzheim proposed that speech was controlled by centers located in the frontal lobes of the cerebrum. What upset the scientific community and eventually led these two scientists into disrepute was their insistence that the shape of the skull reflects the underlying brain tissue and hence the relative strengths of an individual's mental abilities and emotional characteristics. This area was referred to as *phrenology*.

Specifically, it was the work of the French physiologist Pierre Jean Marie Flourens (1794–1867) that spelled the demise of Gall and Spurzheim's phrenology. On the basis of his observations of the behavior of pigeons after the removal of sections of their brain, Flourens held that both common and specific actions are traceable to various portions of the brain, thereby rejecting the notion of exact or precise localization.

This setback to the supporters of the cerebral localization position proved to be only temporary; in 1861, Paul Broca (1824–1880), the noted French surgeon and anthropologist, presented two cases of patients independently diagnosed as *aphasic,* that is, having a loss of articulate speech. Both of Broca's patients had suffered damage to the left frontal part of the brain; the right side of the brain in each case was intact. Broca concluded that the damage to the third convolution of the left frontal lobe, now referred to in the literature as **Broca's area** (see Figure 2.5), had produced the aphasia and therefore was the center of articulate speech, at least for right-handed people. Broca's findings served to sway sentiments away from Flourens's position and back to the position of cerebral localization.

Approximately 10 years later, in 1870, Gustav Theodor Fritsch (1838–1927) and Edward Hitzig (1838–1907), German physiologists, provided further evidence to support the cerebral localization position. By applying a very weak current to specific areas of the cortex of dogs, they were able to observe localized muscle contractions of small muscle groups. With this technique, Fritsch and Hitzig were able to develop maps of brain function.

Finally, by the 1930s, to treat epileptic patients who had not responded to drug therapy regimens, Wilder Penfield (1891–1976) and his colleagues at the Montreal Neurological Institute pioneered the use of surgery to remove a

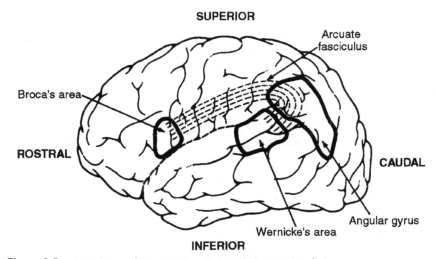

Figure 2.5 • Lateral View of Human Brain with Speech Centers Identified

brain site where abnormal brain wave activity was initiated. While their technique proved to be successful in many cases, most surgeons were hesitant to use it where brain tissue near the parts of the brain controlling speech and language was involved. After all, why substitute one debilitating syndrome (loss of speech) for another (epilepsy)? Clearly, what was needed was a method for determining with great precision the anatomical centers for these functions. To meet this need, Penfield employed direct electrical stimulation to exposed brain tissue to map the precise location of brain centers that controlled speech and language in a given patient (Penfield & Roberts, 1959).

While it is probably not the first thing you think about when you wake up, you are probably aware that humans have a bilaterally symmetrical body plan. Put another way, if we could pass a knife down your body along the median plane, we would have two equivalent halves: a left side and a right side. You already know that you have two legs, two feet, and so on—one on the left side and one on the right. The human brain also gives the appearance of following this same general body plan; the right and left cerebral hemispheres communicate via the several bands of transverse nerve fibers that cross the median plane.

Are these two cerebral hemispheres identical? In 1868 the British neurologist John Hughlings Jackson (1835–1911) responded to this question in the negative, at least as far as function was concerned (Jackson, 1958). In that year, Jackson proposed his notion of the *"leading" hemisphere,* which has been identified as the intellectual precursor of the concept of *cerebral dominance.* On the basis of the earlier work of Broca, which demonstrated that damage to the left cerebral hemisphere left patients without the ability to speak even though the right hemisphere remained intact, Jackson concluded that rather than the two hemispheres being duplicates, one hemisphere—in most people the left—was the leading side.

In the years following Jackson's pronouncement, research efforts were focused on the localization of function in the leading or left hemisphere of the brain. The German neurologist Karl Wernicke (1848–1905) discovered a language loss that differed from that described by Broca. While Broca's patients were unable to produce articulate speech, those of Wernicke were unable to understand the speech of others. The brain area implicated by Wernicke, the back part of the temporal lobe of the left hemisphere, also differed from that identified by Broca (see Figure 2.5).

Early studies also suggested that the left cerebral hemisphere was involved in certain *apraxias* (ideomotor and possibly ideational). **Apraxia** is the inability to perform certain learned or purposeful movements despite the absence of paralysis or sensory loss (Heilman, Rothi, & Kertesz, 1983; Kimura, 1977).

Most early researchers chose to focus their research efforts on localizing functions in the left cerebral hemisphere, while ignoring the right side, despite Jackson's admonition that such a one-sided view of the localization of function was incorrect. Jackson based his warning on his own clinical observation (Jackson, 1958) of a patient with a right parietal lobe tumor who evidenced great difficulty in recognizing people, places, and things. Still other evidence suggested that singing and general musical ability were controlled by the right hemisphere.

Split Brain, Split Consciousness

Although the split-brain procedure was not introduced until the early 1940s, its theoretical effects on consciousness were being argued as early as the mid 19th century by such prominent investigators as Gustav Theodor Fechner (1801–1887), the German experimental psychologist, and William McDougall (1871–1938), the British psychologist and first social psychologist. Fechner argued that such a surgical procedure, were it possible, would result in a doubling of consciousness. Localizing consciousness in the cerebral hemispheres, Fechner argued that the integrity of the brain was necessary to the unity of the consciousness.

McDougall challenged Fechner's position, arguing that the unity of consciousness would remain intact even if the split-brain procedure were performed. To punctuate his point, McDougall offered to undergo such a surgical procedure himself, were he ever to become the victim of some incurable disease. What he hoped to demonstrate by this was that his personality would not be split by such a procedure and that his consciousness would remain intact (Springer & Deutsch, 1997). McDougall never had the opportunity to prove his point, but this was not the last time this argument was to arise.

It was not until the early 1940s that Van Wagenen, a neurosurgeon, performed the first split-brain operations on human patients in a last-ditch effort to control life-threatening seizures in some epileptics (Van Wagenen & Herren, 1940). In the split-brain procedure, the brain is divided into two halves—a left and a right hemisphere. To accomplish this, the transverse bundles of fibers that connect the cerebral hemispheres (the corpus callosum) are surgically severed.

Perhaps the most surprising observation was made by Akelaitis (1941, 1944), who carried out an extensive postoperative study of Van Wagenen's patients. Akelaitis observed that these patients evidenced few, if any, deficits in perceptual and motor abilities, and their everyday behaviors appeared to be unaltered. Unfortunately for some of these patients, the surgical procedure did little to change the condition that was responsible for the operation in the first place. Van Wagenen soon gave up the use of the procedure with epileptics. It should be noted that Van Wagenen's surgical procedure varied considerably from patient to patient but usually consisted of cutting only the anterior half of the corpus callosum and rarely the anterior commissure (Springer & Deutsch, 1997).

These negative results, however, did not dampen research interest in the split-brain procedure and its effects. Thus, in the early 1950s, Myers and Sperry (1958), using cats instead of human subjects, demonstrated that visual information presented to one hemisphere in a cat that had undergone a commissurotomy was not available to the other hemisphere. Each hemisphere functioned independently, as if it were a complete brain. Myers and Sperry concluded that cutting the corpus callosum had kept the information presented to one hemisphere isolated from the other hemisphere. It was only natural that this initial finding was to open up an entirely new set of research questions concerning the extent of the independence of the two hemispheres and the role of the corpus callosum in the integration of the cerebral hemisphere functions in the intact brain.

Encouraged by the Myers and Sperry animal research findings and the Van Wagenen procedure, two California neurosurgeons, Bogen and Vogel (as reported in Springer & Deutsch, 1997), were led to reevaluate the use of the split-brain surgery in the treatment of epileptics with life-threatening seizures who had not responded to drug therapy. In their surgical procedure, sectioning of the corpus callosum was incomplete, leaving the **anterior, hippocampal, habenular**, and **posterior** commissures intact (see Figure 2.6). This left sufficient transverse fibers intact to allow for hemispheric communication.

Over the next several years Bogen and Vogel performed some 24 complete commissurotomies on such patients. Postoperative observations demonstrated that, relative to seizure activity, the results of the surgical intervention exceeded expectations. Additionally, the operation appeared to leave the patients' personality, intelligence, and general behavior unaffected. However, when these patients were more closely scrutinized in Sperry's laboratory at the California Institute of Technology, their everyday behavior and their performance on specialized tests devised by the experimenters revealed some

41

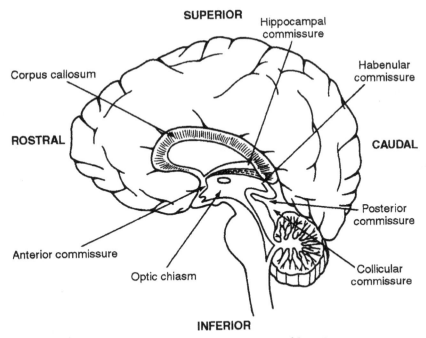

Figure 2.6 • Midsagittal View of the Human Brain with Location of Commissures

distinct behavioral changes. For this work, Sperry received the 1981 Nobel Prize in Physiology/Medicine.

What were some of these important observations? Sperry and his colleagues observed that these patients showed a strong tendency to favor the right side of the body, which, as you will recall, is controlled by the dominant left half of the brain. Spontaneous activity was frequently observed on the right side of the body but appeared to be lacking on the left side. Additionally, responsiveness to sensory stimulation of the left half of the body was diminished.

More specific tests of sensory function initially suggested that, while the dominant left cerebral hemisphere appeared functionally normal with respect to vision and tactile perception, the right side was severely limited. However, when patients were provided with a nonverbal means of reporting their experiences, their visual and tactile perception controlled by the right side was practically as good as that controlled by the dominant left hemisphere. Clearly, the initial sensory differences observed were due to the fact that the speech centers of the brain are located in the left hemisphere.

Specific tests of motor function in these patients showed that, while the hemispheres exercised normal control over the contralateral (opposite-sided) hand, they had less than normal control over the ipsilateral (same-sided) hand. When a conflict develops between the two cerebral hemispheres, their individual inputs dictating distinctly different movements for the same hand, the hemisphere opposite the hand generally takes charge and overrides any input from the ipsilateral hemisphere.

In examining the effects of such surgery on intelligence, perception, and emotion, these investigators observed that the surgery left each patient with two separate minds—that is, with two separate spheres of consciousness. The dominant left hemisphere showed a clear advantage in both verbal and mathematical tasks. However, the right cerebral hemisphere did not prove to be inferior to the left in all respects. On certain spatial tasks, for example, the right hemisphere showed a clear superiority. Such patients, with right-brain superiority, were able to arrange blocks to match a picture design or draw a three-dimensional cube better with their left hand than their right, which had been deprived of input from the right hemisphere (Sperry, 1996). More recent research has replicated these findings, and taken together, these symptoms have become known as the **disconnection syndrome** (Proverbio, Zani, Gazzaniga, & Mangun, 1994; Reuter-Lorenz, Nozawa, Gazzaniga, & Hughes, 1995; Seymour, Reuter-Lorenz, & Gazzaniga, 1994). Additionally, both hemispheres appeared to be equally capable of independently generating an emotional reaction (Sperry, 1966).

Once again, the argument concerning the effect of physically splitting the brain with respect to the unity of the consciousness was raised. This time, however, the adversaries were able to call on a considerable body of empirical evidence. Roger Sperry used this evidence to support his position that the split-brain procedure produced a doubling of the individual's consciousness.

> Everything we have seen so far indicates that the surgery has left these people with two separate minds, that is, two separate spheres of consciousness.
>
> What is experienced in the right hemisphere seems to lie entirely outside the realm of experiencing of the left hemisphere. (Sperry, 1966, p. 121)

According to Sperry, the unity of consciousness in the split-brain patient is an illusion. This illusion exists because the two cerebral hemispheres share a number of things, including the same position in space, the same sensory organs, and the same everyday experiences (Springer & Deutsch, 1997).

The unity of the mind and consciousness in the split-brain patient remained intact according to Eccles (1977). Eccles distinguished between *consciousness*, which both humans and animals share, and *mind*, which is uniquely human and includes language, thought, and culture. For Eccles, all that can be identified as exclusively human resides in the left hemisphere, where thought and the speech centers are housed and where the brain interacts with the mind. In the intact individual, the right hemisphere, which Eccles referred to as the **minor hemisphere**, is an unconscious part of the brain. Under normal conditions the contributions of the right hemisphere to all perceptions, experiences, and memories are transmitted to the **dominant hemisphere**, the left hemisphere, via the corpus callosum.

Additionally, the minor hemisphere may generate special neuronal activities that provide it with some communication to the self-conscious mind. In the split-brain cases in which the communication system is severed, it becomes clear that the right hemisphere is always an unconscious part of the brain that relies on the linkage through the corpus callosum to receive from and give information to the conscious self (Eccles, 1977).

Having reviewed the extensive body of literature dealing with the role of the right hemisphere in language, Gazzaniga (1983) concluded that the right hemisphere of the normal brain is nonlinguistic. Any indications of linguistic ability in the right hemisphere of split-brain patients can be attributed to early left hemisphere damage resulting in a shifting of language functions to the right hemisphere.

Supporting evidence for this position comes from one of a group of split brain patients operated on by Donald Wilson of Dartmouth Medical School and studied by Michael Gazzaniga and his colleagues. This patient, identified as Patient P.S., was a right-handed male, 16 years old at the time of his surgery. His preoperative history indicated considerable damage to the left hemisphere at an early age (Gazzaniga & LeDoux, 1978). Because of the normal location of the speech centers in the left hemisphere, the typical split-brain patient is unable to name objects presented only to his right hemisphere. One can imagine the investigators' surprise upon discovering that, by using his left hand to arrange letters selected from a Scrabble game set, Patient P.S. was able to spell the names of objects flashed to his right hemisphere. Initially, P.S.'s right hemisphere could communicate verbally only by spelling with the Scrabble letters. However, further evidence suggested that P.S. was speaking from his right hemisphere as well (Gazzaniga, Volpe, Smylie, Wilson, & LeDoux, 1979).

The importance of this finding lies in the fact that this procedure was also used with this patient to study the right hemisphere's awareness of the world. The researchers' intention was to ask subjective questions of each hemisphere separately and compare the results. To accomplish this, Patient P.S. was asked a question in which the key word (or words) was replaced by the word "blank." Then the missing part of the question was presented visually to the left or the right cerebral hemisphere. For example, the experimenter might ask, "How much do you like 'blank'?" Then the name "Liz" (the name of his girlfriend) would be presented in the left visual field (to the right cerebral hemisphere), and the subject's response was awaited. When the word was presented to the left hemisphere, the subject responded verbally; when it was presented to the right hemisphere, he was allowed to point to a number from 1 ("like very much") to 5 ("dislike very much") or to spell out his answer with the Scrabble letters when the rating scale was inappropriate.

The results of this study clearly demonstrated that P.S.'s right hemisphere was able to respond to the questions asked of it. The answers and evaluations of this hemisphere, however, sometimes differed from those of the dominant left side. For example, the left hemisphere stated that P.S. wanted to be a draftsman when he grew up, yet his right hemisphere spelled out "automobile race" when asked what job it would pick. During the height of the Watergate affair, the widest divergence between the two hemispheres on the like–dislike scale occurred in response to the item "Nixon"; the right hemisphere expressed "dislike," while the left hemisphere expressed "like."

Gazzaniga and LeDoux also observed that the answers to several questions varied in several different testing sessions. The patient seemed to be in a better mood when the opinions and values of the two hemispheres were similar. On the basis of these observations, these investigators concluded that each of P.S.'s hemispheres had a sense of self as well as its own processing system for the subjective evaluation of current events, the planning for future events, the setting of response priorities, and the production of personal responses (LeDoux, Wilson, & Gazzaniga, 1977).

The findings of both the Sperry (1974) and Gazzaniga (1983) laboratories suggest that the split-brain procedure produces some serious behavioral side effects, not the least of which is that the patient evidences behavior of two separate individuals. Recall, however, that in initially describing the results of this surgery, we observed that without the special behavioral tasks devised by Sperry and his colleagues, these behavioral changes might have gone unnoticed. Such patients' everyday speech, language comprehension, personality, and motor coordination remain remarkably intact.

Clearly, some unifying mechanism or mechanisms must exist that explain how the two separate hemispheres in the split-brain patient act as a unit during the individual's everyday activities. As it turns out, a variety of such mechanisms may well compensate for the lack of intact cerebral commissures. Some of these mechanisms have to do with the concept of decussation. Earlier in this chapter we discussed the fact that many of the ascending and descending fiber tracts within the CNS would decussate, or cross over to the opposite side of the body, at some point between origin and terminus. This may involve a complete crossover of fibers or only a partial crossover. In the case of the visual system, half the fibers from each eye decussate to the contralateral (or opposite) side of the brain. This occurs at the **optic chiasma**. The other half of the fibers from each eye remain on the ipsilateral (or same) side and project only to the ipsilateral hemisphere.

Visual Field

While this seems fairly simple, there is still more, namely, the notion of a **visual field**, which is the surrounding area projecting to the eye and forming an image on the retina. With a subject fixating a point, the part of the visual field to the right of the point of fixation falls on the temporal (toward the side) half of the retina of the left eye and on the nasal (toward the nose) half of the retina of the right eye. At the optic chiasma, the fibers from the nasal half of the retina of the right eye decussate and combine with the fibers from the temporal half of the retina to send information concerning the right visual field to the primary visual cortex of the left cerebral hemisphere. Information concerning the left visual field is projected only to the primary visual cortex of the right hemisphere in the same manner (see Figure 2.7).

Finally, the visual areas of the left and right hemisphere normally communicate through the corpus callosum. If the corpus callosum is cut, however, as it is in the split-brain patient, and if the eyes and head are kept from moving, then each hemisphere would be able to see only half of the visual world. In everyday life, however, how many situations exist in which the head and eyes are not free to move? The conjugate eye movements, combined with the fact that each eye projects to both hemispheres, serve to establish unity of the visual world for the split-brain patient. Thus, even without the communication between the left and right visual cortex, the unity can be maintained, at least in part, as the eye movements initiated by one hemisphere to bring an

FIELDS OF VISION

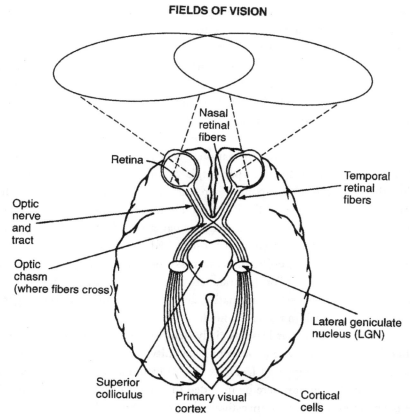

Figure 2.7 • Primary Visual Pathways to the Brain

object into direct view serve to make the information available to the other hemisphere as well.

A study by Levy, Trevarthen, and Sperry (1972) suggests a second mechanism of unity. In this study, an object was placed in the right or left hand of the split-brain patient, who was then asked to identify it on the basis of cutaneous information only. These investigators observed that these patients responded as though they were conscious of stimulation from both sides of space. Touch information, which is primarily responsible for such sensory experiences, is carried principally by the lemniscal tracts, fibers that carry information from the skin receptors to the somatosensory cortex, the part of the cortex responsible for processing cutaneous information. Almost but not all these fibers convey such information to the contralateral hemisphere by decussating at the level of the medulla. The remaining fibers project to the ipsilateral somatosensory cortex; thus, both hemispheres receive touch information.

Once again, even in the case of the split-brain patient, we have a situation in which both hemispheres receive information from both sides of the body. Because this ipsilateral information is generally incomplete and inadequate, the split-brain patient, who has only that information to work with, is generally unable to identify verbally an object held in the left hand. Nonetheless, these ipsilateral pathways do provide at least partial information.

One final way in which information may be made available to both hemispheres, even in the split-brain patient, is through the commissures located below the cortical level. The commissurotomy severs the transverse fibers that connect the cortical level of the brain. While these are the major fibers connecting the hemispheres, there are other, smaller commissures located below the level of the cortex that connect those paired structures that are a part of the brainstem. Thus, the **collicular commissures**, which connect the superior colliculi of the two halves of the brain, are able to provide each hemisphere of the split-brain patient with information about the location of objects, regardless of where they fall in the visual field.

These mechanisms at least partially help to explain why the split-brain patient's everyday behavior appears to have unity. On the basis of their extensive research, Gazzaniga and LeDoux (1978) would argue that the language system of the left hemisphere be included in any list of unity mechanisms in the normal brain. For these investigators, at least, this is the mechanism that makes most of us feel like single, purposeful individuals.

Can Consciousness Be Enhanced by Increasing Hemispheric Communication?

While Sperry, Bogan, Gazzaniga, and others have shown that splitting the brain can essentially "split consciousness," at least to some extent, what would happen if we were to increase signaling across the hemispheres—could that result in a type of "superconsciousness"? A variety of studies have attempted to address this issue. Recent work from Gazzaniga's laboratory has focused on assessing 1) the unique functions of each hemisphere and 2) how the intact corpus callosum integrates information across the hemispheres (Gazzaniga, 2005; Roser & Gazzaniga, 2006). Other research is evaluating differences between strongly handed and weakly handed individuals, as handedness may serve as an index of the degree of brain lateralization (e.g., Witelson, 1985). Recent research from several laboratories has focused on investigating behavioral and cognitive benefits of purposefully promoting bilateral hemispheric activation, by presenting dichotic stimuli. The next section evaluates these latter two experimental paradigms more closely.

Research on Handedness

Hand preference can be measured empirically with a 10-item scale known as the Edinburgh Handedness Inventory (EHI; Oldfield, 1971). The EHI asks the degree to which each hand is used (always right, always left, usually left, usually right, or no preference) when performing tasks including writing, holding a knife, throwing, and using a broom. "Always right" responses are scored with +10 points, "always left" responses are scored as −10 points, "usually right" earns +5 points, "usually left" earns −5 points, and "no preference" earns 0 points. Points are added, and scores greater than +80 indicate strong right handedness, scores greater than −80 indicate strong left handedness, and scores ranging from −80 to +80 indicate mixed handedness, or no strong hand preference (also called "weakly handed"). It should be noted that "mixed handed" is *not* the same as "ambidextrous," since ambidextrous implies an equal preference for both hands in all tasks. Mixed-handed individuals receive scores less than ±80, most often for reporting that they prefer one or the other hand exclusively for certain tasks, as opposed to switching between hands with equal preference.

Based on scores from the EHI and similar handedness inventories, it has been known for some time that mixed-handed individuals have a greater corpus callosum size. Witelson (1985) performed post-mortem analyses on 50 male and female brains, and noted that "non-consistent right handers," that is, individuals with positive scores less than 80 on the EHI, had larger a overall callosal area, primarily in the isthmus, which provides hemispheric connections for the posterior parietal and superior temporal cortices. Interestingly, there were gender and age effects on callosal size; male mixed-handers had larger corpus callosum size compared to females, and this effect decreased with age. Habib and colleagues (1991) confirmed these findings using MRI data in 53 healthy male and females, noting larger corpus callosum size especially in mixed-handed males. While it is unclear why mixed-handedness may affect corpus callosum size differently in males and females, it has been suggested that exposure to sex hormones during development may play a role (e.g., Fitch et al., 1991; Habib et al., 1991).

More recently, a variety of research has noted advantages of mixed-handedness on tasks ranging from memory to causal inference. Let's evaluate some of that research briefly. On tasks of memory, several studies have shown that mixed-handers have better episodic memory recall than strong handers (Christman, 1995; Lyle, McCabe, & Roediger, 2008; Propper & Christman, 2004; Propper, Christman, & Phaneuf, 2005). This research is especially interesting in light of findings demonstrating that episodic memory is disrupted in split-brain patients (e.g., Cronin-Golomb, Gabrieli, & Keane, 1996; Zaidel, 1995). Several tests of episodic memory have been used, including free recall of previously presented words (Lyle et al., 2008; Propper & Christman, 2004; Propper et al., 2005), memory for the source (auditory or visual) of the presented word (Lyle et al., 2008), and recall of autobiographical memories kept in personal journals (Propper et al., 2005). Improvement in episodic memory for mixed-handed individuals is in agreement with that predicted by Tulving's Hemispheric Encoding/Retrieval Asymmetry (HERA) model (Tulving, 1985, 1986; Tulving et al., 1994). The HERA model suggests that encoding of information is differentially processed by the left hemisphere, while retrieval requires right hemisphere. Increased communication between the hemispheres could facilitate performance on explicit tests of episodic memory, by facilitating retrieval by the right hemisphere of information encoded by the left. However, further research is needed to test these and other hypotheses generated by the HERA model (e.g., Owen, 2003).

Gazzaniga and colleagues (Roser, Fugelsange, Dunbar, Corballis, & Gazzaniga, 2005; Fugelsang, Roser, Corballis, Gazzangiga, & Dunbar, 2005) noted that the left hemisphere can draw causal inferences (if you move an object, another object may move), but the right hemisphere was necessary for perceiving causality (whether or not the movement of an object was caused by movement of another object). Interestingly, strongly handed individuals have been found to believe divine-Creator accounts ("creationism") of human origin over evolution, even when presented with scientific facts documenting evolution (Neibauer, Christman, Reid, & Garvey, 2004). It could be that that greater hemispheric integration in mixed-handers affords an advantage for assimilating new information, to update belief systems (causality) more readily.

Taken together, these results suggest some distinct differences between strongly and weakly handed individuals, likely due to increased hemispheric integration for mixed-handers. The next section addresses whether promoting hemispheric integration might provide a benefit, even in strongly handed individuals.

Research on Bilateral Brain Activation

Our discussion here might be remiss if we did not mention, at least briefly, the history of research into bilateral brain activity promoted by eye movements. In 1989, Francine Shapiro published an article in the *Journal of Traumatic Stress* in which she reported decreases in her own negative emotions after engaging in bilateral eye movements (looking side-to-side as she walked in the park, thinking about a distressing event). Ms. Shapiro developed the technique into a standardized clinical treatment she labeled Eye Movement Desensitization (EMD), and later Eye Movement Desensitization and Reprocessing (EMDR), after incorporating cognitive tasks (recalling the distressing memories) users should employ while engaging in the eye movements.

Although controversial, many studies have investigated the efficacy of EMDR therapy in the treatment of anxiety and depressive disorders, and especially in the treatment of post-traumatic stress disorder (PTSD). PTSD is characterized by recurrent distressing thoughts, dreams, or physiological reactions following exposure to an event that involved actual or threatened death or personal injury to one's self, a family member, or a close associate (American Psychiatric Association, 2005). A recent review in the *Annals of the New York Academy of Sciences* (Cukor et al., 2010) reports that although EMDR therapy has demonstrated efficacy in the treatment of PTSD, the reason(s) why the treatment are effective remain unclear. To date, exposure therapy remains the most effective treatment for PTSD and other anxiety disorders, where patients are asked repeatedly to imagine or actually face the threatening event, while trying to remain calm. Similarly, exposure to the memory of the distressing event(s) is a central feature of EMDR therapy. Thus it remains unclear if EMDR facilitates emotional recovery due to exposure to the distressing event, or due to increased hemispheric integration promoted by the eye movement task.

Nonetheless, there is empirical data noting the advantages of hemispheric integration on several tasks, especially those assessing episodic memory. As reviewed by Propper and Christman (2008), saccadic eye movements (but not vertical or smooth-pursuit movements) for 30 seconds can significantly improve episodic memory. Episodic memory tasks included memory for word fragments presented 30 minutes prior to testing (Christman et al., 2003; Parker, Relph, & Dagnall, 2008), and autobiographical memories recorded in a personal journal and recalled one to two weeks later (Christman et al., 2003). Bilateral saccadic eye movements also decreased false memories for words not presented in a list of related words (for example, the list might contain the words *thread, eye, sewing, sharp, thimble, haystack,* and *syringe,* but not the word *needle*. People often report remembering the word *needle* in the list, which would be a false memory; Christman et al., 2004; Parker & Dagnall, 2007). Bilateral eye movements have been found to facilitate earlier autobiographical memories (5.3 vs. 5.9 years of age; Christman, Propper, & Brown, 2006), and increased memory for color and spatial location of previously presented information (Christman, 2001). Other research indicates that the effect is not selective for eye movements; dichotic listening or bilateral tactile tasks (alternate finger or foot tapping) can also produce significant benefits (Propper & Christman, 2008).

Thus there is evidence to suggest that, opposite to the detrimental effects on consciousness caused by splitting the brain hemispheres, increasing communication across the hemispheres can facilitate performance of a variety of tasks, especially those requiring memory or memory "updating." Research suggests that mixed-handed individuals show significant improvements on a several types of episodic memory tasks, and performance on these tasks may also be enhanced in strongly handed individuals following 30 seconds of bilateral saccadic eye movements, which facilitate communication across the hemispheres. Future research should continue to assess benefits in strongly handed individuals following bilateral hemispheric activation.

Neural Correlates of Consciousness

The basic tenet underlying the search for a "neural correlate of consciousness" (NCC) is that our conscious experience is the result of the workings of our brain. Early investigations in humans and animals suggested a wide range of possible NCCs, including 40 Hz oscillations in the cerebral cortex/thalamocortical connections, the extended reticular activating system (ARAS) including connections to the thalamus, or a variety of "comparator" systems, including cortical systems with afferent "back" projections to lower cortical, hippocampal, or thalamic areas (e.g., Chalmers 1998, 2000; Crick & Koch, 1998). The **thalamus, cortex,** and **thalamic-cortical connections** continue to be main targets of investigation.

One challenge, discussed in chapter 1, has been defining consciousness. In the case of measuring the neural correlate(s) of consciousness, how consciousness is defined becomes critical, because that definition determines what aspect of consciousness is being measured. For example, should researchers investigate the neural mechanisms necessary to produce the *contents* of conscious experience (Block's access consciousness)? Or should investigations instead try to determine the neural changes needed to produce consciousness altogether, as in moving a person from an unconscious state to a conscious state (Block's phenomenal consciousness)? Studies investigating the NCCs of the *contents* of conscious experience are usually referred to as ***content-based approaches***, while those investigating neural mechanisms regulating the change between *states* of consciousness/unconsciousness are referred to as ***state-based approaches***.

Many researchers have adopted a **content-based approach**. Studies by Crick and Koch, Logothetis, and Tong and colleagues have all sought to determine the neural mechanisms underlying specific conscious perception, usually of a visual stimulus. This is because much is already known about how the visual system works, and visual perception is amenable to animal studies.

Indeed, early in the 1980s it was proposed that visual information was processed along two paths: a dorsal stream, that processed the "where" of visual information, and a ventral stream that processed the "what" of visual information (Ungerleider & Mishkin, 1982). Many people interpret the "what" of information to be our conscious awareness of visual sensations. The dorsal stream sends projections from visual areas V1, V2, V3A, V4, and V5/MT to the posterior parietal cortex, while the ventral stream sends projections from the visual areas to the inferior temporal cortex (IT). In the mid 1990s Milner and Goodale extended Ungerleider and Mishkin's theory to suggest that dorsal stream not only processes "where," but also provides guidance to perform motor actions necessary to respond to visual stimuli (Milner, 1995). Based on evidence from patients with damage to the dorsal stream, Milner and Goodale noted that dorsal stream neurons are needed to make the necessary hand movements to pick up an object. On this theory, ventral stream neurons function to guide our awareness of objects, so that, for example, we could "unconsciously" grasp an object, were dorsal stream intact. However, ventral stream input is needed to acknowledge what the object is, and possibly to explain why we are picking it up.

A series of studies by Logothetis and colleagues (Leopold & Logothetis, 1996; Logothetis & Schall, 1989; Sheinberg & Logothetis, 1997) investigated the extent to which neural firing along these visual pathways in monkeys corresponded to the physical presentation of a visual stimulus, or the conscious percept. They used several variations of a binocular rivalry task in which two different stimuli, for example, a set of horizontal lines and a set of vertical lines, were presented simultaneously but separately to each eye. Research in humans undergoing binocular rivalry tasks demonstrates that people process both pieces of information, but are only conscious of seeing one stimulus at a time. Furthermore, conscious perception changes between the stimuli automatically and every few seconds, so that there is a constant switch between the perception of each stimulus (e.g., Tong et al., 2006).

Logothetis and colleagues trained monkeys to report via lever press what stimulus was perceived. For example, when the monkey saw horizontal lines, they were to press and hold a lever on their right side. When their perception of the stimulus changed to the vertical lines, the monkey had to switch responses, by pressing and holding the left lever to earn a juice reward. After long and difficult training (apparently monkeys figure out how to "cheat" in this task, so the researchers took several precautions to make sure that the monkeys were being honest), the monkeys underwent surgery to have recording electrodes implanted at various points along the visual pathway. Electrodes were placed along the border of primary and secondary visual cortex (area V1/V2), area V4, and area V5/MT along the dorsal stream, and the **inferior temporal cortex (IT)**, in the ventral stream. Results showed that the majority of neurons in the dorsal stream fired continuously, as long as a visual stimulus was present. However, further through the visual system, and in the ventral stream, neural firing began to correlate more greatly with visual perception, until the IT (and the visual portions of the superior temporal sulcus), where cell firing matched the verbal report. Indeed, unique cells in IT were identified as "horizontal" or "vertical" cells. When monkeys were presented with a grid that had horizontal and vertical lines superimposed on each other, these cells in IT altered their firing rates, so that only "horizontal" cells fired when the monkey reported seeing horizontal lines, and only "vertical" cells fired when monkeys reported seeing vertical lines.

Research by Tong and colleagues has investigated the neural basis of binocular rivalry in humans (e.g., Tong et al., 1998; Tong et al., 2006). In their basic paradigm, participants are shown a picture of a face, a picture of a house, or a binocular rivalry task in which the picture of the house is superimposed on a picture of the face. The human **fusiform face area (FFA)**, located at the base of the **fusiform gyrus in the temporal lobe**, responds to faces, but not to a variety of other types of visual stimuli including houses, birds, flowers, and guitars. Conversely, the **parahippocampal place area (PPA)**, on the border of the **ventromedial temporal lobe**, responds to a variety of "scenes" and places—including houses—but does not respond to faces. Tong and colleagues utilized fMRI scans to determine which area of the brain became active as participants viewed and perceived the face/house images. Participants pressed a 'button box' when their percept changed between the house and the face. Results indicated that all subjects reported a strong tendency to switch between the dominant percept about every 3 seconds. Further, fMRI activity in the FFA and PPA corresponded to the change in perception, not the retinal stimulus. When participants reported seeing the house, fMRI activity in PPA increased, while perception of the face yielded a significant increase in activity in the FFA.

Together, these findings offer evidence that our conscious awareness may lie within select regions of extrastriate cortex, specifically areas in the **temporal lobe** including **IT**, **PPA**, and **FFA**. These findings indicate that areas of visual striate cortex (viz., V1, V2, V4, V5/MT) likely do not mediate consciousness (see also Crick & Koch, 1995, 1996).

While content-based approaches are yielding exciting and important information regarding how the brain regulates conscious perception, at least for visual images, critics emphasize the need for more **state-based approaches**, which should focus on determining the minimal amount of neural activity needed to produce consciousness. For example, Searle (2000) suggests that the scientific study of consciousness should focus on determining how consciousness is possible at all. He proposes that it would be useful to understand the change between "unconscious" and "conscious" states.

Laureys and colleagues have conducted several experiments in which neural activity in conscious people was compared to patients in a "non-conscious" vegetative state. In one study (Laureys, Faymonville, Luxen, Lamy, Franck, & Maquet, 2000), auditory (95 dB tones) and tactile stimuli (electrical stimulation of the wrist) were presented to healthy controls, and to a single patient both during and following recovery from a vegetative coma. A specific pattern of thalamocortical activity (the **intralaminar nucleus of the thalamus** and the **right prefrontal cortex**) was observed in the controls and in the patient following recovery, but was not apparent while the patient was in the vegetative state. Based on these differences, the authors concluded that thalamocortical connections are a likely NCC for the minimally conscious state. However, as pointed out by Hohwy (2009), the pattern of neural activity observed may not reflect *minimal* consciousness, but instead may have been evoked in the conscious patients as a result of learning, expectation, or even planning how to avoid the stimulus (assuming that 95dB tones and electric shocks to the wrist are aversive). Indeed, fMRI data from a second study by Laureys' research group (Owen, Coleman, Boly, Davis, Laureys, & Pickard, 2006) indicated similar brain activity in conscious controls and a patient in a vegetative state, when asked to visualize "playing tennis" or "visiting rooms in her house." Finding similar brain activity in "conscious" and "unconscious" people sheds further doubt on the utility of evaluating patients in a vegetative state. The results suggest that, possibly, a vegetative state is not an unconscious state or minimally conscious state (Laureys, 2005), and certainly, that the neural correlates distinguishing between a vegetative and conscious state need to be further investigated.

Other investigations have sought to elucidate the neural correlates of consciousness using a state-based approach, by assessing changes in brain activity during consciousness and unconsciousness induced by anesthesia. Alkire, Haier, and Fallon (2000) found decreases in thalamocortical glucose metabolism following halothane and isoflourane treatments. Although a PET scan revealed decreased metabolism throughout the brain, including cerebellum and visual cortex (areas not thought to be involved in consciousness), **thalamus and basal forebrain** connections were significantly decreased during anesthesia. Several other studies have found decreases in **thalamic** or **cortical activity** following anesthetics including sevoflourane (Peltier, Kerssens, & Hamann, 2005) and ketamine (Pack, Berezovkii, & Born, 2001; see also Mashour, 2006 for review). Summarized more recently by Alkire, Hudetz, and Tononi (2008), even though not all anesthetics decrease activity in the thalamus (for example, ketamine increases regional brain activity, especially in the thalamus), thalamus or thalamo-cortical connections should not be ruled out as potential NCCs. Indeed, anesthetics appear to cause unconsciousness by deactivating the **posterior corticothalamic complex**, and by producing a functional disconnection between these areas. Thus, while "cortical arousal may occur without the thalamus, consciousness may not" (Alkire et al., 2008, p. 877).

In summary, current research into the neural correlates of consciousness point to important connections between the **thalamus** and **cortical areas**, especially **prefrontal** and **temporal lobe** connections. While a great deal of progress has occurred, future investigations of the NCCs should strive to determine the neural basis of conscious content, across a variety of conscious and unconscious states. Furthermore, future studies should use a wider range of assessment techniques, for example, assessing neurochemical changes in select brain areas during conscious, unconscious, and altered states. We look forward to developing a greater understanding of the neural correlates of consciousness in the near future.

For Further Reading

Carlson, N. R. (2009). *Physiology of behavior* (10th ed.). Boston: Allyn and Bacon.

Damasio, A. (2010). *The self comes to mind: Constructing the conscious brain.* New York: Pantheon.

LeDoux, J. (2003). *The synaptic self: How our brains become who we are.* New York: Penguin.

Ornstein, R. E. (1986). *The psychology of consciousness.* New York: Penguin.

Ramachadran, V. S. (2005). *A brief tour of human consciousness: From imposter poodles to purple numbers.* Boston: Pi Press.

Segalowitz, S. J. (1983). *Two sides of the brain: Brain lateralization explored.* Englewood Cliffs, NJ: Prentice Hall.

Springer, S. P. & Deutsch, G. (1997). *Left brain/right brain* (5th ed.). New York: Freeman.

Consciousness-Altering Drugs

Go to your family medicine cabinet and count the number of drugs stored there. You will probably be as surprised as I was when I recently performed this exercise. Of course, there was the usual family-sized bottle of aspirin for that occasional headache, but that was not all. To begin my count, there was my own medicine for high blood pressure, a barbiturate, and a diuretic. Two bottles of decongestants and several cough syrups (all prescription medications) that had been used last winter in the family's annual bout with the flu were also stored there. A three-year-old bottle of codeine pills prescribed for pain relief following oral surgery, a bottle of muscle relaxants, two containers of antihistamines, and one bottle of eardrops concluded my count. What is your list like?

Clearly, drugs are a part of the American culture.

Traditionally, a **drug** is defined as a compound that, by virtue of its chemical structure, interacts with a specific biological system, perhaps a cell, in ways that change the structure or functions of that system (Hart, Ksir, & Ray, 2011). The problem with this definition is that it is much too broad and all-inclusive for our purposes. For example, food and water interact with biological systems to produce such changes. Under this definition, then, food and water would have to be considered drugs. However, unless one is on the verge of starvation or dehydration, it would be extremely difficult to argue that food and water have much to do with one's state of consciousness.

Definition is not an insurmountable problem, however; all that is needed is greater specificity about the type of drugs. In the present context we are interested only in those drugs that bring about changes in consciousness or affect mood when they are swallowed, inhaled, or injected. These are the **psychoactive** drugs. Although these drugs vary considerably both in chemical structure and in their effects on awareness and mood, Hart, Ksir, and Ray (2011) suggest that several basic principles apply to all of them. First, every psychoactive drug has multiple effects. Thus, while the barbiturate user may seek only one of the drug's effects, such as the euphoria (or high), clearly other aspects of consciousness, such as thinking, solving problems, and remembering, are also altered.

Second, the effects of a psychoactive drug depend on the amount of drug the individual has taken. Changes in the dosage level may alter the drug's effects in two ways. Increasing the amount of the drug taken may result in a heightening of the effects obtained at lower drug levels. Also, different dosage levels may change the effect. Many of us are familiar with the fact that, while a few bottles of beer may relax the drinker and produce euphoria, a pint of whiskey may be sufficient to make the drinker pass out.

Third, the effects of a psychoactive drug depend in part on the user's history and expectations. It seems logical to assume that since these drugs change the level of awareness and the ability to process thoughts, any effect that may be produced in an individual would depend on preexisting conditions. Thus, such factors as attitudes, emotional state, previous drug experiences, and physical setting interact with the drug to alter the user's level of awareness. Smith (1964, p. 78) wrote, "If there is one point about which every student of the drugs agrees, it is that there is no such thing as the drug experience per se—no experience that the drugs merely secrete, as it were. Every experience is a mix of three ingredients: drug, set (the psychological make-up of the individual), and setting (the social and physical environment in which it is taken)." In brief, attempting to describe the effects of a particular drug without specifying these factors is an extremely difficult, if not impossible, task.

Finally, the drug itself is neither "good" nor "bad." For example, morphine, when used to alleviate the pain of a terminal cancer patient, is considered good, but the same drug, when used by an addict to feed a drug habit, is labeled bad. Note, however, that it is not the drug, but rather the use to which it is put, that is labeled.

Pharmacology of Neurotransmission

In chapter 2 we observed that neurons transmit information to each other at junctions called synapses. Initially, it was believed that this process of information transmission at the synapse was electrical. However, in a brilliant series of studies, Dale (1938) conclusively demonstrated the chemical nature of the process and isolated the neurohumural transmitter substances **acetylcholine** and **norepinephrine**. Following this major research step, there has been a concerted effort to identify other neurotransmitter substances. Although many substances have been proposed as neurotransmitters, conclusive evidence is generally lacking. Hebb (1970) suggested that for a substance to be accepted as a neurotransmitter, it must meet the following criteria:

1) The enzymes necessary for synthesis of the substance should be present within the neuron. (An **enzyme** is a protein that causes a particular chemical reaction to take place without becoming a part of the final product.)

2) Direct application of the substance to the postsynaptic element should be equivalent in effect to stimulation of the presynaptic neuron.

3) Drugs that interfere with synthesis of the substance, or its reaction with the postsynaptic membrane, should block the effects of neuronal stimulation.

4) Drugs that block the enzyme that normally inactivates the substance should lead to a prolongation of its effects and of the effects of neuronal stimulation.

In addition to acetylcholine and norepinephrine, a number of other substances have been identified as potential neurotransmitters. These include **dopamine, serotonin, glutamic acid**, and **gamma-amino-butyric acid**.

When an adequate stimulus is applied to a presynaptic neuron, the neuron releases one of these substances into the synapse where it diffuses across the **synaptic cleft** (the space between the neurons). Normally, at this point, the neurotransmitter interacts with the appropriate receptor sites on the postsynaptic neuronal membrane to either increase or decrease the likelihood that the postsynaptic neuron will discharge.

61

Practically all drugs that act on the central nervous system (CNS), and thereby affect consciousness and behavior, do so by somehow influencing some aspect of this neurotransmission process. According to Leavitt (1995), such a drug may interfere with neurotransmission in one of the following ways:

- It may interfere with the synthesis of the neurotransmitter, thereby decreasing the amount of the neurotransmitter substance available at the presynaptic site.

- It may interfere with the release of the neurotransmitter substance.

- A drug may replace the normal neurotransmitter in a presynaptic neuron only to be released later when that neuron is stimulated or in the presence of other drugs. The effects of this **false transmitter** may or may not be similar to those of the normal transmitter.

- A drug may combine with a postsynaptic receptor site where it may elicit the same effect as the normal neurotransmitter or it may have no direct action at all. In either event, by combining with the receptor, it may prevent the action of the normal neurotransmitter.

- A drug may lead to the destruction of the neurotransmitter.

- Most neurotransmitters are inactivated primarily by being taken back up into the presynaptic neurons or into extraneuronal sites. Many drugs act on one or both of these reuptake mechanisms.

- The drug may produce changes in the sensitivity of the receptor cell.

- Finally the drug may serve as a neurotoxic agent. A **neurotoxic agent** is a substance that causes the destruction of neural tissue.

Basic Psychopharmacological Concepts

To understand the following detailed descriptions of the physiological and consciousness-altering effects produced by a sample of psychoactive drugs, it is necessary that you familiarize yourself with a number of common psycho-pharmacological concepts.

Drug abuse refers primarily to the recreational, as opposed to the medical or psychiatric use of drugs. Drug abuse is classified as a disorder by the American Psychiatric Association (APA), which defines it in terms of the resultant maladaptive behaviors that impair social functioning. Also recognized as a disorder by the APA is **drug dependence**, which results from the repeated use of a drug taken in dosages sufficient to elicit a strong desire to continue taking the drug.

Two kinds of drug dependence are recognized: physiological and psychological. The former is frequently referred to as **drug addiction**; this type of dependence is partially or completely organically based. Through the continued use of the drug, the body eventually becomes physiologically dependent on it. Physiological dependence is characteristic of users of such drugs as alcohol, barbiturates, morphine, heroin, and chlordiazepoxide (Librium).

Psychological dependence, sometimes called habituation, is a strong, sometimes overwhelming, desire to continue using a drug. Such dependence is typically caused by the drug's effects on levels of consciousness and mood. The use of such drugs as amphetamines, barbiturates, cocaine, marijuana, and phencyclidine, which relieve anxiety or lead to euphoria, may lead to psychological dependence.

Finally, a pharmacological concept of some importance is that of **drug tolerance**. This is a physiological reaction, which, after prolonged use of a drug, causes the body to require increasingly greater amounts of the agent to experience the same effects. Drug tolerance has been observed in the use of alcohol, barbiturates, amphetamines, and opiate derivatives, such as morphine and heroin. Sometimes the development of tolerance for one drug occurs after the repeated use of another drug. This is known as **cross-tolerance**. Thus, a heroin user may develop a tolerance not only for heroin, but also for morphine.

If our discussion of psychoactive drugs and their effects upon consciousness and behavior is to be coherent, we must adopt some classification scheme. A cursory review of the literature from the many disciplines concerned with drugs (chemistry, pharmacology, law, social work, psychology) clearly demonstrate the existence of a number of drug classification models. Having considered the many choices at some length, it seems reasonable to us that from the standpoint of this chapter, the most realistic classification scheme would be the one described by Julien (1997) on how the drugs affect a user's behavior.

Julien's system involves five classes of psychoactive drugs that alter mood and behavior: (1) **sedative-hypnotic compounds**, or CNS depressants, (2) **behavioral stimulants and convulsants**, (3) **narcotic analgesics (opiates)**, (4) **antipsychotic agents**, and (5) **psychedelics and hallucinogens**.

As Julien observed, even this classification system is not without its limitations. First, the action of psychoactive drugs is seldom restricted to a single functional or anatomical subdivision of the brain. Although there are exceptions, a psychoactive drug will simultaneously affect a variety of processes. This

63

makes the classification process complicated because at different dosage levels, different behavioral actions may predominate.

A second limitation of this scheme has to do with the fact that although a psychoactive drug might have a single effect on a specific neurotransmitter, a variety of effects can be expected because the neurotransmitter is involved in many functions.

Third, it should be recognized that psychoactive drugs simply modify on-going behavioral or physiological responses; they do not create new responses.

Finally the classification scheme we have adopted should not be considered rigid and fixed, because different behavioral responses are observed at different dosage levels. The reader must understand that simply classifying a group of drugs does not fully describe their effects on consciousness and behavior. It only serves as a starting point.

With these limitations in mind we have selected one or more representative agents from each of the major groups for a detailed discussion. The exception is that, for two reasons, we will not discuss antipsychotic drugs.

These drugs are typically not drugs of abuse for the purpose of creating an altered state of consciousness. Second, these drugs are typically used to treat individuals who are already exhibiting hallucinations or altered states. Thus, they are used to reduce the magnitude of or to eliminate entirely the altered state so as to permit the individual to return to a normal, nonaltered, waking state of consciousness.

With regard to the remaining four categories in Julien's system, we will examine some representative drugs from these classes and describe their effects on behavior. Unlike the antipsychotic drugs, the compounds or agents in the remaining categories are often drugs of abuse and do bring about changes in levels or states of consciousness.

Sedative-Hypnotic Compounds

Although the sedative-hypnotic compounds are varied in their chemical structure, all are capable of inducing varying degrees of reduction in both behavioral output and level of consciousness. The behavioral-depressant action of these compounds appears to result from an action on the arousal centers within the brain: the ascending reticular activating system (ARAS) and the diffuse thalamic projection system (Soulairac & Soulairac, 1965; Stern & Morgane, 1974). Included in this class of drugs are alcohol, chloral hydrate, paraldehyde, the bromides, methaqualone (Quaalude), and barbiturates.

Generally, when we think about the effects produced by the members of this category of drugs, we conjure up thoughts of behavioral sedation and sleep. In truth, however, depending on drug dosage level, almost all of these drugs are capable of producing any of the behavioral changes along a continuum of behavioral sedation (see Figure 3.1). In this section we discuss the effects of barbiturates and alcohol on consciousness and behavior.

Barbiturates

In the 1850s a group of new chemical compounds called **bromides** was introduced. These agents gained almost immediate popularity as a sleep-inducing preparation. However, with this popularity came abuse and the realization that excessive use of bromides results in consciousness-altering effects such as delusions, hallucinations, and a variety of neurological disturbances. The toxic psychosis caused by bromide abuse proved to be a major cause of admissions to mental hospitals for some time (Jarvik, 1967).

Participating in the search for a sleep-inducing drug with fewer dangerous side effects, Adolf von Bayer (1835–1917) in Munich, Germany, succeeded in combining urea with malonic acid to produce a new compound called barbituric acid (Sharpless, 1970). Von Bayer's 1862 creation was not a CNS depressant; however, the many barbiturates that came to be derived from barbituric acid proved to be excellent CNS depressants. The first barbiturate to be used clinically, barbital (Veronal), was introduced in 1903.

The medical uses of barbiturates include, but are not limited to, sleep induction, daytime sedation, treatment of epileptic seizures, induction of anesthesia, preanesthetic medication before surgery, and the treatment of anxiety and neurosis. The medical uses for these drugs, however, have declined considerably over the past 20 years primarily because of newer compounds that have less toxicity or dependence liability (Harvey, 1985). At present, the only real advantage of the barbiturates is their low cost, which has come about because they are no longer protected by patent. Social and recreational uses include euphoria and relief from anxiety (Julien, 1997). Despite this, barbiturates have proven to be extremely dangerous and are commonly associated with both physiological and psychological dependence as well as fatalities from overdose.

There are more than 2,500 barbiturates, and they are usually classified on the basis of the duration of their activity (Martindale, 1967). It is the short-acting agents, such as pentobarbital (Nembutal) and secobarbital (Seconal), that are abused. These barbiturates are likely to produce the initial euphoric high within 15 minutes after ingestion. The duration of their action is typically

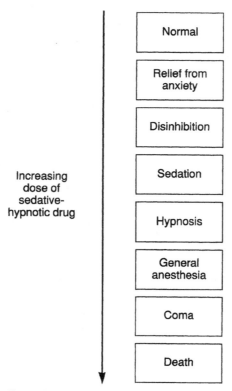

Figure 3.1 • Continuum of Behavioral Sedation

between two and three hours. Tolerance to barbiturates develops gradually, and the dosage must be increased periodically to maintain a constant effect. However, the lethal dosage remains the same. Thus, as tolerance develops, the difference between these two levels becomes dangerously small. Nearly one-third of accidental drug-related deaths are due to barbiturate overdose (Julien, 1997).

Once the individual requires a daily dosage level of about 400 milligrams, he or she will probably experience some withdrawal symptoms if barbiturate use is temporarily interrupted.

It is generally agreed that barbiturates tend to decrease the excitability of neurons throughout the nervous system (Harvey, 1985). The inhibitory influence of barbiturates is thought to be due to enhanced GABA activity at its receptor cites (Skolnick, Noncada, Barker, & Paul, 1981). It has been suggested that the inhibitory effects of barbiturates may also be due to increases in the conductance of potassium ions across the neural membrane (O'Beirne,

Gurevich, & Carlen, 1986). The overall decrease in brain activity probably can best be accounted for by the fact that the pathways of the ascending reticular activating system are among the first of the major brain centers to be affected by barbiturates.

Shortly after dropping some "rainbows" (Tuinal) or "red devils" (Seconal), the individual experiences feelings of relaxation, some behavioral stimulation, and a euphoric high. It is also possible that the individual will exhibit some aggressive behavior, as if he or she were fighting the inevitable drowsiness and sleep. This is especially the case if the barbiturate used is secobarbital (Tinklenberg & Woodrow, 1974). These effects on the user's consciousness level are then replaced by a sense of confusion and cognitive impairment such that problem solving and decision making seem to require great effort; the individual is usually aware that his or her thinking is, at best, "fuzzy." Memory and concentration may also be impaired. Emotionally, the user is likely to be extremely labile, ranging from the euphoric high to severe depression. Finally, loss of motor coordination is reflected in the person's slurred speech, depressed motor activity, and staggering gait (Wesson & Smith, 1971). At dosages between 100 and 200 milligrams, secobarbital and pentobarbital have a hypnotic or sleep-producing effect; therefore, they are often employed in the treatment of certain sleep disorders, including insomnia. This is discussed in some detail in chapter 7. It is sufficient here to note only that these drugs do not bring about a normal sleep in that rapid eye movement, or REM, sleep is suppressed (Dement, 1972).

In addition to the behavioral effects described, barbiturates also produce psychophysiological effects suggestive of parasympathetic arousal, including pupillary constriction, decreased heart rate and blood pressure, and depressed respiratory rate. Excessive dosages are lethal because they result in paralysis of the respiratory centers of the brain.

Cessation of barbiturate administration causes withdrawal symptoms to appear. At normal dosage levels, withdrawal symptoms are not typically serious or life threatening. Among the symptoms is a rebound increase in rapid eye movement (REM) sleep, which causes sleep difficulties. The individual may be quite irritable for days or even weeks after discontinuing the barbiturate. At higher dosage levels, removal of the drug may lead to serious and even lethal withdrawal symptoms, chief among which is convulsions. Associated with these convulsive episodes may be periods of hallucinations, restlessness, and disorientation. Obviously, this is even more serious in the case of the epileptic patient who is already prone to severe convulsions.

Clearly, barbiturate abuse was a significant public health concern through much of the 20th century. However, popularity and abuse of barbiturates has declined, probably due to the increased availability of other prescription drugs. As reported by the U.S. Drug Enforcement Agency (DEA, 2005), barbiturates account for fewer than 10 percent of sedative-hypnotic prescriptions today.

As barbiturate use has declined, benzodiazepine use (and abuse) has increased. Benzodiazepines alter consciousness in a manner similar to the other sedative-hypnotics: low doses decrease anxiety and increase relaxation, while higher doses can induce sleep. Some benzodiazepines also have an amnesiac effect; that is, they can disrupt memory for events that happen while under the influence of the drug. Pharmacologically, benzodiazepines act as allosteric modulators of the neurotransmitter GABA; they increase the ability of GABA to bind to GABAA receptors and, as a result, facilitate the inhibitory effects of GABA (Grilly, 2006).

Benzodiazepines ("benzos," "benz," "downers," "tranks") were developed in the 1960s as an alternative to the potentially addictive barbiturates, for use in the treatment of insomnia and anxiety-related disorders. Yet it was soon realized that benzodiazepines are also addictive, can produce a similar (and life-threatening) withdrawal syndrome, and also carry the potential for abuse (Grilly, 2006; Meyer & Quenzer, 2005; Tan et al., 2010).

Chlordiazepoxide (Librium) was the first benzodiazepine, introduced in 1961. Since then, over 3,000 drugs of this type have been synthesized. Roughly 15 benzodiazepines are currently prescribed in the United States, and more are available overseas (DEA, 2005). Longer-acting benzodiazepines are effective in the treatment of anxiety, and include drugs such as diazepam (Valium), alprazolam (Xanax), lorzepam (Ativan), and clonazepam (Klonopin). Shorter-acting benzodiazepines such as midazolam (Versed) are often used as an adjunct to anesthesia prior to surgical procedures. Other short-acting benzodiazepines are useful in the treatment of insomnia, and include temazepam (Restoril) and triazolam (Halcion). Two newer sleep aids are zolpidem (Ambien) and zaleplon (Sonata), although these are occasionally inaccurately reported as "non-benzodiazepines" (e.g., Hajak, Muller, Wittchen, Pittroch, & Kirch, 2003). While zolpidem and zaleplon have been reported to have a lower abuse and dependence liability than the older-generation benzodiazepines (Soyka, Bottlender, & Moller, 2000), more recent research demonstrates that not only is zolpidem abused (Huang, Lin, & Chen, 2007), it works identically to other benzodiazepines, by facilitating GABA binding to $GABA_A$ receptors, specifically by binding to special "benzodiazepine" receptors, between alpha1 and gamma subunits of the $GABA_A$ sites. It is believed that activation of alpha1 subunits of GABA receptors, especially in the **ventral tegmental area (VTA),** mediates the rewarding and addictive properties of *all* drugs (Tan et al., 2010). Thus, zolpidem (and presumably zaleplon, which has similar pharmacological effects) has the same abuse and addiction potential as other benzodiazepines (and any drug that works via alpha1 subunits of GABA receptors).

While the majority of people prescribed benzodiazepines do not become addicted or abuse these drugs, nonprescription forms of benzodiazepines, though illegal in the U.S., are easily attainable. Abusers can gain "extra" prescriptions by visiting different health care professionals, and nonprescription forms of benzodiazepines are easily purchased via the Internet. According to the National Drug Intelligence Center (NDIC), a division of the U.S. Department of Justice, in 2006, alprazolam (Xanax) was among the top three prescription drugs found illegally in the U.S. (NDIC, 2006). Further, alprazolam has been reported to be the second-most abused prescription drug in Australia, suggesting global abuse (Monheit, 2010). According to the U.S. DEA (2005), benzodiazepines are most often abused by adolescents and young adults to alter consciousness. Benzodiazepines are frequently combined with other drugs, including opiates such as heroin, and other sedative-hypnotics such as alcohol, to potentiate their effects. Although by themselves benzodiazepines have a low potential for lethal overdose, combining benzodiazepines with other sedative-hypnotic drugs can be deadly (Grilly, 2006). Benzodiazepines are also often used to counteract the stimulant and anxiety-producing effects caused by cocaine and amphetamines.

Benzodiazepines can produce a withdrawal syndrome similar to that of alcohol (described fully in a later section) and the barbiturates (described above), including anxiety, tremor, insomnia, and in severe cases, poses a risk of seizures. Abrupt discontinuation of benzodiazepines is not recommended. Instead, a "tapering" regimen should be used, where the dose is gradually reduced over weeks or even months (Vikander, Koechling, Borg, Tonne, & Hiltunen, 2010).

Flunitrazepam (Rohypnol)

Flunitrazepam (Rohypnol) is a type of benzodiazepine known by a variety of street names including "roofies," "rophies," "roche," "roach," "Mexican Valium," "circles," "ruffles," and "rufilin." Flunitrazepam was originally developed in the early 1970s by Roche (now Hoffman-LaRoche) Pharmaceuticals as a powerful sleep aid; it is about 10 times more potent than diazepam (DEA, 2005). Flunitrazepam is currently available in Mexico and Europe, and is primarily used as a sleep aid in hospital settings; this drug is not legal in the United States. According to the U.S. DEA (2005), flunitrazepam is heavily trafficked into the U.S., primarily through Florida and Texas. High school and college students use flunitrazepam as a "party drug" at raves and nightclubs, and often in combination with alcohol, heroin, cocaine, or other drugs.

Perhaps flunitrazepam has gained its greatest notoriety as a "date rape drug." Flunitrazepam is not only powerful and long acting (it has a half-life of 18–26 hours), it frequently produces anterograde amnesia, in which users cannot remember events that happened while they were under the influence of the drug. When dissolved, flunitrazepam is colorless and tasteless; people have reported going out alone or on a "date," possibly having someone unknowingly slip flunitrazepam in their drink, and waking up the next morning in a strange place, perhaps undressed, with no memory of what happened. While it has been difficult to verify instances of sexual assault following flunitrazepam intoxication, likely due to the memory loss experienced by the victim, Hoffman-LaRoche has recently taken precautions against "accidental" ingestion by manufacturing a new tablet that turns blue when dissolved in alcohol (Meyer & Quenzer, 2005). These pharmaceutical alterations, coupled with harsh legal sanctions for possession or use of flunitrazepam in the United States, have resulted in declines in its use here (DEA, 2005).

Gamma-Hydroxybutryrate (GHB)

Although not a benzodiazepine, **gamma-hydroxybutryrate** (GHB) shares many sedative-hypnotic effects in common with the benzodiazepines, especially flunitrazepam (Rohypnol). GHB was identified in the early 1960s as a chemical structurally similar to the neurotransmitter GABA (Meyer & Quenzer, 2005). Not related to its consciousness-altering effects, GHB also stimulates the pituitary gland to release growth hormone; this effect caused the drug to gain popularity in the 1980s as a "natural" supplement to build muscle mass. Throughout the 1980s, GHB was not regulated by the U.S. Food and Drug Administration (FDA), and was readily available in drug stores and nutritional centers. In 1990, following reports of consciousness-altering and other negative physiological effects after ingestion of GHB, the FDA determined the drug was unsafe, and banned over-the-counter sales (Meyer & Quenzer, 2005). However, illicit use continued, and recreational use grew, especially as a "club drug." Some common street names for GHB include "Georgia home boy," "Cherry Meth," "Everclear," "liquid ecstasy" or "liquid X," "Vita-G," "jib," and "grievous bodily harm."

According to the U.S. DEA (2005), abusers of GHB fall into three major categories: 1) body-builders who use GHB to build muscle mass, 2) recreational users who take GHB to produce euphoria or relaxation, or to experience mild hallucinogenic effects, and 3) predators who secretly give victims GHB to facilitate sexual assault. Thus, like flunitrazepam (Rohypnol), GHB is also often referred to as a "date-rape drug." GHB can produce severe intoxication and sedation at high doses, and is also colorless and virtually tasteless when dissolved. Reports of GHB use in sexual assault became so prevalent in the 1990s–2000s, that a company, DrinkSafe Technologies, began marketing the DrinkSafe Coaster, which can detect GHB in drinks. The coasters do not detect flunitrazepam (Rohypnol), due to the manufacturer's belief that flunitrazepam is not a significant risk factor in sexual assault (Meyer & Quenzer, 2005; www.drinksafetechnology.com, 2009). It is unknown at this time how the use of these coasters has impacted GHB-facilitated assault or the recreational use of GHB.

Alcohol

Although few of us probably view alcoholic beverages as drugs in the same way as we do heroin, barbiturates, amphetamines, and tranquilizers, the fact remains that alcohol (more properly, ethyl alcohol) does fit our initial definition of a drug in that its chemical structure interacts with a specific biological system. What is important here is that alcohol alters both the mood and the conscious state of the user. Thus, it is also a psychoactive drug that is every bit as powerful as the more notorious drugs. Although alcohol has all of those qualities, psychological and physical dependency, social disruptiveness, toxicity, and lethality, that our drug-conscious society has deemed unacceptable with respect to drugs, it is so accepted in our culture that it is one of the most widely used and abused drugs known. It has been estimated that alcoholics alone represent about 20 percent of all the patients seen in psychiatric facilities (Guze, Cloninger, Martin, & Clayton, 1986).

From a historical standpoint, it would appear that alcohol has been with us for a very long time. Mead, which is made from honey, is probably the oldest alcoholic beverage, and some authorities (Hart, Ksir, & Ray, 2011) suggest that it first appeared as early as about 8000 BCE. Beer and berry wine were known and used about 6400 BCE. Grape wine first made its appearance about 300–400 BCE. Cambyses, king of Persia in the sixth century BCE, holds the dubious distinction of being one of the first alcoholics on record. His drunken episodes apparently were associated with periods of uncontrollable rage. He behaved much like "a madman not in possession of his senses" (Whitwell, 1936, p. 38). It is reported that on one occasion, without making any plans for feeding his troops, Cambyses set out to thrash the Ethiopians, who had angered the king by referring to the Persians as "dung eaters." Because of his lack of planning, King Cambyses and his troops were forced to retreat to Memphis, where, much to his anger, he found his people celebrating the feast of Apis. Perceiving in his drunken state that the people were rejoicing at his failure, he ordered the entire citizenry taking part in the feast to be executed.

The list of other celebrities, poets, painters, authors, musicians, and leaders who are known to have used alcohol excessively would be endless—Samuel Butler, Lord Byron, Edgar Allan Poe, Ulysses S. Grant, John Barrymore, and Ernest Hemingway, to name a few.

The basis for all alcoholic beverages is a process called **fermentation**. Certain yeasts act on sugar (glucose) in the presence of water so that the yeast recombines the carbon (C), hydrogen (H), and oxygen (O) of the sugar and water into ethyl alcohol and carbon dioxide ($C_6H_{12}O_6 + H_2O \xrightarrow{\text{yeast}} C_2H_6O + CO_2$). Glucose is readily available in most fruits, including grapes. The limitation of this process lies in the fact that yeast generally has only a confined tolerance for alcohol. Thus, when alcohol concentration reaches approximately 15 percent, the yeast cells die and the fermentation process is terminated.

Cereal grains are also used in the production of alcoholic drinks, but here the process is somewhat different. To begin with, grains contain starches, not sugars. Therefore, before fermentation can take place, it is necessary to convert the starches to sugars by the use of enzymes during a process called **malting**. The grain is placed in water and allowed to sprout; afterward, it is dried slowly to kill off the sprouts but preserve the enzymes that formed during the growth. The dried, sprouted grain is then crushed, and when mixed with water, the enzymes convert the starch to sugar. Once yeast is added, fermentation can begin.

However, what if concentrations of alcohol stronger than the 15 percent that can be obtained by fermentation are desired? In this case, it is necessary to resort to a second process called distillation. During this process, an alcohol-containing solution is heated; the resulting vapors are collected and condensed once more into a liquid form. Because the boiling point of alcohol is lower than that of water, the distillation process produces a much higher concentration of alcohol in the distillate (the condensed liquid) than was present in the original solution. While there are any number of variations in the processes leading to the end product (e.g., charcoal fire brewing, storing and aging in special barrels), it is the process of fermentation and distillation that determines the beverage's alcoholic content. In the United States, the alcoholic content of a distilled beverage is indicated on the label by the term **proof**. When a friend gives you a gift bottle of 90-proof rum, you are really getting a distillate from the fermentation of sugar cane molasses, which now contains 45 percent ethyl alcohol. In brief, the percentage of alcohol by volume is one-half the proof number indicated on the label.

Because of the widespread use and frequent abuse of alcohol, it is safe to assume that during your lifetime, many of you have had some personal contact with one or more of the many alcoholic beverages available. These experiences may range from a sip of beer or wine "just to see what it tastes like" to a more dangerous "lost weekend" or (most probably) something in between these two extremes. By comparing your experiences with those of your friends, you may have discovered that alcohol, like most other drugs, produces a variety of behavioral effects.

Some of these effects are general and are experienced by most people; others are peculiar to the individual and may well result from an interaction of the individual's mental set, the setting, and the alcohol. Thus, while some of the behavioral effects are due to pharmacological effects, a large number of the "effects" of alcohol are due to set and expectancy (Critchlow, 1986; Cutter, O'Farrell, Whitehouse, & Dentch, 1986; Hull & Bond, 1986).

It is apparent that there is a gender disparity concerning the ease with which women and men become intoxicated. Because of differences in the content of their stomach enzymes, women absorb alcohol into their bloodstreams more rapidly than men (Frezza et al., 1990). Remember that it is not really a matter of how many drinks you have but rather how much alcohol reaches your brain. Take these two facts and then add the fact that women tend to have a lower volume of fluids in their bodies than do men of equal weight, so the alcohol in women may be more concentrated. York and Welte (1994) suggest that this may explain, in part at least, why women generally become intoxicated more easily than do men.

Alcohol is a consciousness-limiting drug that appears to attack and numb the higher brain centers. See what happens to a fictitious friend, Joe College, whose fraternity pledge class has decided to hold its annual weekend "house-cleaning-and-keg" party. By Friday evening, the fraternity house is spanking clean, the older members have gone their various ways, and now the kegs and other assorted bottles are brought from their hiding places; the party has officially begun. Depending on how tired he is, when he ate last, his body size, his mood, and a host of other factors, the first drink or two may have little effect on Joe's state of awareness. However, with a couple more drinks, Joe's alertness is decreased, and he begins to experience good feelings—feelings of expansiveness, warmth, and well-being. All the unpleasantness, tensions, and worries of the real world begin to melt away. His feelings of self-worth are greatly increased, and everybody is Joe's friend.

With a few more drinks our friend's judgments and other rational processes become impaired, and his self-control diminishes. With the diminution of restraints, more primitive emotional responses are very likely to occur (e.g., the lamp shade on the head, crying, and even aggression), responses that under more normal circumstances he would have kept under control. Most of us are familiar with the crying or belligerent drunk. There are now convincing data that alcohol intoxication, with its resulting disinhibition, also plays a major role in aggressive behavior and violent crimes (Gunn, 1979; Hindman, 1979).

By now, the alcoholic content in Joe's bloodstream has reached or exceeded 0.1 percent, and he is quickly approaching intoxication. Because alcohol is an emetic, users vomit once the blood alcohol level reaches about 0.12 percent. Vomiting is a safety device that may not function if the critical level is approached slowly. Fatal amounts of alcohol may then be ingested. Should our friend decide to return to his room and his studies, he would find the learning process most difficult; learning is impaired in alcoholics and in normal subjects who have had too much to drink (Goldman, 1983; Parker, Chelune, Hamblin, & Kitchens, 1984). On the other hand, some evidence suggests a facilitating effect of small doses of alcohol on difficult intellectual tasks (Keller, 1966).

Chronic alcoholism often leads to severe memory deficits. Evidence suggests that alcohol produces considerable impairment in the ability to convert information from short-term to long-term memory (Nelson, McSpadden, Fromme, & Marlatt, 1986). Until a few years ago, it was pretty much agreed that intoxication resulted in a disruption of the encoding operations involved in attempting to store new information, whereas retrieval of previously learned information was unimpaired. Recent data, however, suggest that retrieval from long-term memory may be affected by acute intoxication and that this effect may be greater for females than for males (Haut, Beckwith, Petros, & Russell, 1989). Depending on the circumstances, memory processes may be so affected that the person experiences blackouts (i.e., complete amnesia for the events that took place during much of the period of intoxication).

Once the blood alcohol level reaches 0.08 percent, Joe is legally intoxicated (according to the laws of most states). His motor coordination is now beginning to show some signs of impairment. This, combined with slowed reaction times and impaired judgment, means that the time has come for one of Joe's sober friends to hide the keys to his car. Should Joe and his motor deficits decide to go for a ride at this point, he would be a menace, not only to himself but also to anyone else on the road. Drivers with a 0.08 percent or greater blood alcohol level can be arrested and removed from the road (Hingson, Hareen, & Winter, 1996).

As the drinking continues and the alcoholic content of Joe's blood increases, his ability to sense pain, cold, and other discomforts is also severely diminished. Alcohol dilates peripheral vessels, so increased amounts of blood circulate through the skin. One consequence is that alcoholics often have red noses. The increased blood flow promotes a feeling of warmth but also leads to a loss of body heat (on cold days, peripheral blood vessels normally constrict so that flow to the skin, and hence heat loss, is minimized). Perhaps you know someone who took a flask of the spirits to a football game or on a winter hunting expedition to help keep warm, only to suffer frostbite or worse because of an inability to sense accurately the severity of the cold weather. Additionally, because of the heat loss caused by blood vessel dilation due to the alcohol, the individual may also have suffered hypothermia, a severe loss of body heat.

Certainly by this point, the clumsiness, staggering, and unsteadiness in standing and walking, all symptomatic of impaired motor coordination and vision, are apparent. Joe's speech is now badly slurred, and his judgment of his own condition and ability is extremely disturbed. His moral judgments become even more immature, and any qualms Joe may have had about driving while drinking have left him. At this point, even if Joe were given a Breathalyzer test and told that he was dangerously intoxicated, he would probably still insist on driving (Denton & Krebs, 1990; MacDonald, Zanna, & Fong, 1995).

When Joe's blood alcohol reaches approximately 0.5 percent, his entire neural balance is upset, and he slowly slides out of his chair, then under the table, and passes out. As blood concentrations above 0.55 percent are considered lethal, it is generally agreed that this lapsing into a state of unconsciousness is simply the body's way of protecting itself. An unconscious drinker is not likely to take another drink, at least for a while. Had Joe College's bout with the demon spirits gone this far, he probably would awaken the next day with an upset stomach, fatigue, headache, thirst, depression, anxiety, and an overall bad feeling, the classic **hangover**.

Exactly how alcohol produces these effects is not yet clear. However, at a cellular level, the best evidence to date suggests that alcohol acts directly on the membrane of the neuron, altering its basic semisolid structure to make it more fluid (Chin & Goldstein, 1977). This may have the effect of inhibiting the movements of the sodium and potassium ions across the membrane. This would interfere with the nerve cell's ability to produce electrical impulses and render it unable to process information normally. Alcohol may change synaptic activity directly. It has been found to depress both excitatory and inhibitory postsynaptic potentials while potentiating presynaptic inhibition. There is also some recent evidence to suggest that alcohol enhances the activity of the neurotransmitter GABA at its receptor cites (Suzdak et al., 1986). Specifically affected, at least initially, are nerve cells that comprise the ascending reticular activating system. Depression of the activity of this system leads in turn to a disruption of cortical activity and the changes in behavior and arousal observed in the drinker.

Should Joe drink himself to sleep, the sleep induced will be abnormal. Slow-wave and REM sleep stages are greatly reduced, and stage shifts occur more frequently than under normal conditions (Ritchie, 1985; Zarcone, 1973). During periods of very heavy drinking, sleep patterns may be profoundly disturbed. Greenberg and Pearlman (1967) note that during withdrawal, sleep is of extremely poor quality, with REM sleep predominating.

Finally, suppose that this is not the first time that Joe C. has used alcohol. Instead, Joe has been using alcohol since his last year of high school, and although he was only a moderate drinker, the "clean-up party" and the hangover the next day have convinced him that it is time for him to give it up. If he were truly a moderate drinker, one or two beers a day, about the only withdrawal symptom he would experience would be limited to prolonged disturbances in brain wave patterns during sleep.

On the other hand, had Joe been consuming larger quantities of alcohol over that period of time he would probably experience a high degree of arousal associated with weakness, tremor, anxiety, and elevated blood pressure, pulse rate, and respiration rate. Very heavy drinkers, those who consume a pint or more of pure ethyl alcohol daily over a protracted period, are likely to experience convulsions and a toxic psychosis, commonly referred to as **delirium tremens**, or the DTs. It includes such symptoms as rapid pulse rate, severe anxiety, headaches, and even death. Vivid hallucinations, especially of small, quickly moving insects or animals, also occur and can heighten the individual's anxiety. The hallucinations may be due to REM rebound, since alcohol suppresses REM; when alcohol is withdrawn, a great deal of REM returns. These, together with irritability, headaches, fever, nausea, agitation, confusion, and visual hallucinations, complete the picture (Grilly, 2006). These withdrawal symptoms can occur even when there is still a fairly high level of blood alcohol (Ritchie, 1985). A second long-term consequence of alcohol use is *Kor-*

sakoff's syndrome, a severe brain impairment characterized by the inability to remember recent events or to learn new information.

Behavioral Stimulants and Convulsants

Drugs such as caffeine, strychnine, pentylenetetrazol (Metrazol), amphetamine (Benzedrine), and cocaine differ widely in their molecular structure and mechanisms of action. However, they share at least one property: They all excite the CNS, which in turn results in an increase in the user's behavioral activity and in the production of a heightened level of arousal. Additionally, these stimulants, including caffeine, can be addictive (Silverman, Evans, Strain, and Griffiths, 1992).

The first part of this section on Stimulants and Convulsants discusses the amphetamines, including Adderall, methylphenidate (Ritalin, Concerta), and methamphetamine. We then discuss an amphetamine derivative, methylenedioxymethamphetamine (MDMA), a popular "club drug," with reputed **neurotoxic** effects. We finish this section by examining the effects of cocaine and "crack" cocaine.

Amphetamines

Amphetamines ("Dexies," "speed," "uppers," "co-pilot," "hearts" or "pink hearts," "footballs," "dominos," "drivers," or "bennies") alter consciousness by increasing subjective feelings of energy, wakefulness, mood, attention, and euphoria. Amphetamines also decrease appetite and the need for sleep. High doses cause rapid or confused speech, agitation, paranoia, aggression, and psychotic symptoms. Physiologically, amphetamines increase heart rate, blood pressure, and body temperature. High doses can cause heart arrhythmia (irregular heart beat), stroke, "shakiness" or tremors, and convulsions.

Amphetamine is a racemic compound, which can be isolated into two mirror images or "isomers," levo-amphetamine (*l*-amphetamine) and dextro-amphetamine (*d*-amphetamine), the more potent isomer. Amphetamine was originally developed as a synthetic substitute for ephedrine, a naturally occurring extract of the *Ephedra vulgaris* ("ma huang") herb, known to have powerful anti-asthmatic effects (Meyer & Quenzer, 2005). The racemic mixture of amphetamine was first marketed in the 1920s as a treatment for asthma, and was sold as Benzedrine in inhaler form by Smith, Kline, and French pharmaceuticals (Grilly, 2006; Meyer & Quenzer, 2005). Evidently, the consciousness altering and reinforcing effects of Benzedrine were readily apparent, and the inhalers were widely abused (Meyer & Quenzer, 2005). Later, in the mid half of the 20th century, the isomers were isolated, and drug companies began marketing *d*-amphetamine under the brand name Dexedrine (hence the street name "Dex," "Dexy," or "Dexies"). Dexedrine and other amphetamines were widely prescribed and used for weight loss, energy-enhancement, and as study aids for students. It sounds surprising today, but women were even given amphetamines by obstetricians to minimize weight gain during pregnancy! A popular book in the 1960s, *Valley of the Dolls* by Jacqueline Susann (1966), illustrates the pervasive use and dependence on amphetamines (and other drugs) in American culture during the mid 1900s; "dolls" has been used as a street name for both amphetamines and barbiturates. Interestingly, that book may be loosely based on the true stories of Hollywood actresses Ethel Merman and Judy Garland, who reportedly grew dependent on amphetamines prescribed for "energy" and to lose weight, and barbiturates to counteract the stimulant and anxiety-promoting effects of the amphetamines and stress.

Amphetamine is structurally similar to the neurotransmitter dopamine, as well as the naturally occurring compounds **ephedrine** and **cathinone** (Meyer & Quenzer, 2005). **Cathinone** ("Khat," qat, Q'at, Quat) is the active ingredient in a shrub indigenous to East Africa and the Arabian peninsula, a stimulant often used (and abused) in those cultures. **Methcathinone** ("cat," "meow"), illegal in the United States, can be readily synthesized from ephedrine, and is abused in the U.S., though not as frequently as other amphetamines including methamphetamine (discussed below). Pharmacologically, amphetamines function as indirect agonists for the catecholamine neurotransmitters dopamine and norepinephrine. Amphetamines both facilitate the release and inhibit reuptake of dopamine and norepinephrine, leaving more in the synaptic cleft to activate post-synaptic neurons (Grilly, 2006).

Amphetamines continue to be available clinically, especially in the treatment of obesity and attention-related disorders including attention-deficit hyperactivity disorder (ADHD). Two drugs commonly prescribed to combat the attention-impairing effects of ADHD are **methylphenidate** (**Ritalin, Concerta**), a drug structurally similar to amphetamine with similar stimulant and euphoric effects, and **Adderall**, a racemic form of amphetamine. According to the National Institute on Drug Abuse (NIDA, 2009), these prescription stimulants are frequently abused, both recreationally and to enhance performance. Often abusers crush prescription tablets and insufflate or "snort" the powder, although some may dissolve the tablets in water and inject the solution into a vein, which can be particularly dangerous due to insoluble particles contained in the pills, which may block small blood vessels. NIDA (2009) reports that prescription stimulant abuse is on the decline from a peak in the mid 1990s, when there were more high school seniors who abused Ritalin than who received prescriptions (DEA, 2005). However, ask any student on a college campus, and you will hear stories suggesting that a significant number of high school and college students continue to abuse these drugs.

Methamphetamine

Methamphetamine ("meth," "crystal," "crank," "glass," "ice," "speed," "tina," "poor man's coke," "zip," and "go") is structurally similar to amphetamine, but is more potent (Meyer & Quenzer, 2005). Methamphetamine is available by prescription for use in the treatment of ADHD and obesity. It is currently sold under the brand name Desoxyn, by Ovation Pharmaceuticals. However, the greatest public health concern surrounds the illicit production of methamphetamine in "meth labs," often residential homes. Methamphetamine is readily (although hazardously) synthesized from ephedrine or pseudoephedrine, chemicals found in many over-the-counter cold preparations. However, by-products of the synthesis of methamphetamine from ephedrine and pseudoephrine are toxic and highly flammable; explosions are common. Nonetheless, easy and affordable availability has caused methamphetamine use to escalate. Not only is methamphetamine abuse a significant problem in the U.S., it has become a major global health concern. According to Cruickshank and Dyer (2009), methamphetamine is the second-most popular illicit drug worldwide (the list is led by cannabis first, followed by opiates third, and cocaine fourth; United Nations Office on Drugs and Crime, 2010).

Methamphetamine can be taken orally, dissolved and injected intravenously, or smoked. The smokeable form of methamphetamine ("ice" or "crystal meth," of the type produced in meth labs) is particularly inexpensive and easily obtained, but highly addictive. In addition to the dangerous convulsive and cardiovascular effects (i.e., increased heart rate, increased blood pressure, and risk of stroke), methamphetamine may selectively destroy dopamine neurons in the brain, making this drug **neurotoxic**. Previous research found significant decreases in the number of dopamine transporters in both animals (McCann & Ricaute, 2004) and human abusers of methamphetamine (McCann et al., 1998; Volkow et al., 2001). While decreases in dopamine transporters do not necessarily mean there is a specific loss of neurons, victims of Parkinson's disease also have significantly fewer dopamine transporters than healthy controls, and it is well established that Parkinson's disease results from the

79

selective loss of dopaminergic neurons (e.g., Ouchi et al., 1999). Furthermore, methamphetamine abusers have been found to have an eight-fold increase in Parkinson's disease, an average of 27 years following drug use (Garwood, Bekele, McCulloch, & Christine, 2006). Thus, there appears to be a link between methamphetamine abuse and dopaminergic cell loss, although further research needs to verify the neurotoxic effects of methamphetamine in humans (Meyer & Quenzer, 2005).

Methylendioxymethamphetamine (MDMA)

Methylendioxymethamphetamine (MDMA) is a type of amphetamine (Meyer & Quenzer, 2005) that, in addition to stimulating effects similar to the other amphetamines, also has mild hallucinogenic effects. Indeed, it has proven extremely difficult to classify this unique drug, as it clearly possesses effects similar to stimulant drugs, as well as to some of the psychedelic and hallucinogenic drugs (described fully below). An early study by Oberlender and Nichols (1988) attempted to determine which consciousness-altering or subjective effect of MDMA was most salient, the stimulant effect or the hallucinogenic effect, by training rats to discriminate either MDMA from saline, or amphetamine from saline, in a two-choice drug-discrimination procedure. **Drug discrimination** is a method by which animals may be trained to respond to the subjective effects of drugs (Colpaert, 1999; Overton, 1974). During training, animals are reinforced for pressing one lever (for example, the right lever) in a two-lever operant-conditioning box when under the influence of a drug, and they are reinforced for pressing the opposite lever when "sober" (that is, following saline administration). Once trained so that animals are accurately reporting when they experience a "drug" versus "no-drug" state, other compounds may be tested. Much research using this paradigm demonstrates that animals reliably identify only subjectively related compounds as the target drug (Colpaert & Balster, 1988; Colpaert & Slgen, 1982; Glennon et al., 1991). That is, a rat trained to discriminate amphetamine from saline will press the "amphetamine" lever following other stimulant drugs like methamphetamine or cocaine, but will press the "saline" lever following administration of nonstimulant drugs like LSD, mescaline, or valium.

Oberlender and Nichols (1988) found that d-amphetamine generalized to the MDMA stimulus cue in animals discriminating MDMA from saline, while the hallucinogenic drugs LSD and DOM did not. Interestingly, MDMA did not substitute for a stimulus cue provided by amphetamine, nor did it substitute for the potent hallucinogenic cues produced by LSD or

DOM in previous studies (Glennon, 1994). These findings make the study of MDMA confusing, since it makes it difficult to assess what consciousness-altering properties of the drug people may find rewarding. Do people take MDMA to experience the stimulant effects or the hallucinogenic effects?

Several studies have tried to address these concerns by training animals to discriminate between 3 (or more) drugs, not just MDMA versus saline (Goodwin & Baker, 2002; Goodwin, Pynnonen, & Baker, 2003; Oswald & Appel, 2006). In one series of studies, Baker and colleagues used an operant chamber equipped with three levers, to train a three-choice drug discrimination, where animals were discriminating MDMA from amphetamine or saline (Goodwin & Baker, 2002), or MDMA from LSD or saline (Goodwin et al., 2003). Training animals to discriminate MDMA from amphetamine forced the animal to focus on the nonstimulant cues of MDMA, because the stimulant cues provided by amphetamine and MDMA are similar. Conversely, training animals to discriminate MDMA from LSD forced animals to focus on the non-hallucinogenic cues, because the hallucinogenic cues provided by MDMA and LSD could be similar. These experiments verified that the stimulant and hallucinogenic effects of MDMA could be teased apart; LSD (but not amphetamine) partially substituted for MDMA in animals discriminating MDMA from amphetamine or saline (Goodwin & Baker, 2002), while d-amphetamine (but not LSD) partially substituted for MDMA when animals were discriminating MDMA from LSD or saline (Goodwin et al., 2003).

To further elucidate the consciousness-altering properties of MDMA, Oswald and Appel (2006) used a 2-level drug discrimination paradigm, but trained animals to discriminate MDMA (on one lever) from a series of other drugs (on the other lever). Four groups were trained in these studies: a traditional MDMA versus saline group; an MDMA versus the stimulants d-amphetamine, cocaine, or saline; MDMA versus the hallucinogens LSD, psilocybin, or saline; and MDMA versus completely dissimilar drugs: the sedative-hypnotic pentobarbital, the convulsant pentelyenetetrazol, and saline. Animals in this study all learned their respective discriminations, but it took animals longer to discriminate between MDMA and stimulant drugs (an average of 59.4 days) than between MDMA and hallucinogenic drugs (an average of 44.6 days). Longer learning times may indicate that the subjective effects are similar; it may have been more difficult to tell the difference between MDMA and the other stimulants, than it was to discriminate MDMA from the hallucinogenic drugs.

Together, these results suggest that although the subjective or consciousness-altering effects of MDMA are different from amphetamine, the effects of MDMA are probably more similar to that of amphetamine than to that of other more potent hallucinogenic drugs. This, coupled with the fact that MDMA is an amphetamine derivative, causes many people to classify MDMA as a stimulant/convulsant, rather than a hallucinogenic drug, although the classification is debatable (e.g., see Grilly, 2006).

While MDMA has a relatively long history of 90 years or more (see Grilly, 2006 and Meyer & Quenzer, 2005 for reviews), it is only within the last two decades that illicit use of the drug has become prevalent. MDMA has a variety of names including "ecstasy," "X," "E," "rolls," "beans," "Adam," and "XTC." The drug is a white crystalline powder, but is usually seen in capsule form, in pressed pills, or as loose powder. It is most commonly swallowed in pill form, but occasionally the powdered form is insufflated, smoked, or dissolved in water and injected (Benzenhofer & Passie, 2009). The physical effects of MDMA include dry mouth, jaw clenching, teeth grinding, nystagmus (eye wiggling), excessive sweating, and nausea. Higher doses result in a pounding heartbeat, dizziness, and restlessness. One dangerous effect of MDMA is that it can make people ignore bodily distress signals, causing them to fail to realize that they are dizzy, dehydrated, or exhausted. Since the drug is frequently used at all-night dance parties or "raves," ignoring signals of dehydration and exhaustion has led to death, possibly due to hyponatremia, or disruption of salt content caused by excessive sweating without appropriate fluid replacement (Schifano, 2004).

Psychological effects of MDMA vary, but most users report that tactile and sensory experiences are heightened, and common things seem especially interesting. Two main effects of MDMA include entactogenesis, a generalized happy feeling that the world is good and peaceful, and empathogenesis, feeling emotionally close to self and others. Many users report they use the drug to experience these empathogenic and entactogenic effects (Bedi, Hyman, & deWit, 2010). Indeed, MDMA has a history of use as an adjunct to psychotherapy, to help patients communicate and gain greater insight into their emotions. Unfortunately, the high abuse potential and other effects of this drug make it an unlikely therapeutic candidate (e.g., see Parrott, 2007 for a review). Furthermore, tolerance to the behavioral and psychological effects of the drug develops rapidly, prompting regular users to "binge" on as many as 15–20 pills per night (Schifano, 2004). Even a single dose of MDMA can produce a "hangover" effect where users report feeling depressed, unpleasant, and unsociable for several days. MDMA can also have long-lasting effects on sleep, mood, and personality (Parrott, 2000). Deficits in long-term memory, attention, and verbal learning have been found in repeat users, even following MDMA abstinence (McCardle, Luebbers, Carter, Croft, & Stough, 2004).

Pharmacologically, MDMA works by stimulating the release and blocking reuptake of the monoamines dopamine and serotonin. MDMA is unique from the other amphetamines in that it affects serotonin to a far greater degree (e.g., Bankson & Cunningham, 2001). Furthermore, MDMA has been found to have **neurotoxic** effects at **serotonin** neurons in rats and nonhuman primates (Green, Cross, & Goodwin, 1995; Ricaurte & McCann, 2001; Steel, McCann, & Ricaurte, 1994). Although some recovery of serotonin neural loss is observed many years following MDMA abstinence, the pattern of recovery does not mimic healthy tissue (Ricaurte & McCann, 2001). It has been difficult to verify neural loss following MDMA use in humans, but there is evidence to suggest that repeat users of MDMA do have significant changes in serotonergic function that may reflect neural loss (Boot et al., 2000; Parrot, 2001).

Cocaine

Cocaine is a natural plant product derived from the leaves of *Erythroxylum coca*, a plant that thrives on the slopes of the Andes Mountains of Bolivia and Peru where the annual rainfall is more than 100 inches (Ray & Ksir, 1987). Research indicates that as early as 500 CE, the native inhabitants of these areas, as well as those of Columbia and northwestern Argentina, chewed on the leaves of this tree to increase their physical stamina (Guerra, 1971).

Before the invasion led by Francisco Pizarro (1476–1541) in the 1500s, the Incas had built a well-developed civilization in Peru. The coca leaves played an important role in Inca culture, functioning initially as a part of the religious ceremonies and later, by the time the Spanish under Pizarro had arrived, as a medium of exchange. The conquistadors also adopted this custom and paid the native laborers in coca leaves for mining and transporting gold and silver. The leaves probably gave the workers an increased sense of strength and endurance and at the same time decreased their appetites (Hart, Ksir, & Ray, 2011).

While historians, through their early writing on Inca civilization, had made available to Europeans the knowledge of the unique properties of the coca leaves, no real interest in the plant was manifested there until the later part of the nineteenth century (Taylor, 1949). Three individuals have been suggested as having played prominent roles in introducing cocaine to Europe (see Hart, Ksir, & Ray, 2011). One was the French chemist Angelo Mariani, who first made coca leaves available to the general public by using their extract in a series of products, including coca tea, coca lozenges, and his famous Mariani coca wine. Uplifted spirits, freedom from fatigue, and an overall good feeling were the major benefits consumers derived from Mariani's coca leaf extract products, which proved so satisfactory that Pope Leo XIII presented Mariani with a medal of appreciation.

The second member of this trio was Sigmund Freud (1856–1939), the founder of psychoanalysis. In the early 1900s, while suffering from a bout of depression and fatigue, Freud read an account of the isolation of cocaine and was determined to experiment with this "new" drug. He found that it not only relieved his own depression and fatigue, but also seemed to provide him with newfound energy to continue his work. It is clear that his personal experiences with the drug, combined with the results he achieved using it in his practice, made Freud an early advocate of cocaine. In his papers on cocaine written in 1885, Freud recited a litany of the drug's supposed therapeutic benefits, which included effectiveness as a local anesthetic, production of exhilaration and aphrodisiac properties, usefulness in treating asthma and digestive disorders of the stomach, and its role in the treatment of alcohol and morphine addiction (Freud, 1970). In regard to the last benefit, Freud wrote:

> It was first discovered in America that cocaine is capable of alleviating the serious withdrawal symptoms in subjects who are abstaining from morphine and of suppressing their craving for morphine. … On basis of my experiences with the effects of cocaine, I have no hesitation in recommending the administration of cocaine for such withdrawal cures in subcutaneous injections of 0.03 to 0.05 grams per dose, without any fear of increasing the dose. On several occasions, I have even seen cocaine quickly eliminate the manifestations of intolerance that appeared after a rather large dose of morphine, as if it had a specific ability to counteract morphine. (1970)

So convinced was Freud of cocaine's effectiveness in this connection that he used it in the treatment of the morphine addiction of a close friend, Dr. Fleischel. What transpired clearly was not anticipated. Freud found that as treatment progressed, increasingly larger doses of the drug were needed, until finally a cocaine-induced psychosis was precipitated. This experience was more than adequate to change Freud's initial attitudes toward cocaine (Jones, 1953–1957).

Finally, in 1890, it was made public that the world's foremost fictitious detective, Sherlock Holmes, advocated the use of cocaine as a means of relieving the boredom of day-to-day existence (Grilly, 2006). In *The Sign of the Four*

(Doyle, 1938), the fictitious Dr. Watson describes the effects of cocaine use on the master detective:

> "It is cocaine," he said, "a seven-percent solution. Would you care to try it?"
>
> "No, indeed," I answered brusquely. "My constitution has not got over the Afghan campaign yet. I cannot afford to throw any extra strain upon it."
>
> He smiled at my vehemence. "Perhaps you are right, Watson," he said. "I suppose that its influence is physically a bad one. I find it, however, so transcendently stimulating and clarifying to the mind that its secondary action is a matter of small moment."
>
> "But consider!" I said earnestly. "Count the cost! Your brain may, as you say, be roused and excited, but it is a pathological and morbid process which involves increased tissue-change and may at least have a permanent weakness. You know, too, what a black reaction comes upon you. Surely the game is hardly worth the candle. Why should you, for a mere passing pleasure, risk the loss of those great powers with which you have been endowed?" ...
>
> He did not seem offended. On the contrary, he put his finger tips together, and leaned his elbows on the arm of his chair, like one who has a relish for conversation.
>
> "My mind," he said, "rebels at stagnation. Give me problems, give me the most abstruse cryptogram, or the most intricate analysis and I am in my own proper atmosphere. I can dispense then with artificial stimulants. But I abhor the dull routine of existence. I crave for mental exaltation." (pp. 91–92)

In the United States, use of cocaine for both medical and quasimedical purposes was widespread around the turn of the century. Traveling salesmen sold their "snake oils," "elixirs of life," and patent medicines, all of which supposedly contained a secret ingredient to bring long life, a sense of exhilaration, and well-being to all its users. Very often, the so-called secret ingredient was cocaine. In fact, cocaine was also at one time an ingredient in cola soft drinks. With the passage of the Harrison Act of 1914, use of cocaine was forced underground, where it was to remain until the emergence of the drug subculture in the late 1960s. Since 1969, use of cocaine in the United States has shown a substantial increase.

Cocaine acts both as a local anesthetic and as a CNS stimulant. The ability of cocaine to numb the area to which it has been applied topically was first discovered in 1860 by Dr. Carl Koller, a Viennese eye surgeon, who used it as a local anesthetic in the eye. Low concentrations of cocaine used in this manner appear to block neural conduction when brought into direct contact with sensory nerve fibers. The drug's ability to increase the user's awareness levels represents the CNS function of cocaine. All available evidence would suggest that the initial central effect occurs at the level of the cerebral cortex, although it is possible that this effect may be mediated by subcortical activity.

The increase in CNS arousal is closely associated with the action of cocaine at noradrenergic synapses—that is, synapses at which norepinephrine serves as the transmitter substance. It is generally accepted that cocaine inhibits the active reuptake of norepinephrine in the brain and the peripheral nervous system. This blockage increases the amount of norepinepherine available in the synaptic cleft, which means that the transmitter will be in contact with postsynaptic receptor sites at higher concentrations and for longer periods of time than would normally be the case.

The gross physiological responses to cocaine are essentially sympathomimetic. During cocaine use, the heart accelerates, the respiration rate increases, the pupils dilate, and blood pressure increases, often to dangerous levels. Sweating and dryness of the throat may also be observed.

Actually, cocaine not only stimulates the sympathetic nervous system, it also suppresses the parasympathetic nervous system, a fact that may help to explain why it can put enough stress on the heart to kill an otherwise healthy young person with just a single use (Cowen, 1990). Use of cocaine can also cause brain atrophy, a form of damage in which the brain actually shrinks (Pascual-Leone, Dhuna, Altafullah, & Anderson, 1990). Despite these functional changes, until the 1980s there was some question as to whether cocaine produces psychological dependence (Jaffe, 1985; Petersen, 1979). Studies during the 1980s suggest that, particularly when administered intravenously or by free-basing (smoking), cocaine can induce a very strong psychological dependence (Perez-Reyes, Guiseppi, Ondrusek, Jeffcoat, & Cook, 1982). Dackis and Gold (1985) suggest that several major biochemical events play a role in cocaine dependency, not the least of which is the fact that cocaine inhibits dopamine reuptake by the presynaptic neuron. This has the effect of prolonging the amount of time that substantial amounts of dopamine are available in the synapse. This biochemical effect seems to be the key to the rewarding property of the drug (e.g., euphoria).

Cocaine, also referred to as "coke," "flake," "snow," "gold dust," "blow," "nose candy," and "Bolivian marching powder," is a white, translucent, flaky substance. It takes more than 200 pounds of coca leaves to produce a little over 2 pounds of pure cocaine, which is distilled into a paste and mixed with hydrochloric acid before being exported for further processing. Importers cut the potency in half by adding agents like procaine, amphetamines, or even strychnine. Before it gets to the street, local dealers and handlers have cut it further, usually with a sugar substance.

About 11 percent of Americans above the age of 12 have used cocaine at least once (U.S. Department of Health and Human Services, 1994), although the number of users has declined since the 1980s. The availability of cocaine has not changed significantly, but perceptions of cocaine's risk and disapproval of its use appear to have increased (Bachman, Johnston, & O'Malley, 1990).

Coke is convenient to use (Ashley, 1976). In the United States, cocaine is most frequently inhaled, or **snorted**, into each nostril (see Figure 3.2). The drug is absorbed from the mucous lining into the bloodstream, reaching the brain almost instantaneously. The **oral method** is another way of ingesting cocaine, although it is often assumed to be ineffective. Van Dyke and his colleagues compared the intranasal and oral rates of ingestion and found that three of four volunteers experienced more intensive highs after oral administration (Van Dyke, Jatlow, Ungeru, Barash, & Byck, 1978). However, the latency of onset was more rapid after snorting. Another, more dangerous method of ingestion is intravenous injection, or **mainlining**.

A typical single dose of cocaine (approximately 30 milligrams) ingested in the most preferred manner (i.e., snorting) usually precipitates a state of euphoria that peaks in a matter of a few minutes. The high typically lasts between 20 and 40 minutes, generally with little or no discernible aftereffects (Hart, Ksir, & Ray, 2011). Thus, the effects of cocaine are similar to those of amphetamines but of shorter duration. A single moderate dose works for about 30 minutes, compared to several hours for amphetamines. The effects are also more subtle and less physical (Julien, 1997).

This altered state of consciousness, however, may be preceded by headache, dizziness, and restlessness. Feelings of fatigue and sleepiness vanish and are replaced by those of exhilaration, newfound energy, and excitement. The individual may have a sense of increased self-confidence, which may be a product of the feelings of enhanced mental abilities. Cocaine has been viewed as

Figure 3.2 • Inhaling Cocaine

Image © ejwhite, 2011. Used under license from Shutterstock, Inc.

87

a social drug, one that has recreational properties; that is, instead of turning inward, the user becomes talkative and seeks the company of others. The cocaine user's sleep is profoundly affected; both REM sleep and total sleep are greatly reduced. Finally, it has been reported that cocaine may enhance the user's sex drive and sexual experience. At least one study (Resnick, Kestenbaum, & Schwartz, 1977) has produced results that suggest a biphasic effect of cocaine—that is, an initial state of euphoria followed by dysphoria. Six of the subjects in this study reported that, following an initial high, they experienced "postcoke blues" or "crashing," which was characterized by feelings of anxiety, depression, fatigue, and a desire for more cocaine.

Crack

Probably the most serious drug problem today is the smoking of a compound produced with cocaine known as crack. **Crack** consists of cocaine and baking soda mixed with water. The mixture is allowed to dehydrate to form a crystalline-like hardness, which then is cracked and broken into small pieces. The term crack derives from the cracking sound that is heard when the drug is mixed with these chemicals and heated (Langton, 1991). These pieces are then heated to degrade the compound, and the result is smoked in a pipe.

Unlike cocaine, which produces a slow euphoria that lasts for several minutes, crack produces a fast euphoria that lasts only seconds. As a result, to continue the euphoric feeling, abusers end up using more crack than cocaine to attain a high. This creates a dangerous situation, and abusers easily overdose on crack, doing damage to the cardiovascular system and often producing death.

Cocaine is also sometimes mixed with tobacco, marijuana, and even heroin and is heated, then smoked in a pipe. Because cocaine hydrochloride is volatile only at extremely high temperatures, during which it is degraded, it must be chemically converted back to its alkaloid state for it to be effective when it is smoked. This is generally referred to as **free-basing** (Jacob, Jones, Benowitz, & Shulgin, 1989; Nelson, 1987). Whatever method of ingestion is selected, the rate of absorption into the system is very rapid (Jeffcoat, Perez-Reyes, Hill, Sadler, & Cook, 1989). Clearly, factors such as how cocaine is ingested and what dosage is used play a major role in determining both the physiological and the psychological effects of the drug (American Society for Pharmacology 1987; Resnick, Kestenbaum, & Schwartz, 1977).

As was alluded to earlier, most users do not habitually take high doses of cocaine (Post, 1975; Siegel, 1985), unless it is the crack variety. However, when coke is chronically abused, it produces a toxic syndrome that is typified by an enhanced sense of physical and mental capacity; loss of appetite; grinding of teeth; stereotyped, repetitious behavior; and paranoia. The addict often carries weapons to use against alleged persecutors. Two commonly reported perceptual changes that occur with cocaine use are the appearance of "cocaine bugs," technically called **formication**, and "snow lights" (Jaffe, 1985). Formication is a tactile disturbance in which the user feels a sensation like bugs crawling under his or her skin; the sensation may become so great that he or she may resort to a knife to cut them out. The physiological basis for this phenomenon is probably drug-induced stimulation of free nerve endings in the skin (Ellinwood, 1969). Snow lights are a visual disturbance in which the user perceives bright flashing lights in his or her visual field.

Until recently, there was some question as to whether tolerance occurs with cocaine use. There were conflicting reports regarding the development of a tolerance to cocaine. Spotts and Schontz (1976), for example, found some support for the then-majority view against development of tolerance when their group of habitual users did not increase dose levels over time. The users did, however, experience a kind of temporary tolerance, in that when they administered cocaine several times in a single day, they had to use increasingly larger doses to achieve the same effect.

Today, however, there is considerable evidence that tolerance does develop to many of the physiological and subjective effects of cocaine, especially crack, and in some cases it develops rapidly (American Society for Pharmacology, 1987; Fischman, Schuster, Javaid, Hatano, & Davis, 1985; Wood & Emmett-Oglesby, 1986). Whether tolerance or sensitization occurs with chronic cocaine use appears to depend on many factors, only some of which are known (Grabowski & Dworkin, 1985).

Withdrawal symptoms following continued high dose use are not dramatic or life threatening. However, cocaine users do experience withdrawal symptoms after extensive cocaine use. Furthermore, the symptoms occur in several phases (Gawin & Kleber, 1986). During the first few hours after heavy use, the cocaine user feels depressed and agitated, lacks an appetite, and experiences high cocaine craving. In the next several hours or days, the user experiences extreme hunger, although cocaine craving is absent. In some individuals there is also a strong abhorrence for cocaine during this time, and the need for sleep is overwhelming. During the next several days the user's sleep patterns and mood return to normal, and there is little cocaine craving.

Subsequently, the user experiences anxiety, a lack of energy, an inability to enjoy normal activities, and high cocaine craving that is enhanced by environmental cues previously associated with cocaine use, such as a particular room, a party, or other friends who also use cocaine. After several weeks, the user's mood and pleasure response return to normal, and he or she experiences only episodic cocaine craving, which again is most common in the presence of specific environmental cues. If the person begins taking cocaine again, he or she generally returns to the first phase of withdrawal.

Although Wetii and Wright (1979) have suggested that only in rare cases does chronic abuse of cocaine prove fatal, today's sports enthusiasts have become tragically aware that cocaine use can be deadly. Obviously, one might predict that extremely high dosage levels of cocaine in pure form would cause problems, but one has to wonder how it is possible that a moderate dose of this drug could kill a world-class athlete such as Leonard Bias of the University of Maryland or Donald Rogers of the Cleveland Browns, who had no known physical weaknesses, while others are able to chronically abuse the drug with no fatal effects. Medical authorities seem to be divided in their explanations of fatal reactions to cocaine but one hypothesis offered by Dr. Grinspoon, a cocaine expert at Harvard University, revolves around the fact that cocaine is a drug. We are all aware of the fact that some people are extremely sensitive to certain drugs (e.g., aspirin, caffeine, penicillin) and cannot take them without severe consequences. Dr. Grinspoon contends that there are some individuals who are especially sensitive to even recreational doses of cocaine and cannot ingest it without suffering severe consequences (Leo, 1986).

Cocaine use may cause sudden death because of cerebral hemorrhaging (Lichtenfeld, Rubin, & Feldman, 1984), convulsion induction (Ellinwood, Kilbey, Fani, & Khoury, 1977), or acute myocardial infarction (sudden insufficiency of blood to the heart muscles), which can occur even in individuals with no preexisting arterial dysfunctions (American Society for Pharmacology, 1987). While the exact mechanism behind sudden deaths is still obscure, recent evidence suggests that even low doses of cocaine can lead to inflammation of the muscular walls of the heart in some individuals (Grilly, 2006).

Narcotic Analgesics (Opiates)

The **opiates** and their derivatives including opium, heroin, morphine, codeine, Percodan, and Demerol, together with their antagonists (e.g., nalorphine) make up the class of consciousness-altering drugs also referred to as **narcotic analgesics** or **strongly addictive analgesics**. Opiates are any natural or synthetic drug that acts on the body in a way similar to that of **morphine**, which is one of the most powerful analgesics derived from the opium poppy plant,

Papaver somniferum (see Figure 3.3). The use of the term **narcotic** by law enforcement agencies, medical personnel, and the general public has led to a proliferation of meanings for this term. However, here it will be used to refer to those drugs that have both a **sedative** (sleep-inducing) and an **analgesic** (pain-relieving) action. This definition restricts the term to the opiates.

The primary medical uses of these drugs include the relief of pain, the treatment of diarrhea, and the relief of a cough. Of course they are also quite capable of inducing sleep. However, because of the euphoria associated with the use of these drugs, which may lead to their abuse, they are seldom, if ever, used for this purpose.

It is hypothesized that the opiates may produce their analgesic effects by interacting with receptor sites for "natural opiate substances" called **endorphins** (Leavitt, 1995). The way the opiate drug acts on these sites is suggested to resemble a lock-and-key mechanism (see Figure 3.4). Thus, the receptors are specific nerve cells that serve as locks into which the appropriate opiate drug (the key) fits.

Figure 3.3 • Opium Poppy Plant (*Papaver somniferum*)
Image © Tatiana Mirlin, 2011. Used under license from Shutterstock, Inc.

Pert and Snyder (1973) were the first to provide experimental evidence that such receptor sites actually exist. They first injected radioactively tagged naloxone into each of their animal subjects. (Naloxone is a drug whose chemical substance so closely resembles morphine that its molecules fit the same receptor locks. Thus, it acts as an opiate antagonist and competes for the same receptor sites.) This afforded the investigators the opportunity to observe the distribution of radioactivity and thus the distribution of opiate receptors. Their findings suggest that the opiate receptor sites are to be found in especially large numbers in the amygdala, the caudate nucleus, the substantia nigra, the medial nuclei of the thalamus, and the periventricular and periacqueductal gray matter that immediately surrounds the ventricles in the lower portion of the brain. Other investigators—Simantov, Goodman, Aposhian, and Snyder (1976)—discovered that only vertebrates possess receptors of this type. However, the degree to which opiate receptors appear to be constant varies among all vertebrates, from the most primitive to the most advanced.

Another reason for suspecting that the opiates may operate on specific receptor sites in the brain was best expressed by Restak (1977). Restak suggested

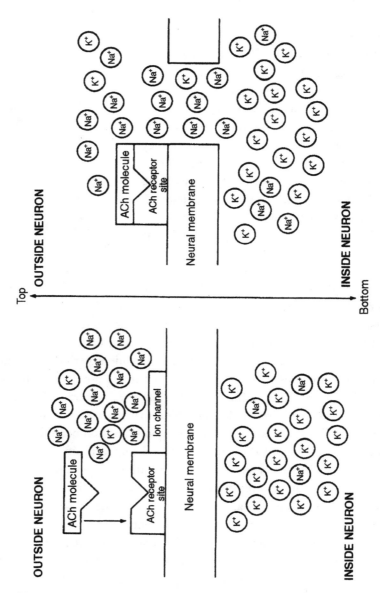

Figure 3.4 • A Lock-and-Key Mechanism

that the existence of a lock strongly suggests the existence of a key or keys in the brain. Stated differently, if there are opiate receptor sites in the brain, then there should also be opiumlike substances that are manufactured in the brain. In 1975, Hughes et al. announced their discovery of two short-chained peptides called **enkephalins** that are produced in the brain and distributed in the same locations as the receptor sites. These results were confirmed in other laboratories (Akil, Watson, Sullivan, & Barchas, 1978). Today, we recognize three distinct families of these opiate-like substances in the brain; in addition to the enkephalins there are the **endorphins** and the **dynorphins** (Akil et al., 1984). Each family is derived from different precursor polypeptides (Marx, 1984).

Such advancement in the understanding of the physiological mechanisms that underlie opium-like drug activity led Snyder (1977) to offer a theory of opiate addiction. According to Snyder, under normal conditions, opiate receptors are exposed to a certain basal level of enkephalin. If an opiate drug is administered to the individual at this time, the drug molecules will proceed to bind the usually unoccupied receptor sites. The net effect is a potentiation of the analgesic effects of the enkephalin system. If the administration of opiates is continued, the opiate receptor sites are soon overloaded with opiate-like material, causing them to transmit a message, probably by some hypothetical neuronal feedback loop, to the enkephalin neurons to cease firing and releasing enkephalin. Once this occurs, the receptor cells are exposed only to the opiate, and they can now tolerate more of it to make up for the enkephalin they are no longer receiving. When the administration of the opiate is terminated, the opiate receptors find themselves with neither the opiate nor the enkephalin. Snyder believes that this lack initiates a sequence of events that result in withdrawal symptoms.

The opiates produce a depression of neural activity in the respiratory and cough centers of the brainstem, along with a depression of neural activity in the cortex. It also appears that they have an excitatory effect on the neural elements that make up the vomiting center of the brainstem.

Heroin is the most frequently abused narcotic. "Horse," "Harry," "smack," "stuff," "junk," and just plain "H" are but a few of the many street names by which this drug is known. The name of the drug is derived from the Greek god Heros, who was the savior of humankind. In a real sense, this is probably how many initially viewed heroin after its discovery in 1874 by Heinrich Dreser. Another opium derivative, morphine, had been used before Dreser's work, both as an analgesic and in the treatment of alcoholism. However, it proved to have one serious side effect: Its use often led to addiction. Dreser, searching for a non-addictive opiate, found that by treating morphine with an inexpensive and readily available chemical called acetic anhydride, he could produce a drug much more potent than morphine without the addictive properties, or so he thought. The new drug rapidly replaced morphine as a painkiller, and by the early 1900s, heroin was being used in the treatment of alcoholism and morphine addiction. Soon it was found, however, that heroin was not only more powerful than morphine but also more addictive. Since 1914 the Harrison Act and subsequent laws and court decisions have progressively restricted the legal use of heroin; today, its use for any purpose is considered illegal.

Opium is derived from the sticky resin produced by the opium poppy plant. Approximately 75 percent of the weight of a given quantity of opium is composed of nonpharmacological organic agents, including oils, sugar, proteins, and resins. The remaining 25 percent includes **morphine**, the major pain-relieving drug found in opium and codeine. Heroin does not occur naturally but is a semisynthetic derivative produced by a chemical modification of morphine, which leads to an increase in the end product's (heroin's) potency. Thus, heroin is approximately three times as potent as morphine (Snyder, 1977). What you might not suspect, however, is that this increase in potency of heroin over morphine has nothing to do with increased activity at the receptor sites in the nervous system, but rather is due to the fact that heroin crosses the blood-brain barrier more rapidly than does morphine. This allows it to accumulate in the brain more quickly. Once in the brain, heroin is metabolized into morphine, but because it gets there so rapidly, it exerts effects that are more rapid and intense than those of morphine (Grilly, 2006).

Manufacturers and distributors of street heroin take little care in its production and cutting. Quinine, milk, sugar, and talc are commonly used to cut the drug (Duvall, Locke, & Brill, 1963). According to Hoffmann and Hoffmann (1975), the heroin content of packets seized by police generally ranges between 1 and 5 percent. As we will see shortly, many of the substances and dilutents are directly harmful.

Heroin is usually introduced into the body by smoking, snorting, eating, skin popping, or mainlining. Oral ingestion leads to a slower and considerably less complete high than that produced by other routes. Mainliners experience a **rush**, an immediate and intense pleasure seconds after the drug is injected into the bloodstream. Current thought suggests that heroin does not reach the brain that quickly and that this rush is most probably due to a powerful action on the peripheral nervous system or on the cardiovascular system. Some of the cutting agents are poorly soluble in the injected solution, and an intravenous injection of incompletely dissolved substances may cause a fatal reaction (Eiseman, Lami, & Rush, 1964). In the case of skin popping, the liquefied heroin is injected just beneath the surface of the skin. Such a technique can lead to the development of severe multiple ulcerating lesions. These lesions most likely are caused by the quinine or other agents used to cut the heroin, and they create a most favorable environment for the development of tetanus (Hirsch, 1972).

On ingesting heroin, the user experiences a restriction of awareness and an almost immediate and intense feeling of pleasure in the abdominal area, which typically lasts about one to five minutes and is often described as resembling a whole-body orgasm (Leavitt, 1995; Mathis, 1970). This brief euphoric spasm, called a "rush," "bang," or "kick," is followed by a sense of euphoria and contentment that may last from four to six hours. During this high period, the heroin user is able to escape reality and experiences the predominantly pleasant feelings of relaxation, euphoria, and reverie. The user feels sedated— "nods"—during which time there may be vivid visions and dreams. Since the heroin user no longer cares about much of anything, he or she does not seem to be bothered by tensions and anxieties. Everything looks rosy and harmonious, at least until the drug effects wear off. As one might predict, heroin has a dramatic effect on pain perception and the response to it. The major effect on pain, however, is not so much to raise the pain threshold as to simply change the response to pain. Heroin makes the pain more bearable.

Along with these behavioral and consciousness-altering effects, heroin also produces some physiological effects. These reactions include pupillary constriction (pinpoint pupils), changes in body temperature, constipation, nausea, and vomiting (Julien, 1997). Clearly, not all of these reactions are pleasant. However, the negative physiological effects seem to be overridden by the euphoria and the escape from reality. As one might expect, individuals vary widely in their reactions to the drug. Thus, for some, the introduction to heroin is anything but pleasant. Such "experimenters" may only experience the discomforts associated with heroin use.

Intermittent use of heroin may be continued indefinitely by some people, who eventually quit without difficulty (Chien, Gerard, Lee, & Rosenfeld, 1964). Continued use of heroin results in the development of both a psychological dependence and a tolerance and physiological craving for the drug. After frequent and repeated administration of smack for two or three weeks, a 10-fold tolerance can easily develop. Although the actual time necessary to establish a drug habit varies considerably from individual to individual, it has been estimated that continued use over one month or longer is sufficient to develop a physiological addiction (Grilly, 2006). The definition of addiction is complicated by the fact that most heroin addicts have tried, and sometimes regularly use, other drugs, including alcohol, amphetamines, barbiturates, and cocaine. When people consume more than one drug, it is hard to classify them as addicts of one drug or another (Istvan & Matarazzo, 1984). The addicts find that the high is followed by a negative phase that produces a desire for more of the drug. If for some reason the drug supply is cut off for even a short time, the heroin addict enters into a phase of withdrawal, during which he or she becomes physically ill. Within four to six hours after stopping, withdrawal discomforts are felt, which turn into agonies by 12 to 16 hours after the last dose. Sweating, shaking, vomiting, running nose and eyes, chills, aching muscles, abdominal pain, and diarrhea are common (Julien, 1997). However, withdrawal from heroin does not cause death.

Psychedelics and Hallucinogens

The drugs included in this class are a highly varied group of chemical compounds, all of which have the ability to induce visual, auditory, somesthetic, or other **hallucination**, a sense perception for which there is no appropriate external stimulus. For this reason these agents have been called **hallucinogens**. These drugs may also produce disturbances in the individual's thoughts and perceptions and in some instances may produce behavioral patterns that have been described as being similar to the components of psychotic behavior. Because they are thought to be able to mimic psychoses or induce a psychotic state, they are often referred to as **psychotomimetic drugs**.

Since both of these terms focus on a single pharmacological action of these drugs rather than their full range of actions, they seem inappropriate. Additionally, there is some question concerning the accuracy of the use of these terms in referring to this category of drugs. For example, these drugs most frequently distort rather than produce sensory images. Thus, the user sees and hears what is going on in his or her world but in strange and different ways. Additionally, a careful analysis of the effects of these drugs suggests that they are really unlike the behavioral patterns observed during psychotic episodes. Osmond (1957), observing that all of the drugs in this category had the ability to alter sensory perception and therefore may be considered mind-expanding, proposed the term **psychedelic drugs** as a label for this group of chemical compounds (Julien, 1997).

As we suggested at the beginning of this section, the category contains a number of drugs that vary considerably in their chemical structure. Like most of the drugs we have discussed to this point, many of these agents produce their effects by changing the synaptic transmission process. Thus, *physostigmine* and *diisopropyl fluorophosphate (DFP)* increase the amounts of *acetylcholine (ACh)* available at the synapse by blocking *acetylcholinesterase's* ability to terminate achetylcholine's transmitter action. Other psychedelic drugs block the neurotransmission activity of ACh. This is the case with both *atropine* and *scopolamine. Muscarine's* effect at the acetylcholinergic synapse is that of directly stimulating the ACh receptor sites on the postsynaptic neuron. Together, these drugs constitute the **acetylcholine psychedelics**.

Norepinephrine psychedelics are those psychedelics that alter synaptic transmission at the norepinephrine synapses. Many of these drugs are closely related in structure to norepinephrine and are thought to exert their effects through changes of transmission at norepinephrine synapses.

A number of the psychedelic drugs, including *dimethyltryptamine (DMT)*, *bufotenin, psilocin, psilocybin, lysergic acid diethylamide (LSD)*, and *diethyltryptamine*, have been found to be structurally similar to the neurotransmitter substance *serotonin* (5-hydroxytryptamine) and are thought to produce their effects by changing the synaptic transmission process at serotonergic synapses.

The **psychedelic anesthetics**, including *phencyclidine (PCP), Sernylan*, and *ketamine (Ketalar)*, represent a unique grouping within this category; they do not resemble structurally any of the known neurotransmitters. This has made it particularly difficult to determine the sites and mechanisms of the action of these drugs.

The final grouping, the **cannabis drugs**, includes *marijuana* and *hashish*. While we have known about the cannabinols for a long time, we have yet to determine exactly how and where these drugs produce their effect. In this section we have selected marijuana and lysergic acid diethylamide (LSD) as representatives of this category.

Marijuana

The earliest known record of marijuana use dates back to 2737 BCE. A description of the drug was found in a book of medicines belonging to the Chinese emperor Shen Nung. Its use as an intoxicant spread to India, where it became a favorite ingredient in Indian cookery. During the 19th century, English ladies visiting India enjoyed their afternoon tea, which was often served with teacakes containing marijuana. From India the use of this drug spread to North Africa and then to Europe. It is believed that one of the major factors involved in this later extension was the return of Napoleon's troops to France after the Egyptian campaign.

Although it had been known in South and Central America for centuries, marijuana did not appear to any significant extent in the United States until about 1920 (Grinspoon, 1969). Snyder (1971) observed that a century ago, cannabis (the common hemp plant from which marijuana comes) was used for medical reasons, much as aspirin is today. It could be found in almost any drugstore, could be purchased without prescription, and was commonly prescribed by physicians for many common medical problems such as ulcers, headaches, cramps, and tooth decay.

In the 1920s the press decided that marijuana was a societal evil that was being used and spread in this country by the underworld element. Claiming an association between marijuana and the increase in crime, a New Orleans newspaper called for outlawing the drug. Shortly thereafter, laws were passed in Louisiana to rid the state of this agent of evil. This push to have marijuana declared illegal was spearheaded by the then-Commissioner of Narcotics Harry Anslinger, who had a strong interest in encouraging the states and the Bureau of Narcotics to enforce rigorously the laws against the drug. His position that marijuana was a narcotic, an agent responsible for crimes of violence, and a great danger to public safety was popularized in the news media. Eventually, this led to the passage of a federal law in 1937, which outlawed marijuana completely. By 1940 the country was convinced that marijuana was a "killer weed" that drove people to insanity and violence. While for several decades use declined due to concern about perceived risk (Bachman, Johnston, O'Malley et al., & Humphrey, 1988), marijuana use is again on the rise, especially among individuals aged 12–17 (NIDA, 2011). The number of people 12 and over reporting marijuana use in the last 30 days increased from 6.0 percent in 2009 to 6.6 percent in 2010. Even more disconcerting are results from the recent 2010 "Monitoring the Future" survey, which sampled nearly 50,000 teens in 400 public and private schools across the US. Data from the survey indicate that 8th, 10th, and 12th graders reporting daily marijuana use has increased nearly 10 percent since 2009 (NIDA, 2011).

Technically, marijuana is not a drug but rather the leaves and buds of the hemp plant, *Cannabis sativa,* which grows in Jamaica, Mexico, India, the Middle East, and most of the United States (see Figure 3.5). These leaves and buds contain over 400 chemicals called *cannabinoids,* most of which are probably not psychoactive even in high doses. The major psychoactive chemical in marijuana is delta-9-tetrahydrocannabinol (THC), a compound that was first synthesized in Israel in the 1960s and is very expensive to manufacture (Grilly, 2006; Grinspoon & Bakalar, 1993). In its naturally occurring form, it is concentrated in the sticky resin of the flowers and seeds of the female plant and, to a much lesser extent, in the leaves and branches of both male and female plants. Besides THC, there are two other cannabinoids, cannabinol and cannabidiol, which may be active at high doses, though not at the levels found in street marijuana. However, Karniol and Carlini (1972) have found that cannabinol and cannabidiol interact with THC to modify its effects; this may help to explain, in part at least, why users experience different effects with different varieties of marijuana grown in different localities. Finally, Stephens (1987) has shown that the concentration of THC in marijuana has slowly increased during the last decade from an average of less than 1 percent before 1974 to an average of nearly 2 percent in samples taken between 1974 and 1979. More recently, some samples with 4 to 5 percent THC have been observed (Grilly, 2006).

Exactly how marijuana produces its effects is not clear. Our lack of understanding of these mechanisms is due to some unique characteristics of THC (Martin, 1986). First, it is highly soluble in lipids (fat) and therefore is absorbed in high concentrations in practically all of the body tissues. Second, it alters just about every biological system in which it is found. Precisely what the significance is of these effects, especially in light of THC's psychoactive properties, is difficult to determine. However, several investigators have called attention to the many behavioral and pharmacological similarities between the effects of marijuana and those of the anticholinergic drugs (Miller & Branconnier, 1983). The latter block activity in a part of the brain called the hippocampus, and it has been argued that marijuana acts via the same mechanism (Campbell, Foster, Hampson, & Deadwyler, 1986).

As evidence for this position, the effects of marijuana, anticholinergics, and hippocampectomy were compared on various behaviors. All three produced decrements in both the acquisition and performance of maze behaviors, impaired sequential behaviors, and impaired short-term memory. They also interfered with the ability to concentrate, reduced conditioned emotional responses, increased resistance to extinction, and produced state-dependent learning. Additionally, many of the physiological effects of marijuana, such as dry mouth and increased heart rate, are the same as those produced by anti-cholinergic drugs.

Figure 3.5 • Cannabis Sativa Leaf
Image © iliuta goean, 2011. Used under license from Shutterstock, Inc.

Finally, in 1992, a natural marijuana-like compound was found in the mammalian brain (Devane et al., 1992). Researchers had known for some time that there exist brain receptor sites that attract the THC of marijuana, but most believed that these receptors had evolved to serve as receptors for a natural brain compound, not a plant derivative. Devane and his colleagues called this new substance *anandamide,* from the Sanskrit *ananda,* which means "bliss." When purified, the natural substance is a little less powerful than THC. It appears that anadamide plays a role in the regulation of mood, memory, pain, movement, and other activities (Dworetzky, 1997).

The physiological effects of marijuana closely resemble those produced by the sympathetic nervous system when it is mildly stimulated. Small to moderate doses of THC usually lead to feelings of well-being and euphoria; large doses can cause paranoia, hallucinations, and dizziness (Fackelmann, 1993). The most common physical effects of THC are an increase in heart rate and a reddening of the eyes. However, attention, short-term memory, and coordination can be impaired (Block, Farinpour, & Braverman, 1992; Block & Ghoneim, 1993; Grinspoon & Bakalar, 1993; Leavitt, 1995). Additionally, gastrointestinal symptoms, such as diarrhea and nausea may occur (Brown, 1971, 1972). Cardiovascular effects include an elevated systolic blood pressure and an increased pulse rate. No change in respiration rate, pupil size, or blood-sugar level is observed (Hollister, 1971; Rossi, Kuehnle, & Mendelson, 1978). The eyes may be bloodshot. Certain spinal reflexes may be elicited more easily than normally, suggesting a lower sensory threshold.

How does the inhalation of marijuana alter the user's awareness? First, it should be noted that the subjective experiences reported by "pot" smokers vary considerably, and it now seems clear that an expectancy effect does operate in this situation. In fact, an *expectancy effect* appears to operate for subjective reports of all consciousness-altering drugs (Barber, 1970). This means simply that the smoker often describes what he or she thinks the experience ought to be. When compared with some of the other drugs discussed in this chapter, marijuana takes effect fairly slowly, and the subjective experiences may take as long as 10 minutes to occur after the user has inhaled the smoke, even longer when the drug is ingested. It is quite possible, however, that these experiences may persist for considerable periods of time. This is because marijuana is metabolized slowly and its half-life in humans has been estimated to be as long as 48 hours (Hart, Ksir, & Ray, 2011).

According to Tart (1972), perhaps the most striking experiences reported by subjects are changes in perception. They observed physical objects to be clearer than they were before using marijuana. They examined shapes and colors very carefully. Their auditory perception underwent a similar change, sounds being more vivid and musical notes being more pure. Some subjects reported that listening to music became a "total experience." Touch, taste, and smell also appeared to be similarly enhanced. Users generally reported increased appetite and appreciation for the flavor of food (Foltin, Brady, & Fischman, 1986).

Marijuana users also regularly report perceptual distortion of space and time. They may judge distances inaccurately and overestimate the passage of time. It is these perceptual changes that may account, at least in part, for the findings reported by Petersen (1977, 1979) and Klonoff (1974). These investigators suggest that smoking the amounts of marijuana that are commonly used is detrimental to performance in automobile driving, whether it is measured in the laboratory or on the road. Miller, McFarland, Cornett, Brightwell, and Wikler (1977) found that marijuana causes a change in attention span, combined with an impairment of driving skills. Whatever the cause, this decrement in driving skills has been firmly established as a contributor to automobile fatalities (Sterling-Smith, 1976). It is interesting to note that over the last several years there has been a significant change in the recognition of these effects by the general population and marijuana users in particular. Before 1975 the majority of marijuana users denied that marijuana impaired driving skills, whereas since 1975 there has been a growing recognition by these individuals that driving skills are impaired by the substance (Grilly, 1981). Hollister (1986) also demonstrated that after getting high on marijuana, airplane pilots evidence a marked decrease in performance in flight simulators.

Sexual pleasure seemed to be increased, although this apparently is due in large part to generally heightened perceptual awareness. In any event, there is little concrete evidence that sexual performance is improved; indeed, with large doses it is likely to be significantly impaired. Recent animal model studies as well as some human studies have demonstrated that prolonged exposure to marijuana exerts significant harmful effects on the male reproductive system, including the development of abnormal sperm cells (Husain, 1989; Husain & Patra, 1989).

Drowsiness and sleep may occur if the marijuana user gets high alone. However, if taken in the presence of others, the drug is more likely to induce a euphoric mood. Feelings of detachment and happiness and preoccupation with simple and familiar things are likely to dominate the individual's conscious awareness. Sometimes the user experiences a paranoid state in which he or she is keenly aware of others watching. If the surrounding company seems unpleasant, the user typically withdraws rather than resorting to antisocial

101

behavior. Marijuana users exhibit antisocial behavior only rarely. While prolonged and regular use of the drug does not bring about the development of a physical dependency, it may result in a feeling of apathy, especially in adolescence; this is often referred to as the *amotivational syndrome*. Such a phenomenon has not been observed in the general population, however.

Marijuana disrupts memory formation, both long term and short term. This is found to occur with both verbal and graphic material. The effect on long-term memory recall is more prominent than with recognition. Much of the memory disruption seems to be due to increased imagery and thought flow due to the intrusion of irrelevant associations (Hooker & Jones, 1987). The drug also interferes with immediate recall of information learned only a few minutes before. Finally, such cognitive effects outlast the period of smoking (Pope & Yurgelun-Todd, 1996; Smith, 1995). It would appear that being stoned is not conducive to learning.

For decades, policymakers have debated whether to legalize marijuana. Many people, scientists and nonscientists alike, have tended to consider marijuana a relatively benign substance—a recreational drug—compared to drugs such as heroin and cocaine. Moreover, it has recently been demonstrated that this agent also has some therapeutic uses, such as in the treatment of the eye disorder glaucoma (Jaffe, 1985) and alleviating the nausea and vomiting caused by chemotherapy in the treatment of cancer as well as the treatment of such ailments as asthma, seizures, and spastic conditions (Grinspoon & Bakalar, 1993; Relman, 1982). Melzack (1990) argued that people typically do not become addicted when using drugs medically. Contrary to this popular view, Wickelgren (1997) reports that there is new evidence that suggests that the effects of marijuana in the brain are similar to those of such hard drugs as cocaine and heroin.

Lysergic Acid Diethylamide (LSD)

Last Friday, April 16, 1943, I was forced to stop my work in the laboratory in the middle of the afternoon and to go home, as I was seized by a particular restlessness associated with a sensation of mild dizziness. On arriving home, I lay down and sank into a kind of drunkenness which was not unpleasant and which was characterized by extreme activity of imagination. As I lay in a dazed condition with my eyes closed (I experienced daylight as disagreeably bright) there surged upon me an uninterrupted stream of fantastic images of extraordinary plasticity and

> vividness and accompanied by an intense kaleidoscope-like play of
> colors. This condition gradually passed off after two hours. (Hofmann,
> 1971, p. 23)

Thus wrote Albert Hofmann, the Swiss chemist, who in 1938 first extracted d-lysergic acid diethylamide (LSD-25). He was describing his experiences following the accidental ingestion of a small amount of this substance. As we noted earlier, "acid," "sugar," "big D," "trips," or "micro-dots," as LSD-25 is called in the language of the streets, is a potent hallucinogen. The average dosage that produces changes in the individual's state of awareness or consciousness—what Barron, Jarvik, and Bunnell (1964) called the **psychomimetic effects**—is approximately 0.5–1.0 micrograms of LSD per kilogram of body weight.

What is even more amazing is the fact that, if such a dosage is taken orally, only about 1 percent of it will ever reach the brain (Freedman & Halaris, 1978). While it is generally agreed that the use of LSD probably does not produce either physical or psychological dependency, the user does quickly develop a tolerance for the drug. After three or four days of use, previously effective dosage levels become ineffective. However, this tolerance appears to be lost after an equal period of abstinence.

Chemical analysis of this white, tasteless, odorless powder reveals that structurally, LSD-25 is composed of a lysergic acid and a diethylamide portion. The former is a natural product of the ergot fungus that can be found

Serotonin

LSD-25

Psilocybin

Figure 3.6 • Indole Ring

103

growing on grains, especially rye. The latter component is related structurally to certain other drugs that are commonly employed as smooth-muscle relaxants. Perhaps the most interesting chemical feature of the LSD molecule, however, is the existence of what chemists refer to as an indole ring. As you can see in Figure 3.6, the indole ring is characteristic, not only of LSD and psilocybin, but also of the neurotransmitter substance serotonin (Sepinwall & Cook, 1980).

At present, exactly how the LSD-25 molecule exerts its effects on an individual's state of consciousness is not completely understood. However, current theory suggests that LSD acts as a blocker of activity of serotonergic neurons in the brain, possibly by activating the serotonergic autoreceptors directly on cell bodies (Rech & Commissaris, 1982; Rech & Rosecrans, 1982). The most recent evidence suggests that LSD induces the majority of these behavioral effects postsynaptically, by acting as agonist at a specific subtype of serotonin receptor (Cunningham & Appel, 1987; Jacobs, 1987). Large numbers of these receptors are located in neocortical, limbic, and brainstem areas. The brainstem consists of two centers in the reticular activating system called the dorsal and medial raphe nuclei. Mokler and his colleagues have demonstrated that these two areas are likely candidates for many of LSD's effects, since microinjections of LSD into these areas produce the most pronounced LSD-type effects in animals (Mokler, Stoudt, Sherman et al., 1986).

What types of changes in consciousness might one expect to experience after ingesting an average dose of LSD? A psychology professor at Harvard University during the height of the drug culture, Dr. Timothy Leary, described his experiences with the drug as being religious-like. Admitting to having used LSD on hundreds of occasions, he believed that the drug made him more creative and gave him insights into daily life, religion, and philosophy that would otherwise not come about. He even advocated to his students that they should try this drug. This got him into trouble with his university, and shortly thereafter he was relieved of his academic responsibilities.

The experiences that individuals report with the abuse of LSD vary from individual to individual. And such variables as the user's mental set, the environmental setting, and the drug itself often contribute to the variety of experiences reported. However, some of the more typical experiences with LSD are described here.

After LSD is applied to a sugar cube and this is ingested, there is generally a period of 30 to 45 minutes during which no effects occur. This is followed by a period of 8 to 10 hours during which the individual goes through changes in sensory perception, lability of emotional experiences, and feelings of depersonalization and detachment. These changes in awareness typically peak between the second and fourth hour of the LSD experience.

Chief among these experiences are the changes reported in sensory perception. Katz, Waskow, and Olsson (1968) observed that while there is a feeling of perceptual sharpness, perceptions of the outer world take on an unreal quality. Vision appears to be the sense affected most profoundly (Levine, 1969). Illusions develop initially as both objects and people in the environment appear to change color, shape, and perspective (Lingeman, 1974). Walls and other objects may become wavy and appear to move; colors seem brighter and more intense. Bizarre shapes and designs that have no basis in reality may be seen (Siegel, 1977). Generally, awareness of time is also affected to the point at which the individual cannot distinguish among past, present, and future. Often, the LSD user reports the visual perception of music or the "warmth" of red and the "icy" feeling of blue. This curious phenomenon, which involves the translation of one type of sensory experience into another, is called **synesthesia**. Such distortions in consciousness, when combined with an emotional state of euphoria, are descriptive of what was labeled a "mind-expanding" trip during the LSD craze of the 1960s.

Many of the early, prominent proponents of the drug, such as author Aldous Huxley (1894–1963), as cited by Hart, Ksir and Ray (2011) suggested that its use allowed them to achieve a degree of personal insight, increased their sensitivity, produced mystical experiences, and helped them develop an understanding of their place in the universe that they could not have achieved in another way. Lilly (1972) observed that the LSD experience may lead not only to mystical or transcendental adventures, but also to profound insights. It has been suggested that LSD experiences can bring about an enhancement of creative activity. One of the problems with relying on a drug for creative production is that the drug does not provide "the checks and balances between intuition and analytic reason required for genuine creation" (Grinspoon & Bakalar, 1979, p. 267). During the drug experience, you are unable to communicate your new insights, partly because of the drug's effects on motor abilities. After taking LSD, users do not show any more creativity than they did beforehand (Dusek & Girdano, 1980).

In addition to altering the state of awareness, LSD produces a number of physiological effects. Ataxia, or loss of muscle coordination, and spastic paralysis are frequently observed. Autonomic effects include an elevated heart rate (tachycardia) and blood pressure, faster and more erratic breathing, excessive amounts of sugar in the blood (hyperglycemia), elevation in body temperature, and pupillary dilation.

Not all LSD experiences can be described as pleasant, mind-expanding trips. In fact, some experiences, referred to as "bad trips," can be harrowing and traumatic. Although the problem has been addressed experimentally (Blacker, Jones, Stone, & Pfefferbaum, 1968), exactly what determines whether a trip will be pleasurable or nightmarish remains unknown. As in the pleasurable trip, hallucinations constitute a dominant feature of the bad LSD experience. Objects and people in the environment, as well as one's own body image, may become so distorted that they are perceived as grotesque and threatening. These perceptions may seem so unreal that they produce a feeling of detachment from the real world. Strange and bizarre thoughts and emotions may creep into consciousness, and the user may have mental experiences causing him or her to feel completely out of control. Such thoughts may represent a major break with reality—a belief that one can fly, walk on water, or perform some other amazing feat. Depression and feelings of acute anxiety or panic are often a part of the bad trip. Occasionally, these feelings may lead to extremely dangerous self-directed behavior, including suicide.

Smith and Rose (1967–1968) observed that a feeling of paranoia may also develop in which the individual fears not only strangers but friends and relatives as well. Because of the fear that accompanies bad LSD trips, Tinklenberg and Stillman (1970) believe that the user's resorting to assaultive behavior would be highly unlikely and that, should it occur, it would be poorly executed. Although these acute effects dissipate within six to 12 hours after the ingestion of LSD, a small minority of individuals continue to experience mental confusion, perceptual distortions, and poor concentration beyond this time—in some cases for days or weeks. In extremely rare cases, individuals have complained about mental and emotional disturbances several years after being exposed to LSD (Jaffe, 1985).

Finally, some individuals experience the phenomenon of flashbacks. The flashback is a spontaneous, involuntary recurrence of perceptual distortions or hallucinations that may follow LSD use weeks or even months later. Abraham (1983) has observed that one of the most common precipitants of these episodes is entering a dark environment. Flashbacks may produce changes every bit as vivid as those experienced during the original trip. However, since the individual is completely unprepared for such an experience, he or she is likely to react to it with fear, anxiety, and in some cases, psychotic behavior (Brecher and the Editors of *Consumer Reports*, 1972; Horowitz, 1969; National Institute of Drug Abuse, 1992).

Cohen (1981) has suggested that flashbacks represent some type of learning phenomenon that occurs in predisposed individuals during acute stress.

Studies of individuals who have experienced flashbacks suggest that these individuals had strong tendencies to fantasize and were highly suggestible before their LSD use (Silling, 1980). Thus, it is possible that, after an LSD experience, they may encounter a situation that reminds them of the experience and elicits a small, conditioned response they are able to elaborate on and interpret as a druglike experience. Others have hypothesized that some flashbacks are a product of visual seizures (Abraham, 1983).

To summarize, many drugs have been, or are being, abused by adults as well as by children as young as four or five years of age. Whenever a "new" drug becomes available, there are individuals who will try it and find that it produces a new consciousness-altering experience. This person will describe the experience to his or her friends, and they may proceed to try it. Thus, we have the makings of a new drug of abuse. Little can be done to protect society from such abuse except to prohibit the use of the drug totally, even for beneficial medical purposes. This is impractical, however; besides, it would not halt the abuse of drugs any more than Prohibition stopped the use of alcohol in the United States. As was mentioned in Weil's (1972) theory in chapter 1, many humans have a drive to experience altered states of consciousness. Unfortunately, this drive may exhibit itself in the abuse of certain drugs such as the ones described in this chapter. Our list is by no means comprehensive or all-inclusive. We have chosen to discuss what we consider the most abused drugs. We hope that this list will not grow with the continued development of the study of consciousness in the years to come. However, in all likelihood, it will, because people inevitably choose these drugs to express their drive to experience different states or levels of consciousness.

As we have seen, drugs affect behavior and have dramatic and immediate effects on consciousness. As human beings ingest drugs, they alter their states of consciousness in profound ways. Sometimes the changes are mild and produce only states of relaxation. At other times the changes are profound and long lasting and produce anywhere from mild to serious changes in mood, temper, personality, and behavior. When psychologists study such changes in behavior, they are studying the effects of how drugs alter consciousness. They have studied particularly carefully both how various dosages of various drugs affect consciousness and the relationship between drug dosage and changes in states or levels of consciousness. If we consider consciousness as a state of awareness, drugs clearly alter that state in significant ways.

For Further Reading
. . . .

Grilly, D. M. (2006). *Drugs and human behavior* (5th ed.). Boston: Allyn & Bacon.

Hart, C. L, Ksir, C. J., & Ray, O. S. (2011). *Drugs, society, and human behavior* (14th ed.). New York: McGraw-Hill.

Jones-Witters, P., & Witters, W. L. (1983). *Drugs and society: A biological perspective.* Belmont, CA: Wadsworth.

Julien, R. M. (1997). *A primer of drug action* (8th ed.). San Francisco: Freeman.

McKim, W. A. (1997). *Drugs and behavior: An introduction to behavioral pharmacology* (4th ed.). Englewood Cliffs, NJ: Prentice-Hall.

Meyer, J. S., & Quenzer, L. F. (2005). P*sychopharmacology: Drugs, the brain, and behavior.* Sunderland, MA: Sinauer.

Milkman, H. B., & Shaffer, H. J. (Eds.). (1985). *The addictions: Multidisciplinary perspectives and treatments.* Lexington, MA: Lexington Books.

Hypnosis

Hypnosis has long been a popular topic of discussion among both psychologists and nonpsychologists. Many individuals' only exposure to hypnosis has been the most stereotyped version, namely, stage hypnosis. In this form of entertainment, audience members are hypnotized and then asked to perform all sorts of strange acts. Some may be made to sing the *Star-Spangled Banner;* others may be asked to act like a turkey and gobble about on stage. It appears to the audience that the hypnotist has complete control over the participant's behavior.

As a result of the popularity of stage hypnosis, the fear of losing control by potential hypnosis subjects, and the many misconceptions concerning the reality of hypnosis and its usefulness off stage, hypnosis has received an inordinate share of bad press. Furthermore, people often ask whether hypnosis is a real manipulation or is simply an act performed by entertainers. If it is a bona fide phenomenon, what is it? Why is it that some people can be hypnotized readily while others cannot? What does it feel like to experience hypnosis? Is hypnosis an altered state of consciousness? These questions and many others are addressed in this chapter as we consider hypnosis as an area of study in the psychology of consciousness.

In the scientific investigation of hypnosis, a clear definition of the phenomenon remains elusive. Several early attempts were made to describe some of the processes that underlie hypnosis. Some have identified hypnosis as a trance state or as an altered state of consciousness (Hilgard, 1965, 1979). Others assert that hypnotized individuals do not behave as they do because they are in a trance; rather, they are striving to enact the role of a hypnotized subject as it is defined by the hypnotist and society in general (Coe, 1978; Coe & Sarbin, 1977; Sarbin & Coe, 1972, 1979). Still others have described hypnosis as a normal state of awareness or consciousness involving the holding of positive attitudes, strong motivations to perform a suggested task, and positive expectancies of the hypnosis situation (Barber, Spanos, & Chaves, 1974).

In 1993, the American Psychological Association, Division of Psychological Hypnosis (APA Division 30) put forth an operational definition of hypnosis, that reflected the multiplicity of viewpoints: "hypnosis is a procedure during which a health professional or researcher suggests that a client, patient, or subject experience changes in sensation, perception, thoughts, or behavior" (APA, 1994). One concern with this definition is that it did not address whether hypnosis produced an altered state. As a result, some believed that it did not provide a definition of hypnosis at all (e.g., Spiegel, 1994).

In response to this and other criticisms, in 2003, the APA Division 30 redefined hypnosis as a procedure in which a subject is guided by a hypnotist to respond to suggestions for changes in experience, perception, sensation, emotion, thought, or behavior. The definition further states that "many believe that hypnotic responses and experiences are characteristic of a hypnotic state" (Green, Barrett, & Montgomery, 2005, p. 262).

Although considered better, there are still concerns with this definition (e.g., Daniel, 2005). One is that the statement "many believe" hypnosis **may** produce a "hypnotic "or altered state, implies that hypnosis might *not* produce an altered state, and biases the definition toward sociological or cognitive theories of hypnosis (described more fully below). According to Christensen (2005), most researchers today reject those "nonstate" theories, and instead view hypnosis as an altered state of consciousness (see also Gruzelier, 1996). Viewing hypnosis as an altered state is important, and may be fundamental for explaining why hypnosis can be clinically useful. Another criticism of the 2003 definition is that it still does not offer an explanation of the phenomenological experience of the subject while hypnotized. Understanding what the subject experiences during hypnosis should help to clarify what hypnosis does, further emphasizing the clinical relevance of hypnosis, and the utility of hypnosis as a tool to elucidate the nature of consciousness and altered states.

Before discussing the contemporary applications of hypnosis in science and behavior, we need to elucidate the role of hypnosis in the study of consciousness. A brief historical overview of this manipulation is then presented, along with a discussion of the theoretical explanations of what hypnosis is and is not, in light of existing experimental evidence.

Hypnosis and Consciousness

As stated in chapter 1, our definition of consciousness is synonymous with the concept of awareness. To be aware of an event is to be fully conscious or cognizant of its occurrence. When we are not aware of an event, this generally indicates the information from its occurrence either is not processed or is being processed at a level below consciousness.

It appears that a different level of awareness operates during hypnosis than during the nonhypnotic state. When individuals are hypnotized, they may or may not feel sleepy, although they usually do feel a bit more relaxed than usual. They report experiencing behavior that differs from their normal state of consciousness or awareness (Hilgard, 1977b, 1987). While hypnotized, individuals have an increased susceptibility to suggestions. They also experience enhanced imagery and imagination, including the availability of visual memories from the past, although many of these memories may be distorted (Loftus, 1979). Hypnotized individuals also experience a loss of initiative and lack the desire to make and carry out plans of their own. This change from their normal state of consciousness is only relative, for the hypnotic subject retains the ability to initiate or terminate actions. In other words, the popular belief that a hypnotized individual experiences a total loss of control is not true. People cannot be made to commit certain acts against their will.

There is also a reduction in reality testing for hypnotized subjects. For example, they accept falsified memories, they may show a change in their own personality, they may modify the rate at which they process time, and they may experience the presence of an object that is physically not present or they may not perceive an object that is present.

Because of the nature of the behavior exhibited by hypnotized subjects, hypnosis is considered to be an integral part of the study of consciousness. Studying the phenomenon of hypnosis may help to unravel many of the mysteries of how, and at what level, information is processed. Furthermore, we will see how hypnosis can be employed to help focus or refocus the processing of information for modifying behavior that is not as easily shaped or changed in the normal state of awareness or consciousness.

Historical Development

The earliest reference to the use of a manipulation resembling hypnosis most probably can be traced (Shor, 1979) to a Viennese physician, Franz Anton Mesmer (1734–1815). In the latter part of the eighteenth century, Mesmer demonstrated that behavior could be affected with the use of magnetic plates that would induce so-called cosmic fluids to react in individuals. He called this reaction *animal magnetism.* Animal magnetism was demonstrated by placing magnetized metal bottles of water in a large wooden tub called a *baquet.* Beneath the bottles in the tub was a surface of powdered glass and iron filings. The tub was subsequently filled with water and covered with a top containing openings through which iron rods were passed. The rods were then applied to a subject's body. Since the tub was, in reality, a crude form of battery, the applications of such rods produced a mild electrical charge.

The *mesmerist* (as early hypnotists were called) would then apply his hands to the subject's body. The result of this was the induction of convulsions and seizures, which in all likelihood were produced by the electrical current. This process was known as **mesmerism**. Afterward, the subject often reported an alleviation of minor aches and pains. In some instances, more severe afflictions, such as blindness and deafness, were reported to have been successfully treated. As you can imagine, the treatments that Mesmer provided were highly controversial and met with considerable disfavor from the medical and scientific communities.

In 1784 a commission headed by Benjamin Franklin, historically referred to as the Franklin Commission, was organized to pass judgment on the value of animal magnetism; this commission disaffirmed the existence and value of the technique. This conclusion did not represent the personal views of Franklin, who believed that mesmerism did have some curative powers (McConkey & Perry, 1985). Other Franklin contemporaries, such as the Marquis de Lafayette and George Washington, also believed that mesmerism had some value.

The Marquis de Puysegur (1751–1825) also saw some promise in the mesmeric demonstrations. Unlike Mesmer, and in agreement with the Franklin Commission, the Marquis did not believe that the results reported and observed were due to the production of seizures and convulsions. Rather, he felt that the presence of a trancelike state was the major reason for the ability to treat afflictions with mesmerism. In such a state, the subject could respond to suggestions made by the mesmerist. For example, since Mesmer performed his "cures" in a darkened room while going from patient to patient and touching each of them, this could suggest to patients that "magnetism" was being transferred from Mesmer to them. Owing to such a belief, patients would have instilled in them the indirect suggestion that a cure was taking place. Such a suggestion was likely a reason why many of Mesmer's patients felt that they had been helped with their various afflictions. As such, animal magnetism was superfluous in the treatment of Mesmer's patients.

With the focus of mesmerism shifted toward a trancelike manipulation and away from the mystical concept of animal magnetism, John Elliotson (1791–1868), a British physician, tried to gain consent to teach mesmerism at University College Medical School in London. Unfortunately, he failed. As a matter of fact, this suggestion met with such furor that he was subsequently forbidden to practice his trade within the confines of his affiliated medical school hospital. As a result of his futile effort, Elliotson resigned his position at the medical school and established the first journal devoted to the study of mesmerism, the *Zoist*.

During the same period, James Esdaile (1808–1859) was making considerable use of mesmerism in India. Mesmerism did not receive the scorn in India that it had in England. As a result, mesmerism became an acceptable manipulation in hospitals during Esdaile's time, especially as a means for inducing analgesia, or anesthesia, during surgery. The first documented case of the use of hypnosis as surgical anesthesia was reported on April 12, 1829, when Jules Cloquet performed a mastectomy in Paris (Gravitz, 1988).

Also during Elliotson's time, James Braid (1785–1860) introduced an important theory that advanced the historical development of hypnosis (mesmerism). He recognized that certain mesmeric phenomena were genuine, but he rejected, as did the Marquis de Puysegur, the influences of external or cosmic forces. Contrary to Mesmer's mystical explanation of animal magnetism, Braid advanced a naturalistic, physiological theory to account for the results of mesmerism. This theory was based on the production of eye-muscle fatigue during a mesmeric induction. Braid observed that subjects who fixated on a bright object for a given period demonstrated a gradual lowering of the eyelids or a closing of the eyes. He postulated that this closure was the result of a general exhaustion of the nerve centers. In other words, an important characteristic of mesmerism was an induced state of relaxation or "near sleep."

In addition to demonstrating this important characteristic of behavior during the process of mesmerism, Braid wanted to remove as much of the stigma associated with the concept as possible. To help with this, he changed the name of mesmerism to **neurhypnotism**. The prefix was later dropped. Braid is credited with coining the term **hypnotism** in 1826. However, it should be pointed out that some credit should be given to Étienne Felix d'Henin de Cuvillers (1755–1841) with coining the term *hypnotism* in 1821, before Braid (Gravitz, 1993; Gravitz & Gerton, 1984).

A few years before Braid changed the name of mesmerism to hypnotism, José Custodi di Faria (1756–1819) advocated a psychological explanation of the phenomenon. Basically, he stressed that "lucid sleep," his term for hypnosis, was produced solely by the subject's heightened expectations and receptive attitudes. Since the subject wanted to be hypnotized and expected something to result from this manipulation, the expectations were, in fact, realized. With the emphasis on psychological factors during the hypnosis process, Faria developed what might be called a standard procedure for inducing lucid sleep. He used a series of soothing and commanding verbal suggestions while the subject was in the receptive hypnotic state. Faria then realized, as did others many years later—for example, Ambroise August Liébeault (1823–1904) and Hippolyte Marie Bernheim (1837–1919)—that verbal suggestion played a major role in hypnosis.

After Faria's discoveries became known and well publicized, Braid extended Faria's ideas and developed a concept he called **monoideism**. Basically, this term refers to a process of focused attention or concentration on a single idea or image during a state of relaxation. Thus, during hypnosis a subject's attention is focused only on this thought while all other thoughts are attenuated, or "put on the back burner." This concept is comparable to what is referred to today as **selective attention** (Haber & Hershenson, 1980; Treisman & Geffen, 1967). According to Braid, the ability to attend readily to a single idea or thought was limited to about 10 percent of his subjects.

Thirty years later, Jean Martin Charcot (1825–1893) described hypnotism as a process involving physiological reflex actions, including eye-muscle relaxation. Although there was, and still is, no evidence that hypnosis has a physiological basis, the eminence of Charcot as a leading authority on neurology gave considerable credence to the phenomenon of hypnosis.

Sigmund Freud (1856–1939) also must be mentioned as having played an important role in the historical development of hypnosis. Actually, some of his early theoretical conceptualizations of psychoanalysis were formalized with information he obtained from his patients while they were hypnotized. For example, he observed that, on awakening, patients did not recall many suggestions given to them during hypnosis. As a result of this demonstration of hypnotic amnesia, Freud believed that many human behaviors were the result of unconscious thoughts or motivations. Freud also discovered that many pent-up emotions and feelings could be uncovered with the aid of hypnosis. With hypnosis it was possible to tap information from the so-called unconscious or subconscious. Freud eventually abandoned the use of hypnosis because he believed that it allowed access to repressed feelings too quickly, suppressed symptoms too easily, and swayed individual responses toward what he perceived the hypnotist wanted.

As you can see, hypnosis has had a controversial historical development (Shor, 1979). However, without the brave experiments and applications of hypnosis by Elliotson, Braid, and others, hypnosis would be only a quaint relic of the past and not an important manipulation in science and medicine.

Assessing Hypnotic Susceptibility

Because hypnosis is a scientifically valid and reliable tool, it has become possible to determine how susceptible given individuals are to this manipulation. In determining whether a subject can be readily hypnotized or is readily susceptible to hypnotic suggestions, several standard tests and nonstandard procedures have been employed. Each standardized test is administered to subjects by beginning with an induction of hypnosis followed by suggestions that represent hypnotic experiences. The standard tests include the **Stanford Hypnotic Susceptibility Scale** (Weitzenhoffer & Hilgard, 1959, 1962), the **Barber Suggestibility Scale** (Barber & Glass, 1962), and the **Harvard Group Scale of Hypnotic Susceptibility** (Shor & Orne, 1962).

The Stanford Hypnotic Susceptibility Scale

The Stanford Hypnotic Susceptibility Scale (SHSS) appears in Forms A, B, and C. The first two emphasize compliance with motor-related suggestions; they are also parallel, permitting test-retest reliability. This means that, for example, Form A can be used interchangeably with Form B. Form C emphasizes cognitive components of hypnotic susceptibility and has become the standard against which all other scales are compared.

Form A of the Stanford Scale consists of 12 parts and is administered to each subject individually. That is, only one person at a time is tested for susceptibility to hypnotic suggestion. The 12 parts of the test are arranged in order of difficulty; the first few parts or tasks are easier, and the last parts the most difficult in terms of subject compliance. Thus, most subjects are capable of performing the first few tasks easily, while only a small number of subjects are capable of performing the last ones.

The first and easiest task on the Stanford scale is referred to as *postural sway*. In this portion of the test, the person giving the test asks the subject to close his or her eyes, after which the test administrator suggests that the subject is slowly falling backward.

The second item is called *eye closure*. In performing this task, subjects, with their eyes wide open, are given the suggestion that their eyelids are becoming very heavy, so heavy that they can no longer keep them open.

Hand lowering is the third item on the scale. Subjects are asked to extend one of their arms out in front of their body. They are then made to feel that their hand is becoming very heavy, so heavy they can no longer keep their arm from falling.

The fourth item is referred to as *arm immobilization*. This task is, in essence, the opposite of the third task. Instead of the administrator suggesting to subjects that their arm is falling, they are told that their arm is becoming so heavy that they cannot lift it from the original position.

The fifth task on the Stanford scale is the *finger lock*. To perform this, subjects are instructed to interlock the fingers of both hands. They are then told that their fingers have become a solid mass and they will not be able to separate them. Individuals are then challenged to separate their hands.

Arm rigidity is the next item on the scale. This task requires subjects to extend their arm out straight in front of their body and then to make it as rigid as possible. Following this procedure, subjects are challenged to bend their arm.

The seventh task is concerned with *hand movement*. Here, subjects are required to move their hands together. To perform this task, individuals first separate their hands, palms facing inward, about 12 inches apart. They are then requested to imagine that a strong, magnetic force is attracting their hands together.

Verbal inhibition is the eighth task on the scale. For this situation the administrator suggests that when a subject is asked his or her name, the subject will be unable to verbalize it.

The next task is perhaps one of the most difficult on the Stanford scale. It is called the *fly hallucination* suggestion. The individual is asked to imagine a fly buzzing about his or her body. The subject is further told that the fly is becoming more and more annoying and that he or she will want to shoo it away. The test administrator tells the subject to get rid of the fly so that it will no longer be a disturbance.

The tenth scale item is called *eye catalepsy*. While the individual's eyes are closed, the administrator suggests that the subject will feel as though his or her eyes have been glued shut and the subject will not be able to open them. Subjects are then challenged to open their eyes.

The next-to-last item is a *posthypnotic suggestion*. Subjects are told that after the testing session is over, to determine their hypnotic susceptibility level, they will, for some reason, feel like changing chairs upon hearing a tapping noise. After the test administration, a tapping noise is sounded.

The final task item on the Stanford scale is the testing for *hypnotic amnesia*. After completing the susceptibility scale items, subjects are first required to enumerate the tasks they remember. Failure to recall more than three such tasks is considered adequate evidence that hypnotic amnesia was successful.

After the Stanford scale has been completed, hypnotic susceptibility level can be determined by adding the total number of task items with which subjects successfully complied. Generally, if they complied with 9 to 12 suggestions, they are considered highly susceptible to hypnotic suggestion. If they complied with 3 or fewer suggestions, this is taken as evidence that they will be difficult to hypnotize and, as such, are considered low in the attribute of hypnotic susceptibility. A score between 5 and 8 is considered to indicate moderate hypnotic susceptibility. Most individuals taking the test fall within this range. The particular items that the subjects successfully complete are not as important as the total test score. However, it is rare to find subjects who successfully complete the most difficult scale items and not the easiest ones.

As a side note, it should be pointed out that a score obtained on a standardized hypnosis test tends to remain stable. That is, on a repeat administration, the subject is likely to score about the same. In fact, a study by Piccione, Hilgard, and Zimbardo (1989) reported that in a 25-year follow-up, hypnosis scores remained stable. While in the short term, hypnotic susceptibility is modifiable (Diamond, 1974, 1977), without intervention procedures, hypnotic susceptibility level seems to be determined by the first administration.

The Barber Suggestibility Scale/Carleton University Responsiveness to Suggestion Scale

Like the Stanford test, the Barber Suggestibility Scale (BSS) is administered on an individual basis. Unlike the Stanford scale, it only consists of eight tasks. Three of the eight items are comparable to items on Form A of the Stanford scale—*arm lowering, hand clasp,* and *verbal inhibition.* The remaining five items are *arm levitation, extreme thirst suggestion, body immobility, posthypnotic response,* and a *selective amnesia.* It is unclear whether the Barber scale is used clinically or in research much anymore; a search of the literature since 1980 revealed fewer than five studies that mentioned the BSS, although this scale was translated into Spanish in 2007 for use in Puerto Rican populations (Guzmán-Hosta, Martínez-Taboas, & Rodríguez-Gómez, 2007). It appears that the Stanford scale, Form C is the preferred individually administered test of hypnotic susceptibility.

Nonetheless, in the 1980s Spanos and colleagues (Spanos, Cross, & De-Groh, 1987; Spanos, Radtke, Hodgins, Bertrand et al., 1983; Spanos, Radtke, Hodgins, Stam, & Bertrand, 1983; Spanos, Radtke, Hodgins, Stam, & Noretti, 1983) introduced a group induction scale based on the Barber Scale, called the Carleton University Responsiveness to Suggestion Scale (CURSS), which is widely used today. Not only can the CURSS be administered in groups, it contains only seven of the eight original BSS items, and the induction takes just over 30 minutes (32 minutes, to be exact). This offers a time advantage over other scales such as the Harvard Group Scale of Hypnotic Susceptibility, Form A (HGSHS: A; described in the next section), which, with questionnaires, can take up to an hour or more (Barnes, Lynn, & Pekala, 2009).

The CURSS, like the SHSS: C, suggests a number of cognitive-perceptual changes like seeing, hearing, smelling, or perceiving things that are not present (positive hallucinations), or ignoring stimuli that are present (negative hallucinations). Cognitive-perceptual changes have been described as the most difficult suggestions to experience during hypnosis (Barnier & McConkey, 2004). As a result, the CURSS and SHSS: C scales are believed to be more challenging than some of the other tests of hypnotic induction, including Forms A and B of the Stanford scale.

It is also important to note that the CURSS was developed by researchers who advocated the social-cognitive theories of hypnosis (described below), which, briefly, emphasize the importance in hypnosis of participant expectations and a desire to comply. Indeed, the CURSS instructs participants prior to induction that their hypnotic experience depends entirely on their willingness to become hypnotized. The instructions further remind participants that they will remain in complete control at all times (Barnes et al., 2009). As a result, one study found that the CURSS seemed to bias respondents to score low on hypnotizability, and produced a high number of reports that the hypnotic experience felt more like a normal waking state or "everyday mentation" (Barnes et al., 2009). Thus, although widely used due to the time savings and ease of administration compared to the lengthy and individually administered SSHS: C, the CURSS may not offer the best method for either measuring hypnotizability or for providing hypnotic induction.

The Harvard Group Scale of Hypnotic Susceptibility

Another widely used and standardized test to determine hypnotic susceptibility is the Harvard Group Scale of Hypnotic Susceptibility, Form A (HGSHS: A). Like the original Barber scale, this test is also based on Form A of the Stanford scale; like the CURSS, it is designed to be administered in groups. Also, subjects taking this test score themselves for their level of hypnotic susceptibility. This is not the case for the Stanford or Barber scales, in which the test administrator does the scoring. Numerical scoring for hypnotic susceptibility on the Harvard scale is comparable to that on the Stanford scale. A score between 9 and 12 indicates high susceptibility to hypnotic suggestion; a score below 3 is considered low susceptibility.

The Group Scale of Hypnotic Ability

Although popular and widely used both clinically and experimentally, the HGSHS: A poses some concerns, primarily due to the length of time it takes to administer (approximately 1 hour). Therefore, an abbreviated version of the HGSHS: A, called the Group Scale of Hypnotic Ability (GSHA), was developed in the late 1990s (Hawkins & Wenzel, 1999). Although some minor word changes were made for clarity and to deemphasize suggestions that the hypnotic experience is similar to sleep, the major difference between the HGSHS: A and the GSHA is that the GSHA contains only six of the 12 suggestions from the HGSHS: A: *eye closure, hand lowering, arm immobilization, arm rigidity, experiencing a fly*, and *post-hypnotic suggestion to touch an ankle*. Also, to maintain consistency between the HGSHS: A, and to make the time to administer compatible with the CURSS, the GSHA includes a pre-induction suggestion for *head falling*. Thus, like the CURSS, the GSHA takes 32 minutes to administer, and even with the addition of questionnaires, induction and susceptibility testing can be completed in well under an hour (Barnes et al., 2009). The GSHA offers similar predictive ability, and appears to be a viable, cost- and time-effective alternative to the lengthy HGSHS (Barnes et al., 2009).

Like the HGSHS: A, the GSHA emphasizes that hypnosis can produce an altered state of consciousness, and takes an authoritative approach to hypnotic induction. This, of course, is different from the CURSS, which emphasizes that participants must be willing to be hypnotized, and that they will remain in control at all times (Barnes et al., 2009).

The Waterloo-Stanford Group C Test of Hypnotic Susceptibility

Another standardized group induction test is based on Form C of the Stanford scale, and is called the Waterloo-Stanford Group C test of hypnotic susceptibility (WSGC; Bowers, 1993). According to Moran, Kurtz, and Strube (2002), "the WSGC is a close copy of the SHSS: C" (p. 222). As a result, the WSGC includes more cognitive questions, including positive and negative hallucinations and age regression, rather than the preponderance of motor items found in the HGSHS: A (Moran et al., 2002). However, as noted by Bowers (1993) and confirmed by others (Cardna & Terhune, 2004), there are concerns regarding risks of the WSGC, including psychological distress (crying) caused in some subjects exposed to the age regression suggestion. Some researchers (e.g., Michael Nash, as cited by Cardena & Terhune, 2009) have reported omitting the age regression suggestion altogether, to avoid these kinds of negative reactions. However, other concerns have been raised with respect to the predictive power of the WSGC. Moran and colleagues (2002) compared how well the SSHS: C and WSGC predicated later hypnotic response to four categories of hypnotic suggestions: positive hallucinations, negative hallucinations, dreams and regression, and cognitive distortion. Results indicated that the WSGC matched the SSHS: C on predictive ability for only one type of suggestion: dreams and regression.

Thus the HGSHS remains the "gold standard" of group hypnotic induction scales, although the GSHA may be a useful alternative in situations (i.e., surgical or dental procedures) where faster induction is preferred. The SHSS: C remains the best and most widely used scale for individual administration.

In addition to the standardized techniques for assessing hypnotic susceptibility, investigators have reported several "quick" methods of assessment. One such technique is the **Hypnotic Induction Profile**, or **HIP** (Spiegel, 1979a; Stern, Spiegel, & Nee, 1979). This test consists of the controversial eye-roll test (Spiegel, 1970) accompanied by a very brief hypnotic induction and test.

Figure 4.1 • Eye-Roll Test

In the eye-roll test (see Figure 4.1) subjects are requested to open their eyes as wide as possible. They are then instructed to roll their eyes to the top of their eyelids and to lower their eyelids very slowly over their eyes without moving their eyes from the upward position. Subjects' ability to perform this simple task is considered as evidence of their susceptibility to hypnotic suggestion.

Although the eye-roll test appears to be a reasonable assessment of hypnotic susceptibility for some subjects (see Frischholz, Spiegel, Trentalange, & Spiegel, 1987), it is far from being a reliable and valid measure (Eliseo, 1974; Orne, Hilgard, Spiegel, Spiegel, & Crawford, 1979; Switras, 1974; Wheeler, Reis, Wolff, Grupsmith, & Mordkoff, 1974). For example, Wheeler et al. (1974) found a very weak relationship between hypnotic susceptibility as assessed by the standardized scales described previously and the ability of a subject to perform the eye-roll procedure. Therefore, the eye-roll test cannot be considered a reliable or valid substitute for the standard testing procedures (Kihlstrom, 1985).

Correlates of Hypnotizability

Cognitive Correlates

A number of investigators have reported cognitive and perceptual correlates of hypnotic susceptibility. For example, Wallace and colleagues (Wallace, 1978b, 1979, 1988; Wallace & Garrett, 1973; Wallace, Garrett, & Anstadt, 1974; Wallace, Knight, & Garrett, 1976) found a relationship between level of hypnotic susceptibility, as assessed by the Harvard scale and frequency of perceiving various visual illusions (see Figure 4.2). Generally, the more susceptible

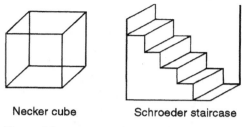

Necker cube   Schroeder staircase

Figure 4.2 • Examples of Reversible Figure Illusions

a subject is to hypnotic suggestions, the greater is his or her susceptibility to visual illusions, especially those involving a frequency report such as viewing the Necker cube, the Schroeder staircase, and the autokinetic effect (the illusory movement of a stationary light source).

Such correlates have been theorized to exist because subjects who are judged high in hypnotic susceptibility generally are better able to selectively attend to a stimulus situation in which there is competition for attention. Thus, when presented with an illusion, high hypnotic subjects are better able than low hypnotic subjects to concentrate on the elements that create the illusion. Their attention is not drawn away to other competing stimuli. As a result, they report a stronger illusory response.

Because of the difference between high and low hypnotics in their response to various illusions, and because this has been reported in a number of independent laboratories (e.g., Crawford, Brown, & Moon, 1993), it might be possible to use such a tool for assessing hypnotic susceptibility. Perhaps in the future, responses to various visual illusions will, in fact, be incorporated in tests of hypnotic responsiveness.

One of the most frequently replicated correlates of hypnotic susceptibility is a high capacity for absorption (e.g., Kumar & Pekala, 1988; Snodgrass & Lynn, 1989; Tellegen & Atkinson, 1974). Absorption involves focused attention, and both classic and recent research demonstrates the importance of focused attention on hypnosis (Crawford, 1994, Crawford, Corby, & Kopell, 1996; Graham & Evans, 1977; Karlin, 1979; Lichtenberg, Bachner-Melman, Ebstein, & Crawford, 2004; Lyons & Crawford, 1997; Raz, 2005).

Recently, Deines and colleagues (2009) performed an experiment to determine whether highly hypnotizable subjects were better at focusing attention, by measuring the ability to inhibit competing information. The experiment used three tests of attention inhibition, two negative priming tasks and a latent inhibition task. In one negative priming task, subjects were presented with 10 words that described animals and 10 words that described fruits and vegetables; subjects were instructed to attend to only one type (viz., either the animal or the fruit and vegetable words), and to ignore the other. In the test phase, subjects were then asked to categorize each of the 20 words, and investigators measured the amount of time it took to categorize each word.

Priming or "positive priming" is a phenomenon in which people respond more quickly to information previously presented, even if they are unaware of the task contingencies or prior exposure (e.g., Higgings, Bargh, & Lombardi, 1985). In negative priming, people should respond more slowly to words they were previously instructed to ignore. Therefore in this experiment, negative priming was indicated by an increased amount of time to categorize a word, while positive priming was defined as a decreased amount of time to categorize a word. It was assumed that subjects would exhibit negative priming (that is, a longer response time) to the words they were instructed to ignore, and positive priming (a shorter response time) to the words to which they were instructed to attend. However, results indicated that there were no significant differences in attentional focus between the groups on this task, nor on any of the three measures of inhibition.

These findings suggest that highly hypnotizable people are not necessarily better at focusing attention. However, further research needs to validate these results, and should specifically include other tests of attention that do not only measure inhibition. Indeed, Raz and Campbell (2010) also found a lack of effect of hypnosis in highly hypnotizable individuals on a negative priming task, although a great deal of other work by Raz and colleagues, suggests that attention is a key correlate of hypnosis (Raz, Fan, & Posner, 2005; Raz, Shapiro, Fan, & Posner, 2002; see also Raz, 2005 for review). As noted by MacLeod (2009), studies of negative priming would benefit from the use of more controlled, standardized procedures, for example, presenting two words on each trial, and instructing subjects to ignore one of them.

Hypnotic susceptibility is also strongly correlated with involvement in imaginative activities outside of hypnosis. Several studies note that hypnotizable subjects are capable of producing vivid mental images or other fantasies (Priebe & Wallace, 1986; Sheehan, 1979, 1982), and with fantasy proneness (Lynn & Rhue, 1986; Rhue & Lynn, 1989). Crawford (1981, 1982, 1983) has argued that what links these correlates is the ability of a hypnotizable subject to use synthetic or holistic thinking. This has been demonstrated in the performance of Gestalt closure tasks (Crawford, 1981) and in tasks requiring subjects to perform a visual search for a hidden letter (Wallace & Patterson, 1984) or object (Priebe & Wallace, 1986).

Nonetheless, according to Kallio and Revonsuo (2003), the strongest cognitive correlate of hypnotizability is how responsive the subject is to suggestion without hypnosis (e.g., Hilgard & Tart, 1966).

Personality Correlates
. . . .

Many people wonder whether hypnotic susceptibility is related to any personality variables. Unfortunately, hypnotizability has not been found to significantly correlate with most of these types of variables. As examples, it does not correlate with test results on the Minnesota Multiphasic Personality Inventory (MMPI) or the California Personality Inventory (CPI) (Hilgard, 1979). However, some support was found for a relationship between greater hypnotizability as assessed by the Harvard scale and relative mental health as assessed by the Rorschach ink-blot test (Zlotogorski, Hahnemann, & Wiggs, 1987).

One study found an increase in persistence in highly hypnotizable subjects, as measured by Cloniger's Tridimensional Personality Questionnaire (Lichtenberg et al., 2004). However, another study found no relationship between hypnotizability and the "Big Five" personality traits of openness, conscientiousness, extroversion, agreeableness, and neuroticism (Nordenstrom, Council, & Meier, 2002).

Physiological Correlates
. . . .

Gur and Gur (1974) have also argued that hypnotizability is correlated to right-brain processing. This conclusion was reached from a body of evidence that has indicated, for example, that hypnotizable subjects are more likely than low-susceptibility subjects to show reflective eye movement shifts to the left. Also, Graham (1977) and Graham and Pernicano (1979) reported that hypnosis led to increases in autokinetic movement to the left, compared to when subjects were not hypnotized. In addition, Sackeim, Paulus, and Weiman (1979) reported that when hypnotizable individuals are asked to find a seat in a room, they tend to find chairs in the right portion of the room. However, Monteiro and Zimbardo (1987) failed to replicate this finding.

Pagano, Akots, and Wall (1988) reported that in a dichotic listening task there was a greater left ear monitoring advantage during hypnosis. A similar finding has been reported by Frumkin, Ripley, and Cox (1978), although there has been difficulty in replicating the effect (Crawford, Crawford, & Koperski, 1983; Levine, Kurtz, & Lauter, 1984).

MacLeod-Morgan and Lack (1982) reported an apparent shift in cortical activation, as measured by alpha EEG activity (see chapter 7), from the left to the right hemisphere when individuals are hypnotized. Recent studies by Gruzelier and colleagues (e.g., Egner, Jamieson, & Gruzelier, 2005; Gruzelier, 2006) support these findings, as they have also found increases in right hemispheric activation during hypnosis. For example, Gruzelier, 2006 noted that in the absence of hypnosis, highly hypnotizable subjects demonstrated dominance by the left hemisphere of their brain. This in itself is probably not that interesting, in that left-hemisphere dominance is typical of most individuals, who are also right-handed. What was more interesting in this study was that highly hypnotizable people switched from left-hemisphere to right-hemisphere dominance following hypnotic induction. Lateralization, or differential activation across the two hemispheres (see chapter 2) has been found to be a function of hypnotizability by others (e.g., Fingelkurts, Fingelkurts, Kalio, & Revonsuo, 2007). Further, Horton and colleagues (2005) found that highly hypnotizable people had a significantly larger rostrum than low hypnotizables, the anterior portion of the corpus collosum. A larger rostrum could indicate greater hemispheric connectivity for high hypnotics, which presumably could facilitate greater contralateral (viz., right hemispheric) activation during hypnosis. These kinds of findings suggest that differences in hemispheric function may explain differences in hypnotic susceptibility.

Naish (2010) recently tested this hypothesis, that hemispheric function mediated hypnotizability. He specifically tested whether highly hypnotizable people could more readily "disconnect" the hemispheres during hypnosis, to activate their nondominant (right) hemisphere. Naish, like Gruzelier (2006) and others, found that highly hypnotizable people had greater hemispheric asymmetry during baseline testing, which was reversed during hypnosis. That is, highly hypnotizable people relied on left hemispheric processing while awake, but shifted to greater right hemispheric processing when hypnotized, more so than people low on hypnotizability. Naish further noted that a majority of low hypnotizability subjects (six out of 10) did not slow left hemispheric processing at all while hypnotized, suggesting a significant difference in hemispheric laterality between hypnotizable and nonhypnotizable people.

Nonetheless, Naish (2010) cautions against using results from this and other studies noting right hemispheric dominance during hypnosis as evidence that hypnosis requires left hemispheric deactivation. This is because both high and low hypnotizable people failed to consistently demonstrate the typical patterns of activation/deactivation in his study. Furthermore, other research shows that hemispheric laterality may be a function of other processes, including the type of stimulus (e.g., noxious or pleasant) used during hypnosis (e.g., Crawford, Clarke, & Kittner-Triolo, 1996; DePascalis, Ray, Tranquillo, & D'Amico, 1998).

In chapter 7 on sleep and dreams we show how EEG activity changes as a function of wakefulness, sleep, and dreaming (e.g., Dement & Kleitman, 1957). Thus other research has investigated the extent to which EEG activity might change during hypnosis, to see if characteristic changes in neural activity accompany the hypnotic state, in a manner similar to that observed for EEG during the sleep state. In an early study, Graffin, Ray, and Lundy (1995) found that high- and low-hypnotizables displayed a differential pattern of EEG activity during both a baseline period and following hypnotic induction. During the baseline period, highly hypnotizable people exhibited greater theta brain wave in frontal areas of the cortex, while low hypnotizables demonstrated the more typical alpha wave patterns. During hypnotic induction, alpha activity significantly increased in both groups all over the brain, while theta activity also increased significantly in posterior cortex in both groups. Based on these findings, the authors suggested that EEG activity could be used to elucidate differences in hypnotizability, although they suggested that differences in overall frontal versus posterior cortical activation might serve as a better marker than hemispheric differences.

Other research has continued to investigate EEG correlates of hypnotizability (e.g., DePascalis, Silveri, & Palumbo, 1988; DePascalis, 1999). Sebastiani and colleagues (2003) compared EEG activity in high and low hypnotizables when imagining neutral or unpleasant stimuli (but not in an hypnotized state). They found significant increases in gamma (36–44 Hz) and theta 1 (4–6 Hz) activity in high hypnotizables, which is similar to that found by Graffin et al. (1995) in their baseline condition. Unfortunately, at least two other studies have failed to replicate differences in baseline theta activity between high and low hypnotizables (White, Ciorciari, Carbis, & Liley, 2009; Williams & Gruzlier, 2001). Future research should continue to examine EEG activity during hypnosis, as well as differences between high- and low-hypnotizable people outside of a hypnotic state.

While EEG offers insight into cortical brain activity during hypnosis, functional brain imaging technology (chapter 2) permits the visualization of brain activity in deep brain structures. Several studies have used fMRI, PET, and SPECT scans to assess brain activity in controls and during hypnosis. Most of these studies note that hypnosis activates or deactivates areas similar to those regulating both consciousness and attention: anterior cingulate cortex (especially in the right hemisphere), thalamus, and pontine regions (Egner et al., 2005; Faymonville, Boly, & Laureys, 2006; Rainville et al., 1999; Rainville, Hofbauer, Bushnell, Duncan, & Price, 2002; Raz et al., 2005).

Other work has looked at a genetic basis for hypnotizability. Two early studies noted significant correlations (r's > 0.50) for monozygotic but not dizygotic twins (r's < 0.20; Morgan, 1973; Morgan, Hilgard, & Davert, 1970), although other studies found a greater concordance rate (as high as

64 percent) even for dizygotic twins (e.g., Bauman & Bul, 1981). These kinds of findings suggest that hypnotizability is inherited, and may be the result of specific genes.

Since the mapping of the human genome in the late 20th century, investigators have been able to evaluate specific genes involved in a variety of behaviors and cognitive functions, including hypnotizability. As mentioned above, Raz and colleagues emphasize the importance of attention for hypnosis. Therefore, their work has focused on evaluating the role of the dopamine system, a neurotransmitter known to regulate attention, in hypnotic susceptibility (e.g., see Raz, 2008 for review). One marker of dopamine turnover in the brain is catechol-O-methyltransferase (COMT), an enzyme that functions to degrade excess dopamine (and all of the catecholamines, including norepinephrine, a neurotransmitter also involved in attention) in the synapse. By breaking down excess synaptic dopamine, COMT provides a primary regulation of overall dopamine concentration in the brain.

COMT had several polymorphisms, or genetic mutations, that affect the function of the enzyme. One of the most widely investigated of these polymorphisms is the substitution of a valine (Val) allele by a methionine (Met) allele at codon 158 (Raz, 2008). Apparently these alleles are codominant, so that expression of the Val/Val alleles yields the greatest COMT activity (and lowest dopamine brain concentrations, since COMT degrades extracellular dopamine), Met/Met yields the least COMT activity (and highest dopamine activity in the brain), and the heterozygous Val/Met condition yields COMT activity intermediate between the two (Raz, 2008; Szekelya et al., (2010).

Several studies have consistently replicated that heterozygous individuals expressing the Val/Met alleles score highest on hypnotizability (Lichtenberg et al., 2004; Lichtenberg, Bachner-Melman, Ebstein, & Gritsenko, 2000; Raz, 2005; Raz et al., 2002). Raz (2005) reported an increase from an average of roughly 6 on the Stanford Scale of Hypnotic Susceptibility, Form C (SSHS: C) for both homozygous Val/Val and Met/Met individuals, to an average of about 7.5 for heterozygous Val/Met individuals. Lichtenberg and colleagues found similar effects, albeit usually a smaller increase of only about a point on the SSHS: C.

Since these previous studies assessed hypnotizablity with the individually-administered SSHS: C, a more recent study (Szekelya et al., 2010) tried to replicate in Hungarian young adults, using the Waterloo-Stanford Group Scale of Hypnotic Susceptibility, Form C (WSGC; described above). As noted above, the advantage of the WSGC is that it is based on the traditional Stanford scale Form C, but it can be administered in groups. Results from

Szekelya and colleagues actually found a linear function between COMT activity and hypnotizability: Individuals with the greatest COMT activity (the homozygous Val/Val group) showed the highest hypnotic susceptibility, while those with the lowest COMT activity (the homozygous Met/Met subjects) showed the lowest susceptibility; heterozygous Val/Met subjects scored in the middle on the WSGC (Szekelya et al., 2010). The authors suggest that their findings support the previous studies of Lichtenberg and Raz and colleagues, even though they did not find the "typical" inverted U-shaped response for homozygous/heterozygous individuals. One shortcoming of the Szekelya study was the inexplicable low mean scores on hypnotizability among their sample, nearly a full point lower (4.84) than the normative mean of 5.77 on the WSGC (Bowers, 1993). Indeed, these scores were possibly significantly lower than the means in the previous studies of genetics using the Stanford scale. Thus, while dopamine in general and COMT function in particular may serve to mediate attention and hypnotizability, research should continue to verify the involvement of the select genes and polymorphisms involved.

Finally, hypnotic susceptibility has also been considered as a function of the time of day when it is assessed, and whether this may be related to the possible existence of ultradian rhythms (regular peaks and valleys in activity). Wallace (1993) and Wallace and Kokoszka (1995) have reported that individuals who are judged to be most alert during daytime hours (day people) show greater susceptibility to hypnosis during the day. Similarly, individuals who are judged to be most alert during late afternoon or evening hours (night people) show greater susceptibility during these periods. In a related study, Mann and Sanders (1995) have reported that subjects who reported the greatest alertness in the morning achieved greater trance depth in the morning than in the evening, whereas those who reported greater evening alertness reported deeper trance depth in the evening than in the morning. However, in assessing hypnotic susceptibility and hypnotic depth, evidence for the presence of ultradian rhythms was not found (see Rossi, 1982).

Thus, a number of physiological/biological correlates of hypnotic susceptibility and hypnosis appear to be emerging. In the mid 1980s (Kihlstrom, 1985) it was concluded that there were no reliable, physiological correlates of hypnotic susceptibility or hypnosis. This conclusion appears to be changing.

Hypnotherapy

Habit Control

Regardless of what hypnosis is or is not, and what variables are associated with hypnotic susceptibility, hypnosis can be a useful tool in dealing with certain behavioral problems, such as the control of an unwanted habit. Hypnosis has been used extensively in dealing with obesity, smoking, stress, and the control of other types of potentially debilitating habits. This application is possible most likely because hypnosis enables individuals to deal with their habit at a level of awareness or consciousness that varies from their normal state of consciousness. In the normal waking state, an individual's habit is in full force and is difficult to alter or reshape. However, at a different level of awareness, at which subjects are more susceptible to suggestions of changing their habit, and thus, perhaps, are more inclined to do so, reshaping or altering becomes easier. Hypnosis, then, is a useful tool for reshaping behavior that can be generalized beyond the altered state to the normal waking state of awareness.

Stanton (1975) has found hypnosis to be a useful technique in the treatment of obesity. Specifically, he employed five procedures to help patients with weight-control problems, all with the aid of hypnosis. These included direct suggestions relating to amount and type of food to be eaten in the future, ego-enhancing suggestions to help patients live their lives more pleasantly, mental imagery to establish a desired goal, self-hypnosis to reinforce the therapist's suggestions, and audiotapes to provide additional support after the completion of formal treatment. Stanton reported that the combined use of these techniques had a marked effect on weight loss as reported by patients who completed the entire process. In other words, hypnosis was a successful procedure in the treatment of obesity.

One factor that appears to be important in determining whether hypnosis will be successful in treating obesity is hypnotic susceptibility level. Andersen (1985) reported a positive association between degree of hypnotizability and success at weight reduction. Subjects who had scored high on the Stanford Hypnotic Susceptibility Scale, Form A (previously described), were aided more by a treatment program designed to help individuals lose weight through hypnosis than were those who had scored in either the medium or low parts of the scale.

Other research verified this effect. For example, Barabasz and Spiegel (1989) found that hypnotizability also correlated with success of hypnosis in the use of weight loss; participants who scored highest on the SHSS: C lost the most weight following hypnotic suggestions that high-calorie foods were toxic to the body. A meta-analysis of data collected from five studies using hypnosis as an adjunct to some other type of cognitive-behavioral therapy (CBT) in the treatment of obesity found that participants using only CBT lost an average of about 6 pounds, compared to over 14 pounds when hypnosis was added to traditional therapy (Kirsch, 1996).

More recently, Barabasz (2007) evaluated research investigating the use of hypnosis in the treatment of three types of eating disorders: obesity, anorexia, and bulimia. However, her main conclusion is that information remains elusive regarding the efficacy of hypnosis as a clinically effective treatment for weight loss or other eating disorders. This is because many studies of hypnosis are not methodologically sound, fail to provide enough information to permit comparison with other research, and/or are not replicated by other laboratories. Thus future research should strive to employ stricter methodological considerations. Future studies must include direct comparisons between hypnosis, other therapies, and combined hypnosis/alternative therapy, and a clearer description of the hypnotic induction process, including how participants were identified as high or low hypnotizables, the length of time of hypnosis, and the length of time and type (if any) of follow-up procedures (i.e., additional guided hypnosis sessions or self-hypnosis).

Hypnosis has also been successful in the treatment of smoking, sometimes requiring no more than one session (Williams & Hall, 1988). However, unlike the treatment of overeating or obesity, smoking control does not require that the person score in the upper range of hypnotizability to achieve success (Holroyd, 1980; Perry, Gelfand, & Marcovitch, 1979; Perry & Mullen, 1975).

Spiegel (1979b) employed a competing-response technique using hypnosis to help individuals stop smoking. After a subject had been hypnotized, he or she was asked to concentrate on three points: (1) that cigarette smoking is a poison to the body, (2) that life is not possible without the body, and (3) that life is possible only if one respects and protects one's body (i.e., by not smoking). These suggestions, administered under hypnosis, were then put in a type of competition with the life process, since Spiegel made it clear that a subject could not maintain both life and the smoking habit. As such, life could be reinforced only if the individual was willing to stop smoking. Thus, smoking became a destructive force in maintaining life.

When subjects were confronted with the life-versus-smoking dilemma, it was up to them to make a choice. They could choose smoking, and thereby decrease life, or they could choose life by abandoning the smoking habit. With the aid of hypnosis and the suggestions, Spiegel reported a 20 percent success rate in the termination of the smoking habit. Although this is not a high percentage, one must keep in mind that subjects received only a single treatment session. With an increase in the number of hypnosis sessions, Hall and Crasilneck (1970) reported a 75 percent cure rate. Jeffrey, Jeffrey, Greuling, and Gentry (1985) reported a success rate of 63 percent in a five-treatment program that combined the use of hypnotic, cognitive, and behavioral interventions. Also, Powell (1980) showed that individuals who had stopped smoking through hypnosis and who subsequently returned to smoking were helped to become more permanent nonsmokers with a flooding of hypnosis and systematic desensitization sessions.

A recent study also found positive effects using intensive hypnotherapy alone (Elkins, Marcus, Bates, Rajab, & Cook, 2006). In this study, 20 participants were randomly assigned to receive either eight one-hour sessions of hypnotherapy (n=10) or to a wait-list control (participants were told they were on a waiting list to receive therapy, but would remain involved in the study until a treatment spot became available; n=10). Intensive hypnotherapy included brief counseling and hypnotic induction on session days 1, 2, 4, and 7, and brief counseling and instruction in self-hypnosis during the other four sessions. Hypnotic suggestions were tailored to each individual based on self-reports of what they believed to be the most aversive images. Both experimental and wait-list controls were contacted by phone for brief (5–10-minute) follow-up "support" sessions three days following the end of the intensive therapy, and at weeks 2, 4, and 5. All participants were then tested for smoking cessation by self-report and carbon monoxide concentrations at weeks 8, 12, and 26. Results indicated significantly greater smoking cessation for the intensive therapy group at weeks 12 and 26; six out of 10 participants in the intensive hypnotherapy were smoke-free at week 12 (compared to zero from the wait-list controls), while four out of 10 remained smoke-free at week 26. While there are definitely limitations of this study (for example, the small sample size employed), the results are promising, especially when compared to other studies of hypnosis in the use of smoking cessation, which typically report only about a 20 percent success rate, compared to the 40 percent success rate reported here. It appears, then, that the smoking habit can be controlled with the help of hypnotic suggestions.

How does hypnosis compare to other techniques as a means of dealing with a smoking habit? In a recent survey, West, Fellows, and Easton (1995) asked professionals to respond to questions about the effectiveness of hypnosis as a therapy. Smoking was seen as one of the habits least successfully treated by hypnosis. However, others disagree. Barkley, Hastings, and Jackson (1977) compared hypnosis to rapid smoking as a method for treating the smoking habit. In rapid smoking, an individual is made to smoke a large number of cigarettes in a short time. Hypnosis was found to be an effective treatment method, although the rapid smoking technique proved slightly more effective. Unfortunately, one must question this advantage because rapid smoking produces severe effects, such as explosive nausea (vomiting) and loss of appetite.

A recent meta-analysis of 11 studies using hypnosis in smoking cessation (including the Elkins et al. 2006 study described above), Barnes and colleagues (2010) concluded that there is limited evidence demonstrating efficacy of the use of hypnosis to stop smoking. For the meta-analysis, they included only studies that followed up with participants for at least six months. They divided the studies into those that assessed hypnosis alone versus no treatment, hypnosis versus an attention/advice control, hypnosis versus psychological treatments, hypnosis versus other therapies such as rapid smoking and drug therapy (including hypnosis versus placebo controls), and hypnosis plus another treatment, versus that treatment alone. While they note that many studies over the years have reported success with hypnosis even at six-month follow-up sessions, the authors suggest that these studies contain methodological flaws or biases favoring the experimental groups, and as such, should not be considered evidence in support of hypnosis. However, it should be emphasized that only 11 studies met the criteria for evaluation by this meta-analysis; indeed, breaking up the studies into the subcategories offered by these authors limited even further the number included for analysis.

Thus, it appears that hypnosis can play an important role in the treatment of overeating and smoking. However, one must ask whether the cure is long lasting. The follow-up data on the treated subjects indicate that some individuals return to their old eating or smoking habits. This was true especially when relatively few hypnosis sessions were employed to treat the habit; that is, hypnosis ceased to serve as a strong motivator to control the habit. Thus, although it has been a successful method of treatment for some individuals, hypnosis alone probably is not a likely method of treatment for control. However, when it is used as an adjunct to behavior modification or cognitive techniques, it appears to be fairly successful (Dengrove, 1976; Jeffrey et al., 1985).

Phobias

With regard to phobia control, if an individual shows an irrational fear of some type of object, event, or environment, a popular method of treating this fear is to use hypnosis along with a process called **systematic desensitization** (Wolpe, 1969). This process creates a hierarchy of stimuli that provoke different levels of fear of the event. For example, if someone is fearful of nonpoisonous snakes, the hierarchy might consist of a series of fear levels ranging from fright on hearing the word "snake" to severe fear of direct contact with a snake. If the hierarchy consists of several steps, desensitization would involve a process of giving the subject muscle relaxation therapy at each step of the hierarchy and continuing this therapy until the subject no longer feared the snake at that level. Thus, the therapist would first try to reduce the fear of hearing the word "snake." Once this was accomplished, the therapist would continue to reduce fear at more, increasingly intense levels until fear at all levels of the hierarchy had disappeared.

Although systematic desensitization is a successful treatment therapy by itself (Carson, Butcher, & Coleman, 1988; Costin & Draguns, 1989; Wolpe, 1969), it can be even more successful when used in conjunction with hypnosis (e.g., Lang & Lazovik, 1963), especially since phobic patients appear to be relatively highly hypnotizable (Frankel & Orne, 1976; John, Hollander, & Perry, 1983). This is because, once a level of fear has been established for a phobic individual, hypnotization before the start of actual desensitization therapy increases the efficacy of the therapy. The irrational fear probably developed at a subconscious level of awareness; hypnosis may help to reinstate this level of consciousness and allow the fear to be treated at the same level of awareness at which it was created.

An example of the joint use of hypnosis and desensitization in the treatment of a phobia is illustrated in an experiment by Lang and Lazovik (1963). The investigators were interested in the success of systematic desensitization in treating people who have a phobia of nonpoisonous snakes. Using the technique illustrated earlier, they found that asking subjects under hypnosis to imagine the fear situation at various levels of the established hierarchy was conducive to producing relaxation and vivid imagery. Therefore, the individual could overcome the fear of snakes through imagery. Thus, the dual use of hypnosis and desensitization can be a potent means of treating phobias.

This treatment procedure sounds fairly impressive, and the results reported are equally impressive. However, what is even more important is that the success reported with imagery held true in actual situations. That is, individuals who used this procedure to overcome fear of snakes under laboratory conditions also showed a diminution or elimination of the fear when they actually encountered a snake. Lang and Lazovik reported that the therapy maintained its effectiveness after six months.

More recent research continues to support the use of hypnosis as a successful adjunct to systematic desensitization, or other types of cognitive-behavioral therapies. Studies by Walters and Oakley (2003), Golden (2006), and others have found positive effects of hypnosis in the treatment of phobias ranging from fear of flying to fear of injections (Medd, 2001) or dental procedures (Gow, 2006).

Sexual Dysfunctions

Another successful use of hypnosis teamed with systematic desensitization is in the treatment of sexual dysfunctions. One such dysfunction that has been treated successfully in this way is vaginismus (Fuchs, Hoch, & Kleinhauz, 1976; Fuchs et al., 1973; Oystragh, 1988). **Vaginismus** is a disorder in which the vaginal opening is constricted so as not to permit entry of the penis. One case involved a 23-year-old woman who had never had sexual intercourse with her husband because her vagina was too constricted to allow his penis to enter. After it was determined that the woman's problem was not physiological in origin, the investigators treated the vaginismus as a fear of pain associated with sexual intercourse. They employed a treatment similar to that used by Lang and Lazovik in the treatment of snake phobia. That is, the woman was taught to relax and to produce vivid imagery under hypnosis. In addition, a fear hierarchy of pain was developed for her. She subsequently was given the hierarchy of events to imagine under hypnosis in order from the least to the most anxiety provoking. The hierarchy ranged from imagining herself going home with her husband and resting with him (least anxiety provoking) to imagining herself having sexual intercourse with him (most anxiety provoking). The therapy continued until the woman felt relaxed imagining the final level of the fear hierarchy.

When the patient no longer felt fearful of having intercourse with her husband (as witnessed by overt signs of relaxation, such as muscle relaxation, and her statement that she felt relaxed), she was asked to try to have intercourse with him. She reported that the treatment had been successful and that, for the first time in two years, her husband had been able to penetrate her vagina. Thus, as with snake phobia, the fear of sex can also be successfully treated with the dual use of hypnosis and systematic desensitization.

Hypnosis has also been successfully used in the treatment of premature ejaculation. Milton Erickson (1973), a pioneer in the use of hypnosis in psychotherapy, reports the case of a 38-year-old who, after trying countless remedies, decided to find out whether hypnosis could help him with his problem.

In a number of sessions with the patient, a posthypnotic suggestion was given to him that no matter how hard he tried and no matter how long coitus endured, an ejaculation would not occur for many minutes. Erickson reported that this technique proved successful and the man no longer experienced his former problem.

In addition to the use of hypnosis in the treatment of sexual problems, it has been found useful in the treatment of other psychological disorders. As examples, it has been used in the treatment of bipolar affective disorders such as manic-depression (Feinstein & Morgan, 1986); bulimia, or the purging of food (Hall & McGill, 1986), and other eating disorders, such as anorexia nervosa (Baker & Nash, 1987; Yapko, 1986); and multiple-personality disorders (Kirsch & Barton, 1988; Kluft, 1988).

It appears, then, that hypnosis is a useful manipulation in the treatment of many psychological problems. Surgeons and dentists also have used hypnosis as an analgesic or an anesthetic. The next section of this chapter considers the use of hypnosis in the relief of pain.

Hypnosis and Pain Control

Before we discuss the role of hypnosis in the control of pain, two terms need to be defined: **analgesia** and **anesthesia**. The former refers to the removal of existing pain; the latter is the prevention of pain that is not currently present.

As was mentioned earlier in this chapter, in the 1800s, Esdaile and others successfully employed hypnosis to create an analgesic effect during surgery. As a matter of fact, hypnosis was used as a means of eliminating pain before chemical agents were discovered. Before Esdaile's important work in this field, surgery without analgesia or anesthesia was so painful that 40 percent of all patients who underwent surgery for the removal of tumors died not long afterward. However, with the advent of hypnotic anesthesia, this rate was reduced to about 5 percent (Fromm & Shor, 1979).

When chemical anesthetics, such as chloroform and sodium thiopental (Pentothal), appeared for use in surgery, hypnosis was effectively eliminated as a procedure to reduce experienced pain, since chemical agents induced an anesthetic effect faster. This development was most unfortunate for several reasons. First, although time-consuming to administer, hypnosis was a successful procedure for reducing pain. Second, hypnotic anesthesia was far safer to use than chemical anesthetics, since the latter were associated with several side effects, including respiratory depression, myocardial depression, cardiac arrhythmias, and prolonged somnolence.

Why does hypnosis play an important role in reducing pain? Mostly because hypnosis helps to dissociate the experience of pain into two levels of awareness (Hilgard, 1973). At one level, the patient is aware of feeling the pain. However, during an altered state of awareness such as hypnosis, the patient does not experience the pain (Hilgard & Hilgard, 1994; Malone, Kurtz, & Strube, 1989). In fact, Crawford, Gur, Skolnick, Gur, and Benson (1993) have provided evidence via PET scans (see chapter 2) that during hypnosis there is increased cerebral blood flow in the frontal cortex to reduce the magnitude of experienced pain. Thus, hypnotic analgesia seems to produce a change in how the brain processes and ultimately reduces the pain experience (see Crawford, 1996).

Surgeons who use hypnosis in their practice today do so primarily when a patient shows allergic reactions to chemical anesthetics, or when the surgeon wishes to reduce the dosage of the chemical agent (Fredericks, 1980; Hogue & Hunter, 1988). Regarding the latter concern, many surgeons believe that there really is no need to rely totally on chemical agents as anesthetics during surgery. Therefore, they might reduce the dosage of the anesthetic by employing hypnotic anesthesia as an adjunct. The more effective the hypnotic anesthesia, the lower the dosage of chemical anesthetic. The dual use of chemical and hypnotic anesthesia effectively reduces many of the drug-related risks mentioned earlier (Nathan, Morris, Goebel et al., 1987).

Unfortunately, not all patients can benefit from the use of hypnotic anesthesia or analgesia. Many are not highly susceptible to hypnotic suggestions and are not readily capable of dissociating various levels of experienced pain. For such patients there is usually no choice but to use a chemical anesthetic or analgesic. Although hypnotic susceptibility may, at least in the short term, improve with practice (Diamond, 1974, 1977; Spanos, 1986), the time required to train individuals to be more hypnotically susceptible becomes a great obstacle to normal operating procedures, both before and during surgery. As a result, relatively few surgeons employ hypnotic anesthesia as either an alternative or an adjunct to chemical agents.

Besides the use of hypnotic anesthesia in surgery, this pain-reducing procedure has been employed in the field of obstetrics. The use of hypnotic anesthesia and analgesia in childbirth is not new; it was used as a means of reducing childbirth pain more than a hundred years ago (Kroger, 1977). As with hypnotic anesthesia in surgery, it is necessary first to determine whether the patient is sufficiently susceptible to hypnotic suggestions. If the expectant mother is susceptible, she can be trained to accept suggestions for hypnotic anesthesia before and during parturition. However, relatively few patients (about 20 percent) can be taught to reduce pain effectively without the aid of some chemical anesthetic or analgesic.

There are some obvious advantages for patients who can profit by the use of hypnotic anesthesia during childbirth. These include a reduction in post-operative side effects that would be present with chemical anesthetics, a reduction in postchildbirth pain, and the elimination of danger to the baby from the administration of a chemical agent to the mother (Kroger, 1977). However, while hypnotic techniques are beneficial during childbirth, procedures for natural childbirth (e.g., the Lamaze technique) are as beneficial as hypnosis (Davenport-Slack, 1975; Weishaar, 1986). Perhaps this is because both procedures enable women to alter their state of awareness temporarily and thus escape the level of pain they would normally experience during the waking state. Additionally, natural childbirth procedures do not differ much from self-hypnosis procedures. During self-hypnosis an individual can temporarily induce an altered state of consciousness. Thus, hypnotically induced pain relief and natural childbirth procedures are equally effective in helping a mother to alter her state of consciousness during childbirth.

Hypnosis has also been employed as a means of dealing with pain during dental procedures. However, hypnosis is rarely used as an anesthetic or analgesic in dentistry. Rather, it is used as a tool to help reduce tension and fear of pain and to allow the patient to become more relaxed (Forgione, 1988). The result of this, of course, is to reduce the magnitude of experienced pain. In general, as with the use of hypnosis in surgery, its use in dentistry is not common. It is time-consuming to administer, and only a limited number of patients can profit by its use. Therefore, neither surgery nor dentistry make considerable use of hypnosis in dealing with experienced pain.

There is a multitude of recent research noting the efficacy of hypnosis either alone or as an adjunct to other treatments (i.e., pharmacological or cognitive-behavioral therapy) in both acute (i.e., childbirth or post-surgery; Cyna, McAuliff, & Andrew, 2004; Montgomery et al., 2007; Montgomery, David, Winkel, Silverstien, & Bovbjerg, 2002) and chronic pain management (Patterson & Jensen, 2003; Stoelb, Molton, Jensen, & Patterson, 2009; Tan, Fukui, Jensen, Thornby, & Walden, 2010). Perhaps with the proven efficacy of some faster induction methods such as the Group Scale of Hypnotic Ability (GSHA; described earlier in this chapter), more clinicians will use hypnosis for pain control and anesthesia.

As an analgesic, hypnosis has been used in the treatment of headaches. Generally, two procedures have been tried in treating this type of pain: glove anesthesia and the hand-warming technique. **Glove anesthesia** (Barber & Adrian, 1982; Kroger, 1977) is a procedure whereby the patient's hand is anesthetized hypnotically. The person is then taught to apply the anesthetized hand to the portion of the head that hurts. The result is to transfer the anesthetic effect to the head. In this manner, individuals can be taught to eliminate or control headaches. Naturally, for this procedure to be maximally beneficial, the individual must be taught self-hypnosis so that he or she can learn to anesthetize the hand to apply it to the head.

The second procedure, **hand warming**, was developed by Sargent, Green, and Walters (1973); it uses hypnosis as well as biofeedback (see chapter 5). In this technique, patients are taught to achieve passive concentration and to relax their entire bodies with hypnotic procedures. Then they receive instructions concerning the use of temperature in the control of pain. Patients are instructed to visualize temperature changes in their hands while watching a temperature trainer, a feedback mechanism by which they can determine whether their hand temperature really has changed. Thus, they think about making their hand warm, and, in fact, it becomes warm. Then they apply the warm hand to the head; in this way the severity of the headache is reduced or the headache is totally eliminated. The principles underlying this phenomenon are discussed in chapter 5.

Success has been reported in the treatment of headaches with the use of both glove anesthesia and hand warming (Andreychuck & Skriver, 1975; Graham, 1975). Therefore, hypnosis can be a beneficial substitute for the chemical agents (e.g., aspirin, buffered aspirin, acetaminophen) that are commonly used to relieve headache pain. Another method for treating headaches is the sole use of biofeedback (see chapter 5) in a manner similar to the hand-warming technique.

Finally, and related to pain control in subjects who are hypnotizable, a number of investigators (Hagemann-Wenselaar, 1988; Hilgard & LeBaron, 1982, 1984; Smith, Barabasz, & Barabasz, 1996; Wall & Womack, 1989) have reported that hypnotizable children who have cancer and are undergoing chemotherapy show significantly more pain control and reduction during bone-marrow aspirations than do those who are not hypnotizable. However, even children who are judged to be low in hypnotic susceptibility benefit by the use of distraction techniques (Smith et al., 1996).

Research continues to support findings of efficacy of hypnosis in pediatric populations (Berberich & Landman, 2009; Richardson, Smith, & Pilkington,

2006; Wild & Espie, 2004). Hypnosis may prove to be especially useful in the treatment of pain in children and adolescents, who may express greater vulnerability than adults to the side effects of pain medications.

Hypnosis and Memory

With regard to memory, investigators have sought to determine whether hypnosis can induce amnesia and hypermnesia. **Amnesia** is defined as a loss of memory. **Hyperamnesia** is concerned with improving an individual's memory for events experienced in the past.

You may recall that on the Stanford and Harvard scales, amnesia through hypnosis is used as a criterion for establishing susceptibility. As such, investigators believe that amnesia can be induced through hypnosis. However, hypnotic susceptibility aside, how effective is this induction in the laboratory? Basically, it appears that hypnotically induced amnesia affects episodic memory (defined, for example, as the ability to recall a word list that was memorized during hypnosis) but not semantic memory. (The ability to use the same word list items as responses on word association tasks would be semantic memory.) This has been demonstrated in a number of experiments (Evans, 1979b; Kihlstrom, 1980; Spanos, Radtke, & Dubreuil, 1982).

With regard to hypermnesia, or improving an individual's memory, several experiments have shown this to be possible through hypnosis (Dhanens & Lundy, 1975; Dywan & Bowers, 1983). There have also been reports in real-world situations of witnesses to a crime providing useful information while hypnotized. For example, in 1976 in Chowchilla, California, a bus filled with children on a field trip was kidnapped. The bus, children, and driver were buried beneath the ground and were to be kept there until a ransom was paid. As the car being driven by the culprits left the scene of the crime, the bus driver observed it. However, he had difficulty remembering important details that would lead to the arrest of the kidnappers. Under hypnosis he was able to recall the license plate of the car. This information ultimately led to the arrest of the kidnappers.

Unfortunately, not all attempts at recovering information from an eyewitness are so successful. Many recall attempts appear to be associated with increases in inaccurate recollection or confabulation (Sheehan, 1988; Worthington, 1979). Thus, in theory, although individuals can recall so-called forgotten information through hypnosis, one cannot be certain that what is being recalled is fact or fiction (McConkey, 1988; Perry, Orne, London et al., 1996).

139

Needless to say, this has presented problems, legal and otherwise, for the use of hypnosis in the courtroom as a means of establishing information about a crime that an individual witnessed (Gianelli, 1995; Laurence & Perry, 1983; Putnam, 1979; Sanders & Simmons, 1983; Sheehan & Tilden, 1983; Zelig & Beidelman, 1981). Despite its problems, hypnosis continues to be a useful tool in forensic psychology and is used as a way to help witnesses to a crime recall some of the detail that they may have forgotten. Yes, there have been instances of confabulation, but there have also been instances in which valuable information has surfaced that has led to the solution of a crime (Beahrs, 1988; Sloan, 1981).

Hypnosis has also been used in an attempt to help individuals remember information about their childhood, information that is normally not available for recall. Examples of such studies are those by Walker, Garrett, and Wallace (1976), Wallace (1978a), and Nash, Johnson, and Tipton (1979). In each of these studies, hypnotically induced age regression was used to help individuals recall or reconstruct information that was no longer available to conscious retrieval. **Hypnotic age regression**, as you might guess, involves taking a subject back in time. For example, an individual might be taken back to the age of 5 to recall events that happened then. He or she might be asked to remember what happened, for example, at a birthday party.

In the Walker et al. study, **eidetic imagery**, or what is popularly referred to as photographic memory, was being investigated. As the researchers noted, this phenomenon is very rare in adults (Stromeyer & Psotka, 1970) although it can be found in about 8 to 10 percent of children around the age of 7 to 8 (Haber, 1979; Haber & Haber, 1964). The investigators reasoned that a good test of hypnotic age regression would be to recreate the process of eidetic imagery in adults who are regressed to the age at which this process is most visible. They also reasoned that if age-regressed adults displayed eidetic imagery in an experimental paradigm in which results could not be faked, they would find evidence to suggest that hypnotic age regression is a valuable tool for investigating the processes involved in memory.

The task that was used was a difficult one and not easily faked. Subjects were asked to perceive, in a binocular fashion, half of a 10,000-dot stereogram for 60 seconds (Julesz, 1971). Immediately after the removal of the first half, they were asked to perceive the second half. Presentation of either half produced a meaningless, unidentifiable composite of dots. Subjects were then asked to combine the memory of the first half with the observed dot composite of the second half and to identify the object formed by such a combination. From a sample of 20 hypnotically age-regressed subjects, two (10 percent) were capable of demonstrating eidetic imagery. This study has been replicated by Wallace (1978a) and Crawford, Wallace, Nomura, and Slater (1986). Spanos, Ansari, and Stam (1979) failed to replicate the phenomenon, but given the rarity of its occurrence in age-regressed adults, this is not surprising. Also, Raikov (1980) believes that some experiments with hypnotic age regression have failed because of the nature of the hypnotist's suggestion and the subject's depth of hypnosis.

It should be mentioned that the concept of hypnotic age regression is controversial. While phenomena with its use have been demonstrated (e.g., rudimentary, childlike handwriting or speaking in a child's voice), thus leading us to believe that it is real, there are many instances in which hypnotic age regression could not be experimentally substantiated as a bona fide event (Ascher, Barber, & Spanos, 1972; Barber, 1962; Fisher, 1962; O'Connell, Shor, & Orne, 1970). Yet experiments, such as those by Walker et al. (1976) demonstrate that while subjects are age regressed, they exhibit behavior that differs from their behavior when they are not regressed. This could, of course, simply be an indication that subjects process information differently when they are asked to be "adults" than when they are asked to be "children." And such processing differences may illustrate age regression in action. However, this issue remains unresolved, and we cannot cite definitive evidence that hypnotic age regression is real. Undoubtedly, an answer to the question of whether hypnotic age regression is real will be a fruitful area for future research.

Hypnosis and Perception

As with the study of memory, hypnosis has also been used to study various perceptual effects. Some of the more dramatic reports include those by Graham and Leibowitz (1972) and Sheehan, Smith, and Forrest (1982), who found that hypnotic suggestions led to improvements in visual acuity in myopic (nearsighted) subjects. That is, hypnosis can be used, at least temporarily, to help improve a nearsighted individual's vision. This improvement takes place without requiring the subject to wear corrective lenses.

The induction of hypnotic deafness has also been reported to affect auditory sensitivity (Crawford, MacDonald, & Hilgard, 1979) and auditory interference on visual choice-reaction time (Blum & Porter, 1974). Thus, hypnosis can temporarily be used to produce a type of artificial deafness, especially for some sound tones. As a simple example, subjects might be taught to selectively attend to the voice of an instructor in a college course while attenuating the distracting voices of fellow students who happen to be conversing during the lecture.

Also, hypnotic anesthesia has been employed in a number of perception experiments. Wallace and his colleagues (Garrett & Wallace, 1975; Wallace & Fisher, 1982; Wallace & Garrett, 1973, 1975) have reported that anesthesia disrupts the ability of individuals to localize visual objects in the environment or to coordinate parts of the body (e.g., arm, leg) with those objects after wearing displacing prisms. Hypnotic anesthesia has also been shown to disrupt the normal ability of subjects to localize their nose when asked to find it with their eyes closed (Wallace & Hoyenga, 1980). Although Spanos, Gorassini, and Petrusic (1981) replicated this latter finding, they failed to replicate the formerly described effect of displacing prisms. However, this failure has been tied to an inadequate control of conditions that would lead to the findings reported by Wallace and his colleagues (Wallace & Fisher, 1982, 1984).

The anesthesia studies imply that hypnosis helps scientists to isolate the factors involved in coordinated motor activities. By doing so, hypnosis gives us some clues about what is going on when, for example, a person suffers a stroke and cannot perform normal (or any) motor activity in a given limb. By isolating the components involved in normal motor functioning, techniques might be devised to more quickly rehabilitate an affected limb or body part in stroke victims.

Hypnosis and hypnotic susceptibility have also been shown to affect performance on the Stroop effect (Sheehan, Donovan, & MacLeod, 1988). The Stroop effect occurs when subjects are asked to name the ink color of an incompatible color word (e.g, the word *yellow* is printed in *blue* and they show strong interference from the word. When provided with an attention-focusing instruction under hypnosis, highly hypnotizable subjects sharply reduced the Stroop effect, whereas less easily hypnotized individuals decreased it slightly.

From the perspective of either a scientist or a student, one can appreciate the usefulness of hypnosis in the study of behavior. Although there is, and will continue to be, controversy concerning the phenomenon of hypnosis, it has proven itself to be a useful tool for scientific research. Hypnosis can be used in a variety of experiments and in professional therapies for habit control, phobias, obsessions, compulsions, and sexual dysfunctions. It can also be used beneficially in the control of pain and in the recall of information that cannot be extracted in the normal waking state of consciousness.

Now that we have seen how hypnosis is measured and used, how has this phenomenon been explained? In other words, what theories describe the phenomenon of hypnosis?

Contemporary Theories of Hypnosis

Today, three theoretical approaches predominate in explaining the phenomenon of hypnosis. These were mentioned briefly at the beginning of this chapter. They include the trance theory of hypnosis (Conn & Conn, 1967; Fromm & Shor, 1979; Hilgard, 1965, 1973, 1977b, 1979), the sociological role theory (Coe, 1978; Coe & Sarbin, 1977; Sarbin & Coe, 1972, 1979), and the task-motivation theory (Barber, 1969; Barber, Spanos, & Chaves, 1974; Spanos, 1982).

The **trance theory** postulates that hypnosis is a process that involves an altered state of consciousness, or a trance, during which the subject is in a heightened state of susceptibility or responsiveness to suggestions or commands. Therefore, in hypnosis an individual must either be temporarily dissociated from the normal waking state of awareness or consciousness or be minimally capable of performing some tasks with hypnosis that are not as easily accomplished or even possible to accomplish at all without hypnosis.

Hilgard (1973, 1979) has presented evidence that a subject is in a special state of consciousness during the reception of hypnotic instructions. In dealing with the perception of pain, Hilgard produced pain by applying extreme cold to a subject's arm. Such application produces what is referred to as *cold-pressor* pain. Hilgard found that hypnotically suggested analgesia can reduce considerably the felt pain sensation associated with the cold pressor. However, if a subject reports feeling no pain and is then asked to write down his or her felt experiences, he or she does indeed report experiencing pain. Therefore, though the subject did not orally report pain, a "hidden part" of the person may report the true level of pain experienced. This "hidden part" has been referred to as the *hidden observer* (Hilgard, 1973; Hilgard, Morgan, & MacDonald, 1975; Knox, Crutchfield, & Hilgard, 1975).

Sometimes, this true level of pain is reported through *automatic writing*, in which it can be suggested to subjects that the hidden observer can communicate with the hypnotist through writing. Subjects orally report no pain but, through this writing, report that they are experiencing pain. Therefore, according to Hilgard, a subject experiences pain at two levels. One level is consciously cognitive; at this level, hypnotic analgesia clearly affects the severity of experienced pain. The subject indicates a cessation or diminution in the level of pain.

However, at the second level the subject does experience pain and reports this via automatic writing. On the basis of these results, Hilgard developed a neodissociation theory of pain reduction in hypnosis. This theory specifies that, at some cognitive level, the subject has experienced the cold and can report its intensity even though the suffering may be reduced. Since Hilgard's theory obviously implies cognitive control of a stimulus event, it suggests that a trance or altered state of consciousness appears to be operating during hypnosis.

Hilgard's neodissociation theory focuses on cognitive changes that occur following hypnotic suggestions. A second theory, by Sarbin and Coe (1972, 1979), focuses on the social context in which hypnosis takes place. Unlike the trance theory, the **sociological theory** does not propose that hypnotized individuals behave as they do because they have undergone a change in the state of consciousness. Rather, it proposes that hypnotized subjects behave as they do because they are striving to enact the role of a hypnotized subject as it is defined by the hypnotist and society in general. Sarbin and Coe have described a number of variables that appear to be important to the success of this role enactment (Kihlstrom, 1985). These include the location of individual participants in their proper roles, perceived congruence between self and role, accuracy of role expectations and sensitivity to role demands, possession of role-relevant skills, and the influence of the audience. Depending on the degree to which these factors are favorable, the subject is capable of giving a performance that is as convincing to observers as to oneself.

Related to Sarbin and Coe's theory, Barber (1969) has suggested that hypnosis does not require a trance or a trance state for the phenomenon to be demonstrated. In other words, according to this **task-motivation theory,** hypnosis is not an altered state of consciousness. Rather, it is a predisposition in a normal state of awareness to attend to commands and suggestions from a hypnotist. Barber believes that most of the phenomena that are purported to come about as a result of hypnosis can be demonstrated in a nonhypnotic, wakeful situation as well. Thus, nonhypnotized subjects are capable of performing tasks that supposedly are possible only under hypnosis. A subject who has positive attitudes about hypnosis, who is sufficiently motivated to perform a given task, and who expects that a given task is possible with hypnosis can perform hypnotic feats without being in an altered state of consciousness.

Some examples of experiments in support of Barber's theory include those by Spanos, Ham, and Barber (1973) and Johnson, Maher, and Barber (1972). In the experiment by Spanos and associates, subjects were asked to hallucinate the presence of an object that in reality was not present. Three conditions were employed in this study. In the first condition, subjects were asked to hallucinate the presence of an object without any special instructions. In the second condition, subjects received task-motivational instructions in which they were told to try as hard as they could to imagine the object. The third condition involved the standardized induction of hypnosis, in which the hallucination of an object was suggested via so-called hypnotic instructions.

The result of the study showed that 98 percent of the control subjects (i.e., those given the first condition) reported imagining the object either vaguely or vividly, but they really did not see it. However, 8 percent of subjects who were given either a hypnotic-induction procedure or task-motivational instructions reported actually seeing the object. This percentage did not differ as a function of receiving hypnotic-induction procedures or task-motivational instructions. Therefore, the investigators concluded that task-motivational instructions were as effective as actual hypnotic-induction procedures in producing a visual hallucination. This finding appears to indicate that a trance or an altered state is not necessary for the production of a phenomenon that theoretically is possible only under a hypnotic trance.

Johnson and associates (1972) reached a similar conclusion. In their experiment they investigated a phenomenon referred to as *trance logic*. Trance logic (Orne, 1959) refers to the use of a special form of reasoning in which it is totally plausible for an individual to report seeing a hallucinated image in a room and at the same time see the same object in another room. Or a person may see a person in one part of the environment and at the same time see a hallucinated image of that person in another part of the environment.

This supposed ability of objects or people to be in two places at the same time does not appear illogical to hypnotized subjects; hence, the term trance logic. Accordingly, it appears, as Orne postulates, that a special trance state exists for a subject to be able to perform trance logic. However, Johnson and associates found that nonhypnotized subjects gave the same kind of reports with the same frequency as subjects who were judged to be deeply hypnotized. Therefore, it appears that the phenomenon of trance logic is possible both for subjects who appear to be in a hypnotic trance and for others who are not hypnotized but who are asked to imagine this form of hallucination under task-motivational instructions. Again, this type of experimental evidence led Barber to postulate that hypnosis is not a trance state, but rather is the result of positive attitudes, positive motivations, and positive expectancies toward the hypnosis-related task.

It appears that, at least for some situations, Barber has found sufficient evidence to support his theory. However, many experiments support the trance theory, so Barber's theory cannot be considered the sole explanation of hypnosis (see Bowers, 1976, and Fromm & Shor, 1979, for reviews of this literature). Also, many experiments have shown that positive attitudes, motivations, and expectancies toward hypnosis may not always be sufficient to produce hypno-sislike results (see Krauss, Katzell, & Krauss, 1974; Walker et al., 1976; Woody, Drugovic, & Oakman, 1997).

It is without question that Barber's research has added considerable in-formation to the study of hypnosis. However, for the nontrance approach to be more acceptable, results such as those obtained by Walker et al. (1976) and Wallace (1978a) in the restoration of eidetic imagery through hypnosis (which, incidentally, could not be produced solely with Barber's conditions) will have to be explained in terms of positive attitudes, motivations, and ex-pectancies. At present this has not been accomplished.

As you can see, the definition or theory of hypnosis is as controversial as the phenomenon itself. Each theory has its advocates and its opponents. In addition, available experimental evidence appears to support, at least to some extent, each side of the argument. To help resolve the controversy, it may be necessary to accept a position similar to that expressed in Hilgard's descrip-tion of the two levels in hypnotically controlled pain. That is, with regard to the phenomenon of hypnosis, at one level, individuals become cognizant of hypnosis, and at another level, they experience hypnosis.

Thus, it is possible that, at one level, individuals have positive attitudes, motivations, and expectancies concerning their ability to be hypnotized. At this level, hypnosis becomes possible even though the individual is still in a normal waking state. At the second level, however, a subject must assume an altered state of consciousness for a hypnotic feat (e.g., hypnotic analgesia) to become effective. With this dual approach to hypnosis, perhaps we can come a bit closer to defining the phenomenon. In fact, something similar to this was proposed by Sheehan and McConkey (1982).

Ultimately, we may discover that hypnosis involves many more levels of consciousness than even Hilgard describes. For example, we know that some hypnotized subjects can be in a so-called light trance at one point and in a deep trance at another. Whether these trance states are actually different levels of awareness or incremental differences in the same level is not known. However, such speculation can be fruitful only if scientists are encouraged to pursue an answer to this possibility.

One unfortunate aspect of the study of hypnosis is our failure to under-stand fully what it is. We also do not know why some individuals are readily hypnotizable while others are not, although many clues are emerging that were previously discussed. Furthermore, we do not know what triggers a state of hypnosis. We think we know that hypnosis is not controlled physiologically, but that idea does not tell us what *does* control hypnosis.

Despite the theories that purport to explain the phenomenon, hypnosis is still a controversial area of study within psychology and medicine, although not nearly as much so as during the days of Mesmer. Only the passage of time, a proliferation of experiments, and an understanding of the general role of hypnosis as an altered state of consciousness will help to place this important scientific tool in the forefront of investigations in the behavioral sciences and medicine. And, at least according to a survey conducted by Nash, Minton, and Baldridge (1988), this is exactly what is happening. There is more scientific interest today (as witnessed by the sheer number of articles in dental, medical, and psychological journals) in hypnosis than there has been since the resurgence of the study of consciousness in the late 1960s and early 1970s. With this increased interest, it is likely that many of the questions surrounding hypnosis may, at least to some extent, be answered.

For Further Reading

Bowers, K. S. (1976). *Hypnosis for the seriously curious.* New York: Norton.

Chapman, R. A. (Ed.). (2006). *The clinical use of hypnosis in cognitive-behavioral therapy.* New York: Springer Publishing.

Green, J., Barabasz, A., Barrett, D., & Montgomery, G. (2005). The 2003 APA Division 30 definition of hypnosis. Reprinted with permission from the *Journal of Clinical and Experimental Hypnosis, 53*(3), 262–264. http://www.asch.net/portals/0/journallibrary/articles/ajch-48/div30definition.pdf

Hilgard, E. R., & Hilgard, J. R. (1994). *Hypnosis in the relief of pain.* New York: Bruner/Mazel.

Jamieson, G. A. (Ed.). (2007). *Hypnosis and conscious states: The cognitive neuroscience perspective.* Oxford: Oxford University Press.

Kallio, S., & Revansuo, A. (2003). Hypnotic phenomena and altered states of consciousness: A theoretical framework. *Contemporary Hypnosis, 20*(3), 111–164.

Kunzendorf, R. G., Spanos, N. P., & Wallace, B. (Eds.). (1996). *Hypnosis and imagination.* Amityville, NY: Baywood.

Naish, P. L. N. (Ed.). (1986). *What is hypnosis? Current theories and research.* Philadelphia: Open University Press.

Nash, M. & Barnier, A. (Eds.). (2007). *The Oxford handbook of hypnosis: Theory, research, and practice.* Oxford: Oxford University Press.

Olness, K., & Kohen, D. P. (1996). *Hypnosis and hypnotherapy with children.* New York: Guilford.

Wallace, B. (1979). *Applied hypnosis: An overview.* Chicago: Nelson-Hall.

Biofeedback

Our bodies have many physiological responses of which we are normally unaware. Some of these include our heart rate, muscle tone, blood pressure, skin-surface temperature, and brain activity. However, through a process called biofeedback, it may be possible to train ourselves to become aware of such involuntary responses. In other words, through biofeedback, we may be capable of learning to attend to responses that normally we cannot control consciously.

Simply defined, **biofeedback** is a behavioral technique that, by use of instrumentation, is meant to increase an individual's level of awareness of his or her biological condition. Such awareness may help people to bring a physiological response (e.g., muscle tone, heart rate, blood pressure) under conscious control. As an example, this might help an individual gain some control over hypertension. The increased level of awareness or consciousness is brought about as the biofeedback instrument detects the physiological activity of the responses in question and simultaneously provides this information to the subject in the form of visual or auditory feedback. Using this feedback, the subject can manipulate and control the physiological response.

In this chapter we attempt to explain the relatively simple and basic principles underlying biofeedback. We also describe the historical development of the manipulation and the basic components of the technique as it helps us to gain access to bodily information of which we are normally unaware. Finally, we assess the importance and validity of biofeedback as a means of helping us bring to consciousness physiological information that we can use in dealing with behavioral and medical problems.

Biofeedback and Consciousness

To explain the process of biofeedback, we first illustrate a basic principle of learning through general feedback. Try to recall the first time you went bowling. Remember when you picked up the ball and discovered how heavy it seemed? Remember how far away the pins appeared and how awkward you felt as you approached the foul line and released the ball for the first time? Finally, remember the embarrassment of watching the ball roll down the gutter or, at best, of leaving all but one or two pins completely unscathed?

If, after all this, you were still determined to continue bowling, you probably found that with time and experience, the ball seemed a bit lighter than before, your feelings of awkwardness as you approached the foul line diminished substantially, and rather than dropping your ball two or three feet from the alley or hurl it into the gutter, you actually released it correctly. As a consequence of these improvements, gutter-ball frames became less frequent as more and more pins fell victim to your ball.

In large part, these improvements in performance were made possible by learning through sensory feedback. Imagine what your improvement would have been had you been forced to wear earplugs and a blindfold each time you went bowling. Lacking visual and auditory input, you would have been completely unaware of your successes and failures, your need or lack of need for correction. For any given frame, your score would be pretty much a function of blind luck. In short, without such feedback, learning to bowl, as measured by improvements in pin count, would be virtually impossible.

Instead of bowling, suppose that you wanted to learn to increase or decrease your heart rate at will. An obvious similarity between the bowling task and the heart rate task is that both involve bringing certain muscles or muscle groups under conscious control. On the basis of the bowling example, you might predict that any improvement in performance (i.e., increasing or decreasing heart rate as desired) would depend, in large part, on your reception of adequate sensory feedback. Herein lies the problem. The human body simply is not designed to provide any but the most rudimentary feedback concerning internal physiological states. As you read this page, you are probably not aware that your heart is beating at a rate between 65 and 75 beats per minute.

At this point, guess what your heart rate is, note the number in the margin, and then take your pulse. (The simplest method of taking one's pulse is to count pulse beats for a 15-second period, multiply this value by 4, and express the answer in terms of beats per minute.) Note your actual pulse rate in the margin and circle it. How accurate was your guess?

Suppose for a moment that our systems were constructed so that we received constant feedback concerning their level of physiological activity and that each system was under voluntary control. If this were the case, our consciousness would be bombarded constantly with information concerning the physiological state of each organ of the body. Simply to stay alive, all our conscious efforts would have to be directed toward making certain that each system functioned properly. Imagine the sensory overload that would occur. With our attention so focused, we would have little or no awareness of our external environment and little or no time to respond to changes in it. As we have already noted, however, under normal conditions our bodily systems continue to function well, despite our lack of awareness of such functioning.

Does this mean that we are never aware of the biological state of an organ system? The answer to this, obviously, is no. From previous experiences at the doctor's office or in a gym class, almost everyone is familiar with the fact that hopping up and down on one foot for one minute produces a perceptible increase in heart rate. However, we are aware of an increase in heart rate under these conditions because the number of beats per minute has almost doubled.

Now stop reading for a minute and check your pulse rate in the same manner as before. When you compare this new value with the one circled earlier, you will probably observe a change of several beats per minute, even though, in all likelihood, you were not aware of any such change because it was so small. Unfortunately for us, at least in terms of the heart rate task, it is these minute changes that are the most valuable as feedback in permitting us to achieve conscious control over the response.

The process of biofeedback training places the individual in a closed feedback loop with an instrument that continually provides information about subtle changes in bodily processes. In turn, the individual or subject who is undergoing biofeedback continually adjusts, corrects, and modifies responses as more and more information is received. The training is continued until it is determined that some final, generally predetermined goal (set by a trainer or clinician after lengthy discussions with the patient) has been achieved (Hart, 1967).

The biofeedback procedure, as it exists today, is a relatively new technique, but one that has substantial historical roots. To place biofeedback in its proper historical perspective, we now examine some of the most important factors that have led to its present state of development.

Historical Development

Many centuries ago, Plato (427–347 BCE) observed that humans possessed a "superior rational soul" located in the head and an "inferior soul" located in the heart and liver. Plato believed that the superior rational soul, which he equated with reason, controlled the voluntary responses of the striated musculature, while the inferior soul controlled the responses of the nonstriated muscles and glands. Plato equated the inferior soul with emotions. This dichotomy between reason and emotion, between voluntary and involuntary responses, was to prove both troublesome to later theorists in the area of learning and extremely persistent in psychological thought.

In the seventeenth century this dichotomy once again gained prominence when M. F. Bichat (1771–1802), a French neuroanatomist, distinguished between the cerebrospinal nervous system, which he labeled the "great brain," and the spinal cord and sympathetic ganglionic chains, which he referred to as the "little brain." To the former, he attributed control of the voluntary skeletal responses; to the latter, he attributed control of the emotional and involuntary visceral or autonomic responses.

The twentieth-century manifestation of this dichotomy was expressed by the European investigators Miller and Konorski (1928). They distinguished between what they called Type I (classical) and Type II (instrumental) conditioning. More important for our discussion, however, is that they proposed, for the first time, that involuntary responses were not subject to instrumental conditioning. The subsequent acceptance of this stance by some of the most prominent psychologists of the day—e.g., Schlosberg (1937), Mowrer (1938), and eventually Skinner (1953)—turned the exclusion of autonomic responses into psychological dogma (Kimmel, 1974). Neal Miller suggested that both classical and instrumental conditioning followed similar laws and that a common mechanism might be found that actually controlled both. As we will see shortly, this hypothesis was at the center of Miller's early research, in which he employed paralyzed animals to determine whether these animals could learn to control their cardiovascular activity for reward or punishment (Dienstfrey, 1991).

This is not to suggest that there were no dissenters. Several independent groups of investigators had begun research programs designed to demonstrate that human involuntary responses could be modified to obtain a desired result. In the former Soviet Union, for example, Lisina (1965) attempted to condition at will the dilation and constriction of the blood vessel in a single finger. Initially, this investigator employed electric shock as a negative reinforcer, but such training failed to change blood vessel activity in either direction (constriction or dilation). When Lisina combined electric shock with a visual feedback display of the subject's vasomotor activity, however, she was able to demonstrate operant conditioning of dilation in the blood vessel.

Meanwhile, in the United States, Harwood (1962) and Shearn (1960) were engaged in attempts to modify heart rate responses using operant learning techniques. Using rats as subjects, Harwood obtained what essentially were negative findings for both acceleration and deceleration of the heart rate. Shearn was somewhat more successful in that he was able to condition an increase in heart rate for human subjects to whom such an increase would postpone the delivery of an electric shock.

Finally, Mandler and colleagues at the University of Toronto and Kimmel and colleagues at the University of Florida were interested in determining whether the galvanic skin response (GSR), or sweat-gland activity, could be operantly conditioned. The results that Mandler, Preven, and Kuhlman (1962) obtained forced these investigators to report negative findings with respect to the possibility of operant autonomic conditioning. However, these results could be considered suggestive; when the workers reviewed the results, subject by subject, they found that six of their nine subjects produced a significantly greater number of GSRs during the training session than they did during the extinction period when behavior was no longer reinforced.

Kimmel and Hill (1960) used pleasant odors as positive reinforcers and unpleasant odors as negative reinforcers in a study designed to detect methodological problems in operant autonomic responding. These investigators obtained results that, at best, only suggested operant modification of the conscious ability to control autonomic responding. Refining the procedures used in the initial study and employing a more conventional reinforcer (a dim white light), Fowler and Kimmel (1962) were able to demonstrate the effects of instrumental conditioning during both the acquisition and extinction phases of the study.

Having demonstrated that autonomic responses were indeed subject to instrumental techniques, contrary to the 1928 dictum of Miller and Konorski, the next logical step was to replicate, refine, and advance this pioneering research. Kimmel (1967), in reviewing the research literature in this area, found that a number of laboratories had focused on this task and that, in general, they had produced supportive findings. Therefore, Kimmel observed that the operant modification of autonomically mediated responses had been adequately demonstrated.

Kimmel's conclusion was almost immediately challenged by Katkin and Murray (1969) and Katkin, Murray, and Lachman (1969). These authors raised the question of skeletal mediation. To explain the hypothesis of skeletal mediation, we can return to the heart rate task that appeared earlier in this chapter. One of the ways in which you might have increased your heart rate would have been to adopt a strategy for altering your respiration. You might want to test this by first taking your pulse rate, next breathing deeply for 30 seconds, and finally taking your pulse rate again. You should observe a sharp increase. According to the Katkin and Murray mediation hypothesis, you have not directly altered your heart rate, over which you had no control before you adopted the breathing strategy. Instead, you actually modified a skeletal-muscle response (i.e., depth of breathing), over which you already had voluntary, conscious control, to produce or mediate the visceral response (the increased heart rate).

Similarly, it could be argued that subjects in the previous operant conditioning studies, who had demonstrated appropriate changes in autonomic responding, had learned to produce those changes not directly, but rather by manipulating the appropriate voluntary-muscle mediators. Of all the studies Katkin and Murray reviewed, they contended that none had employed experimental control procedures that would have eliminated the effects of potential skeletal mediators. They argued that these researchers could not conclude with any degree of certainty that their subjects had learned to operantly modify an autonomic response by manipulating a voluntary response.

A way of achieving experimental control for potential skeletal-muscle mediation is to use the drug curare (d-tubocurarine). The injection of curare at relatively low dosages blocks the action of acetylcholine at the skeletal neuromuscular synapse (Chagas, 1959) while leaving the autonomic nervous system essentially unaffected (Miller & Dworkin, 1974). Such a preparation leaves the subject limp and motionless, so that artificial respiration is needed.

Actually, the problem described by Katkin and Murray was already being addressed in a series of animal studies begun in the laboratories of Neal Miller. In these laboratories, Trowill (1967) was the first to employ deep curarization, which he coupled with electrical stimulation of the pleasure center of the brain as a reinforcer to operantly condition heart rate changes. Using rats as subjects, he was able to demonstrate heart rate increases for 15 of the 19 subjects that were rewarded for fast heart rates and decreases for 15 of 17 subjects that were rewarded for slow heart rates. It should be pointed out that while these average changes were statistically significant, the amount of change was small.

In a subsequent study, Miller and DiCara (1967), again using curarized rats, attempted to replicate the Trowill results while, at the same time, attempting to increase the magnitude of these changes by progressively shifting rats to a more and more difficult criterion after they learned to meet the easier one. Using a discrimination conditioning procedure, these investigators were able to demonstrate remarkable results. Not only were they able to replicate the Trowill results, but after demonstrating achievement of the easy criterion of a small change, their subjects in both the increase and the decrease conditions went on to show significantly larger changes, in the range of 100 beats per minute, as a result of the shaping procedures. It was also clear from the results that the rats had learned to respond discriminatively to the stimuli signaling that cardiac response change would be rewarded.

Black (1966) suggested that even though the subjects in these studies were deeply curarized, it was conceivable that they still might show evidence of action potentials in electromyographic (EMG) recordings. EMG recordings are simply recordings of the electrical activity taking place in the muscles. The implication was that while skeletal-muscular activity had been interrupted by curare, the activity of the motor cortex of the brain was not, and there might be conditioned motor cortex responses that mediated the instrumental conditioning of the autonomic nervous system (ANS).

Miller (1972) reasoned that if such instrumental conditioning of the motor cortex impulses had occurred, the effects would be general rather than specific to a single autonomic response. He then set out to demonstrate that it was possible to instrumentally modify one response independent of other closely related autonomic responses. This study compared the effect of rewarding either heart-rate changes or spontaneous intestinal contractions on the rate of response of both systems in deeply curarized rats. He observed that the subjects that were rewarded for increased or decreased intestinal contraction showed progressive changes in the appropriate direction but that heart rate did not change. Conversely, rats that were rewarded for high or low rates of heartbeat learned to change rates appropriately but showed no changes in intestinal contraction. These findings eliminated Black's alternative explanation.

Other studies from the Miller labs showed that animals could exert specific control over a variety of subtle responses. Miller and DiCara (1968) demonstrated instrumental learning of urine formation independent of other physiological responses. DiCara and Miller (1968) also successfully trained rats to blush in one ear and not the other. It should be pointed out that blushing is brought about by the vasodilation of blood vessels. It was concluded from these studies that there was greater specificity of action in the sympathetic part of the ANS than had previously been attributed to it.

With such experimental success achieved, the idea that operant conditioning of specific autonomic responses could occur independent of skeletal or cognitive mediation gained wide acceptance from the scientific community. Even Katkin and Murray (1969) were willing to accept these findings as adequately controlled examples of operant conditioning of autonomic responses. However, they were not willing to take the necessary next step to conclude that similar processes were involved in human autonomic conditioning.

To date, investigators have failed in attempts to replicate the results of these curare studies. Miller and Dworkin (1974) and other investigators (Hothersall & Brener, 1969; Slaughter, Hahn, & Rinaldi, 1970) have attempted such replication but have reported great difficulty in replicating the large response changes reported in the earlier curare studies.

Actually, one of the studies of operant conditioning that Katkin and Murray reviewed had employed curare with a human subject. After a baseline period and six normal training sessions, an immobilizing but subparalytic dose of curare was administered to the senior author, and only subject, in an electrodermal study reported by Birk, Crider, Shapiro, and Tursky (1966). Although Birk was able to produce more skin-potential responses during the curarized seventh session than during the baseline control period, the results were inconclusive because he was conscious and only partially paralyzed.

In a critical response to the mediation position, Crider, Schwartz, and Shnidman (1969) suggested that Katkin and Murray should identify some of the mediators they had so frequently invoked to discount the earlier examples of human autonomic operant conditioning. It soon became clear, even to Katkin, Murray, and Lachman (1969),that the controversy they had begun was of little more than theoretical importance. From any applied or therapeutic standpoint, how a subject produces an increase or decrease in response magnitude, frequency, or likelihood of occurrence is not nearly as important as the fact that it has been accomplished.

Following some very early training experiments with alpha brain waves in the late 1950s, which became widely known despite the fact that they were not formally published, Kamiya (1968, 1969) turned his attention to a determination of whether subjects could exercise control over the alpha brain wave patterns on command. For this work, many credit Kamiya with initiating the study of biofeedback. Also in 1969 the Biofeedback Research Society was formed at a scientific meeting held in California. Joseph Kamiya served as president of that society from 1975–1976. Other past presidents include Thomas H. Budzynski (1974–1975) and Neal Miller (1984–1985).

In 1989, the Biofeedback Research Society changed its name to The Association for Applied Psychophysiology and Biofeedback (AAPB). According to its website, "The goals of the association are to promote a new understanding of biofeedback and advance the methods used in this practice." Today, AAPB membership includes roughly 2,000 professionals representing psychology, medicine, nursing, social work, counseling, physical therapy, education, and other health care professions. According to the AAPB, "biofeedback has become an accepted form of treatment not only within the medical community, but with consumers as well ... alternative medicine almost equals traditional medicine in total revenues" (http://www.aapb.org/home.html).

In addition to the AAPB, there are several other important organizations dedicated to the scientific study and practice of biofeedback. One of these is the International Society for Neurofeedback and Research (ISNR). Neurofeedback is a type of biofeedback that teaches people how to control electrophysiological processes in the brain. In 1995, researchers and clinicians interested in neurofeedback formed the Society for the Study of Neural Regulation (SSNR). In 1999, this organization changed its name to the Society for Neural Regulation (SNR); in 2002 it changed its name to the INSR. The INSR functions "to promote excellence in clinical practice, educational applications, and research in applied neuroscience in order to better understand and enhance brain function" (http://www.isnr.org/mission.cfm). A second important organization is the Biofeedback Certification International Alliance (BCIA; formerly called the Biofeedback Certification Institution of America). The purpose of this organization is to provide training in how to perform biofeedback (see below under "The Trainer" for more information).

In 2008, the Biofeedback Neurofeedback Alliance (BNA) was formed to pool resources of the AAPB, ISNR, and BCIA on certain related interests. The Alliance offered a definition of biofeedback in 2008, to reflect the diverse interests and findings from each group. Their definition matches ours provided earlier in the chapter, with some elaboration: "Biofeedback is a process that enables an individual to learn how to change physiological activity for the purposes of improving health and performance. Precise instruments measure physiological activity such as brainwaves, heart function, breathing, muscle activity, and skin temperature. These instruments rapidly and accurately 'feed back' information to the user. The presentation of this information—often in conjunction with changes in thinking, emotions, and behavior—supports desired physiological changes. Over time, these changes can endure without continued use of an instrument" (AAPB, 2008).

The Biofeedback Training Process

Today, biofeedback training is the procedure by which a subject is made aware of what was previously an unconscious physiological activity and learns to use this information to gain control over an involuntary process. Because biofeedback training often differs from one laboratory or clinic to another, we need to examine the actual procedure more closely. This variability is probably due to a number of factors, not least of which is the comparative newness of the technique and consequent lack of much-needed methodological research. Another factor that contributes to the differences in biofeedback training is the many applications that have been found for the procedure. Despite the great variability in biofeedback training, however, at least four common elements can be extracted: (1) the trainee, (2) the trainer, (3) the instrument, and (4) the training sessions. To help answer some of the questions you may have about the biofeedback process itself, we consider each of these elements.

The Trainee

The **trainee** is the subject of a biofeedback experiment or the client who seeks biofeedback therapy. In brief, the trainee is the individual who will actually experience the biofeedback process. The selection of a volunteer to serve as a subject in biofeedback research is based primarily on the match between the individual's characteristics and the characteristics demanded by the nature and design of the study. For example, the trainer needs to be aware of how the biosocial characteristics of the subject's race, gender, and age might affect the efficacy of the biofeedback procedure (Roberts & McGrady, 1996). On the other hand, the biofeedback client is someone who has concluded, through reading, study, or consultation with a physician or other primary-care source, that biofeedback may be helpful in dealing with a particular symptom.

Typically, both the biofeedback therapy client and the research subject are requested to submit current health information about themselves. The reasons for this become clear when we recall that the eventual goal of biofeedback training is to increase the trainee's awareness of an involuntary physiological activity to learn to bring the physiological response under voluntary control.

Does the trainee have any health problems that might contraindicate the use of biofeedback? Obviously, one would not want to include a patient with hypertension (high blood pressure) in an experimental group being trained to increase blood pressure.

Perhaps less obvious is the need to consider the trainee's mental health, as well. Sterman (1973) and Fuller (1978), however, have observed that the use of biofeedback is contraindicated if the client suffers from a mental illness in which the biofeedback instrument may become a component of a delusional framework or in which existing feelings of dissociation may be increased by biofeedback-induced relaxation. Biofeedback is also contraindicated for individuals who suffer from depression.

Another reason for obtaining health information is to determine whether the trainee is currently taking drugs, either prescribed or nonprescribed, that might affect performance in biofeedback training. Finally, the biofeedback therapist must be aware of the client's current state of health if he or she is to select the biofeedback technique that will be most effective in dealing with the client's present symptoms.

In chapter 4 we described several standardized tests for determining whether a subject could be readily hypnotized. Although such tests would be of great value in biofeedback, their development remains a task for future investigators. Clearly, however, a highly motivated individual with a positive attitude toward biofeedback has at least two personality characteristics of a potentially successful trainee. Assessment of these factors ought to be considered a necessary feature in any such test designed to predict success or failure in biofeedback training.

The Trainer

The **trainer** is the individual who is responsible for administering the biofeedback training process. In addition to being well trained in his or her area of expertise (e.g., medicine, psychology, physical therapy), the trainer must have a firm understanding of the nature of the physiological processes as they are related to biofeedback training. He or she also should have a working knowledge of biofeedback instrumentation and techniques.

In the biofeedback training process, the trainer and the trainee form the elements of a social dyad. On the basis of research findings in related areas, such as psychophysiology (Christie & Todd, 1975; Fisher & Kotses, 1973) and social psychology (Deutsch, Canavan, & Rubin, 1971; Rosenthal, 1966; Sattler, 1970; Winkel & Sarason, 1964), we might logically predict that the characteristics of one member of the dyad, the trainer, may affect the performance of the other, the trainee.

Using chronic headache patients, Borgeat, Hade, Larouche, and Gauthier (1984) obtained data that suggest that psychophysiological measures, such as those collected in biofeedback research and clinical applications, are indeed sensitive to therapist variables. Gaarder and Montgomery (1977) suggest that the trainer who brings to the training process a cheerful, positive, friendly, and encouraging attitude should have a positive influence on the trainee's performance. It is essential that the trainer, clinician, and researcher have carefully considered their own beliefs as well as those of their colleagues concerning ethical practices in domains such as limits of confidentiality, informed consent, and dealings with minors (Percival & Striefel, 1991).

To address some of these concerns, and to offer some standardization in training, in 1981, the Biofeedback Certification Institute of America (BCIA; now known as the Biofeedback Certification International Alliance) was created (Yucha & Montgomery, 2008). The purpose of the BCIA is to certify and recertify individuals in biofeedback (www.bcia.org, 2011). They offer Board Certification in biofeedback, neurofeedback, and pelvic muscle dysfunction biofeedback. Board certification requires several things, including at least a BA/BS degree from an accredited institution (including at least one college-level course in anatomy and physiology or related biology), the completion of 36 hours of didactic training, and at least 20 or more contact hours with a mentor (consisting of 10 sessions of personal biofeedback demonstrating self-regulation, 50–100 sessions of patient/client treatment, and 10 hours of case conference presentations). Following training and to become board certified, participants must pass a written examination.

The Instrument

We noted earlier that the human body is not designed to provide its owner with the subtle information concerning internal states that would be necessary to develop conscious control over a physiological response. To make the trainee aware of these changes in activity, the biofeedback instrument mirrors the response and feeds the information back to the subject in the form of a tone, lights, meter display, and the like.

A variety of biofeedback instruments are available today; five commonly used types are detailed below. The instruments share in common several basic principles. First, they must have the ability to detect some type of physiological activity. Physiological activity may take the form of a bioelectric signal, such as muscle tonus, heartbeat, neural firing/"EEG brain waves," or skin conductance (described below). Physiological activity may also take the form of a mechanical, thermal, or photoelectric signal, for example, blood pressure, respiration, or skin temperature. To detect a bioelectric signal, the biofeedback instrument may use electrodes attached to the surface of the body. When the physiological signal is some other form like mechanical or thermal, the biofeedback instrument may use transducers to "translate," or convert the signal into an electrical event. Electrical events recorded by electrodes or transducers may be detected by electrical instruments (e.g., the biofeedback machine, for example, a polygraph or EEG).

Whether recording via electrodes or a transducer, the signal is typically very small, and often includes not only the signal of interest, but other activity (noise), as well. Thus, signal refinement is necessary, where the raw signal is amplified and filtered. This is accomplished via a series of electronic circuits that make up a preamplifier and an amplifier. Once the signal is amplified and cleared of noise, the energy from the refined signal can be converted into a signal display that is made available to the subject; this is the feedback.

The signal display can take a variety of forms, including tracings of waveforms on a piece of paper (using machines that have pens activated via the electrical signal to take upward or downward deflections), or graphic waveforms displayed on a computer monitor. To use computer images, the analog electrical signal must be converted into a digital format via an analog-to-digital (A/D) converter. Once in digital format, the signal can be transformed to provide any type of digital output desired, including pictures of waveforms or other graphic images (such as race cars, or bouncing balls). Biofeedback trainees are instructed to try to control some physiological activity by controlling the activity of the object on the screen, for example, make the car go faster or slower, or make the balls bounce higher or lower. The idea is that the graphic image represents the physiological activity, so that faster cars or higher bounces indicate greater physiological activity (and vice versa). Creative graphic images are especially useful for biofeedback training in children.

The following five biofeedback recording techniques are used most frequently today (www.bcia.org; Yucha & Montgomery, 2008):

1) General Muscle Activity: Many types of stress-related and other disorders may be caused by excessive muscle tension. Muscle activity can be recorded with an electromyograph, or EMG. EMG biofeedback gives patients information regarding muscle tension at various sites on the body. Typical recording sites for the purpose of biofeedback include

forehead, neck, shoulders, back, jaws, arms, or legs. EMG biofeedback is used in the treatment of several muscle-tension related disorders including anxiety, asthma, temporomandibular disease, tension headache, and urinary incontinence.

2) Temperature Training: Low skin temperature may be a factor in a variety of disorders including headache, high blood pressure, and Raynaud's disease. Temperature may also vary with changes in anxiety level. Skin temperature may be measured with a thermistor, a thermal sensor that can be taped to the skin. Temperature biofeedback has been used successfully in the treatment of tension and migraine headache, high blood pressure, and Raynaud's disease, and is often used in conjunction with other feedback measures like EMG, in the treatment of anxiety-related disorders.

3) Skin Conductance/Sweat Gland Training: Skin conductance measures the electrical conductance of the skin. Electrical conductance varies with moisture level, so skin conductance offers an index of sweat gland activity. (This is different from skin temperature, which just measures the absolute temperature of the skin). As you can imagine, skin conductance increases under periods of high stress (as in getting "sweaty palms"). Skin conductance is often referred to by other names including electrodermal activity or galvanic skin response (GSR). Although skin conductance increases under periods of stress, it also provides an index of general sympathetic nervous system function (see chapter 2 for a discussion of the nervous system). Thus skin conductance biofeedback has been used in the treatment of sympathetic nervous system disorders, including hyperhidrosis (excessive sweating) and high blood pressure, as well as anxiety-related problems including phobias, which tend to correlate with increased sympathetic activity.

4) EEG Training/Neurofeedback: As noted earlier in this chapter, Kamiya (1968, 1969) realized that feedback regarding brain wave activity provided via EEG recordings could be used to teach people to control brain waves. Today, EEG training has evolved into neurofeedback. Described further in chapter 7, humans typically exhibit four predominant brain waves: alpha, beta, theta, and delta. Research has shown that patients with certain disorders may exhibit atypical patterns of these brain waves. For example, research on attention-deficit/hyperactivity disorder (ADHD) demonstrates that patients often have fewer fast, beta-type brain waves, and a greater incidence of slow, theta

brain waves than normal (e.g., Gevensleben, et al., 2009). Neurofeedback uses EEG recording technology (see chapter 2) to provide information regarding brainwave activity. Neurofeedback has been used successfully in the treatment of ADHD, as well as other disorders including epilepsy, headache, alcoholism/substance abuse, and the loss of neural function due to traumatic brain injury.

5) Heart Rate Variability: Heart rate variability (HRV) refers to changes in the interval between heart beats (Malick, 1996; Moss & Shaffer, 2011). It has been used as an indicator of autonomic nervous system function for many years (e.g., Applehans & Leucken, 2006), although it has gone by different names, including RR variability or cycle length variability. Heart rate activity can be measured via an electrocardiogram (ECG). The ECG can provide a graphic output of the recorded heart rate activity; a single heart beat takes a characteristic waveform, called the QRS complex, which, with the use of an ECG, can be displayed on a screen or piece of paper. The QRS complex represents depolarization of the left and right ventricles. Depolarization and repolarization are regulated by the heart's natural pacemakers, the sinoatrial or SA node, which initiates an electrical signal to start the heart's pumping action (the sympathetic nervous system activation), and the atrioventricular or AV node, which spreads the activation across the ventricles. The Q-wave may record as a rapid downward deflection on a graph, followed by the Rwave, which is an upward deflection, followed by the S-wave, which is another downward deflection. A measurement from one R-wave to the next on an ECG graph (sometimes called RR intervals) provides an index of interbeat interval (IBI). It turns out that IBI, or the time between heart beats, does not occur at a constant rate like a clock, but is quite variable, and depends on a variety of both physiological and psychological factors. Note that "heart rate" and "heart rate variability (HRV)" are referring to two different things: heart rate is the average number of heart beats per minute, while HRV is the difference in time between heart beats during that minute; HRV evaluates the time difference between Heart Beat 1 to Heart Beat 2, compared to the time between Heart Beat 2 to Heart Beat 3, and so on.

It is advantageous to biological systems for heart rate to constantly vary; this allows the heart to conserve energy when needed, but to also increase output as needed. Indeed, high variability in heart rate is best, and may indicate greater functionality between the sympathetic and parasympathetic nervous systems. Low HRV is associated with a variety of cardiac and physiological conditions, especially those involving increased sympathetic activation or inadequate parasympathetic modulation (Malick, 1996).

Researchers have found that low HRV may also be a factor in several types of physical as well as psychological disorders including asthma, high blood pressure, depression, and anxiety. Moreover, there appears to be an "optimal" level of HRV; for humans, optimal HRV appears to be a dominance of low frequency variations in heart rate (approximately 0.1 Hz; Vaschillo, Lehrer, Rishe, & Konstantinov, 2002). HRV biofeedback is designed to train people to maintain overall HRV in this low-frequency range. HRV biofeedback has been used to alleviate symptoms of high blood pressure, asthma, depression, and anxiety (e.g., see Yucha & Montgomery, 2008 for review).

The Training Sessions

Because the physiological changes that occur during biofeedback training are usually beyond the level of conscious experience, it is necessary that in the initial stages of training, the trainee works with a biofeedback machine designed to monitor subtle physiological changes in the system, refine the biological signal, and make the trainee aware of this activity by some type of feedback display. This is the external feedback loop illustrated in Figure 5.1. This increased awareness will enable the trainee to accomplish two major tasks.

The more immediate of the two tasks is to respond to the feedback in ways that will alter the physiological activity of the system in a desired direction. Often, the trainee is instructed to develop, or develops independently, a kind of strategy (e.g., imagining feelings of warmth, calm, and peace) to bring about these changes. Early in the training process, performance may be extremely variable as the trainee attempts first one strategy and then another. A more constant, desirable performance is achieved as the trainee receives more and more positive feedback showing that the physiological changes are in the desired direction) and settles on the particular technique that works best. As the trainee practices the strategy, it is hoped that he or she will become aware of the relationship between the psychological activity and the physiological changes that occur.

The second task that the trainee must accomplish during these sessions is to learn to produce the desired response change without the aid of the machine. Until this point in the training process, the trainee has depended almost exclusively on external feedback. Now, he or she must become aware of internal sensory cues that provide information about the overall physiological state and the relationship between this state and the external feedback. Once these links have been established, the information from the internal sensors can replace the external feedback, thus establishing the internal loop.

The actual biofeedback training process can be broken down into a series of training sessions, the number and nature of which vary considerably, depending on the goal of the investigator or therapist. There are four major types of training sessions: (1) the baseline sessions, (2) the shaping and reinforcement sessions, (3) the test sessions, and (4) the follow-up sessions.

The goal of the initial baseline sessions is to obtain a representative sample of the internal system's activity before training. Measurements obtained during these sessions are used to set training goals and to compare pretraining and posttraining performance levels. If the sample is to be considered truly representative, measurements should be taken during more than one baseline session.

The shaping and reinforcement sessions follow the initial baseline sessions. During the baseline session, with the aid of feedback, the trainee learned to bring about voluntarily a desired change in the physiological activity of a system of which he or she was previously unaware and over which he or she had no control. Because the desired change usually occurs involuntarily and at the unconscious level, the probability of its occurrence is generally very low. Often, the trainer must rely on small spontaneous changes in the response system that represent remote approximations of the desired change and reward their production when they occur. As the trainer rewards progressively better approximations of the desired response, the response eventually can be shaped

Figure 5.1 • Biofeedback Loop

into occurring. Once the trainee has learned to produce the desired response, reinforcement in the form of feedback will occur more and more frequently.

To determine whether the trainee has been able, during these sessions, to replace the external feedback loop with a newly developed internal loop, the trainee is subjected to a test session in which he or she is required to produce the desired physiological changes without the aid of external feedback.

In many respects, follow-up sessions are similar to the test session. The subject must again attempt to produce the desired change in activity without the aid of external feedback. Instead of being administered immediately after the final shaping and reinforcement session, however, follow-up sessions are usually executed some time later. The results of these sessions provide the trainer with information about how well such training holds up over time.

Evaluating Biofeedback Treatments

To evaluate the efficacy of biofeedback and neurofeedback, in 2001, the AAPB and ISNR developed a five-level rating system, which includes strict guidelines for evaluating biofeedback treatment. The evaluation is based on a number of factors including how the treatment was tested (i.e., the research methodology), the number of patients tested, and whether control groups were included (Moss, LaVaque, & Hammond, 2004; Yucha & Montgomery, 2008). According to the AAPB rating system, Level 1 is the lowest, and includes research that is not empirically supported. Level 2 is "Possibly Efficacious," and includes at least one study demonstrating significant effects, but which lacked experimental rigor (like failing to include control groups, or not randomly assigning participants to groups). Level 3 is "Probably Efficacious," and includes multiple studies that demonstrate efficacy, although there may be questions about the research methodology, or there may be contradictory research suggesting a lack of effect. Level 4 is "Efficacious," and includes research that compared biofeedback with no-treatment or other-treatment control groups, randomly assigned patients to groups, and was methodologically sound. Level 5 is "Efficacious and Specific," and includes all of the criteria of Level 4, plus the demonstration from at least two research studies that biofeedback was superior to some other treatment or no treatment at all.

In the next section, we provide a brief sampling of the many applications of biofeedback. Following a brief history of research in each area, we conclude each section with the most recent conclusions offered by the AAPB regarding efficacy.

Biofeedback Applications

How can we use increased awareness of the activity of an internal response system gained with the biofeedback training process? From almost the inception of this technique, applied research has focused on finding answers to this question. As an example, if people's levels of awareness and consciousness are altered through biofeedback, they may be able to better their lives in some important ways. The applications to be considered in this section fall into three broad categories: (1) clinical therapy, (2) exploration of meditative processes, and (3) research.

The obvious potential of biofeedback training to alleviate symptoms has produced a substantial flurry of research activity. To date, biofeedback has been successfully used to treat depressive disorders (Kumano et al., 1996), hyperactivity (Denkowski, Denkowski, & Omizo, 1984; Shouse & Lubar, 1977; Whitmer, 1978), learning disabilities and attention-deficit disorder (Carter & Russell, 1985; Linden, Habib, & Radojevic, 1996), stress-induced urinary incontinence in the elderly (Burns, Clesse-Desotelle, Nochajski, & Pranikoff, 1990), epilepsy in children (Dahl & Melin, 1989; Kay, Shively, & Kilkenny, 1978), and irritable bowel syndrome (Radnitz & Blanchard, 1989; Schwartz, Taylor, Scharf, & Blanchard, 1989).

Researchers have also applied biofeedback techniques to treat speech disorders (Craig & Cleary, 1982; Davis & Drichta, 1980), the acquisition of fine motor movement (French, 1980; LeVine & Irvine, 1984), the control of sexual arousal (Hatch, 1981; Hoon, 1980; Palace, 1995), alcohol dependency (Saxby, 1995; Schneider et al., 1993), essential hypertension (Achmon, Granet, Golomb, & Hart, 1989; Cornish, Blanchard, & Wittrock, 1989; Jurek, Higgins, & McGrady, 1992; Latha, 1991), Raynaud's disease (Freedman, Ianni, & Wenig, 1985; Freedman, Lynn, Ianni, & Hale, 1981; Stroebal & Ford, 1981); stress-induced hyperhydrosis, or excessive sweating (Nigl, 1981), and painful menstrual symptoms (Belick, Elfner, & May, 1982), to name but a few. This section provides only a sample of the many applications of biofeedback.

Headache

Headache is one of the most common disorders known to humankind and was one of the first medical problems to be diagnosed and treated by physicians of early civilizations (Nigl, 1984). Most often headache is related to stress and other benign conditions; however, it may also be due to serious, even life-threatening disorders.

167

Appenzeller (1973) suggested that over 80 percent of all headache sufferers treated in headache clinics have *tension headaches*. According to Budzynski
(1978), the estimates of the number of people in the United States who suffer from tension headache ranges from 50 million to 100 million. While one
must be careful in interpreting such data, it is clear that most professionals
consider tension headache to be the most prevalent pain disorder today.

According to a 1962 report by the Ad Hoc Committee of the National
Institute of Neurological Disease and Blindness (NINDB), tension headache
is described as having the following characteristics (as reported by White and
Tursky, 1982):

1) A gradual onset.

2) A variable duration that may last hours, days, or even months.

3) Steady, nonpulsating pain, often described as being like a vise or a band
   tightening around the head; also there is soreness and a sensation of the
   skin drawing tight.

4) The headache is bilateral in the occipital, suboccipital, or posterior
   cervical area, radiating to the temples and to the frontalis region.

5) The patient frequently awakens with the headache, and it gradually
   becomes worse and more intense as the day progresses.

6) The pain is aggravated by exposure to the cold. It can be relieved by
   massage, heat, or stretching of muscles.

The primary underlying physiological mechanism of tension headache has
been identified as the sustained contraction of skeletal muscles in the scalp,
face, shoulders, and neck, combined with ischemia (less than the required or
normal blood supply) in the affected muscles (Friedman, 1979). These muscles
are identified in Figure 5.2. Contrary to the statement by the NINDB Ad Hoc
Committee, which proposed that the vascular constriction was diagnostic of
migraine but not of tension headache, a number of studies have demonstrated
that it is both of these physiological events, occurring concurrently, that lead
to the development of a tension headache (Budzynski, 1978).

Although the bulk of the empirical evidence suggests that both muscular
contraction and vasoconstriction of the cephalic arteries and arteries carrying
blood to the affected muscles are necessary to trigger the tension headache,
biofeedback techniques have focused primarily on decreasing the activity of
cervical, frontalis, and other muscles of the shoulders, neck, and head.

Figure 5.2 • Skeletal Muscles in the Scalp, Face, Shoulders, and Neck
Illustration by Jamey Garbett. © 2003 Mark Nielsen.

The initial studies were carried out in the laboratories of Budzynski (Budzynski, Stoyva, & Adler, 1970; Budzynski, Stoyva, Adler, & Mullaney, 1973). Rather than attempting to relax specific muscles or muscle groups that are thought to cause the symptom, however, these researchers, as well as many others, have employed a general relaxation process, which we will call **electromyographic** (EMG) feedback-assisted relaxation (Fridlund, Fowler, & Pritchard, 1980).

In this process, the trainee is made conscious of the activity level of a small pair of muscles located near the center of the forehead. These are the frontalis muscles (see Figure 5.2). The subject's task is to reduce the activity level, and thus, the tension of these muscles. The rationale underlying this approach is that, by relaxing this muscle pair, biofeedback training will generalize the relaxation to the untrained muscles, and they, too, will show a decrease in tension.

In reviewing the results of these earlier studies, Budzynski (1978, 1979) observed that subjects who received frontalis EMG biofeedback treatment had significantly lower frontalis EMG levels than did subjects who received noncontingent feedback (feedback unrelated to the muscle activity) or no feedback at all. Additionally, subjects who received contingent EMG biofeedback and relaxation therapy significantly reduced headache activity beyond baseline compared with the subjects who received noncontingent feedback and relaxation. Finally, he found substantial reductions in headache activity for most subjects within an eight-week period involving two EMG feedback sessions a week.

Since Budzynski's studies in the early 1970s, some 40 or more additional studies have been published that have employed some form of biofeedback, usually frontalis muscle activity, in the treatment of tension headache. In reviewing many of these studies, Budzynski (1978) stated that "the evidence appears strong that the use of EMG (primarily frontalis) feedback is effective in the alleviation of tension headaches" (p. 147).

In a study typical of the earlier research efforts in this area, Kondo and Canter (1977), employing EMG-feedback-assisted relaxation and a noncontingent feedback control group, found that after 10 training sessions, the 10 tension headache patients who received the contingent feedback from the frontalis muscles reported a significantly greater decrease in headache frequency than did the 10 tension headache patients who received the noncontingent feedback. Careful analysis of these results suggests that the improvement in headache frequency directly resulted from the EMG biofeedback training and not from expectancy of therapeutic value or attention.

Finally, one year after this treatment, follow-up reports demonstrated that while four of five contingent subjects indicated continued reduction of headache frequency, only two of five noncontingent subjects reported any such reduction. Similar findings have been reported by numerous investigators (Borgeat, Hade, Larouche, & Bedwant, 1980; Hart & Cichanski, 1981).

In the first half of the 1980s, research in this area raised a number of serious questions, including the following: Is EMG-feedback-assisted relaxation more effective than other forms of behavior therapy? Are there certain individual characteristics that might affect the efficacy of biofeedback in the treatment of chronic tension headache?

Concerning the latter question, Friedman (1979) suggests that while most tension headache patients clearly have some emotional problems that are intricately involved with their headache symptoms, few researchers have studied the effects of personality factors on chronic tension headache. Although biofeedback is accepted by most psychiatrists, it is perceived as an adjunct to psychotherapy, not as a primary mode of treatment.

This position seems to have been supported by a study (Levine, 1984) of 48 patients who were given forehead/posterior neck biofeedback therapy for 20 weeks. Half these patients had depression either with or without a previous history of head trauma. Levine reported that headache activity was lowered more for the nondepressed patients than for those who suffered from depression. These findings suggest that there is a probable need for the separation of depressed and nondepressed patients in headache treatment as well as a need for the treatment of the depression itself, aside from the headache.

Another personality variable that has been found to be significant in the treatment of chronic tension headache using biofeedback is introversion-extroversion, or whether one is reserved or outgoing (Merkel, 1979). The results of this study force us to agree with Beaty and Haynes (1979) that far more research and clinical attention be given to who can best benefit by the application of EMG biofeedback to headaches.

As to whether EMG biofeedback is more effective than other forms of behavioral therapy, most reviewers of the research in this area suggest that EMG biofeedback is no more effective than relaxation in reducing headache activity (Silver & Blanchard, 1978; Turk, Meichenbaum, & Berman, 1979; Yates, 1980). Assessing the efficacy of three procedures—relaxation therapy, frontal EMG biofeedback, and thermal biofeedback—in the behavioral treatment of 250 chronic headache patients, Blanchard, Andrasick, Evans, Neff, and Appelbaum (1985) found that relaxation alone led to improvement in 41 percent of the tension headache patients, while the combination of relaxation and thermal biofeedback therapy accounted for the improvement observed in 52 percent of the migraine and combined migraine and tension headache patients. One major dissenting position has been published by Budzynski (1978), who stated that "research indicates that EMG biofeedback can result in greater decreases in EMG at a faster rate than nonbiofeedback relaxation training" (p. 430).

Recent reviews of the research on the use of biofeedback on tension headache suggest that biofeedback is not only effective, it has been shown to be superior to other available treatments in at least two independent research studies (Nestoriuc, Martin, Rief, & Andrasik, 2008; Yucha & Montgomery, 2008).

Biofeedback in the use of tension heading received a Level 5—Efficacious and Specific rating, according to the AABP scale (Nestoriuc et al., 2008).

Migraine Headache

The incidence of the second type of chronic headache, the migraine headache, is reported variously as being between 5 and 8 percent in the U.S. population (Schnarch & Hunter, 1980). Unlike what most nonsufferers think, migraine is not just one kind of chronic headache. Actually, the migraine headache comes in several flavors. To be more precise, Schnarch and Hunter (1980) were able to identify four classifications of migraine headache:

1) *Classic migraine* has two phases, a preheadache, or prodromal, phase and a headache phase. The prodrome is characterized by such symptoms as flashing lights, strange odors, blind spots, tingling or numbness in the limbs, muscular weakness, emotional changes, and dysphasia or disturbances of language function (Olton & Noonberg, 1980). It is generally believed that this prodrome, which has both a sudden onset and a sudden end, is caused by a functional disturbance of intracerebral circulation, which in turn leads to the neurologic disruptions.

2) The *common migraine* is characterized by the absence of the prodrome and may be bilateral, whereas the classic migraine is most often unilateral.

3) *Cluster headaches* are briefer than classic migraines, lasting only 10 to 20 minutes, whereas classic migraines typically last for hours but appear in groups over a time period. Some authorities argue that despite the similarities in both mechanism and subjective report, these headaches should not be included in a migraine classification.

4) *Hemiplegic* or *ophthalmoplegic migraine* is the last type of migraine headache. It leaves those who have it with neurological symptoms still present after the pain is gone. Because of the significance of organic factors in this migraine, it is quite probable that behavioral therapies would be of little consequence.

Migraine is classified as a vascular headache because of the cerebrovascular dysfunction that results in head pain. Theoretically, a migraine is initiated by a complex, intracerebral vascular process that includes excessive vasoconstriction of arteries and arterioles, followed soon after by rebound, excessive vasodilation. Excessive vasodilation, in turn, results in supranormal pulsation and stretching of muscles and elastic fibers within the vessel wall (see Figure 5.3). The corresponding stimulation of stretch receptors surrounding the vessel walls results in pain (Nigl, 1984).

According to Olton and Noonberg (1980), four characteristics of migraine are most often mentioned in the literature:

1) The head pain initially is typically unilateral.

2) The head pain is often relieved, or attacks prevented, by vasoconstricting drugs such as ergotamine tartrate.

3) Migraine is often accompanied or succeeded by gastrointestinal disturbances including nausea, vomiting, diarrhea, or constipation.

4) An aura or prodrome, caused by neurologic disturbances, precedes the migraine attack, except in common migraine.

Olton and Noonberg (1980) indicated that empirical research has not demonstrated a clear-cut dichotomy between migraine and tension headache. Raskin (1980) suggested that both tension and migraine headaches are quantitatively different manifestations of the same phenomenon—instability of vasomotor regulation.

The use of hand temperature biofeedback in the treatment of migraine was discovered by accident when a group of investigators (Schultz & Luthe, 1969) at the Menninger Clinic, in an effort to improve the outcome of autogenic training, combined such training with EMG, alpha brain wave, and temperature feedback. The encouraging results prompted Sargent, Green, and Walters (1973) to carry out a more extensive pilot project. In this project they combined autogenic phases and temperature feedback in the treatment of 19 patients with migraine headache. After their training, all the patients were evaluated clinically by an internist and two psychologists. All three researchers

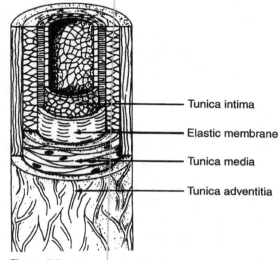

Tunica intima

Elastic membrane

Tunica media

Tunica adventitia

Figure 5.3 • Cross-Section of an Artery

173

considered 12 of the 19 patients treated to have improved and three not to have improved. The researchers did not agree on the clinical evaluation of the remaining four subjects. These successful findings have been confirmed by a number of other investigators (Engel & Rapoff, 1990; Johnson & Turin, 1975; Reading & Mohr, 1976; Stambaugh & House, 1977; Wickramasekera, 1972).

Although the Menninger research stimulated the development of clinical techniques employing skin temperature biofeedback to treat migraine, the findings have been subject to considerable criticism. Some of these methodological inadequacies were corrected in later studies that also obtained successful findings regarding the use of skin temperature biofeedback to treat migraine headaches (Boller & Flam, 1979; Drury, DeRisi, & Liberman, 1979; Fried, Lamberti, & Sneed, 1977; Kewman & Roberts, 1980).

A review of the various research studies suggests that biofeedback methods such as skin temperature and cephalic blood volume feedback are able to reduce headache symptoms effectively for individuals suffering from migraine. Overall, the results of several large-scale follow-up studies suggest that 60 to 80 percent of migraine patients can be expected to show significant improvement with skin temperature biofeedback combined with autogenic training (Aloe, Collings, Wauqwer, McGrady, & Gerard, 1994; Diamond, Diamond-Falk, & Deveno, 1978; Sargent, Green, & Walters, 1977).

A meta-analysis of 56 studies published from 1973–2007 concluded that biofeedback is effective in the treatment of migraine headache, when compared to no treatment at all (Nestroriuc et al., 2008). Patients receiving biofeedback treatment could expect about a 60 percent improvement in their condition, compared to wait-list controls. However, it remains unclear whether biofeedback is superior to any other treatment, including relaxation, or even placebo alone; patients receiving placebo reported an average 44% improvement. Nonetheless, biofeedback in the use of migraine headache has received a Level 4—Efficacious rating, according to the strict AABP standards (Nestroriuc et al., 2008).

Asthma

Biofeedback has been applied in the treatment of asthma. Despite tremendous research efforts, *asthma,* a respiratory disease that affects from 2 to 5 percent of the population, remains a puzzling disorder and the subject of considerable controversy. One of the few points of agreement that has been reached to date concerns the objective characteristics of the asthmatic's breathing patterns. An asthmatic episode appears to be characterized by a changed sensitivity of the bronchial mucosa (mucous membrane lining) and musculature, which in turn produces increased resistance in the airways. Edema (swelling) of the bronchial mucosa, secretions, and spasms of the bronchial muscles finally lead to a constricture or severe narrowing of these airways. The severe bronchial spasm can be a life-threatening event. The relative contributions of the autonomic and central nervous system to these changes are still a matter of some dispute (Yates, 1980).

A review of the literature suggests that asthma is a complex of factors involving allergies, stress, endocrine changes, genetic disposition, and psychological traits. The role of psychological factors in asthma seems to be well established. For example, Weiner (1977) has demonstrated that dependency and fear of separation or rejection are present in a significant number of asthmatics, as well as a wide range of defenses employed to deal with anxiety and the symptoms. For a fuller treatment of the role of psychological factors in asthma, we encourage the reader to read Knapp and Wells (1978).

To date, two distinct biofeedback procedures have been employed in the treatment of asthmatics: skeletal-muscle feedback and direct airways feedback. Yates (1980) suggests that these two approaches are based on divergent views as to the role of anxiety in the asthma attack. The assumption of those employing skeletal-muscle feedback appears to be that asthmatics are characterized by high levels of anxiety and that training in relaxation will help reduce the severity of an attack after it has begun. On the other hand, those who favor a direct airways approach assume that it should be possible to control the events associated with impairment in the control of breathing so that either an attack is less likely to occur or, if it does occur, it can be controlled better. An excellent critical review of both applications and the research in this area can be found in Kotses and Glaus (1981). Our discussion here will be limited to skeletal-muscle, feedback-assisted relaxation.

In a recent series of studies the relationships between changes in muscular tension and respiratory measures in both normal adults and asthmatic children were examined (Glaus, Happ, & Kotses, 1976; Glaus & Kotses, 1976; Kotses, Glaus, Bricel, Edwards, & Crawford, 1978; Kotses, Glaus, Crawford, Edwards, & Scherr, 1976). The results of these studies demonstrated the following:

1) Tension changes in different muscles are not the same insofar as their effects on *peak expiratory flow rate* (PEFR) measures are concerned. PEFR is the maximum flow rate of air in liters per second during the first 0.1 second of a forced expiration. Tension changes in the facial

musculature reliably influence PEFR, whereas limb muscle tension changes do not (Glaus, Happ, & Kotses, 1976).

2) Facial muscle tension changes are inversely related to PEFR behavior, so increases in facial muscle tension result in PEFR decreases, whereas PEFR increases result from decreases in facial muscle tension (Glaus, Happ, & Kotses, 1976; Glaus & Kotses, 1976; Kotses, Glaus, Bricel, Edwards, & Crawford, 1978; Kotses, Glaus, Crawford, Edwards, & Scherr, 1976).

3) Muscle tension changes do not influence respiratory activities in a general manner. Changes in PEFR due to changes in facial muscle tension are not correlated with respiratory rate changes (Glaus & Kotses, 1976).

4) Both clinical (asthmatics) and nonclinical (normal) subjects exhibit comparable changes in PEFR as a function of facial muscle relaxation (Glaus, Happ, & Kotses, 1976; Glaus & Kotses, 1976; Kotses, Glaus, Bricel, Edwards, & Crawford, 1978).

5) Finally, the effects of facial muscle tension change on PEFR can be observed after a single muscle tension training session of relatively short duration (Glaus & Kotses, 1976).

On the basis of these findings, Kotses and Glaus (1981) conclude that the relationship between facial muscle tension and PEFR is mediated by a physiological mechanism, the action of which is fairly specific. Although the precise nature of this mechanism is unknown, Glaus, Happ, and Kotses (1976) argue that it may be convenient to think of this mechanism as a neural reflex. It is assumed that the neural components of such a reflex would include a trigeminal afferent pathway and a vagal efferent pathway. The trigeminal and vagus nerves are cranial nerves whose point of origin lies in the pons and medulla of the brainstem (see chapter 2). Trigeminal and vagal pathways are known to participate jointly in several protective reflexes involving airway resistance changes. This suggests that trigeminal afferent activity is capable of altering airway resistance through modification of vagal efferent activity (Tomori & Widdicombe, 1969).

Further support for a neural reflex mechanism mediator between facial muscle tension and peak expiratory flow rate comes from studies reported by Harver, Kotses, Segreto, and Creer (1984). In the earlier study, healthy adult subjects who evidenced operantly conditioned increases in facial muscle tension also showed increased airway resistance, whereas facial muscle relaxation resulted in decreased airway resistance. Conditioned increases and decreases in limb tension, on the other hand, did not produce such changes in airway resistance. In addition to ruling out general muscular events, this latter finding also weakens the position of possible alternative explanations employing metabolic agents altered or released by muscle tension change.

Harver et al. (1984) provided further evidence that supports the specificity of the relationship between facial muscle activity and pulmonary function. They monitored changes in peek expiratory flow rates (PEFR), respiration rate (RR) and heart rate (HR) while the subjects underwent either facial muscle training or limb muscle training. Increases in facial muscle tension resulted in the predicted decreases in PEFR but produced no related changes in either HR or RR. Increases in limb tension had no such effect.

Harver et al. (1984) also examined the effectiveness of facial muscle biofeedback-assisted relaxation training on asthmatic symptomology in 40 asthmatic children. Each of these children was randomly assigned to one of three treatment conditions: biofeedback training for frontal muscle EMG decreases, biofeedback training for maintaining frontal EMG activity at baseline levels (placebo control), and quiet sitting (no treatment). Children in the first group did reduce frontalis muscle tension as a function of training. The self-reported improvements in asthma severity and in psychological measurements were greater in this group than in the control groups.

It has been clearly demonstrated that biofeedback training for facial muscle relaxation improves short-term pulmonary function in asthmatic individuals. Tibbetts and Pepper (1989) combined both facial EMG relaxation and incentive inspirometer feedback to encourage slow diaphragmatic breathing while decreasing muscular efforts in a group of asthmatic subjects. All subjects were able to increase inhalation volumes and decrease EMG levels. These subjects also reported a 69.4 percent reduction in medication use, a 73 percent increase in sense of control, and 64 percent fewer emergency room visits. Research to date, however, still leaves us with a number of unanswered questions. Chief among them are the following: What are the long-term effects of such therapy? What influence does this treatment have on asthma-related variables other than pulmonary function (Kotses, Hindi-Alexander, & Creer, 1989)? We cannot endorse relaxation assisted by biofeedback of facial muscles as a treatment for asthma—at least not without qualification. Even newer research fails to offer much improvement on the findings from these earlier studies (e.g., Huntley, White, & Ernst, 2000; Ritz, Dahme, & Roth, 2004). The use of biofeedback in the treatment of asthma has received a

Level 2—Possibly Efficacious rating, according to the AABP standards (Yucha & Montgomery, 2008).

Anxiety

Biofeedback has been used in the treatment of anxiety disorders for many years (e.g., Fehring, 1983; Hurley & Meminger, 1992; Roome & Romney, 1985; Scandrett, Bean, Breeden, & Powell, 1986; Wenck, Leu, & D'Amato, 1996). However, many of these early research studies suffered from a variety of methodological problems, including no relaxation-alone comparison groups. Thus it was unclear whether biofeedback offered any benefit in addition to that provided by relaxation alone, for the treatment of anxiety-related disorders.

More recent studies have demonstrated that biofeedback is at least equal to relaxation training alone, and may, in some cases, be superior (see Yucha & Montgomery, 2008 for review). However, many of the studies reviewed by Yucha and Montgomery (2008) did not have control groups, or used concurrent treatments in addition to biofeedback including meditation, guided imagery, and breathing techniques (e.g., Gordon, Staples, Blyta, & Bytyqi, 2004), which may have contributed to decreases in anxiety, independent of the biofeedback treatment.

A more recent test of biofeedback in a group of 49 active-duty service members deployed in combat zones in Iraq or Afghanistan found little benefit of HRV biofeedback training. Although the participants overwhelmingly reported the training to be relaxing and a positive experience, they did not experience significant clinical benefit. The study found only mild declines in anxiety and depression associated with PTSD (Lande, Williams, Francis, Gragnani, & Morin, 2010).

Nonetheless, Yucha and Montgomery (2008) cited two methodologically sound studies comparing biofeedback to other treatments for anxiety, which did report significant improvement following biofeedback: Coy, Cardenas, Cabrera, Zirot, and Claros (2005), who compared the use of the antidepressant drug imipramine alone to the combined effects of imipramine plus biofeedback, and Dong and Bao (2005), who found significant effects of biofeedback versus no treatment for alleviating symptoms of anxiety in 35 high school students in China. Based on these earlier studies, the AAPB has rated biofeedback in the treatment of anxiety disorders a Level 4—Probably Efficacious (Yucha & Montgomery, 2008).

One potentially exciting new application of biofeedback for the use in the treatment of anxiety is the "Intrepid Project"—an evaluation of the efficacy of a mobile biofeedback-enhanced "virtual reality" system (Riva, Gorini, & Gaggioli, 2009). While traditional relaxation training—without biofeedback—has been moderately successful in the treatment of anxiety, often it is difficult for patients to learn, especially if only offered unimodal training (i.e., only auditory suggestions to "relax" or to "imagine yourself in a relaxing place"). Adding a visual "virtual reality" component, for example, having patients actually interact with a relaxing environment such as an island or a calm lake, may further facilitate relaxation. Adding biofeedback regarding physiological changes as patients become relaxed can further facilitate learning, especially in patients amenable to biofeedback training. Riva and colleagues (2009) are testing a home-based system with a mobile phone application that allows patients to receive feedback regarding GSR, HR, skin temperature, and EMG. Feedback can be provided not only while patients interact with the virtual reality scenes (which may be presented via the phone), but also at any other time throughout the day. An exciting component of this system is that not only is it totally portable, so that it may be used in a variety of real-life situations, it also connects patients with their therapist, and can be used in case of emergency. If the emotional level becomes too high while the system is in use, the therapist is contacted immediately by phone to offer intervention. Data regarding clinical trials of 45 patients, 15 in the virtual reality training group, 15 in a nonvirtual reality group who receive traditional relaxation training, and 15 wait-list controls, remains forthcoming.

Attention-Deficit/Hyperactivity Disorder (ADHD)

One of the most exciting potential uses for biofeedback is in the treatment of attention-deficit/hyperactivity disorder (ADHD). As noted in chapter 3, ADHD is particularly difficult disorder to treat. Not only are attention-enhancing drugs like methylphenidate (Ritalin) and amphetamine (Adderall) prone to abuse (see chapter 3), research shows that drug treatments may only help alleviate treatments for a short time (up to 14 months), and that medication treatment alone is not very effective (Harvard Mental Health Letter, 2010; Jensen et al., 2001).

Alternatively, neurofeedback may be a viable treatment for ADHD. Even though Yucha and Montgomery (2008) only rated neurofeedback Level 4—"Efficacious," in the treatment of ADHD, a more recent meta-analysis that includes three randomized studies with blind or double-blind control groups, rates neurofeedback a Level 5—"Efficacious and Specific" treatment for ADHD (Arns, deRidder, Strehl, Breteler, & Coenen, 2009).

The rationale for the use of neurofeedback in the treatment of ADHD comes from studies, as noted above, indicating alterations in cortical EEG for children and adolescents diagnosed with ADHD (see Barry, Clarke, & Johnstone, 2003 for review). Briefly, patients with ADHD exhibit greater theta wave activity relative to beta waves. Thus one proposed treatment for ADHD would be to teach patients to increase alpha and beta waves, and decrease theta waves. Slow-cortical potentials (SCPs) have also been used as an index of neural excitability in the neocortex (Gevensleben et al., 2009). Negative SCPs appear during active neural states, and may relate to cognitive activity. Positive SCPs dominate during decreased neural activity, and may indicate behavioral inhibition (Gevensleben et al., 2009). Thus it might be useful to train children to regulate the ratio of positive and negative SCPs, so they may institute neural activity when needed, but decrease it when high behavioral or cognitive activity (i.e., intrusive thoughts) may be inappropriate.

Gevensleben and colleagues (2009) studied 94 children aged 8–12 years diagnosed with ADHD. Children were enrolled in either a neurofeedback or an attentional skills training program that lasted approximately two months. Most of the children (n=87) had never tried medication for their ADHD; the remaining were drug-free for at least six weeks prior to beginning the program. All participants received thirty-six 50-minute training sessions. Training sessions occurred 2–3 times per week, depending on the families' schedule, and consisted of two 50-minute sessions each day, separated by a short break. Thus families only had to come to the clinic 18 separate times, and training was completed in 6–8 weeks.

Neurofeedback training consisted of both SCP training for 18 sessions, and theta/alpha training for 18 sessions, given in a balanced order for each participant (so half of the participants got the theta/alpha training first, and half got the SCP training first). Neurofeedback was provided via a system that allowed the children to "control a type of computer game by modulating their brain electrical activity" (p. 4). For example, for the SCP training, a ball would move up or down in agreement with their SCP waves (i.e., either positive or negative). For theta/beta training, bars on the left and right would increase and decrease, in correspondence with theta and beta waves. Children were instructed on how to maintain a focused state, which could alter the positions of the balls and the bars on the computer screen. Children were also required to practice their focused states at home at least once a day, and in different situations (while reading, while playing, etc.). Attentional skills training also used a computer-guided training, consisting of games designed to increase sustained attention and reaction times. The games in this case were not guided by brain waves, but required that children pay attention to information on the screen, and click the mouse when appropriate, for example, to change the color of fish so they all matched. Children in the attentional skills group were also trained to focus attention, and were instructed to practice once a day at home.

Results indicated that parent and teacher ratings of ADHD symptoms improved by approximately 26 percent following neurofeedback training; 51.7 percent of children in the neurofeedback group improved at least 25 percent following treatment, compared to 28.6 percent of the children in the attention skills group. Although the results raise concerns regarding the nearly 50 percent of children who did not improve following neurofeedback, this study is significant for several reasons, including the large number of children tested and the use of a control condition that closely matched the treatment condition. There are limitations to the study, for example, the lack of comparison between neurofeedback and medications, and the lack of inclusion of children with severe symptoms. Indeed, a large-scale study funded by the National Institutes of Health-National Institute of Mental Health (NIMH) called the Multi-Modal Treatment study of ADHD (MTA) followed almost 600 children with ADHD for 14 months, and found that the best outcomes were achieved when several treatments, including careful medication management and cognitive-behavioral therapy, were combined. Furthermore, treatment outcomes were only truly successful when children had community- and family-based support (Jensen et al., 2001).

Currently rated at the highest Level 5—"Efficacious and Specific" according to the AAPB, neurofeedback is an exciting alternative to traditional treatments of attentional dysfunction, including medication. However, results from a variety of studies including Gevensleben et al. (2009) and the large-scale MTA study suggest that neurofeedback will likely prove most successful if used in conjunction with other treatments, including carefully managed medication, cognitive-behavioral/attentional training, and family and community support.

Other Conditions

Biofeedback has been found to be Efficacious (Level 4) in treating the following other conditions not specified above: chronic pain (Yucha & Montgomery, 2008), epilepsy (Yucha & Montgomery, 2008), hypertension (Linden & Moseley, 2006), motion sickness (Yucha & Montgomery, 2008), Raynaud's disease (Karavidas, Tsai, Yucha, McGrady, & Lehrer, 2006), and temporomandibular disorders (Crider, Glaros, & Gevirtz, 2005). Biofeedback has been found to Efficacious and Specific (Level 5) in the treatment of urinary incontinence in women, but not in men or children (Glazer & Laine, 2006; Yucha & Montgomery, 2008).

Biofeedback and the Production of Altered States

In addition to being used as a therapeutic technique, biofeedback has been employed as a procedure to alter or change the conscious state indirectly through the manipulation of brain-wave patterns. For example, while the use of alpha biofeedback as a therapeutic technique has met with only limited success to date (Gannon & Sternbach, 1971; Glueck & Stroebel, 1975; Melzack & Perry, 1975), the "alpha state" has received a considerable amount of popular attention. Much of this enthusiasm can be attributed to the early studies of Nowlis and Kamiya (1970) and Brown (1970). These studies suggest that bringing the amount of alpha rhythm to a particular level can produce in the subject a state of meditativeness, serenity, and even happiness. This positive subjective state associated with alpha enhancement led to speculation that the "alpha experience" represented an altered state of consciousness.

Interestingly, those who supported this view also pointed to findings of consistent physiological changes, including alpha wave and occasional theta wave activity, during the practice of certain meditation techniques, as reported by Anand, Chhina, and Singh (1961a); Kasamatsu and Hirai (1969); and Wallace, Benson, and Wilson (1971). These observations are discussed more fully in chapter 6. Finally, the fact that alpha wave activity of the occipital is seen to increase as the individual enters the sleep state (Dement & Kleitman, 1957) has been cited as further support for the notion that the alpha experience represents a state of consciousness that differs from wakefulness, sleep, or dream activity.

Despite these observations, many investigators were skeptical. To begin with, the alpha state simply does not exist. The use of such a term suggests that the brain is an undifferentiated mass of tissue that produces a single brain-wave pattern at any given time. This is not the case. Typically, alpha feedback training involves becoming aware of and learning to increase the amplitude of 8–13 Hz activity reported from the back of the skull immediately superior to the occipital cortex. However, there are several ways to increase the strength of occipital alpha waves without the aid of feedback training. These include relaxing, defocusing, and closing the eyes.

The oculomotor adjustment related to occipital alpha wave production has been demonstrated in the laboratory. In an extremely creative study, Dewan (1967) taught subjects to send Morse code by using their brain waves, which they learned to modify simply by focusing or defocusing their eyes. Defocusing the eyes produced the occipital alpha rhythm, which in turn produced an audible tone. Production of a dot or dash depended on how long the alpha signal was maintained. More recently, Plotkin and Cohen (1976) designed a study to ascertain the extent to which the strength of occipital alpha waves is related to five subjective dimensions most commonly associated with the alpha experience.

The investigators found that visual processing and degree of sensory awareness were involved in control of occipital alpha waves, while the degree of body awareness, deliberateness of thought, and pleasantness of emotion state were not. These findings support the notion that the pleasant, quasi-meditational state of consciousness known as the alpha experience is not associated directly with an increase of alpha wave strength and that the occipital alpha wave strength is a direct function of oculomotor adjustment.

Such findings cast serious doubts on those of earlier alpha feedback studies. First, a close reading of the early studies reveals that only about 50 percent of the subjects actually reported feelings of pleasantness and relaxation associated with alpha wave production. These findings suggest that factors other than alpha wave manipulation may have been operating in these studies. Suggestion, in the form of instructional set, has been considered to be theoretically relevant to alpha feedback because of its demonstrated role, both in hypnosis and in other altered states of consciousness similar to the alpha state (Barber, 1970; Lynch & Paskewitz, 1971; Orne, 1959; Weil, Zinberg, & Nelson, 1968). To observe the individual and combined effects of alpha activity and instructional set, Walsh (1974) paired both alpha and no-alpha feedback with alpha-expectancy and neutral instructions. The alpha-expectancy instructions that were used in this study induced subjects to expect "a special state of consciousness known as the 'alpha state'; a calm, contemplative, dreamlike, or 'high' state." The results showed that for an alpha experience to occur, both alpha activity and alpha set are necessary and neither alone is sufficient.

The findings of meditation studies that are often cited in support of the existence of an alpha experience are also equivocal. The EEG findings of the Kasamatsu and Hirai (1969) study of Zen monks suggest that these monks were, in fact, very much aware of the external environment. In short, although they were in a meditative state, the monks produced brain-wave rhythms that were not alpha. Overall, the research results to date that support a correspondence between an increase in alpha-rhythm production through alpha biofeedback and the alpha experience certainly have been less than convincing.

Research and Biofeedback

It is clear that much of the research in biofeedback and biofeedback therapy is of a pioneering nature. Many investigators appear to have been attracted by the exciting possibility of finding new applications for biofeedback and by biofeedback's potential as a means of helping to understand our states or levels of consciousness. Unlike hypnosis, however, biofeedback enables the subject to perceive directly and rather quickly the physiological consequences of the altered state. Because of this feature, biofeedback is deemed a very useful therapeutic technique as well. It is hoped that the future will lead to even more uses of biofeedback in the treatment of behavioral and physical problems. Biofeedback should also enable us to learn more about humans' capability to control and manipulate involuntary and unconscious responses. Thus, biofeedback at present is one of the most interesting and research-oriented areas in the psychology of consciousness.

For Further Reading

The Association for Applied Psychophysiology and Biofeedback (AAPB). http://www.aapb.org/home.html.

The Biofeedback Certification International Alliance (BCIA). www.bcia.org.

Gatchel, R. J., & Price, K. P. (1979). *Clinical applications of biofeedback: Appraisal and status.* New York: Pergamon Press.

Geyman, J. P., Deyon, R. A., & Ramsey, S. D. (Eds.). (2000). *Evidence-based clinical practice: Concepts and approach.* Boston: Butterworth-Heinemann.

Moss, D., & Gunkelmann, J. (2002). Task force report on methodology and empirically supported treatments: Introduction. *Applied Psychophysiology and Biofeedback, 27*(4), 273–281.

Schwartz, G. E., & Beatty, J. (1977). *Biofeedback theory and research.* New York: Academic Press.

Schwartz, M. S. (Ed.). (1995). *Biofeedback: A practitioner's guide* (2nd ed.). New York: Academic Press.

Thompson, M., & Thompson, L. (2003). *The neurofeedback book: An introduction to basic concepts in applied psychophysiology*. Wheat Ridge, CO: The Association for Applied Psychophysiology and Biofeedback.

White, L., & Tursky, B. (Eds.). (1982). *Clinical biofeedback: Efficacy and mechanisms*. New York: Guilford.

Yucha, C., & Montgomery, D. (2008). *Evidence-based practice in biofeedback and neurofeedback*. Wheat Ridge, CO: The Association for Applied Psychophysiology and Biofeedback. http://www.dol.gov/ebsa/pdf/MHPAEA258.pdf.

Meditation

Some individuals known as *yogis,* from such Eastern countries as India or Tibet, claim they are able to perform some unusual feats. They say that they are able to stop their heart from beating; they show how they can walk on burning coals or sleep on a bed of nails. They demonstrate these abilities, and we watch with amazement and even awe. Have these people really found the secret of controlling pain? Can they really stop the heart from beating? When asked how they can perform these seemingly impossible feats, yogis report that as a result of meditating for many years, they have so learned to control pain that they experience none during such activities. That is, meditation has taught them to concentrate on relaxation, and they do not experience the sensations that you and I might if we were to perform these foolhardy tasks. Has meditation really done this? Can meditation help to achieve such control over bodily functions and sensations? Or are these claims exaggerated? Let's consider these questions.

In many respects, meditation, as a process for altering experiences of consciousness, is similar to hypnosis. In both processes, subjects report being in a relaxed state, far more relaxed than in their normal or waking state of consciousness. Also, meditation and hypnosis both require a form of concentration or attention to a stimulus event.

However, unlike hypnosis, which appears not to have reliable physiological correlates (Evans, 1979a; Kihlstrom, 1985), proponents of meditation claim that it can control physiological events, including brain-wave activity, electrical resistance of the skin, oxygen consumption, and blood-lactate level. Some of these claims have been experimentally verified (Wallace & Benson, 1972). In this respect, meditation appears to be similar to biofeedback; it enables the subject to become aware of and control behavior he or she is not capable of controlling during a normal, waking state of consciousness.

Also, many have assumed that meditation, unlike hypnosis, is associated with religion or religious practices. Specifically, meditation is often believed to be something to do while praying. Thus, it is thought to be something done in a church, synagogue, mosque, or home but not in the laboratory. Because of this association, the lay community (and even some scientists) either look at meditation negatively or at best accept it as an area of study in the physiology of consciousness but relegate it to nonscience. This type of attitude has resulted in a serious lag in the scientific study of meditation.

However, owing partly to the renewed interest in the neuroscience of consciousness, and partly to increasing interest in stress management and the treatment of stress-related disorders, research on the relationship between meditation and consciousness, and the neural correlates of meditation, has rapidly increased in the last decade.

One of the biggest proponents of the scientific study of meditation has been His Holiness Tenzin Gyatso, the XIV Dalai Lama of Tibet. Due to the Dalai Lama's interest in the sciences, in 1987, the first Mind and Life Conference was organized to support conversation between Buddhism and Western science. Conferences have continued every two years, with the most recent (the 22nd) in November 2010. Some neuroscientists involved in past conferences include Antonio Damasio, Larry Squire, and J. Allan Hobson (Houshman, Livingston, & Wallace, 1999). In 2005, the Dalai Lama addressed the Society for Neuroscience, an international organization comprised of more than 30,000 of the world's top neuroscientists, at their annual meeting in Washington, DC. In this address, the Dalai Lama emphasized the utility of meditation for understanding brain function and plasticity (Gyatso, 2005). In 2010, the Dalai Lama donated $50,000 of his personal funds to the Center for Investigating Healthy Minds (CIHM) at the University of Wisconsin–Madison. The center is directed by Richard Davidson, a neuroscientist and professor of psychology. The grant will support Dr. Davidson's research investigating neural correlates of kindness and compassion (Associated Press, 2010).

At this point we need to elaborate on the role of meditation in the psychology of consciousness and to consider the historical roots of the practice. We also examine the possibility of using meditation as a means of helping control behavior and of tapping human potentials that are not usually accessible during the normal, waking state of consciousness or awareness.

Meditation and Consciousness

As mentioned, many forms of meditation are similar to hypnosis. In both situations an individual must concentrate on a stimulus, thereby blocking external interference. In hypnosis the stimulus to which an individual attends is typically the voice of the hypnotist. In meditation the stimulus is a visual object of regard, a physical motion of the body, or a chant.

However, it is possible to induce an altered state of consciousness by hypnotizing oneself. This process is called **autohypnosis**, or self-hypnosis. Individuals concentrate on a stimulus of their own choosing, and the net result is a relaxed feeling. In fact, the behavior exhibited in self-hypnosis approximates that observed in meditation, especially the Zen variety of meditation. Thus, self-hypnosis does not usually involve suggestions of the type discussed with hypnosis induced in other ways (see chapter 4). Self-hypnosis is also reported to involve less steady and less focused attention (Fromm et al., 1981; Johnson, 1981; Kihlstrom, 1985; Orne & McConkey, 1981). Kihlstrom (1985) has described self-hypnosis as emphasizing relaxation and reverie.

Like self-hypnosis, meditation is a procedure a person must learn. The ability to hypnotize oneself or to meditate does not come instantly or easily. It must be practiced repeatedly over a period of time to concentrate effectively on a situation while attenuating potential sources of disturbance. Typically, initial attempts at self-hypnosis and meditation meet with failure because (1) it is difficult to concentrate on only one thing for more than a few minutes and (2) most people have never had to do this or anything like it before. Because the situation is novel to us, we initially resist it. However, with time, the ability to concentrate on a stimulus situation and to isolate ourselves in our environment becomes easier. Eventually, the task does not appear difficult at all. In fact, we start to enjoy it because it helps us relax and escape the world as we experience it in our normal, waking state of consciousness. These effects provide reinforcement, and the result is that we have learned to meditate.

Where did meditation originate? What do we have to do to learn to meditate? What are the different styles of meditation? What benefits can one

189

achieve through meditation? These are some of the questions we address in this chapter. To understand better how the process of meditation relates to altered states of consciousness, let us examine closely how meditation has developed over the decades and why psychologists view it the way they do.

Historical Development

Meditation as an area of psychological study does not have a formal historical development comparable, for example, to hypnosis. No prominent figures in the history of psychology have introduced important methodological or theoretical facets to the study of meditation. Therefore, to search for some of the roots of meditation, we must look to the various Eastern religions and religious practices.

Since many such religions actively encourage the practice of meditation, it is not difficult to understand why many individuals automatically associate meditation with religion. In fact, for many, this association is so strong that to admit to meditating is akin to admitting membership in a strange religious cult. Obviously, this need not be true, since many people who meditate are neither members of cults nor, for that matter, religious in any sense of the word. They simply practice meditation for its beneficial psychological effects (e.g., altering their state of consciousness) or its beneficial physical effects (e.g., reducing tension, anxiety, and blood pressure).

The popular forms of meditation in Western countries—Zen, yoga, and transcendental meditation (TM)—are clearly grounded in, and can trace their origins directly to, Buddhism and Hinduism. Buddhism, founded by Siddhartha Gautama (563–483 BCE), stressed that suffering is caused by desire and that individuals must destroy this desire to achieve peace. Eight paths were described to win freedom from desire, one of these being meditation. Through meditation a person could achieve *nirvana*, or passionless peace. But nirvana could be achieved only if the meditator had reached perfect self-control, unselfishness, knowledge, and enlightenment. It is, in part, through meditating that these goals could be achieved.

In the fifth century the Buddhist monk Buddhaghosa described meditation in his *Visuddhimagga* (a textbook of Buddhist philosophy and psychology) as a "path to purification" (Goleman, 1988; Nanamoli, 1964, 1976). Such purification eventually would lead to an altered state of consciousness, or what was previously referred to as *nirvana*.

Visuddhimagga describes the basic process of meditation, including the various exercises that must be performed to achieve a state of relaxation and eventually the state of nirvana. It details how one learns to focus attention on a specific object or thought and how to begin to attenuate possible sources of interference that can detract from, or prevent achievement of nirvana. As such, *Visuddhimagga* can be considered the first handbook or guide to the practice of meditation.

According to *Visuddhimagga,* meditation consists of breaking with the normal state of awareness or consciousness through absorption, or *jhana.* The book describes eight jhanas, or levels of absorption, ranging from a simple attenuation of thoughts, which occurs during the normal state of consciousness, to total absorption away from normal consciousness to a state of nirvana. Therefore, meditation is not a single altered state of awareness that differs from the normal state of consciousness. Rather, it is a multilevel process involving a continual and progressive change in awareness.

Hinduism also has played an important historical role in the development of contemporary meditation (Goleman, 1988). Hinduism emphasizes a oneness of Brahman, the Supreme World-Soul, or Spirit. To become one with Brahman, it is necessary to discipline one's mind and body. This is accomplished through *yoga.* The Bhagavad-Gita, a devotional poem, describes three ways of reaching Brahman, one of which is the way of thought, or philosophy and meditation.

In the Hindu tradition there is an emphasis on the *mantra,* or the chanting of a harmonious word or phrase on which to concentrate. Such concentration helps a person to become absorbed in the phrase (or, according to Hindu tradition, to become one with the universe or Brahman) and thus to meditate effectively. Although the mantra is not unique to Hindu meditative practices, it is stressed as a means of helping the meditator become aware of his or her thoughts and attenuate external sources of interference. Today, the mantra is an important part of many meditative styles. (This topic is discussed in the next section.)

Christianity and Judaism have also played a role in the historical development of meditation. In these religions, prayer often involves a process that resembles meditation. It is not unusual during prayer to fix one's thoughts on an object or action to aid concentration and to lessen interferences from the materialistic world and the normal state of consciousness. In Christianity a person may fixate on a cross or an image (real or visualized) of the Christ figure. Roman Catholics often use a rosary, or chain of beads, which they manipulate in their hands to count prayers and to attenuate thoughts that might

191

interfere with prayer. In Judaism a prayer book and the Torah serve as objects of fixation. Also, Orthodox Jews may perform a forward-and-backward swaying action during prayer to help them concentrate. The objects of fixation and the movements performed in Judaism and Christianity are similar to actions performed in many Eastern religions and various meditative styles. Therefore, all major religions appear to have played an important role in the development of contemporary meditation.

Probably the most important figure to introduce meditation (in a secularized and popularized form) to the Western world was the Maharishi Mahesh Yogi. He became known to the West through his writings (Maharishi, 1963) and through publicity from visits by the British rock group The Beatles, who, for a while, acclaimed the Maharishi to be a source of inspiration. This belief spread in popularity with the Beatles' music. In fact, many of their recordings included Eastern instruments (e.g., the sitar) and chants (e.g., "Hare Krishna"). Other Eastern traditions, including meditation, became known to the West along with the introduction of Eastern music and chants. Soon the Maharishi was on tour in most Western countries, and many Westerners began to meditate and join meditation societies. These societies flourished, and many still exist with followings as strong today as they were during the 1960s and the 1970s.

In fact, the Maharishi helped to found Maharishi International University in Iowa, which offers a nontraditional curriculum with emphasis on meditative styles and other areas of consciousness. Some of the most controversial claims of meditators have come from professors at this university, including claims of the ability to walk through walls and fly as a result of having meditated. Various psychology and medical journals contain work by professors, and researchers there also claim that world events can be controlled, to some extent, through practicing TM. This is discussed in more detail later in this chapter.

In 1995, Maharishi International University (MIU) officially became Maharishi University of Management (MUM). Within their nontraditional curriculum, MUM offers several Bachelor's and Master's degrees in Business, Computer Science, and Education, as well as nontraditional majors in Sustainable Living or Maharishi Vedic Science; they offer Ph.D. degrees in Management and Maharishi Vedic Science. The University is accredited by the Higher Learning Commission and the International Assembly for Collegiate Business Education (http://www.mum.edu/index.html).

All students and faculty at MUM are required to learn and practice Transcendental Meditation, the meditation style developed by the Maharishi in the 1950s (meditation styles are described more fully in the next section).

Students take only one curriculum course per month, in addition to TM and Vedic science classes. Information regarding TM instruction has traditionally been kept private, in an attempt to prevent students from developing preconceived notions about TM, which could inhibit learning. However, reports suggest that TM is easily learned regardless of age, education level, or cultural background, although TM does require instruction by a qualified teacher (Lindberg, 2005; Ospina et al., 2007).

What Is 'Vedic Science?'

Veda refers to the oldest collections of Hindu literature. The Vedas are written in Vedic Sanskrit. Some orthodox Hindu believers consider the Veda "scriptural authority," and not of human origin. Less orthodox Hindis and other religions including Buddhism acknowledge the existence of the Vedas, but do not view them as religious writings (Witzel, 1997).

While it has been difficult to find peer-reviewed, published information on Vedic science, according to the website "Maharishi's Programmes for Every Area of Science" (http://maharishi-programmes.globalgoodnews.com), Vedic science is the culmination of thousands of years of Vedic literature compiled into one complete source by the Maharishi, who claims that understanding Vedic science is the only way to bring life in harmony with natural law. Transcendental meditation (TM) may be the mechanism by which understanding Vedic science is achieved, although that is not entirely clear from either this source or the MUM website. Nonetheless, as noted above, TM is a requirement of all Vedic scholars.

Indeed, the Marahishi established a program to combine the knowledge of the Vedas with modern-day scientific knowledge—the concept in physics of Unified Field Theory—to create what he called the Unified Field of Consciousness. **Unified field theory of consciousness** tries to apply knowledge of quantum mechanics to explain how consciousness results (Hagelin, 1987; John, 2001). Modern field theories suggest that consciousness may result from neural "resonations" through networks of specific brain structures, in a manner similar to field theory of quantum physics. Proposed brain networks include **prefrontal cortex, thalamus, limbic system,** and **basal ganglia** (John, 2001; see also chapter 2 for a discussion of the neural correlates of consciousness). More on neural correlates of meditation is provided later in this chapter.

Earlier versions of unified field theory may have been used to provide a scientific explanation for the *Maharishi effect* (Pockett, 2009). The **Maharishi**

effect is described as decreases in crime, increases in peaceful unity, and increases in quality of life that have been reported to occur in geographical areas where a proportion—the square root of 1 percent of the total population—practices TM-Sidhi meditation (Orme-Johnson, Alexander, Davies, Chandler, & Larimore, 1988; Pockett, 2009; Schrodt, 1990). Some research (e.g., Dillbeck, 1981; see also Cahn & Polich, 2006) investigating the neural correlates of meditation have found "coherence" in brainwave patterns recorded via an electroencephalogram (EEG). EEG coherence refers to a similarity in brain activity, or the synchronization of neural firing, across a variety of brain structures. According to the unified field theory proposed by the Maharishi, collective TM by a critical mass of people can cause the coherence in brain waves to extend outward, which can produce coherence in nature's "unified field"; this coherence can spread across a limited geographical location to produce harmony and peace among all people in that region.

Orme-Johnson and colleagues (1988) reported that collective meditation by experienced TM-Sidhi meditators meeting in Jerusalem in 1983, caused decreases in conflict (crime rate, auto accidents, fires, and war casualties) in Lebanon during that same time period. However, as noted by Schrodt (1990), several methodological considerations temper enthusiasm for the significance of these results. Methodological problems include incorrect measurement of the independent variable (defined as simultaneous meditation performed by the square root of 1 percent of the population—according to a re-evaluation of the original report, this critical mass was not achieved), as well as inconsistent definitions regarding the geographical boundaries of the Maharishi effect. Furthermore, the study did not control for the time of year, political climate during the testing phase, weather conditions, and other factors that could also impact their dependent measures of criminal activity, fires, war casualties, etc. While a variety of other studies, conducted primarily by faculty at MUM, have further investigated the Maharishi effect, virtually all are plagued by errors in study design, lack appropriate control groups, or perform inappropriate statistical analyses (see Pockett, 2009 for review; see also the end of this chapter under "Other Correlates"). Thus, while the MUM website and other supporters of the Maharishi effect cite a plethora of evidence in support of the benefits of collective meditation, little scientific evidence exists to validate these claims.

Meditative Styles

Concentrative Meditation

Many of the popular forms of meditation require restricting one's attention to achieve the desired state. In essence, meditators concentrate on something while ignoring all else around them. Ornstein (1986) has referred to this as *one-pointedness of mind.* Such activity has also been referred to as *selective attending* (Treisman & Geffen, 1967).

The four most popular forms of concentrative meditation are Zen, yoga, TM, and Sufism. **Zen** is the most classical form of meditation and is often referred to as classical Buddhist meditation (Ornstein, 1972), since it has its origin in the Buddhist religion. In this meditative form, an individual is given instructions to perform several acts. The first is a breath-counting exercise. The meditators count their breaths from 1 to 10, over and over again. If they lose count as a result of inattentiveness, they must start over.

Once they have mastered this exercise in attention, indicating that they are now able to concentrate on a stimulus event (in this case, breaths), they are given a more advanced attention exercise. This time, instead of counting breaths, they concentrate on the breathing process itself. They are requested to concentrate on nothing but their breathing activity and to attend to the movement of air as it fills their lungs via the air passages through the nose and mouth. This exercise enables them to concentrate on their breathing rate, and such activity produces a monotonous, repetitious, rhythmic behavior pattern that enables them to begin meditating.

Some more advanced Zen meditation exercises require the meditators to remain motionless as they sit in the *lotus position* (Figure 6.1). This position entails sitting with the legs crossed and the back as straight and erect as possible. While sitting in this position and attending to their breathing, they are expected to meditate on a *koan,* a type of riddle or thought-provoking question given to them beforehand. The koan is designed to be either difficult or impossible to solve

Figure 6.1 • Example of the Lotus Position
Image © Yuri Arcurs, 2011. Used under license from Shutterstock, Inc.

195

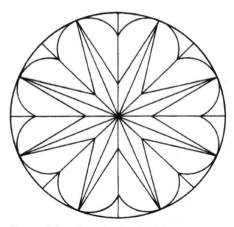

Figure 6.2 • Example of a Mandala

or respond to by rational thought. A few examples of koans, as mentioned by Ornstein (1986), include "Show me your face before your mother and father met" and "What is the sound of one hand clapping?" The basic idea behind the koan exercise is paradox: Concentration is used as a vehicle to shatter, and thus transcend, rational thinking. To solve the koan, meditators must focus their attention on the koan and on nothing else.

In other words, during Zen meditation, individuals perform a type of selective attending (Treisman & Geffen, 1967). Such attending enables them to remove themselves temporarily from their normal state of consciousness or awareness to an altered form. Actually, the ultimate goal of Zen meditation is to attain a *permanent* altered state of consciousness, not a temporary one. In short, living itself becomes a form of meditation.

Yoga is another popular form of meditation, with origins in the Hindu religion. This meditative form differs considerably from Zen or Buddhist meditation. In fact, **yoga meditation** is more closely related to biofeedback training (see chapter 5), though it does not use elaborate electrical/physiological equipment. Individuals who practice yoga attempt to alter their state of consciousness by regulating involuntary or autonomic physiological processes, such as heart rate, blood pressure, blood flow, digestion, and smooth muscle activity. During yoga meditation the practitioner usually assumes a lotus position and gazes on a visual stimulus known as a *mandala* (see Figure 6.2). This object may take one of many forms, such as a circle, a square, a hexagon, or an octagon. The form of the mandala is not as important as its presence. The mandala serves a function similar to that of the mantra: By focusing their thoughts on a single stimulus, practitioners are better able to concentrate and to attenuate external forms of noise or interference. Such focusing becomes more and more elaborate throughout the concentration process. The meditator first focuses on the periphery of the object and gradually moves closer to the center. This technique is a more advanced method for helping the individual concentrate.

In yoga meditation exercises, a **mantra** is commonly used. As was mentioned in the section "Historical Development," a mantra is a word or a set of words that helps meditators to concentrate on a stimulus event. As a result, they are able to attend to the mantra selectively while they attenuate all other forms of information, such as external noise. Thus, in yoga meditation the mantra serves the same function as does breath counting in Zen meditation. Also, as with Zen breath counting, the mantra must be repeated over and over for the individual to attain a state of consciousness that differs from his or her normal, waking state.

Another visual technique for meditation that yoga practitioners use is the **tratakam,** or steady gaze (Ornstein, 1986). This is similar to the mandala, except that anything can serve as an object of a tratakam. For example, one may use a vase, a light from a candle, a star in the sky, the moon, or a flower in a garden. The exact form of the object is not as important as the act of concentrating and focusing on it. As discussed earlier, Western religions rely on a tratakam during prayer (e.g., the cross in Christianity, the Torah in Judaism).

In addition to the use of a mandala and a tratakam, yoga meditators may also practice **mudra**. Mudra consists of repetitive physical movements of the body. The body parts usually used are the arms, the legs, and the fingers. Individuals perform some type of bodily movement on which they are to concentrate. This movement, then, serves the same function as the mandala, the mantra, and the tratakam: It enables the meditator to focus attention on some event and ignore all other sources of stimulation. Some yoga meditators even combine some concentrative stimuli during their practices. For example, one may combine a mudra with a mandala or with a tratakam. Again, the exact form of a concentrative stimulus is not as important as the fact that it enables the practitioner to concentrate.

The stimulus also must be sufficiently salient to prevent the practitioner from redirecting attention to another, interfering source of stimulation. When such interference occurs (as it usually does for most beginning meditators and even for some advanced ones), the task is to bring attention back to the original concentrative stimulus. Attentiveness to a concentrative stimulus and then to an interfering object or event indicates that, in fact, the meditator is moving from one level of awareness or consciousness to another and back again. The goal is to prevent such shifting of consciousness; that is where meditation becomes difficult to master.

Transcendental meditation, or **TM,** is the third form of meditation. In reality, TM is a form of yoga meditation. As in all forms of yoga meditation, TM requires the practitioner to have a mantra on which to meditate silently over and over. Meditators practice this for about a half-hour twice a day, although they can meditate more often. Unlike the traditional form of yoga meditation, TM does not require a specific posture. The practitioner may assume any comfortable position. While in this position, individuals are to concentrate intently on the mantra, focusing all of their thoughts on it. Should their thoughts wander to something else, they are to concentrate on bringing them back to the mantra. Thus, the stimulus serves both as an anchor to which one returns when thoughts drift elsewhere and as a medium on which one concentrates to help keep thoughts from wandering.

TM-Sidhi meditation is a variation of traditional TM in which experienced TM practitioners add a physical component to their mental meditation—bouncing up and down while seated in the lotus position (sometimes referred to as "yogic flying"). TM-Sidhi meditation was developed by the Maharishi in the mid 1970s as a way for meditators to speed the process to enlightenment and "pure consciousness." Pure consciousness is a form of "thoughtless consciousness," where meditation practitioners may transcend normal consciousness to achieve a higher level of thought or experience; pure consciousness has been defined as the least excited state of consciousness (http://www.maharishitm.org/ppaw/tmsidhi.htm). According to the Maharishi, TM-Sidhi meditation yields a faster route to achieving pure consciousness, because this type of meditation can increase EEG coherence in the brain to a greater degree than TM alone (e.g., Orme-Johnson & Hayes, 1981).

According to the Yogic Flying Club website sponsored by MUM, trained meditators can achieve a level of consciousness where their bodies "spontaneously lift up"; this physical change is accompanied by "great clarity of consciousness, energy, exhilaration, and unboundedness" (http://www.yogic-flyingclubs.org/yogic_flying.html). Possibly in an attempt to dismiss criticisms of the practice revealed by defectors from the University, the Maharishi revealed that there are three levels to yogic flying: hopping, floating, and flying.

A variety of evidence negates the existence of Yogic flying, including the inability (or refusal) of the Maharishi himself and other meditators to demonstrate the phenomenon. In a recent exposé, Geoffrey Gilpen (2006) described his personal experiences as a student at MIU 20 years ago, and his voluntary re-immersion into the MUM society 20 years later. Gilpen reported that as a student, he violated the Maharishi's rule for privacy, and secretly observed a group of fellow students practicing yogic flying. Much to his dismay, the "flying" he witnessed amounted to nothing more than a group of students sitting in a circle in the lotus position, bouncing up and down on their bottoms. Previous reports from disenfranchised students of the Maharishi contained corroborating statements (e.g., McCombs, 1987). So, while yogic "hopping," or voluntary bouncing in the lotus position, has been reported in many regions of the world, to date, there have been no verified instances of either floating (level 2) or flying (level 3).

Sufism is the final concentrative, meditation form we discuss. This type of meditation is probably the least known in the United States and the rest of the Western world. There are several reasons for its relative obscurity. First, the exercises for inducing a meditative state in Sufism are different from those of the three types of meditation discussed so far. Second, the principles and styles of Sufi meditation are usually not made public. As a result, even if people with a strong interest in Sufi meditation wished to develop it, they would not be able to do so merely by reading about it. They would have to join a Sufi meditation society and, as members, would be held responsible for keeping the secrets of the society from the general public.

However, on the basis of what is known from writings about Sufi meditation (Goleman, 1988; Ornstein, 1986; Shah, 1970), we do discover some reasons for the secretiveness of Sufi practices. Sufi meditators believe that public knowledge of their practices may lead to faulty applications of the exercises. They are most concerned about this because, to Sufi meditators, meditation exercises vary as a function of time and place. Thus, one Sufi exercise may be appropriate for one individual in a given place and time but totally inappropriate for a different individual at the same place and time. Also, an exercise that is appropriate for a given individual at one time becomes inappropriate at another time. The reasons for these beliefs are neither known to Westerners nor discussed for lay consumption.

Despite the seemingly disparate methods of Sufi meditation and the Sufists' unwillingness to make public their exercises, Sufi meditation exercises share some common features. One exercise calls for the meditator to move in circles. This whirling action is somewhat similar to an individual simply turning about in circles over and over. On the surface, it would appear that this exercise might make the practitioner nauseous at worst and dizzy at best. However, these sensations are eventually overcome and are replaced with a state of relaxation. This state or level of awareness appears to be different from what one experiences in the normal, waking state of consciousness.

The whirling action by some Sufi meditators, most notably the Maulavi, or whirling dervishes of Turkey, is performed as a type of dance that is generally accompanied by the repetition of phrases or sounds, called *zikr* (Goleman, 1988). These sounds begin as oral repetitions and later become silent ones. They are monotonous in tone and are believed to induce an altered state of consciousness.

Because of the vast degree of individual differences in meditative technique used by Sufi meditators, it is only natural that not all such meditators perform the whirling exercise. In fact, many Sufi meditators use exercises that appear similar to those used in the other types of meditation (e.g., the lotus position, chanting a mantra). Other Sufi meditators simply sit in a comfortable position and chant a sound to produce a relaxed or concentrative state.

Since so many differences exist within the Sufi exercises, it seems obvious that Sufi is a nonstandard form of meditation. However, regardless of the types of exercise performed, the goal of all Sufi meditators is the same: to achieve a state of awareness or consciousness that differs from the normal, waking state. This altered state enables meditators to concentrate on a given stimulus situation or environment while effectively blocking all other thoughts and feelings during meditation. Such concentration enables them to achieve a type of bliss or escape from the troubles of the real world.

Opening-Up Meditation

In addition to concentrative meditation, Robert Ornstein (1986) describes a style he refers to as **opening-up meditation**. Here the focus is not on something on which the meditator concentrates. In fact, this form of meditation does not require individuals to isolate themselves nor to fix their gaze upon anyone or anything.

Ornstein describes a form of opening-up meditation in the Zen tradition, which is called *shikan-taza*. In essence, opening-up is a more advanced form of meditation compared to the concentrative forms previously described. After the meditator has mastered concentrative meditation, for example counting breaths, it is possible to achieve a state in which awareness of the external environment is increased. The meditator not only learns to attend to a given object or person of regard, but at the same time pays attention to other things or people around him or her. In this manner, the meditator has expanded his or her horizon or environmental dimensions so that a panorama of stimuli from the environment can be cognitively processed.

An example of opening-up meditation at work might be illustrated by the abilities of a good quarterback in a football game. He must simultaneously concentrate on the position of all of his teammates and the players on the opposing team before, during, and after the snap of the ball. Since the quarterback has decided a play in advance, he may simply rely on what had previously been planned. If all goes as planned, the play is successfully executed. However, we are all aware of the fact that many times things do not go as planned. Therefore, the quarterback has contingencies. He fixes his attention not only on the preplanned actions but also on alternatives. This requires that he open his panoramic horizons to the players who will be rushing him from the opposing team as well as to the position of the members of his own team and, of course, the snap of the ball. When the ball is ultimately snapped, a quick decision must be made. But that decision requires an advanced form of information processing, or an opening-up form of meditation. Such meditating does not and cannot endure for long. But it is necessary to accomplish the desired goal, a successfully executed play.

We need not delve into what would happen if the quarterback were to concentrate only on the ball. The likely outcome would be that he would be tackled or that the play would not be executed properly. By opening up his dimensions and processing multiple actions simultaneously, the quarterback's chances for success are greatly improved.

While the example we have chosen to use to illustrate opening-up meditation may not seem traditional, it is an appropriate example of opening-up meditation at work. (Ornstein [1986] cites other examples.) In any case, opening-up meditation is, by nature, of short duration. To concentrate for a prolonged period of time (greater than 30 minutes) is possible with concentrative meditation. However, to expand one's horizon of attention for a prolonged period is not possible with opening-up meditation. Thus, opening-up meditation usually lasts only a few seconds; it can last longer in situations that permit longer endurance. Needless to say, football or other sport activities do not permit prolonged periods of opening up.

Other Types of Meditation

In recent years, other forms of meditation, or variations in terms used to describe older meditation techniques, have evolved. The following section contains a discussion of some other types of meditation commonly described today:

Relaxation Response

As noted in other sections of this chapter, Herbert Benson, a cardiologist and professor at Harvard University in the 1970s conducted some of the earliest scientific research on the physiological and psychological effects of meditation (e.g., Benson, 1974; Benson, Malvea, & Graham, 1973; Benson, Rosner, Marzetta, & Kelmchuk, 1974; Benson & Wallace, 1972). Benson disagreed that physiological and psychological changes induced by Transcendental Meditation were unique to TM; instead, he argued that any form of behavior that decreased sympathetic nervous system activity could produce effects similar to TM. He coined the term "relaxation response" to refer to a type of meditation he developed that could produce decreased sympathetic activity (Benson, 1983; see also Ospina et al., 2007 for review). The relaxation response (RR) is an actual method of meditation, not to be confused with merely relaxing. It is similar to many of the other concentrative types of meditation discussed earlier, in that it requires practitioners to assume a comfortable position, deeply relax all the muscles, focus on breathing, and repeat a single word (mantra), for example the word "one." Like TM, RR is practiced twice a day for 15–20 minutes each session. What may be unique about RR is that it can be learned very quickly—often in 5 minutes (Benson, 1983; Ospina et al., 2007).

Vipassana

Vipassana (also called "insight meditation") is a type of meditation in the Zen Buddhist tradition, though it probably predates Zen meditation (Chiesa, 2010). Vipassana meditators strive to gain insight into their own thoughts and motivations, while understanding their relation to the world in the present. Vipassana is a type of concentrative meditation. Attention is focused on body posture (which should remain still during the entire meditation process), breathing, emotions, thoughts, and sensory and perceptual processes (Chiesa, 2010; Ospina et al., 2007). Training may take considerable time; it is typically learned and maintained via 10-day "retreats" with other Vipassana meditators (although there may be books or tapes people may purchase to learn the basic practice prior to attending a retreat). Novice meditators are encouraged to limit meditation to short 5–10 minute periods, but advanced meditators may practice for several hours at a time.

Mindfulness Meditation

Although Kabat-Zinn (1991) has been credited with developing an entirely new meditative technique called "mindfulness meditation" (e.g., Wright, 2006), mindfulness meditation is not really a unique meditation technique itself, although sometimes people describe it as such. Instead, the term mindfulness meditation is typically used to refer to any meditation technique that attempts to evoke mindfulness (Chiersa & Seretti, 2010a; Ospina et al., 2007). Examples include Zen meditation and Vipassana, although other clinically based techniques have been developed, including mindfulness-based stress reduction (MBSR), which is probably more accurately credited to Kabat-Zinn (Holzel et al., 2011; Kabat-Zinn, 2003) and mindfulness-based cognitive therapy (MBCT), an 8-week treatment program that combines traditional cognitive therapy with a type of concentrative meditation focused on decreasing stress (Chiesa & Serretti, 2010b; Ospina et al., 2007). Mindfulness techniques do not necessarily require relaxation, and can be employed during many different activities, including states of high cognitive awareness or physical activity. Mindfulness techniques strive to increase perspective and awareness, to permit more rational and less emotional responses to situations (Ospina et al., 2007).

Other Forms of Meditation

Several other types of meditation techniques are used today. One of these is **"open presence"** or **"open monitoring"** (e.g., Lutz, Slagter, Dunne, & Davidson, 2008), a Tibetan practice that may be similar to our description of "opening-up meditation" described earlier, in that it requires "objectless" focus, and "cultivates a state of being," rather than focusing attention on a single object (Lutz, Greischar, Rawlings, Ricard, & Davidson, 2004, p. 16,372; see also Lutz, Dunne, & Davidson, 2007). A second practice is *samatha*, a type of Buddhist concentrative meditation similar in many ways to Vispanna (Lutz et al., 2007). There is also **clinically standardized meditation** (CSM), a variation of TM developed by Carrington in the 1970s (Ospina et al. 2007), **Tai Chi**, the ancient (13th century) martial art that focuses posture and body position to achieve a state of relaxation and concentration (Lutz et al., 2007; Ospina et al., 2007), and **Qi Gong**, or the practice of "energy healing,", which is similar to Tai Chi with its focus on body postures, but without the element of self-defense (if Tai Chi postures are speeded up, they could provide a form of self-defense; Ospina et al., 2007). In addition, Qi Gong emphasizes that practitioners focus on an internal process or consequence, for example, to imagine a pleasant fluid flowing through the body to relieve pain.

In summary, concentrative meditation requires a limiting of input to achieve the goal of attaining a meditative state; opening-up meditation requires an expansion of input. However, regardless of the type of meditative style employed, the goal of *all* meditators is the same: to temporarily alter the state of consciousness or awareness. And by doing so, it is hoped the meditator will achieve some predetermined goal.

Theories of Meditation

The most recent theories or theoretical models concerning the process of meditation are those of Deikman (1966, 1971), Ornstein (1972, 1986), Welwood

(1977), Washburn (1978), and Walsh (1981, 1982). Although these theories or models have much in common in their explanations of the meditation process, they also differ from one another in their manner of explaining what happens during meditation and how a meditative state of consciousness can be achieved.

Deikman and Ornstein

Arthur Deikman and Robert Ornstein explain meditation in terms of a bimodal concept of consciousness. Briefly, the model distinguishes two modes of consciousness: an active mode and a receptive mode.

The *active mode* is concerned with focusing awareness on an object in the environment and distinguishing or isolating the object from the context in which it is found. In addition, the active mode is analytic, sequential, and discursive in nature. According to Deikman and Ornstein, it is the active mode that is involved in concentrative meditation.

The *receptive mode* permits the meditator to be open to experiences in the environment. In other words, rather than concentrating on an object, the meditator eventually (or in some instances, immediately) comes in contact with experiences of the senses. In the receptive mode, the meditator sees parts as they relate to wholes. He or she uses intuition and is not aware of the passage of time. This mode is at work during opening-up meditation.

According to Deikman and Ornstein, we automatically shift from one mode of processing consciousness to another. However, the automatic process can be changed, and we accomplish this through another process called **deautomatization**. Through this process we no longer automatically shift from one mode of processing to another. The principal mode for learning deautomatization is meditation. When we achieve this process successfully, our awareness opens up in a way similar to escaping the bounds that determine our behavior. Instead of being selective about what we attend to or concentrate on, we permit ourselves, in a way, to start from the beginning in the processing of information. Rather than reacting to situations in a learned, automatic fashion, we allow learning to start anew. By doing so, we become more receptive to various stimuli or sensory-input information. This receptivity enables the active mode to take a brief vacation (Ornstein, 1972) from the old, learned, familiar environment of our everyday existence. Afterward, we can return or *dishabituate* to the normal environment and to the normal, waking state of awareness or consciousness fully refreshed and ready to go again (an experience very similar to the relaxed feeling subjects report after hypnosis).

Welwood

Another theory of meditation was proposed by John Welwood (1977), who sees meditation as a means for making ourselves aware of experiences that we do not consciously notice. To explain how meditation helps us become cognizant of previously unnoticed behavior or experiences, Welwood proposes four levels of awareness:

1) the *situational ground,* which Washburn (1978) translates roughly as corresponding to the concept of the preconscious;

2) the *personal ground,* or the conceptualization of an individualized environment;

3) the *transpersonal ground,* in which an individual recognizes that an object of regard is merely an object within a larger and more complex environment; and

4) the *basic ground,* in which an object stands by itself in isolation (e.g., the object is the environment).

These four levels form a system whereby meditation becomes an effective tool for helping an individual become aware of information, potentialities, and abilities that previously had existed at an unconscious level.

In this sense, Welwood's theory is comparable to the Deikman-Ornstein theory; that is, meditation helps to diffuse information so that we become aware of previously unnoticed elements or objects in the environment. However, Welwood goes further by stating that such diffusion is a continuous process; we diffuse to become aware of new information. This information is then diffused further, progressively and repeatedly, until the basic elements in the environment are uncovered for comprehension. Thus, in stepped fashion, meditation enables individuals to become more and more aware of their environment. According to Ornstein (1986), this is exactly what happens in opening-up meditation. Thus on a conceptual basis, Welwood's theory, and that of Deikman and Ornstein, do not appear dissonant.

Washburn

Michael Washburn (1978) has pointed out several weaknesses in Welwood's theory. First, Welwood's theory artificially assumes a single, general unconscious, which may not be the case. Second, his theory postulates that diffusion is a sufficient rather than a necessary condition for bringing information and knowledge from the unconscious state to awareness. In light of these criticisms, Washburn has proposed a three-level theory of meditation. These levels include: (1) defocalization, (2) reduction of the intensity threshold of awareness, and (3) immobilization of psychic operations.

Defocalization is similar to Welwood's concept of diffusion. However, Washburn stipulates that defocalization is a means of focusing on awareness, but in a manner opposite to the process inherent in various forms of concentrative meditation (e.g., yoga, Zen). In concentrative meditation, attention is selective and is restricted to a single object, thought, or action. For a short period, selective attention rules out awareness to all other sources of stimulation in the environment. According to Washburn, such attenuation prevents the meditator from reaching the unconscious, further preventing a tapping of the receptive mode.

In Washburn's theory the second level is a *reduction of the intensity threshold of awareness* by meditation. In the normal waking state, consciousness operates with a relatively high-intensity threshold. Meditation reduces this threshold by "calming the storm on the surface of consciousness" (Washburn, 1978, p. 54), thus permitting the contents of the unconscious to reach awareness. When this occurs, a new threshold is established that is lower in intensity than that of its predecessor. Continued meditation thus becomes progressively easier because it is no longer necessary to reach the previous high threshold. This process is comparable to Welwood's progressive process of diffusion.

The third factor in Washburn's theory, *immobilization of psychic operations*, is the state of complete, motionless attention to the totality of experiences that arise during the meditative process. Through this operation, contact with the unconscious is secured and brought to conscious awareness by interfering with functions of the normal, waking state. This process is automatic; as a result, meditators are unaware that it is happening.

Walsh

In what appears to be a merging of the philosophies of behaviorism and consciousness, Roger Walsh (1981, 1982) has proposed a *stimulus–response*, or S-R, model of meditation. In this, Walsh perceives the meditative practice as representing a stimulus (S) event. This event elicits responses (R) that are considered to be mediated by a variety of psychological, physiological, and chemical mechanisms. The psychological mechanisms include relaxation and global desensitization (Goleman, 1971), deconditioning, behavioral reactivity, heightened awareness (Walsh, 1977), dehypnosis (Walsh, 1982), behavioral self-control skills (Shapiro, 1980), and facilitation of psychological development and maturation (Wilber, 1980, 1982). The physiological mechanisms include reduced arousal, hemispheric lateralization (Earle, 1981; Pagano & Frumkin, 1977), and EEG resonance and coherence or intrahemispheric and interhemispheric synchronisms (Glueck & Stroebel, 1975). Although Walsh (1982) speculates that chemical mechanisms may also be involved in mediating meditation, no such chemicals have to date been discovered. Walsh thus perceives of meditation as being multidetermined and within an S-R framework. In this manner, meditation is perceived as the conscious training of attention aimed at modifying mental processes so as to elicit enhanced states of consciousness and well-being. Or quite simply, meditation, whether of the concentrative or opening-up variety, is something one learns and is helped along by psychological, physiological, and possibly chemical mechanisms.

Theories Compared

In a comparison of the theories discussed, one commonality is evident. The goal in all the discussed approaches is to tap the receptive mode of consciousness. Deikman and Ornstein specify that this comes about through the initial concentration on a stimulus object, thus tapping the active mode. After continual practice with a concentrative meditation exercise, the active mode is replaced eventually by the receptive mode. On the other hand, Welwood, Washburn, and Walsh do not see the need for a concentrative exercise to stimulate the active mode before yielding to the receptive mode. Rather, they see meditation as a response of the receptive mode; concentrative exercise simply detracts or interferes with reaching this mode.

Unfortunately, there is no experimental support for these theories. To date, their predictions have not been tested. However, there is some support for the dishabituation concept of Deikman and Ornstein.

Habituation and Dishabituation

Before discussing dishabituation, we should briefly discuss **habituation**. This phenomenon occurs as a result of continual exposure to a stimulus situation. When we first come in contact with a novel stimulus, we attend to it readily. This produces what Sokolov (1963) referred to as an *orienting response*. As exposure to the stimulus continues, its novelty dissipates and the orienting response disappears. The result is an eventual tuning out of the stimulus event. For example, you may live in an environment where traffic noise is readily apparent. When you first moved to your habitat, the noise probably bothered you; it kept you from sleeping at night or performing your daily activities in an undisturbed manner. After a while, however, you became accustomed to the noise and no longer noticed it, until a friend commented about how noisy it was in your house. Getting used to the noise in this situation is an example of habituation.

Dishabituation means not becoming accustomed to the stimulus (noise) or becoming accustomed to it through some procedure such as meditation. An experimental example of dishabituation through meditation was illustrated in a study by Anand, Chhina, and Singh (1961a, 1961b). A yoga meditator was shown a novel stimulus; his EEG (brain wave) activity was recorded at this time. During meditation the subject produced alpha brain waves. There was no interruption of this wave production on presentation of an external, novel stimulus. Such an interruption would normally occur for a nonmeditator. Also, when the subject was not meditating, the presentation of a novel stimulus did not produce the typical habituation effect. Thus, we can say that in this study, the meditator had successfully dishabituated.

In a study by Kasamatsu and Hirai (1966), habituation to a stimulus was tested on a larger sample than that of Anand and associates. Zen masters and controls (nonmeditating subjects) were exposed to a repeated clicking sound every 15 seconds; their EEG activity was recorded during this time. The control subjects showed the typical habituation to the sound source, and their brain-wave activity indicated reception of the stimulus. After repeated presentations of the sound, brain-wave activity no longer responded to the sound source; that is, habituation had taken place. This was not the case with the meditators. Their brain wave or EEG activity remained constant throughout a 5-minute exposure period.

Thus, it appears that, at least for advanced Zen meditators, dishabituation, as defined by Deikman and Ornstein, does take place. Whether this occurs via the route suggested by Deikman and Ornstein or by the route suggested by Welwood, Washburn, or Walsh is not known. It is hoped that future research will give us the answer to this question.

It seems that no formal contemporary theories of meditation have been proposed (other than perhaps unified field theory mentioned above), although as noted by many researchers including Fell and colleagues (2008), Lutz and colleagues (2007), and the Dalai Lama of Tibet (Gyatso, 2005), one extreme difficulty with scientifically explaining (and studying) meditation is the lack of an accepted definition for the process. The term meditation is frequently used to refer to diverse practices, for example, Sufism and Tai Chi. This is akin to using the word "sport" to refer to any athletic endeavor, while assuming that the requirements needed to successfully perform the activity are identical

(Lutz et al., 2007, p. 498). Nonetheless, it does appear that there is generally widespread acceptance of meditation as a self-regulated practice that can focus attention and possibly induce relaxation (e.g., Cahn & Polich, 2006).

What have instead received a great deal of examination are the physical and psychological correlates of meditation. These are described in detail in the next section.

Correlates of Meditation

Psychological Correlates

Many recent studies have examined the clinical efficacy of mindfulness-based stress reduction (MBSR), rather than try to compare nonspecific meditation types (although some studies have examined benefits of specific types of meditation, for example, TM, Zen, or Vispanna meditation, e.g., Chiesa, 2010). Previous studies reported that meditation could be helpful in the treatment of specific phobias (Boudreau, 1972), as well as nonspecific anxiety (Girodo, 1974; Shapiro, 1976). More recently, Lee and colleagues (2007) compared an 8-week MBSR program to a traditional 12-week cognitive-behavioral group therapy (CBGT), and found significant decreases in anxiety for participants in the MBSR program. However, these investigators did not find significant decreases in several other measures including depression and obsessive-compulsive disorder, and encouraged researchers and clinicians to continue controlled experiments (Lee et al., 2007).

One controlled experiment compared MBSR with CBGT in the treatment of social anxiety disorder (Koszycki, Benger, Shilik, & Bradwejn, 2007). While patients in both groups experienced relief from their symptoms, the CBGT group had significantly lower scores on a number of measures including general social anxiety and remission. These findings suggest that CBGT may actually work better than meditation in the treatment of social anxiety disorders.

Goldin and Gross (2010) found significant decreases in social anxiety following MBSR, but they performed a within-subjects experiment that only compared social anxiety pre- and post-treatment; they did not compare MBSR with any other treatment (or no treatment at all). Thus MBSR may alleviate a variety of symptoms associated with anxiety and/or social anxiety in particular, although further research should continue to replicate these findings. At the very least, MBSR does appear to have potential as an adjunct to traditional therapies.

Meditation has also been reported as useful in dealing with drug and alcohol abuse. A number of investigators (Gelderloos, Walton, Orme-Johnson, & Alexander, 1991; Kus, 1995; Walton & Levitsky, 1994) have shown that dependence on chemical substances was reduced after learning how to meditate. Beneficial effects of meditation have also been reported in enhancing confidence, self-esteem, self-control, empathy, and self-actualization (Hjelle, 1974; Kelly, 1996; Nidich, Seeman, & Dreshin, 1973).

Recent research corroborates the benefits of mindfulness meditation techniques on substance abuse (Garland, Gaylord, Bettiger, & Howeard, 2010; Witkiewitz & Bowen, 2010). A review of 25 studies found that although much of the research on meditation and substance abuse suffered from methodological concerns, mindfulness meditation is probably a safe and effective treatment, which may decrease craving and relapse in substance abuse disorders (Zgierska et al., 2009).

Several studies have also shown that meditation has psychosomatic benefits and is thus useful in rehabilitation following myocardial infarction (Tulpule, 1971), bronchial asthma (Honsberger, 1973; Wilson, Honsberger, Chiu, & Novey, 1975), and insomnia (Miskiman, 1977a, 1977b; Woolfolk, 1975). Others have reported that hypertension, or high blood pressure, has been reduced following instruction and practice in meditation (Benson, Rosner, & Marzetta, 1973; Benson & Wallace, 1972; Blackwell et al., 1975; Dixit, Agrawal, & Dubey, 1994; Michaels, Huber, & McCann, 1976; Patel, 1975; Sudsuang, Chentanez, & Veluvan, 1991). Still others have reported that meditation seems to be beneficial in releasing stress (Dillbeck, Assimakis, Raimondi, Orme-Johnson, & Rowe, 1986; Miller, Fletcher, & Kabat-Zinn, 1995), in leading to better health (Orme-Johnson, 1987), and in enhancing psychological development (Gelderloos, 1987).

A recent review of the literature (Chiesa & Serreti, 2010b) found some support that mindfulness-based cognitive therapy (MBCT), when used in conjunction with traditional therapies, can decrease symptoms of major depression and anxiety, and offered utility in patients with bipolar disorder.

In summary, it appears that meditation is a useful manipulation or intervention in the treatment of a variety of psychologically related problems. However, meditation has also been shown to be effective in influencing physiological responses of the body, as well. We shall now examine some of these.

Physiological Correlates

As we mentioned at the beginning of this chapter, practitioners of meditation have long claimed that they are capable of inducing many changes in their physiological responses to events. For example, they claim they can voluntarily stop their heartbeat temporarily and that they can alter their normal breathing pattern. Are such feats possible? According to a growing body of scientific literature, some physiological changes can be induced with meditation.

As might be expected, most experiments on physiological controls of behavior during meditation have employed well-experienced meditators as subjects. One such study is by Sugi and Akutsu (1964), who used Zen monks from Japan. The researchers found that during meditation the monks were capable of decreasing their consumption of oxygen by 20 percent, which subsequently reduced their output of carbon dioxide. Anand, Chhina, and Singh (1961a, 1961b) reported a similar finding with their yoga meditator.

Changes of brain wave activity have also been noted in well-practiced meditators. Kasamatsu and Hirai (1963) found that Zen monks were capable of producing a predominance of alpha activity with their eyes half open. This brain-wave pattern is usually present only when subjects are very relaxed and have their eyes closed. The Zen monks were also capable of controlling the amplitude and frequency of the alpha brain waves. For example, they demonstrated the ability to slow the frequency of the waves from the normal 8–13 Hz, to 7 or 8 Hz. This seemingly voluntary control of alpha wave production and activity also produced rhythmic theta waves of 6–7 Hz.

Perhaps one of the most comprehensive investigations of the effects of meditation on physiological control was undertaken by Wallace and Benson (1972). Using practitioners of TM as subjects, the researchers were able to support many of the long-standing claims made by meditators. They found that TM practitioners were capable of reducing oxygen consumption as well as carbon dioxide elimination during meditation. The investigators also found a high correlation between TM and a marked reduction in blood-lactate concentration, a rapid rise in the electrical resistance of the skin, an increase in the intensity of alpha brain waves, a slowing of the heartbeat, and an overall decrease in respiratory rate and volume of air breathed. In other words, the results reported by Wallace and Benson substantiated and replicated some of the earlier experiments performed by other investigators with Zen monks and yoga meditators.

Also, as Wallace and Benson pointed out, there is little or no resemblance between the physiological changes noted in meditators and those found in hypnotized or sleeping subjects. For example, whereas after meditation there is a marked drop in oxygen consumption for about 5 to 10 minutes, there is no such drop during hypnosis. Also, decreased oxygen consumption during sleep occurs over several hours.

In light of the results reported by Wallace and Benson and a number of other investigators (Jevning, Wallace, & Beidebach, 1992; Orme-Johnson, 1973) showing that physiological variables are affected by meditation, some have suggested that these effects can be demonstrated with other self-control strategies such as simply resting (Holmes, 1984). Specifically, Holmes suggested that there is nothing unique about meditation and that what can be achieved with it can be achieved by simply teaching an individual the proper techniques of relaxation through resting.

In making his case, Holmes has examined three types of meditation investigations: case studies, own-control studies (in which the effects of meditation versus simply sitting quietly are compared on the same subject), and experimental control studies (in which one group of subjects meditates while another group simply sits quietly). In general, Holmes concluded that simple resting was just as effective as TM and related forms of meditation in achieving control over heart rate, electrodermal activity, respiration rate, systolic blood pressure, skin temperature, oxygen consumption, electromyographic (EMG) activity, and blood flow.

In response to the report by Holmes, a number of investigators criticized his conclusions on several grounds. Benson and Friedman (1985) believed that Holmes misinterpreted much of the meditation literature; in fact, if we examine earlier research, there appear to be consistent and reproducible physiological differences in measures of somatic arousal between subjects who practice relaxation-meditation techniques and those who attain relaxation by simply resting. Also Shapiro (1985), while agreeing that relaxation and control over somatic arousal can be attained by simply resting, thought that Holmes underplayed the role of meditation as an important intervention in the treatment of stress and related problems. While meditation may not be a unique form of achieving relaxation or of dealing with arousal, it is an effective tool and should not be dismissed as valueless simply because other self-control procedures (e.g., deep-muscle relaxation, self-hypnosis, simply resting) produce equivalent results. Shapiro asserted that "there is an important benefit that can be gained from the proper use of meditation as a clinical self-regulation strategy for arousal reduction, as well as an altered state of consciousness for psychotherapy and personal growth" (p. 721).

Also, Dillbeck and Orme-Johnson (1987) noted that a number of studies appearing after the study by Holmes (1984) reported that TM was associated with a significantly greater effect than resting with eyes closed. They considered basal skin resistance, respiration rate, and plasma lactate (Delmonte, 1984; Gallois, 1984; Wolkove et al., 1984).

A number of reports issued from the Maharishi University of Management note significant health benefits following transcendental meditation (TM). These include decreases in arthritis (Nader et al., 2001), and cardiovascular disease (Walton, Schneider, Salerno, & Nidich, 2005), decreases in cardiovascular disease risk factors like smoking, stress, and high cholesterol (Walton, Schneider, & Nidich, 2004), and decreases in basal cortisol level and cortisol release following a stress response (MacLean et al., 1997). A review paper from 2001 boasts significant decreases in several chronic illnesses including chronic back and neck pain, respiratory ailments, digestive problems, arthritis, insomnia, headaches, and eye problems (Nidich et al., 2001).

Research conducted outside of MUM has investigated the effects of meditation strategies other than TM, including the mindfulness-based therapies noted above, and has also found clinical efficacy. One review reports that while many studies have been plagued with methodological problems, in general, mindfulness meditation can produce significant decreases in pain, anxiety, stress, and depression associated with chronic illness (Bonadonna, 2003).

Thus, the controversy concerning whether meditation is more useful and beneficial than other techniques for achieving relaxation and gaining somatic control goes on. We do not try to resolve this issue here. It should be stated, however, that meditation can help individuals to achieve a state of relaxation and that relaxation has been shown by parties on both sides of the controversy to be integrally involved in attaining control over a variety of somatic responses.

However, control over somatic responding is not the major reason individuals learn to meditate. The major reason is that certain benefits, especially relaxation and control over stress or other situations (e.g., Morrell, 1986), appear to result from meditation. In addition, many forms of meditation are easy to learn and are relatively undemanding.

As Holmes (1984) pointed out, a subject does not need to learn to meditate to reach a state of relaxation, which can be achieved through sitting quietly or self-hypnosis. However, for avid meditation practitioners, relaxation will be achieved, and this will result ultimately in a reduced level of tension (Carrington, 1978). The decrease in tension level is manifested by a lessening of anxiety, disappearance of inappropriate startle responses, increased tolerance for frustration, improvement in psychosomatic conditions (e.g., headaches, asthma, hypertension), and a reduced need for psychotropic medication (Carrington, 1977).

With the continued practice of meditative techniques, there also appears to be a heightening in energy level, an improvement in self-esteem, and an elevation and stabilization of mood state (Carrington, 1978). Further, individuals who have meditated for, say, a few weeks at minimum, report that they experience strong feelings of pleasure, sadness, anger, love, and other emotions that they suppressed previously (Glueck, 1973). As a result of the various benefits of practicing meditation, Carrington (1978) advocated incorporating meditation in psychotherapy as an intervention to help individuals with some of the problems mentioned.

Also, Walsh (1978) elaborated on some additional changes that occur during, or as a consequence of, meditation. One such change is in sleep habits. Intensive meditation over time effectively reduces the need for sleep to about four hours per day —a dramatic reduction from the eight hours a nonmeditator usually needs. Since meditation is, in fact, a very relaxing experience and relaxation of the body is one of the consequences of sleep, the decrease in the amount of sleep required by a meditator is not surprising.

Neural Correlates of Meditation

As noted in several chapters throughout this book, interest in the neural correlates of consciousness—including altered states of consciousness—has exploded in the last 20 years. Part of this interest stems from the hope that understanding how the brain produces consciousness will help scientists and clinical professionals find treatments for a host of physical and psychological disorders that plague humans. However, as noted in chapter 2, obstacles pose challenges to studying the neural correlates of consciousness. In many respects, it may be easier to study the neural correlates of altered states of consciousness, to see how the brain changes from "normal" consciousness to the altered state.

To this end, meditation is one altered state of consciousness that is particularly amenable to scientific study (e.g., Fell, Axmacher, & Haupt, 2010). Meditation does not require the administration of drugs, many of which may be illegal or have serious side effects (chapter 3), meditators enter an altered state of consciousness that is more clearly identified than that produced by hypnosis (chapter 4), biofeedback (chapter 5), or sensory deprivation (chapter 8), and meditators probably retain more control over their meditative "altered state" than the altered state achieved during sleep or dreaming (chapter 7), or any of the other altered states previously mentioned. Thus a variety of research has focused on identifying the neural correlates of meditative states, in an attempt to gain insight into not only meditation, but possibly normal consciousness as well. The next section provides an overview of recent knowledge regarding the neural correlates of meditation.

Alpha Waves

As noted previously, early research associated meditation with an "alpha state," or slowing of the alpha rhythm (waves in the 8–12 Hz range), with concomitant increases in alpha power, as measured by EEG (e.g, Kasamatsu & Hirai, 1966; Taneli & Krane, 1987). Unfortunately, probably an equal number of studies failed to find alpha changes during meditation (see Cahn & Polich, 2006 for review). Indeed, alpha waves may show enhanced activation in novice meditators, but not experienced (Davidson et al., 2003; Lutz et al., 2007). While overall changes in alpha rhythm or power were not demonstrated in experienced meditators, Davidson and colleagues (2003) did find asymmetry in alpha waves across the hemispheres. Experienced meditators exhibited greater alpha activation in anterior portions of the left hemisphere during meditation (Davidson et al., 2003). Interestingly, this pattern of alpha asymmetry is similar to that observed when processing emotional stimuli of different valences: left frontal alpha activity is associated with positive emotions, while right frontal alpha is enhanced while processing negative emotions (Davidson, 1992; Davidson, Eckman, Saron, Senulis, & Frieson, 1990). These kinds of findings suggest that long-term meditation may enhance processing in brain areas that regulate positive emotion.

Theta Waves

More recent studies have found significant increases in slower frequency theta waves, in the 3–8 Hz range, during meditation (Aftanas & Golocheikine, 2001, 2005; Slagter, Lutz, Greiscahr, Nieuwenhuis, & Davisdon, 2008; see also Cahn & Polich, 2006 for review). Fell and colleagues (2010) note that theta waves may be representative of or may appear more frequently in advanced rather than beginning meditators. Increases in theta wave activity may therefore indicate greater expertise in meditation; indeed, a variety of human and animal research notes the importance of cortical and hippocampal theta waves in learning and memory (e.g., Schacter, 1977; Seager, Johnson, Asaka, Chabot,

& Berry, 2002). We look forward to continued investigation into the role of theta wave oscillations in meditation.

Gamma Waves

Other recent work has found that experienced meditators exhibit significant increases in high-powered gamma waves (roughly 40 Hz, but ranging anywhere from 20–200 Hz, depending on the study; Cahn, Delorme, & Polich, 2010; Lehmanet al., 2001; Lutz, Greischar, Rawlings, Ricard, & Davidson, 2004; see also Cahn & Polich, 2006 for review). While at least one early study found gamma oscillations in the 40 Hz range in advanced meditators (Banquet, 1973), most early research focused on examining slower waveforms, and did not generally report activity in higher frequencies. In the mid 1990s, with the renewed interest in elucidating the neural correlates of consciousness, researchers began to look again at gamma oscillations in the 40 Hz range, as there was some evidence to suggest the fast-frequency waves may mediate consciousness (e.g., see Chalmers, 1996, 2000; and Crick & Koch, 2003 for reviews). It is possible that this general increase in interest in fast, synchronized brain waves, coupled with increases in recording technology and data extraction capabilities, have led to renewed interest in studying gamma wave involvement in meditation.

One particularly exciting aspect of this analysis is that synchronized firing in the very fast gamma range could provide the neural basis for synaptic plasticity. Neural assemblies firing in fast, synchronized patterns likely promote synaptic connectivity (e.g., Hebb, 1949; Bliss & Lomo, 1973). Fell and colleagues (2010) and Lutz et al. (2004) suggest that synchronized gamma activity provides the basis for neural plasticity, and may explain why experienced meditators demonstrate increases in cortical thickness (discussed below). We look forward to continued investigations into the role of synchronized gamma oscillations in meditation and neural plasticity.

Brain Correlates

Using functional brain imaging technology, several studies have found that meditation increases brain activity in **frontal cortex, parietal cortex, thalamic nuclei,** and **insular cortex**—the deep folds of cortex between the frontal and parietal lobes (Brefczynski-Lewis, Lutz, Schaefer, Levinson, & Davidson, 2007; Lazar et al., 2000; Lutz et al., 2004; see also Rubia, 2009 for review). Not surprisingly, many neural correlates of meditation match the neural correlates of relaxation, sustained attention, and the processing of interoceptive stimuli.

For example, Critchley, Dolan, and colleagues have measured brain activity via fMRI during relaxation. These studies repeatedly note the involvement of the **frontal cortex**—especially **orbitofrontal motor areas** and the **anterior cingulate cortex**—the **insula**, and **thalamus** during relaxation (Critchley et al., 2004; Critchley, Melamed, Featherstone, Mathias, & Dolan, 2001; Nagai, Critchley, Featherstone, Trimble, & Dolan, 2004). However, other research demonstrates that meditation recruits the involvement of select structures not activated by merely relaxing, including **dorsolateral prefrontal cortex** and **limbic** and **paralimbic** brain structures, including **amygdala, hypothalamus,** and **hippocampus** (Lazar et al., 2000). Further, as noted by Rubia (2009), several studies reveal "dose-response" effects in meditation that further differentiate the neural substrates of meditation from relaxation; more experienced meditators, or meditators reporting the deepest levels of meditation, showed the greatest involvement of **fronto-parietal** and **limbic** brain structures (Brefczynski-Lewis, Lutz, Schaefer, Levinson, & Davidson, 2007; Lutz et al., 2004).

Attention appears to require frontal cortex connections with several other networks of brain systems (Posner, 1990, 1994). Thus there is overlap between neural substrates of attention—especially sustained or focused attention—and those involved in meditation, since meditation, at least concentrative meditative styles, require sustained, focused attention. Several studies note the involvement of **fronto-parietal** networks during concentrative meditation (e.g., Aftanas & Golosheykin, 2001; Cahn & Polich, 2006), **fronto-limbic** networks (e.g., Lazar et al., 2005; Lou et al., 1999), and **fronto-striatal** networks, specifically noting the involvement of the **basal ganglia** during meditation (Ritskes, Ritskes-Hoitinga, & Stodklide-Jorgensen, 2003). Pagnoni and colleagues (2008) compared experienced meditators with nonmeditators on a lexical decision task that required conceptual processing. Zen meditators engaged brain areas required for conceptual processing (fronto-cortical areas) to a *lesser* degree than nonmeditators. These findings suggest that experienced meditators may be able to focus attention to minimize their own spontaneous mental activity (Pagnoni, Ceki, & Guo, 2008).

Interoceptive awareness refers to awareness of one's own internal body state or functioning. Several studies note the important involvement of insular cortex for responding to interoceptive cues (Critchley, Wiens, Rotshtein, Ohman, & Dolan, 2004; Khalsa et al., 2008). Khalsa and colleagues (2008) conducted a study to determine whether experienced meditators were more aware of interoceptive cues like heart rate. Interestingly, this study found that meditators were not significantly better than nonmeditators at estimating their own heart rate (Khalsa et al., 2008). Nonetheless, several studies have noted increased insular activity during meditation (Brefczynski-Lewis et al., 2007; Lazar et al., 2000).

In summary, it appears that brain areas involved in processing attention, that is **fronto-parietal** and **fronto-striatal** networks, as well as brain areas involved in emotional processing (**fronto-limbic** structures) mediate the con-sciousness-altering effects of meditation. Specific structures involved include the **prefrontal cortex** (including the **anterior cingulate cortex**), the **insula**, and limbic structures including the **hippocampus**.

Neural Plasticity

Of great interest today are findings suggesting that meditation may facili-tate neural plasticity, that is, increased communication between neurons. As noted above, meditation can facilitate brain activity in structures devoted to attention (fronto-cortical connections), interoceptive awareness (insula), or relaxation (fronto-parietal connections). It is of interest to understand the consequences of this increased brain activity. To this end, several studies have demonstrated morphological changes in experienced meditators, including increases in cortical thickness (Grant, Courtemance, Duerden, Duncan, & Rainville, 2010) and increases in gray matter density (Holzel et al., 2008; Lud-ers, Gaser, Lepore, Narr, & Toga, 2009; Pagnoni & Cekic, 2007; Vestergaard-Poulsen et al., 2009).

Lazar, Benson, and colleagues (2005) used MRI to compare gray matter density in experienced and nonmeditators. Meditators had increased cortical thickness in **right prefrontal cortex, right insula,** and **left auditory cortex**, without significant increases in overall gray matter density (Lazar et al., 2005). Further, participants in this study were compared to age-matched controls, since the most experienced meditators tended to also be the oldest. Finding greater gray matter density in older meditators compared to older controls suggests that meditation may reverse or prevent age-related decreases in corti-cal thickness.

Holzel, Lazar, and colleagues (2011) have recently examined brain density in novice meditators following an 8-week MBSR meditation training pro-gram. This study replicated findings regarding changes in brain morphology, even in these short-term meditators. Increases in gray matter density were found in **left hippocampus, posterior cingulate cortex,** and **cerebellum** (Holzel et al., 2011). These findings suggest that even short-term meditation can produce significant neural changes.

Interestingly, another study found an inverted U-shaped function between meditation expertise and brain activation, such that the most experienced (and also oldest) meditators actually demonstrated the least amount of brain activation (Brefczynski-Lewis et al., 2007). These authors suggested that experienced meditators produced physical changes in neural connectivity or neural reactivity, to minimize neural firing during and following meditation. The significance of decreased neural activity in experienced meditators is unclear, but may be in line with a process proposed to occur during skill learning, whereby neural efficiency may be improved in "experts" (e.g., Grabner, Neubauer, & Stern, 2006; see also Rubia, 2009). Such neural efficiency could result in decreased brain activity of the type observed in skilled meditators.

Thus it appears that meditation can produce significant and long-lasting changes in brain morphology and function, which extends beyond the meditation period. Neural changes may include increases in neural efficiency across networks, and increased synaptic density, possibly due to repeated practice, or the development of expertise.

Other Correlates

A number of investigators have reported that when a group of individuals are collectively involved in meditation, specifically TM, some interesting phenomena seem to occur. For example, a significant improvement in the quality of life was found during a three-month period during which a small group of TM participants in Rhode Island collectively meditated. The improvements included drops in the rates of crime, auto accidents and fatalities, and deaths due to cigarette smoking and alcohol consumption (Dillbeck, Cavanaugh, Glenn, Orme-Johnson, & Mittlefehldt, 1987). Similarly, collective meditation sessions were reported to have reduced the number of hostilities in a Lebanese war (Abou Nader, Alexander, & Davies, 1992; Davies & Alexander, 1989) and other international conflicts including acts of terrorism (Orme-Johnson, Dillbeck, & Alexander, 1989).

Can it really be that when a group of individuals gathers to meditate in a trouble spot somewhere in the world that, in fact, hostilities and other undesirable behaviors decrease? The investigators would argue yes. However, we should not confuse *correlation* with *causation*. While it is interesting that significant correlations have been found between collective meditative sessions and reductions in violence and other undesirable acts, remember that these are only correlations and not causal relations. Also, we must be careful to interpret studies that purport to demonstrate causality when other interpretations are also possible (e.g., lulls in a war, time of meditation vs. time of hostilities, insufficient control techniques and groups). Nonetheless, the correlations that have been reported are interesting.

In summary, it appears that many psychological, physiological, and other changes can occur during and as a consequence of practicing meditation. Thus, meditation is another useful tool for helping us to understand our state of being and to identify various levels of consciousness and awareness. Also, with extensive and intensive practice in meditation (especially yoga and TM), we can become adept at altering many responses under the control of the autonomic nervous system.

This is not to imply that meditation is the only procedure for achieving these results. Simple resting (Holmes, 1984), progressive relaxation (Jacobson, 1938), and biofeedback (see chapter 5) are also beneficial tools for accomplishing this task. In fact, biofeedback and most nonmeditative relaxation procedures do not require as much time to learn, nor does one need to become as adept at them as at meditation. However, conscientious meditators may practice their art or skill for a lifetime and therefore use it in their everyday experiences. This is not the case with biofeedback and other self-control procedures, which are generally employed to treat specific problems at specific times. Thus, meditation can be regarded as a slow, cumulative, long-term procedure for producing an altered state of consciousness.

As far as we know, compared with the use of drugs (see chapter 3), meditation is a relatively safe procedure for bringing about an altered state (see Naranjo & Ornstein, 1976). Many lifelong meditators claim that the "high" they achieve with meditation is as fulfilling as any they could achieve with drugs. In fact, they refer to meditation as a "natural high." If, as Weil (1972) suggested, we have a drive to experience modes of awareness other than the normal waking state, then meditation appears to be a safe outlet for satisfying that drive.

For Further Reading

Gilpen, G. (2006). *The Maharishi effect: A personal journey through the movement that transformed America.* New York: Penguin.

Goleman, D. (1988) *The meditative mind: The varieties of meditative experience.* New York: G. P. Putnam's Sons.

Houshmand, Z., Lingston, R. B, & Wallace, B. A. (Eds.). (1999). *Consciousness at the crossroads: Conversations with the Dalai Lama on brain science and Buddhism.* Ithaca, NY: Snow Lion Publications.

Kabat-Zinn, J. (2005). *Coming to our senses: Healing ourselves and the world through mindfulness.* New York: Hyperion.

Ospina, M. B., Bond, T. K., Karkhaneh, M., Tjosvold L., Vandermeer, B., Liang, Y., Bialy, L., ... Klassen T. P.(2007). *Meditation practices for health: State of the research.* Evidence Report/Technology Assessment No. 155. (Prepared by the University of Alberta Evidence-based Practice Center under Contract No. 290-02-0023, Publication No. 07-E010). Rockville, MD: Agency for Healthcare Research and Quality.

Sapolsky, R. M. (2004). *Why zebras don't get ulcers: An updated guide to stress, stress related diseases, and coping* (3rd Ed.). New York: W. H. Freedman/ Holt.

Zalazo, P. D., Moscovitz, M., & Thompson, E. (Eds.). (2007). *The Cambridge handbook of consciousness.* (especially Ch. 19). New York: Cambridge University Press.

Sleep and Dreams

If you are an average, healthy individual, it is estimated that you will spend about one-third of your life asleep. Thus, when you reach the age of 60, like Washington Irving's Rip van Winkle, you will have slept about 20 years of your life. Moreover, during your 20 years of sleep you will have spent approximately 4 years dreaming.

While sleep and dreams represent a dramatic departure from our normal state of awareness, they are, at the same time, a state of consciousness that each of us has experienced directly. Perhaps this familiarity with sleep and dreams has fostered questions about these phenomena.

Our current state of knowledge concerning sleep and dreams represents the combined research efforts of investigators working in such areas as clinical psychology, physiological psychology, and more recently, psychophysiology. There are several reasons why psychologists and other behavioral scientists have studied sleep and dreams so extensively. Besides the fact that we spend a great portion of our life in the altered states of sleep and dreams, we also often drift into sleep, daydream, and enter states of consciousness in which we are not fully asleep yet not fully awake. And we do so quite frequently. As a result,

Figure 7.1 • Stages of Sleep

it is relatively easy to study these phenomena and to collect a wealth of data about them through introspective reports.

Furthermore, we all have experienced sleep and dreams, while many of us have not experienced altered states, such as hypnosis, meditation, and drug experiences. And it is not considered odd to discuss sleep and dreams with friends, professors, and other acquaintances. Before we survey the results of research efforts in sleep and dreams, let us examine the role of these phenomena in the psychology of consciousness.

Sleep, Dreams, and Consciousness

In terms of our taxonomy of consciousness described in chapter 1, **sleep** is the lowest level of consciousness. However, a quick return to the highest level of our hierarchy is possible when an appropriate stimulus is present, such as the sound of an alarm clock or your mother's voice calling you.

With the advent of modern electroencephalography, Loomis, Harvey, and Hobart (1937) noted that brain-wave recordings could be used to distinguish different stages of sleep. On the basis of electroencephalographic (EEG) records, the investigators were able to identify five distinct stages, ranging from awake to deep sleep. These stages, represented in the Dement-Kleitman (1957) system, are presented in Figure 7.1.

Dreams occur primarily during the stage in Figure 7.1 referred to as Stage REM. We describe this and other stages of sleep in more detail later in the chapter.

It is important now to identify some of the most significant scientific contributions that have led to our current understanding of the phenomena of sleep and dreams. What has history taught us about sleep and dreams?

To help us answer this question, let us examine the historical attempts to study these states of consciousness.

Historical Development

Because sleep and dreams are such common human experiences, it is probably safe to conclude that these phenomena have been of interest since the dawn of humanity. Early humans imbued dreams with magical and mystical properties and viewed them as coming from outside themselves and containing omens of the future. Old Testament references to dreams provide clear examples of these beliefs. Joseph, through Pharaoh's dreams, was able to foretell a time of drought in Egypt, and Daniel was able to predict a period of madness in the life of King Nebuchadnezzar through the king's dreams.

The early Greeks and Romans were also interested in sleep and dreams. In his collection of monographs on the biopsychological characteristics of animals, titled *Parva Naturalia*, Aristotle (384–322 BCE) devoted five chapters to dreams and predictions derived from dreams. On the basis of his own naturalistic observations, Aristotle concluded that dreams were not divine or supernatural but rather followed the laws of the mind. Lucretius (94–50 BCE), the Roman poet and philosopher, suggested that the little movements he observed animals making while asleep were somehow related to dreaming.

According to Webb (1973), surprisingly little scientific inquiry into the nature of sleep and dreams was initiated until the late 1800s. Until that time, most of what was accepted concerning these phenomena had been forged from natural observations, anecdotes, opinions, and a smattering of scientifically based knowledge pertaining to human physiology. It is little wonder that Webb, in describing this "dark age of sleep," refers to this time as an era during which "sleep and dreams were almost exclusively the property of poets and dream diviners" (p. 3).

Much of the early research in the quest for a brain sleep center took the form of clinical anatomical evidence. Gayet in France, in 1875, and Mauthner in Austria, in 1890, worked independently on finding the pathological cause of lethargy syndromes. Both noted the importance of a rostral midbrain lesion. On the basis of his observations, Mauthner proposed one of the earliest sleep center hypotheses. He located this center in the gray matter of the brainstem that forms the walls and floor of the fourth ventricle.

From 1916 through 1926 a worldwide epidemic of encephalitis lethargica developed. More commonly called "sleeping sickness," encephalitis lethargica is a degenerative inflammation of the brain that is thought to be virally produced. The disease is characterized by fever, lethargy, or hypersomnia, and general motor symptoms, such as tremors and body spasms (Marcus, 1972). The search for the pathological basis of this disease led von Economo in 1929 (Marcus, 1972) to conclude that not one, but two brain centers were involved in the control of sleep. A *waking center* served to turn off sleep when properly stimulated and was located in the posterior hypothalamus and mesencephalic tegmentum (the floor of the midbrain). The brain center, which turned on sleep when properly activated, was thought to be located in the basal forebrain structures. This was labeled the *sleep center*.

The late 1930s and the 1940s proved to be a most productive period in the search for the brain centers that controlled the sleep/waking cycle. Partially responsible for this progress was the decision by many investigators to use animals to allow more direct and controlled experiments. Two major research techniques were used. The first involved damaging specific neural structures, then observing changes in behavior (Bremer, 1937). The second technique (Sheer, 1961) involved exciting or activating a specific neural site by applying a series of electrical pulses, then noting changes in the sleep/waking pattern. The pulses were low in voltage and of short duration. Such pulses are not painful.

Bremer believed that sensory input to the cerebrum was responsible for keeping the brain "awake." His argument was based, at least in part, on the effects of lesions that interrupted sensory input via the sensory cranial nerves. He discovered that severing the brainstem at the midbrain level would eliminate all cranial-nerve sensory input to the cerebrum except for vision and olfaction. On the other hand, the more caudal transection would leave all the cranial-nerve sensory input intact.

In studying the effects of various brain lesions on the sleep/waking cycle of the rat, Nauta (1946) found support, not only for the presence of a waking center at the junction of the midbrain and hypothalamus, but also for the existence of a sleep center in the basal preoptic region. Nauta demonstrated that lesions in this area were followed by complete insomnia, motor hyperactivity, and finally, within several days, death.

By the mid 1940s, then, scientists appeared to be on fairly sound footing in proposing the existence of a neural center located somewhere near the rostral midbrain, probably in the posterior hypothalamus, that served as a waking center for the intact organism. More questionable, however, was the notion of a corresponding sleep center. The existence of a sleep center located in a thalamic nucleus, the *massa intermedia*, was suggested by the pioneering study with electrical stimulation reported by Hess (1944). Electrical stimulation of this center in cats induced a state of drowsiness or sleep with all the appropriate behavioral characteristics.

The 1940s closed with the studies of Moruzzi and Magoun (1949), who found that electrical stimulation of the reticular formation in a cat's brainstem produced an EEG pattern of desynchronization and other signs of wakefulness. In the same year, Lindsley, Bowden, and Magoun (1949) provided additional evidence implicating the reticular formation. They showed that midbrain lesions that interrupted the ascending fibers of this structure resulted in a constantly stuporous or sleeping animal. These findings provided an experimental basis for assuming the existence of both sleep centers and waking centers in the brainstem.

As the 1950s came to a close, it was generally accepted that regions necessary for both sleep and waking existed in the parts of the brainstem referred to as the pons and the medulla. It was also evident at this point, in contradiction to Bremer (1937), that sensory input to the brain was not a necessary condition for an organism to demonstrate behavioral signs of wakefulness.

The study of the electrophysiology of sleep and dreams actually originated with the English physiologist Richard Caton, who discovered in 1875 that the brain continually produces low-voltage electrical fluctuations or waves. Using a galvanometer and recording from the exposed cerebral cortex of rabbits, Caton observed these brain wave activities and noted that they ceased upon the animal's death.

Caton's observations went virtually unnoticed by the scientific community until 1929, when the German psychiatrist Hans Berger, using human subjects, reported on a technique he had developed for recording the electrical activity of large populations of cortical neurons lying beneath the intact skull. Berger accomplished this by attaching surface electrodes to the scalp and forehead. This development signaled the advent of modern electroencephalography (EEG). The early 1930s saw the development of EEG as a clinical tool (Gibbs, Davis, & Lennox, 1935; Walter, 1936), but it remained for Loomis, Harvey, and Hobart (1937) to demonstrate that Berger's technique could be used to measure levels of consciousness. As we observed earlier, in the section "Sleep, Dreams, and Consciousness," these investigators showed that cortical brain waves exhibited distinct changes in dominant frequency and amplitude with the onset of sleep and continued to change throughout the sleep period. Loomis and colleagues devised a system for classifying these EEG patterns into five distinct stages, ranging from wakefulness to deep sleep. (See Figure 7.1).

What little understanding scientists had before the 1950s of the nature of dreams was based almost exclusively on clinical observations. Two of the most influential psychoanalysts of the period, Sigmund Freud (1856–1939) and Carl Gustav Jung (1875–1961), paid particular attention to the dreams and dreaming behavior of their clients. Freud referred to the dream as the "royal road to the unconscious." He believed that an understanding of a patient's dreams could provide the therapist with helpful clues as to what the client actually thought and felt. Freud's *The Interpretation of Dreams*, published in 1900, is still regarded as one of the most influential books on the topic. Jung, one of Freud's earliest disciples, eventually separated from Freud and set about developing his own system, which included his own theory of dream interpretation. Both theories receive a more thorough treatment later in this chapter.

In 1892, Ladd speculated that a sleeper's eyeballs moved during dreaming (Aserinsky & Kleitman, 1953). Unfortunately, Ladd failed to pursue the observation, so it went unnoticed for more than 50 years. While carrying out some sleep studies, Kleitman and his graduate student, Aserinsky, noted that periodically during the night, the eyes of the sleeping subject moved rapidly in a generally horizontal fashion. Aserinsky and Kleitman (1953) were able to demonstrate that dreaming occurs during these periods of rapid eye movement (REM). However, before discussing REM activity any further, let us look at the various brain-wave patterns, or EEGs, that commonly accompany sleep and dreams.

Sleep, Dreams, and the EEG

It has been estimated that the human brain consists of as many as 100 billion neurons (Hubel & Wiesel, 1979). These neurons are constantly involved in receiving information about the environment (sensory input), processing such information, and sending neural messages to the muscles and glands of the body so that the individual can respond appropriately (motor output). In carrying out these functions, voltages of the nerve-cell membrane and electrical activity at the synapses are in a state of constant fluctuation. The combined electrical activity from large numbers of neurons and synapses, called *brain waves,* can be recorded by placing electrodes in contact with the scalp and with an instrument called an **electroencephalograph**. The resultant recording of the gross electrical activity of the brain (examples are illustrated in Figure 7.2) is called an **electroencephalogram (EEG)**.

Brain waves differ with respect to at least two major characteristics: *amplitude* (the height of the wave) and *frequency* (rate of occurrence). Much of the pattern of electrical activity in a typical EEG recording can best be described

Excited
(BETA)

Relaxed
(ALPHA)

Drowsy
(COMBINATION)

Asleep
(THETA)

Deep sleep
(DELTA)

1 sec.

Figure 7.2 • Human Brain-Wave Activity

as irregular, low-amplitude activity with no particular pattern. Such activity is described as *desynchronized.* At other times, distinct, very regular patterns of brain waves that are approximately of the same amplitude and occur with a regular frequency can be detected on the EEG. This is called *synchronous* activity. On the basis of the number of waves per second, or Hertz (Hz), different patterns of synchronous activity have been assigned names corresponding to Greek letters.

One of the most common EEG rhythms is the **alpha** frequency, which varies from 8 to 13 Hz and has wave amplitudes ranging from 25 to 100 microvolts (μV). It has been observed most frequently from electrodes situated over the occipital and parietal lobes of the cortex (see chapter 2, Figure 2.5 for an illustration of the lobes of the human brain). Alpha activity occurs in the EEG patterns of healthy individuals when they are awake but in a quiet, resting state with their eyes shut. During sensory stimulation or attentive mental activity, alpha activity is reduced or replaced by desynchronized activity.

Beta waves occur at frequencies between 14 and 30 Hz; their amplitudes seldom exceed 20μV. Such activity is often called "low-voltage, fast" beta activity. Beta activity is recorded most commonly from the parietal and frontal cortical regions. The beta wave is characteristic of wakefulness or arousal (Schneider & Tarshis, 1986).

Among the less frequent patterns of synchronous brain-wave activity are **theta** and **delta** patterns. Theta rhythm was described initially by Walter and Dovey (1944) and includes waves in the range of 4 to 7 Hz, with moderately large amplitudes of less than 20 μV. Theta activity is a common pattern seen in EEG recordings of children under the age of 10, when recorded from frontal and temporal cortical sites. The appearance of midline frontal theta in humans under such conditions as simulated diving, chemical intoxication, sleep, and meditation suggests a relationship between such wave forms and various states of consciousness (Matsuoka, 1990). In people between ages 11 and 20, theta waves decrease in both amplitude and frequency. Delta activity is usually defined as large-amplitude EEG waves of 0.5 to 4 Hz. The presence of delta waves in the EEG of waking adults is considered abnormal.

As we noted earlier, Loomis, Harvey, and Hobart (1935) observed that these cortical brain-wave patterns could be used to identify different stages of consciousness. On the basis of these findings, and using EEG patterns as one criterion, these investigators were able to identify five stages that they believed represented increasing depths of sleep (or consciousness). A classification scheme that is used more frequently, and the one used in this chapter, was developed by Dement and Kleitman (1957). The Dement-Kleitman system identifies four stages of sleep depth and a fifth stage, Stage REM (see Figure 7.1).

Although not pictured in Figure 7.2, gamma waves are high-powered, fast cortical waves that range from 20–200 Hz. The most commonly measured gamma waves are usually in the 40Hz range. These fast waves appear to be involved in attention and may mediate memory formation by promoting neural plasticity and synaptic connectivity (e.g., Bliss & Lomo, 1973; Hebb, 1949; Fell et al., 2010; Lutz et al., 2004). As noted in chapter 6 (Meditation), gamma waves are of interest in the study of consciousness, as they may provide a neural correlate of consciousness, specifically binding (putting together qualities of stimuli to create a coherent awareness; see Chalmers, 1996, 2000; and Crick & Koch, 2003 for reviews). During sleep, very fast gamma oscillations in the 200Hz range may form the basis of the fast-spike waves noted during slow-wave sleep that may accompany memory formation (e.g., Ego-Stengel & Wilson, 2010; Axmacher, Darguhn, Elger, & Fell, 2009). These fast-spike waves or "ripples" are discussed further in the section below, "Sleep and Memory."

Studying Your Sleep

Imagine you have agreed to participate as a research subject in a sleep and dream study and that this is the second night of participation. The second night has been selected for purposes of this discussion because sleep researchers have observed that the data gathered during a subject's first night of participation in such a study are generally atypical. This is the so-called first-night effect (Antrobus, Fein, Jordan, Ellman, & Arkin, 1978). Once you have arrived at the sleep laboratory and completed your nightly ritual of preparing for bed, the researcher attaches surface electrodes to detect brain waves, eye movement, and muscle activity. The standard hook-up for studying sleep activity in the laboratory is shown in Figure 7.3.

Now you can get into bed, get comfortable, relax, and close your eyes. During this state of relaxed wakefulness, brain-wave activity will change from the desynchronized beta type that is commonly observed in the waking, alert individual to the synchronous, alpha type of 8–13 Hz. Should you happen to open your eyes in response to a sudden stimulus or begin to think about some problem of the day at this point, the desynchronized activity will return. On the other hand, should you happen to fall asleep at this time, you will enter the first stage of sleep.

"Drifting off to sleep" and other similar colloquial expressions imply that the process of going to sleep is gradual. While this is the popular view of the onset of sleep, it is far from the truth. Actually, the onset of sleep is instantaneous. One second you are aware, and the next you are not. It is as though someone threw a switch that immediately put the portion of the brain that controls awareness on standby. With the onset of Stage 1 sleep, your body begins to show signs of relaxation; muscle tonus diminishes, heart rate slows, and breathing becomes deeper and more regular. In this stage, brain-wave activity is desynchronous, showing low-voltage, mixed frequencies; 12 to 17 Hz is the

Figure 7.3 • Recording Sites for Sleep Research

most prominent frequency. This stage represents a transition in consciousness between wakefulness and the deeper stages of sleep to follow. During this relatively brief stage, it would be very easy to awaken you.

Against this background of desynchronized EEG activity, brief bursts of sleep spindles and k-complexes begin to occur, signaling the onset of Stage 2 sleep. A *sleep spindle* is a sinusoidal wave with a frequency of between 12 and 14 Hz. The appearance of sleep spindles is associated with the loss of perceptual awareness, and for many researchers the appearance of the first sleep spindle during Stage 2 signals that the individual has truly fallen asleep (Steriade, McCormick, & Segnowski, 1993).

A *k-complex* is a biphasic wave form beginning with an initial, sharp negative wave followed by positive components. Although you are soundly asleep by this stage, you could still be awakened easily. In light of this, it is interesting to note that if you were to be awakened as soon as four minutes into this stage, you would most probably report that you had been asleep (Bonnet & Moore, 1982).

By Stage 3 sleep your physiological signs, such as muscle tonus, heart rate, blood pressure, and body temperature all show signs of decreasing. You are now soundly asleep, and it would take a relatively strong stimulus to awaken you. The onset and termination of this stage are defined by the percentage of delta wave activity on the EEG recording. Against the background of desynchronous cortical brain-wave activity, punctuated by the k-complexes and sleep spindles of Stage 2, delta waves begin to appear. Stage 3 sleep begins when at least 20 percent of the EEG is composed of delta-wave activity.

During Stage 3 the frequency of delta wave activity continues to increase until more than 50 percent of the EEG consists of these slow waves. When this occurs, you have entered Stage 4 sleep. You are now in a very deep state of sleep, and you would be extremely difficult to awaken. If aroused during this stage, you would appear somewhat disoriented, and it would take a little time for you to become conscious of your surroundings. If allowed to sleep uninterrupted, you would begin to drift from Stage 4 into Stage 3 and then into Stage 2.

About every 30 to 90 minutes throughout the night, the sleeping subject passes from Stage 2 into REM sleep, and this passage is announced by both EEG and physiological changes. The EEG during this stage consists of relatively low-voltage, mixed frequencies, punctuated by occasional bursts of alpha activity. If you think that this description of EEG activity sounds familiar, you are correct. In fact, because the EEG of REM sleep resembles that of Stage 1 so closely, this stage of sleep is often called *paradoxical* sleep. Although the EEG pattern is similar to that of Stage 1 sleep, it would be much more difficult to arouse you from Stage REM than it would be from Stage 1.

The term **REM sleep** coined first by Dement, refers to the fact that the sleeper's eyes can be seen darting back and forth beneath closed eyelids at a rate of approximately 50–60 times per minute (Dement & Kleitman, 1957). Since this rapid eye movement occurs during dreaming, one might expect that the eye movements are linked to the visual aspects of the dream. It is almost as if the dreamer were viewing a private movie. Some researchers, however, now believe that rapid eye movements simply reflect the overflow of the individual's activated nervous system (Chase & Morales, 1983).

In addition to changes in the EEG and the *electrooculogram* (EOG), a record of eye movement, other bodily changes also occur during REM sleep. Respiration and pulse rates increase and become irregular during this stage. Blood pressure also increases. Finally, male subjects often experience penile erections during Stage REM sleep. The sleeper shows a profound loss of muscle tonus, although twitches or spasms in the limbs are often observed. That terrifying sensation of being frozen to the spot while someone is chasing you, or of opening your mouth to scream but being unable to utter a sound, may have a basis in the reality that we are, in fact, unable to move our muscles while we are dreaming.

This "dreamer's paralysis" may be due to a brain chemical that inhibits the motor neurons that ordinarily cause our muscles to contract (Chase, 1981a, 1981b). Quite probably, this paralysis is what prevents us from acting out our dream activity, which might be very dangerous (Moore-Ede, Sulzman, & Fuller, 1982). The sleeper's movement, of which all of us who have shared a bed with another are very much aware, takes place between these REM periods. This movement occurs about every 15 minutes, or between 20 and 40 times each night. Although we might think the opposite to be true, poor sleepers tend to move less and spend more time on their backs than do good sleepers (De Koninck, Gagnon, & Lallier, 1983).

Earlier, we mentioned what has come to be one of the most fascinating characteristics of REM sleep: *dreaming*. Having observed that during the course of a night's sleep the subject's eyes periodically moved back and forth rapidly, Aserinsky and Kleitman (1953) began to awaken and question subjects during both REM and non-REM (NREM) sleep. The investigators observed that 74 percent of the subjects reported detailed accounts of their dreams when awakened during REM sleep, while only 7 percent were able to report their dreams when awakened during any other sleep stage. Foulkes (1962b) reported that when people in sleep laboratories were awakened from

Awake

Stage 1

Stage 2

Stage 3

Stage 4

Stage REM

Figure 7.4 • EEG Recordings from the Frontal Lobe of Stages of Wakefulness and Sleep

REM periods, they reported dreaming on the average of 80 percent of the time; in some cases, the percentage was closer to 100.

Hong, Potkin, Callaghan, and Gillin (1997) provided further support for the relationship between REM sleep eye movements and dream visual imagery. They propose that the scanning of the visual imagery in dreams is accomplished in a manner similar to the scanning of real objects during waking visual perception and, as in the case of wakefulness, is an automatic process that normally does not give rise to awareness of the direction of the gaze. Farthing (1992) states that not only are dreams more frequent during REM sleep, they are also more vivid, emotional, and storylike.

While these findings forced the conclusion that dreaming does occur during REM periods, they did not negate the possibility that dreaming could occur during NREM periods as well. Foulkes (1962a) and Rechtschaffen, Verdone, and Wheaton (1963) have provided results indicating that dreaming does in fact occur during NREM states but that these dreams are more difficult to recall on awakening than those that occur during REM periods. EEG records obtained during each of the sleep stages are shown in Figure 7.4.

A number of investigators have suggested that the diverging function, physiology, and mentation of REM and NREM sleep may be related to cortical lateralization, which we discussed in chapter 2 (Goldstein, Stolzfus, & Gardocki, 1972; Gruzelier & Flor-Henry, 1979; McCarley & Hobson, 1979). In an early EEG study, Goldstein et al. (1972) obtained results that were interpreted as indicating greater right-hemisphere involvement in REM sleep and greater left-hemisphere activation during NREM sleep. However, attempts to further substantiate unihemispheric predominance during sleep have been for the most part unsuccessful.

Armitage, Hoffman, Loewy, and Moffitt (1989) found significant differences between slow-wave, Stage 2, and REM sleep, demonstrating that slow-wave sleep evidenced more asymmetrical activity than either Stage 2 or REM sleep. Also, REM sleep was associated with the smallest asymmetries. Such results do not support the notion of a right-hemisphere REM/left-hemisphere NREM relationship. The finding of significant differences in hemispheric asymmetry between Stage 2 and slow-wave sleep may also indicate functional differences within NREM sleep stages.

There are wide, individual variations in patterns of sleep, but most adults complete a full cycle of sleep stages every 90–120 minutes. If a night's sleep in the laboratory is a typical one, most deep sleep (Stages 3 and 4) occurs during the first third of the sleep period, while the bulk of the REM sleep occurs during the final third of the night (Hartmann, 1973). As the night progresses, the length of each REM period increases, while Stages 3 and 4 diminish and all but disappear (see Figure 7.5).

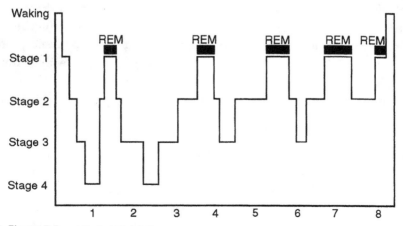

Figure 7.5 • A Typical Night's Sleep

More than 22 million Americans work a shift other than the regular day shift (American Sleep Disorders Association, 1994). Work schedules that include night work greatly interfere with the sleep/waking pattern. Both survey and EEG studies demonstrate that morning sleep after a night shift is short and unrefreshing (Torsvall, Akerstedt, Gillander, & Knutsson, 1989). A few survey studies have also examined compensatory naps during days with short main sleep periods (Akerstedt & Torsvall, 1985; Evans, Cooke, Orne, & Orne, 1977). These naps contained a large proportion of slow-wave sleep and were apparently caused by the sleep deficit after the short main sleep period (Torsvall et al., 1989).

Another major negative effect of night work is the increase in perceived sleepiness, particularly during work. This sleepiness, which is normally at its maximum during the last half of the night shift (Akerstedt, Torsvall, & Gillberg, 1982), can lead to deterioration of performance (Mitler et al., 1988; Torsvall et al., 1989). The latter is of special importance in work situations in which the individual must take responsibility for human lives or for objects of great economic value.

Sleep patterns have also been noted to vary with age. Morewitz (1988), for example, has observed that age-related changes contribute to the excessive daytime sleepiness often observed in the elderly. Despite the fact that they represent only 12 percent of the population, it has recently been observed that the elderly in the United States receive 35–40 percent of the sedative-hypnotic drugs that are prescribed (Moran, Thompson, & Neis, 1988). Webb and Agnew (1971), however, found that the percentage of total time spent in Stage 4 sleep decreases as a function of age. Also, other investigators (Korner, 1968; Roffwarg, Muzio, & Dement, 1966) have observed similar decreases in percentage of total time spent in Stage REM sleep as the individual grows older. Monk, Reynolds, Buysse, and Hoch (1991) compared 34 healthy older adults, aged 80–91 years, who were self-described good sleepers with 30 young controls with regard to sleep habits. Using such measures as the Horne and Ostberg Morningness Questionnaire, the Circadian Type Questionnaire, the Eysenck Personality Questionnaire, a two-week sleep diary, and polysomnographic (e.g., EEG, EOG, and EMG measures), these investigators found that by almost all laboratory measures, the older group slept poorly compared with the young. They also found that compared with the younger subjects, the older subjects evidenced earlier habitual times of waking up and a lack of flexibility in sleep patterns. Correlations between sleep and health status, however, suggested that at least some of these differences might be attributed to illness rather than age. Moran et al. (1988) suggest that before drug intervention is initiated with this particular age group, both physicians and patients need to be made aware of the normal sleep changes that occur as a function of aging.

Finally, it is also known that the sleep pattern can be dramatically altered by ischemic strokes. In 1988, Rakhindzhanov, Gafurov, and Matkhalikov demonstrated that the structure of nocturnal sleep in stroke victims differs significantly from that of normal people in a number of parameters, including greater amounts of dream-state sleep, shorter REM-sleep latency periods, and a shortened sleep-spindle stage. However, strokes or other types of brain damage have not been found to abolish sleep altogether.

Sleep Restriction and Too Much Sleep

Recent data from the National Health and Nutrition Examination Survey (NHANES) suggests that approximately 40 percent of adults 20–59 years of age get fewer than 7 hours of sleep per night (Wheaton, Liu, Perry, & Croft, 2011). There is evidence to suggest that lack of sleep has detrimental consequences. However, it is important to note that harmful effects typically occur only when sleep is restricted to fewer than six hours per night. Some effects of severe sleep restriction (less than six hours per night) include cognitive and behavioral deficits such as the inability to concentrate and remember, impaired driving ability, and reported inability to manage financial affairs (Wheaton et al., 2011). Significant lack of sleep has also been associated with increased mortality and morbidity (National Sleep Foundation, 2010; Youngstedt & Kripke, 2004).

Recently, it has been proposed that lack of sleep can promote obesity. Let's evaluate some of the evidence briefly. Knutson and colleagues (2007) suggest that the increase in diabetes and obesity observed in the United States over the last three decades corresponds with a trend to decrease sleep. Several recent reviews have found evidence to support a relationship between decreased sleep and increased body-mass index (BMI) in both children and adults (Cappuccio et al., 2008; von Kries, Toschke, Wurmser, Sauerwald, & Koletzko, 2002).

Experiments of extreme sleep restriction—limiting sleep to only four to five hours per night—have found altered glucose metabolism, increased insulin resistance, increased appetite, and increased calorie conservation (Knutson, Speigel, Penev, & Van Cauter, 2007). A study of over 1,000 individuals found that people sleeping five hours per night exhibited decreased leptin and increased gherlin levels compared to those sleeping eight hours (Taheri, Lin,

Austin, Young, & Mignot, 2004). Leptin and gherlin play important roles in hunger and satiation, which may stimulate appetite and motivate calorie consumption in short sleepers. Fewer hours asleep may also provide more time awake in which to consume calories.

However, these findings are not always supported. Marshall, Glozier, and Grunstein (2008) reviewed data from 17 studies that together tested over 1 million people worldwide, and found great variability in the data, with only four of the 17 experiments reporting increased BMI or waist circumference for short sleepers. Further, there are no empirical studies demonstrating that more hours asleep can decrease BMI. The remaining 13 studies reviewed by Marshall and colleagues found either no effects, or increased BMI for both short *and* long sleepers.

Indeed, there is evidence suggesting that *too much* sleep can be detrimental. Youngstedt and Kripke (2004) compiled data from over 1 million people followed for six years, and found that people who slept more than eight hours per night had higher mortality rates than people who slept seven hours. It is unclear what mechanisms are responsible for higher mortality found in long sleepers. It may be due to the increased time spent sedentary; long sleepers spend an average of 1–2 more hours asleep and inactive. Long sleepers further tend to lead more sedentary lifestyles overall (Basner et al., 2007), which may contribute to decreased longevity. Whatever the mechanism, it has been recommended that sleep should be purposefully restricted to less than eight hours per night as a preventative health measure, just as calorie restriction might be used to keep weight optimal (Youngstedt & Kripke, 2004).

Based on these and other findings suggesting that both long and short sleep may be detrimental, it appears that adults should strive to achieve an optimal level of 6–7.5 hours of sleep at night. But what about napping—can time lost from sleep at night be regained through daytime naps? This question is addressed in the next section.

Napping

Research shows that naps can decrease sleepiness and improve cognitive function, at least in people who nap regularly. Brief naps (5–15 minutes) increase reports of restfulness, and can improve performance on cognitive tasks learned either before the nap (Takashima et al., 2006) or after the nap (Axmacher, Haupt, Fenandez, Elger, & Fell, 2008). The effects may last 1–3 hours (Lovato & Lack, 2010). Naps longer than 30 minutes usually decrease performance and cognitive function, and also increase reported tiredness, immediately after the nap. However, within 30 minutes of waking, performance is improved, and the benefits of longer naps may last for several hours (Lovato & Lack, 2010). Stickgold and colleagues reported increases in skill-learning following long naps of 60–90 minutes (Mednick, Nakayama, & Stickgold, 2003).

Nonetheless, these findings should be interpreted with caution. Little research has systematically investigated the effects of napping, including timing of the nap (that is, at what time of day, or during what point in a person's circadian rhythm the nap is taken). Also, apparently some people just are not nappers; trying to force naps in nonnappers may actually decrease performance (Lovato & Lack, 2010). Nappers have also been shown to have greater levels of obesity and cardiovascular risk (Owens et al., 2010). The nappers in this study exhibited lower levels of nighttime sleep, so it is possible that overall lack of sleep, or overall decreases in activity level, contributed to these physiological effects. We look forward to additional controlled research on the effects of napping.

Sleep Deprivation

Most of us try to allow ourselves between six and eight hours of sleep per night, and recent research notes the benefits of trying to achieve this optimal level of sleep (Knudson et al., 2007; Youngstedt & Kripke, 2004). But what happens if we pull an "all-nighter," or totally deprive ourselves of sleep? Sleep deprivation occurs when we have gone without sleep for 24 hours.

If we miss a night's sleep or greatly reduce the amount of sleep for any reason, we feel ill-used and tend to express such feelings the next day in the form of irritability, inattentiveness, and generally lackluster performance. If we can agree that this is a common experience when we have been deprived of a single night's repose, then the next question might well be: What are the consequences of more prolonged periods of sleep deprivation?

Sleep deprivation studies with both human and animal subjects were performed as early as the 1890s. However, it was not until the 1950s that sleep researchers began to focus attention on this problem. Certainly, one major impetus to this sudden surge of research had to be newly acquired knowledge that in certain countries, prolonged periods of sleep deprivation, combined with emotional and physical abuse, were being used to induce personality disorders in noncooperative prisoners of the state.

Can prolonged periods of "sleep starvation" actually alter our normal state of consciousness? If such effects do occur, what is their nature? Are they relatively transitory or permanent? These are the sorts of questions that the sleep researchers tried to answer in a variety of ways.

A frequently cited example of sleep deprivation is Peter Tripp's bid in the early 1960s to stay awake for 200 consecutive hours to raise money for the March of Dimes. Tripp, a New York disk jockey, made daily broadcasts from his booth at Times Square, where crowds gathered to watch him. During the course of his self-imposed sleep starvation, Tripp was given medical and neurological examinations, performance tests, and psychological tests. He was watched closely by a number of sleep researchers, including Dement, Lubin, and Wolff. Almost from the beginning, Tripp had to fight off a strong tendency to go to sleep. As he neared the halfway mark (100 hours), it became evident that he was experiencing great difficulty in terms of memory, attention, and even simple mental tasks. He also had visual hallucinations. Luce (1965) described the last day of Tripp's 200-hour sleepless period:

> By 170 hours the agony had become almost unbearable to watch. At times Tripp was no longer sure he was himself, and frequently tried to gain proof of his identity. Although he behaved as if he were awake, his brain patterns resembled those of sleep. In his psychotic delusions he was convinced that the doctors were in a conspiracy against him to send him to jail. On the last morning of his wakeathon, Tripp was examined by Dr. Wolff of Cornell. The late Dr. Wolff had a somewhat archaic manner of dress, and to Tripp he must have appeared funereal. Tripp undressed, as requested, and lay down on the table for medical examination, but as he gazed up at the doctor he came to the gruesome decision that the man was actually an undertaker, about to bury him alive. With this grim insight, Tripp leapt for the door, and tore into the Astor hall with several doctors in pursuit. At the end of the 200 sleepless hours, nightmare, hallucination, and reality had merged, and he felt he was the victim of a sadistic conspiracy among the doctors.
>
> With some persuasion, Tripp managed to make a final appearance in the glass-windowed booth in Times Square, and after his broadcast he went to sleep for 13 hours. (pp. 19–20)

When Tripp awoke from his recovery sleep, the terrors, hallucinations, and mental deterioration had vanished. A three-month mild depression was the only residual effect he experienced.

Five years later, a 17-year-old high school student, Randy Gardner, made an effort to break the record for consecutive hours of wakefulness. He was highly motivated and in excellent health. The attempt was made in the familiar confines of his own home, and he had the aid of two schoolmates and Dr. William Dement. Under these conditions, Gardner was able to exceed the *Guinness Book of World Records* listing of 260 hours by four hours. Although Randy experienced some memory lapses, irritability, and difficulty in concentrating, he demonstrated no psychotic behavior or serious emotional change during the entire period. Dement and his colleagues did note that Randy experienced some neurological difficulties, including blurred vision, involuntary eye movements, and an EEG pattern that resembled a sleeping person, regardless of whether his eyes were open or closed (Johnson, Slye, & Dement, 1965).

Having set his record, Randy held a press conference and then went to bed, where he spent the next 14½ hours in a sleep dominated by Stages 4 and REM. On awakening, he appeared to have suffered no ill effects from his ordeal.

Why the differences in the effects of sleep deprivation between Peter Tripp and Randy Gardner? The lack of experimental controls in these observations makes it extremely difficult to pinpoint any single factor. However, a list of possible explanations would include age, physical health, prestudy psychological make-up, setting, and the kinds of demands placed on the subjects during their ordeals.

Laboratory research suggests that during total sleep deprivation, subjects may evidence decrements in performance. To account for such performance deficits, Williams and Lubin (1959) proposed a lapse hypothesis. They suggested that a subject under total sleep deprivation demonstrated an uneven slowing of performance that led to an eventual absence of the appropriate task-related response. Edwards (1941) observed that highly motivated sleep-deprived subjects were able to maintain an acceptable level of task performance, but only with tremendous difficulty. Goleman (1982) observed that when confronted with complex and interesting tasks, sleep-deprived subjects may evidence a very small drop in performance level.

While the underlying mechanisms still are not fully understood, it is clear from laboratory findings that sleep starvation is accompanied by impairment of memory. Though it generally has been accepted that sleep deprivation affects short-term memory (Lubin, Moses, Johnson, & Naitoh, 1974), Vojtechovsky, Safratova, Votava, and Feit (1971) have presented evidence to suggest that long-term memory also may be impaired.

Finally, laboratory research (Hartmann, Baekeland, Zwilling, & Hop, 1971; Webb & Agnew, 1974) has shown that when total sleep time is reduced, the amount of time actually spent in Stage 4 does not decrease. In fact, if the reduction is severe, Stage 4 time may actually increase (Dement & Greenberg, 1966; Johnson & MacLeod, 1973). Therefore it should not be surprising to find that the better predictor of slow-wave sleep rebound following sleep reduction is not the amount of slow-wave sleep lost but rather the total duration of sleep (Lucidi, Devoto, Violani, Mastraceli, & Bertini, 1997).

Until now, we have dealt with the effects of total sleep loss. One might also ask what would be the effects of a more selective deprivation—say, deprivation of a single stage of sleep. Dement (1960) was one of the first researchers to deprive subjects selectively of Stage REM sleep. In his research, adults were allowed to sleep normally in the laboratory, except that whenever a subject entered Stage REM, he or she was awakened by the investigator, then allowed to return to sleep. Dement continued this procedure for five successive nights. He observed that with the passage of time, subjects had to be awakened more frequently, indicating that progressive deprivation of REM sleep increases the tendency to enter REM sleep. During their first normal night's sleep the REM-deprived subjects spent approximately 60 percent more time in REM sleep than they had during a comparable prestudy baseline period. This phenomenon was called the **REM-rebound effect**, since it appeared as though subjects were trying to make up for the lost Stage REM sleep. The REM-rebound effect has since been replicated many times (Brunner, Kijk, Tobler, & Borbely, 1990; Clemes & Dement, 1967; Dement, Greenberg, & Klein, 1966; Sampson, 1966).

Fisher (1966) noted that penile erections, which normally occur during Stage REM sleep, begin to occur during NREM sleep in REM-sleep-deprived male subjects. Tilley and Empson (1978) found that human memory may be affected subtly by Stage REM deprivation. Nevertheless, Webb (1974) suggested that, contrary to early studies (Dement & Greenberg, 1966), REM-sleep deprivation studies have failed to demonstrate any harmful psychological effects.

Sleep Learning

Passing from a conscious state of wakefulness to one of sleep does not mean a sudden cessation of brain activity. It has been demonstrated that we are not completely unaware of our environment during sleep (Arkin & Antrobus, 1978; Goodenough, Witkin, Koulack, & Cohen, 1975).

This knowledge that the brain still functions during sleep was probably all the impetus researchers needed to explore the possibility of learning during sleep, **hypnopedia**. Wouldn't it be wonderful if you could turn on a cassette by your bed at night and wake up the next morning with a head full of facts? While a great many claims have been made for the effectiveness of sleep learning, laboratory findings have failed to offer much support for such claims (Emmons & Simon, 1956). Webb and Cartwright (1978) observed that "no study has been able to show convincingly an ability to learn complex verbal material during sleep" (p. 227). Reviewing the research literature on hypno-pedia, Aarons (1976) and Webb and Cartwright (1978) observed that many of these studies were poorly controlled. Adequately controlled studies do in-dicate, however, that while the subject does not actually learn material that is presented during sleep (with accompanying sleep brain-wave patterns), learn-ing such material when awake (beta waves) appears to be facilitated slightly as compared with the rate at which similar, but new, material is learned. In short, there appears to be a positive savings score on learning similar material.

Sleep and Memory

While little research supports the idea that people can learn in their sleep, a great deal of evidence points to the importance of sleep for memory. Thus, one primary function of sleep may be to consolidate and store information that is learned throughout the day.

It has been known for a long time that retention of recently learned in-formation is generally better when learning is followed by a brief period of sleep rather than a period of wakefulness (Benson & Feinberg, 1977). Once paradoxical sleep was discovered, a strong interest developed in its possible role. A large body of evidence now establishes relations between paradoxi-cal sleep and memory. It has been demonstrated in a variety of animals that increases in paradoxical sleep over normal levels occur following successful learning (Bloch, Hennevin, & Leconte, 1979; Gisquet-Verrier, & Smith, 1989; Hennevin, Hars, & Bloch, 1989; Smith, 1985). Also, deprivation of par-adoxical sleep, at the times of extraparadoxical sleep following training, result in learning deficits (Gisquet-Verrier, & Smith, 1989; Hennevin et al., 1989; Pearlman, 1979; Smith, 1985). Unfortunately, any such theory attempting to explain the function of REM sleep must be able to adequately explain why *tricyclic antidepressant drugs* do not severely disrupt behavior. A class of drugs that is commonly prescribed for the treatment of depression and for some REM-sleep-related disorders, tricyclic antidepressants prevent the individual from experiencing REM sleep for months at a time, yet no side effects are experienced that can be explained by REM sleep loss (Pinel, 1997).

Several recent reviews eloquently describe the state of research on sleep and memory (Axmacher et al., 2009; Maquet, 2001; Poe, Walsh, & Bjorness, 2010; Stickgold, Hobson, Fosse, & Fosse, 2001; Stickgold & Walker, 2005; Walker & Stickgold, 2004). One thing is clear: sleep deprivation can disrupt memory, while periods of sleep can facilitate memory. Less clear is the exact influence that sleep has on memory. Not all research replicated those early studies of the effects of REM and NREM sleep deprivation and memory.

As a result, recent research has focused on elucidating the specific role that REM and NREM sleep may have for consolidating procedural and declarative memory, respectively. Procedural or nondeclarative memory involves skill learning. In the laboratory, skill learning tasks often involve visual discrimination (distinguishing between two or more visual stimuli), mirror-tracing, or learning finger tapping sequences. Declarative memory refers to purposeful memory for events or facts, and in the laboratory, often involves remembering lists of words.

Research investigating procedural learning including has found that REM sleep is critically involved. Disrupting REM (Axmacher et al., 2009; Smith, 2001; Stickgold, James, & Hobson, 2000; Stickgold, Scott, Rittenhouse, & Hobson, 1999) but not NREM slow-wave sleep (Smith & Butler, 1982) decreased performance on procedural memory tasks. Long naps that contained a REM period also enhanced procedural memory (Backhaus & Junghanns, 2006).

Alternatively, NREM sleep appears necessary for consolidating declarative memories. Declarative memory tasks, such as learning lists of words or remembering spatial locations, are disrupted by loss of sleep early in the night (when sleep is dominated by NREM periods), but are not generally affected by loss of REM sleep (Axmacher et al., 2009; Plihal & Born, 1997). Brief naps that include only NREM sleep have been found to facilitate declarative but not procedural memory (Tucker et al., 2006).

As mentioned above, one significant anomaly that has plagued research on the involvement of REM sleep and memory are antidepressant drugs. Most antidepressant medications significantly disrupt REM sleep, but they do not impair memory (Pinel, 1997). Indeed, one recent study found increases in both procedural and declarative memory following REM-suppression induced by selective serotonin and noradrenergic antidepressants (Rasch, Pommer, Diekelman, & Born, 2008).

These findings regarding antidepressant drugs, REM sleep disruption, and memory represent a continuous challenge to interpreting results from studies on the involvement of sleep and memory formation. Thus, while there are supporters of a REM–NREM dissociation between procedural and declarative memory (Axmacher et al., 2009), memory may depend on a rich association between both slow-wave NREM and REM periods during sleep (Smith, 2001; Walker & Stickgold, 2004). As described below, much memory formation may depend on fast-wave neural oscillations in the hippocampus, which seem to occur primarily during early stages (stages 1–2) of NREM sleep.

Neural Correlates of Sleep and Memory

A variety of neural evidence from both animals and humans supports memory formation during sleep. In animals, single-cell recording studies have demonstrated patterns of neural activity during sleep that mimic patterns of activity that occurred during learning (Wilson & McNaughton, 1994). These findings have led to a "replay hypothesis"—that during sleep, when stimulation by external information is at a minimum, neuronal assemblies activated while we were awake become reactivated in a similar, albeit quicker, pattern, to promote memory consolidation and storage. Phase synchronization of neural assemblies—that is, collections of neurons that fire rhythmically together, likely form the neural basis for memory. Rhythmic firings of neuronal assemblies are referred to as oscillations, and recent research is demonstrating the importance of neural oscillations for learning and memory, both while awake and asleep (Axmacher et al., 2009; Fell & Axmacher, 2011). Synchronization of neural oscillations provides a mechanism for neurons to communicate with each other. Phase-locked oscillations represent qualities (e.g., post-synaptic firing within 20ms of presynaptic discharge) necessary for long-term potentiation (LTP) and long-term depression (LTD), the mechanisms by which neurons increase and decrease their synaptic connectivity to promote learning and memory (e.g., Bliss & Collingridge, 1993). This process has also been referred to as *synaptic scaling*, and it may be the mechanism by which the brain develops integrated neural networks (Krueger et al., 2008).

One interesting finding is that while we sleep, and especially while we're in slow-wave sleep, very fast (~200Hz) spike-waves called ripples can be observed in the hippocampus in very brief bursts (less than 20ms). Ego-Stengel and Wilson (2010) showed that disrupting the onset of these spike-wave ripples disrupted memory for a spatial task in rats. Thus it appears that activation or reactivation of these fast-spike hippocampal neural assemblies during sleep is important for memory.

In humans, it is difficult to study hippocampal spike waves due to the subcortical location of the hippocampus (non-invasive recording techniques like EEG can only record from cortical areas). However, some studies have examined hippocampal activity in epileptic patients who had subcortical electrodes implanted for the purpose of examining their seizures (Clemens et al., 2007; Urrestarazu, Chander, Debeau, & Gottman, 2007; Staba et al., 2004). These studies have verified that humans also exhibit hippocampal fast ripples between 40–180Hz. Ripples occur during both wakefulness and NREM sleep, especially during stages 1 and 2 (Clemens et al., 2007; Staba et al., 2004). Axmacher and colleagues (2009) suggest that the fact that ripples occur during wakefulness and sleep indicates that neural reactivation works to promote memory consolidation both while awake and during NREM sleep. This may explain why disrupting sleep does not totally abolish memory; some memory formation may happen while awake. However, memory consolidation during wakefulness is probably limited by processing of incoming information, which limits the time neurons may devote to storing learned information.

To summarize, it appears that neuronal activation during sleep may function to promote memory consolidation. Sleep deprivation can inhibit memory, while learning may lead to longer periods of REM sleep. It remains unclear exactly what role NREM and REM sleep have on memory consolidation. However, it may be that our brain takes advantage of minimal input while asleep to do some "off-line" reprocessing that may promote neural plasticity. This neural plasticity may form the basis of memory consolidation and storage. Evidence in both animals and humans note that neuronal assemblies activated during learning become reactivated during NREM sleep. Fast-spike ripples—brief bursts of 80–200 Hz brainwaves in the hippocampus, may provide the neural basis for this memory formation.

Sleep Disorders

Before closing this discussion of sleep, we need to take a sample from what is, perhaps, the most dramatic aspect of this phenomenon: sleep disorders; that is, disorders of consciousness.

One of the most common of the sleep disorders is insomnia. On the average, 33 percent of American adults complain of insomnia to some degree and 17 percent believe that their symptoms are serious (Pressman, 1991). Dement (1972) refers to insomnia as "an illness that is caused by the treatment." The very sleeping pill the doctor prescribes to regulate the patient's sleep may well produce the sleep disturbance. Initially, the sleep medication may cause a suppression of REM sleep; but if the dosage is not increased, this effect will eventually habituate. As you might expect, once medication is discontinued, the individual experiences a tremendous REM-rebound effect. The sudden increase in REM sleep leads to sleeplessness that is often accompanied by vivid nightmares (Oswald, 1968). Now the patient is convinced that he or she has a bad case of insomnia and so returns to the sleeping pill, and the cycle begins once more. Over-the-counter drugs do no more good than sugarcoated pills and are only as effective as people's faith that they will help (Webb & Bonnet, 1979). The danger with these drugs is that people who regularly use sleeping pills also run the risk of psychological and physical drug dependence (Spielman & Herrera, 1991). Because they may not produce the desired effect, the frustrated insomniac may take more than what is recommended. This can lead to serious medical problems.

While insomnia may take several forms, each form results in the same thing: a loss of sleep. The individual may experience great difficulty in initially falling asleep. This is sometimes referred to as a *sleep-onset disorder.* Other forms of insomnia include a tendency to wake up repeatedly during the night and to wake up very early in the morning, then be unable to go back to sleep. Regardless of the form, people with insomnia typically feel very sleepy during the daytime, and many sufferers consider this the most serious aspect of their problem (Coleman et al., 1982).

Approximately 25 percent of all insomniacs complain that they get little sleep, even though when they are brought into the sleep laboratory, their EEGs show normal sleep patterns. These patients suffer from a condition called *subjective insomnia.* If these people are aroused during Stage 2 sleep, they are more likely to say that they were awake when called than sound sleepers are (Borkovec, Lane, & VanDot, 1981; Trinder, 1988). They are able to give detailed accounts of their thoughts during sleep and often can describe accurately any sounds that occurred while they were sleeping (Engle-Friedman, Baker, & Bootzin, 1985). It seems clear that these insomniacs monitor the environment as normal sleepers do, but they are unable to shut these stimuli out of their sleeping consciousness.

As we have already observed, problems arise when sleeping pills are used to treat insomnia. It is only logical, then, that investigators would eventually begin the search for a more effective therapy with fewer side effects. Comparing the effectiveness of various behavioral therapies, Espie, Lindsay, Brooks, and Hood (1989) discovered that the techniques of progressive relaxation and stimulus control both produced significant improvement; however, the nature of the treatment gains varied. Stimulus control procedures improved the patient's sleep pattern, whereas progressive relaxation affected the patient's perception of the quality of his or her sleep.

Morawetz (1989), in a controlled study designed to evaluate a commercially available self-help treatment for insomnia based on stimulus control and progressive relaxation principles, observed that for individuals who were not taking sleep medication, this self-help program was clinically effective. However, for those taking sleep medication, the program had to be supplemented by professional assistance to be fully effective. Other investigators have demonstrated that various behavioral strategies are effective in alleviating insomnia (Lacks & Powlishta, 1989).

Another sleep disorder, *sleep apnea,* was identified first by Gastaut and Broughton (1965) in patients who complained of hypersomnia. Sleep apnea has been found to occur in about 40 percent of elderly people but is less common in younger adults (Coleman et al., 1981). As the name suggests, sleep apnea is characterized by brief periods during which the sleeping person stops breathing. These periods generally last from 15 to 60 seconds.

For the person who suffers from sleep apnea, the change from the waking to the sleeping state has the effect of turning off the respiratory centers of the brain. This causes the muscles necessary for breathing, the diaphragm and the intercostal muscle, to stop working. Under such conditions there can be no exchange of oxygen and carbon dioxide, so the amount of oxygen carried by the red blood cells decreases to extremely low levels while the carbon dioxide in the blood continues to increase. In response to these changes in blood-gas levels, the respiratory centers of the central nervous system and the respiratory muscles begin to function once more.

However, there is yet another problem. Because the loss of muscle tonus that normally accompanies sleep is exaggerated in sleep apnea, the throat collapses, effectively cutting off the flow of air to the lungs. Thus, oxygen levels continue to decrease and carbon dioxide levels increase until they reach dangerous levels and the individual is briefly aroused. After a series of gasping breaths, during which time the blood gases return to normal levels, the patient goes back to sleep, and the cycle begins again (Dement, 1972). The specific cause of sleep apnea is as yet unknown. Major treatments may include a *tracheotomy* (a surgical opening in the windpipe), major weight loss, and drugs (Kalat, 1992).

Narcolepsy is another common sleep disorder. It is more technically known as *disorder of excessive somnolence* (Levinthal, 1990). Generally, narcolepsy shows up for the first time between ages 10 to 25 and may last throughout life. There are approximately 250,000 narcoleptics in the United States (Dement

& Baird, 1977; Fenton, 1975). The individual suffering from narcolepsy experiences sudden and recurrent attacks of sleep and the desire to sleep during the waking hours. Many narcoleptics have difficulty differentiating between sleep and waking states (Browman & Mitler, 1988), and most experience other periodic disorders that occur frequently enough to be included as part of the narcolepsy syndrome. These disorders include cataplexy, sleep paralysis, and hypnogogic hallucinations.

Cataplexy refers to a sudden loss of muscle tonus and postural reflexes. During these seizures the patient is fully awake and aware of what is happening in the environment. *Sleep paralysis* is an inability to move that occurs while falling asleep or awakening. *Hypnogogic hallucinations* are very vivid, often frightening dreams that occur at the onset of sleep. Some three to four hours after waking, the narcoleptic feels overcome by sleepiness and often falls asleep while talking, standing, or simply moving about. Initially, a number of episodes that might be described as microsleep, or sleep periods lasting from five to 15 seconds, will be experienced, but eventually, the narcoleptic is forced to take a nap.

Earlier in this chapter, we noted that the normal onset of sleep is characterized by NREM brain-wave activity. Laboratory studies have demonstrated that narcoleptics begin their night's sleep with a REM phase (Rechtschaffen, Wolpert, Dement, Mitchell, & Fisher, 1963). These results led Rechtschaffen and colleagues to predict that the narcoleptic's daytime sleep attacks may well be attacks of REM sleep—a prediction that was later confirmed in the laboratory (Rechtschaffen & Dement, 1969). The exact cause of this condition is unknown. However, findings such as those cited above led Dement, Holman, and Guilleminault (1976) to suggest that narcolepsy may be a physiological defect in the REM sleep-control mechanism. Although we do not at present know the precise cause of or the adequate treatment for narcolepsy, we do know that it is not associated with any kind of emotional disorder, runs in families, and may be a genetic disturbance.

Nocturnal panic, another sleep disorder, involves a sudden awakening from sleep in a state of panic characterized by various somatic sensations of sympathetic arousal and intense subjective fear (Craske & Barlow, 1989). Despite the fact that approximately 18 percent of all spontaneous panic attacks occur from a sleeping state, the phenomenon of nocturnal panic has received little research attention (Taylor, Sheikh, & Agras, 1986). Empirical evidence of this phenomenon has been based largely on accidental findings from the examination of naturally occurring panic attacks over 24-hour periods (Margraf, Taylor, & Ehlers, 1987; Taylor et al., 1986) and from sleep laboratory studies

(Hauri, 1985; Lesser, Poland, Holcomb, & Rose, 1985). Nocturnal panics have been found to occur during light, non-REM sleep (Gastaut, Dongier, Broughton, & Tassinari, 1964) and during delta sleep (Hauri, Friedman, Ravaris, & Fisher, 1985; Lesser et al., 1985).

Several sleep disorders predominantly affect children, including sleepwalking, bed-wetting, and night terrors. Some 15 percent of all children between the ages of 5 and 12 sleepwalk at least once, and some 1 to 6 percent do it regularly (Anders, Carskado, & Dement, 1980). Children who suffer from sleepwalking, or *somnambulism,* usually go to sleep normally, but sometime during the night, they arise and walk in their sleep. Because the skeletal muscles are paralyzed during REM sleep, sleepwalkers do not actually act out their dreams. Instead, sleepwalking occurs during Stage 3 and Stage 4 sleep and therefore is more likely to occur during the first third of the night (Kefauver & Guilleminault, 1994). If unchecked, sleepwalkers may go from room to room, leave the house, and even perform rather complex tasks. During sleepwalking the child's eyes are partially or fully open, and he or she is able to avoid obstacles, listen when spoken to, and obey commands. After 15 to 30 minutes of such behavior, the sleepwalker will return to bed on his or her own. In the morning the child usually remembers none of these nocturnal events. Children of somnambulists are likely to have the same problem, a finding suggesting that this sleep disturbance has a hereditary component (Abe, Amatomi, & Oda, 1984).

Although we have been discussing sleep disorders that affect children, *REM-sleep behavior disorder* (RBD), which is similar to sleepwalking, occurs primarily in older men, the average age of onset being approximately 50 (Schenck, Hurwitz, & Mahowald, 1993). This syndrome consists of injurious or disruptive behavior that occurs during REM sleep (Schenck & Mahowald, 1990).

Nocturnal enuresis, or bed-wetting, is a childhood sleep problem that affects some 5 million children in the United States. Sleep specialists do not consider bed-wetting a disorder if the child is under the age of 5 (Friman & Warzak, 1990). This sleep disorder is often associated with dreams in which the child is urinating into a toilet. The child awakens to discover that he or she has wet the bed. Turner and Taylor (1974) estimate that as many as 4–5 million children and adolescents in the United States suffer from this embarrassing condition. Because about 15 percent per year pass through this and become continent, the older the child is, the more important treatment becomes. The guilt and shame that often accompany enuresis are also important factors in determining whether or not to treat the condition (Scharf & Jennings, 1988).

Night terrors, or *incubus attacks*, normally occur during the early part of the night and leave a child in an apparent state of terror, thrashing and screaming, unable to communicate what is wrong and completely inconsolable. Concomitant with the night terror attack is a severe physiological upheaval. Kahn, Fisher, and Edwards (1978) suggest that during severe attacks, the heart rate may almost triple. Increases in heart rate, magnitude of respiration, and skin conductance are also observed. Such episodes are generally short in duration, and the child characteristically returns to sleep once the attack passes. Despite the apparent intensity of the experience, the child often forgets it by morning.

Because at least some dream content is associated with these night terrors, it may come as a surprise that they normally occur near the end of one of the first Stage 4 (deep sleep) periods. Although the exact causes of these disorders remain unknown, a review of the literature suggests at least two hypotheses. Since night terrors are most common among children between three and eight years old, Hartmann (1981) suggests that they are linked with the development of the nervous system and may indicate a mild neurological disorder due to faulty maturation in the brainstem. Since these episodes generally disappear by adolescence, other sleep researchers (Mitler et al., 1975) recommend that when night terrors in children have no apparent cause, they should be allowed to run their course. Still other investigators say that the behavior observed in such disorders may be an expression of emotional conflicts that the child represses during the waking hours (Freud, 1933).

Night terrors and somnambulism seem to be present in young children and some adults under extreme stress. For this reason, patience, support, and reassurance at the time of sleep disruption are the treatment of preference (Arkin, 1991).

Theories of Sleep

In discussing sleep as the lowest state in our hierarchy of consciousness, we need to ask: Why do we sleep? This question has long puzzled both the layperson and the researcher. Theoretical responses to the question why we sleep have been many and varied. Rather than attempt to identify each theoretical explanation that has been offered—a task that is well beyond the scope of this chapter—we have attempted to classify these explanations into representational categories.

With the advent of new data about, and increased interest in, hematology (the study of blood) came the first categories of sleep theory, the *humoral theories.* Such theories suggest that some substance in the blood causes a dysfunction in the central nervous system that results in sleep. One theory that is representative of this category, the *circulatory theory,* suggests that sleep is a result of the brain being deprived of its normal amount of oxygen.

Several investigators, such as Bartley and Chute (1947), proposed a *reparative theory* of sleep, arguing that cortical activity that occurs during the waking period brings about cortical cellular changes. Since such cortical functions as processing sensory information, processing memory, and thinking diminish or cease during sleep, the investigators conclude that the necessary cellular repairs are made during the sleep period. A study in the early 1980s, which found an increase in slow-wave sleep and in total sleep time after running a 92-kilometer road race, seems to support this theory (Shapiro, Bortz, Mitchell, Bartel, & Jooste, 1981). Because sleep research has shown continual brain and body activity during sleep, this is probably not the entire picture.

Naturally occurring chemicals in the central nervous system have been studied to determine their possible effects on waking and sleeping. However, a "sleep toxin" has not yet been discovered (Groves & Schlesinger, 1982).

A number of years ago, sleep was described simply as a cessation of the active condition of wakefulness, not unlike the state of unconsciousness. This view of sleep has been incorporated into some modern theories. Of the modern *passive theories* of sleep, perhaps one of the best known is Lindsley's (1961) *reticular hypothesis.* According to this explanation, sleep results from the cessation of ascending impulses in the ascending reticular activating system.

In sharp contrast to the passive theories stand the *active theories* of sleep, which suggest that sleep is an active process produced by the activation of a sleep-producing system. All active theories of sleep contend that different neural mechanisms are involved in the control of wakefulness and sleeping.

Finally, some theories suggest that sleep is an evolved mechanism that has a particular survival function. One such evolutionary theory, proposed by Zepelin and Rechtschaffen (1974), contends that the sleep process evolved as a system of conserving energy. Studies of brain metabolism during sleep show that people use less energy while asleep than while awake (Madsen, 1993).

Whether it is simply energy conservation or something more important, there must be some evolutionarily adaptive function achieved by sleep. This is because sleep itself is so evolutionarily *maladaptive;* time asleep prevents organisms from engaging in other survival behaviors including mating, eating, and drinking, and makes organisms vulnerable to predators. Krueger and colleagues (2008) suggest that sleep permits the brain to make important synaptic changes, called *synaptic scaling.* As described earlier in the chapter, these neural networks may serve as the basis for learning and memory observed while organisms are awake (Ego-Stengel & Wilson, 2009; Fell & Axmacher, 2011; Maquet, 2001; Stickgold & Walker, 2005; Walker & Stickgold, 2004).

In fact, and in contrast to the earlier theories of why we sleep, evidence is accumulating to suggest that sleep is a fundamental and global property of the brain, not the result of any active or passive processes (see Kumar, 2010 for review). One main reason for this shift in view is the fact that even large lesions or strokes affecting proposed "sleep centers" of the brain do not totally abolish sleep (Datta & Maclean, 2007; John & Kumar, 1998).

Instead, the emerging view is that sleep and wakefulness are promoted by neural oscillations that occur within collections of neural assemblies or networks in the brain (Krueger et al., 2008; see also Maquet, 2001). One line of research demonstrates that columns of integrated neurons, extending through several layers of the cortex, display coherence in neural firing that correspond with EEG recordings of sleep and wakefulness. These cortical columns of neural assemblies may be in a waking or sleep state at any given time. A waking state of a cortical column exhibits neural oscillations in the high-frequency, low-amplitude range (i.e., beta waves). A sleep state is determined by neural oscillations in the low-frequency, high-amplitude (delta wave) range. Whether or not a cortical column will enter a sleep state is determined by how long that column has been in the waking state (Krueger et al., 2008). Subjective feelings of sleep may arise when a significant proportion of cortical columns are in the sleep state.

Have you ever had the feeling that you've barely slept, even though your alarm clock suggests otherwise? Laboratory studies verify that subjective bouts of insomnia are often accompanied by normal sleep EEG patterns. These discrepancies between subjective feelings of "barely sleeping" and EEG evidence reporting otherwise may be due to differential activation of the cortical columns described by Krueger and colleagues (2008). On this view, a person could have some threshold number of cortical columns in the sleep state required to induce sleep. However, a significant number of other cortical columns may remain in the awake state, which could produce subjective feelings of not really sleeping. Feelings of deep, restful sleep would be explained by a large proportion of cortical columns in the sleep state, relative to columns in the awake state.

Related to the idea that neuronal assemblies control sleep and wakefulness, are the theories suggesting that sleep is the result of neurotransmitters, hormones, or other neurochemicals that might promote sleep. If sleep is controlled by activation and deactivation of neuronal assemblies, then it makes sense that chemicals that alter the firing rates of neurons would impact sleep. Several chemicals have been identified as "sleep-regulatory substances," including adenosine, nitric oxide, prostaglandin D., tumor-necrosis factor, interleukin-1, and growth-hormone-releasing hormone (Krueger et al., 2008).

Several lines of evidence note alterations in the accumulation of these substances during sleep. For the sake of brevity, only adenosine and nitric oxide are considered here. In a recent review, Porkka-Heiskanen and Kalinchuk (2011) explain how adenosine, the "A in ATP" (adenonsine triphosphate, p. 19), the basic energy molecule of the mammalian body, accumulates while organisms are awake; accumulation of adenosine inhibits firing of "awake" neurons in the basal forebrain. Once a critical threshold of inhibition of these neurons by adenosine is achieved, sleep ensues. Interestingly, caffeine, a drug that can promote wakefulness, works by blocking adenosine in the brain.

The data from nitric oxide studies are less clear. A recent review suggests that several studies of nitric oxide agonists find increases in slow-wave sleep following treatment (Gautier-Sauvigne et al., 2005). However, these effects are muddied because nitric oxide antagonists have not always been found to inhibit sleep (Gautier-Sauvigne et al., 2005). Thus additional research is needed to verify the role of nitric oxide in sleep and wakefulness.

Kier (2008) proposes that nitrogen, which makes up 78 percent of our air, is key for promoting sleep. While awake, normal breathing causes an accumulation of nitrogen. Too much nitrogen in tissues causes sleep onset. Decreased respiration during sleep causes nitrogen levels to fall, which then promotes wakefulness. According to Kier (2008), several studies demonstrate that nitrogen itself can promote anesthesia, and sleep-deprived individuals (who presumably would have increased nitrogen levels due to greater respiration while awake) are more susceptible to the effects of volatile anesthetics like isoflourane.

From the foregoing discussion, it should be obvious that there are many suggested explanations of why we sleep. Several of the theories have yet to be clearly substantiated by the rigors of laboratory research. The more recent theories suggesting that sleep is a global property of the brain which results from decreases in firing among neuronal assemblies (which is motivated by increases and decreases in sleep-promoting neurochemicals) holds promise. However, we must await further research before concluding for certain that this why we sleep.

On Dreams and Dreaming

When we dream, what do we dream about? Research has demonstrated that dream content is infinitely varied. Obviously, dream content is also a very private experience. Through EEG and EOG recordings it may be possible for the experimenter to determine whether a sleeping subject is dreaming. However, the only way researchers can discover what subjects are dreaming about is to ask them.

Although it presents certain methodological problems (Schwartz, Weinstein, & Arkin, 1978), *daytime dream recall* is one way of studying dream content. As its name suggests, the subject, on awakening, is requested to give an account of the dream or dreams he or she had during the previous night's sleep. The procedure is a bit like keeping a dream diary. Another approach to the study of dream content involves using EEG and EOG recordings to determine when the subject is dreaming, awakening him or her immediately after the dream period, and asking for a verbal report of the dream. One advantage of this research technique over daytime dream recall is that it eliminates dependency on the subject's memory.

Some researchers (Hall, 1951; Hall & Van de Castle, 1966; Snyder, 1970), using the dream logs of a large number of college students as their database, have tabulated the themes of these dreams to analyze dream content. Most dreams involve two or three people, usually strangers, and one or two familiar objects. Men dream about other men almost twice as often as they dream about women; women dream about men and other women with equal frequency.

Despite what your friends may have told you about their dreams, the probability is very low that their dreams are populated by famous figures. Animals appear in dreams; however, the ever-popular dream monster is almost never encountered. Generally, some kind of activity, most frequently a form of movement, is found in dreams. The second most common activity is talking, followed in frequency by sitting, watching, socializing, and playing. Dream themes more often portray bad news, misfortune, and failure than success; aggressive encounters are slightly more frequent than friendly ones. Although sex-related dream themes are certainly not uncommon, their observed frequency of approximately 10 percent is far less than one might predict in view of the importance attached to sex by Freudian psychoanalysts. In fact, we rarely dream about sexual encounters and almost never about sexual intercourse (Kiester, 1980).

Evans and Evans (1983) suggest that about 50 percent of our dreams are in color; the percentage for women is a few points higher than it is for men. Kahn, Dement, Fisher, and Barmack (1962) obtained results that suggest that all dreams are in color. The researchers explain that only a small number of dreams are reported to have been in color because color is forgotten between the time of the dream experience and recall. The database for this study was obtained by awakening the subject immediately after the dream and carefully questioning him or her about the color content of the dream.

Finally, it would appear that the cognitive processing involved in dream production is not unique to the sleeping state. Cavallero and Natale (1988) first collected 36 mental activity reports provided by six subjects during experimental sessions, then collected an equal number of invented dreams from awake subjects. Next, three groups of 30 judges were asked to distinguish real from artificial dreams on the basis of seven structural dimensions: self-involvement, continuity, temporal attributes, implausibility, and three types of bizarreness. The judges were unable to distinguish real from artificial reports at a rate greater than chance.

In discussing the topic of dreams and dreaming in my psychology classes, I often ask students to estimate the frequency with which they dream. In almost every class, I have found one or two students who swear that they never dream. Such a claim must fly in the face of the REM evidence, which makes it clear that everyone dreams every night (Faraday, 1972). However, as in the case of almost all human behavior, there are individual differences in the clarity with which we recall our dreams. Dreams may be difficult to recall because of some characteristic of the dream's content. Thus, exciting dreams are easier to recall than dull ones, and bizarre dreams are easier to recall than ordinary ones. It is also possible that some property of sleep that distinguishes it from other levels of consciousness, can explain why dream recall is so difficult (Goodenough, 1978).

Webb and Kersey (1967) have suggested that habitual dream recallers tend to wake up from REM sleep, whereas those who rarely recall dreams generally awaken from NREM sleep. Finally, it appears that the individual's presleep mood may affect dream recall. In a study designed to examine the relationship between depression and dream reporting, negative moods were related to an increase in dream recall (Cohen, 1979). This finding is probably due to the fact that the subject's unpleasant mood before sleep leads to poor sleep, which, in turn, results in the sleeper's awakening from REM sleep instead of NREM sleep. More recently, Robbins and Tanck (1988) obtained results that supported the earlier study. They discovered that it more frequently happened that subjects had been depressed before the nights in which they had dreams they were able to recall and describe than before the nights in which they had no memory of dreaming.

Most of you have probably experienced a dream that occurs over and over again with little or no change. The *recurrent dream* is typically one in which the dreamer is being threatened or pursued and is trying to hide. These anxiety dreams may be reported more often than others because they are so disturbing and therefore more likely to be remembered (Robbins & Houshi, 1983).

Research suggests close parallels between dreaming and wakefulness. Foulkes (1982) carried out a longitudinal study of some 42 children from the time they were 3 until they were 15 years of age. Every year, each child spent nine nights in Foulkes's sleep laboratory, where dream reports from both ordinary and REM sleep were obtained. Foulkes discovered that the nature of children's dreams at different ages closely paralleled cognitive development, as described by Piaget (1970). Thus, the dreams of a preoperational child were very egocentric, those of a five- to seven-year-old were increasingly more concrete, and those of the adolescent were more abstract.

A second line of research attempted to gain awareness and control of dreams. Some people report having dreams in which they become aware that they are dreaming; such dreams are referred to as *lucid dreams.* By experimenting with a number of self-suggestive techniques, LaBerge, Nagel, Dement, and Zarcone (1981) demonstrated that it was possible to develop a self-suggestive technique called MILD (mnemonic induction of lucid dreams), by which subjects were able to increase the frequency of lucid dreams by some 400 percent to a maximum of approximately 26 lucid dreams a month over a three-year period. More recently, LaBerge (1992) reported on a training technique in which sleepers are trained to signal when they are dreaming by voluntarily moving their eyes and clenching their fists. The importance of this technique is that it provides researchers with the possibility of immediate rather than after-the-fact reporting. Some lucid dreamers report that once they become aware that they are dreaming, they are able to change the course of the dream (LaBerge, 1992; Weinstein, Schwartz, & Arkin, 1991).

Along the same lines, Carpenter (1988) presented data suggesting that presleep stimuli may have an effect on the dream experience. She found that simply having her college students look at pictures that produced positive, neutral, or negative effects before going to bed would produce corresponding dream effects as reported in their morning dream reports. She also observed that the physical elements of the dreams and pictorial stimuli were not related.

Theories of Dream Activity

Similar to the question posed earlier—Why do we sleep?—we can also ask: Why do we dream? Two prominent individuals who addressed this issue were Sigmund Freud and Carl Jung. Through their clinical observations, they each suggested a possible answer.

Sigmund Freud

Freud suggested that the function of dreams is twofold. First, dreams prevent the sleeper from being awakened by minor environmental disturbances. In this regard, Freud wrote, "The dream is the guardian of sleep" (Freud, 1913). Freud's theory seems to be supported by the fact that many disturbances during the night often find their way into dreams. For example, once I dreamed of being chased through the desert by bandits who were shooting at me. In my dream, I was hot and thirsty. When I awoke the next morning, I was indeed hot and thirsty. I had forgotten to turn down the thermostat before retiring, and the indoor thermometer read almost 80°. I have not yet determined the source of the gunshots. Perhaps they were produced by the window blinds slapping against the wall. Possibly you can recall having a similar dream experience.

Wish fulfillment is the second function proposed by Freud. He believed that unconscious impulses were responsible for dreams and that the goal of dreams was to gratify some drive. Thus, the hungry person dreams of food; the student, of graduating; and the failure, of success. According to Freud, dreaming is unconscious and reflects sexual and aggressive instincts that cannot be expressed during waking hours. These impulses are always pressing for activation, and dreams provide an occasion for their expression. In its final form, the dream is seen as a distorted and symbolic version of the impulses that triggered it. In fact, Freud (1900) put great emphasis on the symbolism contained in dreams, especially those related to repressed sexual desires. For example, when a woman dreamed about straight objects, this was interpreted as symbolic representation of the male penis. Similarly, a male dreaming about round objects was symbolically representing the female vagina. In addition to phallic

Figure 7.6 • Sigmund Freud
Courtesy of Library of Congress

representations in dreams, the raw materials the individual used to construct dreams were traces of prior perceptual experiences, particularly those of the day preceding the dream. Additionally, dreams contained repressed memories of infancy or childhood.

Dreams are not logically organized, but rather appear as a strange patterning of the aforementioned elements. The bizarre patterning is believed to occur so that the repressed impulses can be successfully disguised. Freud referred to this transformation as *dream work*, and because of it, the dream becomes progressively detached from sensory memory and less intelligible to waking consciousness. This strange organization of elements makes up the dream's *manifest content*—namely, what you remember and are able to convey to others—and disguises the dreamer's unconscious desires that give the dream its meaning. The unconscious component of the dream is called the *latent content*. It often rises from unresolved early emotional conflicts regarded by the dreamer as too evil or too frightening to be openly expressed (Fisher & Greenberg, 1977).

Carl Jung

Jung, as discussed by Hall and Lindzey (1978), also believed that dreams had several functions, but he suggested that dreams were more than unconscious wishes. First, he believed that dreams are *prospective*, or that they help the dreamer prepare for events anticipated in the immediate future. For instance, the test you must take tomorrow or the next day may be the main feature of your dream tonight. A second aspect of Jung's proposed function of dreams is closely tied to his theory of personality, which suggests that personality is composed of a number of subsystems. The goal of personality development is to unify these parts into an integrated whole. For this to be accomplished, Jung believed that all the parts of the personality had to develop fully. If the development of any one subsystem is neglected, it will find expression in the form of dreams.

Other Theories

We all encounter various problems during the course of the day. Some of these problems lend themselves to immediate solutions, while others require considerably more thought. French and Fromm (1964) suggested that dreams are simply the individual's attempts to solve such problems. The function of dreams is to help the dreamer define the problem more clearly.

A **cognitive** or **problem-solving theory** of dreaming was proposed by Cartwright (1977). On the basis of studies in sleep laboratories, Cartwright suggested that the several dreams that occur during a single night are related and may deal with the same theme or problem. The night's first dream is the most realistic; the middle dreams are the most distorted and fantastic; and the last dream is often focused on the solution of the problem. This led Cartwright to propose that dreams may have two major functions. First, the dream appears to afford the individual an opportunity to solve daily problems. Whether the solution that is arrived at in the dream carries over into waking life is as yet unknown. Second, dreams appear to provide the dreamer with an opportunity to attend to fantasy and to personal impulses. Cartwright argued that this opportunity enables the subject to focus more clearly on the world of reality during the waking hours.

More recent neurocognitive theories have been proposed by David Foulkes and William Domhoff (e.g., Domhoff, 2003, 2011; Foulkes, 1990). Even more recently, Continuity Theory (Kahan & LaBerge, 2011) proposes that dreaming and waking activate the same cognitive and perceptual systems. If this is true, then cognitive activity while we dream and while we are awake is not fundamentally different, and may serve a purpose of "problem-solving." Recent evidence demonstrates that REM dreams can exhibit high-level cognitive abilities, including rational thought, executive control, and analytical ability (Kahan & LaBerge, 2011; Wolman & Kozmova, 2007).

Engaging in higher-order cognitive processing during dreaming complements neurobiological evidence demonstrating off-line reactivation of neuronal assemblies during sleep (e.g., Wilson & McNaughton, 1994). However, we await evidence demonstrating that dream content mimics whatever content may be represented by this neural activation. There is no evidence suggesting that we cognitively "replay" events of the day during REM or any other period of sleep. In fact, several studies investigating procedural skill learning (which you'll recall from the section on Sleep and Memory in this chapter, is known to require REM sleep) have found that while people do report hypnogogic presleep images of skills they learned during the day, they do not report REM dreams containing this content (Stickgold et al., 2001; Stickgold, Malia, McGuire, Roddenberry, & O'Connor, 2000).

The **activation-synthesis hypothesis** of Hobson and McCarley (1977) represents a radical departure from those theories of dreaming previously discussed. Rather than viewing dreams as problem-solving mechanisms or as a vehicle to express sexual and aggressive instincts, this hypothesis suggests that dreams have no inherent meaning at all. Rather, they reflect efforts of the cortex to make sense out of the neural activity ascending from the brainstem during REM sleep. According to this theory, during sleep, cholinergic (acetylcholine) stimulation of the REM sleep regulatory center, the paramedian pontine reticular formation, sends impulses to the cerebral cortex via the thalamus. This activates the cortical neurons, which elicit well-known images or emotions, and the cortex then tries to synthesize the disparate images into a meaningful whole. As one might expect, the dream product may be quite strange, even nonsensical, because it is triggered by the semirandom activity of the pons (Hobson, 1993). Evidence for this activation-synthesis is at best mixed (Bear, Conners, & Paradiso, 1996).

Hobson's Activation-Input-Modulation (AIM) model of dreaming is an extension of the activation-synthesis model, based on new data demonstrating additional mechanistic functions of REM sleep (Hobson, 1992, 2009). According to the AIM model, REM sleep evolved in mammals as a way to perform "off-line" analysis of the environment. As such, REM sleep is a type of protoconsciousness that emerges as a property of the conscious state depending on three factors: activation, input-output, and modulation. Activation (A) involves the subcortical brain stem and neocortical areas that are active during waking and REM sleep, but not during slow-wave sleep. The brainstem decreases activity during slow-wave sleep to regulate I, or input-output gating, which keeps the brain from responding to external stimuli during sleep. This minimizes neural processing that might occur from external stimulation, to permit neurons to focus on other important duties, one of which may be to reprocess information learned during the day (e.g., Wilson & McNaughton, 1994). Modulation (M) is controlled by neurotransmitters, specifically increases in acytelcholine and dopamine, accompanied by decreases in serotonin and norepinephrine, during REM. These neurotransmitters may be essential for either mediating neural activity or storing memories or both. Hobson (2009) proposes that increases in dopamine during REM sleep may explain why REM dreams usually involve vivid hallucinations and a bizarre quality; dopamine is a neurotransmitter implicated to cause hallucinations in schizophrenics.

A newer theory of dreams is the threat simulation theory proposed by Revonsuo. Threat simulation theory explains how threatening or recurring dreams could serve a biological function (Revonsuo, 2000; Valli & Revonsuo, 2009). According to this theory, dreams evolved as a way for organisms to engage in off-line reprocessing of threatening and dangerous situations. This would allow organisms to "rehearse" avoidance strategies while asleep, which could promote survival. Although today our environment does not usually

261

involve threats like wild beasts chasing us, akin to our ancient relatives, Revonsuo points out that many dream studies demonstrate that typical dreams today do contain specific social and emotional content (e.g., Domhoff, 1996; Strauch & Meier, 1996), but rarely contain common activities like writing or using a computer (Hartmann, 2000; Schredl & Hofmann, 2003). According to Revonsuo, social and emotional situations could represent modern-day "threats" (Valli & Revonsuo, 2009).

Malcolm-Smith and Solms (2004) attempted to find evidence in support of threat simulation theory, by assessing the proportion of physically threatening images in dreams. Although more than 44 percent of their sample had experienced physical threats in real life, fewer than 9 percent of them had dreams representing threat. Valli and Revonsuo (2009) explain that tests on hundreds of nontraumatized and traumatized volunteers using their Dream Threat Scale, a content analysis system designed specifically to objectively measure dream threats, suggests the opposite. They've found that a significant majority of dreams do contain threatening content. Threat simulation or replaying critical events of the day certainly corresponds with recent neural evidence indicating that neural patterns may be replayed during sleep. We look forward to additional research investigating threat simulation theory.

As with sleep theories, dream theories differ widely. The classical theories, such as those of Freud and Jung, are so vague that subjecting them to experimental scrutiny would be extremely difficult. Attempts to test more recently developed theories in the research laboratory have generally produced results that are contradictory and often confounded by uncontrolled variables. In summary, then, the questions of why we sleep and why we dream must, for now, remain unanswered.

Daydreaming: Another Level of Consciousness

In addition to night dreams or those generated during sleep, we also experience so-called daydreams. How many times have you caught yourself thinking about the great weekend party you and your friends are planning while sitting in class listening to the definitive lecture on "Epigone—The Seven Against Thebes?" Whether it is "woolgathering," "castles in Spain," or "looking into the middle distance," **daydreaming** is an activity that everyone appears to engage in almost daily (Singer, 1975).

Undoubtedly, you are very much aware of the highly private nature of this process. It is this characteristic that makes daydreaming so difficult to research and define. Perhaps the single most acceptable definition of day dreaming is as follows:

> Daydreaming represents a shift of attention away from some primary physical or mental task we have set for ourselves, or away from directly looking at or listening to something in the external environment, toward an unfolding sequence of private responses made to some internal stimulus. (Singer, 1975, p. 3)

Daydreaming is an activity that lies between our active consciousness and the dreams we have while we are asleep. During daydreams, as our awareness is turned inward, we lose awareness of our external world. For a very large number of people, daydreams take the form of fairly clear visual images of people, objects, or ongoing events.

Singer (1975) observed that daydreams fall into one of two general categories. The first group includes the dramatic, recurrent, self-consistent, and fairly elaborate fantasies that persist from early childhood. The second category consists of the individual's ongoing stream of consciousness, the private interior monologues and sometimes more elaborate fantasies, all of which seem to occur spontaneously in association with events observed in the outside world or in the chains of sequence to early memories. This latter type of daydream can be further categorized (Singer, 1975):

1) *Self-recriminating:* Daydreams are initiated by the statement, "What I should have done (or said) ..."

2) *Well-controlled and thoughtful:* Planning daydreams in which the day is planned, a party is organized, and so forth.

3) *Autistic:* Material usually associated with night dreams breaks through and disrupts consciousness.

4) *Neurotic or self-conscious:* Fantasy daydreams: "How I can guess the winning lottery number and retire to Tahiti?" or "How I can be elected President of the United States?"

Despite the common belief that daydreams are often romantic, sexual, and violent, this is simply not the case. Although most people have such daydreams at times, they make up a very small proportion of the total.

Although you might expect men's and women's daydreams to be quite different, they are remarkably similar in frequency, vividness, spontaneity, and realism. The differences usually reflect contrasts in women's and men's concerns and stereotypical roles in our society (Klinger, 1987).

Daydreams usually occur when events in the external environment become boring or unchanging. When this happens, there is a tendency for our consciousness to turn toward the inner or private world. Our need for what Fiske and Maddi (1961) have called *varied experience* demands that, when novel stimuli are absent in the external environment, we create our own.

Most people report that daydreaming occurs chiefly when they are alone, although some individuals indicate that they find themselves daydreaming even when they are engaged in conversation with others. Results of early studies suggest that late adolescence is a peak period for daydreaming frequency and that there is a gradual decline with age through the 50s. There are also indications that elderly people, even into their 80s, daydream.

Daydreaming probably occurs most often when people are preparing to go to sleep at night. Under these circumstances, as we settle down for the night, consciously excluding varied external stimulation by shutting our eyes, there is probably increased awareness of innerworld activity. This increase in imagery and fantasy at this time may be so vivid and varied as to maintain alertness, even when sleep is much desired.

Consider the following situation, which I am certain many of you have experienced. It is the day before a major exam. You have spent most of the day in heavy study and preparation, and now, at 11:30 p.m., you decide that it is time to go to bed and get a good night's sleep. You get ready for bed, cover up, and get into that favorite sleeping position. You close your eyes and begin to daydream about all the possible questions that might appear on the test the next day. All of a sudden, you find yourself caught up in a stream of visual images. Even though you are tired and desperately want to go to sleep, chances are good that you will stay awake for hours.

What are the functions of this mental process that causes us to lose consciousness of the external world and, in so doing, become less effective in our work and study? Until recently, psychologists turned to the psychoanalytic model for answers to this question. According to this model, the daydream acts as a kind of safety valve; it allows for a socially acceptable expression of sexual needs or aggressive tendencies before they create severe psychological or psychosomatic symptoms. Thus, even the most socially accepted daydreams, such as seeing oneself as a servant of the poor and the downtrodden, can be reduced to basic sexual or aggressive tendencies that must be defended against and thus expressed in more socially acceptable forms (Freud, 1933).

A modern-day alternative is that daydreams are the function of a default-mode network of the brain (Domhoff, 2011; Mason et al., 2007). The default mode network is characterized by slow-wave oscillations (< 1 Hz) in medial prefrontal cortex, medial temporal lobe, and posterior parietal cortex. It is generally engaged during rest, mind-wandering, and creativity. According to Mason and colleagues (2007), our brain is wired to remain in the default mode network, as a baseline resting state. When not exposed to an explicit, attention-demanding task, our default mode network functions to generate spontaneous thoughts, which we call daydreams. The default mode network only shuts down and shifts processing to other areas of the brain when a task requires explicit attention. One question that remains, however, is Why? Why does the brain have a mechanism to promote daydreaming or mind-wandering? Mason et al. (2007) suggest that it may have evolved as a way to "multitask," or to train the mind to divide attention. We await further research investigating daydreaming and the purpose of daydreaming for consciousness and attention.

Sexual Fantasies

Fantasies or daydreams appear to play an important role in human sexual functioning. According to a National Health and Social Life Survey, 19 percent of women and 54 percent of men spend at least a part of each day fantasizing about sex (Laumann, Gagnon, Michael, & Michaels, 1994). Studies have demonstrated that these self-created fantasies afford their creator the ability to control their sexual excitement or arousal as well as to spice up and add novelty to a relationship (Kelly, 1996).

Meuwissen and Over (1991) have suggested that on the basis of their theme, fantasies fall into one of the following four groups:

1) *Exploratory sexual fantasies:* Includes fantasies that have as their major theme group sex, mate-swapping, and homosexual behavior.

2) *Intimate sexual fantasies:* These fantasies have themes such as passionate kissing, oral sex, and mutual masturbation.

3) *Impersonal sexual fantasies:* Looking at pornography, having sex with a stranger, and watching others engage in sex represent the kinds of themes of fantasies belonging to this category.

4) *Sadomasochistic sexual fantasies:* Fantasies with themes such as whipping, spanking, and forceful sex are included in this category.

The most common sexual imagery in the above fantasies involve having sex with a past, new, or imaginary partner or having sex in various settings and positions. Both men and women show fewer fantasies of the impersonal and sadomasochistic type (Leitenberg & Henning, 1995).

Many questions concerning the study of sleep and dreams have not been answered, either by theory or by research. This is the present state of the science. However, we have discovered much information concerning sleep and dreams as states of consciousness. For example, we know that sleep is not one state of consciousness but rather several states, or at least, sleep consists of several levels. These levels are defined by differences in recorded brain-wave activity (EEG) that correspond to each stage of sleep. We know that each stage is different, not only in terms of EEG activity, but also in terms of consciousness experiences. For example, one stage may correspond to light sleep, while another may correspond to deep sleep. While in these stages, we have distinctly different experiences of consciousness or awareness. During another stage of sleep, dreams generally occur.

Therefore, when we discuss sleep and dreams as states of consciousness, it is clear that we do not simply have a wakeful state of consciousness and a sleep state of consciousness. The process is more complex. We hope that, in time, science will reduce some of the complexity and help us better understand the role of sleep and dreams, not only as physiological events, but also as unique experiences that comprise altered states of consciousness.

For Further Reading

Barrett, D. (Ed.). (1996). *Trauma and dreams.* Cambridge, MA: Harvard University Press.

Dement, W. C. (1972). *Some must watch while some must sleep: Exploring the world of sleep.* San Francisco: Freeman.

Hobson, J. A. (1995). *Sleep.* New York: Freeman.

Hobson, J. A. (2002). *Dreaming: An introduction to the science of sleep.* New York: Oxford University Press.

Kryger, M. H., Roth, T., & Dement, W. C. (Eds.). (2005). *Principles and Practice of Sleep Medicine* (4th Ed.). Philadelphia: Elsevier.

Kerkoff, D. A., & Van Dogen, H. F. A. (Eds.). (2010). *Human Sleep and Cognition: Part I Basic Research.* New York: Elsevier.

Lavie, P., & Berris, A. (1996). *The enchanted world of sleep.* New Haven, CT: Yale University Press.

Singer, J. L. (1975). *The inner world of daydreaming.* New York: Harper & Row.

Webb, W. B. (1975). *Sleep: The gentle tyrant.* Englewood Cliffs, NJ: Prentice-Hall.

Sensory Deprivation

Sitting here looking out the window of my study, I can see my 7-year-old daughter providing two of her playmates with an explanation, complete with elaborate gestures and gory details, of her most recent loss—her two upper front teeth. This backyard drama is being played out against a background of rock music that emanates from my teenage son's bedroom. I have yet to discover a way of shutting out sound waves. The day is clear and sunny, and the sunshine pours through the study window and feels warm and pleasant on my back. Since noon, I have been nursing along with great care the main course for this evening's dinner: stuffed cabbage rolls. Only now has the aroma begun to escape the confines of the kitchen to stimulate my sense of smell. Being the chef in our home carries certain advantages. The one I exercise most frequently is that of official taster. On my last trip to the kitchen to coax my creation, I paused long enough to satisfy my taste buds with the cream sauce. The movement of my arm as I write, the noise of the cars driving past the house, the light touch of my shirt against my skin, and the hunger pangs I feel are among the many environmental stimuli, both internal and external, of which I am currently aware.

In large part this stimulation will govern my behavior. The stimuli serve to initiate, maintain, or sustain certain physiological processes and bring about certain behavioral consequences. If the noise of my son's latest rock music becomes too loud, I will cease writing, open the doors of my study, and in my stern, fatherly voice, explain to him the imminent danger his CD and stereo system face if the sound is not immediately diminished.

The environment I have described fairly teems with stimulation, but the important point to remember is that it is a brief and incomplete description of a typical environment. This will become evident if you put down your book for a minute and make a partial list of stimuli in your present environment. Now imagine that you are transported to another kind of environment, one that does not contain any of the stimulation that you normally encounter in your daily life.

Consider the small life raft of a lone crash survivor, adrift under a cloudless sky with nothing but endless ocean in sight. Or think of the small, dark, quiet cell of a prisoner in isolation or the water tank in a sensory deprivation laboratory in which the subject, blindfolded and nude, is immersed. These environments all have at least one thing in common: The normal daily exposure to stimulation is absent. After several days in such a strange new environment, how might you function? Can an environment so devoid of stimulation actually affect your level of consciousness and thus your perceptual judgments, learning, and problem-solving behavior? These questions, as well as others you may have thought of, are addressed in this chapter.

Before we plunge into a discussion of sensory deprivation, it is necessary to have a clear understanding of what this term means. Actually, it is impossible to create a situation of complete sensory deprivation for a human subject. Even by using a well-ventilated, soundproof, and lightproof room, we would not be able to eliminate all possible stimulation. Our nude subject would still hear the pounding of the heart, the sounds generated by breathing, and perhaps an occasional growl of the stomach. Additional sensory stimulation may come from muscle activity involved in movement, body odors, and skin contact with another surface. In a sense, then, the term **sensory deprivation** is a misnomer; it implies that none of the senses can be stimulated at all.

The term *sensory deprivation* is not only scientifically imprecise, but through repeated associations with such notions as stress and brainwashing, it has come to carry a connotation of threat, disturbance, and adversiveness. For these reasons, Suedfeld (1980) has suggested that it is time to deemphasize this term, and to this end he proposes **Restricted Environmental Stimulation Technique (REST)** as an alternative. Throughout the remainder of this chapter we will adopt Suedfeld's terminology to indicate that the level of stimulation has been reduced or altered in such a way as to no longer conform to an individual's normal variety or range of exposure.

Sensory Deprivation and Consciousness

In chapter 6 we observed that certain meditative techniques involve the use of some external stimulus upon which the meditator learns to focus attention to exclude from consciousness all other external forms of stimulation. In the case of REST, an altered state of consciousness also appears to be achieved through a reduction in perceived external stimulation. However, unlike meditation, this reduction is not brought about by a mental process; rather it is accomplished by the direct experimental manipulation of the environment. Research data to date make it clear that manipulation in restricted environmental stimulation technique leads to an altered state of awareness. For example, REST may produce visual sensations (Zuckerman, 1969b) like those occurring just before dreams or increased proneness to being persuaded of something. These changes occur only under certain conditions (Suedfeld & Vernon, 1966; Myers, Murphy, & Smith, 1963). Many of these changes are described in detail in this chapter.

We have noted that, in general, individuals enter situations that typically produce an altered state of consciousness to achieve a desired goal. For example, a person may enter a biofeedback training program to heighten his or her awareness of specific bodily responses to develop conscious control over them. For the person who can master a technique, meditation affords an opportunity to enter an altered state of consciousness and, in doing so, bring about a mystical experience. Finally, a person who experiences chronic pain may choose to undergo hypnosis or biofeedback in hopes of reducing the pain.

What can REST offer the individual? Why would a person decide to enter a sensory-deprived situation? At first glance your response to both of these questions might be negative. Certainly, any review of the literature on sensory deprivation, both natural observations and experimental research data, prior to 1975 would suggest very little to be gained by individuals who undergo such an experience. In the final section of this chapter, however, we focus on some of the therapeutic possibilities that are a positive outgrowth of research on sensory deprivation and the altered state of awareness it establishes. Before discussing the ways in which REST changes states or levels of consciousness, let us trace the development of this manipulation.

Historical Background

The topic of sensory deprivation certainly is not new to those interested in human behavior. The Bible provides a number of references to such isolation experiences. Moses, withdrawing from the multitudes, ascended Mount Sinai, where he spent 40 days and nights alone; there he received the Commandments from God. John the Baptist spent much of his early life in the isolation of the desert, where he developed the mystical qualities he would need to fulfill his ministry. Jesus, after being baptized by John, went out into the wilderness alone, where he overcame the temptations of the devil.

More detailed descriptions of the experiences of prisoners, writers, explorers, mystics, and others under conditions of extreme isolation have been made public. For example, Admiral Richard Byrd (1938) chronicled his experiences of being isolated for six months in a small hut buried beneath the snows of the Antarctic. The small, unchanging surroundings of his hut, combined with the quiet of the seemingly unending polar nights that served as Byrd's environment for this period, can best be described as monotonous, confining, and unchanging.

Although he undertook the ordeal voluntarily, Byrd soon discovered that life under such conditions was anything but peaceful and serene. His early reactions centered on a fear that his rescuers would not reach him in time; these fears gave way to an overwhelming apathy. It took an almost Herculean effort for Byrd to attend to life-sustaining necessities of eating, drinking, and keeping warm. He also experienced hallucinations. By the fourth month he had entered severe depression. He reported an extremely strong need for the kinds of stimulation we normally take for granted—sounds, odors, human touch, and so on. During this time, Byrd also reported feelings of loss of identity

Figure 8.1 • Admiral Richard Byrd
Courtesy of Library of Congress

and of floating freely though space. Such descriptions undoubtedly served to attract the interest of psychological researchers as well as the general public.

Shurley (1961) has suggested that the experimental approach to sensory deprivation resulted from the convergence of three major lines of influence. First, the developments in neurophysiological techniques provided an avalanche of new findings and led to a revised model of the central nervous system. Instead of viewing the brain as a switchboard for connecting an appropriate response to a stimulus, the new model, using new electrophysiological methods, took into account such phenomena as reverberating circuits, neural feedback systems, and arousal centers (Hebb, 1949).

The second major influence was based on numerous investigations by psychological researchers into the effects of sensory deprivation on the developmental processes and learning of nonhuman subjects. The impetus for this research came, at least in part, from the many case reports of feral humans. Carl von Linnaeus (1707–1778) first introduced the term *feral man* in his 1758 edition of the *Systema Naturae*. He used it to describe cases in which a human child had been cared for, in complete social isolation from other human beings, either by animals or by only indirect contact with human caretakers. One of the best known of these cases is that of the Wild Boy of Aveyron (Itard, 1932).

By the early 1950s it had become apparent that, for the sake of national security, American researchers needed to investigate and attempt to understand the factors involved in thought-reform movements, indoctrination programs, and brainwashing techniques. This became the third push toward sensory deprivation research. Disturbing newspaper accounts of captured U.S. soldiers defecting to the enemy and confessing to all sorts of war atrocities began to appear. The publication of General William F. Dean's (1954) account of his own experiences at the hands of his Communist captors, combined with the newspaper reports, served to heighten public as well as government interest and speculation that the enemy had developed a new, secret method of breaking the mind.

It was at Canada's McGill University in 1953 that these three major influences—development of neurophysiological techniques and electrophysiological methods, research in sensory deprivation effects on subhumans, and the need to combat a threat to national security—finally brought about the development of a research program conducted by Donald O. Hebb and his students, focusing on stimulus reduction and decreased sensory variability. Besides formalizing the question of sensory deprivation, which they labeled *perceptual isolation*, the McGill University studies opened a whole new track

Figure 8.2 • McGill University
Courtesy of Library of Congress

for psychological research, theory, and speculation (Brownfield, 1965).

The McGill Studies

Historically, there have been any number of recorded natural observations of REST experiences. However, the initial, experimentally controlled attack on this problem was carried out in the 1950s at McGill University (Bexton, Heron, & Scott, 1954; Doane, Mahatoo, Heron, & Scott, 1959; Heron, Bexton, & Hebb, 1953; Heron, Doane, & Scott, 1956; Scott, Bexton, Heron, & Doane, 1959). Because this series of studies defined the problem and set the tone for future research in this area, it is important to review some of the details here.

In these studies, the researchers' goal was to reduce or alter the patterns or relationships in the sensory input from the environment by providing an experimental setting much like the one described in the section "Experimental Procedures" later in this chapter. Brief time-out periods were allowed for meals and going to the restroom, but subjects otherwise remained in this very restricted environment until they asked to end the experience. As an incentive, each was offered $20 each day they remained in this strange environment. (This might not seem like much money, but in the 1950s, $20 had much greater buying power than it does today.) Despite the potential financial gains, the experimental conditions were so intolerable that most subjects asked to get out within four days.

Most subjects spent the early part of the test period asleep. Later they slept less, became bored, and seemed to need some stimulation. To this end they began singing and talking to themselves, tapping together the cylinders in which their arms and legs were placed, or using the cylinders to explore the cubicle. They became restless and engaged in a great deal of random movement. When the experiment ended, subjects described their experience as extremely unpleasant. Upon leaving, they reported a number of aftereffects, including disturbances in visual perception, confusion, headaches, mild nausea, and fatigue.

Subjects reported some cognitive and perceptual disturbances during their time in the cubicle. Many were unable to concentrate on a single topic for any length of time. Some subjects, desperate for stimulation, attempted to review their studies or solve self-initiated intellectual problems. However, they found such activity extremely difficult and soon gave it up, lapsing instead into daydreaming and simply allowing their minds to wander. Several subjects reported blank periods during which they were unable to think of anything at all.

Reports such as these prompted some members of the McGill group to try to measure the cognitive and perceptual effects of sensory deprivation. Some 28 perceptual and cognitive tasks were administered to subjects before, during, and after their deprivation experience. While the group results suggested that certain of the tested functions were impaired after sensory deprivation, some subjects appeared to be completely unaffected. Certainly, one interpretation of these findings is that the REST experience causes deterioration of certain perceptual and cognitive skills. However, these same results can also be accounted for, at least in part, by a decrease in the subject's motivation.

Several of these researchers (Scott et al., 1959) found that with the passage of time, their subjects became extremely persuasible. For example, they requested to hear normally boring and childish passages over and over again. After hearing a message supporting the reality of psi (psychical research), they indicated substantially greater acceptance of this possibility than did control subjects hearing the same material.

During the experimental sessions the researchers observed an unusual degree of emotional fluctuation on the part of most subjects. In the early phase of the session, subjects reported being elated; however, as time passed, they became irritable. Perhaps the most interesting and certainly the most widely reported finding of the McGill studies was the occurrence of hallucinations. Visual hallucinations varied considerably in their degree of complexity, ranging from simple light flashes and geometric forms to much more complex, dreamlike scenes, such as "a procession of squirrels with sacks over their shoulders marching purposefully across a snow field and out of the field of vision" (Bexton et al., 1954). The hallucinatory experiences were not all visual. Subjects also reported auditory, kinesthetic, and somesthetic hallucinations. For example, one subject described a "miniature rocketship" shooting pellets at his arm; another reported hearing a music box. Finally, feelings of "otherness" and bodily "strangeness" were also reported. One subject indicated that his mind seemed to be a ball of cotton wool floating above his body.

Sensory Deprivation Research After McGill

The McGill research was followed by a number of studies that can best be described as exploratory rather than rigorous and authoritative (Zuckerman, 1969a, 1969b). These studies typically used relatively few subjects, who were drawn from restricted populations. They also introduced such variations as placing the subject in a small box with no room to move or having the subject sit in a reclining chair, lie in an inoperative iron lung, or lie on a bed in a dark, soundproof room. Or a subject might be entirely submerged in water using underwater breathing apparatus. Because of the introduction of these different research techniques, the term perceptual isolation gave way to a new term: *sensory deprivation* (Rossi, 1969). Finally, to explain the findings of this research, theories ranging from the psychoanalytic to the neurological were adopted (Brownfield, 1965).

As the second decade of research into sensory deprivation dawned in the mid 1960s, it had become clear that things were not always as they appeared. Put another way, the effects attributed to sensory deprivation during the previous decade were not nearly as clear-cut and replicable as had been thought at first. For example, although it was one of the most widely cited results, visual sensations continued to be reported. Zuckerman (1969b), having surveyed 33 separate reports, concluded that the number of subjects reporting any visual sensation in any given experiment was most frequently zero. Suedfeld and Vernon (1964) suggested that if we define hallucinations as perceptions that the subject thought were real and over which he or she had no control, then they were practically a nonexistent finding in such research.

Other early findings had to be substantially modified as a result of new findings (Myers, Murphy, & Smith, 1963; Suedfeld & Vernon, 1966; Robertson & Walter, 1963; Zubek, Sansom, & Prysianiuk, 1960). For example, it had been supposed that sensory deprivation had a negative impact on cognition and that subjects undergoing sensory deprivation were more susceptible to persuasion than in normal circumstances.

It is also important to note that a few studies were published during this decade that explored the applicability of the effect of sensory deprivation in the context of clinical treatment (Adams, Robertson, & Cooper, 1963; Gibby & Adams, 1961).

Some methodological changes also were made during this second decade of REST research. Of the many techniques that were tried in the first 10 years, only two survived in active research programs: sensory reduction in a dark, soundproof chamber and the original perceptual isolation technique used at McGill. Even these were modified by instituting set durations of sessions, removing panic buttons, and orienting the subjects to the environment before initiating the session. These changes were effected to minimize the confounding effects of expectancy, uncertainty, and stress (Suedfeld, 1980).

As the second decade of research continued, it became evident that the popularity of sensory deprivation research was waning. Suedfeld (1980) suggested several reasons for this change. First, many scientists working in the field had only a limited interest in the dramatic phenomena associated with REST research and either had exhausted their concern or had decided to move on to other questions. Second, REST research is expensive, and any systematic program in this area would require substantial funding at a time when research support generally had begun to erode. Third, researchers in the area had failed to integrate the results of their research. Therefore, specialists in clinical psychology, perception, cognition, and so on were generally unaware of the relevance of sensory deprivation findings to these areas.

Finally, between the late 1960s and the early 1970s, a period of great political unrest, several sensory deprivation investigators came under attack from political activists who viewed sensory deprivation as analogous to solitary confinement and torture. These attacks ranged from hostile publications in both the popular media and professional journals, in which the deleterious effects reported during the first years of research were emphasized and exaggerated, to actual physical attack against these researchers. As a result some investigators left while others probably avoided the field. There is also anecdotal evidence to suggest that journal editors and perhaps even grant reviewers were not very receptive to sensory deprivation research and proposals (Suedfeld & Coren, 1989).

In addition to the reasons put forth by Suedfeld, Reed (1962) suggested at least one more reason for the decline of research on reduced environmental stimulation. He suggested that workers in the area became increasingly aware of the complexity of the variables involved and the even greater complexity of their interactions. It was frustrating to generate exact hypotheses to be tested.

Thus, for whatever reason, as the second decade (roughly mid 1960s to mid 1970s) came to a close, there were only three major research centers carrying out programmatic research in sensory deprivation with another few laboratories producing occasional papers. This represented a substantial decrease from the 20 such centers that were identified during the first decade of research (Suedfeld, 1969).

As the third decade opened, it was clear that something had to happen to rekindle attention and attract researchers back to the area of sensory deprivation. While researchers began to focus their attention on further extension and application of the best-established basic findings, two major events occurred that went a long way toward reestablishing sensory deprivation as a major research area.

First, there was the discovery that stimulus reduction, either alone or combined with other techniques, was a highly effective treatment in giving up smoking (Best & Suedfeld, 1982; Suedfeld & Ikard, 1974). The second was the discovery and publication by John C. Lilly (1977) of the method of floating in a warm solution of Epsom salts. This technique was generally reported to induce deep relaxation and enjoyment. This was completely contrary to the then-prevalent notion that immersion in water and stimulus reduction led to extreme stress. The increased number of research projects in sensory deprivation focused on applications of this altered environment to modify habits. The flotation method was quickly adopted as a component of stress management and the treatment of stress-related disorders (Fine & Turner, 1982; Jacobs, Heilbronner, & Stanley, 1985; Koula, Kemp, Keane, & Belden, 1987; Suedfeld, Ballard, & Murphy, 1983; Suedfeld & Kristeller, 1982).

There were also some changes in methodology. While the darkened, soundproof chamber continued to be used, the use of the flotation tank replaced the perceptual isolation technique employed in the McGill studies. It was also during this decade that Suedfeld (1980) coined the term REST to which we have previously referred, *Restricted Environmental Stimulation Technique* (or *Therapy*, depending on the context).

Both the public and the professional image of this research area improved greatly between the mid 1970s and the mid 1990s. The release of the highly successful science fiction movie *Altered States*, which presents an exciting, although inaccurate, picture of flotation, did much to bring about an increased public interest and awareness of REST. Additionally, in response to public demand, commercial flotation centers charging about $60 per hour in the tank sprang up across North America. These pay-to-float facilities continue to be popular and offer both enjoyment and a way to beat the day's stresses. In light of this public response, it was difficult to maintain the notion, popular during the 1970s, of sensory deprivation or REST as an aversive, damaging form of torture (Suedfeld & Coren, 1989). Professional acceptance of this technique also began to increase, and as we have already seen, there was a substantial increase in the number of scientific publications. The International REST

Investigators' Society (IRIS) was formed in 1983 in Denver to disseminate information to researchers and therapists through its bulletin and conferences.

It is unclear whether IRIS remains active today, although popular interest in sensory deprivation appears to be again on the rise. In 2008, a television station in London (BBC Two) hosted a reality TV series called *Horizon*, in which six volunteers spent 48 hours completely isolated in light- and sound-attenuated rooms. According to a news report issued from the station, the show recreated the original isolation experiments by Donald Hebb from the 1950s and 60s (http://www.bbc.co.uk/sn/tvradio/programmes/horizon/broadband/tx/isolation). Further, the series producers likened the experience to that of prisoners of war including Brian Keenan, who spent eight months in isolation during his four-year captivity in Beirut until 1990, as well as more recent detainees of Guantanamo Bay, who reported isolation as a form of torture.

According to a news report by Simon Crompton (2008), volunteers on the TV show experienced some profound negative reactions. While two of the six coped well by sleeping most of the 48 hours, all six reported the experience to be extremely boring and distressing, and half (three of six) experienced unpleasant visual and auditory hallucinations. All of the volunteers experienced decreased memory or other cognitive declines following isolation (for example, difficulty in thinking of words that begin with the letter F). The four men who participated (but neither of the women) showed increases in suggestibility as a result of their isolation experience.

Experimental Procedures

Although the specific conditions of REST vary from experiment to experiment, it is possible to identify at least three distinct, basic procedures that researchers use to reduce sensory input. The first of these approaches attempts to achieve an absolute reduction of sensory stimulation. To accomplish this, researchers, such as Lilly (1956) and Shurley (1960), used a large tank filled with continuously flowing water maintained at a temperature of 93.5° F (34.5° C). Shurley (1963) labeled his water-immersion technique a hydro-hypodynamic environment. The subject, nude except for a blacked-out face mask attached to breathing tubes, was immersed in the tank. This technique substantially diminishes gravity, light, and temperature stimuli. The tank itself is usually located in a room constructed so that light, sound, vibration, odor, and taste sensations are markedly reduced. The overall system provides a constant environment with maximal reduction of ambient physical stimuli.

Once the subject is immersed in the tank, he or she is requested to get comfortable and to remain motionless for several hours. Either during or after the study, a subject may be requested to report on his or her experiences. Subjects were allowed to terminate their participation in the study at any time and for any reason.

The movie *Altered States*, which we have mentioned, and the popularity of commercial centers that employ a variation of the flotation tank technique have undoubtedly made this technique the most generally known of the sensory reduction methods.

The use of a dark, silent chamber is also a sensory reduction technique and dates back to the first decade (1955–1965) of REST investigation (Suedfeld & Coren, 1989). This technique employs a completely dark, sound-attenuated room that is typically furnished with a bed, a chemical toilet, an intercom for communication with the experimenter in the next room, and a food box containing thermos bottles of water and liquid diet food. Before entering this experimental environment, the subject is instructed to lie as still as possible on the bed and to refrain from getting up and walking about, singing, talking, or making any other kind of unnecessary noise. Once in the room, the subject remains there until the end of the session or until he or she requests that the session be terminated prematurely (Suedfeld, Ballard, Baker-Brown, & Borrie, 1986).

The second major approach employed by researchers in stimulus deprivation (e.g., Bexton et al., 1954) is to reduce or alter the patterns and relationships in sensory input from the environment. This technique, which was used by the McGill University group, was originally labeled *perceptual isolation*, was later called *pattern reduction*, and now is commonly referred to as **perceptual monotony**. The techniques employed do not decrease the absolute levels of stimulation and, in fact, may even increase them. Rather, they interfere with normal pattern perception.

The McGill subjects were required to lie on a comfortable bed located in a lighted, semisoundproof cubicle. Subjects wore translucent goggles that allowed the passage of only a diffuse light. Auditory stimulation was held constant by placing the subject's head on a U-shaped pillow of foam rubber and by using the sound of an exhaust fan located in the ceiling directly above the subject's head to provide a continuous masking noise. Each subject was required to wear gloves, and his or her hands and arms were encased in cardboard tubes to reduce the possibility of tactile stimulation. To allow subjects to communicate their needs to the experimenter, a two-way speaker system was embedded in the foam rubber pillow. Subjects were fed and permitted to go to the restroom when necessary and were able to terminate their participation in the experiment whenever they desired.

The third and least commonly used approach to the study of sensory deprivation is to impose highly structured or monotonous conditions in the sensory environment rather than reduce the levels of stimulation. It is termed *variation reduction* (Suedfeld, 1968). The subject, with arms and legs encased in rigid but comfortable cylinders to limit movement and tactile stimulation, is placed in a tank respirator (iron lung) containing a specially built mattress. Although the subject breathes normally, the respirator motor is turned on to provide a dull, monotonous masking noise. Room lighting is kept at a minimum. A large hood placed around the respirator prevents the subject from seeing anything but the front of the tank and the blank white walls and ceiling. Food in the form of an eggnog mixture is available through a tube placed near the subject's mouth, and a bedpan or urinal is provided upon request. This technique probably provides an environment that is closer to normal than any we have discussed so far. However, the mechanical elimination of bodily movement introduces a new dimension of deprivation that is far more stringent than the equivalent in other methods (Zubek, Bayer, Milstein, & Shephard, 1969).

A newer technique uses blindfolding to produce visual sensory deprivation. This technique may have resulted from findings of rare clinical cases of Charles Bonnet Syndrome, a condition where visually impaired individuals experience profound visual hallucinations (Kester, 2009; Menon, Rahman, Menon, & Dutton, 2003). Visual impairment in Charles Bonnet Syndrome is due to deterioration within the visual system, and primarily affects the elderly. Patients typically experience complex visual hallucinations, for example, visions of people, animals, buildings, and landscapes. The patient is aware that the visual sensations they experience are not real (Menon et al., 2003).

As a sensory deprivation paradigm, blindfolding attempts to completely deprive subjects of visual input. Blindfolding may last anywhere from 3 days to 3 weeks or more, and participants may stay in the laboratory, or they may be asked to engage in their normal activities while blindfolded (e.g., Proulx, Stoerig, Ludowig, & Knoll, 2008). Merabet and colleagues (2004) asked 13 healthy individuals to wear a special blindfold that permitted no visual stimulation for five consecutive days (96 hours). After one day, 10 out of 13 participants (77 percent) reported visual hallucinations, which ranged in complexity from simple dots of light, to faces or scenes. Participants reported that the hallucinations were not disturbing, and all 10 reported knowing that the hallucinations were unnatural reactions to the lack of visual input (Merabet et al., 2004). These results suggest that prolonged limitation of visual input in normally sighted individuals can alter consciousness to produce nonthreatening visual disturbances.

A later study examined fMRI activity in a single subject following three weeks of blindfolding (Sireteanu, Oertel, Mohr, Linden, & Singer, 2008). Near the end of the blindfolding period, the subject was assessed with fMRI, which revealed high activation in **extrastriate** (visual) cortex, **posterior parietal**, and some **prefrontal** regions. Following the fMRI measurements, the participant was asked to provide detailed descriptions of her hallucinations, during which she described seeing flashes of light, colors, and patterns. Several weeks following recovery from the blindfolding, the participant was assessed via fMRI again, and asked to imagine the same perceptions she remembered from the blindfolding experience. Brain imaging revealed significant activation in **prefrontal** areas, but not occipital or parietal cortex. The authors suggested that these findings indicate that visual hallucinations activate visual pathways in extrastriate and parietal cortex, while visual imagery only invokes activation of "voluntary" prefrontal brain areas, without relying on actual visual areas of the brain to produce the memory of the visual image. To further support this notion, the participant in the study reported that the hallucinations were far more vivid than her mental imagery of the events. It is unclear if people who reliably produce highly vivid mental images might invoke activation of visual structures to a greater degree. There is some evidence to suggest that vivid visual imagers do activate extrastriate cortex and other visual areas during an imaging task, although this study also noted greater activation in frontal areas than occipital regions (Ganis, Thompson, & Kosslyn, 2004). Future research should continue to investigate the consciousness-altering effects of restricted visual input with blindfolding, as well as the neural correlates of visual imagery.

In summary, to study the effects of sensory deprivation, the investigator is faced with the selection of one of the following major methodological approaches: (1) absolute reduction of sensory stimulation, (2) reduction or change in the patterns and relationships in the sensory input, or (3) imposition of highly structured or monotonous conditions in the sensory environment. Whichever approach is selected, an extremely complex experimental environment is required. Having reviewed the common experimental methodologies employed in the study of sensory deprivation, we are now ready to determine what effects, if any, this phenomenon may have upon consciousness or arousal.

Restricted Environmental Stimulation Theory

The preceding sections of this chapter have referred to both naturalistic and experimental observations of the effects of REST on human behavior. At some point in such a discussion, it is reasonable to expect that the curious student will question how these effects can best be explained within the framework of psychology. To account for these findings, investigators of this phenomenon have posited a number of interesting theoretical statements.

Concentrating on the hallucinatory experiences reported by some REST subjects, Rosenzweig (1959) suggested that the condition of sensory deprivation is somewhat analogous to that of schizophrenia. Rosenzweig contends that the schizophrenic's symptoms are brought about by disruptions in internal processes that, in turn, destroy the orderly associations of sensory and perceptual material. Thus, even though the schizophrenic may experience considerable stimulation, he or she simply is unable to establish the relevance of such input to ongoing cognitive processes.

Subjects of REST studies also find it difficult to attach meaning to sensory input. In this case, however, the problem does not stem from any disruption of internal processes, but rather from the manipulation of external environmental conditions such that sensory stimuli are restricted, depatterned, or redundant. To Rosenzweig, then, it is not the lack of external stimuli, but rather that they are not relevant or meaningful, that leads to the effects, especially hallucinations, observed. Because of its concentration on the hallucinatory-like experiences reported by REST subjects, the current status of this theory is very much in question. As we have already seen in this chapter, the idea that REST leads to hallucinations has been pretty well exploded.

Robertson (1961) assumes that under normal conditions an individual's response is a result of the interaction between external and internal stimuli. As we use the terms here, external stimuli refer to those that the senses experience (e.g., sights, sounds, tastes); internal stimuli refer to feelings, memories, images, and thoughts. It follows that under conditions of restricted environmental stimulation technique, the hypothesized interaction between external and internal stimuli is substantially reduced, and behavior is determined almost completely by various internal stimuli. This leads to preoccupation, during which the subject's perceptual and cognitive activities are considerably restricted and internally directed. Robertson suggests that, faced with diminished external stimulation and with internal stimuli for which there is no normal background of external stimulation, the subject experiences a heightened suggestibility, and the behavioral effects of sensory deprivation are manifested.

To provide a somewhat different explanation for the effects of REST, Lindsley (1961) looked to the neurophysiology of the organism and, more specifically, to the functioning of the **ascending reticular activating system (ARAS)**. Under normal conditions, two major functions are subserved by the neurons of the lower brainstem that make up the ARAS. First, the ARAS acts as a kind of relay station. It receives information in the form of neural impulses from each of the sensory receptors and in turn transmits messages centrally to other structures of the brain, especially the cortex. The ARAS neural impulses alert or arouse the cortex, which plays an essential role in the occurrence of normal perception. If for any reason the ARAS is not functioning, sensory information from the receptors will still reach the appropriate cortical projection centers. However, the cortex will not be sufficiently activated to allow the processes of sensory discrimination and perception to occur.

The second major function of the ARAS, under normal conditions, can best be described as a self-regulating or adjustive function. On the basis of its own neural activity and that of the cortex, which it monitors, the ARAS regulates the amount of its own sensory input. Put another way, the ARAS is functionally capable of monitoring its own input-output levels of neural excitation.

This regulatory function led Lindsley to the concept of an adaptation level. According to this concept, the ARAS, on the basis of the amount of input from various sensory receptors, adjusts the neural output of the cortex so as to establish a correspondingly high, neutral, or low level of arousal. As you might expect, under conditions of sensory deprivation, this level of arousal decreases markedly, with attendant boredom, inactivity, and finally sleep. A characteristic of the compensatory adjustment process is that it is limited. If these limits are exceeded, as they most certainly are in the case of REST, behavior deteriorates and becomes disorganized.

Ziskind (1965) suggests that the psychological symptoms that occur during the restricted environmental stimulation technique do not result from reduced sensory input per se, but rather from the reduced level of arousal that is also present during such an experience. Ziskind sees this reduction in awareness level as the condition necessary for the development of sensory-deprived mental symptoms. The reduction in awareness occurs in conjunction with internal and external stimuli and goal-directed actions, which Ziskind calls the *sufficient condition*. The sufficient condition apparently is related, in part at least, to the instructions and psychological set or demand characteristics of the experiment (Orne, 1959, 1979).

More recent theoretical accounts rely upon Bayesian theory, the idea that perception is "unconscious inference," based on expectation (Barlow, 1990; Helmholtz, 1871/1971; from Corlett, Frith, & Fletcher, 2009, p. 516; see also Fletcher & Frith, 2009 and Shanks, 2006). According to this view, delusions—that is, false beliefs that do not match information from the incoming stimulus—may be produced if **bottom-up processing**, or the stimulus set from the environment, does not match a person's prior knowledge or expectation (**top-down processing**). In this case, a delusional person may rely too heavily on top-down processing (expectation), instead of using the stimulus set to guide their perception. Similarly, hallucinations may be produced in otherwise normal people forced to rely on top-down processing, when there is no bottom-up processing available. This may happen during sensory deprivation; bottom-up processing cannot occur since there is no stimulus set to produce a signal (or the stimulus set is "noisy" or unpredictable; Corlett et al., 2009).

A recent study by Granqvist and Larsson (2006) could be explained in this respect. Granqvist and Larsson found that during a 30-minute light- and sound-deprivation period, highly religious people interpreted their experiences as more "mystical" or "religious" compared to nonreligious people. Although this experiment suffered from a variety of methodological considerations, including demand characteristics and priming effects (they asked participants about religion and religiosity prior to the sensory deprivation experience), it is interesting that more religious people were primed to interpret their experiences as religious; these same people were not more prone to mystical experiences during a 30-minute control period. These findings offer some support that prior expectation (for example, a religious explanation) directs interpretation of incoming information, especially when incoming information is minimal.

Mason and Brady (2009) have further gained empirical support for the hypothesis that hallucinatory experiences may be due to a disconnect between incoming information and prior expectations. This study compared healthy people, either prone or not prone to hallucinations, exposed to short-term (15 minutes) light and sound sensory deprivation. Two hundred and eleven people took the Revised Hallucinations Scale, a test that measured predisposition to experience hallucinations. Twenty-eight high scorers and 29 low scorers (representing the upper and lower 20th percentiles, respectively) were selected to complete the sensory deprivation experiment. Participants were told they would remain alone in the sensory deprivation room for several minutes, and were instructed to hit a "panic button" nearby if the experience became too stressful or aversive; the panic button would turn on the lights and

Figure 8.3 • panic button

Image © studio 58, 2011. Used under license from
Shutterstock, Inc.

activate an intercom to communicate with the experimenter. After 15 minutes, participants were removed from the chamber and asked to immediately complete the Psychotomimetic States Inventory (PSI), a 48-question test measuring "psychotic-like" symptoms (p. 784). Participants spent 20 minutes completing the test and talking with the experimenter, which served as a post-sensory deprivation rest period prior to completing the PSI again.

While none of the participants activated the panic button, all participants reported increases in perceptual distortions, anhedonia (depression), and paranoia, that dissipated by the 20-minute post-test. Participants highly prone to hallucinations reported experiencing significantly more psychotic-like symptoms. Mason and Brady interpreted their findings to support those of Fletcher and Frith (2009) and Corbett et al. (2009), that hallucinations are due to a greater reliance on top-down processing, or a lack of integration between incoming stimulation and prior knowledge (which Mason and Brady called *source monitoring*). On this view, sensory deprivation produced a lack of sensory input, so sensory stimulation was internally generated. Hallucination-prone individuals do not realize that the stimulation is internally generated, and instead perceive the stimulation as "real," or externally generated.

However, as noted by Bell (2010), there are some issues with the conclusions of Mason and Brady (2009), due to errors in their experimental design. Mason and Brady employed the use of a "panic button," and instructed participants to push the button if they experienced any adverse or frightening effects. As discovered in early research by Orne and Scheibe (1964), demand characteristics may be produced by giving participants a "panic button"—participants may assume the experience will be so aversive, that they perceive a need to "panic," which could produce extremely negative reactions. Orne and Scheibe demonstrated that offering participants a panic button, compared to telling them to knock on a window if they wanted to leave the room, resulted in greater anxiety and more negative perceptual and cognitive effects for participants in the panic button condition. Thus Bell (2010) advises replication of the Mason and Brady (2009) experiment with a "nonpanic button" control, to ensure that any perceptual distortions were not the result of expectation or demand characteristics.

Taking a slightly different approach, Steel and Suedfeld (1994) recognized that there are certain natural working environments that closely resemble the restricted environment (e.g., the polar regions of the earth). Using a standardized personality test, they attempted to ascertain what effects, if any, such an environment would have upon personality. Comparing a group of polar workers with a normal sample of workers, they reported that polar workers were less conscientious, less extroverted, less agreeable, and more open to experiences than their normal counterparts were.

Recent work corroborates these findings, that personality factors may impact the magnitude of experience following sensory deprivation (Kjellgren, Lindahl, & Norland, 2009). People identified as "highly sensitive" personalities experienced more mystical experiences and a greater altered state of consciousness following 45 minutes of flotation REST, compared to less "sensitive" personalities. Furthermore, the highly sensitive personalities reported greater anxiety prior to the experimental session (Kjellgren et al., 2009). This may have further impacted the experience in highly sensitive individuals; as noted in earlier sections, prior expectations can influence reactions in sensory deprivation experiments (e.g., Bell, 2010; Orne & Scheibe, 1964; Mason & Brady, 2009).

As you might have surmised, there certainly is no lack of theoretical speculation and explanation for the behavioral phenomena associated with the sensory deprivation experience. The major problem is one of accumulating critical evidence in support of one or more of these theoretical positions.

Sensory Deprivation and Altered States of Consciousness

Traditionally, seekers of a transcendental or spiritual experience have used solitude and stimulus restriction as means to that end. From the beginning, both Eastern and Western religious traditions have maintained that spiritual experiences are best sought in solitude. The uniformity that underlies many of the practices of yoga, Zen, Tao, Sufism, and Christian monasticism reinforces this idea (Goleman, 1977; Pelletier & Garfield, 1976). Not only did Moses and Jesus first achieve the insights that led to their ministries while isolated in the wilderness, but so did Mohammed and the Buddha. Thus, there is a noteworthy similarity among the founders of the four great religions of the world. Today, modern mystics use periods of isolation in the desert or in other remote locations to achieve altered states of consciousness and transcendence. Religious retreats for laity and clergy also frequently incorporate periods of

Figure 8.4 • ancient sitting Buddha image
Image © Markuso, 2011. Used under license from Shutterstock, Inc.

solitude for the same purpose (Havens, 1969; Lilly, 1972).

A second example is to be found in the initiation rites of countless societies. As Tyre (1978) has observed, one of the six defining characteristics of this ritual of passage is solitude. The anthropological literature suggests that a period of solitude or isolation has been a central feature of the initiation rite of societies in North America, the Middle East, Africa, Asia, and Australia. Such a finding suggests a universal appreciation of the possible values of being alone in a natural environment. Accounts of these culturally imposed periods of solitude also suggest that the participants often experienced what could best be described as an altered state of consciousness. Whether such experiences were due to long periods of fasting, use of drugs, or self-inflicted pain—often a part of the initiation rite—or solely to the isolation experience is impossible to determine.

Researchers using REST typically have not concerned themselves with the question of altered states of consciousness. Probably the one major exception to this is John C. Lilly. Lilly's original starting point was a logical one: He concluded that the appropriate way to study the body-brain-mind system was to isolate it from the influences of the external world, thus permitting examination of the system by itself. His early work in the area includes the description of his own spiritual experiences while undergoing water immersion. Frequently, these early experiences in the tank occurred while he was under the influence of LSD (Lilly, 1960, 1972).

Lilly's later work is characterized by the concept that the current view of the mind, as essentially contained within the brain, is inadequate and that the tank immersion environment, more than any other setting, has the potential for allowing the mind to operate at a much higher level of freedom.

The subjects involved in this work were volunteers who requested an opportunity to experience the tank and who often paid for the use of the facilities as a part of a workshop in self-exploration. The isolation tank, which was much smaller than the rather large ones used in the original immersion research, was located in a dark, soundproof environment, with body-temperature water mixed with Epsom salts to make it easier to float. No monitors were provided, so each tank was completely isolated. After the immersion session, each person was asked to write a report concerning the phenomena encountered during isolation.

According to Lilly, the immersion tank has two major uses, depending on the individual's orientation. If the individual is satisfied and thoroughly tied into Western concepts about the relationship between the external world and the individual, the isolation tank can be used as a place to rest and relax as well as to think over problems and work out solutions with a minimum of distraction. For those who do not find that much distinction between the external world and internal processes, the isolation environment is useful because it minimizes interactions with external reality and allows the internal process to be more fully explored.

As Lilly says, "The tank experience is a very refreshing one, a resting one. If one wants to push further than this, one can do so to the limits of one's mental discipline and to the limits of one's imagination" (Lilly, 1977, p. 31).

Lilly argues that the tank enables a person to separate the mind from the body and to become aware of many other states of being in which consciousness is unimpaired and apparently disconnected from the brain and body. These states include dream travel to other worlds, the appearance of extraterrestrial organisms, and the transformation of individuals into such organisms. Although the experiences are dreamlike, awareness, consciousness, and participation are much more vivid than usual.

Some 78 post-immersion reports are presented in Lilly's (1977) book *The Deep Self.* These indicate that in the beginning, subjects concentrate on the environment and on their own physical and psychological reactions. However, as tank time increases, the participants become more aware of relaxation, feelings of love and warmth, and vivid and novel imagery. The aftereffects appear to be very positive, consisting primarily of vivid memories, deep relaxation, restfulness, and pleasant sleep. Many, but not all, of the participants wanted to repeat the experience.

Clearly, the changes reported by Lilly and his subjects match our definition of an altered state of consciousness. Such events have also been reported in the course of more traditional research using REST. Altered states of consciousness develop gradually in such an environment (Taylor, 1973). The initial reaction is heightened alertness to features of the environment and to bodily sensations. For some subjects, the focus of attention then switches to internal cognitive and emotional experiences. Some subjects go further and develop vivid images that Taylor calls "visual translation and projection of cognitive and emotional states" (Taylor, 1973, p. 125).

Suedfeld and Mocellin (1987) report that subjects in the REST condition report experiencing the *sensed presence,* the perception or feeling that another person is present. This phenomenon can be explained in terms of Jaynes's bicameral mind (see chapter 1). Beyond this phase comes a state of flowing imagery, interspersed with mental blankness and eventually a state of detachment, serenity, tranquility, and unity with the infinite (Suedfeld, 1980; Suedfeld et al., 1986).

More recent research by Kjellgren, Norlander, and colleagues suggests that REST can indeed induce an altered state of consciousness. In a series of studies investigating the clinical effects of REST (described more fully in the next section), these investigators show clinical benefits result specifically from altered consciousness produced by flotation REST (e.g., Bood, Kjellgren, & Norlander, 2009; Edebold, Bood, & Norlander, 2008; Kjellgren, Lyden, & Norlander, 2008; Kjellgren, Sunderquist, Norlander, & Archer, 2001; Kjellgren, Sundequist, Sundholm, Norlander, & Archer, 2004).

Indeed, an early study reported that flotation REST produced a pleasurable change in consciousness that was not the result of either the setting, or previous experiences with altered consciousness (e.g., drugs; Norlander, Kjellgren, & Archer, 2001). A comparison of flotation REST with chamber REST demonstrated that consciousness was altered to a greater degree by flotation REST (Kjellgren et al., 2004; Norlander, Kjellgren, & Archer, 2003). Flotation REST produced feelings of "cosmic unity" and out-of-body experiences, not experienced during chamber REST (see also Kjellgren et al., 2008 for review).

Findings by Gordeeva and Finikova (2005) further emphasize how even short-term sensory deprivation—as little as 10 minutes—can result in altered consciousness. These authors suggest that sensory deprivation can produce a type of "analytical introspection" which can promote changes in perception, self-awareness, and greater imagery. Short-term sensory deprivation produced alterations in body image and alertness. These findings, coupled with previous results described above, suggest that sensory deprivation can produce an altered state of consciousness, similar to that produced by drugs, hypnosis, sleep and dreams, biofeedback, or meditation.

Neural Correlates of Sensory Deprivation

It appears that only a few studies have examined the neural correlates of sensory deprivation, especially the consciousness-altering aspects of sensory deprivation. This is unfortunate, in that understanding the neural correlates of the altered state of consciousness produced by sensory deprivation may help elucidate the neural correlates of normal, waking consciousness. Nonetheless, research conducted to date appears to suggest the following:

One early study examined brain glucose metabolism via PET scan in volunteers exposed to either auditory, visual, or both auditory and visual sensory deprivation (Mazziotta, Phelps, Carson, & Kuhl, 1982). Results noted an overall decrease in glucose metabolism following sensory deprivation. The greatest decreases occurred in **right hemisphere**, and in **occipital** and **parietal cortex** relative to frontal cortex. The authors found the greatest hemispheric differences specifically within **lateral occipital cortex, inferior prefrontal cortex, and cortical areas near the Sylvian fissure**. While medial occipital cortex also had demonstrated decreases, these could be attributed to eye closure; activity nearly doubled bilaterally when subjects opened their eyes. Later research with EEG examination validated greater **right hemispheric** processing following flotation REST (Hayashi, Morikawa, & Hori, 1992; Raab & Gruzelier, 1994). Hayashi and colleagues (1992) further implicated **alpha waves** as guiding hallucinatory experiences produced by 72 hours of isolation sensory deprivation.

Iwata and colleagues (1999) specifically compared **alpha** and **theta waves** produced during sensory deprivation with those occurring during sleep. They did this based on previous reports during flotation REST, where participants stated that they felt like they were on the border between wakefulness and sleep, and felt like they were dreaming, even though they knew they were awake. In this study, five participants (three males, two females) were exposed to one hour flotation REST while EEG measurements were taken. Participants were asked to report their experiences after the sensory deprivation period ended. The researchers reported only visual images or sleep that occurred during the sensory deprivation experience, although they note that other "aspects of the experiences" were found (p. 129), though the quality or typology of these other aspects remains unclear. For participants who either did not sleep, or only fell into "light sleep" (stage 1-2), EEG revealed a predominance of alpha waves with theta waves apparent for over five minutes. For participants who reported falling asleep, delta waves predominated. However, one participant reported experiencing visual images related to the sensory deprivation experience, prior to falling asleep in the

Figure 8.5 • EEG (brain waves)
Image © dusan964, 2011. Used under license from Shutterstock, Inc.

latter 30 minutes of the experiment. His EEG data revealed an alteration ("zigzag") in eye movements following the hallucination, in which the participant reported bringing himself back to reality. Just prior to the changes in eye movements, the EEG demonstrated **alpha** and **theta** waves, as well as **rapid eye movements** associated with the hallucination. The authors suggested that the rapid eye movements may have been invoked as a way to visually scan the hallucination. The authors stated that these findings suggest that EEG analysis during sensory deprivation may be used to elucidate sensory deprivation–produced hallucinations from "conventional" states of consciousness such as wakefulness and sleep (Iwata, Yamamoto, Nakao, & Kimura, 1999).

A more recent study used a multimodal ganzfeld technique to produce sensory deprivation (Putz, Braeunig, & Wackermann, 2006). In this technique, monotonic visual and auditory stimuli were presented via goggles that displayed red light, and headphones that played a constant waterfall sound. Participants were first selected as "high responders" to the environment, that is, they produced frequent and vivid visual images during a 50-minute test phase. In the second half of the test phase, participants were told that they may experience hallucination-like images, and were instructed to hit a button on a microswitch held in their right hand every time they experienced a visual image. They were to hit the button at the moment the image was most intense, and to hit the button again when the image vanished. The button press signaled the experimenter, who then interrupted the auditory ganzfeld to get a verbal report of the imagery. From these screening tests, seven high responders were identified, who were invited back for the EEG experiments. For the EEG portion, the procedure was identical, except that participants wore EEG recording devices, ganzfeld sessions lasted 45 minutes, and the button press also triggered an EEG event marker, in addition to starting the verbal report sessions.

Results indicated that exposure to the ganzfeld produced accelerated **alpha waves** (10–12 Hz) that were not similar to those produced by a hypnogogic state (Putz et al., 2006). The authors suggested that accelerated alpha waves may indicate active inhibition by cortical areas processing sensory information. Inhibiting cortical activity during ganzfeld (or sensory deprivation, as found by Hayashi et al., 1992) may be necessary to focus on the internally directed cues. These findings appear to be in line with those proposed above by Corlett et al. (2009) and Fletcher and Frith (2009), who suggest that minimal external stimuli may produce hallucinations, due to greater reliance on top-down processing. A neural correlate of this top-down processing may be inhibition of cortical activity, to minimize responsiveness to externally generated cues. We look forward to future research investigating this hypothesis.

Clinical Potential of Sensory Deprivation

Earlier in this chapter we posed the question: Are there any positive aspects of the sensory deprivation experience? Now that we have reviewed the effects of a sensory-deprived environment as observed under controlled experimental conditions, you may find it difficult to view this phenomenon positively. Keep in mind, however, that these studies have demonstrated that by limiting or modifying environmental stimuli, it is possible to produce marked changes in consciousness levels, and subsequently in behavior, without the use of drugs or other medical techniques.

From our earlier discussion you should remember that as far back as the early 1960s there was some research to determine whether or not REST might have a future as a therapeutic technique. It remained for Suedfeld and Ikard (1974) to provide a major demonstration of the effectiveness of REST as a treatment for cigarette smoking. In this study, four groups of subjects were used: a group in which the restricted environmental stimulation therapy was combined with the presentation of substantive messages and reinforcers, a group that received REST only, another that received messages only, and a control group. All subjects were psychologically addicted smokers; that is, their smoking habit was more than nicotine addiction. Eisinger (1972) notes that such subjects are the least likely to quit smoking.

Smoking rates of subjects in all four groups were compared over a two-year follow-up period. These findings not only pointed to the efficacy of REST in the treatment of cigarette smoking, but also led the investigators to make several other significant observations. They noted that even though the messages were more elaborate and appeared more helpful than the previously used messages of Suedfeld, Landon, Pargament, and Epstein (1972), they had only a minimal additive effect when combined with REST. In other words, there was no significant difference between the REST-plus-message group and the REST-only group.

One major problem that is constantly found in literature on how to stop smoking is that while almost any treatment can reduce smoking rate for a while, almost none has resulted in significant reductions over a long period (Levenberg & Wagner, 1976). Suedfeld and Ikard (1974) found that almost every subject abstained completely for at least the first week following REST

293

but that the number of cigarettes smoked per day later increased as it does in all smoking cessation techniques.

However, subjects who had received REST as part of a smoking cessation program frequently reported long-term maintenance of smoking rates that were significantly below their baseline, even though they were not able to abstain completely. This contrasts with the experience of many smoking-control clinics, which show that baseline smoking rate levels are rapidly reattained if the subject begins smoking again after treatment. Many of these findings have been replicated by more recent studies employing REST alone or in conjunction with hypnosis (Barabasz, Baer, Sheehan, & Barabasz, 1986; Suedfeld & Baker-Brown, 1986). Such research has spurred other researchers to look at other habitual problems for which REST therapy may be useful.

Precisely how REST is able to bring about this substantial reduction in cigarette smoking rate is a question, the answer to which must await more definitive research. We do know, however, that sensory deprivation induces an altered state of consciousness. Perhaps this state helps the subject learn to relax in certain anxiety-inducing situations or to come to grips with a habit, such as smoking.

Barabasz and Barabasz (1989) have demonstrated that REST can be used to enhance hypnotic susceptibility in patients suffering pain. Not only were they able to demonstrate increased hypnotic susceptibility using REST but also that subjects then were able to use hypnosis daily to reduce pain with a substantial decrease in pain medication.

Ramirez, Suedfeld, and Remick (1993) investigated the effect of electroconvulsive shock therapy (ECT) and environmental stimulation on memory complaints of clinically depressed patients. After recovering from ECT, patients were randomly assigned to spend time in a REST condition (lying on a bed in a sparsely furnished, dimly lit, quiet room), or a control condition (free to go to anyplace accessible to patients after receiving ECT). Objective and subjective measures of memory were taken before the first ECT session, after the last, and at one-week and one-month follow-ups. Subjective and objective memory measures showed significant memory improvements from baseline to last follow-up in both groups. However, the control group reported significantly less improvement in subjective memory over time than did the REST patients.

Clearly, we are a long way from being able to explain fully how REST can bring about a reduction in smoking or the enhancement of hypnotic susceptibility. Substantial clinical research will be required before we are able to provide answers to these questions. For now we can only accept the data that suggest that REST has a future as a part of the behavior therapist's arsenal.

Most recent research on REST has focused on the clinical efficacy of flotation REST for pain and stress. This may be due to the popularity of flotation REST "clinics" across the country, as well as increased accessibility of home-use devices (which are affordable, costing around $40,000). A recent meta-analysis of 27 studies concluded that flotation REST had beneficial effects on stress indicators including cortisol levels, blood pressure, and verbal reports (Van Dierendonck & Nijenhuis, 2005). One study demonstrated that people with chronic neck and back pain could experience relief from pain symptoms following nine flotation REST treatments over 3 weeks (three treatments/week). Those reporting the highest levels of pain experienced the greatest relief in symptomology, while patients reporting less pain did not find much relief from flotation REST (Kjellgren et al., 2001).

A later study investigated gender differences in the effects of flotation REST (Bood et al., 2009). This study examined previous data collected from 69 women and 19 men who received flotation REST treatment 12 times over seven weeks for stress-related pain. Results indicated that while women reported greater levels of depression prior to treatment, depression scores were equal between genders following treatment. Further, while men exhibited greater pain thresholds before and after REST treatment, REST treatment increased pain threshold in women (Bood et al., 2009).

Flotation REST appears to be a safe and efficacious method for both stress management (e.g., Van Dierendock & Nijenhuis, 2005) and pain control (Bood et al., 2009; Kjellgren et al., 2001), and possibly habit control (e.g., Adams, 1988; Forays, 1987). Although there has been one reported death in a home flotation-REST chamber, cause of death was attributable to other factors; the victim had a blood-alcohol level of 0.27 percent, and other drugs were found in her system (Lann & Martin, 2010). We hope renewed interest into the neural correlates of consciousness will yield new and interesting studies on both the consciousness-altering effects and clinical efficacy of REST.

As a technique for helping us understand the psychology of consciousness, REST has staged a significant comeback, and as it becomes more popular with the research community, we can expect that it may well provide us with new insights into consciousness. Clearly, REST does produce a change in the states or levels of consciousness. Earlier, we saw that sleep and "sensed presence" may be produced when persons are deprived of changes in sensory input. Therefore, although historically REST has had its ups and downs as a research technique, it still has much to offer.

For Further Reading
. . . .

Brownfield, C. A. (1965). *Isolation: Clinical and experimental approaches.* New York: Random House.

Dean, W. F. (1954). *General Dean's story.* New York: Viking Press.

Hutchinson, M. (1984/2003). *The book of floating: Exploring the private sea.* Nevada City, CA: Gateway Books.

Lilly, J. C. (1977/2006). *The deep self: Consciousness exploration in the isolation tank.* Nevada City, CA: Gateway Books.

Suedfeld, P. (1980). *Restricted environmental stimulation: Research and clinical applications.* New York: Wiley-Interscience.

Suedfeld, P., & Borrie, R. A. (1995). *Therapeutic applications of chamber and floatation restricted environment stimulation therapy (REST).* Vancouver: University of British Columbia Press.

Zubek, J. P. (Ed.). (1969). *Sensory deprivation: Fifteen years of research.* New York: Appleton-Century-Crofts.

Parapsychology

Historically, parapsychology, or **psychical research (psi)**, has been one of the most interesting and controversial areas of study in the realm of consciousness. Many individuals who are not psychologists admit to an interest in this area. The topic is often written about in popular magazines and discussed on television and radio programs. Many people would like nothing better than to be able to "read minds" or to make objects move in space by mental control. Can you imagine how nice it might be to read someone's mind, such as the brightest student's during an exam? Or your boyfriend's or girlfriend's? However, few admit to being able to perform these feats, although many believe that some people possess such abilities. Among scientists, especially psychologists and other behavioral scientists, a small minority admit to the possibility of **extrasensory perception (ESP)** or **psychokinetic (PK) abilities** (McClenon, 1982). In fact, to express a belief in such possibilities is often to risk being labeled a scientific heretic, a believer in the occult.

Why is the study of parapsychology so controversial? Is there any scientific evidence to support some people's claims that they can read minds or perform other such feats? If so, do such claims indicate that these people possess a special ability to control mind over matter? These issues as well as others are discussed here.

Parapsychology and Consciousness

Parapsychology literally means "alongside psychology." As this root definition implies, this area of interest is not within the mainstream of psychological study. However, those who conduct scientific investigations in psi claim that some people on some occasions are capable of processing information without relying on the five senses (vision, hearing, taste, smell, and touch). Such people supposedly can relate information to an investigator in ways beyond the normal limits of consciousness or awareness. Although you and I may not be able to sense or detect consciously a phenomenon or event, people with this ability theoretically can experience it. If such abilities do exist and can be isolated and controlled for scientific study, they may help us to understand yet another piece of information within the workings of the human system. These abilities supposedly enable one to consciously control or alter behavior that we once believed could not be so controlled. If some behavior can be manipulated or controlled outside the normal limits of our senses, the discovery would be remarkable indeed and might enable us to tighten our grasp on the limits of our abilities and potentialities. As we discuss psi as an area of investigation within the psychology of consciousness, we shall discover whether this is possible.

Historical Development

Although stories about the ability to read minds or move objects by thought have circulated for centuries, it was not until 1882 that scientists organized to study parapsychology. In that year the Society for Psychical Research was founded in London by F. W. H. Myers (1843–1901), Edmund Gurney (1847–1888), and Henry Sidgwick (1838–1900), who became the first president of the organization. One of the most notable members of the society was Sir Arthur Conan Doyle (1859–1930), author of the Sherlock Holmes detective stories. An American version of this society was organized in Boston in 1885 with the purpose of investigating claims of telepathy, clairvoyance, precognition, and other forms of paranormal cognition (Mauskopf, 1989). Some prominent members of the Boston society were psychologists Gardner Murphy (1895–1980) and William James (1842–1910). The two societies later merged, and James eventually became president.

The most prevalent investigation in the early scientific years of parapsychology centered around **mediumship,** or communication with the dead. In fact, several prominent psychologists were attracted to parapsychology because of their interest in communicating with a dead person. These individuals included William James (Murphy & Ballou, 1969), who played a major role in the early development of the psychology of consciousness (see chapter 1), and William McDougall (1871–1938).

James believed that psychic research was an important and little-understood area of the human mind and its powers. He thought it necessary that this area be investigated by "any means at our disposal if progress in understanding was to be achieved" (Murphy & Ballou, 1969, p. 12). He further believed that a phenomenon was not necessarily untrue simply because it conflicted with known principles of science. (Many people view parapsychology as conflicting with such principles.)

McDougall probably played the most important role in developing the scientific investigation of parapsychology in the United States. In 1927, while at Duke University, McDougall set up the first laboratory devoted to the investigation of psi—specifically to study telepathy, clairvoyance, precognition, and psychokinesis. McDougall was also at the time an influential force in the council of the Society for Psychical Research.

McDougall brought to Duke two botanists, Joseph B. Rhine (1895–1980), who is often credited with coining the term *parapsychology* (Wallechinsky & Wallace, 1975), and his wife, Louisa E. Rhine (1891–1983), who had been experimenting with psi at Harvard University.

The Rhines' major area of interest did not fall within the categories of study for which McDougall had organized his laboratory. Rather, they were interested in the area that was the impetus for the development of psi research, the question of survival after death. Their research involved having a medium in one room try to read the thoughts of a subject in another room; they could not deduce how such thought transference could take place. They hypothesized that either a dead person was communicating with the medium by acting as an intermediary to relay information or telepathy was taking place between the medium and the subject. The latter hypothesis seemed more reasonable to them (and far easier to test experimentally) than the former. Thus, they commenced their investigation of mental telepathy with the aid of research support from the Rockefeller Foundation and the U.S. Navy. They published the first formal report of their findings in a book titled *Extrasensory*

Perception (1934). This important publication, reprinted in 1964 (see the References), described the Rhines' many experiments with subjects' abilities to deduce symbols on a deck of cards. These cards were called *Zener cards* after the originator of the deck, Karl Zener (1903–1964).

A Zener deck consisted of 25 cards with 5 identical cards in each of five different suits (see Figure 9.1). The suits consisted of crosses, circles, stars, wavy lines, and squares. The probability of guessing the correct suit of a particular card was 1 in 5. Thus, a typical subject would correctly guess the suit of 5 cards out of 25 presented. The odds of guessing all 25 correctly were 298,023,223,876,953,125 to 1. According to the Rhine report, one subject named Hubert Pearce, a divinity student at Duke, remarkably beat those odds and guessed all 25 cards correctly. Unfortunately, he was unable to repeat his phenomenal performance.

Ever since scientists began to investigate parapsychological phenomena, card-guessing ability has been one of the most researched areas. The technical term for this ability is telepathy. This term is used when the experimenter can see the cards while the subject tries to guess their identity.

Precognition is the attempt by the subject to guess the order in which the cards will be arranged before the experimenter arranges them. When the experimenter does not know the identity or order of the cards but the subject nevertheless guesses their identity, the subject's ability is known as clairvoyance. Each of these powers is discussed under the general heading of "Extrasensory Perception." Extrasensory perception is distinguished from psychokinesis, which describes the ability to move objects by thought. Both ESP and PK have been scientifically investigated by many researchers (Moss & Butler, 1978; Rao, 1966, 1979; Rao & Palmer, 1987; J. B. Rhine, 1964; L. E. Rhine, 1964, 1970; Rhine & Pratt, 1957); many positive as well as negative findings have been reported (Alcock, 1987; Rao & Palmer, 1987).

Figure 9.1 • The Five Suits Depicted on Zener ESP Cards

Extrasensory Perception

Extrasensory perception, or ESP, generally refers to the phenomena of clair-voyance, precognition, and telepathy. Each of these is now described.

Clairvoyance

Clairvoyance, broadly defined, is the ability to experience the occurrence of an event without physically perceiving it (without using the senses)—in other words, in an "extrasensory" manner. Pratt (1973a, 1973b) reports an example of an individual who claimed to have such ability. His name was Pavel Ste-panek, and he lived in Prague, Czechoslovakia. In an experiment designed to test clairvoyant abilities, Stepanek was requested to guess on many trials whether a given card placed in a covered container was white or colored. Be-fore the testing session, all of the cards and covers were ordered randomly so that in no event did the experimenter know what type of card was in a given container. Thus, the experimenter could not convey any information regarding the card's identity to the subject. This procedure is necessary for conducting a scientific experiment in clairvoyance.

After examining Stepanek's guesses over a series of trials, researchers dis-covered that he significantly exceeded chance in correctly identifying the color of cards hidden from both himself and the experimenter. Pratt mentions that this ability was not random or spurious, for Stepanek was able to demonstrate this feat over and over again, not only for Pratt but for other investigators, as well (Beloff, 1968).

The case of Pavel Stepanek is interesting. Here is a demonstration of the ability of an individual to experience an event accurately (above chance) with-out relying on his five senses. Does this finding scientifically establish the existence of an ESP component in clairvoyance? Although the evidence seems to be convincing in the case of Stepanek, it is still unclear how he performed his feat. Learning as a function of trials cannot be totally discounted as an alternative to the possibility of ESP. For example, if one guesses (correctly or incorrectly) the same color of a card for a series of responses, one probably will switch to another color after a while.

In a similar manner, if someone is flipping a coin and asks you if you wish to pick "heads" or "tails," you have a 50 percent chance of being correct on each and every flip of the coin. However, let us say that by coincidence or chance, a "head" appears three times in a row. Might you switch to saying "tails" on the fourth trial simply because "heads" appeared on the previous trials? Might you do this even if you know that the probability of a "head" has remained the same?

In essence, subjects often develop a strategy for performing or guessing, often in the face of probability. Could it be that Stepanek became very skilled in developing a strategy for producing accurate guesses? After all, it is known that some card players often develop strategies that help them to win more money than would be the case if they had not developed a winning strategy. With regard to Stepanek, it is not possible to determine whether he developed a successful strategy for performing in a clairvoyance task because Pratt did not discuss this issue. However, this is not unusual, since investigators in this area generally tend to ignore alternatives to psi as an explanation for results. Perhaps future investigators will make a greater effort to consider such explanations.

Precognition

Another area of ESP is *precognition,* the ability to predict a future event. Did you ever predict a future occurrence? Do you remember how shocked or surprised you were when the event really happened? Did it occur by coincidence, or is precognition possible? Such a possibility formed the basis of an experiment by Friedman, Schmeidler, and Dean (1976). Subjects were asked to predict which of five possible targets would be selected by an experimenter on each of 20 calls or trials. This assignment differs from the one employed in clairvoyance experiments because the experimenter knows the identity of the targets to be guessed. Also, the subject predicts what an experimenter *will do* rather than saying what he or she did. In this experiment, subjects scored significantly above chance, but only if they were in a nonaggressive mood and didn't need social affection. Mood states were determined before the experiment by having subjects complete the Nowlis (1965) Mood Adjective Checklist.

It is not clear why these mood states were necessary for subjects to score above chance. There seems to be no logical reason why precognition would require these states. There also is no definitive evidence that the data of Friedman and associates support the existence of precognitive abilities. Perhaps, as we discussed in the case of clairvoyance, subjects became skillful at developing a strategy for guessing on the basis of a learning experience over 20 trials. Obviously, there is no way to resolve the controversy over whether Friedman and associates really demonstrated precognition. However, they did make a scientific attempt to determine the possible existence of the phenomenon. It is hoped that, with many more such attempts, science will be able to give us some clues as to whether precognition is a bona fide phenomenon.

Recently, Daryl J. Bem, professor emeritus of Cornell University, published a paper in the highly respected *Journal of Personality and Social Psychology* reporting significant *psi*, or precognitive abilities, based on a sample of more than 1,000 students (Bem, 2011). This paper has sparked extreme controversy regarding both the way in which Professor Bem conducted and analyzed the research (Alcock, 2011; Miller, 2011; Bem, Utts, & Johnson, 2011; Wagenmakers, Wetzels, Borsboom, & van der Maas, 2011; Wagenmakers, Wetzels, Borsboom, Kievit, & van der Maas, 2011), as well as raising questions as to why a top-tier journal would publish such results (Judd & Gawronski, 2011). Indeed, publication of the paper has called the entire scientific peer-review process into question (see http://www.nytimes.com/roomfordebate/2011/01/06/the-esp-study-when-science-goes-psychic for a debate between scientists, started January 6, 2011).

Although probably best known for *self-perception theory*, the idea that people form attitudes based on their behaviors rather than performing behaviors that conform with their attitudes (e.g., Bem, 1972), Bem has held a long interest in paranormal phenomena, publishing papers as early as 1994—with parapsychologist Charles Honorton—on the existence of psi (Bem & Honorton, 1994). In that paper, Bem and Honorton express frustration with the lack of scientific research on the paranormal. They suggest that excessive and unfair skepticism prevents scientists from objectively considering reports of supranormal abilities, most of which occur in the popular press. Excessive skepticism prevents validation under the controlled conditions of the laboratory, and the scientific study of psi phenomena fails to advance (Bem & Honorton, 1994).

In his more recent paper, Bem (2011) suggests that there is increasing evidence regarding psi abilities in both humans and two animal studies demonstrating **"presentiment"**—increases in physiological arousal to aversive and erotic pictures, that occur *prior* to the actual presentation of the pictures (e.g., Bierman & Scholte, 2002; Radin, 1997, Radin, 2006, as cited by Bem, 2011; the animal studies were reported as personal communication with D. I. Radin on December 20, 2009).

Bem suggests the ability to predict highly aversive or erotic stimuli offers an evolutionary advantage. Correct precognition of aversive stimuli allows organisms to avoid potentially dangerous situations. Precognition for erotic stimuli would permit organisms to approach viable mating opportunities.

In an attempt to validate results from presentiment studies, and to demonstrate the existence of psychic "predictive" abilities, Bem (2011) conducted nine experiments. In general, each experiment consisted of at least 100 trials (100 pairs of pictures chosen from the International Affective Picture System, a standardized set of pictures frequently used in psychological tests of emotion), and included data from at least 100 undergraduates per study (approximating 50 men and 50 women) who volunteered for a 30-minute experiment through an online registration system at Cornell University, in exchange for either financial compensation ($5) or course credit. Bem chose 100 as the target number for both participants and trials based on previous studies of psi phenomena reporting effect sizes around 0.25; with such small effect sizes, a minimum of 100 subjects is needed to achieve statistical power of 0.8 in a one-tailed t-test with significance at the 0.05 level (Bem, 2011). For the sake of brevity, we summarize highlights of the first two experiments.

Experiment 1 (Bem, 2011) was called Precognitive Detection of Erotic Stimuli. In this task, an equal number of non-emotional, emotion-arousing, and erotic pictures were used. Pictures were randomly selected, with the exception that each trial consisted of a pair of one emotional or erotic picture, and one neutral picture. Location (right or left on a computer screen) was also randomized. Participants were seated in front of the screen, and were asked to predict, 100 times, under which of two "curtains" on the screen, right or left, the emotionally-arousing or erotic picture would be presented.

Data analysis revealed that participants correctly identified the location of the erotic (but not the emotional) pictures 53.1 percent of the time, which Bem found significantly greater than chance (under a binomial distribution created by this twochoice task, chance "guessing" would yield 50 percent correct).

In Experiment 2, "Precognitive Avoidance of Negative Stimuli," Bem (2011) assessed the ability to avoid future negative stimuli based on precognitive cues. In this study, only non-emotional pictures were shown to participants, and each trial asked participants to indicate their preference between a picture and its mirror image. Target pictures were randomly determined, but if participants reported a preference for the target picture, an emotionally pleasant picture was then presented subliminally three times. If participants reported a preference for the nontarget picture, then a highly aversive picture was presented subliminally three times. A "hit" was defined as selecting the target picture, which would prevent the future subliminal presentation of the aversive photos. This measured precognition, in that being able to "psychically" identify the target could prevent the aversive (albeit subliminal) stimulus.

Results revealed that participants were able to identify the targets correctly to avoid aversive pictures 51.7 percent of the time. With 150 participants in this study, 51.7 percent was significantly greater than 50 percent chance.

All but one of the other seven experiments reported similar small, but significant, effects (Bem, 2011). These results have raised concern among both scientists and skeptics regarding the validity of the studies. Significant methodological problems have been noted (see Alcock, 2011), and there is confusion why data were analyzed with the statistics employed (one-tailed t-tests; discussed below).

As scientists and students of psychology, we learn to critically evaluate all research. One obvious concern with Bem's research is the small overall differences: As noted above, probability dictates 50 percent correct guessing at chance level in a 2-choice task, while participants in Bem's research increased their correct selections to, at most, 53 percent. David Krantz, a statistician at Columbia University, offers the following caution: "One can't expect statistics to do the job of human inductive inference" (Miller, 2011, p. 273). It should be difficult to convince anyone that 53 percent correct is much better than 50 percent (chance). Would you take a medication that only worked 53 percent of the time? Skepticism should be even greater when evaluating paranormal abilities. The very nature of psi research, and the plausibility that extrasensory abilities exist, should prompt people to hold evidence for the paranormal to an even higher standard (e.g., Wagenmakers et al., 2011a).

A second issue with Bem's research is the number of participants tested in each experiment. Some experiments appear to have sampled closer to 200 than 100 people, and reasons for adding additional participants to the experiments are not always clear (see Alcock, 2011 for further discussion). The primary issue here is that if enough participants are tested, it is not difficult to demonstrate statistical significance with a t-test. Further, interpretation of a p-value, or the probability that an effect will not be found by chance, is often misunderstood. This is the gist of the concerns raised by Miller (2011) and Wagenmakers et al. (2011).

Instead of the "traditional" statistics Bem used, Wagenmakers and colleagues argued that these data needed to be analyzed with Bayesian statistics. Bayesian methods determine the likelihood that results are true, given the data collected in the present study, and also taking into consideration prior findings. Moreover, Bayesian statistics are particularly useful for accurately analyzing large datasets like those collected by Bem, since they do not compute significance based on sample size. Wagenmakers and colleagues reanalyzed Bem's dataset using Bayesian statistics, and found that if anything, Bem's data demonstrated that psi does not exist (Wagenmakers, Wetzels, Botsboom, & van der Maas, 2011).

Bem, Utts, and Johnson (2011) addressed these concerns by suggesting that Wagenmakers and colleagues applied Bayesian analyses too stringently. Rouder and Morey (2011) reanalyzed Bem's data with Bayesian t-tests, and have validated Bem's statistical support for psi, at least for experiments 1, 2, 3, and 4; Rouder and Morey did not include data from experiments 5, 6, and 7, as they reported being "unconvinced that the data are interpretable" (p. 12) from those experiments. Already one set of researchers have reported failing to replicate results of Experiment 8, which assessed retroactive facilitation ("psychic") recall (Galak & Nelson, 2010).

It will be interesting to see how concerns raised by the Bem studies are addressed. Perhaps it will stimulate future controlled experiments into paranormal phenomena; Bem has offered to make his experimental paradigm and stimuli available to anyone interested in replicating his research (Bem et al., 2011).

History of science teaches us that future research will not offer much insight or validation of paranormal ability. For over 80 years, good scientists have made bold claims regarding paranormal abilities, all of which have been refuted (see Alcock, 1981, 2011). Indeed, Alcock (2011) warns that publication of the experiments by Bem has ultimately been destructive:

> "The publication of this set of experiments will serve no one well. Parapsychology is not honored by having this paper accepted by a mainstream psychology journal. Neither does Bem's paper serve the public well, for it only adds to confusion about the scientific case for the existence of psi." (p. 14)

Telepathy

The third major area of ESP, *telepathy*, is the ability to read someone's mind and to tell others the thoughts perceived in this fashion. As with precognition and clairvoyance, the possible existence of telepathic skills has been scientifically investigated. But telepathy differs from both clairvoyance and precognition in that it requires the experimenter to look at a target while the subject tries to guess the target's identity (see Figure 9.2). Therefore, telepathy is akin to mind reading.

Tart (1966, 1977b) researched telepathy in a manner similar to Rhine's experiments with Zener cards (1964). Tart hypothesized that giving a subject immediate feedback in a repeated card-guessing task would stabilize psi performance by permitting talented individuals to develop a strategy for learning which cards had a greater chance of appearing on subsequent guesses. This strategy of research was based in part on a memory theory of ESP proposed by Roll (1966). Roll suggested that ESP responses are in fact revived memory traces that are activated by an external ESP target stimulus.

According to Tart, Palmer, and Redington (1979a, 1979b), such learning could take place via internal processes that enable the subject to gain conscious control of ESP functioning. In essence, the subject makes "mental snapshots" in reaching a response decision, stores such snapshots in memory along with the feedback knowledge of the success or failure of each response, and then examines the stored data to determine which internal events constituted a guide for a useful ESP guessing strategy.

Although their results are not as impressive as those produced by Hubert Pearce in the Rhine report (1964), the experiments conducted by Tart and colleagues do present evidence that card-guessing above chance definitely is possible. The question is whether this skill requires ESP. It seems that Tart's data can easily be explained in nonparapsychological terms, namely, that good subjects have the ability to memorize card sequences, much as good poker players can remember which cards have been played previously in an expended deck.

Figure 9.2 • A Person Reading Another's Mind

Because of the feedback manipulation, the assertion that ESP was necessary for above-chance performance is at best tenuous. As Irwin (1978a, 1978b) and Kennedy (1980) have demonstrated in their card-guessing experiments, and as Vitulli (1983) has demonstrated in a computer-assisted psi test, the ability to be an above-chance guesser may relate more to the subject's ability to process available information, as in a perception or cognition task (see Kahneman, 1973; Lindsey & Norman, 1977) than to possession of ESP abilities.

Remote Viewing

Related to the phenomena of clairvoyance, precognition, and telepathy is a reported experience referred to as *remote viewing* (Targ & Puthoff, 1974a; 1977). This refers to the ability of subjects to describe places being visited by other people without having any normal form of communication with the visitors. Unfortunately, attempts at replicating this phenomenon have been unsuccessful (Marks & Kammann, 1978; 1980). The major reason given for a failure to replicate concerns the judging procedure used by Targ and Puthoff.

In the Targ and Puthoff studies, judges were asked to match a series of subject responses to a set of target responses. (*Target responses* means those that were determined before the experiment to be the ones most likely to be given by subjects.) Marks and Kammann argued that the transcripts of the subjects' reports should have been edited to remove cues that would assist the judges in identifying the target responses. Since this was not done, the judging procedure was biased and produced above-chance matching of transcripts with targets. As a result, Marks and Kammann and, later, Marks and Scott (1986) argued that remote viewing is only another example of a psi phenomenon that can be explained by experimenter bias.

Factors Influencing Experimental Findings

Ganzfeld Controls

In an attempt to partially address the issue of experimenter bias, some researchers have studied psi phenomena in a *ganzfeld*. This term refers to a condition of reduced sensory stimulation that can, for example, be produced by applying halved Ping-Pong balls to a subject's eyes and shining a light onto them while playing white noise (a combination of all sound frequencies) into the subject's ears via headphones. Some researchers have indicated that this control procedure, when applied, produces about a 50 percent replication rate of psi experiments (Blackmore, 1980).

However, in an exhaustive analysis of virtually all psi ganzfeld research between 1974 and 1981, Hyman (1985) concluded that the replication rate was really close to chance, primarily because of detected experimental flaws in all studies examined. Honorton (1985) argued that Hyman's conclusion was inaccurate and that many of the studies, in which so-called flaws were detected, were really free of such experimenter error or bias. In a joint paper, Hyman and Honorton (1986) finally agreed that a conclusion on the viability of the ganzfeld as a control procedure for psi experiments was premature and that the value of this procedure could be determined only by continuing its use in future research.

Interestingly, the debate continues. Storm, Tressoldi, and Risio (2010a) published a meta-analysis of psi experiments conducted between 1992 and 2008. Their analysis revealed that true ganzfeld experiments did demonstrate significant paranormal abilities. Hyman (2010b) again responded, expressing concerns reminiscent of those issued many years ago to Honorton: Storm et al. considered non-ganzfeld studies as true ganzfeld. Further, they combined data in their meta-analysis inappropriately, by selectively including and excluding data as outliers, which produced an inaccurate inflation of the effects. This created an illusion that scientific studies have reliably reproduced paranormal activity in the laboratory when, in fact, they have not (Hyman, 2010b).

Storm et al. (2010b) responded to Hyman (2010b) by explaining that they followed standard meta-analytic statistical procedures that have been applied—and accepted—in areas other than parapsychology. So, while Storm et al. (2010b) acknowledged that their evidence for psi is "largely statistical," they emphasize that statistics do demonstrate a significant effect of psi from well-controlled ganzfeld experiments. Storm and colleagues acknowledge that further research is needed to determine the nature of psi. It is hoped that further research will encourage the development of a theory that may explain paranormal phenomena and generate replicable hypothesis testing (e.g., Hyman, 2010b).

Individual Differences

Regardless of the type of ESP experiment a researcher is conducting, subjects are classified into two types—sheep (believers in ESP) and goats (disbelievers or doubters.) Research has tended to show that sheep generally score better than chance on ESP tasks, while goats tend to score at or below random chance (Palmer, 1971; Schmeidler & McConnell, 1958). However, such differences between sheep and goats are not always found. For example, Smith (1992) investigated belief in the paranormal and how this affects the observation of a "psychic" demonstration. Individuals were shown a videotaped demonstration of ostensible psychic ability. Subjects were told that the demonstration was authentic or that it involved trickery. Sheep and goats did not differ in their observation and subsequent report of the demonstration.

Interestingly, belief in paranormal phenomena has been correlated with manic-depressive illness (Thalbourne & French, 1995), with neurotic disorders (Thalbourne, Dunbar, & Delin, 1995), and with childhood trauma (Irwin, 1994). Also, Snel, van der Sijde, and Wiegant (1995) found that believers (sheep) are more field-dependent (influenced by external stimuli) than nonbelievers (goats). As a result, they concluded that believers tend to interpret paranormal phenomena and information in the context in which they are presented, while nonbelievers tend to abstract the context and interpret paranormal phenomena and information analytically.

Besides being a sheep or goat, are other factors important in demonstrating ESP abilities? This is not an easy question to answer. However, L. E. Rhine (1961) and J. B. Rhine (1964) have reported that subjects who demonstrated ESP in their experiments did not fall into one particular age group. Their subjects have ranged in age from 4 to 60 years. For college students who have served as subjects, grades have not been a predictive factor in determining who can demonstrate ESP. In addition, no evidence exists to demonstrate that ESP ability is related to gender.

Factors that appear to improve ESP abilities include one's level of confidence (people who are more confident demonstrate greater abilities) and concentration. Krippner, Hickman, Auerhahn, and Harris (1972) also discovered that for some subjects, ESP abilities were improved when there was a full moon. We can only speculate why any of these factors influence ESP abilities. Does a person's level of consciousness change when he or she is more confident about performing a certain task and concentrates on the task? In chapter 4 we learned that both these factors appeared to be important in determining who was hypnotizable. Therefore, it is also conceivable that these factors play a role in determining who can demonstrate certain ESP abilities. However, this is only a matter of conjecture.

As for the influence of moon phase on ESP abilities, a physical force may be working on behavior and consciousness in a manner similar to that which controls tide levels. Because this suggestion is highly speculative and is supported by no evidence, a scientific conclusion is not possible. However, would it not be interesting if such a phenomenon were taking place?

Hypnotic Influences

Is hypnotic susceptibility related to ESP performance or belief? Pekala, Kumar, and Cummings (1992) investigated hypnotic susceptibility in relation to a variety of parapsychological and anomalous feelings, beliefs, and experiences. Over 500 students completed the Harvard Group Scale of Hypnotic Susceptibility (see chapter 4) and two questionnaires that dealt with altered state and cognitive experiences. Individuals with high hypnotic susceptibility endorsed far more psi-related items and anomalous beliefs and experiences than did those with low hypnotic susceptibility.

In reviewing the literature on hypnotic suggestions and ESP performance, Honorton and Krippner (1969) and Hinds (1995) reported some interesting findings. Some of the studies reviewed were those by Grela (1945), Fahler and Cadoret (1958), and Casler (1962, 1967), in which hypnosis appears to be a facilitator in clairvoyance and telepathy.

Grela (1945) undertook the first systematic investigation of the effects of hypnosis on ESP performance. In this study, one group of subjects, who were judged high in hypnotic responsiveness, were hypnotized and asked to guess symbols displayed on a deck of cards that were visible only to an experimenter. While hypnotized, they were told that they possessed ESP abilities and that these abilities would be displayed more than adequately when they were asked to guess the symbols. A second group of subjects, who were judged low in hypnotic susceptibility and therefore not hypnotized, was asked to perform the same task with the same instructions. Although Grela's results did not prove to be statistically significant, a trend was exhibited in which hypnosis tended to facilitate card-guessing accuracy.

In a related card-guessing study by Fahler and Cadoret (1958), subjects who were judged high in hypnotic susceptibility participated in an ESP experiment during a waking state and again during a state of hypnosis. During the waking state, the number of correct guesses did not exceed chance. However, in the hypnotized state, a very high level of performance was achieved, statistically exceeding chance.

Casler (1962, 1967) also found that subjects demonstrated ESP card-guessing abilities that were significantly better with hypnotic facilitation than during the waking state. In these studies, subjects were asked to generate, during hypnosis, whatever suggestions of their own they felt would help them perform better in an ESP task. Results indicated that self-induced suggestions during hypnosis significantly improved card-guessing performance.

In addition to the studies we have discussed, Krippner (1968) reported a study concerned with the effects of hypnotic imagery on ESP performance. When subjects were instructed to concentrate on an image that they could not physically see but that the experimenter could, Krippner found that hypnotized subjects were better able to accurately report the content of the image. He concluded that hypnosis may have served to accelerate the processing of the extrasensory material.

Clairvoyant dreams have also been examined by Honorton (1972). In this study, subjects who were judged highly susceptible to hypnotization were hypnotized and given suggestions to dream about the contents of an envelope. Results indicated that content guessing was significantly improved in subjects experiencing clairvoyant dreams under hypnosis. However, such a finding is not consistently reported in the literature (e.g., Honorton & Stump, 1969). Unfortunately, when positive findings are reported in one laboratory, they are soon met with negative or disconfirming findings from another laboratory (see Alcock, 1987). Thus, although hypnosis would appear to facilitate ESP abilities, especially telepathy and clairvoyance, results are far from conclusive.

In general, despite many failures to replicate a variety of phenomena labeled extrasensory perception, and despite the continuing controversy over whether ESP even exists, many reports continue to be published that demonstrate that clairvoyance, telepathy, and precognition can be produced in a laboratory situation (e.g., Radin, 1988; Schmeidler, 1985; Sondow, 1988).

Psychokinesis

In addition to telepathy, precognition, and clairvoyance, another interesting area of research in parapsychology is what is referred to as **psychokinesis (PK),** or the ability to make an object move by mind control—that is, without being in physical contact with it. We have witnessed such an occurrence in a number of movies using the film industry's expertise in special effects, but can people actually demonstrate such an ability? We now examine this possibility in terms of reported laboratory findings.

There are several examples of PK in the parapsychology literature. One classic case was reported by Aylesworth (1975). An Englishman, Harry Price, observed a young girl who appeared to be able to depress a telegraph key without touching it. Doubting the girl's PK abilities, Price had her repeat the performance under some very stringent controls. He blew a soap and glycerin bubble over the telegraph key and placed the setup in a glass enclosure. After this, he further enclosed the apparatus in a wire cage. He hoped that all of these precautions would guarantee the girl's not having physical contact with the telegraph key. Price was astonished to see that she nonetheless depressed the telegraph key.

Other examples of PK have been reported in the Duke University laboratories of the Rhines (L. E. Rhine, 1970). Basically, the Rhines' (J. B. and L. E.) study of PK grew out of their concern for methodological control during investigations of parapsychological phenomena. They wondered, for example, whether the number of Zener cards a subject could accurately report, in excess of chance guessing, might be due to clairvoyant or telepathic abilities. Or could it be that the subject used PK to control the order in which the cards were presented? To help answer these questions, the Rhines used as a subject in a PK experiment a man who had previously demonstrated clairvoyant abilities with the Zener cards. This time, instead of having the subject report the symbol on each card, he was to report the exact order of the cards before and after they were shuffled. The researchers observed no difference between these two sessions; in both instances the subject exceeded chance guessing. As a result, it appeared that the ability to name Zener card symbols might be multidetermined. That is, it could be attributed to clairvoyance, telepathy, PK, or perhaps just good guessing.

It was obvious to the Rhines that isolating the various ESP and PK phenomena in the card-guessing task would not be possible. Although several subjects in the Duke experiments demonstrated the ability to guess Zener cards accurately above the chance guessing level, no conclusion could be made concerning the reasons for their ability to do so.

Therefore, the Rhines began another experiment to determine whether PK could exist. This was a dice-throwing task. In one such experiment (Rhine & Brier, 1968), subjects were asked to throw two dice and attempt to have their sum total greater than 7. Of a possible 36 combinations of two dice, 15 combinations are greater than 7. Subjects threw the dice a total of 6,744 times, and managed to accumulate 3,110 throws in which the total of the dice exceeded 7. The odds against doing so are about a billion to 1 when 2,810 throws of the dice totaling more than 7 are expected by chance. Again, however, a question arose regarding whether subjects were controlling the dice by PK or whether they knew via precognition how the dice would land. This question frequently arises in experiments like this and must be dealt with if such experiments are to be conducted in a controlled fashion.

Although Rhine and colleagues have studied PK in the laboratory for many years, examples of PK phenomena also happen in the natural environment. Pratt and Roll (1958) report the case of the James H. Herrmann family of Seaford, New York. For several weeks this family complained of rather strange occurrences in their home. Objects moved for no apparent reason: a figurine flew through the air and a bottle of shampoo moved across the bathroom shelf. Sixty-seven such events occurred before the Herrmanns sought assistance.

Retroactive PK is a newer term, used to describe the ability to control, via psychokinesis or PK, the outcome of random events *before* they are generated. In this view, people with precognitive ability—the ability to predict the outcome of a random event—are really employing PK before the start of the experiment, to control the order in which the "random" events will occur. It is then easy for these people with PK abilities to "predict" the order of events, since they established the order beforehand, using their PK abilities. Several researchers have attempted to demonstrate the existence of retroactive PK, primarily using evidence from studies with random event generators (e.g., Hootkouper, 2002; Jahn & Dunne, 2005). Studies of random event generation will be described more fully in a later section of this chapter.

Poltergeist Phenomena

Poltergeist is a German word meaning "noisy spirit" and generally refers to strange happenings such as objects moving in space (see Figure 9.3) and other things that occurred in the Herrmann home. Pratt and Roll discovered that objects never moved in the home when it was unoccupied. However, when the Herrmann son, James, Jr., was present, objects began to move. Pratt and Roll observed five of these so-called PK movements, and they did not believe that trickery or deception was involved.

In fact, Pratt (1973a) reported several additional instances of poltergeist events similar to the Herrmann example. In one case a court reporter from Oakland, California, named James Hazlewood reported some strange happenings in his office. A Dictaphone foot pedal moved from a cabinet; light bulbs in a fixture became unscrewed, fell, and broke; and the metal top of a typewriter went through an open window and fell to the street below.

Are these poltergeist phenomena examples of PK in the real world? This question is not easy to answer, because many of the PK or poltergeist events are reported after the fact and therefore cannot be verified scientifically. However, similar examples continue to be reported and therefore cannot be dismissed

Figure 9.3 • Objects Floating in Space

lightly. Until more examples can be demonstrated under controlled laboratory settings, the scientific community will not accept the poltergeist phenomenon.

Some of the most interesting demonstrations of PK were exhibited by Uri Geller. Geller claimed to be able to break metal rings simply by concentration and to start broken clocks by concentrating on them. As reported by Aylesworth (1975), Geller demonstrated bending a ring that belonged to Friedbert Karger of the Max Planck Institute in Berlin. While Geller visited the space scientist Werner von Braun, von Braun's calculator ceased functioning. This also happened at the Stanford Research Institute in California when Geller appeared as a subject for an experiment by two physicists, Russell Targ and Harold Puthoff.

Targ and Puthoff (1974b) conducted several experiments on Geller. All the experiments were filmed or videotaped to ascertain that the scientists would not miss anything, such as a sleight-of-hand trick or other deception. In one experiment, Geller unbalanced a precision scientific scale. He also bent a steel band to an angle that would have required about 100 pounds of pressure. Geller accomplished this without coming into physical contact with the objects.

Needless to say, the PK demonstrations by Geller and others are highly controversial. Can some or all of the feats performed by Geller be magic? In other words, could a magician replicate the so-called PK demonstrations? One magician, the Amazing Randi, says yes. In fact, Randi (1975, 1982) has written two books in which he detailed exactly how Geller performed his so-called feats. As an example, it is possible to demonstrate the bending of forks or spoons on television if one uses utensils made of sterling silver. With the heat generated by the lights required for television cameras, silver will begin to bend, especially if exposed to intense light for a prolonged period. Thus, the research in the area of PK, especially the feats demonstrated by Geller, does not appear to have a sound methodological base. It is difficult to take research on the aforementioned PK phenomena seriously when magicians can replicate the demonstrated feats.

Interestingly, James Randi continues to debunk proclaimed psychics. He has a standing offer of $1 million dollars to any person who can successfully demonstrate psi abilities. Visit http://www.youtube.com/watch?v=sesamjLNHlU&NR=1&feature=fvwp for a brief clip of Randi's "Million Dollar Challenge." Though hundreds have tried, no one has yet claimed the money—Randi has been able to recreate each psychic "feat," showing how they are nothing more than clever magic tricks. Randi has specifically invited two self-proclaimed mediums, Sylvia Brown and James van Praagh (a coproducer of the TV show *Ghost Whisperer*, which aired on the CBS network from 2005–2010). Sylvia Brown said, in 2001, that she would prove Randi was wrong and would collect the money. She has not yet shown up for testing, saying she "doesn't know how to reach Randi." Randi, amusingly, replied to this by noting that she is a medium—if she knows how to reach dead people, she should be able to reach him (also—he's in the phone book).

Kirlian Photography

Another PK phenomenon is called **Kirlian photography**. This process was discovered by two Russian scientists, Semyon and Valentina Kirlian (Krippner & Rubin, 1974; Moss & Johnson, 1974). The notion behind this phenomenon is that a form of energy flows, or can be made to flow, by PK from acupuncture points on the human body. The Kirlians believe they have discovered a process that can photograph this energy. (Such photography has also been demonstrated with plants.)

The actual Kirlian process involves the use of an electric tesla coil (a type of transformer) connected to two metal plates. An object (usually a finger) is placed between the plates, where a piece of film touches the object. Electricity is turned on, generating a high-energy frequency that causes the film to record an "aura" or "halo." Variations in the color and form of the halo are considered descriptors of mood states. For example, a red, blotchy halo is indicative of anxiety; a glowing halo indicates relaxation (the greater the glow, the more relaxed the person is). Since the energy flow does not appear to be controlled by the five senses, parapsychologists believe that it is controlled by PK.

Whether this is really the case cannot be stated at this time. Montandon (1977), however, believed that Kirlian photography and the resultant auras were related to palmar sweating. If so, such photography has a physical basis that is autonomically controlled. That is, it is controlled involuntarily by the autonomic nervous system (ANS) (see chapter 5). If this is the case, and if Kirlian photography is an accurate recording of ANS activity, the potential uses of Kirlian photography are limitless. For example, the technique might someday serve as a lie detector in recording levels of anxiety or nervousness. Or it might be used to help individuals understand their level of anxiety and subsequently decrease or control this level, much as in biofeedback training. Of course, these suggestions are speculative and are based on the assumption that Kirlian photography is not an illustration of PK. Only time will help us to understand this process more fully.

Random Event Generation

A final example of PK is illustrated by Schmidt, Morris, and Rudolph (1986) and by Schmidt (1970a, 1970b, 1973) in their random-event generator studies. Their method basically involved asking subjects to predict or influence the radioactive emission of subatomic particles. While Schmidt reported positive results indicating that subjects can have control over such particles, Alcock (1987) argued that Schmidt's procedure suffered from less-than-optimal experimental control. For example, subjects were usually unsupervised, and the control of experimental conditions was not rigorous. In addition, Alcock argued that Schmidt's random-event generator was not truly random and that, since subjects were provided with immediate feedback concerning their performance, it was possible that they learned how to respond on subsequent performances. Needless to say, Schmidt (1987) disagreed with Alcock's assessment.

Another example of extensive work with random event generators comes from the Princeton Engineering Anomalies Research (PEAR) lab. Although closed in 2007, the PEAR lab conducted controlled studies on paranormal activity using random event generators (REGs) for 30 years. The PEAR lab was led by Robert Jahn, an aerospace engineer, and managed by Brenda Dunne. Research began in the mid 1970s, when a student proposed to develop a mechanical device—a random event generator—to test whether people could use telekinetic and psychic abilities to control the outcome of random events.

While Jahn had no inherent interest in testing psychic or telekinetic abilities, he was interested in engineering a random event device, and so the lab began.

Numerous studies have shown that when left alone, mechanical or electrical random event generators are truly random. However, when an operator is imposed, slight deviations from random chance occur. For example, if you flip a coin 10 times, chance suggests you should get five heads and five tails. While you might not be too alarmed if you found six heads and four tails after only 10 coin flips, if you flipped the coin 10 million times and got 6 million heads and only 4 million tails, you would be very surprised; it is highly unlikely that you would get an "extra" 1 million heads with an unbiased coin.

In the traditional REG experiments, participants are asked to use their mental abilities to try to get the machines to select specific events at random. This is actually an example of psychokinesis (PK), in that participants are controlling the outcome, or "selecting" random events, rather than being clairvoyant about the occurrence of a future event. Results from hundreds of participants engaging with millions of random events have verified slight shifts above or below chance occurrence. For example, one series of studies asked participants to control the outcome of 10,000 coin flips, and found slight changes above or below 5,000 "expected" heads.

Jahn and Dunne (e.g., Jahn, 1982; Jahn & Dunne, 2005; Jahn, Dunne, & Nelson, 1987) suggest that there is something about the people engaging with the machinery that causes these slight deviations in chance. Indeed, the idea of "retroactive PK" (above), or the notion that they were using their PK abilities to select the outcome of the random events *before* the experiment emerged from these studies. Despite the dozens of articles, meticulous development and testing of sensitive machinery, methodologically sound, controlled experiments, and extensive statistical analyses, it has been difficult to gain acceptance among the scientific community for precognitive or retroactive PK ability using Jahn's random event generators (e.g., Jahn & Dunne, 2005). Thus, as with other psi phenomena, evidence for the control of random events is inconclusive.

Paranormal Phenomena and "Anomolies" in Science

Due to the fact that PK and other psychic abilities cannot be produced "on demand," and because there is difficulty replicating it in the laboratory, any accumulated evidence in support of parapsychological phenomena may be considered anomalous. What makes modern science so successful is how it deals with these kinds of anomalous findings (e.g., Hyman, 2003, 2010a; 2010b; Kuhn, 1962).

All science progresses under a governing theory that can produce specific, testable hypotheses. If one of the hypothesis tests suggests that the theory is not accurate, findings are examined for flaws. If flaws in methodology or data analyses are not identified, then further research is conducted. If additional research by independent laboratories confirms evidence for the new finding, then the prevailing theory may be revised. If the anomalous findings cannot be reliably reproduced, then the governing theory remains, and the new hypothesis is rejected (e.g., Kuhn, 1962).

In an attempt to emphasize why reports of successful paranormal activity should not be considered, Hyman (2010a, 2010b) applies this process to parapsychology. Hyman notes how "meteorites, general relativity, quantum mechanics, and the planet Neptune" (Hyman, 2010b, p. 488), each, in their day, began as anomalous findings to a prevailing theory. Clear, testable hypotheses were generated, and unambiguous explanations were offered regarding how the existing theory might be revised to accommodate the new findings. Independent confirmation of the existence of these events occurred, the existing theory was revised, and today we consider these things to be true, scientific fact.

In contrast, other scientific claims, including those of "N-rays" and water canals on Mars, have not been justified. Hyman (2010a, 2010b) eloquently describes the search for "N-rays" in the early 20th century. At least 180 articles were published between 1903–1907 on the successful isolation of N-rays. By 1907, at least 100 contradictory papers had also emerged, reporting failures to replicate the results. In spite of the fact that more reports of the existence of N-rays were published than not, due to inconsistent results and the failure to replicate, Nrays were soon rejected by the scientific community. Hyman asks why a similar rejection of psychic phenomena has not yet occurred in psychological science?

Indeed, in the case of parapsychology, the same researcher often cannot replicate their own results; this has been referred to as the **"decline effect"** or **"unsustainable"** nature of psi (e.g., Bierman, 2001; Kennedy, 2003; see also Alcock, 2010 and Hyman, 2010a for discussion). Indeed, the decline effect has been proposed as a governing mechanism of psi ability; the **decline effect** is defined as the reduction in psi ability caused by the interaction of observers with experimenters and the experimental environment. This means that the same psychic will experience decrements in their psychic powers as a function of using their abilities. Further, experimenters will not be able to replicate previous results even with new participants, due to a reduced ability to detect psi ability following previous demonstrations of psi ability within their lab.

What this means is that due to the nature of psi, a decline effect should be *expected*—it should not appear anomalous when psi cannot be replicated, or when a previously validated psychic cannot accurately predict or control an event. Hyman's point is well taken in this regard; if physicists accepted such a proposition, then we would still be searching for N-rays. Physicists would merely suggest that failure to replicate results was an "inherent" property of N-rays—once identified, the quality of N-rays made them elusive for some period of time. It is our hope that the reader can readily grasp the ludicrous nature of this type of argument, and how it seriously undermines the very nature of scientific endeavor.

The Out-of-Body Experience

In addition to the study of clairvoyance, precognition, telepathy, and PK, parapsychologists have also developed an interest in what are referred to as the **out-of-body experience (OBE)** and the **near-death experience (NDE)**. The OBE is the experience of a subject who has been separated from his or her physical body (Alvarado, 1992). The NDE refers to a number of experiences, including an out-of-body experience, reported by individuals who have been pronounced clinically dead and then resuscitated. What they say they perceived or witnessed while "dead" is the NDE.

The OBE, the feeling that one has been separated from one's body, is generally accompanied by a number of other phenomena. For example, some subjects, who have reported that they have experienced leaving their bodies or have seen themselves as a type of spirit floating above their physical bodies (see Figure 9.4) also report that they have experienced accompanying physical paralysis or catalepsy (Morris, Harary, Janis, Hartwell, & Roll, 1978; Muldoon & Carrington, 1977). Others have reported that separation from the body is frequently accompanied by strong vibrational sensations (Monroe, 1971). A pronounced clarity of consciousness also seems to be common among those reporting OBEs (Crookall, 1966; Fox, 1962; Monroe, 1971). Other separation experiences include hearing unexplained noises (Crookall, 1966; Monroe, 1971) and a heightened sexual arousal (Monroe, 1971). And some of these experiences seem to be associated with REM or rapid eye movement activity

Figure 9.4 • An Out-of-Body Experience

(see chapter 7), indicating that perhaps the person is asleep and dreaming in a conscious state (Salley, 1982).

How common is it for individuals to report that they have been separated from their physical body? In a survey of college students, Blackmore (1982) reported that around 13 percent had such experiences. Before her report, a number of investigators reported OBEs ranging from around 8 percent (Haraldsson, Gudmundsdottir, Ragnarsson, Loftsson, & Jonsson, 1977) to around 34 percent (Green, 1967).

What produces this strange experience? Salley (1982) has suggested that OBEs may merely be vivid hallucinatory dreams and that the paralysis and sexual arousal simply reflect the physiology of REM sleep. (Incidentally, the other symptoms also seem to fall into what might be considered typical symptomology of dream or REM activity). However, Tart (1968) reported that during an OBE some subjects are capable of demonstrating extrasensory perception. Needless to say, this cannot be accounted for by the REM hypothesis.

Exactly what OBEs are, and what produces them, is not known. As we mentioned, Salley believes that they are related to the onset of REM activity. Blackmore (1982) has likewise reported that OBEs appear to be related to lucid dreams. Whether they are related to sleep, dreams, or whatever cannot be answered at this time. Some have speculated that they result from a blockage in the perception of body-relevant stimulation at a sensory level and that they are emotionally neutral or even pleasant experiences (Irwin, 1988; Nash, Lynn, & Stanley, 1984).

However, this is not the case. In fact, Nash et al. have shown that OBEs are reported to be troubling and unpleasant. Also, they found little support for their own contention that they are the result of a sensory blockage. Clearly, more controlled laboratory experiments than have been reported thus far are needed to answer the question of what produces OBEs. It is clear, however, that they are interesting experiences, and regardless of what they are and what produces them, they continue to be reported in the scientific literature (e.g., Alvarado, 1984).

Bunning and Blanke (2005) reviewed the literature on out-of-body experiences. They argued that understanding the neural correlates of OBEs will permit a great understanding of how self-consciousness and embodiment arise in the normal brain. This more recent report estimates about 10 percent of the normal population experiences OBEs. OBEs are reported in virtually all cultures, although individuals typically only experience one or two OBEs in a lifetime. This makes it extremely difficult to verify experimentally.

Nonetheless, certain conditions seem to precipitate OBEs. In addition to those mentioned above (e.g., sleep and certain drugs), high altitudes can induce OBEs. Seventy-five percent of experienced mountain climbers report OBEs (Bunning & Blanke, 2005). Airplane pilots also report a "disembodied" sensation, feeling not only similar to an OBE, but often stating that they feel like they are watching themselves fly from *outside* of the airplane! This occurs especially when flying alone at very high altitudes (greater than 10,000 feet).

Based on the findings that the most frequent OBEs were observed either when people were in the supine position (laying down), right before sleep or general anesthesia, at high altitudes or following acceleration or deceleration changes (as when mountain climbing or flying), OBEs may be caused by alterations in vestibular sensation (Bunning & Blanke, 2005). We look forward to future research on the mechanisms underlying OBEs.

Related to the out-of-body experience is the so-called near-death experience (NDE). In fact, as previously mentioned, one quality of a near-death experience is an out-of-body report. What exactly are NDEs? Are these potential indicators that there is life after death? These are some of the issues we now consider.

The Near-Death Experience

The scientific study of the NDE began with the appearance of two books on the subject by Moody (1975, 1988). In these books, Moody reported a number of interviews he conducted with individuals who had narrowly escaped death or who had been brought back to life after experiencing clinical death. These people reported a variety of happenings, including the following (see Figure 9.5):

1) Seeing oneself leave one's physical body, often from a distance (the out-of-body experience)
2) Seeing spirits of relatives and friends who had already died
3) Seeing light or an illuminated apparition
4) Seeing what appeared to be a review of the major events of one's life
5) Feeling warmth, joy, happiness, and peace
6) Having psi experiences, especially precognition

After these reports, a number of scientific studies were conducted to determine how universal these experiences were and to what, if anything, they were related. Foremost among the studies on the NDE were those of Ring (1980, 1985,

Figure 9.5 • A Near-Death Description of "Entering the Light"

1993, 1995), who studied a number of individuals who had been brought back to life after experiencing clinical death. From his sample, half had reported NDEs that were practically identical to those reported by Moody. Ring subsequently categorized the NDEs as follows:

60 percent reported feeling at peace.

53 percent reported "entering the darkness."

37 percent had experienced leaving one's body.

33 percent "saw the light" (of this percentage, 20 percent actually entered it).

33 percent reported that they had chosen or willed themselves back to life.

25 percent reviewed the highlights of their life.

As further evidence for the universality of NDEs, Kellehear (1996) has indicated that reports garnered by researchers such as Ring are remarkably similar all over the world. Individuals in India, China, Guam, Australia, and New Zealand report experiences similar to those obtained in the United States and Canada.

Several explanations have been offered concerning the NDE. Palmer (1978) believed that sensory deprivation (see chapter 8) and stress, which can produce hallucinations, might, to some extent, be involved in producing NDEs. If one conceives that being near death is a state of sensory deprivation and that dying is a stressful event, then Palmer's explanation may have some validity.

Another explanation for the NDE was proposed by McHarg (1978). He believed that the NDE resulted from cerebral anoxia or a shortage of oxygen in the brain metabolism and temporal lobe or epileptic seizures. Cerebral anoxia involves symptoms of anxiety, disorientation, and distortions of perception; temporal lobe seizures are sometimes associated with seeing visions of objects or people not physically present. While such visions may be associated with the anoxia and temporal lobe seizures, it is difficult to imagine that all NDE reports are associated with the combination of these two events. Also, as Grosso (1981) pointed out, the match between symptoms associated with NDE and those associated with anoxia, temporal lobe, and epileptic seizures was not sufficiently similar. One study (Audette, 1979) also indicated that many NDE reports come from individuals who displayed flat EEGs. This, of course, precludes the possibility of universal temporal lobe involvement.

Palmer (1978) suggested that religious expectations may influence the NDE. That is, highly religious individuals who are dying may expect to see or to be taken away by an apparition. However, many individuals who report NDEs are not religious in any sense of the term (Moody, 1975, 1977, 1985, 1988; Ring, 1980, 1985, 1993, 1995). As Grasso (1981) has nicely summarized, "the empirical findings across the board so far indicate that religious beliefs influence the *interpretation*, not the *content*, of experiences of this nature" (p. 48).

Attribution has also been offered as an explanation for the NDE (Norton & Sahlman, 1995). In essence, it is argued that personal belief systems influence coding and interpreting NDEs. Thus, individuals who report experiencing an NDE might first simplify the experience to help interpret its meaning. Ambiguities are then resolved, and the NDE is eventually attributed to a cause. While this may be going on during an NDE, attribution, in and of itself, cannot be argued as the sole cause for such an experience.

Susan Blackmore published a review describing six common NDE "theories" of what causes NDEs and why the experience is so similar across individuals and cultures (Blackmore, 1996). The six theories include expectation, drugs, endorphins, anoxia, temporal lobe stimulation, and life after death. Blackmore suggests that evidence is both abundant and lacking for each of these theories; it becomes a matter of personal preference if one chooses to define an NDE as a physiological by-product of the dying brain, or as a type of divine intervention. Blackmore further suggests that belief in NDEs is a type of divine intervention that may function to decrease fear of death.

To date, there is really no universal explanation for the NDE (Corcoran, 1988; Perry, 1988; Schroter-Kunhardt, 1993). It is an interesting phenomenon, and many of us have heard of individuals who have had this type of experience. Some have even interpreted the NDE as an indication that there is life after death or as evidence to confirm the existence of a deity. Unfortunately, these, like other explanations, must fall into the category of speculations.

Psychic Healing

Another topic that has sparked the interest of many in the area of parapsychology is *psychic healing*, or what is also sometimes referred to as faith healing. With this phenomenon, we generally envision a type of mystical or religious ceremony in which someone is helping an afflicted person to overcome a disease or medical problem. Those who seek a faith cure generally do so either when a medical cure has failed or when this may be their only means of treatment. Does this form of healing really work? Is it possible that an altered state of consciousness accompanies the psychic healing process? These are some of the questions we address here.

Although psychic or faith healing is generally associated with some sects of Protestant Christianity, it is also found in various forms in Catholicism, Judaism, and even societal organizations that do not adhere to an organized religion. As examples, exorcism was and still is practiced to some extent by some Catholics. This form of healing requires the presence of a priest to rid the person's body of a supposed evil spirit that possesses it. In Judaism, psychic healing has been employed in what has been referred to as Jewish Science (Meyer, 1965), a counterpart to Christian Science. In both Jewish and Christian Science, believers feel that a variety of maladies can be treated through prayer to a deity who has power to cure them of their affliction. Strong prayer may induce the person to experience a change in the normal, waking state of consciousness.

Those who seek cures primarily with prayer often report that, during such prayer, they felt removed from their normal, waking state. This distance helped them come closer to their deity, who helped to cure their illness or problem. In all likelihood, major physical illnesses could not be treated successfully with psychic healing alone, although many adherents to such beliefs would disagree with us (Ricalla, 1975). However, a variety of psychosomatic problems can be alleviated, and many individuals find relief from their troubles through the power of prayer and a strong belief in psychic healing as a way to deal with illness and other problems.

The most popularized form of psychic healing is the type we often see on Sunday morning television or at revival meetings at which a religious leader "lays hands" on an afflicted believer and tries to cure him or her of a malady. In a stereotyped example, a physically incapacitated person confined to a wheelchair is brought to a stage, where a preacher lays his hands on the individual's head or sometimes another part of the body. The preacher then begins to pray and asks the invalid to pray along with him. He may then ask whether the person believes in Jesus and believes that Jesus can cure the person's problems. After receiving an affirmative response, the preacher applies some pressure through the laying on of hands as a gesture of transferring psychic healing power from Jesus to the afflicted individual.

While continuing to pray and while experiencing the pressure being applied to his or her body, the believer then is observed to experience either a sense of euphoria or, in many instances, a loss of waking consciousness. If the believer does not faint, he or she appears to at least have experienced some transformation in consciousness from the normal, waking state. The audience may then sometimes observe the afflicted individual beginning to walk after being confined to the wheelchair for many years. Of course, this produces a definite religious high, both for the afflicted person and for those observing this miracle example of psychic healing.

Did psychic healing really occur? Was there a change in consciousness by which healing was achieved? Believers in psychic healing may experience relief from an affliction or, in some instances, a bona fide cure (Whitlock, 1978). However, most who have experienced a psychic cure probably suffered from a psychosomatic illness. Therefore, if they truly believed that Jesus, through the aid of the psychic healer, could help them, it is very possible that they indeed were helped.

What about those who truly believed that Jesus could help them and yet were not cured? Often, they are simply accused of not being true believers. Since Jesus could detect lack of true faith, the cure did not come about. A more realistic suggestion is that their illness was not psychosomatic. Therefore, a psychic cure could not be as effective for them.

Targ (1997) conducted a review of what he called "distant healing" studies. Targ noted that there were many well-controlled studies demonstrating significant effects of distant healing in people, animals, and other biological systems (viz., plants). The main problem is that virtually none of these studies controlled for potentially psychological influences including expectancy and placebo effects, hope, or relaxation.

A more recent meta-analysis of 23 clinical-type trials of distant healing note that while many of the studies suffered from methodological problems, roughly 57 percent of the trials showed beneficial effects (Astin, Harkness, & Ernst, 2000). Atwood (2001) and others (e.g., Courcey, 2001; Kaptchuk, 2001) suggest that the limited evidence (57 percent) should not lead people to believe in the power of distant healing; "extraordinary claims demand extraordinary evidence" (Atwood, 2001, p. 1150).

Although there are numerous informal reports of psychic healing, there has been little controlled scientific research into this area of parapsychology. This is unfortunate, since there appears to be some promise that this form of healing may be beneficial for some individuals. No doubt, as interest in this area continues, research will be forthcoming.

General Theories of Parapsychology

For science to progress in a particular area of concern, it is essential that theories either exist or can be established to explain the various phenomena considered. In an area such as psi, which has many critics and doubters, this requisite is especially crucial. Some researchers (Moss & Butler, 1978; Scriven, 1976) have argued that there exist no bona fide theories of parapsychology. There is surely an absence of a general, comprehensive theory that is considered scientifically adequate to integrate and explain some psi phenomena; this matter is elaborated on at length by Rao (1977). Some general, theoretical accounts of psi include those by Walker (1975, 1984), Stanford (1974, 1977a, 1977b), and Schmidt (1975).

Walker

Walker's theory was based on the notion that ESP and PK are products of hidden variables in quantum mechanics. He stated that this is possible because the mathematical formalism of quantum mechanics does not specify exactly what constitutes an observation or measurement of an event. Because of this deficiency, hidden variables are conceived that are essentially inaccessible to physical measurement. These variables function independently of space and time constraints.

Walker believed that hidden variables exist in consciousness as a part of one's "will" and, as a result, may not be directly observable or measurable. The hidden variables could then produce physical changes in the environment that cannot be accounted for by any physical variables. Thus, phenomena such as ESP and PK could take place even though science is unable to determine their physical or biological loci.

The attempt to explain psi as a function of physics, specifically a measurement problem of quantum mechanics, is an interesting avenue in parapsychology. Unfortunately, Walker's theory is not scientifically testable because of the impossibility of locating these hidden variables for manipulation. Also, Walker's assumption that ESP and PK are the result of physical events remains unproven. Furthermore, to argue that something occurs as a result of something "hidden" is like trying to catch a ghost with an invisible net. To look for psi by proposing "hidden variables" is a poor approach to explaining a supposed scientific relationship.

Houtkooper

An extension of Walker's quantum mechanics theory, Houtkooper (1977, 2002) proposed the Observational Theory (OT). OT is an attempt to address the problem of a lack of a mechanistic explanation for how paranormal phenomena could occur. The "central axiom" of OT is the following: "The act of observation by a motivated observer of an event with a quantum mechanically uncertain outcome influences that outcome" (Houtkooper, 2002, p. 172). OT suggests that psychics are "motivated observers" who can influence the outcome of an event. This is an example of "retroactive PK," where the observer manipulates the events prior to predicting what will happen. Since observers or participants in psi experiments have created the outcome beforehand, they are able to predict successfully what the outcome may be.

Although Houtkooper (2002) specifies ways in which OT may be used to predict and measure paranormal events, this theory continues to be plagued by the same problems as Walker's: There is no way to measure the hidden "quantum" events mediating the ability to perform retroactive PK.

Stanford

Stanford (1974, 1977a, 1977b) proposed a theory of psi that appears to incorporate and elaborate on the idea of mind projection (Rhine, 1945, 1953). Specifically, in addition to using other sense modalities, the individual also employs psi to scan the environment. In this way, psi may be considered a "sixth sense." In a particular need situation, an individual uses ESP as well as other senses to gather necessary information about the world. When the individual obtains extrasensory information, he or she may use it to satisfy a need or what Stanford calls the *psi-mediated instrumental response* (PMIR). Stanford explained PK as "a response mode for PMIR." Thus, PMIR may be a kind of goal-relevant response that comes about as a result of extrasensory means via PK.

Basically, Stanford proposed that all psi responses are mediated, are instrumental, and serve to satisfy a need. Unfortunately, as with Walker's theory, there is no scientific basis or evidence for his conclusions. If psi functions as Stanford has predicted, it should be possible to test his assumptions with basic instrumental learning techniques, such as shaping and extinction. This is not possible, however, because we do not know what behavior to shape or extinguish. Until Stanford can define this "sixth sense" more operationally and explain how it functions, his theory will not help to advance our knowledge of parapsychology.

Schmidt

Probably the most sophisticated attempt to develop a theory of psi was made by Schmidt (1975). He proposed a mathematical explanation that postulates the existence of "psi sources." These mathematically derived sources, according to Schmidt, act similar to the behavior exhibited by successful PK subjects. His theory proposes a psi axiom that leads mathematically to the spatial and temporal independence of psi. Also, the different forms of psi, such as PK, precognition, and clairvoyance, appear as logical consequences of one psi axiom.

Although Schmidt's theory sounds impressive, Schmidt applied mathematics to things we cannot observe. There is nothing intrinsically wrong with doing so, except that mathematical models of behavior often do not have a basis in the real world. To date, Schmidt has not shown such a basis; until he does, his model will remain interesting but not scientifically predictive.

For the time being, it is safe to say that all existing theories of psi have received little or no experimental support. This unfortunate state in the science of parapsychology is undoubtedly one of the major reasons why a large number of scientists, especially psychologists, do not take research in parapsychology very seriously.

Contemporary Theories of Parapsychology

As mentioned several times throughout this chapter (and addressed more completely in the final section), one cornerstone of successful science is that an overarching theory explains the phenomena in question. A good theory will generate testable hypotheses. This is a major pitfall for parapsychology— there remains a lack of theory to explain how and why paranormal phenomena exist (assuming they do). One recent theory attempts to address this concern: May's Decision Augmentation Theory (May, 2004; May, Utts, & Spottiswoode, 1995).

May

Decision Augmentation Theory (DAT) tries to provide a means by which paranormal phenomena may not only be explained, but may be statistically verified (May, 2004; May, Utts, & Spottiswoode, 1995). May and colleagues offer DAT as an extension of Stanford's "elegant" (May et al., 1995, p. 4) psi-mediated instrumental response (PMIR) model described above. According to DAT, psi is a function of a (potentially learned) "favorable bias" established by *experimenters* investigating the paranormal.

DAT suggests that experimenters use their own psi abilities to randomly select only the most able participants. They further randomly engage the experimental situation to present stimuli most favorable to accurate detection (May, 2004; May et al., 1995). In this way, DAT may explain both how a person may acquire future knowledge, as well as telekinetic abilities; experimenters merely use their own psychic ability to find able participants, and then test them at appropriate times, on tasks for which they are most suited (see also Dobyns & Nelson, 1998). May and colleagues present a variety of evidence in support of DAT theory, especially that accumulated through the Princeton Engineering Anomalies Research program (PEAR), described earlier in this chapter.

Dobyns and Nelson (1998) refute the evidence for DAT, based on data from the PEAR database. As noted above, many reports of significant deviations from random chance were published from the PEAR lab, which tested participants interacting with random event generators. May et al. (1995) used those reports as evidence in support of DAT. May and colleagues suggested that there is no other logical or physical explanation for why random events should occur at anything other than chance levels, unless the experimenters are using their own psi abilities to set up a favorable bias. Dobyns and Nelson (1998) explain that May and colleagues analyzed only a subset of the immense dataset accumulated by the PEAR lab, and thus incorrectly gained support for DAT. In other words, DAT does not necessarily provide the only explanation for the small but significant effects found in the PEAR studies.

However, May (2004) suggests that other evidence for DAT comes from presentiment studies. As noted earlier in the chapter, presentiment studies found that participants exhibited physiological responses (changes in skin conductance) before emotional stimuli were actually presented (e.g., Bierman & Radin, 1997; Radin 1997).

May (2004) explains that DAT, unlike other theories, explains the mechanism that allows participants to predict stimuli presented in the future. DAT proposes that the participants themselves probably are not doing anything—they are exhibiting random skin conductance levels. However, the experimenter uses their psi abilities to elicit changes within the participant at the start of each trial, before the stimuli are actually presented. This establishes a favorable bias, so participants can accurately "guess" what will happen next. In this way,

DAT theory is similar to PMIR, in that individuals themselves are guiding their behavior, rather than some immeasurable, inexplicable, external "force."

Radin (e.g., Radin, 2008; Radin, Hayseen, Emoto, & Kizu, 2006) calls the ability to correctly predict future events "intuition." Radin (2008) cites several examples from medicine, science, and the arts, where successful predictions are made with intuition. Radin (2008) suggests that intuition presents an "embarrassing" challenge to science (p. 25) in that there is no rational explanation for how intuition occurs. However, it is unclear from Radin's arguments how intuition is more than skilled guessing by highly trained individuals. Even though we may not be able to consciously describe how we arrive at a correct solution, our accumulated knowledge undoubtedly causes our successful "predictions," or intuition. It appears that Radin (2008) attempts to impose an inappropriate psychical explanation for skilled, educated guessing. It remains to be seen whether other support will be gained for DAT.

Neural Correlates of Paranormal Ability

In an effort to maintain consistency with the previous eight chapters of this text, we discuss in this section data regarding possible neural and physiological correlates of psi.

As reviewed by Bunning and Blanke (2005), although several early studies conducted in the 1970s, including those by Charles Tart, investigated changes in EEG expression during one form of paranormal ability, the out-of-body experience (OBE), none reported significant alterations in EEG waveforms between normal rest and the OBE. This lack of reported effect may have been due to limitations in EEG technology of the time (Bunning & Blanke, 2005). There was also a trend in the 1970s, noted in earlier chapters (e.g., chapter 6) for research to focus on evaluating brainwave changes only in the lower frequency range (e.g., alpha or theta waves). Thus these earlier studies may have overlooked important changes in EEG coherence, amplitude, or latency that could explain OBEs.

Steven Kosslyn recently conducted a study evaluating brain areas involved in psi using fMRI (Moulton & Kosslyn, 2008). In this study, pairs of emotionally close or biologically related individuals were randomly assigned to act as either "senders" or "receivers" of psychic information. The sender would look at either an arousing or neutral picture from the IAPS (the same set of affective picture stimuli used in the Bem (2011) studies described earlier in this chapter). The receiver would try to detect which of two pictures the sender was viewing. The picture the sender viewed was called the "psi" stimulus, while the distracter picture was the "non-psi" stimulus. IAPS pictures were chosen based on previous presentiment studies noting greater psi abilities with emotional and erotic pictures (e.g., Radin, 1997). Receivers were motivated by the potential to earn $1 for every correct choice (250 pairs of pictures were presented, so receivers could earn up to $125). Whole brain images were recorded via fMRI during the experimental session.

Results revealed, first, that participants did not demonstrate any psi abilities; receivers predicted the psi pictures exactly 50 percent of the time (chance guessing). Further, no differences in brain activity following presentation of the "psi" and "non-psi" images were noted at all. Both types of stimuli "evoked widespread but indistinguishable" BOLD responses (Moulton & Kosslyn, 2008, p. 187). Interestingly, one participant out of 32 in the study did demonstrate significant differences in brain activity, in left superior temporal gyrus; this participant also demonstrated very slight alterations in their ability to detect the psi pictures (approximately 52 percent). However, Moulton and Kosslyn (2008) present evidence that this result was not due to psychic ability, but was the effect of individual differences in reactivity to the arousing effects of pictures from the IAPS. Another study (Kensinger & Schacter, 2006; cited in Mouton & Kosslyn, 2008) also reported a single participant with similar, unexplained, elevated activity in left superior temporal gyrus, just while viewing emotionally arousing pictures from the IAPS.

It is not surprising that Moulton and Kosslyn (2008) did not find brain differences between "psi" and "non-psi" stimuli, since none of their participants could effectively detect the psi stimuli. Nonetheless, Moulton and Kosslyn suggest that fMRI should offer utility for scientifically verifying paranormal ability; researchers who can successfully demonstrate psi should concurrently measure brain activity, so a neural correlate may be elucidated. Finding a neural correlate of paranormal ability will surely lend credibility to the notion that psi exists.

To this end, Raz and colleagues (2008) also suggest that determining a biological or genetic process underlying psi could facilitate validation of the paranormal. In chapter 4, we discussed research by Raz demonstrating that highly suggestible people have an elevated genetic marker for COMT, the enzyme that degrades dopamine (e.g., see Raz, 2005 for a review). Raz and colleagues measured this genetic marker in a study of psi. Their argument for this line of research was that, as explained earlier in the chapter, people with a propensity for paranormal activity tend to be highly hypnotizable. As a result, believers in psi may display a genetic marker similar to that observed in highly hypnotizable people.

Although their test of 107 students proved inconclusive—COMT alleles did not differ between believers in the paranormal and nonbelievers—Raz and colleagues (2008) suggest that future studies should continue to assess neural and physiological correlates of psi ability. Identifying a genetic marker could offer proof of paranormal ability. It could also serve as the basis for developing a fundamental theory of psi.

General Problems

Alcock (1987) and Moss and Butler (1978) summarized the major problems that haunt parapsychology as an area of study in the psychology of consciousness. These include:

- Inadequate reporting of test procedures and experimental designs
- Failure to replicate most parapsychology experiments
- Absence of psychological, predictive laws and theories of psi
- Lack of harmony between psi and established physical and biological laws and theories
- Absence of generally observable (i.e., by most of us) psi phenomena in the real world and, therefore, an absence of practical applications of psi
- General absence of scientific evidence in the laboratory to establish the existence of psi phenomena
- Absence of internal consistency (Berkowitz, 1986) essential to convince other scientists that extraneous variables did not influence the outcome of the experiment

In response to these criticisms, Rao (1979) and Rao and Palmer (1987) accused Moss, Butler, and Alcock of bias in reaching their conclusions. They believe that an accumulation of evidence reported in two scientific publications for psi research, the *Journal of Parapsychology* and the *Journal of the American Society for Psychical Research,* basically contradicted each of the points made by these critics. Rao and Palmer went on to say that although the critics' points might be true for a small number of psi experiments, they were no less true for psychology experiments in general. For example, Rao and Palmer stressed that most experimental psychologists do not attempt to replicate their studies (see Bozarth and Roberts, 1972), and, as a result, it is often not known whether they are replicable. Psi experiments, however, are often replicated successfully (Honorton, 1978).

Despite Rao and Palmer's arguments in defense of psi and psi research, there are problems with their defense. For instance, it is simply not true that experimental psychologists do not attempt to replicate their findings. Also, other problems face investigators in the field of parapsychology in addition to those enumerated by the critics (and many of these are still valid, despite Rao and Palmer's defense). There is the problem of the inability of good ESP and PK subjects to replicate their own performance. On one day or trial they exhibit an above-chance performance, while on another day or trial the performance is below chance. This has been dubbed the "decline effect" (Anderson, 1959; Pratt, 1973b; Pratt & Woodruff, 1939; Woodruff & Rhine, 1942). Does this observation indicate that ESP and PK performances are spurious or occur by coincidence? Many believe so (see Tart, 1996). However, those who defend psi findings (e.g., Rao, 1979) believe that it is not possible to set up controls for psi performances, and therefore they are not predictable. Thus, it is not unusual to discover an individual manifesting strong psi abilities on some occasions and reduced or nonexistent abilities on others. As Stanford (1974) has theorized, psi is a sixth sense; sometimes we use it and sometimes we do not.

In the final analysis the study of parapsychology may simply reveal that strange things happen in the laboratory and in the real world that cannot be explained by traditional laws and theories of science. Such investigators as Stanford, Schmidt, Walker, the Rhines, and others have proposed explanations for these happenings. Some believe that these explanations may help us ultimately to understand these occurrences; others believe that such happenings are spurious events that might be attributable to physical, biological, or psychological laws that we have not yet been able to discover. And some (Randi, 1975, 1982) believe that there simply are no real strange happenings that cannot be explained by a magician.

As you can see, a conclusion concerning the validity of psi is not possible. As with many areas of consciousness we have discussed (e.g., hypnosis, meditation, biofeedback), there will always be critics and disbelievers. With regard to parapsychology, most researchers today maintain a fairly healthy skepticism (see Krippner, 1995). While they keep an open mind, they have many doubts about the likelihood of this area becoming an important part of psychological study. Also, the other areas of consciousness have provided us with practical applications, regardless of whether scientists believe the manipulations are totally valid. This has not been the case with parapsychology, and until this happens, the study of psi will remain as controversial as it is now.

For Further Reading

Edge, H. L., Morris, R. L., Palmer, J., & Rush, J. H. (1986). *Foundations of parapsychology.* London: Routledge & Kegan Paul.

Hansel, C. E. M. (1980). *ESP and parapsychology: A critical evaluation.* Buffalo: Prometheus.

Kane, B., Millay, J., & Brown, D. H. (Eds.). (1993). *Silver threads: 25 years of parapsychology research.* Westport, CT: Praeger.

Kellehear, A. (1996). *Experiences near death: Beyond medicine and religion.* New York: Oxford University Press.

Krippner, S., & Friedman, H. L. (Eds). (2010). *Debating psychic experience.* Santa Barbara, CA: Praeger.

Moody, R. A., Jr. (1988). *The light beyond.* New York: Bantam.

Radin, D. (2006). *Entangled minds: extrasensory experiences in a quantum reality.* New York: Paraview Pocket Books.

Rhine, J. B., & Brier, R. (Eds.). (1968). *Parapsychology today.* New York: Citadel Press.

Targ, R. (2004). *Limitless mind: A guide to remote viewing and transformation of consciousness.* Novato, CA: New World Library.

Tart, C. T., Puthoff, H. E., & Targ, R. (Eds.). (1979). *Mind at large.* New York: Praeger.

Thalbourne, M. A., & Storm, L. (Eds.). (2010). *Essays on the future of psychical research: The future of parapsychology.* Jefferson, NC: McFarland & Company, Inc.

The New York Times (2011, January 6). When science goes psychic. *The Opinion Pages, Room for Debate.* http://www.nytimes.com/roomfordebate/2011/01/06/the-esp-study-when-science-goes-psychic.

Wolman, B. B. (Ed.). (1977). *Handbook of parapsychology.* New York: Van Nostrand Reinhold.

Conclusion

Having discussed the psychology of consciousness, we wish to spend a few pages summarizing the status of this field of inquiry. Although much of what you read here will be our own opinions, remember that this area of psychology is timely.

It is indeed an exciting era. Recent advances in neuroscience have prompted interest by psychologists, biologists, and physicists to move the study of consciousness from the realm of philosophy into the hard sciences. Understanding how the brain produces consciousness holds great promise for understanding what makes us human. Moreover, identifying correlates of consciousness should aid the development of better treatments for disorders affecting consciousness, including traumatic brain injury and coma, sleep disorders, memory problems, and addictive disorders. Future research will allow clinicians to perfect the practical use of therapies based on altering consciousness, including hypnosis, biofeedback/neurofeedback, and meditation. Determining the neural correlates of consciousness will allow us to either confirm, or finally put to rest, claims of the paranormal, as it will allow for an empirical validation of any mechanisms underlying psychic ability.

Although tremendous gains have occurred, science must continue to address problems facing the study of consciousness. These include the development of methods for assessing and describing levels of consciousness. Developing adequate procedures for summarizing the vast individual differences in levels of experience is also necessary. It is mandatory that scientifically testable theories improve so that experiments can be derived. Without strong and empirically testable theories of consciousness, this area cannot progress.

We realize that all the topics in this book represent controversial areas of study. Yet these areas are what many people believe psychology is all about. This observation can be verified by reading certain popular magazines and weekly tabloids. If most people believe such notions, which are known to be distortions of the total picture, investigators must put to rest these misconceptions through empirical experimentation. In the scientific community, a strong bias still exists that prevents researchers from engaging in such investigations. However, the psychology of consciousness has much to offer, and perhaps the development of strong theories and experiments will break down this bias.

Future Applications of Consciousness

The future of each area we have discussed will depend on many factors. We would like to indicate what we see happening in these areas.

In chapter 1, we addressed the "hard problem" of studying consciousness, and in chapter 2 we described how determining the neural correlate(s) of consciousness may aid this age-old endeavor. Great strides have been made in understanding the neural correlates of visual awareness (Leopold & Logothetis, 1996; Tong et al., 1998), as well as neural properties mediating conscious and unconscious states (Alkire et al., 2008; Laureys, 2005; Owen et al., 2006). We expect future research to continue to elucidate the brain structures and specific neuronal mechanisms necessary to produce consciousness. Greater knowledge regarding how the brain mediates conscious experience will lead to the development of stronger theories of consciousness. Stronger theories will guide future research, which will lead to the development of more effective treatments for disorders affecting consciousness.

In chapter 3, we addressed how consciousness-altering drugs have been used for a variety of beneficial purposes. This was the reason they were originally produced. Unfortunately, many of these drugs are abused, due to their consciousness-altering effects. Our knowledge has advanced tremendously regarding the specific receptor mechanisms underlying the subjective effects of abused drugs such as LSD, marijuana, cocaine, methamphetamine, and heroin. This research has lead to the development of opioid receptor antagonist drugs including naloxone and naltrexone, and the mixed opioid agonist/antagonist buprenorphine, which are used successfully in the treatment of opiate and alcohol addiction. Abuse of the stimulant drugs cocaine and methamphetamine pose a significant worldwide public health concern. Research has determined that the neurotransmitter dopamine is in large part responsible for the pleasurable feelings elicited by these drugs. Although dopamine antagonists may seem like an obvious treatment for stimulant drug addiction, the side effects produced by these drugs often outweigh the benefit (and make it difficult to motivate addicts to take the treatment drugs). It is our hope that future research on the neural mechanisms underlying pleasure and craving will determine safe and efficacious ways to help addicts without drugs. For example, non-invasive but selective brain stimulation produced via technologies like transcranial magnetic stimulation may be useful for altering consciousness without the use of drugs. We anticipate future research on these possibilities.

Chapter 4 addressed hypnosis. Recent research with better controls points to the utility for hypnosis in clinical populations. Although not always effective on its own, adding hypnosis to other types of cognitive-behavioral therapy has been shown to increase weight loss (Kirsch, 1996), facilitate smoking cessation (Elkins et al., 2006), and decrease fear and anxiety in phobic patients (Golden, 2006; Walters & Oakley, 2003). Hypnosis has been found to significantly decrease pain during childbirth or post-surgery (Cyna et al., 2004; Montgomery et al., 2007). Hypnosis has also been found to be effective for managing chronic pain (Patterson & Jensen, 2003; Stoelb et al., 2009; Tan et al., 2010).

Although many recent studies have investigated the role of attention on hypnotizability (Lichtenberg et al., 2004; Raz, 2005), there remains a lack of research investigating whether hypnosis could be used clinically to enhance attention. As suggested by Wallace (1979), hypnosis could help individuals with poor concentration. Future research should examine hypnosis as an aid to improving attentional focus in clinical populations.

In chapter 5, we examined biofeedback. Advances in technology, coupled with demonstrations of clinical efficacy, have led to significant increases in biofeedback therapy. Many clinics and hospitals now have biofeedback clinics where patients can receive treatment for headaches, anxiety-related problems, and hypertension. Although not yet covered by most health insurance plans, neurofeedback in the treatment of attention-deficit disorder holds great promise as an alternative or adjunct to other therapies; we predict increases in the use of neurofeedback for attentional dysfunction in the future. We also see increases in the use of home-based and portable virtual reality biofeedback systems to aid in the treatment of anxiety and stress-related disorders.

We predict that controlled studies of the effects of meditation (chapter 6) will be increasingly used to elucidate the neural correlates of consciousness. This is because meditation provides a safe, relatively easy way to compare how the brain changes as a person moves from normal consciousness to an altered, meditative state. Research indicates that experienced meditators display different patterns of brain wave activity than novices, which can help elucidate neural mechanisms underlying practice, focused attention, and learning. Recent evidence noting that experienced meditators display increased cortical thickness (Grant et al., 2010; Holzel et al., 2011) offers great promise for the use of meditation as a way to promote brain function. We see increases in the use of meditation to stave off the natural effects of aging, or to facilitate improvement in the cognitively impaired. We predict an exciting future for the scientific study and clinical applications of meditation.

Recent research has led to significant improvements in our understanding of sleep and dreams (chapter 7). The purpose of sleep has long eluded science, and advances in neural recording technology have led to the discovery that sleep appears to be a global property of the brain, regulated by functional networks of neuronal assemblies (Krueger et al., 2008; Kumar, 2010; Maquet, 2001). We anticipate a great deal of future research to focus on the specific neuronal activities that take place during sleep, which may function to develop integrated neural networks or to form memories (Wilson & McNaughton, 1994). Understanding why we sleep and what motivates sleep will inevitably help with the development of treatments for sleep disorders. Future research will surely focus on determining the role that sleep plays in memory, as well as how sleep functions to maintain overall health.

As predicted by Wallace and Fisher (1999) in the earlier edition of this text, sensory deprivation (chapter 8) induced by flotation restricted environmental stimulation technique (REST), or "tank therapy" (Daniel, 1981; Lilly, 1977) has indeed been shown to have clinical efficacy. Flotation REST clinics are widespread across the country, and home flotation tanks are available. Flotation REST has been shown to have benefits in the treatment of anxiety and stress-related disorders (Van Dierendock & Nijenhuis, 2005), substance abuse and addictive disorders (Adams, 1988; Forays, 1987, and pain control (Bood et al., 2009; Kjellgren et al., 2001). With the recent rise in media coverage surrounding the negative effects of prolonged isolation experienced by hostages and prisoners, we predict that public awareness of sensory deprivation will again increase. This increased interest will prompt improved controlled studies of both the positive and negative effects of isolation.

Parapsychology (chapter 9) is an area of consciousness that will continue to interest laypeople. The last decade has seen an explosion in media attention devoted to the paranormal, including popular television shows like *Ghost Whisperer, Ghost Hunters,* and *Medium.* A recent article published by the social psychologist Daryl Bem (2011) reporting significant precognitive ability in normal undergraduate students has sparked intense debate in the scientific community. We predict that overexposure of paranormal phenomena in the media, coupled by the lack of scientific evidence supporting psychic ability, will lead to a temporary decrease in public interest in the paranormal (possibly by the printing of this text). However, future controlled experiments will continue, in an attempt to support or refute Bem's (2011) claims. We believe the focus of these studies will shift to elucidate a neural (Mouton & Kosslyn, 2008) or genetic (Raz et al., 2008) correlate of psi. We do not perceive that this will necessarily improve the lot or status of the study of the paranormal.

As predicted in the previous edition of this text, research in consciousness and altered states has progressed and flourished. We are excited to see a renewed interest in the psychology of consciousness and behavior. It has been our pleasure to present here the latest information regarding advances made in the scientific study of consciousness and behavior. We look forward to continued research, and a new generation of critical thinkers devoted to understanding the scientific underpinnings of consciousness and altered states.

For Further Reading

Koch, C. (2011). *The Quest for Consciousness: A Neurobiological Approach.* Engelwood, CO: Roberts & Company.

Adams, H. B. (1988). Studies in REST. III. REST, arousability, and the nature of alcohol and substance abuse. *Journal of Substance Abuse Treatment, 5*(2), 72–81.

Aftanas, L. I., & Golocheikine, S. A., (2001). Human anterior and frontal midline theta and lower alpha reflect emotionally positive state and internalized attention: high–resolution EEG investigation of meditation. *Neuroscience Letters, 310,* 57–60.

Aftanas, L. I., & Golocheikine, S. A. (2005). Impact of regular meditation practice on EEG activity at rest and during evoked negative emotions. *International Journal of Neuroscience, 115,* 893–909.

Alcock, J. E. (1987). Parapsychology: Science of the anomalous or search for the soul? *Behavioral and Brain Sciences, 10,* 553–643.

Alcock J. (2003). Give the null hypothesis a chance: reasons to remain doubtful about the existence of psi. *Journal of Consciousness Studies, 10*(6–7), 29–50.

Alcock, J. (2010). Attributions about impossible things. In Krippner, S., & Friedman, H. L. (Eds.). *Debating Psychic Experience: Human Potential or Human Illusion?* (pp. 29–41). Santa Barbara, CA: Praeger.

Alcock, J. (2011). Back from the future: parapsychology and the Bem affair. *Skeptical Inquirer,* March/April.

Alkire, M. T., Haier, R. J., & Fallon, J. H. (2000). Toward a unified theory of narcosis: brain imaging evidence for a thalamocortical switch as the neurophysiologic basis of anesthetic–induced unconsciousness. *Consciousness and Cognition, 9*, 370–376.

Alkire, M. T., Hudetz, A. G., & Tononi, G. (2008). Consciousness and anesthesia. *Science, 322*, 876–880.

Aloe, L., Collings, B., Wauqwer, A., McGrady, A., & Gerard, G. (1994). Effect of biofeedback-assisted relaxation on migraine headaches and changes in cerebral blood flow velocity. Paper presented at the 25th annual meeting of the Association for Applied Psychophysiology and Biofeedback, Atlanta.

Alvarado, C. S. (1984). Phenomenological aspects of out-of-body experiences: A report of three studies. *Journal of the American Society for Psychical Research, 78*, 219–240.

Alvarado, C. S. (1992). The psychological approach to out-of-body experiences: A review of early and modern developments. *Journal of Psychology, 126*, 237–250.

Ambrosini, M. V., Mariucci, G., Colarieti, L., Bruschelli, G., Carobi, C., & Giuditta, A. (1993). The structure of sleep is related to the learning ability of rats. *European Journal of Neuroscience, 5*, 269–275.

American Psychiatric Association (2005). *Diagnostic and statistical manual of mental disorders* (4th ed., text revision). Washington, DC.

American Society for Pharmacology and Experimental Therapeutics and Committee on Problems of Drug Dependence. (1987). Scientific perspectives on cocaine abuse. *The Pharmacologist, 29*, 20–27.

Anand, B. K., Chhina, G. S., & Singh, B. (1961a). Some aspects of electroencephalo-graphic studies in yogis. *Electroencephalography and Clinical Neurophysiology, 13*, 452–456.

Anand, B. K., Chhina, G. S., & Singh, B. (1961b). Studies on Shri Ramanand Yogi during his stay in an air-tight box. *Indian Journal of Medical Research, 49*, 82–89.

Anders, T. P., Carskado, M. A., & Dement, W. C. (1980). Sleep and sleepiness in children and adolescents. *Pediatric Clinics of North America, 27*, 29–43.

Andersen, M. S. (1985). Hypnotizability as a factor in the hypnotic treatment of obesity. *International Journal of Clinical and Experimental Hypnosis, 33*, 150–159.

Anderson, M. (1959). A precognition experiment comparing time intervals of a few days and one year. *Journal of Parapsychology, 23*, 81–89.

Andreychuck, T., & Skriver, C. (1975). Hypnosis and biofeedback in the treatment of migraine headaches. *International Journal of Clinical and Experimental Hypnosis, 23*, 172–183.

Antrobus, J. S., Fein, G., Jordan, L., Ellman, S. J., & Arkin, A. M. (1978). Measurement and design in research on sleep reports. In A. M. Arkin, J. S. Antrobus, & S. J. Ellman (Eds.), *The mind in sleep: Psychology and psychophysiology*. Hillsdale, NJ: Erlbaum.

APA (American Psychological Association, Division of Psychological Hypnosis) (1994). Definition and description of hypnosis. *Contemporary Hypnosis 11*, 142–162. (Released in 1993, reproduced with commentaries in *Contemporary Hypnosis* in 1994.)

Appenzeller, O. (1973). Getting a sore head from banging it on the wall. *Headache, 13*, 131–132.

Applehans, B. M. & Luecken, L. J. (2006). Heart rate variability as an index of regulated emotional responding. *Review of General Psychology, 10*, 229–240.

Arkin, A. M. (1991). Sleeptalking. In S. A. Ellman & J. S. Antrobus (Eds.), *The mind in sleep: Psychology and psychophysiology* (2nd ed., pp. 415–436). New York: Wiley.

Arkin, A. M., & Antrobus, J. S. (1978). The effects of external stimuli applied to and during sleep on sleep experience. In A. M. Arkin, J. S. Antrobus, & S. J. Ellrnan (Eds.), *The mind in sleep: Psychology and psychophysiology*. Hillsdale, NJ: Erlbaum.

Armitage, R., Hoffman, R., Loewy, D., & Moffitt, A. (1989). Variations in period-analysed EEG asymmetry in REM and NREM sleep. *Psychophysiology, 26*, 329–336.

Arns, M., deRidder, S., Strehl, U., Breteler, M., & Coenen, A. (2009). Efficacy of neurofeedback treatment in ADHD: the effects on inattention, impulsivity, and hyperactivity: a meta–analysis. *Clinical EEG and Neuroscience, 40*(3), 180–189.

Ascher, L. M., Barber, T. X., & Spanos, N. P. (1972). Two attempts to replicate the Parrish-Lundy-Leibowitz experiment on hypnotic age regression. *American Journal of Clinical Hypnosis, 14*, 178–185.

Aserinsky, E., & Kleitman, N. (1953). Regularly occurring periods of eye motility and concomitant phenomena during sleep. *Science, 118*, 273–274.

Ashley, R. (1976). *Cocaine: Its history, uses, and effects*. New York: Warner Books.

Associated Press (2010, September 8). Dalai Lama makes donation to support brain research. *The Richmond-Times Dispatch*, http://www2.timesdispatch.com/news/2010/sep/08/dlgat08-ar-492345.

Association for Applied Psychophysiology and Biofeedback (2008). What is biofeedback? http://www.aapb.org/. Retrieved January 12, 2011.

Astin, J. A., Harkness, E., & Ernst, E. (2000). The efficacy of "distant healing": a systematic review of renadomized trials. *Annals of Internal Medicine, 132,* 903.–910.

Atkinson, R.C., & Shiffrin, R. M. (1968). Human memory: a proposed system and its control processes. in Spence, K.W. & Spence, J.T. (Eds.). *The Psychology of Learning and Motivation (Volume 2).* New York: Academic Press, pp. 89–195.

Atwood, K. C. (2001). The efficacy of spiritual healing. *Annals of Internal Medicine, 134*(12), 1150.

Audette, J. R. (1979). Denver cardiologist discloses findings after 18 years of near-death research. *Anabiosis, 1,* 1–2.

Axmacher, N., Draguhn, A., Elger, C. E., & Fell, J. (2009). Memory processes during sleep: beyond the standard consolidation theory. *Cellular and Molecular Life Sciences, 66,* 2285–2297.

Axmacher, N., Haupt, S., Fernandez, G., Elger, C. E., & Fell, J. (2008). The role of sleep in declarative memory consolidation—direct evidence by intracranial EEG. *Cerebral Cortex, 18,* 500–507.

Aylesworth, T. G. (1975). *ESP.* New York: Watts.

Baars, B. J. (1983). Conscious contents provide the nervous system with coherent, global information. *Consciousness and Self-Regulation, 3,* 45–76.

Baars, B. J. (1988). *A cognitive theory of consciousness.* Cambridge, UK: Cambridge University Press.

Baars, B. J. (1997). *Consciousness regained: The new science of human experience.* Oxford, UK: Oxford University Press.

Baars, B. J., Newman, J., & Taylor, J. G. (1998): Neuronal mechanisms of consciousness: a relational global workspace framework. In S. Hameroff, A. Kaxzniak, J. Laukes (Eds.). *Toward a Science of Consciousness II: the Second Tucson Discussions and Debates.* Cambridge, MA: MIT Press, pp. 269–278.

Bachman, J. G., Johnston, L. D., & O'Malley, P. M. (1990). Explaining the recent decline in cocaine use among young adults: Further evidence that perceived risks and disapproval lead to reduced drug use. *Journal of Health and Social Behavior, 31,* 173–184.

Bachman, J. G., Johnston, L. D., O'Malley, P. M., & Humphrey, R. H. (1988). Explaining the recent decline in marijuana use: Differentiating the effects of perceived risks, disapproval, and general lifestyle factors. *Journal of Health and Social Behavior, 29,* 92–112.

Backhaus, J., & Junghanns, K. (2006). Daytime naps improve procedural motor memory. *Sleep Medicine, 7,* 508–512.

Bakan, P. (1969). Hypnotizability, laterality of eye movements, and functional brain asymmetry. *Perceptual and Motor Skills, 28,* 927–932.

Baker, E. L., & Nash, M. R. (1987). Applications of hypnosis in the treatment of anorexia nervosa. *American Journal of Clinical Hypnosis, 29,* 185–193.

Balster, R. L. (1988). Drugs as chemical stimuli. In: Colpaert, F. C., & Balster, R. L. (eds.). *Transduction mechanisms of drug stimuli.* Springer: Berlin. Bankson, M.G., Cunningham, K.A. (2001). 3,4–methylenedioxymethamphetamine (MDMA) as a unique model of serotonin receptor function and serotonin–dopamine interactions. *The Journal of Pharmacology and Experimental Therapeutics, 297*(3), 846–852.

Banks, W. P. (1993). Problems in the scientific pursuit of consciousness. *Consciousness & Cognition, 2,* 255–263.

Banquet, J. P. (1973). Spectral analysis of the EEG in meditation. *Electroencephalography and Clinical Neurophysiology, 35,* 143–151.

Barabasz, A. F., Baer, L., Sheehan, D. V., & Barabasz, M. (1986). A three-year follow-up of hypnosis and restricted environmental stimulation therapy for smoking. *International Journal of Clinical and Experimental Hypnosis, 34,* 169–181.

Barabasz, A. F., & Barabasz, M. (1989). Effects of restricted environmental stimulation: Enhancement of hypnotizability for experimental and chronic pain control. *International Journal of Clinical and Experimental Hypnosis, 36,* 217–231.

Barabasz, M. (2007). Efficacy of hypnotherapy in the treatment of eating disorders. *International Journal of Clinical and Experimental Hypnosis, 55*(3), 318–335.

Barabasz, M., & Spiegel, D. (1989). Hypnotizability and weight loss in obese subjects. *International Journal of Eating Disorders, 8*(3), 335–341.

Barber, J., & Adrian, C. (1982). *Psychological approaches to the management of pain.* New York: Brunner-Mazel.

Barber, T. X. (1962). Hypnotic age regression: A critical review. *Psychosomatic Medicine, 24,* 286–299.

Barber, T. X. (1969). *Hypnosis: A scientific approach.* Princton, NJ: Van Nostrand.

Barber, T. X. (1970). *LSD, marihuana, yoga, and hypnosis.* Chicago: Aldine.

Barber, T. X., & Glass, L. B. (1962). Significant factors in hypnotic behavior. *Journal of Abnormal and Social Psychology, 64,* 222–228.

Barber, T. X., Spanos, N. P., & Chaves, J. F. (1974). *Hypnotism, imagination, and human potentialities.* New York: Pergamon.

Barkley, R. A., Hastings, J. E., & Jackson, T. L., Jr. (1977). The effects of rapid smoking and hypnosis in the treatment of smoking behavior. *Journal of Clinical and Experimental Hypnosis, 25,* 7–17.

Barnes, J., Dong, C.Y., McRobbie, H., Walker, N., Mehta, M., & Stead, L.F. (2010). Hypnotherapy for smoking cessation. *Cochrane Database of Systematic Reviews, 10.* Art. No.: CD001008. doi: 10.1002/14651858.CD001008.pub2.

Barnes, S. M., Lynn, S. J., & Pekala, R. J. (2009). Not all group hypnotic suggestibility scales are created equal: individual differences in behavioral and subjective responses. *Consciousness and Cognition, 18,* 255–265.

Barnier, A., & McConkey, K. M. (1999). Absorption, hypnotisability, and context: nonhypnotic contexts are not all the same. *Contemporary Hypnosis, 16,* 1–8.

Barron, F., Jarvik, M. E., & Bunnell, S. (1964). The hallucinogenic drugs. *Scientific American, 210,* 29–37.

Bartley, S. H., & Chute, E. (1947). *Fatigue and impairment in man.* New York: McGraw-Hill.

Baruss, I. (1987). Metanalysis of definitions of consciousness. *Imagination, Cognition and Personality, 6,* 321–329.

Basner, M., Fomberstein, K.M., Razavi, F.M., Banks, S., William, J.H., Rosa, R.R., & Dinges, D.F. (2007). American time use survey: sleep time and its relationship to waking activities. *Sleep, 30*(9), 1085–1095.

Bauman, D. E., & Bul', P. I. (1981). Human inheritability of hypnotizability. *Genetika, 17,* 352–356.

Beahrs, J. O. (1988). Hypnosis cannot be fully nor reliably excluded from the courtroom. *American Journal of Clinical Hypnosis, 31,* 18–27.

Bear, M. F., Conners, B. W., & Paradiso, M. A. (1996). *Neuroscience: Exploring the brain.* Baltimore: Williams & Wilkins.

Beatty, J. (1982). Biofeedback in the treatment of migraine: Simple relaxation or specific effects? In L. White and B. Tursky (Eds.), *Clinical biofeedback: Efficacy and mechanisms* (pp. 211–221). New York: Guilford.

Beaty, T., & Haynes, S. (1979). Behavioral intervention with muscle-contraction headache: A review. *Psychosomatic Medicine, 41,* 165–180.

Bedi, G., Hyman, D., deWit, H. (2010). Is Ecstasy an "empathogen"? Effects of +3,4 methylenedioxymethamphetamine on prosocial feelings and identification of emotional states in others. *Biological Psychiatry,* doi:10.1016/j.biopsych.2010.08.003.

Belick, L., Elfner, L., & May, J. (1982). Biofeedback treatment of dysmenorrhea. *Biofeedback and Self-Regulation, 7,* 499–520.

Bell, V. (2010). An alternative interpretation of "The psychotomimetic effects of short–term sensory deprivation." *The Journal of Nervous and Mental Disease, 198*(2), 166.

Beloff, J. (1968). ESP: Proof from Prague? *New Scientist, 40,* 76–77.

Bem, D. J. (1972). Self–perception theory. *Advances in Experimental Social Psychology, 6,* 1–62.

Bem, D. J. (2011). Feeling the future: experimental evidence for anomalous retroactive influences on cognition and affect. *Journal of Personality and Social Psychology, 100*(3), 407–425.

Bem, D. J., & Honorton, C. (1994). Does psi exist? Replicable evidence for an anomalous process of information transfer. *Psychological Bulletin, 115*(1), 4–18.

Bem, D.J., Utts, J., & Johnson, W. O. (2011). Must psychologists change the way they analyze their data? A response to Wagenmakers, Wetzels, Borsboom, & Van der Maas (2011) Under Editorial Review. Please do not quote without permission. (Revised 2/13/2011). Most recent revision can be downloaded from http://dl.dropbox.com/u/8290411/ResponsetoWagenmakers.pdf.

Benson, H., & Friedman, R. (1985). A rebuttal to the conclusions of David S. Holmes's article: "Meditation and somatic arousal reduction." *American Psychologist, 40,* 725–728.

Benson, H., Rosner, B. A., & Marzetta, B. R. !1973). Decreased blood pressure in hypertensive subjects who practiced meditation. *Journal of Clinical Investigation, 52,* 8a–lla.

Benson, H., & Wallace, R. K. (1972). Decreased drug abuse with transcendental meditation: A study of 1862 subjects. In C. Zarafonetis (Ed.), *Drug abuse: Proceedings of the International Conference* (pp. 239–252). Philadelphia: Lea and Febiger.

Benson, K., & Feinberg, I. (1977). Beneficial effect of sleep in an extended Jenkins and Dallenbach paradigm. *Psychophysiology, 14,* 375–384.

Benson, H. (1974). Decreased alcohol intake associated with the practice of meditation: a retrospective investigation. *Annals of the New York Academy of Sciences, 233*, 174–177.

Benson, H. (1983). The relaxation response: its subjective and objective historical precedents and physiology. *Trends in Neuroscience, 6*(7), 281–284.

Benson, H., Rosner, B.A., Marzetta, B.R., Klemchuk, H.P. (1974). Decreased blood pressure in borderline hypertensive subjects who practiced meditation. *Journal of Chronic Disease, 27*(3), 163–169.

Benson, H., Malvea, B.P., Graham, J.R. (1973). Physiologic correlates of meditation and their clinical effects in headache: an ongoing investigation. *Headache, 13*(1), 23–24.

Benzenhofer, U. & Passie, T. (2009). Rediscovering MDMA (ecstasy): the role of American chemist Alexander T. Shulgin. *Addiction, 105*(8) 1355–1361.

Berberich, F. R., & Landman, Z. (2009). Reducing immunization discomfort in 4- to 6-year old children: a randomized, clinical trial. *Pediatrics, 124*, 203–209.

Berkowitz, L. (1986). *A survey of social psychology* (3rd ed.). New York: Holt, Rinehart & Winston.

Best, J. A., & Suedfeld, P. (1982). Restricted environmental stimulation therapy and behavioral self-management in smoking cessation. *Journal of Applied Social Psychology, 12*, 408–419.

Bexton, W. H., Heron, W., & Scott, T. H. (1954). Effects of decreased variation in the sensory environment. *Canadian Journal of Psychology, 8*, 70–76.

Bierman, D. J. (2001). On the nature of anaomalous phenomena: another reality between the world of subjective consciousness and the objective world of physics? In P. Van Lock (Ed.). *The Physical Nature of Consciousness* (pp. 269–292). New York: Benjamins.

Birk, L., Crider, A., Shapiro, D., & Tursky, B. (1966). Operant electrodermal conditioning under partial curarization. *Journal of Comparative and Physiological Psychology, 62*, 165–166.

Black, A. H. (1966). The operant conditioning of heart rate in curarized dogs: Some problems of interpretation. Paper presented at the meetings of the Psychonomic Society, St. Louis.

Blacker, K. H., Jones, R. T, Stone, G. C., & Pfefferbaum, D. (1968). Chronic users of LSD: The acidheads. *American Journal of Psychiatry, 125*, 97–107.

Blackmore, S. J. (1980). The extent of selective reporting of ESP ganzfeld studies. *European Journal of Parapsychology, 3,* 213–219.

Blackmore, S. J. (1982). Out-of-body experiences, lucid dreams, and imagery: Two surveys. *Journal of the American Society for Psychical Research, 76,* 301–317.

Blackmore, S. J. (1996). Near-death experiences. *Journal of the Royal Society of Medicine, 89,* 73–76.

Blackwell, B., Hanenson, I. B., Bloomfield, S. S., Magenheim, N. G., Nidich, S. I., & Gartside, P. (1975). Effects of transcendental meditation on blood pressure: a controlled pilot experiment. *Psychosomatic Medicine, 37,* 86.

Blanchard, E. B., Ahles, T, & Shaw, E. (1979). Behavioral treatment of headaches. In M. Hersen, R. Eisler, and P. Miller (eds.), *Progress in behavior modification.* New York: Academic Press.

Blanchard, E. B., Andrasick, F., Evans, D. D., Neff, D. F., & Appelbaum, K. A. (1985). Individual predictors of self-regulating treatment outcome in tension headache. Paper presented at the annual meeting of the Biofeedback Society of America, New Orleans.

Blanchard, E. B., & Epstein, L. H. (1978). *A biofeedback primer.* Reading, MA: Addison-Wesley.

Bliss, T. V. P., & Collingridge, G. L. (1993). A synaptic model for memory: long-term potentiation in the hippocampus. *Nature, 361,* 31–39.,

Bliss, T. V., & Lomo, T. (1973). Long lasting potentiation of synaptic transmission in the dentate gyrus of the anesthetized rabbit following stimulation of the perforant path. *Journal of Physiology, 232*(2),331–356.

Bloch, V., Hennevin, E., & Leconte, P. (1979). Relationship between paradoxical sleep and memory processes. In M. A. B. Brazier (Ed.), *Brain mechanisms in memory and learning: From the single neuron to man* (pp. 329–343). New York: Raven.

Block, N. (1995). On a confusion about a function of consciousness. *Behavioral Brain Science, 18,* 227–247.

Block, N. (2005). Two neural correlates of consciousness. *Trends in Cognitive Neurosciences, 9*(2), 46–52.

Block, N. (2009). Comparing the major theories of consciousness. In: Gazzangia, M. (ed.), *The Cognitive Neurosciences IV.* Cambridge, MA: MIT Press.

Block, R. I., Farinpour, R., & Braverman, K. (1992). Acute effects of marijuana on cognition: Relationships to chronic effects and smoking techniques. *Pharmacology Bulletin, 43,* 907–917.

Block, R. L, & Ghoneim, M. M. (1993). Effects of chronic marijuana use on human cognition. *Psychopharmacology, 110,* 219–228.

Blum, G. S., & Porter, M. L. (1974). Effects of the restriction of conscious awareness in a reaction-time task. *International Journal of Clinical and Experimental Hypnosis, 22,* 335–345.

Boiler, J., & Flam, B. (1979). Treatment of the common migraine: Systematic application of biofeedback and autogenic training. *American Journal of Clinical Biofeedback, 2,* 63–64.

Bonadonna, R. (2003). Meditation's impact on chronic illness. *Holistic Nursing Practice, 17*(6), 309–319.

Bonnet, M. H., & Moore, S. E. (1982). The threshold of sleep: Perception of sleep as a function of time asleep and auditory threshold. *Sleep, 5,* 267–276.

Bood, S. A., Kjellgren, A., & Norlander, T. (2009). Treating stress–related pain with the flotation restricted environmental stimulation technique: are there differences between women and men? *Pain Research Management, 14*(4), 293–298.

Boot, B. P., McGregor, I. S., & Hall, W. (2000). MDMA (Ecstasy) neurotoxicity: assessing and communicating the risks. *Lancet, 355,* 1818–1821.

Borgeat, F., Hade, B., Larouche, L., & Bedwant, C. (1980). Effect of therapist's active presence on EMG biofeedback training of headache patients. *Biofeedback and Self-Regulation, 5,* 275–282.

Borgeat, F., Hade, B., Larouche, L., & Gauthier, B. (1984). Psychophysiological effects of therapist's active presence during biofeedback as a simple psychotherapeutic situation. *Psychiatric Journal of the University of Ottawa, 9,* 132–137.

Boring, E. G. (1929). *A history of experimental psychology.* New York: Appleton-Century-Crofts.

Borison, H. L., McCarthy, L. E., & London, S. W. (1981). Cannabinoids and emesis. *New England Journal of Medicine, 298,* 1480–1481.

Borkovec, T. D., Lane, T. W., & VanDot, P. H. (1981). Phenomenology of sleep among insomniacs and good sleepers: Wakefulness experience when cortically asleep. *Journal of Abnormal Psychology, 90,* 607–609.

Bosinelli, M. (1995). Mind and consciousness during sleep. Special Issue: The function of sleep. *Behavioural Brain Research, 69,* 195–201.

Boudreau, L. (1972). Transcendental meditation and yoga as reciprocal inhibitors. *Journal of Behavior Therapy and Experimental Psychiatry, 3,* 97–98.

Bowers, K. S. (1976). *Hypnosis for the seriously curious.* New York: Norton.

Bozarth, J. D., & Roberts, R. R. (1972). Signifying significant significance. *American Psychologist, 27,* 774–775.

Braud, W., and Schlitz, M. (1983). Psychokinetic influence on electrodermal activity. *Journal of Parapsychology, 47,* 95–120.

Brecher, E. M., & the Editors of Consumer Reports. (1972). *Licit and illicit drugs.* Mount Vernon, NY: Consumers Union.

Brefcynzski-Lewis, J. A., Lutz, A., Schaefer, H. S., Levinson, D. B., & Davidson, R. J. (2007). Neural correlates of expertise in long-time meditation practitioners. *Proceedings of the National Academy of Sciences, 104*(27), 11483–11488.

Brerner, F. (1937). L'activite cerebrale au cours du sommeil et de la narcose: Contribution a l'etude du mecanisme du sommeil. *Bulletin de l'Academie Royale de Belgique, 4,* 68–86.

British Broadcasting Company (BBC). (2008). Total isolation. *Science & Nature: TV and Radio Follow Up.* http://www.bbc.co.uk/sn/tvradio/ programmes/horizon/broadband/tx/isolation.

Broughton, R. (1984). Quoted in "Is sleep a waste of time?" *Science Digest, 92,* 4.

Browman, C. P., & Mitler, M. M. (1988). Hypersomnia and the perception of sleep-wake states: Some preliminary findings. *Perceptual and Motor Skills, 66,* 463–470.

Brown, B. B. (1970). Recognition of aspects of consciousness through association with EEG alpha activity represented by a light signal. *Psychophysiology, 6,* 442–452.

Brown, H. (1971). Some anticholinergic-like behavioral effects of trans(-)-delta[8] tetrahydocannabinol. *Psychopharmacologia, 21,* 294–301.

Brown, H. (1972). Possible anticholinesterase-like effects of trans(-)-delta[8] and -delta[9] tetrahydrocannabinol as observed in the general motor activity of mice. *Psychopharacologia, 27,* 111–116.

Brownfield, C. A. (1965). *Isolation: Clinical and experimental approaches.* New York: Random House.

Bruner, J. (1965). *On knowing: Essays for the left hand.* New York: Atheneum.

Brunner, D. P., Kijk, D. J., Tobler, I., & Borbely, A. A. (1990). Effect of partial sleep stages and EEG power spectra: Evidence for non-REM and REM sleep homeostasis. *Electroencephalography and Clinical Neurophysiology, 75,* 492–499.

Budzynski, T. H. (1978). Biofeedback strategies in headache treatment. In J. V. Basrnjian (Ed.), *Biofeedback: Principles and practice for clinicians* (pp. 132–152). Baltimore: Williams and Wilkins.

Budzynski, T. H. (1979). Biofeedback and the twilight states of consciousness. In D. Goleman and R. J. Davidson (Eds.), *Consciousness: Brain states of awareness and mysticism.* New York: Harper and Row.

Budzynski, T. H., Stoyva, J. M., & Adler, C. (1970). Feedback-induced muscle relaxation: Application to tension headache. *Journal of Behavioral Therapy and Experimental Psychiatry, 1,* 205–211.

Budzynski, T. H., Stoyva, J. M., Adler, C., & Mullaney, B. J. (1973). EMG biofeedback and tension headache: A controlled outcome study. *Psychosomatic Medicine, 35,* 484–496.

Bunning, S., & Blanke, O. (2005). The out-of-body experiences: precipitating factors and neural correlates. In Laureys, S. (Ed.). *The boundaries of consciousness: neurobiology and neuropathology* (Progress in Brain Research, 150), pp. 331–351.

Burns, P. A., Clesse-Desotelle, P.M., Nochajski, T., & Pranikoff, K. (1990). Biofeedback procedure for stress urinary incontinence. *Clinical Gerontologist, 10,* 51–54.

Byrd, R. E. (1938). *Alone.* New York: Putnam.

Byrne, A. (1997). Some like it HOT: consciousness and higher–order thourhgts. *Philosophical Studies, 86,* 103–129.

Cahn, B. R., Delorme, A., & Polich, J. (2010). Occipital gamma activation during Vipassana meditation. *Cognitive Processes, 11,* 39–56.

Cahn, B. R. & Polich, J. (2006). Meditation states and traits: EEG, ERP, and neuroimaging studies. *Psychological Bulletin, 132*(2), 180–211.

Campbell, K. A., Foster, T. C., Hampson, R. E., & Deadwyler, S. A. (1986). Effects of delta-9-tetrahydrocannabinol on sensory-evoked discharges of granule cells in the dentate gyrus of behaving rats. *Journal of Pharmacology and Experimental Therapeutics, 239,* 941–945.

Cappuccio, F. P., Taggart, F. M., Kandala, N-B., Currie, A, Peile, E., Stranges, S., & Miller, M. A. (2008). Meta-analysis of short sleep duration and obesity in children and adults. *Sleep, 31*(5), 619–626.

Carlson, N. R. (2009). *Physiology and behavior* (10th ed.). Boston: Allyn and Bacon.

Carpenter, K. A. (1988). The effects of positive and negative pre-sleep stimuli on dream experiences. *Journal of Psychology, 122,* 33–37.

Carrington, P. (1977). *Freedom in meditation.* New York: Doubleday.

Carrington, P. (1978). The uses of meditation in psychotherapy. In A. A. Sugarman & R. E. Tarter (Eds.), *Expanding dimensions of consciousness.* New York: Springer.

Carson, R. C., Butcher, J. N., & Coleman, J. C. (1988). *Abnormal psychology and modern life* (8th ed.). Glenview, IL: Scott Foresman.

Carter, J. L., & Russell, H. L. (1985). Use of EMG biofeedback procedures with learning disabled children in a clinical and an educational setting. *Journal of Learning Disabilities, 18,* 213–216.

Cartwright, R. D. (1977). *Nightlife: Explorations in dreaming.* Englewood Cliffs, NJ: Prentice-Hall.

Casler, L. (1962). The improvement of clairvoyance scores by means of hypnotic suggestion. *Journal of Parapsychology, 26,* 77–87.

Casler, L. (1967). Self-generated hypnotic suggestions and clairvoyance. *International Journal of Parapsychology, 9,* 125–128.

Cavallero, C, & Natale, V. (1988). Was I dreaming or did it really happen? A comparison between real and artificial dream reports. *Imagination, Cognition and Personality, 8,* 19–24.

Chagas, C. (1959). Studies on the mechanisms of curarization. *Annals of New York Academy of Sciences, 81,* 345–357.

Chalmers, D. J. (2000). What is a neural correlate of consciousness? In T. Metzinger (ed.). *Neural Correlates of Consciousness: Empirical and Conceptual Questions,* MIT Press.

Chalmers, D. (1995). Facing up to the problem of consciousness. *Journal of Consciousness Studies, 2*(3), 200–219.

Chalmers, D. (2000). What is a neural correlate of consciousness? In T. Metzinger (ed.). *Neural Correlates of Consciousness: Empirical and Conceptual Questions.* Cambridge, MA: MIT Press.

Chalsma, A. L., & Boyum, D. (1994). *Marijuana situation assessment.* Washington, DC: Office of National Drug Control Policy.

Chase, M. H., & Morales, F. R. (1983). Subthreshold excitatory activity and motoneuron discharge during REM periods of active sleep. *Science, 221,* 1195–1198.

Chien, I., Gerard, D. L., Lee, R. S., & Rosenfeld, E. (1964). *The road to H: Narcotics, delinquency, and social policy.* New York: Basic Books.

Chiesa, A. (2010). Vipassana meditation: systematic review of current evidence. *Journal of Alternative and Complementary Medicine, 16*(1), 37–46.

Chiesa, A., & Serretti, A., (2010a). A systematic review of neurobiological and clinical features of mindfulness meditations. *Psychological Medicine, 40,* 1239–1252.

Chiesa, A., & Serretti, A. (2010b). Mindfulness based cognitive therapy for psychiatric disorders: a systematic review and meta-analysis. *Psychiatry Research,* doi: 10.1016/j.psychres.2010.08.011.

Chin, J. H., & Goldstein, D. B. (1977). Drug tolerance in biomembranes: A spin label study of the effects of ethanol. *Science, 196,* 684–685.

Christensen, C. (2005) Preferences for descriptors of hypnosis: a brief communication. *International Journal of Clinical and Experimental Hypnosis, 53,* 281–289.

Christie, M. J., & Todd, J. L. (1975). Experimenter-subject-situational interactions. In P. H. Venables & M. J. Christie (Eds.), *Research in Psychophysiology.* London: Wiley.

Christman, S. D. (1995). Independence versus integration of right and left hemisphere processing: effects of handedness. In F. L. Kitterle (Ed.), *Hemispheric communication: Mechanisms and models* (pp. 231–253). Hillsdale, NJ: Erlbaum.

Christman, S. D. (2001). Individual differences in Stropp and local–global processing: a possible role of interhemispheric interaction. *Brain and Cognition, 45,* 97–118.

Christman, S. D., & Propper, R. E. (2001). Superior episodic memory is associated with interhemispheric processing. *Neuropsychology, 15,* 607–616.

Christman, S. D., Garvey, K. J., Propper, R. E., & Phaneuf, K. A. (2003). Bilateral eye movements enhance the retrieval of episodic memories. *Neuropsychology, 17,* 221–229.

Christman, S. D., Propper, R. E., & Dion, A. (2004). Increased interhemispheric interaction is associated with decreased false memories in a verbal converging semantic associates paradigm. *Brain and Cognition, 56,* 313–319.

Christman, S. D., Propper, R. E., & Brown, T. J. (2006). Increased interhemispheric interaction is associated with earlier offset of childhood amnesia. *Neuropsychology, 20,* 336–345.

Cicero, T. J. (1978). Tolerance to and physical dependence on alcohol: Behavioral and neurobiological mechanisms. In M. A. Lipton, A. DiMascio, & K. F. Killman (Eds.), *Pharmacology,* New York: Raven.

Clemes, S. R., & Dement, W. C. (1967). Effects of REM sleep deprivation on psychological functioning. *Journal of Nervous and Mental Disease, 144,* 488–491.

Coe, W. C. (1978). The credibility of posthypnotic amnesia: A contextualist's view. *International Journal of Clinical and Experimental Hypnosis, 26,* 218–245.

Coe, W. C., & Sarbin, T. R. (1977). Hypnosis from the standpoint of a contextualist. In W. E. Edmonston (Ed.), *Conceptual and investigative approaches to hypnosis and hypnosic phenomena. Annals of the New York Academy of Science, 296,* 2–13.

Cohen, D. (1979). Remembering and forgetting dreaming. In J. F. Kihlstrom & F. J. Evans (Eds.), *Functional disorders of memory.* Hillsdale, NJ: Erlbaum.

Cohen, S. (1971). Statement before the Subcommittee to Investigate Juvenile Delinquency of the U.S. Senate Committee on the Judiciary on Drug Abuse, December 15.

Cohen, S. (1981). *The substance abuse problems.* New York: Haworth.

Coleman, R. M., Miles, L. E., Guillemineult, C. C., Zarcone, V. P., Jr., Vanden Hoed, J., & Dement, W. C. (1981). Sleep-wake disorders in the elderly: A polysomno-graphic analysis. *Journal of the American Geriatrics Society, 29,* 289–296.

Coleman, R. M., Roffwag, H. P., Kennedy, S. J., Guillemineult, C. C., Cinque, J., Cohn, M. A., Karacan, I., Kupfer, D. J., Lemmi, H., Miles, L. E., Orr, D., & Dement, W. C. (1982). Sleep-wake disorders based on a polysomnographic diagnosis. *Journal of the American Medical Association, 247,* 997–1003.

Colpaert, F. C., (1999). Drug discrimination in neurobiology. *Pharmacology, Biochemistry, and Behavior, 64*(2), 337–345.

Conn, J. H., and Conn, R. N. (1967). Discussion of T. X. Barber's 'Hypnosis as a causal variable in present-day psychology': A critical analysis. *International Journal of Clinical and Experimental Hypnosis, 16,* 106–110.

Corcoran, D. K. (1988). Helping patients who've had near-death experiences. *Nursing 88,* 18, 34–39.

Corlett, P. R., Frith, C. D., & Fletcher, P. C. (2009). From drugs to deprivation: a Bayesian model for understanding psychosis. *Psychopharmacology, 206,* 515–530.

Cornish, P. J., Blanchard, E. B., & Wittrock, D. (1989). Relation of subjective experiences to clinical outcome in the thermal biofeedback treatment of essential hypertension. Paper presented at the meetings of the Association of Applied Psychophysiology and Biofeedback, San Diego.

Costin, F., & Draguns, J. G. (1989). *Abnormal psychology: Patterns, issues, interventions.* New York: Wiley.

Courcey, K. (2001). Distant healing. *Annals of Internal Medicine, 134*(6), 532.

Cowen, R. (1990, April 14). Cocaine and the nervous system. *Science News, 56*, 449–456.

Coy, P.C., Cardenas, S.J., Cabrera, D.M., Zirot, G.Z., & Claros, M.S. (2005). Psychophysiological and behavioral treatment of anxiety disorder. *Salud Mental, 28*(1), 28–37.

Craig, A. R., & Cleary, P. J. (1982). Reduction of stuttering by young male stutterers using EMG feedback. *Biofeedback and Self-Regulation, 7*, 241–255.

Craske, M. G., & Barlow, D. H. (1989). Nocturnal panic. *Journal of Nervous and Mental Disease, 177*, 160–167.

Crawford, H. J. (1981). Hypnotic susceptibility as related to gestalt closure tasks. *Journal of Personality and Social Psychology, 40*, 376–383.

Crawford, H. J. (1982). Hypnotizability, daydreaming style, imagery vividness, and absorption: A multidimensional study. *Journal of Personality and Social Psychology, 42*, 915–926.

Crawford, H. J. (1983). Enhanced visual memory during hypnosis as mediated by hypnotic responsiveness and cognitive strategies. *Journal of Experimental Psychology: General, 112*, 662–685.

Crawford, H. J. (1996). Cerebral brain dynamics of mental imagery: Evidence and issues for hypnosis. In R. G. Kunzendorf, N. P. Spanos, & B. Wallace (Eds.), *Hypnosis and imagination* (pp. 253–282). Amityville, NY: Baywood.

Crawford, H. J., Brown, A. M., & Moon, C. E. (1993). Sustained attentional and disattentional abilities: Differences between low and highly hypnotizable persons. *Journal of Abnormal Psychology, 102*, 534–543.

Crawford, H. J., Crawford, K., & Koperski, B. J. (1983). Hypnosis and lateral cerebral function as assessed by dichotic listening. *Biological Psychiatry, 18*, 415–427.

Crawford, H. J., Gur, R. C., Skolnick, B., Gur, R. E., and Benson, D. M. (1993). Effects of hypnosis on regional cerebral blood flow during ischemic pain with and without suggested hypnotic analgesia. *International Journal of Psychophysiology, 15*, 181–195.

Crawford, H. J., Macdonald, H., and Hilgard, E. R. (1979). Hypnotic deafness: A psychophysiological study of responses to tone intensity as modified by hypnosis. *American Journal of Psychology, 92,* 193–214.

Crawford, H. J., Wallace, B., Nomura, K., and Slater, H. (1986). Eidetic-like imagery in hypnosis: Rare but there. *American Journal of Psychology, 99,* 527–546.

Crawford H.J. (1994) Brain dynamics and hypnosis: attentional and disattentional processes. *International Journal of Clinical and Experimental Hypnosis, 42,* 204–32.

Crawford, H.J., Corby, J.C., & Kopell, B. (1996) Auditory event-related potentials while ignoring tone stimuli: attentional differences reflected in stimulus intensity and latency responses in low and highly hypnotizable persons. *International Journal of Neuroscience, 85,* 57–69.

Crick, F., and Mitchison, G. (1983). The function of dream sleep. *Nature, 304,* 111–114.

Crick F. & Koch C. (1995). Are we aware of neural activity in primary visual cortex? *Nature, 375*(6527), 121–123.

Crick, F. (1996). Visual perception: rivalry and consciousness. *Nature, 379*(6565), 485–486.

Crick, F., & Koch, C. (1998). Consciousness and neuroscience. *Cerebral Cortex, 8,* 97–107.

Crick, F. & Koch, C. (1995). Are we aware of neural activity in primary visual cortex? *Nature, 375*(6527), 121–123.

Crick, F., & Koch, C. (2003). A framework for consciousness. *Nature Neuroscience, 6*(2), 119–126.

Crider, A., Schwartz, G. E., and Shnidman, S. R. (1969). On the criteria for instrumental autonomic conditioning: A reply to Katkin and Murray. *Psychological Bulletin, 71,* 455–461.

Crider, A., Glaros, A.G., & Gevirtz, R.N. (2005). Efficacy of biofeedback-based treatments for temporomandibular disorders. *Applied Psychophysiology and Biofeedback, 30*(4), 333–345.

Critchley, H.D., Wiens, S., Rotshtein, P., Ohman, a., & Dolan, R. J. (2004). Neural systems supporting interoceptive awareness. *Nature Neuroscience, 7,* 189–195.

Critchley, H.D., Melmed, R. N., Fetherstone, E., Mathias, C.J., & Dolan, R.J. (2001). Brain activity during biofeedback relaxation: a functional neuroimaging investigation. *Brain, 124*(5), 1003–1012.

Critchley, H.D., Melmed, R. N., Featherstone, E., Mathias, C. J., & Dolan, R. J. (2002). Volitional control of autonomic arousal: a functional magnetic resonanace study. *Neuroimage, 16*, 909–919.

Critchlow, B. (1986). The powers of John Barleycorn: Beliefs about the effects of alcohol on social behavior. *American Psychologist, 41*, 751–763.

Cronin–Golomb, A., Gabrieli, J.D., & Keane, M.M. (1996). Implicit and explicit memory retrieval within and across the disconnected cerebral hemispheres. *Neuropsychology, 10*(2), 254–262.

Crookall, R. (1966). The study and practice of astral projection. Secaucus, NJ: University Books.

Crumpton, S. (2008, Jan. 19). Sensory deprivation: the story behind Horizon's TV experiment. *The Times* (London), http://women.timesonline.co.uk/tol/life_and_style/women/body_and_soul/article3209803.ece

Cruickshank, C.C. & Dyer, K.R. (2009). A review of the clinical pharmacology of methamphetamine. *Addiction, 104*, 1085–1099.

Cunningham, K. A., & Appel, J. B. (1987). Neuropharmacological reassessment of the discriminative stimulus properties of d-lysergic acid diethylamide (LSD). *Psychopharmacology, 91*, 67–73.

Cutter, H. S. G., O'Farrell, T. J., Whitehouse, J., & Dentch, G. M. (1986). Pain changes among men from before to after drinking: Effects of expectancy set and dose manipulations with alcohol and tonic as mediated by prior experience with alcohol. *International Journal of the Addictions, 21*, 937–945.

Cyna, A. M., McAuliffe, G. A., & Andrew, M. I. (2004). Hypnosis for pain relief in labour and childbirth: a systematic review. *British Journal of Anaesthesia, 93*(4), 505–511.

Dackis, C. A., & Gold, M. S. (1985). New concepts in cocaine addiction: The dopamine depletion hypothesis. *Neuroscience and Biobehavioral Reviews, 9*, 469–477.

Dahl, J., & Melin, L. (1989). The psychological treatment of epilepsy: A behavioral approach. Paper presented at the meetings of the Association of Applied Psychophysiology and Biofeedback, San Diego.

Dale, H. H. (1938). Acetylcholine as a chemical transmitter substance of the effects of nerve impulses. The William Henry Welch Lectures, 1937. *Journal of Mount Sinai Hospital, 4*, 401–429.

Daniel, A. (1981, January 12). Off the couch and into the tub. *Time*, p. 45.

Daniel, S. A. (2005). *American Journal of Clinical Hypnosis, 48*, 141–143.

Datta, S., & Maclean, R. R. (2007). Neurobiological mechanisms for the regulation of mammalian sleep-wake behavior: reinterpretation of historical evidence and inclusion of contemporary cellular and molecular evidence. *Neuroscience and Biobehavioral Reviews, 31,* 775–824.

Davenport-Slack, B. (1975). A comparative evaluation of obstetrical hypnosis and antenatal childbirth training. *International Journal of Clinical and Experimental Hypnosis, 23,* 266–281.

Davidson, R. J. (1992). Anterior cerebral asymmetry and the nature of emotion. *Brain & Cognition, 20,* 125–151.

Davidson, R. J., Ekman, P., Saron, C. D., Senulis, J. A., & Frieson, W.V. (1990). Approach-withdrawal and cerebral asymmetry: emotional expression and brain physiology. I. *Journal of Personality and Social Psychology, 58*(2), 330–341.

Davidson, R. J., Kabat-Zinn, J., Schumacher, J., Rosenkranz, M., Muller, D., Santorelli, S.F., Urbanowski, F., Harrington, A., Bonus, K., Sherrington, A. F. (2003) Alterations in brain and immune function produced by mindfulness meditation. *Psychosomatic Medicine, 65,* 564–570.

Davies, J. L., & Alexander, C. N. (1989). Alleviating political violence through reduction of collective stress: Impact assessment analysis of the Lebanon war. Paper presented at the annual meeting of the American Political Science Association, Atlanta.

Davis, S. M, & Drichta, C. E. (1980). Biofeedback theory and application in allied health speech pathology. *Biofeedback and Self-Regulation, 5,* 159–174.

Dean, W. F. (1954). *General Dean's story.* New York: Viking Press.

Deepak, K. K., Manchanda, S. K., & Maheshwari, M. C. (1994). Meditation improves clinicoelectroencephalographic measures in drug-resistant epileptics. *Biofeedback & Self-Regulation, 19,* 25–40.

Dehaene, S., & Nacchache, L. (2001). Towards a cognitive neuroscience of consciousness: basic evidence and a workspace framework. *Cognition, 79,* 1–37.

Dehaene, S., Changeux, J.-P., Nacchache, L., Sackur, J., & Sergent, C. (2006). Conscious, preconscious, an dsubliminal processing: a testable taxonomy. *Trends in Cognitive Neurosciences, 10,* 204–211.

Deikman, A. J. (1966). Deautomatization and the mystic experience. *Psychiatry, 29,* 324–338.

Deikman, A. J. (1971). Bimodal consciousness. *Archives of General Psychiatry, 45,* 481–489.

De Koninck, J., Gagnon, P., & Lallier, S. (1983). Sleep positions in the young adult and their relationship with the subjective quality of sleep. *Sleep, 6,* 52–59.

De Koninck, J., Lorrain, D., Christ, G., Proulx, G., & Coulombe, D. (1989). Intensive language learning and increases in rapid eye movement sleep: evidence of a performance factor. *International Journal of Psychophysiology, 8,* 43–47.

Delmonte, M. M. (1984). Physiological responses during meditation and rest. *Biofeedback and Self-Regulation, 9,* 181–200.

Dement, W. C. (1960). The effect of dream deprivation. *Science, 131,* 1705–1707.

Dement, W. C. (1972). *Some must watch while some must sleep.* San Francisco: Freeman.

Dement, W. C., & Baird, W. P. (1977). *Narcolepsy: Care and treatment.* Stanford, CA: American Narcolepsy Association.

Dement, W. C, & Greenberg, S. (1966). Changes in total amount of stage four sleep as a function of partial sleep deprivation. *Electroencephalography and Clinical Neurophysiology, 20,* 523–526.

Dement, W. C., Greenberg, S., & Klein, R. (1966). The effect of partial REM sleep deprivation and delayed recovery. *Journal of Psychiatric Research, 4,* 141–152.

Dement, W. C., Holman, R. B., & Guilleminault, C. (1976). Neurochemical and neuropharmacological foundations of the sleep disorders. *Psychopharmacology Communications, 2,* 77–90.

Dement, W. C., & Kleitman, N. (1957). Cyclic variations in EEG during sleep and their relation to eye movement, body motility, and dreaming. *Electroencephalography and Clinical Neurophysiology, 9,* 673–690.

Dengrove, E. (1976). *Hypnosis and behavior therapy.* Springfield, IL: Charles C. Thomas.

Denkowski, K. M., Denkowski, G. C., & Omizo, M. M. (1984). Predictors of success in the EMG biofeedback training of hyperactive male children. *Biofeedback and Self-Regulation, 9,* 253–264.

Dennett, D. C. (1988) Quining qualia. In: Marcel, A. & Bisiach, E. (eds.) *Consciousness in Modern Science,* Oxford University Press.

Dennett, D. C. (1995). Animal consciousness: what matters and why. *Social Research, 62*(3), 691–710.

Denton, K., & Krebs, D. (1990). From the scene to the crime: The effect of alcohol and social context on moral judgment. *Journal of Personality and Social Psychology, 59,* 242–248.

DePascalis, V., Silveri, A., & Palumbo, G. (1988). EEG asymmetry during covert mental activity and its relationship with hypnotizability. *International Journal of Clinical and Experimental Hypnosis, 36*, 38–52.

DePascalis, V. W. J., Ray, I., Tranquillo, D., & D'Amico, D. (1998). EEG activity and heart rate during recall of emotional events in hypnosis: relationships with hypnotizability and suggestibility. *International Journal of Psychophysiology, 29*, 255–275.

Deutsch, M., Canavan, D., & Rubin, J. (1971). Effects of size of conflict and sex of experimenter upon interpersonal bargaining. *Journal of Experimental Social Psychology, 7*, 258–267.

Devane, W. A., Hanus, L., Brauer, A., Pertwee, R. G., Stevenson, L. A., Griffin, G., Gibson, D., Mandelbaum, A., Etinger, A., & Mechoulam, R. (1992). Isolation and structure of a brain constituent that binds to the cannabinoid receptor. *Science, 258*, 1946–1949.

Dewan, E. D. (1967). Occipital alpha rhythm, eye position, and lens accommodation. *Nature, 214*, 975–977.

Dhanens, T. P., and Lundy, R. M. (1975). Hypnotic and waking suggestions and recall. *International Journal of Clinical and Experimental Hypnosis, 23*, 68–79.

Diamond, M. J. (1974). Modification of hypnotizability: a review. *Psychological Bulletin, 81*, 180–198.

Diamond, M. J. (1977). Hypnotizability is modifiable: an alternative approach. *International Journal of Clinical and Experimental Hypnosis, 25*, 147–166.

Diamond, S., Diamond-Falk, J., and Deveno, T. (1978). Biofeedback in the treatment of vascular headache. *Biofeedback and Self-Regulation, 3*, 385–408.

DiCara, L., & Miller, N. E. (1968). Instrumental learning of vasomotor responses by rats: Learning to respond differentially in the two ears. *Science, 159*, 1485–1486.

Dienes, Z., Brown, E., Hutton, S., Kirsch, I., Mazzoni, B., & Wright, D. B. (2009). Hypnotic suggestibility, cognitive inhibition, and dissociation. *Consciousness and Cognition, 18*, 837–847.

Dienstfrey, H. (1991). Neal Miller, the dumb autonomic nervous system, and biofeedback. *Advances, 7*, 33–44.

Dillbeck, M. C, Assimakis, P. D., Raimondi, D., Orme-Johnson, D. W., & Rowe, R. (1986). Longitudinal effects of the Transcendental Meditation and TM-Sidhi program on cognitive ability and cognitive style. *Perceptual and Motor Skills, 62*, 731–738.

Dillbeck, M. C., Cavanaugh, K. L., Glenn, T., Orme-Johnson, D. W., & Mittlefehldt, V. (1987). Consciousness as a field: The Transcendental Meditation and TM-Sidhi program and changes in social indicators. *Journal of Mind and Behavior, 8,* 67–104.

Dillbeck, M. C., & Orme-Johnson, D. (1987). Physiological differences between transcendental meditation and rest. *American Psychologist, 42,* 879–881.

Dixit, S. P., Agrawal, A., & Dubey, G. P. (1994). Management of essential hypertension by using biofeedback technique. *Pharmacopsychoecologia, 71,* 17–19.

Doane, B. K., Mahatoo, W., Heron, W., & Scott, T. H. (1959). Changes in perceptual function after isolation. *Canadian Journal of Psychology, 13,* 210–219.

Dobyns, Y. H., & Nelson, R. D. (1998). Empirical evidence against decision augmentation theory. *Journal of Scientific Exploration, 12*(2), 231–257.

Domhoff, G. W. (1996). *Finding meaning in dreams: a quantitative approach.* New York: Plenum

Domhoff, G. W. (2003). *The scientific study of dreams: neural networks, cognitive development, and content analysis.* Washington, DC: American Psychological Association.

Domhoff, G. W. (2011). The neural substrate for dreaming: is it a subsystem of the default network? *Consciousness and Cognition,* doi: 10.1016/j.concog.2011.03.001.

Dong, W., & Bao, F. (2005). Effects of biofeedback therapy on the intervention of examination-caused anxiety. *Chinese Journal of Clinical Rehabilitation, 9*(32), 17–19.

Doyle, A. C. (1938). The Sign of the Four. In *The Complete Sherlock Holmes.* New York: Garden City Publishing.

Drink Safe Technology (2009). http://www.drinksafetech.com/products.htm. Accessed November 15, 2010.

Drury, R., DeRisi, W., & Liberman, R. (1979). Temperature biofeedback treatment for migraine headache: A controlled multiple baseline study. *Headache, 19,* 278–284.

Duggins, A. J. (2010). A complex vector space model of single neuronal coding and experience. *BioSystems.* doi: 10.1016/j.biosystems.2010.08.005.

Dusek, D., & Girdano, D. A. (1980). *Drugs: A factual account.* Reading, MA: Addison-Wesley.

Duvall, H., Locke, B., &Brill, L. (1963). Follow-up study of narcotic drug addicts five years after hospitalization. *Public Health Service Reports, 78,* 185–193.

Dworetzky, J. P. (1997). *Psychology* (6th ed.). Pacific Grove, CA: Brooks Cole.

Dywan, J., & Bowers, K. S. (1983). The use of hypnosis to enhance recall. *Science, 222,* 184–185.

Earle, J. (1981). Cerebral laterality and meditation: A review of the literature. *Journal of Transpersonal Psychology, 13,* 155–173.

Eccles, J. C. (1977). *The understanding brain.* New York: McGraw-Hill.

Edebol, H., Bood, S. A., & Norlander, T. (2008). Chronic whiplash–associated disorders and their treatment using flotation REST (restricted environmental stimulation technique). *Qualitative Health Research, 18*(4), 480–488.

Edmonston, W. E., Jr. (1986). *The induction of hypnosis.* New York: Wiley.

Edwards, A. S. (1941). Effects of the loss of one hundred hours of sleep. *American Journal of Psychology, 54,* 80–91.

Egner, T., Jamieson, G., & Gruzelier, J. (2005). Hypnosis decouples cognitive control from conflict monitoring processes of the frontal lobe. *Neuroimage, 27,* 969–978.

Ego–Stengel, V., & Wilson, M. A. (2010). Disruption of ripple–associated hippocampal activity during rest impairs spatial learning in the rat. *Hippocampus, 21,* 1–10.

Ehrlichman, H., & Weinberger, A. (1979). Lateral eye movements and hemispheric asymmetry: A critical review. P*sychological Bulletin, 85,* 1080–1101.

Eiseman, B., Lam, R., & Rush, B. (1964). Surgery on the narcotic addict. *Annals of Surgery, 159,* 748–757.

Eisinger, R. A. (1972). Psychosocial predictors of smoking behavior change. *Social Sciences and Medicine, 6,* 137–144.

Eliseo, T. S. (1974). The Hypnotic Induction Profile and hypnotic susceptibility. *International Journal of Clinical and Experimental Hypnosis, 22,* 320–326.

Elkins, G., Marcus, J., Bates, J., Rajab, H. M., & Cook, T. (2006). Intensive hypnotherapy for smoking cessation: a prospective study. *International Journal of Clinical and Experimental Hypnosis, 54*(3), 303–315.

Ellinwood, E. H. (1969). Amphetamine psychosis: a multi-dimensional process. *Seminars in Psychiatry, 6,* 208–226.

Ellinwood, E. H., Kilbey, M. M., Castellani, S., & Khoury, C. (1977). Amygdala hyper-spindling and seizures induced by cocaine, In E. H. Ellinwood & M. M. Kilbey (Eds.), *Cocaine and other stimulants.* New York: Plenum.

Emmons, W. H., & Simon, C. W. (1956). The non-recall of material presented during sleep. *American Journal of Psychology, 69,* 79–81.

Engel, J. M., & Rapoff, M. A. (1990). Biofeedback-assisted relaxation training for adult and pediatric headache disorders. *Occupational Therapy Journal of Research, 10,* 283–299.

Engle-Friedman, M., Baker, E. A., and Bootzin, R. R. (1985). Reports of wakefulness during EEG identified stages of sleep. *Sleep Research, 14,* 152.

Erickson, M. H. (1973). Psychotherapy achieved by a reversal of the neurotic processes in a case of ejaculatio precox. *American Journal of Clinical Hypnosis, 15,* 217–222.

Espie, C. A., Lindsay, W. R., Brooks, D. N., & Hood, E. M. (1989). A controlled comparative investigation of psychological treatments for chronic sleep-onset insomnia. *Behavior Research and Therapy, 27,* 79–88.

Evans, C., & Evans, P. (Eds.). (1983). *Landscapes of the night.* New York: Viking.

Evans, F., Cook, M., Cohen, H., Orne, E., & Orne, M. (1977). Appetitive and replacement naps: EEG and behavior. *Science, 197,* 687–689.

Evans, F. J. (1979a). Hypnosis and sleep: Techniques for exploring cognitive activity during sleep. In E. Fromm & R. E. Shor (Eds.), *Hypnosis: Developments in research and new perspectives.* New York: Aldine.

Evans, F. J. (1979b). Contextual forgetting: posthypnotic source amnesia. *Journal of Abnormal Psychology, 88,* 556–563.

Eysenck, M. W, & Keane, M. T. (1995). *Cognitive psychology: A student's handbook.* Hills-dale, NJ: Erlbaum.

Fackelmann, K. A. (1993). Marijuana and the brain. *Science News, 143,* 88–94.

Fahler, J., & Cadoret, R. J. (1958). ESP card tests of college students with and without hypnosis. *Journal of Parapsychology, 22,* 125–136.

Faraday, A. (1972). *Dream power.* New York: Coward, McCann and Geoghagen.

Farthing, G. W. (1992). *The psychology of consciousness.* Englewood Cliffs, NJ: Prentice-Hall.

Faymonville, M–E., Boly, M., & Laureys, S. (2006). Functional neuroanatomy of the hypnotic state. *Journal of Physiology Paris, 99,* 463–469.

Fehring, R.J. (1983). Effects of biofeedback-aided relaxation on the psychological stress symptoms of college students. *Nursing Research, 32*(6), 362–366.

Feinstein, A. D., & Morgan, R. M. (1986). Hypnosis in regulating bipolar affective disorders. *American Journal of Clinical Hypnosis, 29,* 29–38.

Fell, J., Axmacher, N., & Haupt, S. (2008). From alpha to gamma: electrophysiological correlates of meditation-related states of consciousness. *Medical Hypotheses, 75,* 218–224.

Fell, J., & Axmacher, N. (2011). The role of phase synchronization in memory processes. *Nature Reviews Neuroscience, 12,* 105–118.

Fenton, G. W. (1975). Clinical disorders of sleep. *British Journal of Hospital Medicine,* August, 120–144.

Fine, T. H., & Turner, J. W., Jr. (1982). The effect of brief restricted environmental stimulation therapy in the treatment of essential hypertension. *Behavior Research and Therapy, 20,* 567–570.

Fingelkurts, Andrew A., Fingelkurts, Alexander A., Kalio, S., & Revonsuo, A. (2007). Cortex functional connectivity as a neuropsychological correlate of hypnosis: an EEG case study. *Neuropsychologica, 45,* 1452–1462.

Fischman, M. W., Schuster, C. R., Javid, J., Hatano, Y., & Davis, J. (1985). Acute tolerance development to the cardiovascular and sujective effects of cocaine. *Journal of Pharmacology and Experimental Therapeutics, 235,* 677–682.

Fisher, C. (1966). Dreaming and sexuality. In L. Lowenstein, M. Newman, M. M. Schur, & A. Solnit (Eds.), *Psychoanalysis: A general psychology.* New York: International University Press.

Fisher, L. E., & Kotses, H. (1973). Race differences and experimenter race effect in galvanic skin response. *Psychophysiology, 10,* 578–582.

Fisher, S. (1962). Problems of interpretation and controls in hypnotic research. In G. H. Estabrooks (Ed.), *Hypnosis: Current problems.* New York: Harper and Row.

Fisher, S., & Greenberg, R. P. (1977). *Scientific credibility of Freud's theory and therapy.* New York: Basic Books.

Fiske, D. W., & Maddi, S. R. (1961). *Functions of varied experience.* Homewood, IL: Dorsey.

Fitch, R. H., Cowell, P.E., Schrott, L. M., & Denenberg, V. H. (1991). Corpus collosum: ovarian hormones and feminization. *Brain Research, 542*(2), 313–317.

Fletcher, P. C., & Frith, C. D. (2009). Perceiving is believing: a Bayesian approach to explaining the positive symptoms of schizophrenia. *Nature Neuroscience, 10*, 48–58.

Foltin, R. W., Brady, J. V., & Fischman, M. W. (1986). Behavioral analysis of marijuana effects on food intake in humans. *Pharmacology, Biochemistry, and Behavior, 25*, 577–582.

Forays, D. G. (1987). Flotation REST as a smoking intervention. *Addictive Behaviors, 12*(1), 85–90.

Forgione, A. G. (1988). Hypnosis in the treatment of dental fear and phobia. *Dental Clinics of North America, 32*, 745–761.

Foulkes, D. (1962a). Cognitive processes during sleep: Evolutionary aspects. In A. Mayes (Ed.), *Sleep mechanisms and functions.* Wokingham, England: Van Nostrand Reinhold.

Foulkes, D. (1962b). Dream reports from different stages of sleep. *Journal of Abnormal and Social Psychology, 65*, 14–25.

Foulkes, D. (1982). *Children's dreams: Longitudinal studies.* New York: Wiley. Fowler, R. L., & Kimmel, H. D. (1962). Operant conditioning of the GSR. *Journal of Experimental Psychology, 63*, 563–567.

Foulkes, D. (1990). Dreaming and consciousness. *European Journal of Cognitive Psychology, 2*(1), 39–55.

Fox, O. (1962). *Astral Projection: A record of out-of-the-body experiences.* Secaucus, NJ: University Books. (Originally published 1939).

Frankel, F. J., & Orne, M. T. (1976). Hypnotizability and phobic behavior. *Archives of General Psychiatry, 33*, 1259–1261.

Fredericks, L. E. (1980). The value of teaching hypnosis in the practice of anesthesiology. *International Journal of Clinical and Experimental Hypnosis, 28*, 6–15.

Freedman, D. X., & Halaris, A. E. (1978). Monoamines and the biochemical mode of action of LSD at synapses. In M. A. Lipton, A. DiMascio, & K. F. Killam (Eds.), *Psychopharmacology.* New York: Raven.

Freedman, R., Ianni, P., & Wenig, P. (1985). Beta-adrenergic vasodilating mechanisms in biofeedback. Paper presented at the annual meeting of the Biofeedback Society of America, New Orleans.

Freedman, R., Lynn, S., Ianni, P., & Hale, P. (1981). Biofeedback treatment of Raynaud's phenomenon. *Biofeedback and Self-Regulation, 6*, 355–365.

French, S. N. (1980). Electromyographic biofeedback for tension control during fine motor skill acquisition. *Biofeedback and Self-Control, 5,* 221–228.

French, T., & Fromm, E. (1964). *Dream interpretation: A new approach.* New York: Basic Books.

Freud, S. (1900). *The interpretation of dreams.* London: Hogarth.

Freud, S. (1913). *Totem and taboo.* London: Penguin.

Freud, S. (1933). *New introductory lectures on psychoanalysis.* London: Hogarth.

Freud, S. (1970). On the general effect of cocaine. Lecture given at Psychiatric Union, March 5,1885. Reprinted in *Drug Dependence, 5,* 17.

Frezza, M, di Padova, C, Pozzato, G., Terpin, M., Baraona, E., & Lieber, C. S. (1990). High blood alcohol levels in women: The role of decreased gastic alcohol dehydrogenase activity and first-pass metabolism. *New England Journal of Medicine, 322,* 95–99.

Fridlund, A. J., Fowler, S. C., & Pritchard, D. A. (1980). Striate muscle tension patterning in frontalis EMG biofeedback. *Psychophysiology, 17,* 47–55.

Fried, F., Lamberti, J., & Sneed, P. (1977). Treatment of tension and migraine headaches with biofeedback techniques. *Missouri Medicine, 74,* 253–255.

Friedman, A. (1979). Characteristics of tension headache: A profile of 1420 cases. *Psychosomatic Medicine, 20,* 451–461.

Friedman, R. M., Schmeidler, G. R., and Dean, E. D. (1976). Ranked-target scoring for mood and intragroup effects in precognitive ESP. *Journal of the American Society for Psychical Research, 70,* 195–206.

Friman, P. C., & Warzak, W. J. (1990). Nocturnal enuresis: A prevalent, persistant, yet curable parasomnia. *Pediatrician, 1,* 38–45.

Frischholz, E. J., Spiegel, D., Trentalange, M. J., & Spiegel, H. (1987). The Hypnotic Induction Profile and absorption. *American Journal of Clinical Hypnosis, 30,* 87–93.

Fromm, E., & Shor, R. E. (Eds.). (1979). *Hypnosis: Developments in research and new perspectives.* New York: Aldine.

Fromm, E., Brown, D. P., Hurt, S. W., Oberlander, J. Z., Boxer, A. M., & Pfeifer, G. (1981). The phenomena and characteristics of self-hypnosis. *International Journal of Clinical and Experimental Hypnosis, 29,* 189–246.

Frumkin, L. R., Ripley, H. S., & Cox, G. B. (1978). Changes in cerebral lateralization with hypnosis. *Biological Psychiatry, 13,* 741–750.

Fuchs, K., Hoch, Z., & Kleinhauz, M. (1976). Hypno-desensitization therapy of vaginismus. Paper presented at the International Congress of Hypnosis and Psychosomatic Medicine, Philadelphia.

Fuchs, K., Hoch, Z., Paldi, E., Abromovici, H., Brandes, J. M., Timor-Tritsch, L, & Kleinhauz, M. (1973). Hypno-desentization therapy of vaginismus. I. In vitro method. II. In vivo method. *International Journal of Clinical and Experimental Hypnosis, 21,* 144–156.

Fugelsang, J. A., Roser, M. E., Corballis, P. M., Gazzaniga, M. S., & Dunbar, K. N. (2005). Brain mechanisms underlying perceptual causality. *Cognitive Brain Research, 24*(1), 41–47.

Fuller, G. D. (1978). Current status of biofeedback in clinical practice. *American Psychologist, 33,* 39–48.

Gaarder, K. R., and Montgomery, P. S. (1977). *Clinical biofeedback: A procedural manual.* Baltimore: Williams and Wilkins.

Gabel, S. (1989). Dreams as a possible reflection of a dissociated self-monitoring system. *Journal of Nervous and Mental Disease, 177,* 560–568.

Galak, J. & Nelson, L. D. (2010). A replication of the procedures from Bem (2010, Study 8) and a failure to replicate the same results. Available at SSRN: http://ssrn.com/abstract=1699970. (While the authors refer to Bem (2010), this is only an online version of what ultimately became Bem (2011).

Galin, D., & Ornstein, R. E. (1972). Lateral specialization of cognitive mode: An EEG study. *Psychophysiology, 9,* 412–418.

Gallois, P. (1984). Modifications neurophysiologiques et respiratoires lors de la pratique des techniques de relaxation. *L'Encephale, 10,* 139–144.

Ganis, G., Thompson, W. L., & Kosslyn, S.M. (2004). Brain areas underlying visual mental imagery and visual perception: an fMRI study. *Cognitive Brain Research, 20*(2), 226–241.

Gannon, L., and Sternbach, R. A. (1971). Alpha enhancement as a treatment for pain: A case study. *Behavior Therapy and Experimental Psychiatry, 2,* 209–213.

Garland, E.L., Gaylord, S. A., Boettiger, C.. A., & Howard, M. O. (2010). Mindfulness training modifies cognitive, affective, and physiological mechanisms implicated in alcohol dependence: results of a randomized controlled pilot trial. *Journal of Psychoactive Drugs, 42*(2), 177–192.

Garrett, J. B., & Wallace, B. (1975). A novel test of hypnotic anesthesia. *International Journal of Clinical and Experimental Hypnosis, 23,* 139–147.

Garwood, E. R., Bekele, W., McCulloch, C. E., & Christine, C. W. (2006). Amphetamine exposure is elevated in Parkinson's disease. *Neurotoxicology, 27,* 1003–1006.

Gastaut, H., & Broughton, R. (1965). A clinical polygraphic study of episodic phenomena during sleep. In J. Wortis (Ed.), *Recent Advances in Biological Psychiatry,* (Vol. 7), New York: Plenum.

Gastaut, H., Dongier, M., Broughton, R., & Tassinari, C. A. (1964). Electroencephalographic and clinical study of diurnal and nocturnal anxiety attacks. *Electroencephalography and Clinical Neurophysiology, 17,* 475–481.

Gautier–Sauvigne, S., Colas, D., Parmantier, P., Clement, P., Gharib, A., Sarda, N., & Cespuglio, R. (2005). Nitric oxide and sleep. *Sleep Medicine Reviews, 9*(2), 101–113.

Gawin, F. H., & Kleber, H. D. (1986). Abstinence symptomatology and psychiatric diagnosis in cocaine abusers. *Archives of General Psychiatry, 43,* 107–113.

Gazzaniga, M. S. (1983). Right hemisphere language following brain bisection: A 20 year perspective. *American Psychologist, 38,* 525–537.

Gazzaniga, M. S., Bogen, J. E., & Sperry, R. W. (1965). Observations on visual perception after disconnection of the cerebral hemispheres in man. *Brain, 8,* 221–236.

Gazzaniga, M. S., Volpe, B., Smylie, C., Wilson, D. H., & LeDoux, J. E. (1979). Plasticity in speech organization following commissurotomy. *Brain, 102,* 805–816.

Gazzaniga, M. A., & LeDoux, J. E. (1978). *The integrated mind.* New York: Plenum.

Gazzaniga, M. A., & Sperry, R. W. (1967). Language after section of the cerebral commissures. *Brain, 90,* 131–148.

Gazzaniga, M.S. (2005). Forty–five years of split–brain research and still going strong. *Nature Reviews Neuroscience, 6,* 653–659.

Gelderloos, P. (1987). *Valuation and transcendental meditation.* Lelystad, Netherlands: Soma Scientific Publishers.

Gelderloos, P., Walton, K. G., Orme-Johnson, D, & Alexander, C. N. (1991). Effectiveness of the transcendental meditation program in preventing and treating substance misuse: A review. *International Journal of the Addictions, 26,* 293–325.

Gevensleben, H., Holl, B., Albecht, B., Vogel, C., Schlamp, D., Kratz, O., Studer, P., Rotherneberger, A., Moll, G. H., & Heinrich, H. (2009). Is neurofeedback an efficacious treatment for ADHD? A randomized controlled clinical trial. *Journal of Child Psychology and Psychiatry,* doi: 10.1111/j.1469–7610.2008.02033.x.

Giannelli, P. C. (1995). The admissibility of hypnotic evidence in U.S. courts. *International Journal of Clinical and Experimental Hypnosis, 43,* 212–233.

Gibbs, F. A., Davis, H., & Lennox, W. G. (1935). The electroencephalogram in epilepsy and in conditions of impaired consciousness. *Archives of Neurology and Psychiatry, 34,* 1133–1148.

Gibby, R. G., & Adams, H. B. (1961). Receptiveness of psychiatric patients to verbal communication: An increase following partial sensory deprivation. *Archives of General Psychiatry, 5,* 366–370.

Girodo, M. (1974). Yoga meditation and flooding in the treatment of anxiety neurosis. *Journal of Behavior Therapy and Experimental Psychiatry, 5,* 157–160.

Gisquet-Verrier, P., & Smith, C. (1989). Avoidance performance in rats enhanced by postlearning paradoxical sleep deprivation. *Journal of Behavioral and Neural Biology, 52,* 152–169.

Glaus, K. D., Happ, A., & Kotses, H. (1976). Airway resistance changes associated with conditioned frontalis and bronchioradiolis EMG. Paper presented at the meeting of the Society for Psychophysiological Research, San Diego.

Glaus, K. D., & Kotses, H. (1976). Conditioned frontalis muscle tension effects on airway resistance. Paper presented at the meeting of the Society for Psychophysiological Research, San Diego.

Glaus, K. D., & Kotses, H. (1983). Facial muscle tension influences lung airway resistance: Limb muscle tension does not. *Biological Psychology, 17,* 105–120.

Glazer, H.I., & Laine, C.D. (2006). Pelvic floor muscle biofeedback in the treatment of urinary incontinence: a literature review. *Applied Psychophysiology and Biofeedback, 31*(3), 187–201.

Glennon, R. A. (1994). Classical hallucinogens: an introductory overview. In: G.C. Lin and R.A. Glennon Editors, *Hallucinogens: An update U.S. Department of Health and Human Services,* Washington, DC, pp. 4–32.

Glennon, R. A., Jarbe, T. U. C., & Frankenheim, J. (1991). Drug discrimination: applications to drug abuse research. *NIDA Research Monograph, 116.* National Institute on Drug Abuse, Rockville.

Glueck, B. (1973, May 27). Quoted in the *Hartford Courant,* p. 6.

Glueck, B. C, & Stroebel, C. F. (1975). Biofeedback and meditation in the treatment of psychiatric illnesses. *Comprehensive Psychiatry, 16,* 303–321.

Golden, W. L. (2006). Hypnotherapy for phobias, anxiety, and psychotherapy. In Chapman, R. A (Ed.). *The Clinical Use of Hypnosis in Cognitive–Behavioral Therapy,* pp. 101–138. New York: Springer Publishing.

Goldin, P. R., & Gross, J. J. (2010). Effects of mindfulness-based stress reduction (MBSR) on emotion regulation in social anxiety. *Emotion, 10*(1), 83–91.

Goldman, M. S. (1983). Cognitive impairment in chronic alcoholics: Some cause for optimism. *American Psychologist, 38,* 1045–1054.

Goldstein, L., Stolzfus, N., & Gardocki, J. (1972). Changes in interhemispheric amplitude relations in the EEG during sleep. *Physiology and Behavior, 8,* 811–815.

Goleman, D. (1971). Meditation as a meta-therapy: Hypotheses toward a proposed fifth state of consciousness. *Journal of Transpersonal Psychology, 3,* 1–25.

Goleman, D. (1977). *The varieties of the meditative experience.* New York: Dutton.

Goleman, D. (1982). Staying up: The rebellion against sleep's gentile tyranny. *Psychology Today, 16,* 24–35.

Goleman, D. (1988). *The meditative mind: The varieties of the meditative experience.* New York: G. P. Putnam's Sons.

Goleman, D., & Davidson, R. J. (1979). *Consciousness: Brain, states of awareness, and mysticism.* New York: Harper and Row.

Goodenough, D. R. (1978). Dream recall: History and current status of the field. In A. M. Arkin, J. S. Atrobus, & S. J. Ellman (Eds.), *The mind in sleep: Psychology and psychophysiology.* Hillsdale, NJ: Erlbaum.

Goodenough, D. R., Witkin, H. A., Koulack, D., & Cohen, H. (1975). The effects of stress filds on dream affect and on respiration and eye movement during rapid-eye movement sleep. *Psychophysiology, 15,* 313–320.

Goodwin, A. K., & Baker, L. E. (2002). A three–choice discrimination procedure dissociates the discriminative stimulus effects of d–amphetamine and MDMA in rats. *Experimental and Clinical Psychopharmacology, 8*(3), 415–423.

Goodwin, A. K., Pynnonen, D. M., & Baker, L.E. (2003). Serotonergic–dopaminergic mediation of MDMAs discriminative stimulus effects in a three–choice discrimination. *Pharmacology, Biochemistry, and Behavior, 74,* 987–945.

Gordeeva, O. V., & Finikova, G. N. (2005). Analytical introspection and short–term sensory deprivation as means of modifying consciousness. *Voprosy Psychologii, 6,* 72–81 (abstract only).

Gordon, H. W., & Sperry, R. W. (1968). Olfaction following surgical disconnection of the hemisphere in man. Paper presented at the annual meetings of the Psychonomic Society, Austin, TX.

Gordon, J.S., Staples, J.K., Blyta, A., & Bytyqi, M. (2004). Treatment of posttraumatic stress disorder in postwar Kosovo high school students using mind-body skills groups: A pilot study. *Journal of Traumatic Stress, 17*(2), 143–147.

Gow, M. A. (2006). Hypnosis with a blind 55-year-old female with dental phobia requiring periodontal treatment and extraction. *Contemporary Hypnosis, 23*(2), 92– 100.

Grabner, R. H., Neubauer, A. C. & Stern, E. (2006). Superior performance and neural efficiency: the impact of intelligence and expertise. *Brain Research Bulletin, 69*(4), 422–439.

Grabowski, J., & Dworkin, S. E. (1985). Cocaine: An overview of current issues. *International Journal of the Addictions, 20,* 1065–1088.

Graffin, N. F., Ray, W. J., & Lundy, R. (1995). EEG concomitants of hypnosis and hypnotic susceptibility. *Journal of Abnormal Psychology, 104,* 123–31.

Graham, C., & Evans, F. J. (1977). Hypnotizability and the development of waking attention. *Journal of Abnormal Psychology, 86,* 631–638.

Graham, C., & Leibowitz, H. W. (1972). The effect of suggestion on visual acuity. *International Journal of Clinical and Experimental Hypnosis, 20,* 169–186.

Graham, G. W. (1975). Hypnotic treatment for migraine headaches. *International Journal of Clinical and Experimental Hypnosis, 23,* 165–171.

Graham, K. R. (1977). Perceptual processes and hypnosis: Support for a cognitive-state theory based on laterality. In W. E. Edmonston (Ed.), *Conceptual and investigative approaches to hypnosis and hypnotic phenomena. Annals of the New York Academy of Science, 296,* 274–283.

Graham, K. R., & Pernicano, K. (1979). Laterality, hypnosis, and the autokinetic effect. *American Journal of Clinical Hypnosis, 22,* 79–84.

Graham, R. B. (1990). *Physiological psychology.* Belmont, CA: Wadsworth.

Granqvist, P. & Larsson, M. (2006). Contribution of religiousness in the prediction and interpretation of mystical experiences in a sensory deprivation context: activation of religious schemas. *The Journal of Psychology, 140*(4), 379–327.

Grant, J. A., Courtemanche, J., Duerden, E. G., Duncan, G. H., & Rainville, P. (2010). Cortical thickness and pain sensitivity in Zen meditators. *Emotion, 10*, 43–53.

Gravitz, M. A. (1988). Early uses of hypnosis as surgical anesthesia. *American Journal of Clinical Hypnosis, 30*, 201–208.

Gravitz, M. A. (1993). Etienne Felix d'Henin de Cuvilleres: A founder of hypnosis. *American Journal of Clinical Hypnosis, 36*, 7–11.

Gravitz, M. A., & Gerton, M. I. (1984). Origins of the term hypnotism prior to Braid. *American Journal of Clinical Hypnosis, 27*, 107–110.

Green, A. R., Cross, A. J., & Goodwin, G. M. (1995). Review of the pharmacology and clinical pharmacology of 3,4-methylenedioxymethamphetamine. *Psychopharmacology, 119*(3), 247–260.

Green, C. E. (1967). Ecsomatic experiences and related phenomena. *Journal of the American Society for Psychical Research, 44*, 111–131.

Green, E., & Green, A. (1979). General and specific applications of thermal biofeed-back. In J. Basmajian (Ed.), *Biofeedback: Principles and practice for clinicians*. Baltimore: Williams and Wilkins.

Green, J., Barabasz, A., Barrett, D., & Montgomery, G. (2005). The 2003 APA Division 30 definition of hypnosis. *Journal of Clinical and Experimental Hypnosis, 53*(3), 262–264.

Green, K. (1979). *The ocular effects of cannabinoids: Vol. 1. Current topics in eye research*. New York: Academic Press.

Greenberg, R., & Pearlman, C. (1967). Delirium tremens and dreaming. *American Journal of Psychiatry, 124*, 37–46.

Greenwood, P., Wilson, D. H., & Gazzaniga, M. S. (1977). Dream report following com-missurotomy. *Cortex, 13*, 311–316.

Grela, J. J. (1945). Effect on ESP scoring of hypnotically induced attitudes. *Journal of Parapsycholgy, 9*, 194–202.

Grilly, D. M. (1981). People's views on drugs and driving: An update. *Journal of Psychoactive Drugs, 13*, 377–379.

Grilly, D. M. (2006). *Drugs and human behavior* (5th ed.). Boston: Allyn and Bacon.

Grinspoon, L. (1969). Marihuana. *Scientific American, 221*, 17–25.

Grinspoon, L., & Bakalar, J. (1979). A kick from cocaine. *Psychology Today, 12*, 36–39, 77–78.

Grinspoon, L., & Bakalar, J. (1993). *Marihuana, the forbidden medicine*. New Haven, CT: Yale University Press.

Grosso, M. (1981). Toward an explanation of near-death phenomena. *Journal of the American Society for Psychical Research, 75,* 37–60.

Groves, P. M., & Schlesinger, K. (1982). *Biological psychology.* Dubuque, IA: William C. Brown.

Gruzelier, J., & Flor-Henry, P. (Eds.). (1979) *Hemisphere asymmetries offunctin in psychopathology.* Amsterdam: Elsevier.

Gruzelier, J. (1996). The state of hypnosis: evidence and applications. *Quarterly Journal of Medicine, 89,* 313–317.

Gruzelier, J. (2006). Frontal functions, connectivity and neural efficiency underpinning hypnosis and hypnotic susceptibility. *Contemporary Hypnosis, 23,* 15–32.

Guerra, F. (1971). *The pre-Columbian mind.* New York: Seminar Press.

Guglielmi, R. S., Roberts, A. H., & Patterson, R. (1982). Skin temperature biofeedback for Raynaud's disease: A double-blind study. *Biofeedback and Self-Regulation, 7,* 99–120.

Gunn, J. (1979). Drugs in the violence clinic. In M. Sandier (Ed.), *Psychopharmacology of aggression.* New York: Raven.

Gur, R. C., & Gur, R. E. (1974). Handedness, sex, and eyedness as moderating variables in the relation between hypnotic susceptibility and functional brain asymmetry. *Journal of Abnormal Psychology, 83,* 635–643.

Gur, R. E., Gur, R. C., & Harris, L. J. (1975). Cerebral activation as measured by subjects' lateral eye movements is influenced by experimenter location. *Neuropsychologia, 13,* 35–44.

Guze, S. B., Cloninger, C. R., Martin, R., & Clayton, P. J. (1986). Alcoholism as a medical disorder. *Comprehensive Psychiatry, 27,* 501–510.

Guzmán–Hosta, L., Martínez–Taboas, A., & Rodríguez–Gómez, J. (2007). A Spanish version of the barber suggestibility scale for the Puerto Rican population. *International Journal of Clinical and Experimental Hypnosis, 55*(1), 59–66.

Gyatso, T. (2005). *Science at the crossroads.* Boulder, CO: Mind & Life Institute.

Haber, R. N. (1979). Twenty years of haunting eidetic imagery: Where's the ghost? *Behavioral and Brain Sciences, 2,* 583–629.

Haber, R. N., & Haber, R. B. (1964). Eidetic imagery. I. Frequency. *Perceptual and Motor Skills, 19,* 131–138.

Haber, R. N., & Hershenson, M. (1980). *The psychology of visual perception.* New York: Holt, Rinehart, and Winston.

Habib, M., Gayraud, D., Olivia, A., Regis, J., Salamon, G., & Khalil, R. (1991). Effects of handedness and sex on the morphology of the corpus callosum: A study with brain magnetic resonance imaging. *Brain & Cognition, 16*, 41–61.

Hageman-Wenselaar, L. H. (1988). Hypnosis for pain control during lumbar puncture and bone marrow aspirations in children with cancer. *Tijdschr Kindergeneeskd, 56*, 120–123.

Hajak, G., Muller, W. E., Wittchen, H. U., Pittrow, D., & Kirch, W. (2003). Abuse and dependence potential for the non–benzodiazepine hypnotics zolpidem and zopiclone: a review of case reports and epidemiological data. *Addiction, 98*(10), 1371–1378.

Hall, C. S. (1951). What people dream about. *Scientific American, 184*, 60–63.

Hall, C. S., & Lindzey, G. (1978). *Theories of personality* (3rd ed.). New York: Wiley.

Hall, C. S., & Van de Castle, R. L. (1966). *The content analysis of dreams.* New York: Appleton-Century-Crofts.

Hall, J. R., & McGill, J. C. (1986). Hypnobehavioral treatment of self-destructive behavior: Trichotillomania and bulimia in the same patient. *American Journal of Clinical Hypnosis, 29*, 39–46.

Hall, J. S., & Crasilneck, H. B. (1970). Development of a hypnotic technique for treating chronic cigarette smoking. *International Journal of Clinical and Experimental Hypnosis, 18*, 283–289.

Hamilton, W. (1880). *Lectures on metaphysics.* New York: Sheldon.

Hansel, C. E. M. (1980). *ESP and parapsychology: A critical evaluation.* Buffalo: Prometheus.

Haraldsson, E., Gudmundsdottir, A., Ragnarsson, A., Loftsson, J., & Jonsson, S. (1977). National survey of psychical experiences and attitudes towards the paranormal in Iceland. In J. D. Morris, W. G. Roll, & R. L. Morris (Eds.), *Research in Parapsychology 1976.* Metuchen, NJ: Scarecrow Press.

Hart, C. L., Ksir, C. J., & Ray, O. S. (2011). Drugs, society, & human behavior (14th edition). New York: McGraw-Hill.

Hart, J. T. (1967). Autocontrol of EEG alpha. Paper presented at the annual meeting of the Society for Psychophysiological Research, San Diego.

Hart, J. T., & Cichanski, K. (1981). A comparison of frontal EMG biofeedback and neck EMG biofeedback in the treatment of muscle-contractin headache. *Biofeedback and Self-Regulation, 6*, 63–74.

Hartmann, E. L. (1973). *The functions of sleep.* New Haven: Yale University Press.

Hartmann, E. L. (1981). The strangest sleep disorder. *Psychology Today, 15,* 14–18.

Hartmann, E., Baekeland, F., Zwilling, G., & Hop, P. (1971). Sleep need: How much sleep and what kind? *American Journal of Psychiatry, 127,* 1001–1008.

Hartmann, E. (2000). We do not dream of the 3 R's: implications for the nature of dreaming mentation. *Dreaming, 10,* 103–110.

Harvard Mental Health Letter (March, 2010). Neurofeedback for attention deficit hyperactivity disorder. Pages 4–5. www.health.harvard.edu.

Harver, A., Kotses, H., Segreto, J., & Creer, T. L. (1984). Impact of facial relaxation training on asthma symptoms. Paper presented at the Fifth International Symposium on Respiratory Psychophysiology, Nijmegen, The Netherlands.

Harvey, S. C. (1985). Hypnotics and sedatives. In A. G. Gilman, L. S. Goodman, T. W. Rail, & F. Murad (Eds.), *The pharmacological basis of therapeutics.* New York: Macmillan.

Harwood, C. W. (1962). Operant heart rate conditioning. *Psychological Record, 12,* 279–284.

Hashrroudi, S., Parker, E. S. Yablick, L., DeLisi, L. E., & Wyatt, R. J. (1981). Generation is a better "antidote" for alcohol amnesia than semantic elaboration. Paper presented at the meetings of the Psychonomic Society, Philadelphia.

Hatch, J. P. (1981). Voluntary control of sexual responding in men and women: Implications for the etiology and treatment of sexual dysfunctions. *Biofeedback and Self-Regulation, 6,* 191–206.

Hauri, P. J. (1985). Primary sleep disorders and insomnia. In T. Riley (Ed.), *Clinical aspects of sleep and sleep disturbance.* Boston: Butterworth.

Haut, J. S., Beckwith, B. E., Petros, T. V, & Russell, S. (1989). Gender differences in retrieval from long-term memory following acute intoxication with ethanol. *Physiology and Behavior, 45,* 1161–1165.

Havens, J. (1969). Psychology and religious retreats. *Pastoral Psychology, 20,* 45–52.

Hayashi, M., Morikawa, T., & Hori, T. (1992). EEG alpha activity and hallucinatory experience during sensory deprivation. *Perceptual and Motor Skills, 75*(2), 403–412.

Hebb, C. (1970). CNS at the cellular level: Identity of transmitter agents. *Annual Review of Physiology, 32,* 165–192.

Hebb, D. O. (1949). *The organization of behavior.* New York: Wiley.

Heilman, K. M., Rothi, L., & Kertesz, A. (1983). Localization of apraxia-producing lesions. In A. Kertesz (Ed.), *Localization in neuropsychology* (p. 381). New York: Academic Press, p. 381.

Helmholtz, H. (1871/1971). The facts of perception. In Russell, K. (Ed.). *Selected writings of Hermann von Helmholtz.* Connecticut: Wesleyn University Press.

Helper, R. S., & Frank, I. M. (1971). Marijuana smoking and intraocular pressure. *Journal of the American Medical Association, 217,* 1392.

Hennevin, E., Hars, B., & Block, V. (1989). Improvement of learning by mesencephalic reticular stimulation during postlearning paradoxical sleep. *Journal of Behavioral and Neural Biology, 51,* 291–306.

Heron, W., Bexton, W. H., & Hebb, D. O. (1953). Cognitive effects of decreased variation to sensory environment (abstract). *American Psychologist, 8,* 366.

Heron, W., Doane, B. K., & Scott, T. H. (1956). Visual disturbances after prolonged perceptual isolation. *Canadian Journal of Psychology, 10,* 13–18.

Hess, W. R. (1944). Das Schlafsyndrom als Folgedienzephaler Reizung. *Helvetica Physiologica et Pharmacologica Ada, 2,* 305–344.

Hilgard, E. R. (1965). *The experience of hypnosis.* New York: Harcourt, Brace and World.

Hilgard, E. R. (1973). A neodissociation interpretation of pain reduction in hypnosis. *Psychological Review, 80,* 396–411.

Hilgard, E. R. (1976). Neodissociation theory of multiple cognitive controls. In G. E. Schwartz & D. Shapiro (Eds.), *Consciousness and self-regulation: Advances in research.* New York: Plenum.

Hilgard, E. R. (1977a). Controversies over consciousness and the rise of cognitive psychology. *Australian Psychologist, 12,* 7–27.

Hilgard, E. R. (1977b). *Divided consciousness: Multiple controls in human thought and action.* New York: Wiley.

Hilgard, E. R. (1979). Divided consciousness in hypnosis: The implications of the hidden observer. In E. Fromm & R. E. Shor (Eds.), *Hypnosis: Developments in research and new perspectives.* New York: Aldine.

Hilgard, E. R. (1987). Research advances in hypnosis: Issues and methods. *International Journal of Clinical and Experimental Hypnosis, 35,* 248–264.

Hilgard, E. R., & Hilgard, J. R. (1994). *Hypnosis in the relief of pain* (2nd ed.). Los Altos, CA: Kaufmann.

Hilgard, E. R., Morgan, A. H., & MacDonald, H. (1975). Pain and dissociation in the cold pressor test: a study of hypnotic analgesia with "hidden reports" through automatic keypressing and automatic talking. *Journal of Abnormal Psychology, 84,* 280–289.

Hilgard, J. R., & LeBaron, S. (1982). Relief of anxiety and pain in children and adolescents with cancer: Quantitative measures and clinical observations. *International Journal of Clinical and Experimental Hypnosis, 30,* 418–442.

Hilgard, J. R., & LeBaron, S. (1984). *Hypnosis in the treatment of pain and anxiety in children with cancer: A clinical and quantitative investigation.* Los Altos, CA: Kaufmann.

Hindman, M. H. (1979, Fall). Family violence: An overview. *Alcohol Health and Research World* (NIAA A, Public Health Administration, Department of Health, Education, and Welfare), p. 4.

Hinds, J. (1995). A model of the mind that explains subject and experimenter expectancy effects. *Journal of the American Society for Psychical Research, 89,* 51–72.

Hingson, R., Hareen, T., & Winter, M. (1996). Lowering state legal blood alcohol limits to 0.08%: The effect on fatal motor vehicle crashes. *American Journal of Public Health, 86*(9), 1297–1299.

Hirsch, C. (1972). The dermatopathology of narcotic addiction. *Human Pathology, 3,* 45–52.

Hjelle, L. A. (1974). Transcendental meditation and psychological health. *Perceptual and Motor Skills, 39,* 623–628.

Hobson, J. A. (1993). Sleep and dreaming. *Current Opinion in Neurobiology, 10,* 371–382.

Hobson, J. A. (1995). *Sleep.* New York: Freeman.

Hobson, J. A., & McCarley, R. W. (1977). The brain as a dream state generator: An activation-synthesis of the dream process. *American Journal of Psychiatry, 134,* 1335–1348.

Hobson, J. A., & Strickgold, R. (1995). The conscious state paradigm: A neurocognitive approach to waking, sleeping, and dreaming. In M. S. Gazzaniga (Ed.), *The cognitive neurosciences.* Cambridge, MA: MIT Press, pp. 1373–1389.

Hobson, J. A. (1992). A new model of brain-mind state: activation level, input source, and mode of processing *(AIM). The neuropsychology of sleep and dreaming.* Antrobus, J S. & Bertini, M. (Eds.). pp. 227–245. Hillsdale, NJ, England: Lawrence Erlbaum Associates, Inc.

Hobson, J. A. (1997). Consciousness as a state–dependent phenomenon. In J. Cohen & J. Schooler (eds.). *Scientific Approaches to Consciousness.* Hillsdale, NJ: Lawrence Erlbaum.

Hobson, J. A. (2009). REM sleep and dreaming: toward a theory of protoconsciousness. *Nature Reviews Neuroscience, 10,* 803–813.

Hofmann, F., & Hofmann, A. (1975). *A handbook on drug and alcohol abuse.* New York: Oxford.

Hogue, D. R., & Hunter, R. E. (1988). The use of hypnosis in orthopaedic surgery. *Contemporary Orthopaedics, 16,* 65–68.

Hohwy, J. (2009). The neural correlates of consciousness: new experimental approaches needed? *Consciousness and Cognition, 18,* 428–438.

Hollister, L. (1971). Marihuana in man: Three years later. *Science, 172,* 21–29.

Hollister, L. E. (1986). Health aspects of cannabis. *Pharmacological Reviews, 38,* 1–20.

Holmes, D. S. (1984). Meditation and somatic arousal reduction: A review of the experimental evidence. *American Psychologist, 39,* 1–10.

Holroyd, J. (1980). Hypnosis treatment for smoking: An evaluative review. *International Journal of Clinical and Experimental Hypnosis, 28,* 341–357.

Holzel, B. K., Carmody, J., Vangel, M., Congleton, C. Yerramsetti, S. M., Gard, T., & Lazar, S. W. (2011). Mindfulness practice leads to increases in regional brain gray matter density. *Psychiatry Research: Neuroimaging, 191,* 36–43.

Holzel, B.K., Ott, U., Gard, T., Hempel, H., Weygandt, M., Morgan, K., & Vaitl, D. (2008). Investigation of mindfulness meditation practitioners with voxel–based morphometry. *Social Cognitive and Affective Neuroscience, 3,* 55–61.

Holzel, B.K., Ott, U., Hemel, H., Hackl, A., Wolf, K., Stark, R., & Vaitl, D. (2007). Differential engagement of anterior cingulated and adjeacent medial frontal cortex in adept meditators and non–meditators. *Neuroscience Letters, 421,* 16–21.

Hong, C. C., Potkin, J. S., Antrobus, M. D., Callaghan, G. M., & Gillin, C. (1997). REM sleep eye movement counts correlate with visual imagery in dreaming: A pilot study. *Psychophysiology: The International Journal of the Society for Psychophysiological Research, 34,* 377–381.

Honorton, C. (1972). Significant factors in hypnotically induced clairvoyant dreams. *Journal of the American Society for Psychical Research, 66,* 86–102.

Honorton, C. (1978). Replicability, experimenter influence, and parapsychology: An empirical context for the study of mind. Paper presented at the Annual Meeting of the American Association for the Advancement of Science, Washington, D.C.

Honorton, C. (1985). Meta-analysis of psi ganzfeld research: A response to Hyman. *Journal of Parapsychology, 49,* 51–91.

Honorton, C., & Krippner, S. (1969). Hypnosis and ESP performance: A review of the experimental literature. *Journal of the American Society for Psychical Research, 63,* 214–253.

Honorton, C., & Stump, J. P. (1969). A preliminary study of hypnotically induced clairvoyant dreams. *Journal of the American Society for Psychical Research, 63,* 175–184.

Honsberger, R. (1973). The effect of transcendental meditation upon bronchial asthma. *Clinical Research, 21,* 368.

Hooker, W. D., & Jones, R. T. (1987). Increased susceptibility to memory intrusions and the stroop interference effect during acute marijuana intoxication. *Psychopharmacology, 91,* 20–24.

Hoon, E. F. (1980). Biofeedback-assisted arousal in females: A comparison of visual and auditory modalities. *Biofeedback and Self-Regulation, 5,* 175–191.

Hoppe, K. D. (1977). Split brains and psychoanalysis. *The Psychoanalytic Quarterly, 46,* 220–224.

Horowitz, M. J. (1969). Flashbacks: Recurrent intrusive images after the use of LSD. *American Journal of Psychiatry, 126,* 147–151.

Hothersall, D., & Brener, J. (1969). Operant conditioning of changes in heart rates in curarized rats. *Journal of Comparative and Physiological Psychology, 68,* 338–342.

Houshmand, Z., Lingston, R. B, & Wallace, B. A. (Eds.). (1999). *Consciousness at the crossroads: conversations with the Dalai Lama on brain science and Buddhism.* Ithica, NY: Snow Lion Publications.

Houtkooper, J. M. (1977). A study of repeated retroactive psychokinesis in relation to random PK effects. *European Journal of Parapsychology, 1*(4), 1–20.

Houtkooper, J. M. (2002). Arguing for an observational theory of paranormal phenomena. *Journal of Scientific Exploration, 16*(2), 171–185.

Huang, M.C., Lin, H. Y., & Chen, C. H. (2007). Dependence on zolpidem. *Psychiatry and Clinical Neuroscience, 61,* 207–208.

Hubel, D. H., & Wiesel, T. N. (1979). Brain mechanisms of vision. In *The Brain* (Scientific American Reprints). San Francisco: Freeman.

Hughes, J., Smith, T. W., Kosterlitz, H. W., Fothergill, L. A., Morgan, B. A., & Morris, H. R. (1975). Identification of two related pentapeptides from the brain with potent opiate agonist activity. *Nature, 258,* 577–579.

Hull, J. G., & Bond, C. F. (1986). Social and behavioral consequences of alcohol consumption and expectancy: A meta-analysis. *Psychological Bulletin, 99,* 347–359.

Humphrey, M. E., & Zangwill, O. L. (1951). Cessation of dreaming after brain injury. *Journal of Neurology, Neurosurgery and Psychiatry, 14,* 322–325.

Hunt, H. T. (1995). *On the nature of consciousness: Cognitive, phenomenological, and transpersonal perspectives.* New Haven, CT: Yale University Press.

Huntley, A., White, A.R., & Ernst, E. (2002). Relaxation therapies for asthma: a systematic review. *Thorax, 57*(2), 127–131.

Hurley, J.D., & Meminger, S.R. (1992). A relapse–prevention program: Effects of electromyographic training on high and low levels of state and trait anxiety. *Perceptual and Motor Skills, 74*(3, Pt. 1), 699–705.

Husain, S. (1989). Effects of delta-9-tetrahydrocannabinol on in vitro energy substrate metabolism in mouse and rat testes. *Physiology and Behavior, 46,* 65–68.

Husain, S., & Patra, P. B. (1989). Delta-9-tetrahydrocannabinol on spermatogenesis in mice. *Physiology and Behavior, 46,* 60–64.

Hyman, R. (1985). The ganzfeld/psi experiment: A critical appraisal. *Journal of Parapsychology, 49,* 3–49.

Hyman, R., & Honorton, C. (1986). A joint communique: The psi ganzfeld controversy. *Journal of Parapsychology, 50,* 351–364.

Hyman, R. (2010a). What's wrong with materialism? In Krippner, S., & Friedman, H. L. (Eds.). *Debating Psychic Experience: Human Potential or Human Illusion?* (p. 42–52). Santa Barbara, CA: Praeger.

Hyman, R. (2010b). Meta-analysis that conceals more than it reveals: comment on Storm et al. (2010). *Psychological Bulletin, 136*(4), 486–490.

Irwin, H. J. (1978a). ESP and the human information processing system. *Journal of the American Society for Psychical Research, 72,* 111–126.

Irwin, H. J. (1978b). Psi, attention, and processing capacity. *Journal of the American Society for Psychical Research, 72,* 301–313.

Irwin, H. J. (1988). Out-of-body experiences and attitudes to life and dealth. *Journal of the American Society for Psychical Research, 82,* 237–251.

Irwin, H. J. (1994). Childhood trauma and the origins of paranormal belief: A constructive replication. *Psychological Reports, 74,* 107–111.

Istvan, J., & Matarazzo, J. D. (1984). Tobacco, alcohol, and caffeine use: A review of their interrelationships. *Psychological Bulletin, 95,* 301–326.

Itard, J. M. G. (1932). *The Wild Boy of Aveyron* (G. Humphrey & M. Humphrey, Trans.). New York: Appleton-Century-Crofts.

Iwata, K., Yamamoto, M., Nakao, M., & Kimura, M. (1999). A study on polysomnographic observations and subjective experiences under sensory deprivation. *Psychiatry and Clinical Neurosciences, 53,* 129–131.

Jackson, J. H. (Ed.). (1958). *Selected writings of John Hughlings Jackson.* New York: Basic Books.

Jacob, P., Jones, R. T, Benowitz, N. L., & Shulgin, A. T. (1989). Cocaine smokers inhale a pyrolysis product: Anhydroecgonine methyl ester. Paper presented at the meetings of the American Society for Clinical Pharmacology and Therapeutics, Nashville.

Jacobs, B. L. (1987). How hallucinogenic drugs work. *American Scientist, 75,* 386–392.

Jacobs, G. D., Heilbronner, R. L., & Stanley, J. M. (1985). The effects of short term flotation REST on relaxation: A controlled study. In T. H. Fine & J. W. Turner, Jr. (Eds.), *Proceedings of the First International Conference on REST and Self-Regulation* (pp. 86–102). Toledo, OH: IRIS.

Jacobson, E. (1938). *How to relax and have your baby: Scientific relaxation in childbirth.* New York: McGraw-Hill.

Jaffe, J. H. (1985). Drug addiction and drug abuse. In A. G. Gilman, L. S. Goodman, T. W. Rall, & F. Murad (Eds.), *The pharmacological basis of therapeutics.* New York: Macmillan.

Jahn, R. G. (1982). The persistent paradox of psychic phenomena: an engineering perspective. *Proceedings of the IEEE, 70*(2), 136–170.

Jahn, R. G., & Dunne, B. (2005). The PEAR project. *Journal of Scientific Exploration, 19*(2), 195–245.

Jahn, R. G., Dunne, B., & Nelson, R. D. (1987). Engineering anomalies research. *Journal of Scientific Exploration, 1*(1), 21–50.

James, W. (1890). *Principles of psychology* (Vol. 1). New York: Holt.

James, W. (1904). Does consciousness exist? *Journal of Philosophy, Psychology, and Scientific Methods, 1,* 477–491.

Jarvik, M. E. (1967). The psychopharmacological revolution. *Psychology Today, 1,* 51–58.

Jaynes, J. (1976). *The origin of consciousness in the breakdown of the bicameral mind.* Boston: Houghton Mifflin.

Jaynes, J. (1986a). Hearing voices and the bicameral mind. *Behavioral and Brain Sciences, 9,* 526–527.

Jaynes, J. (1986b). Consciousness and voices of the mind. *Canadian Psychology, 27,* 128–148.

Jeffcoat, R. A., Perez-Reyes, M., Hill, J. M., Sadler, B. M., & Cook, E. (1989). Cocaine disposition in humans after intravenous injection, nasal insufflation (snorting), or smoking. *Drug Metabolism and Disposition, 17,* 153–159.

Jeffrey, T. B., Jeffrey, L. K., Greuling, J. W., & Gentry, W. R. (1985). Evaluation of a brief group treatment package including hypnotic induction for maintenance of smoking cessation: A brief communication. *International Journal of Clinical and Experimental Hypnosis, 33,* 95–98.

Jensen, P. S., Hinshaw, S. P., Swanson, J. M., Greenhill, L. L., Conners, C. K., Arnold, L. E., Abikoff, H. B., Elliott, G., Hechtman, L., Hoza, B., March, J. S., Newcorn, J. H., Sever, J., Vitiello, B., Wells, K., & Wigal, T. (2001). Findings from the NIMH multimodal treatment study of ADHD (MTA): implications and applications for primary care providers. *Journal of Developmental and Behavioral Pediatrics, 22*(1), 60–73.

Jevning, R., Wallace, R. K., & Beidebach, M. (1992). The physiology of meditation: A review: A wakeful hypometabolic integrated response. *Neuroscience & Biobehavioral Reviews, 16,* 415–424.

John, E. R. (2001). A field theory of consciousness. *Consciousness and Cognition, 10,* 184–213.

John, J., & Kumar, V. M. (1998). Effect of NMDA lesion of the medial preoptic neurons on sleep and other functions. *Sleep, 21,* 587–598.

John, R., Hollander, B., & Perry, C. (1983). Hypnotizability and phobic behavior: Further supporting data. *Journal of Abnormal Psychology, 92,* 390–392.

Johnson, L. C., & MacLeod, W. L. (1973). Sleep and awake behavior during gradual sleep reduction. *Perceptual and Motor Skills, 36,* 87–97.

Johnson, L. C., Slye, E., & Dement, W. C. (1965). EEG and autonomic activity during and after prolonged sleep deprivation. *Psychosomatic Medicine, 27,* 415–423.

Johnson, L. S. (1981). Current research in self-hypnotic phenomenology: The Chicago paradigm. *International Journal of Clinical and Experimental Hypnosis, 29,* 247–258.

Johnson, R. F. Q., Maher, B. A., & Barber, T. X. (1972). Artifact in the "essence of hypnosis": An evaluation of trance logic. *Journal of Abnormal Psychology, 79,* 212–220.

Johnson, W. G., and Turin, A. (1975). Biofeedback treatment of migraine headache: A systematic case study. *Behavior Therapy, 6,* 394–397.

Jones, E. (1953–1957). *The life and work of Sigmund Freud* (3 vols.). New York: Basic Books.

Jones-Witters, P., & Witters, W. L. (1983). *Drugs and society: A biological perspective.* Belmont, CA: Wadsworth.

Judd, C. M., & Gawronski, B. (2011). Editorial comment on Bem, D. J. *(2011). Feeling the future: experimental evidence for anomalous retroactive influences on cognition and affect. Journal of Personality and Social Psychology, 100(3), 407–425, Journal of Personality and Social Psychology,* 100(3), 406.

Julesz, B. (1971). *Foundations of cyclopean perception.* Chicago: University of ChicagoPress.

Julien, R. M. (1997). *A primer of drug action* (8th ed.). New York: Freeman.

Jurek, I. E., Higgins, J. T., & McGrady A. (1992). Interaction of biofeedback-assisted relaxation and diuretic in treatment of essential hypertension. *Biofeedback & Self-Regulation, 17,* 125–141.

Kabat-Zinn, J. (1991). *Full catastrophe living: using the wisdom of your body and mind to face stress, pain, and illness.* New York: Bantam Dell/ Random House.

Kabat-Zinn J. (2003). Mindfulness-based stress reduction (MBSR). *Constructivism and Human Science, 8*(2), 73–107.

Kahan, T. L., & LeBerge, S. P. (2010). Dreaming and waking: similarities and differences revisited. *Consciousness and Cognition,* doi: 10.1016/j. concog.2010.09.002.

Kahn, E., Dement, W. C., Fisher, C., & Barmack, J. L. (1962). The incidence of color in immediately recalled dreams. *Science, 137,* 1054.

Kahn, E., Fisher, C., & Edwards, A. (1978). Night terrors and anxiety dreams. In A. M. Arkin, J. S. Antrobus, and S. J. Ellman (Eds.), *The mind in sleep: Psychology and psychophysiology.* Hillsdale, NJ: Erlbaum.

Kahneman, D. (1973). *Attention and effort.* Englewood Cliffs, NJ: Prentice-Hall.

Kalat, J. W. (1992). *Biological psychology* (4th ed.). Belmont, CA: Wadsworth

Kallio, S., & Revansuo, A. (2003). Hypnotic phenomena and altered states of consciousness: a theoretical framework. *Contemporary Hypnosis, 20*(3), 111–164.

Kamiya, J. (1968). Conscious control of brain waves. *Psychology Today, 1,* 57–60.

Kamiya, J. (1969). Operant control of the EEG alpha rhythm and some of its reported effects on consciousness. In C. T. Tart (Ed.), *Altered states of consciousness*. New York: Wiley.

Kane, B., Millay, J., & Brown, D. H. (Eds.) (1993). *Silver threads: 25 years of parapsychology research*. Westport, CT: Praeger.

Kaptchuk, T. J. (2001). Distant healing. *Annals of Internal Medicine, 134*(6), 532.

Karavidas, M., Tsai, P.–S., Yucha, C., McGrady, A., & Lehrer, P.M. (2006). Thermal biofeedback for primary Raynaud's phenomenon: a review of the literature. *Applied Psychophysiology and Biofeedback, 31*(3), 203–216.

Karlin, R. A. (1979). Hypnotizability and attention. *Journal of Abnormal Psychology, 88,* 92–95.

Karniol, J. G., & Carlini, E. A. (1972). The content of delta-9-trans-tetrahydrocannabi-nol (delta-9-THC) does not explain all biological activity of some Brazilian marihuana samples. *Journal of Pharmacy and Pharmacology, 24,* 833–835.

Kasamatsu, A., & Hirai, T. (1963). Science of Zazen. *Psychologia, 6,* 86–91.

Kasamatsu, A., & Hirai, T. (1966). An electroencephalographic study on the Zen meditation. *Folia Psychiatrica et Neurologia Japonica, 20,* 315–336.

Kasamatsu, A., & Hirai, T. (1969). An electroencephalographic study of the Zen meditation (Zazen). *Psychologia, 12,* 205–225.

Kasamatsu, A., & Hirai, T. (1966). An electroencephalographic study on the zen meditation (zazen). *Folia Psychiatriatry and Neurology Japan, 20*(4), 315–336.

Katkin, E. S., & Murray, E. N. (1969). Instrumental conditioning of autonomically mediated behavior: Theoretical and methodological issues. *Psychological Bulletin, 70,* 52–68.

Katkin, E. S., Murray, E. N., & Lachman, R. (1969). Concerning instrumental auto-nomic conditioning: A rejoinder. *Psychological Bulletin, 71,* 462–466.

Katz, M. M., Waskow, E. E., & Olsson, J. (1968). Characteristics of the psychological state produced by LSD. *Journal of Abnormal Psychology, 73,* 1–14.

Kay, J., Shively, M., & Kilkenny, J. (1978). Training of sensorimotor rhythm in devel-opmentally disabled children through EEG biofeedback. *Biofeedback and Self-Regulation, 3,* 197–198.

Kefauver, J. S. P., & Guilleminault, C. (1994). Sleep terrors and sleepwalking. In M. Kyger, T. Roth, & W. C. Dement (Eds.), *Principles and practices of sleep medicine* (2nd ed.). Philadelphia: Saunders, pp. 567–573.

Kellehear, A. (1996). *Experiences near death: Beyond medicine and religion.* New York: Oxford University Press.

Keller, M. (1966). Alcohol in health and disease. *Annals of the New York Academy of Science, 133,* 820.

Kelly, G. F. (1996). Using meditative techniques in psychotherapy. *Journal of Humanistic Psychology, 36,* 49–66.

Kennedy, J. E. (1980). Learning to use ESP: Do the calls match the targets or do the targets match the calls? *Journal of the American Society for Psychical Research, 74,* 381–393.

Kennedy, J. E. (2003). The capricious, actively evasive, unsustainable nature of psi: a summary and hypotheses. *Journal of Parapsychology, 67,* 53–74.

Kensinger, E. A., & Schacter, D. L. (2006). Processing emotional pictures and words: effects of valence and arousal. *Cognitive, Affective, and Behavioral Neuroscience, 6,* 110–126.

Kester, E. M. (2009). Charles Bonnet syndrome: case presentation and literature review. *Optometry, 80,* 360–366.

Kewman, D., & Roberts, A. H. (1979). Skin temperature biofeedback and migraine headaches. Paper presented at the annual conference of the Biofeedback Society of America, San Diego.

Kewman, D. G., & Roberts, A. H. (1980). Skin temperature biofeedback and migraine headaches: A double-blind study. *Biofeedback and Self-Regulation, 5,* 327–345.

Kewman, D. G., & Roberts, A. H. (1983). An alternative perspective on biofeedback efficacy studies: A reply to Steiner and Dince. *Biofeedback and Self-Regulation, 8,* 487–503.

Khalsa, S. S., Rudrauf, D., Damasio, A. R., Davidson, R. J., Lutz, A., & Tranel, D. (2008). Interoceptive awareness in experienced meditators. *Psychophysiology, 45,* 671–677.

Kier, L. B. (2008). A review of recent studies relating ligand diffusion, general anesthesia, and sleep. *American Association of Nurse Anesthetists (AANA) Journal, 76*(2), 109–112.

Kiester, E., Jr. (1980). Images of the night. *Science 80, 1,* 36–43.

Kihlstrom, J. F. (1980). Posthypnotic amnesia for recently learned material: Interactions with episodic and semantic memory. *Cognitive Psychology, 12,* 227–251.

Kihlstrom, J. F. (1985). Hypnosis. *Annual Review of Psychology, 36,* 385–418.

Kihlstrom, J. F. (1994). The rediscovery of the unconscious. In H. Morowitz & J. L. Singer (Eds.), *The mind, the brain, and complex adaptive systems* (pp. 123–143). Reading, MA: Addison-Wesley.

Kihlstrom, J. F. (1996). Unconscious processes in social interaction. In S. R. Hameroff, A. W. Kaszniak, & A. C. (Eds.), *Toward a science of consciousness* (pp. 93–104). Cambridge, MA: MIT Press.

Kimmel, H. D. (1967). Instrumental conditioning of autonomically mediated behavior. *Psychological Bulletin, 67,* 337–345.

Kimmel, H. D. (1974). Instrumental conditioning of autonomically mediated responses in human beings. *American Psychologist, 29,* 325–335.

Kimmel, H. D., & Hill, F. A. (1960). Operant conditioning of the GSR. *Psychological Reports, 7,* 555–562.

Kimura, D. (1977). Acquisition of a motor skill after left hemisphere damage. *Brain, 100,* 527–542.

Kirsch, I. (1996). Hypnotic enhancement of cognitive–behavioral weight loss treatments—another meta–reanalysis. *Journal of Consulting and Clinical Psychology, 64,* 317–319.

Kirsch, L, & Barton, R. D. (1988). Hypnosis in the treatment of multiple personality. *British Journal of Clinical and Experimental Hypnosis, 5,* 131–137.

Kjellgren, A., Lyden, F., & Norlander, T. (2008). Sensory isolation in flotation tanks: altered states of consciousness and effects on well–being. *The Qualitative Report, 13*(4), 636–656.

Kjellgren, A., Sundequist, U., Norlander, T., & Archer, T. (2001). Effects of flotation–REST on muscle tension pain. *Pain Research Management, 6*(4), 181–189.

Kjellgren, A., Sundequist, U., Sundholm, U., & Norlander, T. (2004). Altered consciousness in flotation–REST and Chamber–REST: Experience of experimental pain and subjective stress. *Social Behavior and Personality, 32*(2), 103–116.

Klinger, E. (1987). The power of daydreams. *Psychology Today, 21,* 36–44.

Klonoff, H. (1974). Marijuana and driving in real-life situations. *Science, 186,* 317–324.

Kluft, R. P. (1988). The simulation and dissimulation of multiple personality disorder. *American Journal of Clinical Hypnosis, 30,* 104–118.

Knapp, T. J., & Wells, L. A. (1978). Behavior therapy for asthma: A review. *Behaviour Research and Therapy, 16,* 103–115.

Knox, V. J., Crutchfield, L., & Hilgard, E. R. (1975). The nature of task interference in hypnotic dissociation: An investigation of hypnotic behavior. *International Journal of Clinical and Experimental Hypnosis, 23,* 305–232.

Knutson, K. L., Speigel, K., Penev, P., & Van Cauter, E. (2007). The metabolic consequences of sleep deprivation. *Sleep Medicine Reviews, 11,* 163–178.

Kokoszka, A. (1988). An integrated model of the main states of consciousness. *Imagination, Cognition, and Personality, 7,* 285–294.

Kokoszka, A. (1992). An evolutionary-psychodynamic model of the main states of consciousness. *Imagination, Cognition, and Personality, 12,* 387–394.

Kondo, C., & Canter, A. (1977). True and false electromyographic feedback: Effect on tension headache. *Journal of Abnormal Psychology, 36,* 93–95.

Korner, A. F. (1968). REM organization in neonates: Theoretical implications for development and the biological functions of REM. *Archives of General Psychiatry, 19,* 330–340.

Koszycki, D., Benger, M., Shlik, J., & Bradwejn, J. (2007). Randomized trial of a meditation-based stress reduction program and cognitive behavior therapy in generalized social anxiety disorder. *Behavioral Research Therapy, 45*(10), 2518–2526.

Kotses, H., & Glaus, K. (1981). Applications of biofeedback to the treatment of asthma: A critical review. *Biofeedback and Self-Regulation, 6,* 573–594.

Kotses, H., Glaus, K. D., Bricel, S. K., Edwards, J. E., & Crawford, P. L. (1978). Operant muscular relaxation and peak expiratory flow rate in asthmatic children. *Journal of Psychosomatic Medicine, 22,* 17–23.

Kotses, H., Glaus, K. D., Crawford, P. L., Edwards, J. E., & Scherr, M. S. (1976). Operant reduction of frontalis EMG activity in the treatment of asthma in children. *Journal of Psychosomatic Medicine, 20,* 453–459.

Kotses, H., Hindi-Alexander, M., & Creer, T. L. (1989). A reinterpretation of psychologically induced airway changes. *Journal of Asthma, 26,* 53–63.

Koula, G. M, Kemp, J. C, Keane, K. M., & Belden, A. D. (1987). Replication of a clinical outcome study on a hospital-based stress management and behavioral medicine program utilizing flotation REST (Restricted Environmental Stimulation Technique) and biofeedback. In T. H. Fine & J. W. Turner, Jr. (Eds.), *Proceedings of the Second International Conference on REST* (pp. 127–135). Toledo, OH: IRIS.

Krauss, H. H., Katzell, R., & Krauss, B. J. (1974). Effect of hypnotic time distortion upon free-recall learning. *Journal of Abnormal Psychology, 83,* 140–144.

Kreuger, J. M., Rector, D. M., Roy, S., VanDongen, H. P. A., Belenky, G., & Panksepp, J. (2008). Sleep as a fundamental property of neuronal assemblies. *Nature Reviews Neuroscience, 9,* 910–919.

Krippner, S. (1968). Experimentally induced telepathic effects in hypnosis and non-hypnosis groups. *Journal of the American Society for Psychical Research, 62,* 387–398.

Krippner, S. (1995). Psychical research in the postmodern world. *Journal of the American Society for Psychical Research, 89,* 1–18.

Krippner, S., Hickman, J., Auerhahn, N., & Harris, R. (1972). Clairvoyant perception of target material in three states of consciousness. *Perceptual and Motor Skills, 35,* 439–446.

Krippner, S., & Rubin, D. (Eds.). (1974). *The Kirlian aura.* New York: Anchor Books.

Kroger, W. S. (1977). *Clinical and experimental hypnosis,* Philadelphia: Lippincott.

Kumano, H., Horie, H., Shidara, T, Kuboki, T, Suematsu, H., & Yasushi, M. (1996). Treatment of a depressive disorder patient with EEG-driven photic stimulation. *Biofeedback & Self-Regulation, 21,* 323–334.

Kumar, V. K., & Pekala, R. J. (1988). Hypnotizability, absorption, and individual differences in phenomenological experience. *International Journal of Clinical and Experimental Hypnosis, 36,* 80–88.

Kumar, V. M. (2010). Sleep is neither a passive nor an active phenomenon. *Sleep and Biological Rhythms, 8,* 163–169.

Kunzendorf, R. G., Spanos, N. P., & Wallace, B. (Eds.). (1996). *Hypnosis and imagination.* Amityville, NY: Baywood.

Kus, R. J. (1995). Prayer and meditation in addiction recovery. In R. J. Kus, *Spirituality and chemical dependency* (pp. 101–115). New York: Harrington Park Press.

LaBerge, S. P. (1992). *Physiological studies of lucid dreaming.* Hillsdale, NJ: Erlbaum.

LaBerge, S. P., Nagel, L. E., Dement, W. C., & Zarcone, V. (1981). Lucid dreaming verified by volitional communication during REM sleep. *Perceptual and Motor Skills, 52,* 727–732.

Lacks, P., & Powlishta, K. (1989). Improvement following behavioral treatment for insomnia: Clinical significance, long-term maintenance, and predictors of outcome. *Behavior Therapy, 20,* 117–134.

Lang, P. J., and Lazovik, A. D. (1963). Experimental desensitization of a phobia. *Journal of Abnormal and Social Psychology, 66,* 519–525.

Langenbucher, J. W., & Nathan, P. E. (1983). Psychology, public policy, and the evidence for alcohol intoxication. *American Psychologist, 38,* 1070–1077.

Langton, P. A. (1991). *Drugs and the alcohol dilemma*. Boston: Allyn and Bacon.

Lann, M. A. & Martin, A. (2010). An unusual death involving a sensory deprivation tank. *Journal of Forensic Sciences, 55*(6), 1638–1640.

Lanyon, R. I., Barrington, C. C., & Newman, A. C. (1976). Modification of stuttering through EMG biofeedback: A preliminary study. *Behavior Therapy, 7*, 96–103.

Latha, K. K. V. (1991). Yoga, pranayama, thermal biofeedback techniques in the management of stress and high blood pressure. *Journal of Indian Psychology, 9*, 36–46.

Laumann, E. O., Gagnon, J. H., Michael, R. T, & Michaels, S. (1994). *The social organization of sexuality*. Chicago: University of Chicago Press.

Laurence, J. R., & Perry, C. (1983). Hypnotically created memory among highly hypnotizable subjects. *Science, 222*, 523–524.

Laureys, S. (2005). The neural correlate of (un)awareness: lesions from the vegetative state. *Trends in Cognitive Sciences, 9*,(12), 556–559

Laureys, S., Faymonville, M. E., Luxen, A., Lamy, M., Franck, G., & Maquet, P. (2000). Restoration of thalamocortical connectivity after recovery from a persistent vegetative state. *Lancet, 355*, 1790–1791.

Lavie, P., & Berris, A. (1996). *The enchanted world of sleep*. New Haven, CT: Yale University Press.

Lazar, S. W., Bush, G., Gollub, R. L., Fricchione, G. L., Khalsa, G., & Benson, H. (2000). Functional brain mapping of the relaxation response and meditation. *Neuroreport, 11*(7), 1581–1585.

Lazar, S. W., Kerr, C. E., Wasserman, R.H., Gray, J.R., Greve, D. N., Treadway, M. T., McGarvey, M, Quinn, B. A., Dusek, J. A., Benson, H., Rauch, S. L, Moore, C. I., & Fischl, B. (2005). Meditation experience associated with increased cortical thickness. *Neuroreport, 16*(17), 1893–1897.

Leavitt, F. (1995). *Drugs and behavior* (3rd ed.). Newbury Park, CA: Sage.

LeDoux, J. E., Wilson, D. H., & Gazzaniga, M. S. (1977). Manipulospatial aspects of cerebral lateralization: Clues to the origin of lateralization. *Neuropsychologia, 15*, 743–750.

Lee, S. H., Ahn, S. C., Lee, Y. J., Choi, T., K., Yook, K. H., & Suh, S. Y (2007). Effectiveness of a meditation-based stress management program as an adjunct to pharmacotherapy in patients with anxiety disorder. *Journal of Psychosomatic Research, 62*(20), 189–195.

Lehman, D., Faber, P. L., Achermann, P., Jeanmonod, D., Gianotti, L. R., & Pizzagalli, D. (2001). Brain sources of EEG gamma frequency during volitionally meditation–induced, altered states of consciousness, and experience of the self. *Psychiatry Research, 108*, 111–121.

Leitenberg, H., & Henning, K. (1995). Sexual fantasy. *Psychological Bulletin, 117*, 469–496.

Leo, J. (1986). How cocaine killed Leonard Bias. *Time, 128*, 52.

Leopold, D. A., & Logothetis, N. K. (1996). Activity changes in early visual cortex reflect monkeys' percepts during binocular rivalry. *Nature, 379*, 549–553.

Leskowitz, E. (1988). The "third eye": A psychoendocrine model of hypnotizability. *American Journal of Clinical Hypnosis, 30*, 209–215.

Lesser, I. M., Poland, R. E., Holcomb, C., & Rose, D. E. (1985). Electrocephalographic study of nighttime panic attacks. *Journal of Nervous and Mental Disorders, 173*, 744–746.

Levenberg, S. B., & Wagner, M. K. (1976). Smoking cessation: Long-term irrelevance of mode of treatment. *Journal of Behavior Therapy and Experimental Psychiatry, 7*, 93–95.

Levine, B. A. (1984). Effects of depression and headache type on biofeedback for muscle-contraction headaches. *Behavioral Psychotherapy, 12*, 300–307.

Levine, J. (1969). LSD: A chemical overview. In P. Black (Ed.), *Drugs and the brain*. Baltimore: Johns Hopkins Press.

Levine, J. L., Kurtz, R. M., & Lauter, J. L. (1984). Hypnosis and its effects on right and left hemisphere activity. *Biological Psychiatry, 19*, 1461–1475.

LeVine, W. R., & Irvine, J. K. (1984). In vivo EMG biofeedback in violin and viola pedagogy. *Biofeedback and Self-Regulation, 9*, 161–168.

Levinthal, C. F. (1990). *Introduction to physiological psychology*. Englewood Cliffs, NJ: Prentice-Hall.

Levy, J. Trevarthen, C., & Sperry, R. W. (1972). Perception of bilateral chimeric figures following hemispheric disconnection. *Brain, 95*, 61–78.

Li, X., & Shen, Z. (1985). Positive electron emission layer scanning technique and its application in psychological research. *Information on Psychological Sciences, 3*, 54–58.

Lichtenberg, P., Bachner-Melman, R., Ebstein, R. P., & Crawford, H. J. (2004). Hypnotic susceptibility: multidimensional relationships with Cloninger's Tridimensional Personality Questionnaire, COMT polymorphisms, absorption, and attentional characteristics. *International Journal of Clinical and Experimental Hypnosis, 52*, 47–72.

Lichtenberg, P., Bachner–Melman, R., Gritsenko, I., & Ebstein, R. P. (2000). Exploratory association study between catechol–O–methyltransferase (COMT) high/low enzyme activity polymorphism and hypnotizability. *American Journal of Medical Genetics, 96,* 771–774.

Lichtenfeld, P. J., Rubin, D. B., & Feldman, R. S. (1984). Subarachnoid hemorrhage precipitated by cocaine snorting. *Archives of Neurology, 41,* 223–224.

Lilly, J. C. (1956). Mental effects of reduction of ordinary levels of physical stimuli in intact, healthy persons. *Psychiatric Research Reports, 5,* 1–28.

Lilly, J. C. (1960). Discussion of paper by J. T. Shurley. Profound experimental sensory isolation. *American Journal of Psychiary, 117,* 544–545.

Lilly, J. C. (1972). *Center of the cyclone: An autobiography of inner space.* New York: Julian.

Lilly, J. C. (1977). *The deep self.* New York: Simon and Schuster.

Linden, M., Habib, T., & Radojevic, V. (1996). A controlled study of the effects of EEG biofeedback on cognition and behavior of children with attention deficit disorder and learning disabilities. *Biofeedback & Self-Regulation, 21,* 35–49.

Linden, W., & Moseley, J.V. (2006). The efficacy of behavioral treatments for hypertension. *Applied Psychophysiology and Biofeedback, 31*(1), 51–63.

Lindsey, P. H., & Norman, D. A. (1977). *Human information processing: An introduction to psychology* (2nd ed.). New York: Academic Press.

Lindsley, D. B. (1961). Common factors in sensory deprivation, sensory distortion, and sensory overload. In P. Solomon, P. Kubzansky, P. Leiderman, J. Mendelson, R. Trumbull, & D. Wexler (Eds.), *Sensory deprivation: A symposium.* Cambridge: Harvard University Press.

Lindsley, D. B., Bowden, J., & Magoun, H. (1949). Effect upon the EEG of acute injury to the brain stem activating system. *Electroencephalography and Clinical Neurophysiology, 1,* 475–486.

Lingeman, R. (1974). *Drugs from A to Z: A dictionary.* New York: McGraw-Hill.

Lisina, M. I. (1965). The role of orientation of the transformation of involuntary reactions into voluntary ones. In L. G. Veronin, A. H. Leontiev, A. R. Luria, C. N. Sokolov, & O. S. Vinogradova (Eds.), *Orienting reflex and exploratory behavior.* Washington, DC: American Institute of Biological Sciences.

Locke, J. (1975). *An essay concerning human understanding.* Oxford: Oxford University Press. (Originally published 1690)

Loftus, E. F. (1979). *Eyewitness testimony.* Cambridge, MA: Harvard University Press.

Lofrus, E. F. (1980). *Memory.* Reading, MA: Addison-Wesley.

Logothetis, N. K., Pauls, J., Augath, M., Trinath, T., & Oeltermann, A. (2001). Neurophysiological investigation of the basis of the fMRI signal. *Nature, 412,* 150–157.

Logothetis, N. K., & Schall, J. D. (1989). Neuronal correlates of subjective visual perception. *Science, 245,* 761–763.

London, P., Hart, J. T., & Leibovitz, M. P. (1968). EEG alpha rhythms and susceptibility to hypnosis. *Nature, 219,* 71–72.

Loomis, A. L., Harvey, E. N., & Hobart, G. A. (1935). Potential rhythms of the cerebral cortex during sleep. *Science, 81,* 597–598.

Loomis, A. L., Harvey, E. N., & Hobart, G. A. (1937). Cerebral states during sleep, as studied by human brain potentials. *Journal of Experimental Psychology, 21,* 127–144.

Lou, H. C., Kjaer, T. W., Friberg, L., Wildschiodtz, G., Holm, S., & Nowak, M. (1999). A 150–H2O PET study of meditation and the resting state of normal consciousness. *Human Brain Mapping, 7,* 98–105.

Lovato, N., & Lack, L. (2010). The effects of napping on cognitive function. *Progress in Brain Research, 185,* 155–166.

Lubin, A., Moses, J., Johnson, L. C., & Naitoh, P. (1974). The recuperative effects of REM sleep and stage 4 sleep on human performance after complete sleep loss: experiment 1. *Psychophysiology, 2,* 125–132.

Luce, G. G. (1965). *Research on sleep and dreams.* Bethesda, MD: National Institute of Mental Health.

Lucidi, F., Devoto, A., Violani, C, Mastraceli, P., & Bertini, M. (1997). Effects of different sleep duration on delta sleep in recovery nights. *Psychophysiology: The International Journal of the Society for Psychophysiological Research, 32,* 227–233.

Ludesr, E., Gaser, C., Lepore, N., Narr, K. L, & Toga, A. W. (2009). Larger gray matter volumes in long–term meditators. *NeuroImage, 47*(Suppl1), S39–S41.

Luria, A. R. (1966). *Higher cortical functions in man.* New York: Basic Books.

Lutz, A., Dunne, J. D., & Davidson, R. J. (2007). Meditation and the neuroscience of consciousness: an introduction. In: *The Cambridge Handbook of Consciousness.* Zalazo, P. D., Moscovitz, M., & Thompson, E. (Eds.). New York: Cambridge University Press.

Lutz, A., Greischar, L. L., Rawlings, N. B., Ricard, M., & Davidson, R. J. (2004). Long–term mediatators self–induce high–amplitude gamma synchrony during mental practice. *Proceedings of the National Academy of Sciences, 101*(46), 16369–16373.

Lutz, A., Slagter, H. A., Dunne, J. D., & Davidson, R. J. (2008). Attention regulation and monitoring in meditation. *Trends in Cognitive Neurosciences, 12*(4), 163–169.

Lyle, K. B., McCabe, D. P., & Roediger, H. L. III (2008). Handedness is related to memory via hemispheric interaction: evidence from paired associate recall and source memory tasks. *Neuropsychology, 22*(4), 523–530.

Lynch, J. J., & Paskewitz, D. A. (1971). On the mechanism of the feedback control of human brain wave activity. *Journal of Nervous and Mental Disease, 153,* 205–217.

Lynn, S. J., & Rhue, J. W. (1986). The fantasy-prone person: Hypnosis, imagination, and creativity. *Journal of Personality and Social Psychology, 51,* 404–408.

Lyons, L. C., & Crawford, H. J. (1997). Sustained attentional and disattentional abilities and arousability: factor analysis and relationship to hypnotic susceptibility. *Personality and Individual Differences, 26,* 1071–1084.

MacCloud, C. M. (2009). Hypnosis and the control of attention: where to from here? *Consciousness and Cognition,* doi:10.106/j.concog.2009.10.007.

MacDonald, T. K., Zanna, M. P., & Fong, G. T. (1995). Decision making in altered states: Effects of alcohol on attitudes toward drinking and driving. *Journal of Personality and Social Psychology, 68,* 973–985.

MacLean, C. R. K., Walton, K. G, Wenneberg, S. R., Levitsky, D. K., Mandarino, J. P., Waziri, R., Hillis, S. L., & Schneider, R. H. (1997). Effects of the transdendental meditation program on adaptive mechanisms: changes in hormone levels and response to stress after 4 months of practice. *Psychoneuroendocrinology, 22*(4), 277–295.

MacLennan, B. J. (1995). The investigation of consciousness through phenomenoogy and neuroscience. In J. Ring & K. H. Pribram (Eds.), *Scale in conscious experience: Is the brain too important to be left to specialists to study?* (pp. 25–43). Mahwah, NJ: Erlbaum.

MacLeod-Morgan, C., & Lack, L. (1982). Hemispheric specificity: A physiological concomitant of hypnotizability. *Psychophysiology, 19,* 687–690.

Madsen, P. L. (1993). Bloodflow and oxygen uptake in the human brain during various states of sleep and wakefulness. *Ada Neurologica Scandinavica, 88*, 1–27.

Maharishi Mahesh Yogi. (1963). *The science of being and art of living.* London: Unwin.

Maharishi Health Education Center. http://www.maharishitm.org/ppaw/tmsidhi.htm. Accessed February 16, 2011.

Maharishi's Programmes for Every Area of Science. http://maharishi–programmes.globalgoodnews.com. Accessed February 11, 2011.

Maharishi University of Management (MUM). http://www.mum.edu/index.html. Accessed February 9, 2011.

Malcolm, N. (1964). Behaviorism as a philosophy of psychology. In T. W. Warm (Ed.), *Behaviorism and phenomenology: Contrasting bases for modern psychology.* Chicago: University of Chicago Press.

Malcolm–Smith, S., & Solms, M. (2004). Incidence of threat in dreams: a response to Revonsuo's threat simulation theory. *Dreaming, 14*(4), 220–229.

Malick, M. (1996). Heart rate variability: standards of measurement, physiological interpretation, and clinical use. *Circulation, 93*, 1043–1065.

Malone, M. D., Kurtz, R. M., & Strube, M. J. (1989). The effects of hypnotic suggestion on pain report. *American Journal of Clinical Hypnosis, 31*, 221–230.

Mandler, G., Preven, D. W., & Kuhlman, C. K. (1962). Effects of operant reinforcement on the GSR. *Journal of the Experimental Analysis of Behavior, 62*, 552–559.

Mann, B. J., & Sanders, S. (1995). The effects of light, temperature, trance length, and time of day on hypnotic depth. *American Journal of Clinical Hypnosis, 37*, 43–53.

Maquet, P. (2001). The role of sleep in learning and memory. *Science, 294*, 1048–1052.

Marcus, E. M. (1972). Clinical considerations of the cerebral hemispheres and a general survey of neuropathology. In B. A. Curtis, S. Jacobson, & E. M. Marcus (Eds.), *An introduction to the neurosciences.* Philadelphia: Saunders.

Margraf, J., Taylor, C. B., & Ehlers, A. (1987). Panic attacks in the natural environment. *Journal of Nervous and Mental Disorders, 175*, 558–565.

Marks, D., & Kammann, R. (1978). Information transmission in remote viewing experiments. *Nature, 272,* 680–681.

Marks, D., & Kammann, R. (1980). *The psychology of the psychic.* New York: Prometheus.

Marks, D., & Scott, C. (1986). Remote viewing exposed. *Nature, 319,* 444.

Marshall, N. S., Glozier, N. & Brunstein, R. R. (2008). Is sleep duration related to obesity? A critical review of the epidemiological evidence. *Sleep Medicine Reviews, 12*(4), 289–298.

Martin, B. (1986). Cellular effects of cannabinoids. *Pharmacological Reviews, 38,* 45–74.

Martindale, W. (1967). *Extrapharmacopoeia* (25th ed.). London: Pharmaceutical Press.

Marx, J. L. (1984). "Anxiety peptide" found in brain. *Science, 227,* 934.

Mashour, G. A. (2006). Integrating the science of consciousness and anesthesia. *Anesthesia & Analgesia, 103,* 975–982.

Mason, O. J., & Brady, F. (2009). The psychotomimetic effects of short–term sensory deprivation. *The Journal of Nervous and Mental Disease, 197*(10), 783–785.

Mathis, J. L. (1970). Sexual aspects of heroin addiction. *Medical Aspects of Human Sexuality, 4,* 98–109.

Matsuoka, S. (1990). Theta rhythms: State of consciousness. *Brain Topography, 3,* 203–208.

Mauskopf, S. H. (1989). The history of the American Society for Psychical Research: An interpretation. *Journal of the American Society for Psychical Research, 83,* 7–30.

Maxon, M. F., Norton, M. I., Van Horn, J. D., Wegner, D. M., Grafton, S. T., & Macrae, C. N. (2007). Wandering minds: the default network and stimulus–independent thought. *Science, 315,* 393–395.

May, E. C. (2004). *Anticipatory skin conductance responses: a possible example of decision augmentation theory.* Paper presented at The Parapsychological Association 47th Annual Convention, http://archived.parapsych.org/papers/10.pdf.

May, E. C, Utts, J. M., & Spottiswoode, S. J. P. (1995). Decision augmentation theory: toward a model of anomalous mental phenomena. *Journal of Parapsychology, 59,* 195–220.

Mazziotta, J. C., Phelps, M. E., Carson, R. E., & Kuhl, D. E. (1982). Tomographic mapping of human cerebral metabolism: sensory deprivation. *Annals of Neurology, 12*(5), 435–444.

McCann, U. D., & Ricaurte, G. A. (2004). Amphetamine neurotoxicity: accomplishments and remaining challenges. *Neuroscience and Biobehavioral Reviews, 27*, 821–826.

McCann, U. D., Wong, D. F., Yokoi, F., Villemange, V., Dannals, R.F., Ricaurte, G. A. (1998). Reduced striatal dopamine transporter density in abstinent methamphetamine and methcathinone users: evidence from positron emission tomography studies with [^{11}C]WIN–35,428. *Journal of Neuroscience, 18*, 8417–8422.

McCardle,K., Luebbers, S., Carter, J. D., Croft, R. J., & Stough, C (2004). Chronic MDMA (ecstasy) use, cognition and mood. *Psychopharmacology, 173*, 434–439.

McCarley, R., & Hobson, A. (1979). The form of dreams and the biology of sleep. In B. Wolman (Ed.), *Handbook of dreams.* New York: Van Nostrand Reinhold.

McCarthy, L. E., & Borison, H. L. (1977). Antiemetic activity of nabilone, a cannabinol derivative, reversed by naloxone in awake cats. *Pharmacologist, 19*, 230.

McClenon, J. (1982). A survey of elite scientists: Their attitudes toward ESP and parapsychology. *Journal of Parapsychology, 46*, 127–152.

McCombs, P. (1987, July 2). Group says movement a cult. *The Washington Post*, p. C03. http://www.washingtonpost.com/wp–srv/national/longterm/cult/trans_med/tm2.htm.

McConkey, K. M. (1988). A view from the laboratory on the forensic use of hypnosis. *Australian Journal of Clinical and Experimental Hypnosis, 16*, 71–81.

McConkey, K. M., & Perry, C. (1985). Benjamin Franklin and mesmerism. *International Journal of Clinical and Experimental Hypnosis, 33*, 122–130.

McHarg, J. F. (1978). Review of At the hour of death by K. Osis and E. Haraldsson. *Journal of the American Society for Psychical Research, 49*, 885–887.

McKim, W. A. (1997). *Drugs and behavior: An introduction to behavioral pharmacology* (4th ed.). Englewood Cliffs, NJ: Prentice-Hall.

Medd, D. (2001). Fear of injections: the value of hypnosis in facilitating clinical treatment. *Contemporary Hypnosis, 18*(2), 100–106.

Mednick, S., Nakayama, K., & Stickgold, R. (2003). Sleep-dependent learning: a nap is good as a night. *Nature Neuroscience, 6*, 697–698.

Melzack, R. (1990). The tragedy of needless pain. *Scientific American, 262*, 27–33.

Melzack, R., & Perry, C. (1975). Self-regulation of pain: The use of alpha-feedback and hypnotic training for the control of chronic pain. *Experimental Neurology, 46,* 452–469.

Menon, G. J., Rahman, I., Menon, S. J., & Dutton, G. N. (2003). Complex visual hallucinations in the visually impaired: the Charles Bonnet syndrome. *Survey of Ophthalmology, 48*(1), 58–72.

Merabet, L. B., Maguire, D., Warde, A., Alterescu, K., Stickgold, R., & Pascual–Leone, A. (2004). Visual hallucinations during prolonged blindfolding in sighted subjects. *Journal of Neuroopthalamology, 24*(2), 109–113.

Merkel, J. (1979). A study of individual differences in eletromyograph feedback treatment for muscle contraction headache. *Dissertation Abstracts, 40,* 1904.

Meuwissen, L, & Over, R. (1991). Multidimensionality of the content of female sexual fantasy. *Behaviour Research and Therapy, 29,* 179–189.

Meyer, D. (1965). *The positive thinkers.* New York: Doubleday.

Meyer, J. S., & Quenzer, L. F. (2005). *Psychopharmacology: drugs, the brain, and behavior.* Sunderland, MA: Sinauer.

Michaels, R. R. Huber, M. J., & McCann, D. S. (1976). Evaluation of transcendental meditation as a method of reducing stress. *Science, 192,* 1242–1244.

Milkman, H. B., & Shaffer, H. J. (Eds.). (1985). *The addictions: Multidisciplinary perspectives and treatments.* Lexington, MA: Lexington.

Miller, G. (2011). ESP paper rekindles discussion about statistics. *Science, 331,* 272–273.

Miller, J. J., Fletcher, K., & Kabat-Zinn, J. (1995). Three-year follow-up and clinical implications of a mindfulness meditation-based stress reduction intervention in the treatment of anxiety disorders. *General Hospital Psychiatry, 17,* 192–200.

Miller, L. L., & Branconnier, F. (1983). Cannabis: Effects on memory and the cholinergic limbic system. *Psychological Bulletin, 87,* 441–457.

Miller, L. L., McFarland, D., Cornett, T., Brightwell, Dv & Wikler, L. (1977). Marijuana and memory impairment: Effect of free recall and recognition memory. *Pharmacology, Biochemistry, and Behavior, 7,* 99–103.

Miller, N. E., & DiCara, L. (1968). Instrumental learning of urine formation by rats: Changes in ural blood flow. *American Journal of Physiology, 215,* 677–683.

Miller, N. E., & Dworkin, B. R. (1974). Visceral learning: Recent difficulties with curarized rats and significant problems for human research. In P. A. Obrist, A. H. Black, J. Brener, & L. V. DiCara (Eds.), *Cardiovascular psychophysiology*. Chicago: Aldine.

Miller, S., & Konorski, J. (1928). On a particular type of conditioned reflex. *Proceedings of the Biological Society (Polish Section, Paris), 99*, 1155–1157.

Milner, A. D. (1995). Cerebral correlates of visual awareness. *Neuropsychologia, 33*, 1117–1130.

Milner, B. (1965). Visually guided maze learning in man: Effects of bilateral, frontal, and unilateral cerebral lesions. *Neuropsychologia, 3*, 317–338.

Miskiman, D. E. (1977a). The treatment of insomnia by the transcendental meditation program. In D. Orme-Johnson & J. Farrow (Eds.), *Scientific research on the transcendental meditation program* (Vol. 1, pp. 296–298). Los Angeles: Maharishi European Research University Press.

Miskiman, D. E. (1977b). Long-term effects of the transcendental meditation program in the treatment of insomnia. In D. Orme-Johnson & J. Farrow (Eds.), *Scientific research on the transcendental meditation program* (Vol. 1, pp. 299–300). Los Angeles: Maharishi European Research University Press.

Mitler, M. M., Carskadon, M. A., Czeisler, C. A., Dement, W. C, Dinges, D. F., & Graeber, R. C. (1988). Catastrophes, sleep, and public policy: Consensus report. *Sleep, 11*, 100–109.

Mokler, D. J., Stoudt, K. W., Sherman, L. C., & Rech, R. H. (1986). The effects of intracranial administration of hallucinogens on operant behavior in the rat. I. Lysergic acid diethylemide. *Pharmacology, Biochemistry, and Behavior, 25*, 717–725.

Monheit, B. (2010). *Prescription drug misuse. Australian Family Physician, 39*(8), 540–546.

Monk, T. H., Reynolds, C. F., Buysse, D. J., & Hoch, C. C. (1991). Circadian characteristics of healthy 80-yr-olds and their relationship to objectively recorded sleep. *Journal of Gerontology, 46*, M171-M175.

Monroe, R. A. (1971). *Journeys out of the body*. Garden City, NY: Doubleday.

Montandon, H. E. (1977). Psychophysiological aspects of the Kirlian phenomenon: A confirmatory study. *Journal of the American Society for Psychical Research, 77*, 45–49.

Monteiro, K. P., & Zimbardo, P. G. (1987). The path from classroom seating to hypnotizability: A dead end. *International Journal of Clinical and Experimental Hypnosis, 35*, 83–86.

Montgomery, G. H., Bovbjerg , D. H., Schnur , J. B., David , D., Goldfarb, A., Weltz, C. R., Schechter, C., Graff–Zivin, J., Tatrow, K., Price, D. D., & Silverstein, J. H. (2007). A randomized clinical trial of a brief hypnosis intervention to control side effects in breast surgery patients. *Journal of the National Cancer Institute, 99,* 1304–1312.

Montgomery, G. H., David, D., Winkel, G., Silverstein, J. H., & Bovbjerg, D. H. (2002). The effectiveness of adjunctive hypnosis with surgical patients: a meta–analysis. *Anesthesia and Analgesia, 94,* 1639–1645.

Moody, R. A., Jr. (1975). *Life after life.* Atlanta: Mockingbird.

Moody, R. A., Jr. (1977). *Reflections on life after life.* New York: Bantam.

Moody, R. A., Jr. (1985). *Reflections on life after life* (2nd ed.). Atlanta: Mockingbird.

Moody, R. A., Jr. (1988). *The light beyond.* New York: Bantam.

Moore-Ede, M. C., Sulzman, F. M., & Fuller, C. A. (1982). *The clocks that time us.* Cambridge, MA: Harvard University Press.

Moran, M. S., Thompson, T. L., & Neis, A. S. (1988). Sleep disorders in the elderly. *American Journal of Psychiatry, 145,* 1369–1378.

Morawetz, D. (1989). Behavioral self-help treatment for insomnia: A controlled evaluation. *Behavior Therapy, 20,* 365–379.

Morewitz, J. H. (1988). Evaluation of excessive daytime sleepiness in the elderly. *Journal of the American Geriatrics Society, 36,* 324–330.

Morgan, A. H. (1973). The heritability of hypnotic susceptibility in twins. *Journal of Abnormal Psychology, 82,* 55–61.

Morgan, A. H., Hilgard, E. R., & Davert, E. C. (1970). The heritability of hypnotic susceptibility of twins: a preliminary report. *Behavior Genetics, 1,* 213–224.

Morrell, E. M. (1986). Meditation and somatic arousal. *American Psychologist, 41,* 712–713.

Morris, R. L., Harary, S. B., Janis, J., Hartwell, J. & Roll, W. G. (1978). Studies of communication during out-of-body experiences. *Journal of the American Society for Psychical Research, 72,* 1–21.

Moruzzi, G., & Magoun, H. W. (1949). Brainstem reticular formation and activation of the EEG. *Electroencephalography and Clinical Neurophysiology, 1,* 455–473.

Moss, D., LaVaque, T. J., & Hammond, D. C. (2004). Introduction to white paper series—guest editorial. *Applied Psychophysiology and Biofeedback, 29*(3), 151–152.

Moss, D., & Shaffer, F. (n.d.) Heart rate variability training. http://www.bfe.org/articles/hrv.pdf. Accessed January 14, 2011.

Moss, S., & Butler, D. C. (1978). The scientific credibility of ESP. *Perceptual and Motor Skills, 46*, 1063–1079.

Moss, T., & Johnson, K. (1974). Bioplasma or corona discharge? In S. Krippner & D. Rubin (Eds.), *The Kirlian aura*. New York: Anchor Books.

Mouton, S. T., & Kosslyn, S. M. (2008). Using neuroimaging to resolve the psi debate. *Journal of Cognitive Neuroscience, 20*(1), 182–192.

Mowrer, O. H. (1938). Preparatory set (expectancy): A determinant in motivation and learning. *Psychological Review, 85*, 61–91.

Muldoon, S., & Carrington, H. (1977). *The projection of the astral body*. London: Rider. (Originally published 1929)

Murphy, G., & Ballou, R. O. (1969). *William James on psychical research*. New York: Viking Press.

Myers, T. L, Murphy, D. B., & Smith, S. (1963). The effect of sensory deprivation and social isolation on self-exposure to propaganda and attitude change. Paper read at the meetings of the American Psychological Association, Chicago.

Myers, R. E., & Sperry, R. W. (1958). Interhemispheric communication through the corpus callosum: Mnemonic carryover between the hemispheres. *Archives of Neurology and Psychiatry, 80*, 298–303.

Naagai, Y., Critchley, H. D., Featherstone, E., Trimble, M. R., & Dolan, R. J. (2004). Activity in ventromedial prefrontal cortex covaries with sympathetic skin conductance level: a physiological account of a "default mode" of brain function. *NeuroImage, 22*, 243–251.

Nader, T. A., Smith, D. E., Dillbeck, M. C., Schanbacher, V., Dillbeck, S. L., Gallois, P., Beall–Rougerie, S., Schneider, R. H., Nidich, S. I., Kaplan, G. P., & Belock, S. (2001). A double blind randomized controlled trial of Maharishi Vedic vibration technology in subjects with arthritis. *Frontiers in Bioscience, 6*, H7–H17.

Nagel, T. (1974). What is it like to be a bat? *Philosophical Review, 83*, 435–450.

Naish, P. L. N. (2010). Hypnosis and hemispheric asymmetry. *Consciousness and Cognition, 19*, 230–234.

Nanamoli, T. (1964). *Mindfulness of Breathing*. Kandy, Sri Lanka: Buddhist Publication Society.

Nanamoli, T. (1976). *Visuddhimagga: The Path of Purification*. Berkeley: Shambala.

Naranjo, C., & Ornstein, R. E. (1976). *On the psychology of meditation*. New York: Penguin.

Nash, J. M. (1997). The chemistry of addiction. *Time, 149,* 68–77.

Nash, M. R., Johnson, L. S., & Tipton, R. D. (1979). Hypnotic age regression and the occurrence of transitional object relationships. *Journal of Abnormal Psychology, 88,* 547–555.

Nash, M. R., Minton, A., & Baldridge, J. (1988). Twenty years of scientific hypnosis in dentistry, medicine and psychology. *International Journal of Clinical and Experimental Hypnosis, 36,* 198–205.

Nathan, R. G., Morris, D. M., Goebel, R. A., & Blass, N. H. (1987). Preoperative and intraoperative rehearsal in hypnoanesthesia for major surgery. *American Journal of Clinical Hypnosis, 29,* 238–241.

National Drug Intelligence Center (2006). Prescription drug fast facts. Product No. 2003–L0559–013. http://www.justice.gov/ndic/pubs5/5140/index.htm#What

National Institute on Alcolol Abuse and Alcoholism. (1994). Alcohol and minorities. *Alcohol Alert, 23* (PA 347).

National Institute on Drug Abuse (2009). Stimulant ADHD medications: methylphenidate and amphetamines. *NIDA InfoFacts.* http://www.drugabuse.gov/infofacts/ADHD.html.

National Institute on Drug Abuse (2011). Teenage marijuana use is on the rise. *NIDA Notes, 23*(4), 15.

National Sleep Foundation (2010). How much sleep do we really need? Washington, DC. Available at: http://www.sleepfoundation.org/article/how-sleep-works/how-much-sleep-do-we-really-need. Accessed April 6, 2011.

Natsoulas, T. (1978a). Consciousness. *American Psychologist, 33,* 906–914.

Natsoulas, T. (1978b). Toward a model for consciousness in the light of B. F. Skinner's contribution. *Behaviorism, 6,* 139–176.

Natsoulas, T. (1979). The unity of consciousness. *Behaviorism, 7,* 45–63.

Natsoulas, T. (1987). The six basic concepts of consciousness and William James's stream of thought. *Imagination, Cognition and Personality, 6,* 289–319.

Nauta, W. J. H. (1946). Hypothalamic regulation of sleep in rats: Experimental study. *Journal of Neurophysiology, 9,* 285–316.

Nelson, J. (1987). Cracking up. *Essence,* 65–66,100–101.

Nelson, T. O., McSpadden, M., Fromme, K., & Marlatt, G. A. (1986). Effects of alcohol intoxication on metamemory and on retrieval from long-term memory. *Journal of Experimental Psychology: General, 115,* 247–254.

Nestoriuc,Y, Martin, A., Rief, W., & Andrasik, F. (2008). Biofeedback for headache disorders: a comprehensive efficacy review. *Applied Psychophysiology and Biofeedback, 33,* 125–140

Nidich, S., Seeman, W., & Dreshin, T. (1973). Influence of transcendental meditation: A replication. *Journal of Counseling Psychology, 20,* 565–566.

Nidich, S. I., Schneider, R. H., Nidich, R. J., Rainforth, M., Salerno, J., SCharf, D., Smith, D. E., Dillbeck, M. C., & Nader, T. A. (2001). Maharishi Vedic vibration technology on chronic disorders and associated quality of life. *Frontiers in Bioscience, 6,* H1–H6.

Nigil, A. J. (1981). A comparison of binary and analog EMG biofeedback techniques in the treatment of low back pain. *American Journal of Clinical Biofeedback, 4,* 24–31.

Nigil, A. J. (1984). *Biofeedback and behavioral strategies in pain treatment.* Jamaica, NY: Spectrum.

Nordenstrom, B. K., Council, J. R., & Meier, B. P. (2002). The "big five" and hypnotic suggestibility. *International Journal of Clinical and Experimental Hypnosis, 50*(3), 276–281.

Norlander, T., Kjellgren, & Archer, T. (2001). The experience of flotation-REST as a function of setting and previous experience of altered state of consciousness. *Imagination, Cognition and Personality, 20*(2), 161–178.

Norlander, T., Kjellgren, A., & Archer, T. (2003). Effects of flotation-versus chamber-restricted environmental stimulation technique (REST) on creativity and realism under stress and non–stress conditions. *Imagination, Cognition and Personality, 22*(4), 343–359.

Norton, M. C, & SahLman, J. H. (1995). Describing the light: Attribution theory as an explanation of the near-death experience. *Journal of Near-Death Studies, 13,* 167–184.

Nowlis, D., & Kamiya, J. (1970). The control of electroencephalographic alpha rhythms through auditory feedback and the associated mental activity. *Psychophysiology, 6,* 476–484.

Nowlis, V. (1965). Research with the mood ajective checklist. In S. S. Tomkins & C. E. Izard (Eds.), *Affect, cognition and personality.* New York: Springer.

O'Beirne, M., Gurevich, N., & Carlen, P. L. (1986). Pentobarbital inhibits hippocampal neurons by increasing potassium conductance. *Canadian Journal of Physiological Pharmacology, 65,* 36–41.

O'Connell, D. N., Shor, R. E., & Orne, M. T. (1970). Hypnotic age regression: An empirical and methodological analysis. *Journal of Abnormal Psychology Monograph Supplement, 76,* 1–32.

Odajnyk, V. W. (1993). *Gathering the light: A psychology of meditation.* Boston: Shambhala.

Oldfield, R. (1971). The assessment and analysis of handedness: the Edinburgh Inventory. *Neuropsychologia, 9,* 97–113.

Olness, K., & Kohen, D. P. (1996). *Hypnosis and hypnotherapy with children.* New York: Guilford.

Olton, D., & Noonberg, A. R. (1980). *Biofeedback: Clinical applications in behavioral medicine.* New York: Prentice-Hall.

Orme-Johnson, D. W. (1973). Autonomic stability and transcendental meditation. *Psychosomatic Medicine, 35,* 341–349.

Orme-Johnson, D. W. (1987). Medical care utilization and the Transcendental Meditation program. *Psychsomatic Medicine, 49,* 493–507.

Orme-Johnson, D. W., Dillbeck, M. C., & Alexander, C. N. (1989). Strategic interventions reducing international conflicts and terrorism: Time series analysis of coherence creating groups. Paper presented at the meetings of the American Political Science Association, Atlanta.

Orme–Johnson, D. W., & Hayes, C. T. (1981). EEG phase coherence, pure consciousness, creativity, and TM–Sidhi experiences. *International Journal of Neuroscience, 13*(4), 211–217.

Orme–Johnson, D.W., Alexander, C.N., Davies, J.L., Chandler, H.M., & Larimore, W.E. (1988). International peace project in the Middle East: The effects of the Maharishi technology of the unified field. *Journal of Conflict Resolution, 32,* 776–812.

Orne, M. T. (1959). The nature of hypnosis: Artifact and essence. *Journal of Abnormal and Social Psychology, 58,* 277–299.

Orne, M. T. (1979). On the simulating subject as a quasi-control group in hypnosis research: Why, what and how. In E. Fromm & R. E. Shor (Eds.), *Hypnosis: Developments in research and new perspectives.* New York: Aldine.

Orne, M. T., Hilgard, E. R., Spiegel, H., Spiegel, D., & Crawford, H. J. (1979). The relation between the Hypnotic Induction Profile and the Stanford Hypnotic Susceptibility Scales, Forms A and C. International *Journal of Clinical and Experimental Hypnosis, 27,* 85–102.

Orne, M. T., & McConkey, K. M. (1981). Toward convergent inquiry into self-hypnosis. *International Journal of Clinical and Experimental Hypnosis, 29,* 313–323.

Orne, M. T., & Scheibe, K. E. (1964). The contribution of nondeprivation factors in the production of sensory deprivation effects: the psychology of the "panic button". *Journal of Abnormal Social Psychology, 68,* 3–12.

Ornstein, R. E. (1972). *The psychology of consciousness.* San Francisco: Freeman.

Ornstein, R. E. (1986). *The psychology of consciousness* (2nd ed.). New York: Penguin.

Osmond, H. (1957). A review of the clinical effects of psychotomimetic agents. *Annals of the New York Academy of Science, 66,* 418–434.

Ospina, M.B., Bond, T.K., Karkhaneh, M., Tjosvold L., Vandermeer, B., Liang, Y., Bialy, L., Hooton, N., Buscemi, N., Dryden, D.M., & Klassen T.P.(2007). *Meditation practices for health: state of the research.* Evidence Report/Technology Assessment No. 155. (Prepared by the University of Alberta Evidence–based Practice Center under Contract No. 290–02–0023, Publication No. 07–E010). Rockville, MD: Agency for Healthcare Research and Quality.

Oswald, B. B. & Appel, J. B. (2006, October). *Using a 'Drug vs. Other' Discrimination Procedure to Elucidate the Stimulus Properties of (+)MDMA ("Ecstacy").* Paper presented at the Society for Stimulus Properties of Drugs (SSPD) 2006 Satellite Meeting of the Society for Neuroscience. Georgia World Congress Center, Atlanta, GA.

Oswald, I. (1968). Drugs and sleep. *Pharmacological Review, 20,* 272–303.

Overton, D. A. (1974). Experimental methods for the study of state–dependent learning. *Federal Proceedings of the National Academy of Sciences, 33*(7), 1800–1813.

Owen, A. M. (2003). HERA today, gone tomorrow? *Trends in Cognitive Sciences, 7*(9), 383–384.

Owen, A., M., Coleman, M. R., Boly, M., Davis, M. H., Laureys, S., & Pickard, J. D. (2006). Detecting awareness in the vegetative state. *Science, 313*(5792), 1402.

Owens, J.F., Buysee, D.J., Hall, M., Kamarck ,T.W., Lee, L., Strollo, P.J., Reis, S.E., Matthews, K.A. (2010). Napping, nighttime sleep, and cardiovascular risk factors in mid-life adults. *Journal of Clinical Sleep Medicine, 6*(4), 330–335.

Oxford English Dictionary. (1933). Oxford: Oxford University Press.

Oystragh, P. (1988). Vaginismus: A case study. *Australian Journal of Clinical and Experimental Hypnosis, 16,* 147–152.

Pack, C. C., Berezovskii, V. K., & Born, R. T. (2001). Dynamic properties of neurons in cortical area MT in alert and anaesthetized macaque monkeys. *Nature, 414,* 905–908.

Pagano, R., & Frumkin, L. (1977). Effects of TM in right hemispheric functioning. *Biofeedback and Self-Regulation, 2,* 407–415.

Pagano, R. R., Akots, N. J., & Wall, T. W. (1988). Hypnosis, cerebral laterality and relaxation. *International Journal of Clinical and Experimental Hypnosis, 36,* 350–358.

Pagnoni, G., Cekic, M., & Guo, Y. (2008). "Thinking about not thinking": neural correlates of conceptual processing during Zen meditation. *PLoS One, 3*(9), 1–10.

Palace, E. M. (1995). Modification of dysfunctional patterns of sexual response through autonomic arousal and false physiological feedback. *Journal of Consulting and Clinical Psychology, 63,* 604–615.

Palmer, J. (1971). Scoring in ESP tests as a function of belief in ESP: 1. The sheep-goat effect. *Journal of the American Society for Psychical Research, 65,* 373–408.

Palmer, J. (1978). Correspondence: Deathbed apparitions and the survival hypothesis. *Journal of the American Society for Psychical Research, 72,* 392–395.

Palmer, J. (2004). *Synchronicity and psi: how are they related?* Paper presented at The Parapsychological Association 47th Annual Convention, http://archived.parapsych.org/papers/15.pdf.

Parker, A., & Dagnall, N. (2007). Effects of bilateral eye movements on gist based false recognition in the DRM paradigm. *Brain and Cognition, 63,* 221–225.

Parker, A., Relph, S., & Dagnall, N. (2008). Effects of bilateral eye movements on the retrieval of item, associative, and contextual information. *Neuropsychology, 22,* 136–145.

Parker, J. B., Chelone, G. J., Hamblin, D. K., & Kitchens, E. M. (1984). Verbal impairment in alcoholics. *Addictive Behavior, 9,* 287–290.

Parrott, A. C. (2000). Human research on MDMA (3,4–methylene-dioxymethamphetamine) neurotoxicity: cognitive and behavioural indices of change. *Neuropsychology, 42,* 17–24.

Parrott, A. C. (2001). Human psychopharmacology of Ecstasy (MDMA): a review of 15 years of empirical research. *Human Psychopharmacology: Clinical and Experimental, 16,* 557–577.

Parrott, A. C. (2007). The psychotherapeutic potential of MDMA (3,4-methylenedioxymethamphetamine): an evidence–based review. *Psychopharmacology (Berl.), 191*(2), 181–193.

Pascual-Leone, A., Dhuna, A., Altafullah, L, & Anderson, D. C. (1990). Cocaine-induced seizures. *Neurology, 40,* 404–407

Paskewitz, D. A. (1975). Biofeedback instrumentation: Soldering closed the loop. *American Psychologist, 30,* 371–378.

Patel, D. H. (1975). Twelve-month follow-up of yoga and biofeedback in the management of hypertension. *Lancet, 1,* 62–65.

Patterson, D. R. & Jensen, M. P. (2003). Hypnosis and clinical pain. *Psychological Bulletin, 129*(4), 495–521.

Pearlman, C. (1979). REM sleep and information processing: Evidence from animal studies. *Neuroscience and Biobehavioral Review, 3,* 57–68.

Pekala, R. J., Kumar, V. K., & Cummings, J. (1992). Types of high hypnotically-susceptible individuals and reported attitudes and experiences of the paranormal and the anomalous. *Journal of the American Society for Psychical Research, 86,* 135–150.

Pelletier, K. R., & Garfield, G. (1976). *Consciousness East and West.* New York: Harper and Row.

Peltier, S. J., Kerssens, C., & Hamann, S. B. (2005). Functional connectivity changes with concentration of sevoflurane anesthesia. *Neuroreport, 16,* 285–288.

Penfield, W., & Roberts, L. (1959). *Speech and brain mechanisms.* Princeton, NJ: Princeton University Press.

Percival, G., & Striefel, S. (1994). Ethical beliefs and practices of A.A.P.B. members. *Biofeedback & Self-Regulation, 19,* 67–93.

Perez-Reyes, M., Guiseppi, S. D., Ondrusek, G., Jeffcoat, A. R., & Cook, C. E. (1982). Free-base cocaine smoking. *Clinical Pharmacology and Therapeutics, 32,* 459–465.

Perry, C., Gelfand, R., & Marcovitch, P. (1979). The relevance of hypnotic susceptibility in the clinical context. *Journal of Abnormal Psychology, 88,* 592–603.

Perry, C., & Mullen, G. (1975). The effects of hypnotic susceptibility on reducing smoking behavior treated by an hypnotic technique. *Journal of Clinical Psychology, 31,* 498–505.

Perry, C., Orne, M. T, London, R. W., & Orne, E. C. (1996). Rethinking per se exclusions of hypnotically elicited recall as legal testimony. *International Journal of Clinical and Experimental Hypnosis, 44,* 66–81.

Perry, P. (1988). Brushes with death. *Psychology Today, 22,* 14–17.

Pert, C. B., and Snyder, S. H. (1973). Opiate receptor: Demonstration in nervous tissue. *Science, 179,* 1011–1014.

Petersen, R. C. (Ed.). (1977). *Marijuana research findings.* National Institute of Drug Abuse Research Monograph No. 14, Rockville, MD: National Institute of Drug Abuse.

Petersen, R. C. (1979, July 24.) *Cocaine.* Statement of R. C. Petersen (NIDA, Alcohol, Drug Abuse, and Mental Health Administration Public Health Service, DHEW) Before the Select Committee on Narcotics Abuse and Control, House of Representatives.

Phelps, M. E., & Mazzietta, J. C. (1985). Positron emission tomography: Human brain function and biochemistry. *Science, 228,* 799–809.

Piaget, J. (1970). Piaget's theory. In P. H. Mussen (Ed.), *Carmichael's manual of child psychology* (Vol. 1). New York: Wiley.

Piccione, E., Hilgard, E. R., & Zimbardo, P. G. (1989). On the degree of stability of measured hypnotizability over a 25-year period. *Journal of Personality and Social Psychology, 56,* 289–295.

Pinel, J. P. J. (1997). *Biopsychology* (3rd ed.). Needham Heights, MA: Allyn and Bacon.

Plihal, W., & Born, J. (1997). Effects of early and late nocturnal sleep on declarative and procedural memory. *Journal of Cognitive Neuroscience, 9,* 534–547.

Plotkin, W. B., and Cohen, R. (1976). Occipital alpha and attributes of the "alpha experience." *Psychophysiology, 13,* 16–21.

Pockett, S. (2009). *The philosophy of global consciousness: a brief history of God.* http://www.scholarpedia.org/article/Field_theories_of_consciousness/ Field_theories_of_global_consciousness. Last updated April 19, 2009. Accessed February 10, 2011.

Poe, G. R., Walsh, C. M., Bjorness, T. E. (2010). Cognitive neuroscience of sleep. *Progress in Brain Research, 185,* 1–19.

Posner, M. I. (1990). The attention system of the human brain. *Annual Review of Neuroscience, 13,* 25–42.

Posner, M. I. (1994). Attention: the mechanisms of consciousness. *Proceedings of the National Academy of Sciences, 91,* 7398–7403.

Pope, H. G., & Yurgelun-Todd, D. (1996). The residual cognitive effects of heavy marijuana use in college students. *Journal of the American Medical Association, 275,* 521–527.

Porkka–Heiskanen, T., & Kalinchuk, A. V. (2011). Adenosine as a sleep factor. *Sleep and Biological Rhythms, 9*(Suppl. 1), 18–23.

Post, R. M. (1975). Cocaine psychosis: A continuum model. *American Journal of Psychiatry, 132,* 225–231.

Powell, D. H. (1980). Helping habitual smokers using flooding and hypnotic desensitization techniques. *International Journal of Clinical and Experimental Hypnosis, 28,* 192–196.

Pratt, J. G. (1973a). *ESP research today: A study of developments in parapsychology since 1960.* Metuchen, NJ: Scarecrow Press.

Pratt, J. G. (1973b). A decade of research with a selected ESP subject: An overview and reappraisal of the work with Pavel Stepanek. *Proceedings of the American Society for Psychical Research, 30,* 1–78.

Pratt, J. G., & Roll, W. G. (1958). The Seaford disturbances. *Journal of Parapsychology, 22,* 79–124.

Pratt, J. G., & Woodruff, J. L. (1939). Size of stimulus symbols in extrasensory perception. *Journal of Parapsychology, 3,* 121–158.

Pressman, M. R. (1991). Whatever happened to insomnia (and insomnia research)? *American Journal of Psychiatry, 148,* 419–420.

Priebe, F. A., & Wallace, B. (1986). Hypnotic susceptibility, imaging ability and the detection of embedded objects. *International Journal of Clinical and Experimental Hypnosis, 34,* 320–329.

Propper, R. E., & Christman, S. D. (2004). Mixed– versus strong right handedness is associated with biases towards "remember" versus "know" judgements in recognition memory: role of interhemispheric interaction. *Memory, 12,* 707–714.

Propper, R. E., Christman, S. D., & Phaneuf, K. A. (2005). A mixed–handed advantage in episodic memory: a possible role of hemispheric interaction. *Memory & Cognition, 33*(4), 751–757.

Proulx, M. J., Stoerig, P., Ludowig, E., & Knoll, I. (2008). Seeing 'where' through the ears: effects of learning-by-doing and longer-term sensory deprivation on localization based on image–to–sound substitution. *PLoS One, 3*(3), 1840.

Proverbio, A. M., Zani, A., Gazzaniga, M. S., & Mangun, G. R. (1994). ERP and RT signs of a rightward bias for spatial orienting in a split-brain patient. *Neuroreport: An International Journal for the Rapid Communication of Research in Neuroscience, 5,* 2457–2461.

Putnam, W. H. (1979). Hypnosis and distortions in eyewitness memory. *International Journal of Clinical and Experimental Hypnosis, 27,* 437–448.

Putz, P., Braeunig, M., Wackermann, J. (2005). EEG correlates of multimodal ganzfeld induced hallucinatory image. *International Journal of Psychophysiology, 61,* 167–178.

Pykett, I. L. (1982). NMR imaging in medicine. *Scientific American, 246,* 78–88.

Raab, J., & Gruzelier, J. (1994). A controlled investigation of right hemispheric processing enhancement after restricted environmental stimulation (REST) with floatation. *Psychological Medicine, 24,* 457–462.

Radin, D. I. (1988). Effects of a priori probability on psi perception: Does precognition predict actual or probable futures? *Journal of Parapsychology, 52,* 187–212.

Radnitz, C. L., & Blanchard, E. B. (1989). Bowel sound biofeedback as a treatment for irritable bowel syndrome: A 2-year follow-up study. Paper presented at the meetings of the Association for Applied Psychophysiology and Biofeedback, San Diego.

Raikov, V. L. (1980). Age regression to infancy by adult subjects in deep hypnosis. *American Journal of Clinical Hypnosis, 22,* 156–163.

Rainville, P., Hofbauer, R. K., Bushnell, M. C., Duncan, G. H., & Price, D. D. (2002). Hypnosis modulates activity in brain structures involved in the regulation of consciousness. *Journal of Cognitive Neuroscience, 14*(6), 887–901.

Rainville, P. Hofbauer, R. K., Paus, T., Duncan, G. H., Bushnell, M. C., & Price, D. D. (1999). Cerebral mechanisms of hypnotic induction and suggestion. *Journal of Cognitive Neuroscience, 11*(1), 110–125.

Rakhindzhanov, A. R., Gafurov, V. G., & Matkhalikov, A. F. (1988). The pathogenesis of nocturnal and diurnal cerebral strokes. *Soviet Neurology and Psychiatry, 21,* 50–57.

Ramirez, C. E., Suedfeld, P., & Remick, R. (1993). Reducing post-ECT memory complaints by REST. Paper presented at the meetings of the 54th annual convention of Canadian Psychological Association, Montreal.

Randi, J. (1975). *The magic of Uri Geller.* New York: Ballatine.

Randi, J. (1982). *Truth about Uri Geller.* Buffalo, NY: Prometheus.

Rao, K. R. (1966). *Experimental parapsychology.* Springfield, IL: Charles C. Thomas.

Rao, K. R. (1977). On the Nature of psi: An examination of some attempts to explain ESP and PK. *Journal of Parapsychology, 41,* 294–351.

Rao, K. R. (1979). On "the scientific credibility of ESP." *Perceptual and Motor Skills, 49,* 415–129.

Ras, K. R., & Palmer, J. (1987). The anamoly called psi: Recent research and criticism. *Behavioral & Brain Sciences, 10,* 539–643.

Rasch, B., Pommer, J., Diekelman, S., & Born, J. (2008). Pharmacological REM sleep suppression paradoxically improves rather than impairs skill performance. *Nature Neuroscience, 12,* 396–397.

Raskin, N. (1980). Migraine, tension Headache: Same disorder. *Clinical Psychiatric News,* May 15.

Raz, A., Hines, T., Fossella, J., & Castro, D. (2008). Paranormal experience and the COMT dopaminergic gene: a preliminary attempt to associate phenotype with genotype using an underlying brain theory. *Cortex, 44,* 1336–1341.

Raz, A. (2005). Attention and hypnosis: neural substrates and genetic associations of two converging processes. *International Journal of Clinical and Experimental Hypnosis, 53*(3), 237–258.

Raz, A. (2008). Genetics and neuroimaging of attention and hypnotizability may elucidate placebo. *International Journal of Clinical and Experimental Hypnosis, 56*(1), 99–116.

Raz, A., & Campbell, N. K. J. (2010). Can suggestion obviate reading? Supplementing primary Stroop evidence with exploratory negative priming analyses. *Conscious and Cognition,* doi: 10/1016/j.concog. 2009.09.013.

Raz, A., Fan, J., & Posner, M. I. (2005). Hypnotic suggestion reduces conflict in the human brain. *Proceedings of the National Academy of Sciences, 102*(28), 9978–9983.

Raz, A., Shapiro, T., Fan, J., & Posner, M. I. (2002). Hypnotic suggestion and the modulation of Stroop interferences. *Archives of General Psychiatry, 59*(12), 1155–1161.

Reading, C., & Mohr, P. D. (1976). Biofeedback control of migraine: A pilot study. *British Journal of Social and Clinical Psychology, 15,* 429–433.

Rech, R. H., & Commissaris, R. L. (1982). Neurotransmitter basis of the behavioral effects of hallucinogens. *Neuroscience and Biobehavioral Reviews, 6,* 521–528.

Rech, R. H., & Rosecrans, J. A. (1982). Review of mechanisms of hallucinogenic drug action. *Neuroscience and Biobehavioral Reviews, 6,* 481–482.

Rechtschaffen, A., & Dement, W. C. Narcolepsy and hypersomnia. (1969). In A. Kales (Ed.), *Sleep: Physiology and pathology.* Philadelphia: Lippincott.

Rechtschaffen, A., Verdone, P., & Wheaton, J. (1963). Reports of mental activity during sleep. *Canadian Psychiatric Association Journal, 8,* 409–414.

Rechtschaffen, A., Wolpert, E. A., Dement, W. C., Mitchell, S. A., & Fisher, C. (1963). Nocturnal sleep of narcoleptics. *Electroencephalography and Clinical Neurophysiology, 15,* 599–609.

Reed, G. K. (1962). Preparatory set as a factor in the production of sensory deprivation phenomena. *Proceeding of the Royal Society of Medicine, 55,* 1010–1014.

Reed, S. K. (1996). *Cognition: Theory and applications* (4th ed.). Monterey, CA: Brooks/Cole.

Reiman, E. M., Lane, R. D., Ahern, G. L., Schwartz, G. E., & Davidson, R. J. (1996). Positron emission tomography, emotion, and consciousness. In S. R. Hameroff, A. W. Kaszniak, & A. C. Scott (Eds.), *Toward a science of consciousness: The first Tucson discussions and debates* (pp. 311–320). Cambridge, MA: MIT Press.

Reiman, A. S. (1982). Marijuana and health. *New England Journal of Medicine, 306,* 603–605.

Resnick, R. B., Kestenbaum, R. S., & Schwartz, L. K. (1977). Acute systematic effects of cocaine in man: A controlled study by intranasal and intravenous routs of administration. *Science, 195,* 696–698.

Restak, R. (1977, March 5). The brain makes its own narcotics. *Saturday Review,* pp. 8–11.

Reuter-Lorenz, P. A., Nozawa, G., Gazzaniga, M. S., & Hughes, H. C. (1995). Fate of neglected targets: A chronometric analysis of redundant target effects in the bisected brain. *Journal of Experimental Psychology: Human Perception and Performance, 21,* 211–230.

Revonsuo, A. (2000). The reinterpretation of dreams: an evolutionary hypothesis of the function of dreaming. *Behavioral and Brain Sciences, 23,* 877–901.

Rhine, J. B. (1945). Parapsychology and dualism (editorial). *Journal of Parapsychology, 9,* 225–228.

Rhine, J. B. (1953). *New world of the mind.* New York: William Sloan.

Rhine, J. B. (1964). *Extrasensory perception.* Boston: Bruce Humphries. (Originally published 1934)

Rhine, J. B., & Brier, R. (Eds.). (1968). *Parapsychology today.* New York: Citadel Press.

Rhine, J. B., & Pratt, J. G. (1957). *Parapsychology: Frontier science of the mind.* Springfield, IL: Charles C. Thomas.

Rhine, L. E. (1961). *Hidden channels of the mind.* New York: Sloan Associates.

Rhine, L. E. (1970). *Mind over matter.* New York: Macmillan.

Rhue, J. W., & Lynn, S. J. (1989). Fantasy proneness, hypnotizability and absorption: A reexamination. *International Journal of Clinical and Experimental Hypnosis, 37,* 100–106.

Ricalla, L. M. (1975). Healing by laying on of hands: Myth or fact? *Ethics in Science and Medicine, 2,* 167–171.

Ricaurte, G.A. & McCann, U.D. (2001). Assessing long–term effects of MDMA (Ecstasy). *The Lancet, 358,* 1831–1832.

Richardson, J., Smith, J. E., & Pilkington, K. (2006). Hypnosis for procedure–related pain and distress in pediatric cancer patients: a systematic review of effectiveness and methodology related to hypnosis interventions. *Journal of Pain and Symptom Management, 31*(1), 70–84.

Ring, K. (1980). *Life at death: A scientific investigation of the near-death experience.* New York: Morrow.

Ring, K. (1985). *Heading toward omega: In search of the meaning of the near-death experience.* New York: Morrow.

Ring, K. (1993). Near-death experiences: Implications for human evolution and planetary transformation. In B. Kane, J. Millay, & D. H. Brown (Eds.), *Silver threads: 25 years of parapsychology research* (pp. 242–257). Westport, CT: Praeger.

Ring, K. (1995). The impact of near-death experiences on persons who have not had them: A report of a preliminary study and two replications. *Journal of Near-Death Studies, 13,* 223–235.

Ritchie, J. M. (1985). The aliphatic alcohols. In A. G. Gilman, L. S. Goodman, T. W. Rail, & F. Murad (Eds.), *The pharmacological basis of therapeutics.* New York: Macmillan.

Ritskes, R., Ritskes,-Hoitinga, M., & Stodklide-Jorgenson, H. (2003). MRI scanning during meditation: the picture of enlightenment? *Constructivism in the Human Sciences, 8,* 85–90.

Ritz, T., Dahme, B., & Roth, W.T. (2004). Behavioral interventions in asthma: biofeedback techniques. *Journal of Psychosomatic Research, 56*(6), 711–720.

Robbins, P. R., & Houshi, F. (1983). Some observations on recrurrent dreams. *Bulletin of the Menninger Clinic, 47,* 262–265.

Robbins, P. R., & Tanck, R. H. (1988). Depressed mood, dream recall and contentless dreams. *Imagination, Cognition and Personality, 8,* 165–174.

Roberts, A. H. (1985). Biofeedback: Research, training, and clinical roles. *American Psychologist, 40,* 938–941.

Roberts, G., & McGrady, A. (1996). Racial and gender effects on the relaxation response: Implications for the development of hypertension. *Biofeedback & Self-Regulation, 21,* 51–61.

Robertson, M. H. (1961). Theoretical implications of sensory deprivation. *Psychological Records, 11,* 33–42.

Robertson, M. H., & Walter, D. J. (1963). The effect of sensory deprivation upon scores on the Wechsler Adult Intelligence Scale. *Journal of Psychology, 56,* 213–218.

Roffwarg, H. P., Muzio, J. N., & Dement, W. C. (1966). Ontogenetic development of the human sleep-dream cycle. *Science, 152,* 604–619.

Roll, W. G. (1966). ESP and memory. *International Journal of Neuropsychiatry, 2,* 505–521.

Roome, J.R., & Romney, D.M. (1985). Reducing anxiety in gifted children by inducing relaxation. *Roeper Review, 7*(3), 177–179.

Rosenthal, D. (2000). Metacognition and higher–order thoughts. *Consciousness and Cognition, 9*(2), 231–242.

Rosenthal, R. (1966). *Experimenter effects in behavioral research.* New York: Appleton-Century-Crofts.

Rosenzweig, N. (1959). Sensory deprivation and schizophrenia: Clinical and theoretical similarities. *American Journal of Psychiatry, 116,* 326–329.

Roser, M. E., Fugelsang, J. A., Dunbar, K.N., Corballis, P. M., & Gazzaniga, M. S. (2005). Dissociating processes supporting causal perception and causal inference in the brain. *Neuropsychology, 19*(5), 591–602.

Roser, M. & Gazzaniga, M. S. (2006). Automatic brains–interpretative minds. *Current Directions in Psychological Science, 13*(2), 56–59.

Rossi, A. M. (1969). General methodological considerations. In J. P. Zubek (Ed.), *Sensory deprivation: Fifteen years of research* (pp. 16–46). New York: Appleton-Century-Crofts.

Rossi, A. M., Kuehnle, J. C., & Mendelson, J. H. (1978). Marijuana and mood in human volunteers. *Pharmacology, Biochemistry, and Behavior, 8,* 447–453.

Rossi, E. L. (1982). Hypnosis and ultradian cycles: A new state(s) theory of hypnosis? *American Journal of Clinical Hypnosis, 25,* 21–32.

Rouder J.N.& Morey R.D. (2011). An assessment of the evidence for feeling the future with a discussion of Bayes factor and significance testing/A Bayes–factor meta analysis of Bem's ESP claim. *Psychonomic Bulletin & Review,* submitted. http://people.psych.cornell.edu/~jec7/pcd%20pubs/rouder&morey.pdf.

Rubia, K., (2009). The neurobiology of meditation and its clinical effectiveness in psychiatric disorders. *Biological Psychology, 82,* 1–11.

Sackheim, H. A., Paulus, D., & Weiman, A. L. (1979). Classroom seating and hypnotic susceptibility. *Journal of Abnormal Psychology, 88,* 81–84.

Salley, R. D. (1982). REM sleep phenomena during out-of-body experiences. *Journal of the American Society for Psychical Research, 76,* 157–165.

Sampson, H. (1966). Psychological effects of deprivation of dreaming sleep. *Journal of Nervous and Mental Disease, 143,* 305–317.

Sanders, G. S., & Simmons, W. L. (1983). Use of hypnosis to enhance eyewitness accuracy: Does it work? *Journal of Applied Psychology, 68,* 70–77.

Sarbin, T. R., & Coe, W. C. (1972). *Hypnosis: A social psychological analysis of influence communication.* New York: Holt, Rinehart, Winston.

Sarbin, T. R., & Coe, W. C. (1979). Hypnosis and psychopathology: Replacing old myths with fresh metaphors. *Journal of Abnormal Psychology, 88,* 506–526.

Sargent, J. D., Green, E. E., & Walters, E. D. (1973). Preliminary report on the use of autogenic feedback techniques in the treatment of migraine and tension headaches. *Psychosomatic Medicine, 35,* 129–135.

Sargent, J. D., Green, E. E., & Walters, E. D. (1977). The use of autogenic feedback training in a pilot study of migraine and tension headaches. *Headache, 12,* 120–124.

Sattler, J. M. (1970). Racial "experimenter effects" in experimentation, testing, interviewing and psychotherapy. *Psychological Bulletin, 73,* 137–160.

Saxby, E. (1995). Alpha-theta brainwave neurofeedback training: An effective treatment for male and female alcoholics with depressive symptoms. *Journal of Clinical Psychology, 51,* 685–693.

Scandrett, S.L., Bean, J.L., Breeden, S., & Powell, S. (1986). A comparative study of biofeedback and progressive relaxation in anxious patients. *Issues in Mental Health Nursing, 8*(3), 255–271.

Schacter, D. L. (1977). EEG theta waves and psychological phenomena: a review and analysis. *Biological Psychology, 5*(1), 47–82.

Scharf, M. B., & Jennings, S. W. (1988). Childhood enuresis: Relationship to sleep, etiology, evaluation, and treatment. *Annals of Behavioral Medicine, 10,* 113–120.

Schenck, C. H., Hurwitz, T. D., & Mahowald, M. W. (1993). REM sleep behaviour disorder: An update on a series of 96 patients and a review of the world literature. *Journal of Sleep Research, 2,* 224–231.

Schenck, C. H., & Mahowald, M. W. (1990). Polysomnographic, neurologic, psychiatric, and clinical outcome report on 70 consecutive cases with REM sleep behavior disorder (RBD). Sustained clonazepam efficiency in 84.5% of 57 treated patients. *Cleveland Clinic Journal of Medicine, 57* supplement, S9–S23.

Schifano, F. (2004). A bitter pill. Overview of ecstasy (MDMA, MDA) related fatalities. *Psychopharmacology, 173,* 242–248.

Schlosberg, H. (1937). The relationship between success and the laws of conditioning. *Psychological Review, 44,* 379–394.

Schmeidler, G. R. (1984). Further analyses of PK with continuous termperature recording. *Journal of the American Society for Psychical Research, 78,* 355–362.

Schmeidler, G. R. (1985). Field and stream: Background stimuli and the flow of ESP responses. *Journal of the American Society for Psychical Research, 79,* 13–26.

Schmeidler, G. R., & McConnell, R. A. (1958). *ESP and personality patterns.* New Haven: Yale University Press.

Schmidt, H. (1970a). A PK test with electronic equipment. *Journal of Parapsychology, 34,* 175–181.

Schmidt, H. (1970b). A quantum mechanical random number generator for psi tests. *Journal of Parapsychology, 34,* 219–224.

Schmidt, H. (1973). PK tests with a high-speed random number generator. *Journal of Parapsychology, 37,* 105–118.

Schmidt, H. (1975). Toward a mathematical theory of psi. *Journal of the American Society for Psychical Research, 69,* 301–319.

Schmidt, H. (1987). Alcock's critique of Schmidt's experiments. *Behavioral and Brain Sciences, 10,* 609.

Schmidt, H., Morris, R. L., & Rudolph, L. (1986). Channeling evidence for a PK effect to independent observers. *Journal of Parapsychology, 50,* 1–15.

Schnarch, D., & Hunter, J. (1980). Migraine incidence in clinical and nonclinical populations. *Psychosomatic Medicine, 21,* 314–325.

Schneider, A. M., & Tarshis, B. (1986). *An introduction to physiological psychology.* New York: Random House.

Schneider, R, Elbert, T., Heimann, H., Welker, A., Stetter, F., Mattes, R., Birbaumer, N., & Mann, K. (1993). Self-regulation of slow cortical potentials in psychiatric patients: Alcohol dependency. *Biofeedback & Self-Regulation, 18,* 23–32.

Schredl, M., & Hofmann, F. (2003). Continuity between waking activities and dream activities. *Consciousness and Cognition, 12,* 298–308.

Schrodt PA. (1990) A methodological critique of a test of the effects of the Maharishi technology of the unified field. *Journal of Conflict Resolution, 34,* 745–755.

Schroter-Kunhardt, M. (1993). A review of near death experiences. *Journal of Scientific Exploration, 7,* 219–239.

Schultz, J. H., & Luthe, W. (1969). *Autogenic therapy* (Vol. 1). New York: Grune and Stratton.

Schwartz, D. G., Weinstein, L. N., & Arkin, A. M. (1978). Qualitative aspects of sleep mentation. In A. M. Arkin, J. S. Antrobus, & S. J. Ellman (Eds.), *The mind in sleep: Psychology and psychophysiology*. Hillsdale, NJ: Erlbaum.

Schwartz, G. E., & Beatty, J. (1977). *Biofeedback theory and research*. New York: Academic Press.

Schwartz, M. S. (Ed.). (1995). *Biofeedback: A practitioner's guide* (2nd ed.). New York: Guilford.

Schwartz, S. P., Taylor, A. E., Scharf, L. P., & Blanchard, E. B. (1989). Behavioral treatment of irritable bowel syndrome: A 3- and 4-year follow-up study. Paper presented at the meetings of the Association for Applied Psychophysiology and Biofeedback, San Diego.

Scott, T. H., Bexton, W. H., Heron, W., & Doane, B. K. (1959). Cognitive effects of perceptual isolation. *Canadian Journal of Psychology, 13*, 200–209.

Scriven, M. (1976). The frontiers of psychology: psychoanalysis and parapsychology. In J. M. O. Wheatley & H. L. Edge (Eds.), *Philosophical dimensions of parapsychology*. Springfield, IL: Charles C. Thomas.

Seager, M. A., Johnson, L. D., Chabot, E. S., Asaka, Y., & Berry, S. D. (2002). Oscillatory brain states and learning: impact of hippocampal theta–contingent learning.

Searle, J. R. (1995). The problem of consciousness. In J. King & K. H. Pribram (Eds.), *Scale in conscious experience: Is the brain too important to be left to specialists to study?* Mahwah, NJ: Erlbaum, pp. 13–22.

Searle, J. R. (2000). Consciousness. *Annual Review of Neuroscience, 23*, 557–578.

Segalowitz, S. J. (1983). *Two sides of the brain: Brain lateralization explored*. Englewood Cliffs, NJ: Prentice-Hall.

Sepinwall, J., & Cook, L. (1980). Relationship of gamma-aminobutyric acid (GABA) to antianxiety effects of benzodiazepins. *Brain Research, 5*, 839–848.

Seymour, S. E., Reuter-Lorenz, P. A., & Gazzaniga, M. S. (1994). The disconnection syndrome: Basic findings reaffirmed. *Brain, 117*, 105–115.

Shah, I. (1970). *The way of the Sufi*. New York: Dutton.

Shanks, D. R. (2006). Bayesian associative learning. *Trends in Cognitive Science, 10*, 477–478.

Shapiro, C. M., Bortz, R., Mitchell, D., Bartel, P., & Jooste, P. (1981). Slow wave sleep: A recovery after exercise. *Science, 214*, 1253–1254.

Shapiro, D. H. (1976). Zen meditation and behavioral self-control strategies applied to a case of generalized anxiety. *Psychologia, 9,* 134–138.

Shapiro, D. H. (1980). *Meditation: Self-regulation strategy and altered state of consciousness.* New York: Aldine.

Shapiro, D. H. (1985). Clinical use of meditation as a self-regulation strategy: Comments on Holmes's conclusions and implications. *American Psychologist, 40,* 719–722.

Shapiro, D. H., & Walsh, R. (Eds.). (1984). *Meditation: Classic and contemporary perspectives.* New York: Aldine.

Sharpless, S. K. (1970). Hypnotics and sedatives. In J. Goodman & A. Gilman (Eds.), *The pharmacological basis of therapeutics.* New York: Macmillan.

Shearn, D. W. (1960). *Operant conditioning of heart rate.* Unpublished doctoral dissertation, Indiana University.

Sheehan, E. P., Smith, H. V, & Forrest, D. W. (1982). A signal detection study of the effects of suggested improvement on the monocular visual acuity of myopes. *International Journal of Clinical and Experimental Hypnosis, 30,* 138–146.

Sheehan, P. W. (1979). Hypnosis and the process of imagination. In E. Fromm & R. E. Shor (Eds.), *Hypnosis: Developments in research and new perspectives.* Chicago: Aldine.

Sheehan, P. W. (1982). Imagery and hypnosis: Forging a link, at least in part. *Research Communication in Psychology, Psychiatry, and Behavior, 7,* 257–272.

Sheehan, P. W. (1988). Memory distortion in hypnosis. *International Journal of Clinical and Experimental Hypnosis, 36,* 296–311.

Sheehan, P. W., Donovan, P., & MacLeod, C. M. (1988). Strategy manipulation and the Stroop effect in hypnosis. *Journal of Abnormal Psychology, 97,* 455–460.

Sheehan, P. W., & McConkey, K. M. (1982). *Hypnosis and experience: The exploration of phenomena and process.* Hillsdale, NJ: Erlbaum.

Sheehan, P. W., & Tilden, J. (1983). Effects of suggestibility and hypnosis on accurate and distorted retrieval from memory. *Journal of Experimental Psychology: Learning, Memory and Cognition, 9,* 283–293.

Sheer, D. E. (Ed.). (1961). *Electrical stimulation of the brain.* Austin: University of Texas Press.

Sheinberg, D. L., & Logothetis, N. K. (1997). The role of temporal cortical areas in perceptual organization. *Proceedings of the National Academy of Sciences, 94,* 3408–3413.

Shor, R. E. (1979). The fundamental problem in hypnosis research as viewed from historic perspectives. In E. Fromm & R. E. Shor (Eds.), *Hypnosis: Developments in research and new perspectives.* New York: Aldine.

Shor, R. E., & Orne, E. C. (1962). *The Harvard Group Scale of Hypnotic Susceptibility: Form A.* Palo Alto, CA: Consulting Psychologists Press.

Shouse, M. N., & Lubar, J. F. (1977). Management of the hyperkinetic syndrome with methylphenidate and SMR biofeedback training. *Biofeedback and Self-Regulation, 2,* 290.

Shurley, J. T. (1960). Profound experimental sensory isolation. *American Journal of Psychiatry, 117,* 539–545.

Shurley, J. T. (1961). *Problems and methods in experimental sensory input alteration and variance.* Unpublished paper.

Shurley, J. T. (1963). The hydro-hypodynamic environment. *Proceedings of the Third World Congress of Psychiatry, Vol. 3.* Toronto: University of Toronto.

Siegel, R. K. (1977). Hallucinations. *Scientific American, 237,* 132–140.

Siegel, R. K. (1985). Quoted in Cocaine use: Disturbing signs. *Science News, 128.*

Silling, S. M. (1980, January). LSD flashbacks: An overview of the literature for counselors. *American Mental Health Counselors Association Journal,* 39–45.

Silver, B., & Blanchard, E. (1978). Biofeedback and relaxation training in the treatment of psychophysiological disorders: Or are the machines really necessary? *Journal of Behavioral Medicine, 1,* 217–239.

Silver, B., Blanchard, E., Williamson, D., Theobald, D., & Brown, D. (1979). Temperature biofeedback and relaxation training in the treatment of migraine headaches. *Biofeedback and Self-Regulation, 4,* 359–366.

Silverman, K., Evans, S. M., Strain, E. C, & Griffiths, R. R. (1992). Withdrawal syndrome after the double-blind cessation of caffeine consumption. *New England Journal of Medicine, 327,* 1109–1114.

Simantov, R., Goodman, R., Aposhian, D., & Snyder, S. H. (1976). Phylogenetic distribution of a morphine-like ligand "enkephalin." *Brain Research, 111,* 204–211.

Simon, D. B., Oparil, S., & Kimball, C. P. (1977). The transcendental meditation program and essential hypertension. In D. Orme-Johnson & J. Farrow (Eds.), *Scientific research on the transcendental meditation program* (Vol. 1). Los Angeles: Mahar-ishi European Research University Press.

Singer, J. L. (1975). *The inner world of daydreaming.* New York: Harper & Row.

Sireteanu, R., Oertel, B., Mohr, H., Linden, D., Singer, W. (2008). Graphical illustration and functional neuroimaging of visual hallucinations during prolonged blindfolding: a comparison to visual imagery. *Perception, 37*(12). 1805–1821.

Skinner, B. F. (1964). Behaviorism at fifty. In T. W. Warm (Ed.), *Behaviorism and phenomenology: Contrasting bases for modern psychology.* Chicago: University of Chicago Press.

Skinner, B. F. (1974). *About behaviorism.* New York: Knopf.

Skolnick, P., Noncada, V., Barker, J. L., & Paul, S. M. (1981). Pentobarbital: Dual actions to increase brain benzodiazepine receptor affinity. *Science, 211,* 1448–1450.

Slagter, H. A., Lutz, A., Greischar, L. L., Nieuwenhuis, S., Davidson, R. J. (2008). Theta phase synchrony and conscious target perception: impact of intensive mental training. *Journal of Cognitive Neuroscience, 21,* 1536–1549.

Slaughter, J., Hahn, W., & Rinaldi, R. (1970). Instrumental conditioning of heart rate in the curarized rat with varied amounts of pretraining. *Journal of Comparative and Physiological Psychology, 72,* 356–359.

Sloan, M. C. (1981). *A comparison of hypnosis vs. waking state and visual vs. nonvisual recall instructions for witness/victim memory retrieval in actual major crimes.* Unpublished doctoral disseration, Florida State University.

Smith, C. (1985). Sleep states and learning: A review of the animal literature. *Neuroscience and Biobehavioral Review, 9,* 157–168.

Smith, C. (2001). Sleep states and memory processes in humans: procedural versus declarative memory systems. *Sleep Medicine Reviews, 5,* 491–506.

Smith, C., & Butler, S. (1982). Paradoxical sleep at selective times following training is necessary for learning. *Physiology & Behavior, 29,* 469–473.

Smith, D. E., & Rose, A. J. (1967–1968). LSD: Its use, abuse, and suggested treatment. *Journal of Psychelic Drugs, 1,* 117–123.

Smith, J. (1964). Do drugs have religious import? In D. Soloman (Ed.), *LSD: The consciousness-expanding drug.* New York: Putnam's Sons.

Smith, J. C., Ellenberger, H. H., Ballanyi, K., Richter, D. W., & Feldman, J. L. (1991). Pre-Botzinger complex: A brainstem region that may generate respiratory rhythm in mammals. *Science, 254,* 726–729.

Smith, J. T., Barabasz, A., & Barabasz, M. (1996). Comparison of hypnosis and distraction in severely ill children undergoing painful medical procedures. *Journal of Counseling Psychology, 43,* 187–195.

Smith, M. D. (1992). The effect of belief in the paranormal and prior set upon the observation of a "psychic" demonstration. *European Journal of Parapsychology, 9,* 24–34.

Smith, P. F. (1995). Cannabis and the brain. *New Zealand Journal of Psychology, 24,* 5–12.

Smith-Donals, L., & Klitzner, M. D. (1985). Self-reports of youthful drinking and driving! Sensitivity analyses of sensitive data. *Journal of Psychoactive Drugs, 17,* 179–190.

Snel, F. W. J. J., van der Sijde, P. C, & Wiegant, F. A. C. (1995). Cognitive styles of believers and disbelievers in paranormal phenomena. *Journal of the Society for Psychical Research, 60,* 251–257.

Snodgrass, M., & Lynn, S. J. (1989). Music absorption and hypnotizability. *International Journal of Clinical and Experimental Hypnosis, 37,* 41–54.

Snyder, F. (1970). The phenomenology of draining. In H. Madlow & T. H. Snow (Eds.), *The psychodynamic implications of the physiological studies on dreams.* Springfield, IL: Charles C. Thomas.

Snyder, S. H. (1971). Cannabis. *Psychology Today, 4,* 37–40.

Snyder, S. H. (1977). The brain's own opiates. *Chemical and Engineering News, 55,* 26–35.

Sokolov, E. N. (1963). *Perception and the conditioned reflex.* New York: Pergamon.

Sondow, N. (1988). The decline of precognized events with the passage of time: Evidence from spontaneous dreams. *Journal of the American Society for Psychical Research, 82,* 33–52.

Soulairac, A., & Soulairac, M. (1965). Effects of certain steroid hormones on the sexual behaviour of the male rat and an analysis of their effect on the central nervous system. *Hormonal steroids, biochemistry, pharmacology and therapeutics: Proceedings of the First International Congress on Hormonal Steroids* (Vol. 2). New York: Academic Press.

Spanos, N. P. (1982). A social psychological approach to hypnotic behavior. In G. Weary & H. Mirels (Eds.), *Integration of clinical and social psychology.* New York: Oxford University Press.

Spanos, N. P. (1986). Hypnosis and the modification of hypnotic susceptibility: A social psychological perspective. In P. Naish (Ed.), *What is hypnosis? Current theories and research,* (pp. 85–120). Philadelphia: Open University Press.

Spanos, N. P., Ansari, F., & Stam, H. J. (1979). Hypnotic age regression and eidetic imagery: A failure to replicate. *Journal of Abnormal Psychology, 88,* 88–91.

Spanos, N. P., Cross, W. P., & de Groh, M. M. (1987). Measuring resistence to hypnosis and its relationship to hypnotic susceptibility. *Psychological Reports, 60,* 67–70.

Spanos, N. P., Gorassini, D. R., & Petrusic, W. (1981). Hypnotically induced limb anesthesia and adaptation to displacing prisms: A failure to confirm. *Journal of Abnormal Psychology, 90,* 329–333.

Spanos, N. P., Ham, M. W., & Barber, T. X. (1973). Suggested ("hypnotic") visual hallucinations: Experimental and phenomenological data. *Journal of Abnormal Psychology, 81,* 96–106.

Spanos, N. P., Radtke, H. L., & Dubreuil, D. L. (1982). Episodic and semantic memory in posthypnotic amnesia. *Journal of Personality and Social Psychology, 43,* 565–573.

Spanos, N. P., Radtke, H. L., Hodgins, D. C., Bertrand, L., Stam, H. J., & Dubreuil, D. L. (1983). The Carleton University Responsiveness to Suggestion Scale: Stability, reliability, and relationships with expectancy and hypnotic experience. *Psychological Reports, 53,* 555–563.

Spanos, N. P., Radtke, H. L., Hodgins, D. C., Stam, H. J., & Bertrand, L. (1983). The Carleton University Responsiveness to Suggestion Scale: Normative data and psychometric properties. *Psychological Reports, 53,* 523–535.

Spanos, N. P., Radtke, H. L., Hodgins, D. C, Stam, H. J., & Noretti, P. (1983). The Carleton University Responsiveness to Suggestion Scale: Relationships with other measures of susceptibility, expectancies, and absorption. *Psychological Reports, 53,* 723–734.

Sperry, R. W. (1966). Brain bisection and consciousness. In J. Eccles (Ed.), *Brain and conscious experience.* New York: Springer-Verlag.

Sperry, R. W. (1974). Lateral specialization in the surgically separated hemispheres. In F. O. Schmitt & F. G. Wordon (Eds.), *The neurosciences: Third study program,* Cambridge: MIT Press.

Spiegel, D., & Barabasz, A. F. (1988). Effects of hypnotic instructions on P300 event-related-potential amplitudes: Research and clinical implications. *American Journal of Clinical Hypnosis, 31,* 11–17.

Spiegel, D., Bierre, P., & Rootenberg, J. (1989). Hypnotic alteration of somatosensory perception. *American Journal of Psychiatry, 146,* 749–759.

Spiegel, D. (1994). A definition without a definition. *Contemporary Hypnosis, 11,* 151–152.

Spiegel, H. (1970). An eye-roll sign for hypnotizability. Paper presented at the annual meeting of the Society for Clinical and Experimental Hypnosis, Philadelphia, October.

Spiegel, H. (1979a). The Hypnotic Induction Profile (HIP): A review of its development. In W. E. Edmonston (Ed.), *Conceptual and investigative approaches to hypnosis and hypnotic phenomena. Annals of the New York Academy of Science, 296,* 129–142.

Spiegel, H. (1979b). A single-treatment method to stop smoking using ancillary self-hypnosis. *International Journal of Clinical and Experimental Hypnosis, 18,* 235–250.

Spielman, A., & Herrera, C. (1991). Sleep disorders. In S. A. Ellman & J. S. Antrobus (Eds.), *The mind in sleep: Psychology and psychophysiology* (2nd ed., pp. 25–80). New York: Wiley.

Spotts, J., & Schontz, F. (1976). *The life styles of nine American cocaine users.* Washington, DC: Department of Health, Education, and Welfare.

Springer, S. P., & Deutsch, G. (1997). *Left brain/right brain: Perspectives from cognitive neuroscience* (5th ed.). New York: Freeman.

Stambaugh, E. E., & House, A. E. (1977). Multimodality treatment of migraine headache: A case study utilizing biofeedback, relaxation, autogenic and hypnotic treatments. *American Journal of Clinical Hypnosis, 19,* 235–240.

Stanford, R. G. (1974). An experimentally testable model for spontaneous psi events. I. Extrasensory events. *Journal of the American Society for Psychical Research, 68,* 34–57.

Stanford, R. G. (1977a). Are parapsychologists paradigmless in psiland? In B. Shapin & L. Coly (Eds.), *The Philosophy of parapsychology.* New York: Parapsychology Foundation.

Stanford, R. G. (1977b). Conceptual frameworks of contemporary psi research. In B. Wolman (Ed.), *Handbook of Parapsychology.* New York: Van Nostrand Reinhold.

Stanton, H. E. (1975). Weight loss through hypnosis. *American Journal of Clinical Hypnosis, 18,* 34–38.

Steiner, S., & Dince, W. (1981). Biofeedback efficacy study: A critique of critiques. *Biofeedback and Self-Regulation, 6,* 275–288.

Steel, G. D., & Suedfeld, P. (1994). The "big five" personality dimensions in polar sojourners. Paper presented at the meetings of the 55th annual convention of the Canadian Psychological Association, Penticton, BC.

Steele, T. D., McCann, U.D., & Ricaurte, G.A.(1994). 3,4-methylenedioxymethamphetamine (MDMA, "Ecstasy"): pharmacology and toxicology in animals and humans. *Addiction, 89*(5), 539–551.

Stephens, R. C. (1987). *Mind-altering drugs.* Newbury Park, NY: Sage.

Steriade, M., McCormick, D. A., & Segnowski, T. J. (1993). Thalmocortical oscillations in sleeping and aroused brain. *Science, 262,* 679–685.

Sterling-Smith, R. S. (1976). A special study of drivers most responsible in fatal accidents. *Summary for Management Report,* Contract DOT HS 310-3-595. Washington, DC: Department of Transportation.

Sterman, M. B. (1973). Neurophysiological and clinical studies of sensorimotor EEG biofeedback training: Some effects on epilepsy. *Seminars in Psychiatry, 5,* 507–525.

Stern, D. B., Spiegel, H., & Nee, J. C. (1979). The Hypnotic Induction Profile: Normative observations, reliability, and validity. *American Journal of Clinical Hypnosis, 21,* 109–133.

Stern, W., & Morgane, P. (1974). Theoretical view of REM sleep functions: Maintenance of catecholamine systems in the central nervous system. *Behavioral Biology, 11,* 1–32.

Sternberg, R. J. (1996). *Cognitive psychology.* Ft. Worth, TX: Harcourt Brace.

Stickgold, R., Hobson, J. A., Fosse, R., & Fosse, M. (2001). Sleep, learning, and dreams: off–line memory reprocessing. *Science, 294,* 1052–154.

Stickgold, R., James, L., & Hobson, J. A. (2000). Visual discrimination learning requires sleep after training. *Nature Neuroscience, 3,* 1237–1238.

Stickgold, R., Malia, A., MacGuire, D., Roddenberry, D., & O'Conner, M. (2000). Replaying the game: hypnogogic images in normals & amnesiacs. *Science, 290,* 350–353.

Stickgold, R., Scott, L., Rittenhouse, C., & Hobson, J. A. (1999). Sleep–induced changes in associative memory. *Journal of Cognitive Neuroscience, 11*(2), 182–193.

Stoelb, B.L., Molton, I. R., Jensen, M. P., & Patterson, D. R. (2009). The efficacy of hypnotic analgesia in adults: a review of the literature. *Contemporary Hypnosis, 26*(1), 24–39.

Storm, L., Tressoldi, P. E., & DiRisio, L. (2010a). Meta-analysis of free-response studies, 1992–2008: assessing the noise reduction model in parapsychology. *Psychological Bulletin, 136*(4), 471–485.

Storm, L., Tressoldi, P. E., & DiRisio, L. (2010b). A meta–analysis with nothing to hide: reply to Hyman (2010) *Psychological Bulletin, 136*(4), 491–494.

Strauch, I., & Meier, B. (1996). *In search of dreams: results of experimental dream research.* Albany: State University of New York Press.

Stroebal, C., & Ford, M. (1981). Quieting response training: Five-year evaluation of a clinical biofeedback practice. *Proceedings of the Biofeedback Society of America, 8,* 78–81.

Stromeyer, C. F., & Psotka, J. (1970). The detailed texture of eidetic images. *Nature, 225,* 346–349.

Sudsuang, R., Chentanez, V., & Veluvan, K. (1991). Effect of Buddhist meditation on serum cortisol and total protein levels, blood pressure, pulse rate, lung volume and reaction time. *Physiology & Behavior, 50,* 543–548.

Suedfeld, P. (1968). Anticipated and experienced stress in sensory deprivation as a function of orientation and ordinal position. *Journal of Social Psychology, 76,* 259–263.

Suedfeld, P. (1969). Changes in intellectual performance and in susceptibility to influence. In J. P. Zubek (Ed.), *Sensory deprivation: Fifteen years of research.* New York: Appleton-Century-Crofts.

Suedfeld, P. (1980). *Restricted environmental stimulation: Research and clinical applications.* New York: Wiley.

Suedfeld, P., & Baker-Brown, G. (1986). Restricted environmental stimulation therapy and aversive conditioning in smoking cessation. *Behavior Research and Therapy, 24,* 421–428.

Suedfeld, P., Ballard, E. J., Baker-Brown, G., & Borrie, R. A. (1986). Flow of consciousness in restricted environmental stimulation. *Imagination, Cognition, and Personally, 5,* 219–230.

Suedfeld, P., Ballard, E. J., & Murphy, M. (1983). Water immersion and flotation: From stress experiment to stress treatment. *Journal of Environmental Psychology, 3,* 147–155.

Suedfeld, P., & Coren, S. (1989). Perceptual isolation, sensory deprivation, and REST: Moving introductory psychology texts out of the 1950s. *Canadian Psychology, 30,* 17–29

Suedfeld, P., & Ikard, F. F. (1974). The use of sensory deprivation in facilitating the reduction of cigarette smoking. *Journal of Consulting and Clinical Psychology, 42,* 888–895.

Suedfeld, P., & Kristeller, J. L. (1982). Stimulus reduction as a technique in health psychology. *Health Psychology, 1,* 337–357.

Suedfeld, P., Landon, P. B., Pargament, R., & Epstein, Y. M. (1972). An experimental attack on smoking: Attitude manipulation in restricted environments. III. *International Journal of the Addictions, 7,* 721–733.

Suedfeld, P., & Mocellin, J. S. P. (1987). The sensed presence in unusual environments. *Environment and Behavior, 19,* 33–52.

Suedfeld, P., & Vernon, J. (1964). Visual hallucinations during sensory deprivation: A problem of criteria. *Science, 145,* 412–413

Suedfeld, P., & Vernon, J. (1966). Attitude manipulation in restricted environments. II. Conceptual structure and the internalization of propaganda received as a reward for compliance. *Journal of Personality and Social Psychology, 3,* 586–589.

Sugi, Y., & Akutsu, K. (1964). *Science of Zazen—Energy metabolism.* Tokyo: University Press of Tokyo.

Surwit, R. S. (1982). Biofeedback and the behavioral treatment of Raynaud's disease. In L. White & B. Tursky (Eds.), *Clinical biofeedback: Efficacy and mechanisms* (pp. 222–232). New York: Guilford.

Susann, J. (1966). *Valley of the dolls.* Grove Press: NY.

Suzdak, P. D., Glowa, J. R., Crawley, J. N., Schwartz, R. D., Skolnick, P., & Paul, S. M. (1986). A selective imidazobenzodiazepine antagonist of ethanol in the rat. *Science, 234,* 1243–1248.

Switras, J. E. (1974). A comparison of the eye-roll test for hypnotizability and the Stanford Hypnotic Susceptibility Scale: Form A. *American Journal of Clinical Hypnosis, 17,* 54–55.

Syrjala, K. R., & Abrams, J. L. (2002). Hypnosis and imagery in the treatment of pain. In Turk, D. C., & Gatchel, R.J. (Eds.). *Psychological Approaches to Pain Management: A Practitioner's Handbook (2nd ed.),* pp. 187–209. New York: Guilford Press.

Szekelya, A., Kovacs-Nagyb, R., Bányaia, E. I., Gősi-Gregussa, A. C., Vargaa, K., Halmaia, Z., Ronaib, R., & Sasvari-Szekelyb, M. (2010). Association between hypnotizability and the catechol-O-methyltransferase (COMT) polymorphism. *International Journal of Clinical and Experimental Hypnosis, 58*(3), 301–315.

Taheri, S., Lin, L., Austin, D., Young, T., & Mignot, E. (2004). Short sleep duration is associated with decreased leptin, increased gherlin, and elevated body–mass index. *PLoS Med 1*(3), e62. doi:10.1371/journal.pmed.0010062.

Takashima, a., Petersson, K. M., Rutters, F., Tendolkar, I., Jenson, O., Zwarts, M. J., McNaughton, B. L., & Fernandez, G. (2006). Declarative memory consolidation in humans: a prospective functional magnetic resonance imaging study. *Proceedings of the National Academy of Sciences USA, 103,* 756–761.

Tan, G., Fukui, T., Jensen, M. P., Thornby, J., & Walsman, K. L. (2010). Hypnosis treatment for chronic low back pain. *International Journal of Clinical and Experimental Hypnosis, 58*(1), 53–68.

Tan, K. R., Brown, M., Labouebe, G., Yvon, C., Creton, C., Fritschy, J-M., Rudolph, U., & Luscher, C. (2010). Neural bases for addictive properties of benzodiazepines. *Nature, 463,* 769–775.

Taneli, B., & Krahne, W. (1987). EEG changes of transcendental meditation practitioners. *Advanced Biological Psychiatry, 16,* 41–71.

Targ, R., & Puthoff, H. (1974a). Information transfer under conditions of sensory shielding. *Nature, 251,* 602–607.

Targ, R., & Puthoff, H. (1974b). ESP experiments with Uri Geller. In W. G. Roll, R. L. Morris, & J. D. Morris (Eds.), *Research in parapsychology.* Metuchen, NJ: Scarecrow Press.

Targ, R., & Puthoff, H. (1977). *Mind-read.* New York: Delacorte.

Tart, C. T. (1966). Card guessing tests: Learning paradigm or extinction paradigm? *Journal of the American Society for Psychical Research, 60,* 46–55.

Tart, C. T. (1968). A psychophysiological study of out-of-the-body experiences in a selected subject. *Journal of the American Society for Psychical Research, 62,* 3–27.

Tart, C. T. (Ed.). (1972). *Altered states of consciousness.* Garden City, NY: Doubleday.

Tart, C. T. (1975). *States of consciousness.* New York: Dutton.

Tart, C. T. (1977a). Putting the pieces together: A conceptual framework for understanding discrete states of consciousness. In N. E. Zinberg (Ed.), *Alternate states of consciousness: Multiple perspectives on the study of consciousness.* New York: Free Press.

Tart, C. T. (1977b). Toward conscious control of psi through immediate feedback training: some considerations of internal processes. *Journal of the American Society for Psychical Research, 71,* 375–407.

Tart, C. T. (1996). Parapsychology and transpersonal psychology. In B. W. Scotton, A. B. Chinen, & J. R. Battista (Eds.), *Textbook of transpersonal psychiatry and psychology* (pp. 186–194). New York: Basic Books.

Tart, C. T, Palmer, J., and Redington, D. J. (1979a). Effects of immediate feedback on ESP performance: *A second study. Journal of the American Society for Psychical Research, 73,* 151–165.

Tart, C. T., Palmer, J., & Redington, D. J. (1979b). Effects of immediate feedback on ESP performance over short time periods. *Journal of the American Society for Psychical Research, 73,* 291–301.

Tart, C. T, Puthoff, H. E., & Targ, R. (Eds.). (1979). *Mind at large.* New York: Praeger.

Taylor, C. B., Sheikh, J., & Agras, W. S. (1986). Self report of panic attacks: Agreement with heart rate changes. *American Journal of Psychiatry, 143*, 478–482.

Taylor, E. I. (1973). Psychological suspended animation. Unpublished master's thesis, Southern Methodist University.

Taylor, N. (1949). *Flight from reality.* New York: Duell, Sloan and Pearce.

Tellegen, A., & Atkinson, G. (1974). Openness to absorbing and self-altering experiences ("absorption"), a trait related to hypnotic susceptibility. *Journal of Abnormal Psychology, 83*, 268–277.

Thalbourne, M. A., Dunbar, K. A., & Delin, P. S. (1995). An investigation into correlates of belief in the paranormal. *Journal of the American Society for Psychical Research, 89*, 215–231.

Thalbourne, M. A., & French, C. C. (1995). Paranormal belief, manic-depressiveness, and magical ideation: A replication. *Personality and Individual Differences, 18*, 291–292.

Tibbetts, V., & Pepper, E. (1989). Follow-up study on EMG/incentive inspirometer training to reduce asthmatic symptoms. Paper presented at the meetings of the Association for Applied Psychophysiology and Biofeedback, San Diego.

Tilley, A. J., & Empson, J. A. C. (1978). REM sleep and memory consolidation. *Biological Psychology, 6*, 293–300.

Tinklenberg, J. R., & Stillman, R. (1970). Drug use and violence. In D. Daniels, M. Gilula, & F. Ochberg (Eds.), *Violence and the struggle for existence.* Boston: Little, Brown.

Tinklenberg, J. R., & Woodrow, K. M. (1974). Drug use among youthful assultive and sexual offenders. In S. H. Frazier (Ed.), *Aggression research publication.* Association for Research in Nervous and Mental Disease.

Titchener, E. B. (1909). *Experimental psychology of the thought process.* New York: Macmillan.

Tomori, Z., & Widdicombe, J. G. (1969). Muscular bronchomotor, and cardiovascular reflexes elicited by mechanical stimulation of the respiratory tract. *Journal of Physiology, 200*, 25–49.

Tong, F., Meng, M., & Blake, R. (2006). Neural bases of binocular rivalry. *Trends in Cognitive Sciences, 10*(11), 502–511

Tong, F., Nakayam, K., Vaughan, J. T., & Kanwisher, N. (1998). Binocular rivalry and visual awareness in human extrastriate cortex. *Neuron, 21*, 753–759.

Torsvall, L., Akerstaedt, T, Gillander, K., & Knutsson, A. (1989). Sleep on the night shift: 24-hour EEG monitoring of spontaneous sleep/wake behavior. *Psychophysiology, 26,* 352–358.

Treisman, A., & Geffen, G. (1967). Selective attention: Perception or response? *Quarterly Journal of Experimental Psychology, 19,* 1–18.

Trinder, J. (1988). Subjective insomnia without objective findings: A pseudo diagnostic classification? *Psychological Bulletin, 103,* 87–94.

Trowill, J. A. (1967). Instrumental conditioning of heart rate in curarized rat. *Journal of Comparative and Physiological Psychology, 63,* 7–11.

Tucker, M. A., Hirota, Y., Wamsley, E. J., Lau, H., Chaklader, Al, & Fishbein, W. (2006). A daytime nap containing solely non–REM sleep enhances declarative but not procedural memory. *Neurobiology of Learning and Memory, 86,* 241–247.

Tulpule, T. E. (1971). Yogic exercises in the management of ischaemic heart disease. *Indian Heart Journal, 23,* 259–264.

Tulving, E. (1985). Memory and consciousness. *Canadian Psychologist, 26,* 1–12.

Tulving, E. (1986). What kind of a hypothesis is the distinction between episodic and semantic memory? Journal of Experimental Psychology: Learning, *Memory, & Cognition, 12,* 307–311.

Tulving, E., Kapur, S., Craik, F. I.M., Moscovitch, M., & Houle, S. (1994). Hemispheric encoding/retrieval asymmetry in episodic memory: positron emission tomography findings. *Proceedings of the National Academy of Sciences, 91,* 2016–2020.

Turk, D. C., Meichenbaum, D., & Berman, W. H. (1979). Application of biofeedback for the regulation of pain: A critical review. *Psychological Bulletin, 86,* 1322–1338.

Turner, R. K., & Taylor, P. D. (1974). Conditioning treatment of nocturnal enuresis in adults: Preliminary findings. *Behavioral Research and Therapy, 12,* 41–52.

Tyre, R. H. (1978). Teaching "The Lord of the Rings." *Media and Methods, 15,* 18–20.

Ungerleider, L. G., & Mishkin, M. (1982). Two cortical visual systems. In D. J. Ingle, M. A. Goodale, and R.J.W. Mansfield (Eds.). *Analysis of Visual Behavior.* MIT Press: Cambridge, MA.

United Nations Office on Drugs and Crime (2010). *World Drug Report.* United Nations Publication, Sales No. E.10.XI.13. NY. http://www.unodc.org/documents/wdr/WDR_2010/World_Drug_Report_2010_lo–res.pdf

United States Drug Enforcement Agengy (2005). *Drugs of abuse.* http://www.justice.gov/dea/concern/depressants.html.

U.S. Department of Health and Human Services. (1994). *Preliminary estimates for the 1993 National Household Survey on Drug Abuse.* Washington, DC: U.S. Government Printing Office.

Valli, K., & Revonsuio, A. (2009). The threat simulation theory in light of recent empirical evidence: a review. *American Journal of Psychology, 122*(1), 17–38.

Van Dierendonck, D., & Nijenhuis, J. T. (2005). Flotation restricted environmental stimulation therapy (REST) as a stress–management tool: a meta–analysis. *Psychology and Health, 20*(3), 405–412.

Van Dyke, C., Jatlow, P., Ungerer, J., Barash, P., & Byck, R. (1978). Oral cocaine: Plasma concentrations and central effects. *Science, 200,* 211–213.

Van Wagenen, W., & Herren, R. (1940). Surgical division of commissural pathways in the corpus callosum. *Archives of Neurology and Psychiatry, 44,* 740–759.

Vaschillo, E., Lehrer, P., Rishe, N., & Konstantinov, M. (2002). Heart rate variability biofeedback as a method for assessing baroreflex function: a preliminary study of resonance in the cardiovascular system. *Applied Psychophysiology and Biofeedback, 27,* 1–27.

Vestergaard–Poulsen, P., vanBeek, M., Skewes, J., Bjarkam, C.R., Stubberup, M., Bertelsen, J., Roepstorff, A. (2009). Long–term meditation is associated with increased gray matter density in the brain stem. *Neuroreport, 20,* 170–174.

Vikander, B., Koechling, U. M., Borg, S., Tonne, U., & Hiltunen, A. J. (2010). Benzodiazepine tapering: a prospective study. *Nordic Journal of Psychiatry, 64*(4), 273–282.

Vitulli, W. F. (1983). Immediate feedback and target-symbol variation in computer-assisted psi test. *Journal of Parapsychology, 47,* 37–17.

Vojtechovsky, M., Safratova, V, Votava, Z., & Feit, V. (1971). The effects of sleep deprivation on learning and memory in healthy volunteers. *Activitas Nervosa Superior, 13,* 143–144.

Volkow, N. D., Chang, L., Wang, G-J., Fowler, J. S., Leonido-Yee, M., Franceshi, D., Sedler, J. J., Gatley, S. J., Hitzemann, R., & Ding, Y.-S. (2001). Association of dopamine transporter reduction with psychomotor impairment in methamphetamine abusers. *American Journal of Psychiatry, 158,* 377–382.

Von Kries, R., Toschke, A. M., Wurmser, H., Sauerwald, T., Koletzo, B. (2002). Reduced risk for overweight and obesity in 5– and 6–y–old children by duration of sleep—a cross–sectional study. *International Journal of Obesity and Related Metabolic Disorders, 26*(5), 710–716.

Wagenmakers, EJ., Wetzels, R., Borsboom, D., & van der Maas, H. (2011). Why psychologists must change the way they analyze their data: The case of psi. *Journal of Personality and Social Psychology, 100,* 426–432. Wagenmakers, E–J., Wetzels, R., Borsboom, D., Kievit, R., & van der Maas, H. L. J. (2011). Yes, psychologists must change the way they analyze their data: clarifications for Bem, Utts, and Johnson (2011). http://www.ruudwetzels.com/articles/ClarificationsForBemUttsJohnson.pdf. Accessed March 7, 2011.

Walker, E. H. (1975). Foundations of paraphysical and parapsychological phenomena. In L. Oteri (Ed.), *Quantum physics and parapsychology.* New York: Parapsychology Foundation.

Walker, E. H. (1984). A review of criticisms of the quantum mechanicial theory of psi phenomena. *Journal of Parapsychology, 48,* 277–332.

Walker, M. P., & Stickgold, R. (2004). Sleep–dependent learning and memory consolidation. *Neuron, 44,* 121–133.

Walker, N. S., Garrett, J. B., & Wallace, B. (1976). Restoration of eidetic imagery via hypnotic age regression: A preliminary report. *Journal of Abnormal Psychology, 85,* 335–337.

Wall, V. J., & Womack, W. (1989). Hypnotic versus active cognitive strategies for alleviation of procedural distress in pediatric oncology patients. *American Journal of Clinical Hypnosis, 31,* 181–191.

Wallace, B. (1978a). Restoration of eidetic imagery via hypnotic age regression: More evidence. *Journal of Abnormal Psychology, 87,* 673–675.

Wallace, B. (1978b). Hypnotic susceptibility and the perception of afterimages and dot stimuli. *American Journal of Psychology, 92,* 681–691.

Wallace, B. (1979). *Applied hypnosis: An overview.* Chicago: Nelson-Hall.

Wallace, B. (1988). Hypnotic susceptibility, visual distraction, and reports of Necker cube apparent reversals. *Journal of General Psychology, 115,* 389–396.

Wallace, B. (1993). Day persons, night persons, and variability in hypnotic susceptibility. *Journal of Personality and Social Psychology, 64,* 827–833.

Wallace, B., & Fisher, L. E. (1982). Hypnotically induced limb anesthesia and adaptation to displacing prisms. *Journal of Abnormal Psychology, 91,* 390–391.

Wallace, B., & Fisher, L. E. (1984). Prism adaptation with hypnotically-induced limb anesthesia: The critical roles of head position and prism type. *Perception and Psychophysics, 36,* 303–306.

Wallace, B., & Garrett, J. B. (1973). Hypnotic susceptibility and autokinetic movement frequency. *Perceptual and Motor Skills, 36,*1054.

Wallace, B., & Garrett, J. B. (1975). Perceptual adaptation with selective reductions of felt sensation. *Perception, 4,* 437–445.

Wallace, B., Garrett, J. B., & Anstadt, S. P. (1974). Hypnotic susceptibility, suggestion and reports of autokinetic movement. *American Journal of Psychology, 87,* 117–123.

Wallace, B., & Hoyenga, K. B. (1980). Reduction of proprioceptive errors with induced hypnotic anesthesia. *International Journal of Clinical and Experimental Hypnosis, 28,* 140–147.

Wallace, B., Knight, T. A., & Garrett, J. B. (1976). Hypnotic susceptibility and frequency reports to illusory stimuli. *Journal of Abnormal Psychology, 85,* 558–563.

Wallace, B., & Kokoszka, A. (1995). Fluctuations in hypnotic susceptibility and imaging ability over a 16-hour period. *International Journal of Clinical and Experimental Hypnosis, 43,* 20–33.

Wallace, B., & Patterson, S. L. (1984). Hypnotic susceptibility and performance on various attention-specific cognitive tasks. *Journal of Personality and Social Psychology, 47,* 175–181.

Wallace, R. K., & Benson, H. (1972). The physiology of meditation. *Scientific American, 226,* 85–90.

Wallace, R. K., Benson, H., & Wilson, A. F. (1971). A wakeful hypometabolic physiological state. *American Journal of Physiology, 221,* 795–799.

Wallechinsky, D., & Wallace, I. (1975). *The people's almanac.* Garden City, NY: Doubleday.

Walsh, D. H. (1974). Interactive effects of alpha feedback and instructional set on subjective state. *Psychophysiology, 11,* 428–435.

Walsh, R. N. (1977). Initial meditative experiences. I. *Journal of Transpersonal Psychology, 9,* 151–192.

Walsh, R. N. (1978). Initial meditative experiences. II. *Journal of Transpersonal Psychology, 10,* 1–28.

Walsh, R. N. (1981). *Towards an ecology of brain.* Jamaica, NY: Spectrum.

Walsh, R. N. (1982). A model for viewing meditation research. *Journal of Transpersonal Psychology, 14,* 69–84.

Walter, W. G. (1936). The location of cerebral tumors by electroencephalography. *Lancet, 2*, 305–308.

Walter, W. G., & Dovey, V. J. (1944). Electro-encephalography in cases of subcortical tumour. *Journal of Neurology, Neurosurgery, and Psychiatry, 7*, 57–65.

Walters, V.J., & Oakley, D.A. (2003). Does hypnosis make in vitro, in vivo? Hypnosis as a possible virtual reality context in cognitive behavioral therapy for an environmental phobia. *Clinical Case Studies, 2*(4), 295–305.

Walton, K. G., & Levitsky, D. (1994). A neuroendocrine mechanism for the reduction of drug use and addictions by Transcendental Meditation. *Alcoholism Treatment Quarterly, 11*, 89–117.

Walton, K. G., Schneider, R. H., & Nidich, S. I. (2004). Review of controlled research on the transcendental meditation program and cardiovascular disease. *Cardiology Reviews, 12*(5), 262–266.

Walton, K. G., Schneider, R. H., Salerno, J. W., & Nidich, S. I. (2005). Psychosocial stress and cardiovascular disease. Part 3: clinical and policy implication of research on the transcendental meditation program. *Behavioral Medicine, 30*(4), 173–183.

Washburn, M. C. (1978). Observations relevant to a unified theory of meditation. *Journal of Transpersonal Psychology, 10*, 45–65.

Watson, J. B. (1913). Psychology as the behaviorist views it. *Psychological Review, 20*, 158–177.

Webb, W. B. (1973). Sleep research past and present. In W. B. Webb (Ed.), *Sleep: An active process.* Glenview, IL: Scott, Foresman.

Webb, W. B., & Agnew, H. W, Jr. (1971). Stage 4 sleep: Influence of time course variables. *Science, 174*, 1354–1356.

Webb, W. B., & Agnew, H. W., Jr. (1974). The effects of a chronic limitation of sleep length. *Psychophysiology, 11*, 265–274.

Webb, W. B., & Bonnet, M. H. (1979). Sleep and dreams. In M. E. Meyer (Ed.), *Foundations of contemporary psychology.* New York: Oxford University Press.

Webb, W. B., & Cartwright, R. D. (1978). Sleep and dreams. *Annual Review of Psychology, 29*, 223–252.

Webb, W. B., & Kersey, J. (1967). Recall of dreams and the probability of stage 1-REM sleep. *Perceptual and Motor Skills, 24*, 627–630.

Weil, A. T. (1972). *The natural mind: A new way of looking at drugs and the higher consciousness.* Boston: Houghton Mifflin.

Weil, A. T. (1996). Pharmacology of consciousness: A narrative of subjective experience. In S. R. Hameroff, A. W. Kaszniak, & A. C. Scott (Eds.), *Toward a science of consciousness* (pp. 677–689). Cambridge, MA: MIT Press.

Weil, A. T., Zinberg, N. E., & Nelson, J. N. (1968). Clinical and physiological effects of marihuana in man. *Science, 162,* 1234–1242.

Weiner, H. (1977). *Psychobiology and human disease.* New York: Elsevier.

Weinstein, L. N., Schwartz, D. G., & Arkin, A. M. (1991). Qualitative aspects of sleep mentation. In S. A. Ellman & J. S. Antrobus (Eds.), *The mind in sleep: Psychology and psychophysiology* (2nd ed., pp. 172–213). New York: Wiley.

Weishaar, B. B. (1986). A comparison of Lamaze and hypnosis in the management of labor. *American Journal of Clinical Hypnosis, 28,* 214–217.

Weitzenhoffer, A. M., & Hilgard, E. R. (1959). S*tanford Hypnotic Susceptibility Scale, Forms A and B.* Palo Alto: Consulting Psychologists Press.

Weitzenhoffer, A. M., & Hilgard, E. R. (1962). *Stanford Hypnotic Susceptibility Scale, Form C.* Palo Alto: Consulting Psychologists Press.

Welwood, J. (1977). Meditation and the unconscious. *Journal of Transpersonal Psychology, 9,* 1–26.

Wenck, L.S., Leu, P.W., & D'Amato, R.C. (1996). Evaluating the efficacy of a biofeedback intervention to reduce children's anxiety. *Journal of Clinical Psychology, 52*(4), 469–473.

Wesson, D. R., & Smith, D. E. (1971). Barbiturate use as an intoxicant: A San Francisco perspective. Testimony given to the Subcommittee to investigate Juvenile Delinquency, San Francisco, December 15.

West, M. A. (Ed.). (1987). *The psychology of meditation.* New York: Oxford University Press.

West, V, Fellows, B., & Easton, S. (1995). The British Society of Experimental and Clinical Hypnosis: A national survey. *Contemporary Hypnosis, 12,* 143–147.

Wetii, C. V., & Wright, R. K. (1979). Death caused by recreational cocaine use. *Journal of the American Medical Association, 241,* 2519–2522.

Wheaton, A. F., Liu, Y., Perry, G. S., & Croft, J. B. (2011). Effect of short sleep duration on daily activities—United States, 2005–2008. *Morbidity and Mortality Weekly Report (MMWR), 60*(8), 239–242.

Wheeler, L., Reis, H. T., Wolff, E., Grupsmith, E., & Mordkoff, A. M. (1974). Eye-roll and hypnotic susceptibility. *International Journal of Clinical and Experimental Hypnosis, 22,* 327–334.

White, D., Ciorciari, J., Carbis, C., & Liley, D. (2009) EEG correlates of virtual reality hypnosis. *International Journal of Clinical and Experimental Hypnosis, 57*(1), 94–116.

White, L., & Tursky, B. (Eds.). (1982). *Clinical biofeedback: Efficacy and mechanisms.* New York: Guilford.

Whitlock, F. A. (1978). The psychiatry and psychopathology of paranormal phenomena. *Australian and New Zealand Journal of Psychiatry, 12,* 11–19.

Whitmer, P. G. (1978). EMG biofeedback manipulation of arousal and the test of the oversarousal and underarousal areas of childhood hyperactivity. *Disseratation Abstracts International, 38,* 3423.

Whitwell, J. R. (1936). *Historical notes on psychiatry.* London: H. K. Lewis.

Wickelgren, I. (1997). Marijuana: Harder than thought? *Science, 276,* 1967–1968.

Wickramasekera, I. E. (1972). Electromyographic feedback training and tension headache: Preliminary observations. *American Journal of Clinical Hypnosis, 15,* 83–85.

Wilber, K. (1980). *The Atman project.* Wheaton, IL: Quest.

Wilber, K. (1982). Odyssey: A personal inquiry into humanistic and transpersonal psychology. *Journal of Humanistic Psychology, 22,* 57–90.

Wild, M. R., & Espie, C. (2004). The efficacy of hypnosis in the reduction of procedural pain and distress in pediatric oncology: a systematic review. *Journal of Developmental and Behavioral Pediatrics, 25*(3), 207–213.

Williams, H. L., & Lubin, A. (1959). *Impaired performance in a case of prolonged sleep loss.* Mimeographed paper. Washington, DC: Walter Reed Army Institute of Research.

Williams, J. D., & Gruzelier, J. H. (2001). Differentiation of hypnosis and relaxation by analysis of narrow band theta and alpha frequencies. *International Journal of Clinical and Experimental Hypnosis, 49,* 185–205.

Williams, J. M., & Hall, D. W. (1988). Use of single session hypnosis for smoking cessation. *Addictive Behavior, 13,* 205–208.

Wilson, A. F., Honsberger, R., Chiu, J. T., & Novey, H. S. (1975). Transcendental meditation and asthma. *Respiration, 32,* 74–80.

Wilson, M. A., & McNaughton, B. L. (1994). Reactivation of hippocampal ensemble memories during sleep. *Science, 265,* 676–679.

Winkel, G. H., & Sarason, I. G. (1964). Subject, experimenter and situational variables in research on anxiety. *Journal of Abnormal and Social Psychology, 68,* 601–608.

Witelson, S. F. (1989). Hand and sex differences in the isthmus and genu of the human corpus callosum: a postmortem morphological study. *Brain, 112*, 799–835.

Witkiewitz, K., & Bowen, S. (2010). Depression, craving, and substance use following a randomized trial of mindfulness-based relapse prevention. *Journal of Consulting and Clinical Psychology, 78*(3), 362–374.

Witzel, M. (Ed.) (1997). *Inside the texts, beyond the texts: new approaches to the study of the Vedas.* Harvard Oriental Series, Opera Minora vol. 2, Cambridge: Harvard University Press

Wolkove, N., Kreisman, H., Darragh, D.; Cohen, C., & Frank, H. (1984). Effect of Transcendental Meditation on breathing and respiratory control. *Journal of Applied Physiology, 56*, 607–612.

Wolman, B. B. (Ed.). (1977). *Handbook of parapsychology.* New York: Van Nostrand Reinhold.

Wolman, B. B., & Ullman, M. (Eds.) (1986). *Handbook of states of consciousness.* New York: Van Nostrand Reinhold.

Wolman, R. N., & Kozmova, M. (2007). Last night I had the strangest dream: varieties of rational through processes in dream reports. *Consciousness and Cognition, 16*(4), 838–849.

Wolpe, J. (1969). For phoria: A hair of the hound. *Psychology Today, 3*, 34–37.

Wood, D. M., & Emmett-Oglesby, M. W. (1986). Characteristics of tolerance, recovery from tolerance and cross-tolerance for cocaine used as a discriminative stimulus. *Journal of Pharmacology and Experimental Therapeutics, 237*, 120–125.

Woodruff, J. L., & Rhine, J. B. (1942). An experiment in precognition using dice. *Journal of Parapsychology, 6*, 243–262.

Woody, E. Z., Drugovic, M., & Oakman, J. M. (1997). A reexamination of the role of nonhypnotic suggestibility in hypnotic responding. *Journal of Personality and Social Psychology, 72*, 399–407.

Woolfolk, R. L. (1975). Psychophysiological correlates of meditation. *Archives of General Psychiatry, 32*, 1326–1333.

Worthington, T. S. (1979). The use in court of hypnotically enhanced testimony. *International Journal of Clinical and Experimental Hypnosis, 27*, 402–416.

Wright, L. D. (2006). Meditation: a new role for an old friend. *American Journal of Hospice and Pallative Medicine, 23*(4), 323–327.

Yapko, M. D. (1986). Hypnotic and strategic interventions in the treatment of anorexia nervosa. *American Journal of Clinical Hypnosis, 28*, 224–232.

Yates, A. J. (1980). *Biofeedback and the modification of behavior.* New York: Plenum.

York, J. L., & Welte, J. W. (1994). Gender comparisons of alcohol consumption in alcoholic and nonalcoholic populations. *Journal of the Study of Alcohol, 55,* 743–750.

Youngstedt, S. D., & Kripke, D. F. (2004). Long sleep and mortality: rationale for sleep restriction. *Sleep Medicine Reviews, 8,* 159–174.

Yucha, C., & Montgomery, D. (2008). *Evidence–based practice in biofeedback and neurofeedback.* Wheat Ridge, CO: The Association for Applied Psychophysiology and Biofeedback.

Zaidel, D. (1995). Separated hemispheres, separated memories: lesions on long–term memory from split–brain patients. In R. Campbell & M. A. Conway (Eds.). *Broken memories: case studies in memory impairment.* Oxford: Blackwell.

Zarcone, V. (1973). Marijuana and ethanol: Effects on sleep. *Psychiatry and Medicine, 4,* 201–212.

Zelig, M., & Beidelman, W. B. (1981). The investigative use of hypnosis: A word of caution. *International Journal of Clinical and Experimental Hypnosis, 29,* 401–412.

Zepelin, H., & Rechtschaffen, A. (1974). Mammalian sleep, longevity, and energy metabolism. *Brain, Behavior, and Evolution, 10,* 425–470.

Zgierska, A., Rabago, D., Chawla, N., Kushner, K., Koehler, R., & Marlatt, A. (2009). Mindfulness meditation for substance use disorders: a systematic review. *Substance Abuse, 30*(4), 266–294.

Zinberg, N. E. (1977). *Alternate states of consciousness: Multiple perspectives on the study of consciousness.* New York: Free Press.

Ziskind, E. (1965). An explanation of mental symptoms found in acute deprivation: Researches, 1958–1963. *American Journal of Psychiatry, 121,* 939–946.

Zlotogorski, Z., Hahnemann, L. E., & Wiggs, E. A. (1987). Personality characteristics of hypnotizability. *American Journal of Clinical Hypnosis, 30,* 51–56.

Zubek, J. P. (1969). *Sensory deprivation: Fifteen years of research.* New York: Appleton-Century-Crofts.

Zubek, J. P., Bayer, L., Milstein, S., & Shephard, J. M. (1969). Behavioral and physiological changes during prolonged immobilization plus perceptual deprivation. *Journal of Abnormal Psychology, 74,* 230–236.

Zubek, J. P., Sansom, W, & Prysianiuk, A. (1960). Intellectual changes during prolonged perceptual isolation (darkness and silence). *Canadian Journal of Psychology, 14,* 233–243.

Zuckerman, M. (1969a). Variables affecting deprivation results. In J. P. Zubek (Ed.), *Sensory deprivation: Fifteen years of research* (pp. 47–84). New York: Appleton-Century-Crofts.

Zuckerman, M. (1969b). Hallucinations, reported sensations, and images. In J. P. Zubek (Ed.), *Sensory deprivation: Fifteen years of research* (pp. 85–125). New York: Appleton-Century-Crofts.

B

H

CPSIA information can be obtained
at www.ICGtesting.com
Printed in the USA
FSHW010757241019
63324FS

9 780757 593512